J.M.W. TURNER

Andrew Wilton

J.M.W. TURNER

His Art and Life

POPLAR BOOKS

Frontispiece:
J.T. Smith   (1766–1835)
J.M.W. Turner in the Print Room of the British Museum   ? *c.* 1825
Watercolour over pencil, 222 × 184
Coll.: British Museum

Published by
POPLAR BOOKS, INC.
A Division of **BOOK SALES, INC.**
110 Enterprise Avenue
Secaucus, New Jersey 07094

© 1979 by Office du Livre S.A., Fribourg, Switzerland

Reprinted with permission by William S. Konecky Associates, Inc.

Poplar Books, Inc. is a division of Book Sales, Inc., 110 Enterprise Ave.
Secaucus, N.J. 07904

ISBN: 0-89009-905-7

Printed and bound in Hong Kong.

TABLE OF CONTENTS

FOREWORD

Among the many studies of Turner that have appeared in recent years, two in particular have placed his art in fresh light and offered new approaches to it. One was the exhibition and catalogue compiled for the Museum of Modern Art in New York in 1966 by Lawrence Gowing under the title 'Imagination and Reality'; the other, John Gage's study of 'Colour in Turner' published in 1969. The first of these provided an opportunity to see Turner as a forerunner of twentieth-century abstraction, a romantic who slipped out of the mould and became so avant-garde that his originality did not fall into its rightful place until over a hundred years after his death. The second had the very reverse effect: instead of presenting Turner as an abstract painter, it tended to show that he was almost obsessively concerned with an inner meaning, with symbolism, literary allusion, and analogy.

Each of these points of view has proved enormously beneficial in its own way, and has brought home the immense scope of Turner's art, the range of his means of expression. But each has also been responsible for the dissemination of an approach to Turner which, by itself, fails to do the artist justice. 'Imagination and Reality' has prompted the wholesale reinterpretation of his work as a series of mighty leaps 'forward' towards a kind of pictorial 'truth', as represented by the spaceless and climateless canvases of, say, Mark Rothko; 'Colour in Turner' has generated a school of students eager to prove that Turner's mind was a labyrinth of abstruse learning, the clue to which was a crossword-puzzle capacity for pun and association, all of which was transferred by the artist image for image, as it were, to his canvases.

The truth of the matter is, of course, to be found neither in the one extreme nor in the other. Turner, far from being a deliberately revolutionary innovator in painting, was almost neurotically concerned with the problem of communicating with his public and obsessed with the perpetual measuring of himself against the yardstick of others — his successful contemporaries and the masters of the past. He was equally far from being the sort of intellectual and 'literary' artist whose work needs detailed verbal analysis to be understood. That he was highly intelligent is not in doubt, and that he could, on occasion, bring the fruits of his historical and technical reading to bear on his art is likewise clear; but that he was primarily a cerebral painter his works themselves strenuously deny. They are full of the deep thought and subtle design that we expect from a great creative intellect — but that is a very different thing from saying that his creativity was intellectual.

The learning that Turner displays in his paintings, his watercolours and his drawings and prints is the learning of the eye and the heart: the science that accrues to the passionate observer of nature — and of human nature. The apparent 'abstraction' some have glibly found in his statements of that passion is the glimpse of an inner reality in nature itself — not an attempt to render nature down into the manageable quantities of form and tone with which so many abstract artists are content to play. We are perhaps too ready to judge the works of the past by the values of our own age, and in doing so we often forget to ask whether those values are adequate to assess the weight and height and depth of their significance. Turner was certainly an artist of his own

7

time, however he may have transcended the performances of his contemporaries; and his art must be seen in the early nineteenth-century context. Only by establishing what he himself, as well as his intended audience, understood as communication can we arrive at a just conception of what he meant his pictures to convey.

Turner's world was one in which the beauty of nature exercised a more compulsive sway over men's minds than it does now: it was capable of prompting outbursts of incandescent brilliance and intensity; the mystical grandeur of Goethe and Wordsworth, the private ecstasies of Keats and Constable, the melodrama of Chateaubriand and Byron. At the same time it was a world in which the values and purposes of art were still clearly established: the great masters, from Raphael to Reynolds, had determined the parameters of inspired communication, and all respected their example — Turner most conspicuously. Art was a perpetual discourse on the subject of man and his world. Reynolds proclaimed it in his advocacy of the depiction of noble episodes from history, displaying the human passions; and this emphasis was transmitted to landscape as an inevitable feature of its rise to favour. Ruskin, long after Turner's death, could define the art of landscape as 'the thoughtful and passionate representation of the physical conditions appointed for human existence', while a fellow-artist, Samuel Palmer, thought that 'landscape is of little value, but as it hints or expresses the thoughts and doings of man'. The unanimity that existed on this all-important matter in the early nineteenth century has suffered setbacks in the last hundred years; but although the assumption has been challenged it has not been entirely lost sight of, and indeed many people still make it unconsciously, simply because, as human beings, they feel a recurrent need to do so. A recent commentator, J. W. Lambert, has expressed the survival of the notion forcibly: 'One of our leading art critics wrote only the other day that the arts are about selection, exaggeration, distortion, distillation. But they are not. They are about people and the world they live in, physical and spiritual.' That world was the substance of which Turner's art was created; it is our world, and for that reason his marvellous illuminations of it are interesting to us. In so far as time has radically changed it, we must distinguish what means and motives were accessible to him, and assess his work accordingly.

Because of Turner's exceptionally self-conscious relationship with other artists, past and present, I have thought it worth while to illustrate their work more copiously than is usual in accounts of him. A token Claude, a more or less

representative Poussin, are all that the reader is normally permitted; I hope that the opportunity to see examples of several other artists' work alongside Turner's will prove helpful. The text itself cannot, of course, comprehend all of even the principal matters of interest that are raised by the immense body of his output, but it tries to explain, as I see it, how his art came to be the phenomenon that it is, and to pursue some of the technical and conceptual problems that emerge from it, as well, perhaps, as offering some account of why the sheer physical beauty of the paintings and water-colours — not their 'meaning' or their social or historical significance, but their capacity to move us as the works of nature itself do — is, in the end, their main claim to our admiration.

Despite these arguments, I have devoted some space to the reproduction and discussion of a number of Turner's more abstruse pictures. This is because they are generally rather unsuccessful and are tactfully omitted from most accounts, the problems they raise glossed over. Nevertheless, they have occasioned considerable controversy over the years, and they need, I am sure, to be given their rightful place. They can tell us a good deal about Turner's personality which the greater works do not; that is really why they are unsuccessful. They also contrast most tellingly with the paintings that are masterpieces, and make it clear that such obscurities and complexities are emphatically not Turner's usual and preferred language.

If I have given prominence to the watercolours, I have done so for two reasons. First, because they have been my special field of study. Second, because, though long admired, they have not often been given the place they rightfully hold in Turner's output as the key to his whole life's work, and the area in which he was actually able to say most clearly and accurately what he meant to say about the world about him. Only Ruskin and Finberg, I believe, have provided a view of Turner in which the watercolours take a fully integrated place; and neither of them ever attempted a general, consecutive survey of his art of the kind that I, very hesitantly, present here as a slight introduction to its manifold wonders.

As far as the catalogues are concerned, I knew there was no need for a full catalogue of the paintings, for that task has just been completed with great success by Martin Butlin and Evelyn Joll; it would have been physically impossible, as well as futile, to attempt to cover the same ground again in the time available, and I am therefore immensely grateful to them, and to their publishers, Christopher White of the Paul

Mellon Center for British Studies, John Nicoll of Yale University Press and Iain Bain of Tate Gallery Publications, for allowing me to use the head-matter from their entries in my list. I have adhered to their numbering primarily in order to avoid confusion, using the prefix 'P' to distinguish that series from the numbering of the watercolour catalogue.

This second catalogue, although unwieldy, represents only a small portion of Turner's output as a draughtsman; though it does include all exhibited or engraved subjects, as well as most of the other finished works and a large number of the watercolour studies and sketches outside the artist's Bequest. Lack of space has forced me to draw rather arbitrary boundaries: there are a few finished, though unengraved and, apparently, unexhibited subjects in the Bequest that have been omitted; and all other drawings in the Bequest are excluded. Pencil drawings with or without monochrome wash are excluded — a group that comprehends the *Liber Studiorum* drawings; copies after other artists are not catalogued; this means principally those after Cozens made in the mid-1790s, and other drawings for Dr. Monro and John Henderson. A welter of dubious, or very unimportant, work dating from about 1792-6 has been omitted, and I have tried to avoid cataloguing any drawing which seemed to me of doubtful authenticity. This does not, I am afraid, mean that drawings outside the categories mentioned above which happen not to be listed are necessarily rejected by me as inauthentic: I may have overlooked them from ignorance of their existence, or because they came to my attention too late for inclusion. A number of minor studies identifiable only from vague references in sales catalogues and other lists have been left out because without seeing them it was impossible to determine where they should be placed. The catalogue is divided into sections, within which, as far as possible, everything has been allocated a logical niche. Here, too, there are some exceptions, and I have distended a group here and there to make room for some important, but stray, item. The concordances and indexes will give further access to the catalogue. In both the main text and the catalogues I have used the titles that appear in Turner's own catalogue entries as a rule, adjusting their somewhat erratic spelling only when necessary to avoid confusion.

The collection of all the information this book contains could not have been accomplished single-handed, and I am immensely grateful to numerous friends and colleagues whose interest in the project and concern for its progress have been continuously encouraging. The book could certainly not have been compiled without the goodwill and co-operation of hundreds of people whose ownership or custodianship of works by Turner has necessitated my bothering them repeatedly for information and photographs. With few exceptions they have proved incredibly prodigal of their time and trouble. I cannot name them all, but should like to mention Frances Butlin, Edward Casassa, Timothy Clifford, Judy Egerton, John Harris, Edward King, Rodney Merrington, Angelina Morhange, David Posnett, Anthony Reed, Dudley Snelgrove, Stephen Somerville, Lindsay Stainton, Selby Whittingham and Andrew Wyld. I owe still more emphatic thanks to a few people whose uncomplaining hard work and generous imparting of information has been a source of embarrassment to me: especially Anthony Browne, Margie Christian, Priscilla Copeman, Julia Hett, James Holloway, James Miller, Peter Moore, Eric Shanes, Stanley Warburton and Robert Yardley have put themselves out frequently for my benefit and have been gratifyingly willing to draw my attention to new discoveries. In America, I have encountered equal kindness, and must extend particular thanks to Jacob Bean, Beverly Carter, Roy Davis, Joyce Giuliani, Joseph Goldyne, Cynthia Lambros, Perry Rathbone, Charles Ryskamp, Marilyn Simms, Kristin Spangenberg, Bob Wark and John Wisdom. Kurt Pantzer has allowed me to benefit considerably from the great generosity that springs from his long-standing love of Turner, and to him and to Grace Ritchie at Indianapolis I am especially grateful. Above all, I acknowledge the unstinted help of Evelyn Joll of Agnew's, whose unique acquaintance with the history of the Turner market has been vital to the compilation of the watercolour catalogue, and whose advice and support have often been crucial. He and his assistant, Sue Valentine, have also dedicated many hours to the pursuit of truant drawings which I could never have retrieved without their unselfish zeal.

The production of the book has been no less arduous than its compilation, and I again owe much to the co-operation of others, including Marigold Benn, Dolores Gall, and, among the many photographers involved, Christopher Ridley and Joe Szaszfai. At Office du Livre, the prodigious tasks of editing the illustrations and the text have been dispatched with quite amazing fearlessness by the Editor and by Ingrid de Kalbermatten. Ronald Sautebin has brought the mass of material into splendid visual order; and Jean Hirschen has watched over the birth of the book with patience and indulgence. Throughout, Ann Forsdyke has toiled selflessly and unremittingly as researcher, secretary, typist, switchboard operator, and public relations officer. It is she who has gathered much of the material and rendered it intelligible; and she has worked extensively on the watercolour provenances, which owe much to her assiduity. Her contribution to this book cannot be adequately assessed: without her efforts, it could never have been either begun or finished. To her I offer thanks in the knowledge that nothing can ever repay the many months of hard work she has devoted to the tasks involved. At the same time I must make it clear that neither she nor any of my kind helpers is responsible for the errors and omissions from which, I am all too conscious, this book is not exempt.

New Haven,
February 1979

The Master and the Tyro

By tradition the painter of *Calais Pier, Dido building Carthage,* the *Fighting Temeraire* and *Rain, Steam and Speed* has been regarded as a somewhat dim figure, obscured by the effulgence of his own works. He was born in obscurity, and he died in almost greater obscurity, hiding himself from the world with a jealousy that seemed to court rumours of misanthropy and squalor. A. J. Finberg, at the beginning of his *Life of J. M. W. Turner,* now the standard biography, remarks that 'The records of his life are few and scattered. The paucity of facts and the difficulties of finding them stimulate the intellectual curiosity inspired by his works.'[1] But that biography is nearly 450 pages long; and from the material that Finberg, and many other researchers, have gathered together over the 130 years since Turner's death, the artist emerges as vividly as the best documented figures in the history of English painting.

Turner's fame as an artist naturally induced many people to observe and note his behaviour and conversations on the occasions when they met him; several men incorporated their reminiscences of him into their memoirs and other writings; and his first full biographer, the journalist Walter Thornbury, was able to assemble a mass of anecdote, of every degree of authenticity, for his *Life and Correspondence of J. M. W. Turner,* first published in 1862. Thornbury himself later admitted that it was a 'careless book', though he claimed that it included 'much curious, authentic, and original anecdote';[2] and he revised it for a second edition in 1876. His work remains a prime source for the detail of Turner's character and way of life, especially in the accounts supplied by old friends of the artist. It is substantially amplified by the evidence of John Ruskin, whose reputation as a critic was established by his *Modern Painters,* an explicit and lengthy defence of the art of Turner, published in 1843. Here, and in subsequent volumes of the same work[3], as well as other parts of his large output, Ruskin offered many insights into the

artist whom he made every effort to know and understand in the interval between their first meeting in 1840 and Turner's death in 1851.

Ruskin, passionately committed to his belief that Turner was the greatest of all modern painters, knew at their first meeting that he was a man fully the equal of his art. He wrote in his diary: 'Everybody had described him to me as coarse, boorish, unintellectual, vulgar. This I knew to be impossible. I found in him a somewhat eccentric, keen-mannered, matter-of-fact, English-minded—gentleman: good-natured evidently, bad-tempered evidently, hating humbug of all sorts, shrewd, perhaps a little selfish, highly intellectual, the powers of his mind not brought out with any delight in their manifestation, or intention of display, but flashing out occasionally in a word or a look.'[4]

Ruskin had the insight, and the interest, to perceive the whole of Turner's personality: but, as he says, Turner himself made no attempt to impress himself on others as a luminary, intellectually or socially. He was a man of great integrity, content to be himself and to let other people take him as they found him. Although he made every effort to forward his career as a painter, he never pretended to be anything other than what he was—a Londoner of simple origins and unprepossessing background. Here lies the central paradox of Turner's career: the monumental aspiration and achievement of the artist; the independent, modest and unpretentious life of the man.

There is, of course, nothing unusual in great men springing from humble families, and indeed an example providing a very close parallel can be found in the immediate neighbourhood of Turner's early home: another great landscape artist, Thomas Girtin, was born in Southwark, on the south side of the Thames in London, on 18 February 1775; his father was a brush-maker.[5] Turner was born two months later, on 23 April, just to the north of the river, by Covent Garden market, the son of a barber and wig-maker.[6] The two were to develop along such similar paths that the coincidence of their close birth-dates prompted much comparison and (no doubt entirely imaginary) stories of rivalry. By the end of the century they led the English school of watercolour painting and, despite Turner's fast maturing practice in oil, which Girtin more rarely used, many felt that Girtin was the superior genius. But he died in 1802, leaving them to guess at what he might have become. Their hopes for him are enshrined in the undoubtedly apocryphal story of Turner's saying 'If Tom Girtin had lived, I should have starved.'[7] Turner must have known perfectly well that, whatever his colleague's success, it would not have competed in any way with the entirely personal art that he himself had evolved. It is a tale that, like many such anecdotes, takes no account of the down-to-earth simplicity and integrity of Turner's character.

Not only was he brought up in a small house in a narrow street, with a barber's shop on the premises, near a large and busy vegetable market: Turner suffered the misfortune of having a mother who was mentally very unstable. She had been born Mary Marshall, grand-daughter of Joseph Mallord, a prosperous butcher. Three years after the birth of her son she had a daughter, Mary Ann, who died at the age of eight. In 1800 she was committed to the London asylum for the insane, Bethlem Hospital, where she probably remained until her death in April 1804. Her son's childhood must have been one of emotional strain, cramped both physically and psychologically as far as life at home was concerned. But his father foreshadowed many years of devotion to his son's art by allowing the boy to exhibit his drawings in the window of his shop, and encouraging him in every way that he could. The two contrasting facets of Turner's personality are indeed symbolized by his parents: on the one hand quiet, industrious and keenly desirous of success; on the other withdrawn, eccentric and imaginative to the point of frenzy.[8]

His relations played a considerable role in Turner's upbringing, and, in a sense, in the development of his art. He was sent to stay with relatives of his mother's at Margate, perhaps in the early 1780s, and Margate exercised a fascination for him which lasted throughout his life: some of his earliest and his latest drawings were made from, or inspired by, its scenery. Not very much later, in 1786, he went to live with his mother's brother at Brentford in Middlesex, and there too, on the reaches of the Thames west of London, he formed predilections which affected a great deal of his art; they dictated where he should live, and what he should draw,

even many years afterwards. The same uncle moved from Brentford shortly after this, to live at Sunningwell near Oxford, and when Turner stayed with him in 1789 he became acquainted with another of the crucial locales for his painting: the city of Oxford, and the gentle hills which surround it and the higher reaches of the Thames.

A further family connection was the occasion of his first really long sketching tour: his father's friend John Narraway, a fell-monger and glue-maker of Bristol, who was his host in 1791 and 1792, introduced him to the splendours of the Avon gorge, and acted as intermediary between the young artist and the picturesque beauties of the South Welsh coast, the mountains of the border country, and the Wye valley, which he could easily reach from Bristol. The pattern of his sketching tours, which were to dominate his programme and output all his life, was set up at a very early date by the network of his family and their friends in the South of England.

On these people Turner made the impression that he was to make on everyone all his life: he did not attempt to cultivate the usual social accomplishments, being far too intensely involved in pursuing and fostering the great and real accomplishment he knew was in him. The Narraways, for instance, thought him 'not like young people in general, he was singular and very silent, seemed exclusively devoted to his drawing, would not go into society...' 'He was very difficult to understand, he would talk so little.' Nevertheless, his lack of affectation recommended him: 'People... could not help but like him because he was so good humoured...He...did not make himself otherwise than pleasant...' But, of course, it was annoying for his hosts that he was so utterly absorbed: 'Turner during his visits would sometimes go out sketching before breakfast, and sometimes before and after dinner...he was not particular about the time of returning to his meals.'[9] The Narraways, however, were glad to have in return for their hospitality the drawings that Turner gave them, which they could sell. Later in the 1790s, on one of his excursions into Wales, Mr. Narraway lent Turner a pony; the animal was never returned. The family formed a poor opinion of the young man's reliability and honesty, which was not alleviated by his failure to write letters of thanks after his visits.

By this time Turner was exhibiting at the Royal Academy rather than in his father's window, and his circle of acquaintances was widening, through the various architects' offices in which he had employment, through his attendance at the Royal Academy Schools, where he began to study in 1789, and through other professional connections. The disenchanted Narraways saw him as a 'plain uninteresting youth both in manners and appearance, ...very careless and slovenly in his dress, not particular what was the colour of his coat or clothes, and... anything but a nice looking young man. ...He was not at table polite, he would be helped, sit and lounge about, caring little for anyone but himself.'[10] It seems that he may well have taken these family or near-family connections for granted, taking advantage of them as stages in his tours; but as he began to make adult friendships more attractive aspects of his personality emerged. One of the closest and most long-lasting of those he contracted in the 1790s was with the watercolour painter William Frederick Wells. Wells had a house in Mount Street, Grosvenor Square, and later moved to a cottage at Knockholt in Kent; at both places Turner seems to have felt very much at home. When Wells died, Turner was to describe him as 'the best friend I have ever had in my life'.[11] Wells's daughter Clara, later Mrs. Wheeler, is a rich source of intimate recollection of Turner, recollection plainly coloured by a deep affection. 'Of all the light-hearted, merry creatures I ever knew, Turner was the most so; and the laughter and fun that abounded when he was an inmate in our cottage was inconceivable, particularly with the juvenile members of the family. I remember one day coming in after a walk, and when the servant opened the door the uproar was so great that I asked her what was the matter. "Oh, only the young ladies (my young sisters), ma'am, playing with the young gentleman (Turner)." When I went into the sitting-room, where Turner was seated on the ground, with the children winding his ridiculously large cravat round his neck, he exclaimed: "See here, Clara, what these children are about."... He was a firm, affectionate friend to the end of his life: his feelings were deep and enduring. No one would have imagined, under that rather rough and cold exterior, how very strong were the affections which lay hidden beneath.'[12]

Those affections were formed not only towards people, but towards ideas and institutions. A man of profound thoughtfulness—truly intellectual (as his art demonstrates) in spite of the coarseness of manner and expression that resulted from his lack of formal education—Turner could conceive and grasp with passion an idea which seemed to him of real human benefit. The strongest motive force in his life was that of his art, and he expressed that not only in his rather surly 'one-track-mindedness' with others, but in an intense and total professionalism that characterized all his actions as an artist. His working day, which began 'when you were still in bed', as he told an enquirer;[13] his carefully planned tours;

the very functional cultivation of a long thumb-nail with which to scratch out highlights in his watercolours: all speak of a life wholly subordinated to the demands of art, not abandoned to an extravagant and wild romantic creativity, but controlled and ordered within the principles of a workmanlike and disciplined profession. The central and most prestigious expression of that profession was the Royal Academy in London, which had been founded under the patronage of George III in 1768, and until 1792 was presided over by one of the most articulate art theorists of the age, Sir Joshua Reynolds.[14] Turner recognized the Academy as the professional institution that it was, and throughout his career dedicated his unswerving loyalty to it.

The measure of his dedication is clear from the amount of social activity into which it forced him, against his instincts and inclinations. He began by small, inevitable steps: first a student at the Academy's Schools, and soon afterwards an exhibitor at its Spring exhibitions—he first showed a watercolour in 1790. These were essential stages in the promotion of his own career, in the furthering of his own reputation. Equally essential, and indeed inevitable for an artist of such astounding talent, were his election to an Associateship in 1799, and to full membership as Royal Academician at the early age of 27 in 1802. But this honour, while it introduced him into a circle of distinguished men, did not necessarily entail much or extensive further participation in its affairs. Turner quite deliberately and conscientiously embraced the responsibilities involved in holding a regular position on the Academy's Council, and later, in taking the office of Professor in the Schools.

Turner was appointed to the Royal Academy Council for the first time in 1803, and he continued to attend its meetings with regularity during all his terms of office until the end of his career;[15] he also regularly sat on the hanging committees which annually chose and hung pieces submitted for the exhibition. He himself sent work to the Academy almost every year, often showing six or more pictures there at once. Even in the last years of his life he sent work, sometimes pictures painted long before, sometimes earlier canvases modified in some way; only in 1848 did he fail altogether to be represented, and in 1850, the year before his death, he submitted four entirely new pictures. He was by that date the oldest surviving Academician; but he never attained to the Presidency. In 1845 he was acting president during the illness of the President, Sir Martin Archer Shee; and there can be little doubt that he would have relished the position, in so far as it represented the highest point to which his profession could aspire. But his gruff, unprepossessing manner (and, no doubt, his Cockney accent) restrained his colleagues from selecting him for so socially conspicuous a post, and indeed, in one sense at least, he would surely have been loath to undertake it. He was happy to serve the Academy as actively as possible, and would have welcomed tangible recognition, but it was precisely at that point that the opposing aspects of his nature—his reticence and his eagerness for success—clashed, and it was no doubt a satisfactory dispensation which prevented him from having to cope with the task.

His desire to serve was literally filial; he thought of the Academy as a 'mother': when the earnest and desperate historical painter Benjamin Robert Haydon, who had publicly attacked the Academy for its corruption, killed himself in June 1846 Turner's comment was, 'Why did he stab his Mother?'[16] Although not a member of the Academy, Haydon should nevertheless have regarded it as the sacred fount and heart of his profession simply because he was a painter. Turner himself ventured much for the institution: when he accepted the Professorship of Perspective in 1807, he took upon himself to give a course of lectures each year to the students in the Schools; he had no natural gift for public speaking—his notebooks occasionally have the tentative beginnings of remarks he wished to make at Council meetings or annual dinners[17]—he nevertheless undertook an extended programme of public exposition, which involved him in much research. It was not until 1811 that he delivered the first course, of six papers, which he evidently tried to model on the Discourses of Sir Joshua and other Professors, especially those of painting—Fuseli and Opie,[18] for instance. In them he disclosed a wide knowledge of aesthetic theory and theorists from Algarotti and Lomazzo, Felibien and Du Fresnoy, to modern writers such as Joshua Kirby on Perspective and Moses Harris on Colour Systems.[19] To begin with, the lectures were fairly well received; the first paper, it was reported, 'was written throughout in a nervous and elegant style and was delivered with unaffected modesty'. But gradually attendances fell off, on account of Turner's uncertain delivery and general lack of showmanship, and the series ended by attracting a good deal of ridicule. The papers were considered 'ignorant and ill-written', and sometimes criticized for being off the point: Turner's comprehensive interest in the problems of the artist overrode his concern for the particular discipline he was supposed to teach. Each talk was accompanied by Turner's own superb sketches and diagrams, often very beautiful complete watercolour draw-

ings. His colleague Thomas Stothard, though very deaf, regularly attended, and when asked why, said, 'Sir, there is so much to *see* at Turner's lectures—much that I delight in seeing; though I cannot hear him.'[20] He continued to give the course until 1828, though its recurrence in January of each year became less and less predictable and sometimes it did not take place at all. Towards the end of this period his audience was often very small—sometimes only his old father was present: he loyally attended every one. Turner retained the title of Professor of Perspective until 1838; he was proud of it, as a badge of his active participation in the Academy's business, and appended the initials 'P. P.' to his normal signature, 'J M W Turner R. A.', in many paintings and drawings.

The Perspective lectures demonstrate clearly that, as Ruskin realized, Turner was 'highly intellectual', capable of perceiving the nature of large and complex problems; they also reveal, in spite of the clumsiness of their language, a serious attempt to grapple with the difficulty of expressing abstract ideas in words. In fact Turner was by no means unused to the written word, and employed it as a subsidiary mode of expression all his life. The form in which he preferred to exploit it, however, was that of verse. A notebook in use in 1798 contains a number of nautical ballads—some presumably transcribed from broadsheets, but others perhaps improvised by Turner himself; and there are snatches of invention to be found even earlier. Soon afterwards he was drafting love poems between pages of drawings, and such exercises appear often in the sequence of his sketchbooks. The verses vary in type from the simplest of lyrics to more personal reflections on love, life, death and ambition. The majority of them are couched in conventional forms, often of a light-hearted cast, but what is striking is that they vary considerably in mood and technique, indicating a real adventurousness and freshness of thought on Turner's part.

'Come oh Time (nay that is stuff)
Gaffer thou comest on fast enough
Wingd foe to feathered Cupid
But tell me Sandman ere thy trains
Have multiplied upon my brains
So thick to make me stupid'[21]

attempts very creditably the verse-form (though not the dialect) of Burns; while on another occasion he polishes away at lines imitating the satire of Pope (this is on the back of a drawing showing an amateur artist at work):

'Pleased with his work he views it oer & oer
And finds fresh Beauties never seen before.
The Tyros mind another feat controls
....
The Master loves his Art, the Tyro butterd rolls'[22]

Here is a pithy statement (Turner was trying hard to get it pithier) of his own attitude to professionalism: 'thė Master loves his Art' sums up his whole life, and provides explanation enough for his shortcomings, his failures of tact or of temper. It is no coincidence that the drawing of the amateur artist has a companion, showing an unsuccessful Pl.118 poet (*The garreteer's petition*), which embodies Turner's doubts of his own achievements in the literary field. He knew himself to incorporate the 'Tyro' as well as the 'Master'; hence the intensity, the nervous tension that characterized his ambition. The poems express this in other ways:

'O Gold thou parent of Ambition's ardent blush
Thou urge the brave to utmost danger rush
The rugged terrors of the Northern main
Where frost with untold rage does widely reign
The long lost sun below the horizon drawn
Tis twilight dun, no crimson blush of morn
The deepning air in frozen fetters bound
Gives up to cheerless night the Expanses round'[23]

This passage tells us unequivocally that Turner's ideas about money and ambition spring from a core of real concern in his own nature. The siren call of fame and wealth reached his ears very clearly, as these lines also imply:

'What can the song of greatness be
Can it resist (?) that fated shock
High towring like the beechen tree
Which long the rudest blast does mock...'[24]

We cannot doubt that Turner gave vent to very private and personal thoughts and feelings in his verses; and that he read with critical attention the work of poets such as Milton, Thomson, Gray and, a little later, Byron and Shelley, is evident not only from his attempts to imitate them and from reports that 'he was fond of talking of poetry',[25] but from his quoting from them in the exhibition catalogue entries for his pictures.

Quotations of this sort, amplifying the titles of exhibited works, were first permitted by the Royal Academy in 1798;

and at once, in that year, Turner contributed three fairly long citations, from *Paradise Lost* and Thomson's *Seasons*. The coupling of his picture titles with lines of verse became a life-long habit; and at one point, while he was working on his series of watercolours of *Picturesque Views on the Southern Coast of England*, he planned an accompanying text consisting of descriptive verse.[26] This was never published; indeed, his preoccupation with poetry was very much a *violon d'Ingres*, and drew upon him much ridicule during his lifetime and after. For he did contrive to publicize some of it: from about 1800 onwards he regularly introduced his own, rather than other people's, verse into the subtitles of his Academy entries. In 1809 he accompanied his picture of *Thomson's Aeolian Harp*[27] with a further tribute to the poet consisting of no less than 32 lines of rhyming pentameters, for which there is evidence of much careful work among the drafts in his notebooks. And in 1812 there appeared, with the entry for *Snow storm: Hannibal and his army crossing the Alps*,[28] eleven lines from a 'manuscript poem', *Fallacies of Hope*.[29] Although Turner later frequently made citations from other poets, he just as often contributed his own lines, usually ascribing them to the *Fallacies of Hope*, which, as far as is known, never attained a complete or even a unified form. Some of these fragments contain material of real beauty: nothing coherent, but a telling and often moving use of words, suggestive of a great mind ponderously struggling to give voice to its ideas. Nothing points up the pictorial concreteness of Turner's visual output so well as these efforts to frame abstract conceptions in words, or, indeed, as the success with which he sometimes presents a visual image in verse: for instance, *The Fountain of Fallacy* of 1839[30] is thus described:

'Its rainbow—dew diffused fell on each anxious lip
Working wild fantasy, imagining,
First, Science in the immeasurable abyss of thought,
Measured her orbits slumbering.'

A typical late example is that accompanying the *Evening of the Deluge*[31] of 1843:

'The moon put forth her sign of woe unheeded;
But disobedience slept; the dark'ning Deluge closed
    around
And the last token came: the giant framework floated,
The roused birds forsook their nightly shelters
    screaming,
And the beasts waded to the ark.'

When, in 1851, the Comte d'Orsay published a lithograph of his drawing of the aged Turner stirring a cup of tea,[32] he entitled the print 'The Fallacy of Hope': Turner had come to be identified with the idea that he reiterated in his 'manuscript poem'; and the insistence on delusion and disappointment, doom and decay which the verses transfer to the pictures themselves is a significant thread in the pattern of Turner's personality as a whole. As we shall see, it is not always a theme that can easily be related to Turner's art; but it takes a perfectly natural place in his psychology. The professional dedication that was the mainspring of his life took it for granted that that dedication worked towards the ultimate goal of professional success. The Academy stood for that, and at the same time made success possible by affording artists the platform on which to publicize themselves. But Turner, for all his loyalty to the Academy, did not limit his search for professional success to its arena alone. All his life, and, what is especially significant, in the later part of his life, he undertook work for publishers, making illustrations for books that he knew would reach an audience far wider than that commanded by the Academy. Even more revealingly, as soon as he had attained to the dignity of membership, he set up his own gallery in rivalry, as it were, with the Academy. It opened in 1804, at No. 64 Harley Street, where Turner had been in lodgings since 1799; in 1805 he sent no pictures at all to the Academy, and for a year or two year thereafter, his submissions were relatively few. In 1819 he began work on the rebuilding and enlarging of the gallery, round the corner into Queen Anne Street; it reopened in 1822.[33] These activities betray a tireless concern with professional advancement, the corollary of which, inevitably, was unceasing anxiety about professional failure. For a man of this temperament no amount of success can dissolve the permanent dissatisfaction with present achievement, or the fear of inadequate recognition. As for this last, Turner knew well enough that recognition, however it came, could not measure up to his achievement. His 'hope', therefore, was bound to be 'fallacious'. He could only be a disappointed man.

This was not, of course, the only significance of his poem, as his habit of linking it to his pictures makes clear. A further element in its evolution was Turner's palpable failure on the social level: however little he may have had the wish, or the ability, to 'advance' himself in this respect, he was by nature a man who made few, if close, friends. We have seen how his personality prevented him from attaining the highest office in his profession. He lived a sufficiently reclusive and solitary life to have time to ponder often and bitterly the fate by which some men are gregarious, and superficially happy; others condemned to a loneliness which is the necessary condition for their exploration of the profounder channels of existence. He was, consequently, very dependent on the few intimate friends that he had; it was when these began to be taken from him by death that he most felt the force of his fears; it is no coincidence that he published extracts from his manuscript poem most frequently in his last decade, the 1840s.

By then nearly all his close friends were dead, including many of the academicians with whom he had formed warm friendships born of professional respect. These included Sir Thomas Lawrence, whose death in 1830 deeply affected him; the architect Sir John Soane, who died in 1837; Sir Francis Chantrey, the sculptor, who died in 1841; and Sir Augustus Calcott, who died in 1844. His father, an unfailing companion from the time of his retirement, had died in September 1829. Thornbury was told that 'Turner never appeared the same man after his father's death; his family was broken up.'[34] Not only his family: old Mr. Turner had been his son's studio assistant for many years, following his wife's death, and had acted as housekeeper, gardener, secretary and general factotum in all his enterprises, notably in the building and maintaining of a little villa which Turner designed and lived in from 1813. This was 'Solus Lodge', aptly named, at Twickenham, on his favourite stretch of the Thames; it was later rechristened Sandycombe Lodge, and still exists under that name. Turner and his father lived there together until about 1825, when they moved back to Queen Anne Street.

Turner never married. If the Academy was his mother, he was wedded to his art, and there would have been no place in his overwhelmingly professional existence for a wife and children. But he was nevertheless a man, and there are pages in his sketchbooks—rough scribbles of nude figures—which offer evidence enough that he was prone to erotic fantasies.

Thornbury printed a story of his frequenting the brothels of the London Docks—of furtive visits to Wapping where Turner, among other things, made drawings of prostitutes.[35] This report may well have been a fabrication based on the fact that Turner regularly visited Wapping to collect rents from property he had there, inherited from his mother's family; though of course, he could have used the rent-collecting as an excuse to go for other reasons. In any case, drawings of the kind described have not survived. Ruskin testified that a parcel of sketchbooks containing 'grossly obscene drawings' was burnt at the behest of the National Gallery Trustees in his presence in December 1858;[36] but it is difficult to be certain what that parcel consisted of—whether of studies from the life such as he might have made at Wapping, or private fantasies invented for his own passing gratification. Apart from the scribbles in the sketch-books, only one sheet now exists which might indicate what sort of drawings were burnt: it is a sheet of studies[37] that appear to have been made early in Turner's career, perhaps about 1800–1805, in pen and ink rather in the manner of the figure studies that he made for his large academic paintings of that period. The drawings depict erotic activities more or less explicitly, but can hardly be said to count as interesting works of art. We can only accept Ruskin's word for it that they were of little aesthetic value, though we may regret on principle that such potentially revealing documents were destroyed, and contest his assertion that they were 'drawn under a certain condition of insanity'—a less than ingenuous expla-nation from the champion of Turner's supreme sanity in all other respects.

Turner's private life was destined to be secret, and largely surreptitious. Thornbury tells of a youthful engagement to a Margate girl in the 1790s, which Finberg rejects as nonsense; but certainly by about 1798 he had contracted an intimate relationship with Sarah Danby, the widow of John Danby, a composer of glees, who died in that year. She had four children, and later was to bear two more, fathered by Turner, girls whose names were Evelina and Georgianna. At first Turner arranged for them all to be accommodated in a separate house, but by 1809 Sarah was living at Harley Street, and was joined there about that time by her husband's niece Hannah, who later became chatelaine of the little establish-ment that Turner maintained there, and, after his father's death, studio assistant too. It is not known how long Sarah lived, or whether she remained on close terms with Turner; but it appears that by the late 1820s their relationship was at an end. Throughout he had kept himself aloof from her and her brood, retiring for much of the time to his retreats on the Thames—first at Upper Mall, Hammersmith; then, from 1811, briefly, at Sion Ferry House, Twickenham; and later at Solus Lodge.

His two daughters do not seem to have grown up with much fondness for him. He is said to have painted portraits of them as the two girls in *Crossing the brook* of 1815,[38] while Evelina had already appeared as the child in the *Frosty Morning* of 1813.[39] Georgianna died during Turner's lifetime; she was named in his first will of 1829, but later codicils omit

her, as they do Evelina, who in 1817 married a man named Joseph Dupuis and went to live abroad. It is clear that, whatever his feelings about this 'family' of his, it occupied relatively little of his life, and was never—could never be—the repository of his most enduring affections. It should come as no surprise that Turner's most important and enduring friendships sprang directly out of his work: they related to his professional career.

Oddly enough, in the context of his life as an artist he found it possible to contract intimate friendships which completely flouted the notion that he was uneasy outside his own social sphere. A most unexpected class of men provided him with friends that were to prove of the highest significance to him both as an artist and as a man. These were the landed gentlemen and noblemen who first came into contact with him as his patrons. It was the regular practice for artists to stay in the houses of such men, making drawings for commissioned views; Turner had been in this capacity to Harewood in Yorkshire, to Hafod in Wales, and to Fonthill and Stourhead in Wiltshire, among other country seats, before the turn of the century. Later he was to visit Sir John Swinburne at Capheaton in Northumberland, Lord Lonsdale in Cumberland, Lord Darlington at Raby in Durham, John Nash at Cowes, and Sir Walter Scott at Abbotsford. In the first decade of the new century he acquired three new patrons of special importance: Sir John Fleming-Leicester, later Lord de Tabley, with whom Turner stayed in 1808; the third Earl of Egremont, who first commissioned work from him in 1809, and Walter Fawkes, who began to buy Turner's watercolours in 1803. Leicester's collection of paintings was the most extensive and discerning modern collection of its time, and his Turners were outstanding; they were sold at his death in 1827, when Turner bought back his own *Sun rising through vapour*. Lord Egremont was to reappear as a patron much later in Turner's life; Fawkes, however, quickly became a dear friend, one of the best friends the artist ever had.

Walter Ramsden Fawkes owned a fine sixteenth-century house, enlarged in the eighteenth century, which stands on a hillside in the valley of the Wharfe at Farnley, near Leeds in Yorkshire. Turner first went to stay with him and his family at Farnley Hall in 1810, and revisited them frequently thereafter until Fawkes's death in 1825, which he felt as so bitter a blow that he could not bring himself to go there again. At Farnley he could enjoy the outdoor pleasures of the country gentleman; Fawkes was a conscientious landowner, keenly interested in agriculture, and in the breeding of exotic animals. He had much fishing and shooting, and Turner was able to indulge his love of angling, which indeed he pursued wherever he stayed; and at Farnley too he was introduced to the joys of the grouse moor. His first bag was a cuckoo.[40] He became one of the family, more palpably and genuinely than anywhere else, with the exception perhaps of Wells's cottage at Knockholt. Fawkes was a Whig, and between 1802 and 1807 represented the county of York in Parliament. He actively supported the movement for the abolition of slavery, on which Turner was to make his own wry comment in his famous picture of the *Slavers* of 1840.[41] It may be that there was a strong bond between the two men on the matter of politics, but we do not know for certain of what shade Turner's opinions were, though both Thornbury and Ruskin agreed that he had no religious belief.[42]

In 1819 and 1820 Fawkes displayed his collection of watercolours publicly at his London house, 45 Grosvenor Place. It contained work by many artists, but the sixty or seventy items by Turner were patently the centre-piece of the show. A catalogue was printed, and dedicated by Fawkes to Turner as follows: 'My dear Sir,—The unbought and spontaneous expression of the public opinion respecting my Collection of Water Colour Drawings, decidedly points out to whom this little Catalogue should be inscribed. To you, therefore, I dedicate it; first, as an act of duty; and, secondly, as an Offering of Friendship: for, be assured, I never can look at it without intensely feeling the delight I have experienced, during the greater part of my life, from the exercise of your talent and the pleasure of your society. That you may year after year reap an accession of fame and fortune, is the anxious wish of Your sincere Friend, W. Fawkes.'[43] Although he discontinued his visits to Farnley after 1825, Turner kept in touch with Fawkes's family, and at the end of his life was still corresponding with his son, Hawksworth, who regularly sent him a Christmas present of game.

Turner's relationship with Lord Egremont was necessarily less intimate, though the Earl was 'much attracted to him', as we are told.[44] At his great house, Petworth in Sussex, Egremont was openly and lavishly hospitable to a varied gathering of guests, including many artists. Turner first visited the place in 1809, but began to go there regularly only after about 1827. It seems unlikely that he and Egremont evolved any very intimate relationship: but the Earl was master of the art of making his guests feel at home; Turner clearly felt free to do as he liked. 'I really never saw such a character as Lord Egremont!' wrote Haydon; '"Live & let live" seems to be his motto. He has placed me in one of the most magnificent bedrooms I ever saw!... The very flies at Petworth seem to know there is room for their existence; that the windows are theirs. Dogs, horses, cows, deer, pigs, Peasantry & the Servants, the guests & the family, the children & the parents, all share alike his bounty & opulence & luxuries.'[45] In such an atmosphere Turner had no need to feel shy or awkward. His standing as an artist was enough to confer on him a real status in the group, as Egremont proclaimed in his gallery of paintings and sculpture where several pictures of Turner's hung. The little coloured sketches that Turner made of life at Petworth, in the great house, at church and in the park,[46] bear witness to his sense of being at liberty to express himself, to create as he pleased.

When Egremont died, in November 1837, another of Turner's surrogate 'families' was dissolved. (His old friend Wells had died a year previously.) On the 21st he travelled down to Petworth for the funeral: 'A group of artists walked before the hearse with Turner at their head.'[47] From this moment he moved into a new phase of his existence: that of old age. The loneliness that had oppressed him since the deaths of Fawkes and his father now settled densely round him, and he became more and more withdrawn from the world. He began to assume the character that Ruskin, who was to meet him for the first time in 1840, tried to know and to fathom. At about this date, it is not known precisely when, Turner took a small house in what is now Cheyne Walk, Chelsea, where, from a bedroom window or a terrace that he constructed on the roof, he could sit and watch the Thames, or see the firework displays across the river at Vauxhall Gardens. His housekeeper was a Mrs. Sophia Caroline Booth, whom he had first met some years earlier—she lived in Cold Harbour, Margate from 1827 until her husband's death in 1833, and probably continued there, with Turner as an intermittent lodger, until he moved her to Chelsea. Their relationship was reputed to be close; it has been supposed that Mrs. Booth replaced Sarah Danby in Turner's affections; it is certain that in her he found a motherly, comforting, domestic soul who could efficiently and tenderly minister to him in his decline. At Chelsea he allowed himself to be known as Mr. Booth; even, by some, as 'Admiral Booth'; he hid his true identity from his closest neighbours, and from the doctors who came to treat him for the digestive complaints from which he continuously suffered. He lost his teeth, and was unable to eat in a civilized manner; his diet became limited; he lived largely on rum and milk; and his self-consciousness in society became greater than ever.

Meanwhile, at Queen Anne Street, his gallery with its piles of pictures and portfolios of drawings was falling into neglect. Elizabeth Rigby, who was later to marry Turner's friend and colleague Charles Lock Eastlake, visited the house in 1846: 'The door was opened by a hag of a woman, for whom one hardly knew what to feel most, terror or pity—a hideous woman is such a mistake [this was Hannah Danby]. She showed us into a dining-room, which had penury and meanness written on every wall and article of furniture. Then up into the gallery; a fine room—indeed, one of the best in London, but in a dilapidated state; his pictures the same. The great *Rise of Carthage* all mildewed and flaking off... he uncovered a few matchless creatures, fresh and dewy, like pearls just set—the mere colours grateful to the eye without reference to the subjects... The old gentleman was great fun...'[48]

Another visitor, J. A. Hammersley, told Ruskin: 'I was placed in what I suppose was Turner's dining-room. I waited there for a short time... I heard a shambling, slippered footstep down a flight of stairs... When the door opened, I nobody, stood face to face with, to my thinking, the greatest man living. I shall attempt no description; you know how he looked. I saw at once his height, his breadth, his loose dress, his ragged hair, his indifferent quiet—all, indeed, that went to make his *physique* and some of his mind: but, above all, I saw, felt (and still feel) his penetrating grey eye! Remaining only a moment longer in the cold and cheerless room, at his request I followed him into his gallery... the room was even less tidy than the one we had left... most of the pictures, indeed all those resting against the wall, being covered with uncleanly sheets or cloths of a like size and character.'[49]

It is hardly surprising that Turner acquired the reputation of a miser. He was known to be very rich, and many stories circulated of his unwillingness to part with money, of his stickling for high prices for his work, and so on. But these amount to very insubstantial evidence of his meanness. In reality he was a careful, often an acute, businessman—such as will always irritate those who envy wealth. As early as 1799 he had declined Lord Elgin's invitation to accompany him as draughtsman on his expedition to Athens, since Elgin would not accede to the salary Turner stipulated. This was firm-minded, practical sense in a young man, and the same tone characterized all his business dealings. He built up a handsome fortune from the sale of his works and, more especially, from the publication of his designs as engravings. He invested on the stock market and in property—not only his own houses, but in land, some of which, at Twickenham, he proposed to develop for the typically professional purpose of providing almshouses for indigent artists. Such charitable

gestures were not rare in him; his friends knew him as a generous man; Thornbury claims that he helped the Fawkes family after the financial crash of 1825–6, to the tune of 'many, many thousands of pounds', and one of the most enduring of all his commitments was to the Artists' General Benevolent Institution, which he helped to found in 1814, and supported all his life.[50] Money, as his poetry reveals, was significant to him as a gauge of his professional success, the only sure measure (given the ignorance and waywardness of public taste) of his achievement. If he hoarded money, he did so, as a recent biographer has remarked,[51] as he hoarded his pictures: these things were the tangible achievement that justified his existence. And when he gave money in charity to other artists he expressed his profound fear of failure.

In rather the same way, he was always willing to help the fumbling amateur along the right path. He knew only too well the awful futility of the 'Tyro': his own poeticizing was a painful example, in which, however he wished to believe otherwise, he knew he could not take a true professional pride. So, while he was touring Switzerland with H. A. J. Munro of Novar—one of those patrons with whom he struck up a warm friendship—he tacitly but unmistakably gave him a kindly lesson in drawing. Here is Ruskin's account of it: 'One of the points in Turner which increased the general falseness of impression respecting him was a curious dislike he had to *appear* kind. Drawing, with one of his best friends, at the bridge of St. Martin's, the friend got into great difficulty over a coloured sketch. Turner looked over him a little while, then said, in a grumbling way—"I haven't got any paper I like, let me try yours." Receiving a block book, he disappeared for an hour and a half. Returning, he threw the book down, with a growl, saying—"I can't make anything of your paper." There were three sketches on it, in three distinct states of progress, showing the process of colouring from beginning to end, and clearing up every difficulty which his friend had got into.'[52]

The obliquity of his approach as 'tutor' here is the direct consequence of his poignant sense of the humiliation attendant on professional inadequacy. It is from what he imagines to be that humiliation that he seeks to shield his friend. In just the same way he would try to help younger artists to realize their intentions in their pictures; in the 1840s this became a common feature of his appearances at the Academy's 'varnishing days' before the annual exhibitions. In 1847 his *Hero of a hundred fights*[53] hung next to a grandiose canvas of Daniel Maclise, the *Sacrifice of Noah*.[54] Turner 'suggested to Maclise an alteration in his picture with the following colloquy: "I wish Maclise that you would alter that lamb in the foreground, but you won't." "Well, what shall I do?" "Make it darker to bring the lamb out, but you won't." "Yes, I will." "No you won't." "But I will." "No you won't." Maclise did as his neighbour proposed... Turner (stepping back to look at it) "It is better, but not right," he then went up to the picture, took Maclise's brush, accomplished his wish and improved the effect. He also introduced a portion of rainbow, or reflected rainbow, much to the satisfaction of Maclise...'[55]

By such gestures as these Turner signalled his indissoluble sense of identity with his brother artists, an identity which dictated that he assist them in their search for success just as he must do everything in his power to further his own.

He remained sound of mind and alert to the world until the end. He searched out the American photographer J. J. E. Mayall, cross-examined him on the principles and practice of photography, and repeatedly listened to Mayall's descriptions of Niagara, which he said he would like to see.[56] He was much concerned over the fate of works of art in Rome during the siege of the city by the French under General Oudinot in 1849.[57] In the last year of his life F. T. Palgrave could report that 'Turner talked of the mysteries of bibliography and the tangle of politics neither wittily, nor picturesquely, nor technically; but as a man of sense before all things... He appeared as secure in health, as firm in tone of mind, as keen in interest, as when I had seen him years before; as ready in his dry short laugh, as shrewd in retort, as unsoftened in that straightforward bearing which seems to make drawing-room walls start and frightens diners-out from their propriety.'[58]

But he was not as 'secure in health' as Palgrave imagined, and he had no hope of visiting Rome, or any part of Europe again. He had made his last continental tour in 1844; prior to that he had been abroad almost every summer since the Continent was reopened after the peace with France in 1815. The doctor he summoned in his final illness, a Mr. W. Bartlett, said that 'he offered should he recover to take me on the continent and shew me all the places he had visited.'[59] Travel had played an essential role in his life, and, more important, in his art; and the confinement of his old age evidently irked him. Despite his infirmities, which occasioned him much discomfort, he did not want to die: he was still actively pursuing his compulsive path. When his Margate doctor, Price, was called for to the Chelsea cottage, and told him that death was near, 'Go downstairs,' he exclaimed, 'take a glass of sherry, and then look at me again.'[60] On the morning of

19 December 1851, Bartlett recorded, 'it was very dull and gloomy, but just before 9 a. m. the sun burst forth and shone directly on him with that brilliancy which he loved to gaze on ...He died without a groan.'[61] The cause of death was certified as 'natural decay'.

His body was taken to Queen Anne Street and many people paid tribute to him there before the funeral, which was on December 30th. It took place at St. Paul's Cathedral, where Turner was buried in the crypt, beside several other artists. On the same day his will was read to his executors, among whom were his patron Munro of Novar, his fellow academician George Jones, and his agent Thomas Griffith. Others, not present, were Charles Turner, the engraver, Henry Scott Trimmer, an old friend from Twickenham, and the poet Samuel Rogers. Ruskin had been named as an executor, but declined the responsibility. With the exception of Trimmer these were all men whom Turner had come to know through his profession: there was no representative of his family. The will was quickly disputed by his relatives, and a long-drawn-out Chancery suit followed. None of Turner's stipulations for the use of his money was acted upon. He had bequeathed two of his paintings, the *Sun rising through vapour* and *Dido building Carthage,* to be hung in the National Gallery beside works by Claude Lorrain; this was done; but the remainder of the contents of his studio—some 100 finished pictures and 182 oil studies and sketches, together with over 19,000 drawings in sketchbooks or on loose sheets—were intended by Turner to be kept and displayed in a 'Turner Gallery' built for the purpose by the Trustees of the National Gallery; pending this, they were to be stored and exhibited at Queen Anne Street. But the Queen Anne Street house was transferred to his next-of-kin, and the works of art deposited in the National Gallery. This development was ratified by a decree of the Vice-Chancellor of March 1856, by which all Turner's works 'pictures, drawings and sketches... without any distinction of finished or unfinished' were given into the possession of the Trustees of the National Gallery. The foundation of the Tate Gallery in 1897 led to the transfer of the national collection of British art to a new building on Millbank, where paintings and drawings alike were housed, until 1928 when a flooding of the Thames severely damaged the sketchbooks stored in the basement. Shortly after that date all the works on paper in the bequest were transferred to the British Museum Print Room.

These arrangements, following one another haphazardly and without plan, are far removed from Turner's intentions for his works. Still, Turner's burning preoccupation has been posthumously gratified: his art has, ever since his death, been held in the highest esteem; the vicissitudes of his will and his Bequest have in no way obscured it. Indeed, it must be in his works themselves that we seek a complete enlightenment of the gloom and obscurity in which he, largely deliberately, wrapped his life.

NOTES

1   Finberg, *Life,* p. 6.

2   Thornbury, *Haunted London,* 1865, p. 84. Finberg, *Life,* pp. 2–5, gives his reasons for dismissing much of Thornbury's book as a 'mass of turgid fiction'.

3   The five volumes of *Modern Painters* appeared in 1843, 1846, 1856 and 1860. They are vols. III–VII of the complete *Works* of Ruskin, ed. E. T. Cook and A. Wedderburn, 1903–5.

4   Ruskin, *Works,* XXXV, p. 305.

5   Thomas Girtin (1775–1802). See T. Girtin and D. Loshak, *The Art of Thomas Girtin,* 1954.

6   He was christened Joseph Mallord William. Turner even contrived to confuse the record as to his date of birth: this is discussed in Charles F. Stuckey, *Turner—His Birthday and related Matters,* unpublished paper, Johns Hopkins University.

7   See Thornbury, *Life of J. M. W. Turner,* revised ed., p. 71.

8   Finberg, *Life,* chap. II, gives the basic facts of Turner's family. Much colourful detail about his private life is supplied by Jack Lindsay, *J. M. W. Turner,* 1966, pp. 20–22 and *passim.*

9   Ruskin, *Works,* XIII, p. 473.

10   Ruskin, *Works,* XIII, p. 473.

11   Thornbury, p. 236 (Here and subsequently, all references to 'Thornbury' are to his *Life* of Turner.)

12   Thornbury, p. 236.

13   Ruskin, *Works,* XXXVIII, p. 36.

14   See Sidney C. Hutchison, *The History of the Royal Academy, 1768–1968,* 1968.

15   Detailed accounts of some of the Council's proceedings, including periodic quarrels, are given by Finberg, *Life,* pp. 94–7 etc.

16   See W. P. Frith, *My Autobiography and Reminiscences,* 1887, vol. I, p. 333.

17   C. R. Leslie called Turner's speeches 'confused and tedious'; see Thornbury, p. 269.

18   Johann Heinrich Fuseli (1741–1825) was Professor of Painting in the Academy Schools from 1799 to 1805; John Opie (1761–1807) succeeded him, holding the post until his death.

19   See J. Gage, *Colour in Turner,* 1969, chap. 6, and below, chap. 5.

20   See R. and S. Redgrave, *A Century of Painters,* 1866, vol. II, p. 95.

21   T.B., C (inside cover).

22   T.B., CXXI-B verso.

23   T.B., CII-1 verso.

24   T.B., CXII-85 verso.

25   Thornbury, p. 302.

26   See Finberg, *Life,* p. 183.

27   Cat. No. P86.

28   Cat. No. P126.

29   The title was perhaps suggested by Thomas Campbell's *Pleasures of Hope,* first published in 1799, a poem which Turner was to illustrate in 1837.

30   Cat. No. P376.

31   Cat. No. P404.

32   The print was lithographed by Hullmandel & Walton, and published by J. Hogarth on 1 January 1851.

33   For Turner's gallery see Finberg, *Life,* pp. 107, 267–70; and Gage, 1969, chap. 9.

34   Thornbury, p. 117.

35   Thornbury, p. 314, where it is stated that these episodes took place in Turner's old age. The passage was attacked in the *Quarterly Review* for April 1862; Finberg dismisses the idea (*Life,* p. 4).

36   Letter from Ruskin to R. N. Wornum, 3 May 1862, now in the National Gallery Library.

37   In the British Museum Print Room; not included by Finberg in his *Inventory.*

38   Cat. No. P130.

39   Cat. No. P127.

40   See Turner's letter to Hawksworth Fawkes, 31 January 1851, quoted by Finberg, *Life,* p. 431.

41   Cat. No. P385.

42   Thornbury, p. 303.

43   A copy of this catalogue, decorated with watercolours by Turner, is still in the possession of the Fawkes family.

44   Thornbury, p. 233.

45   Willard Bissell Pope, ed., *Benjamin Robert Haydon's Diary,* 1963, vol. III, pp. 166–7.

46   Cat. Nos 906–12.

47 W. T. Whitley, *Art in England 1821–1837,* p. 344.

48 Lady Eastlake, *Journals,* quoted by Finberg, *Life,* p. 414.

49 Finberg, *Life,* p. 404. The date of this visit was 1844.

50 Thornbury, pp. 353–6.

51 Lindsay, *J. M. W. Turner,* 1966, p. 263.

52 Ruskin, *Works,* VII, p. 446 (note).

53 Cat. No. P427.

54 Now in the City Art Galleries, Leeds.

55 George Jones, *Reminiscences,* MS., Bodleian Library, Oxford.

56 See Thornbury, p. 349.

57 See Turner's letter to Hawksworth Fawkes, 24 December 1849, quoted by Finberg, *Life,* p. 426.

58 Letter from F. T. Palgrave to Ruskin, quoted by Finberg, *Life,* p. 434.

59 Letter from Bartlett to Ruskin dated 7 August 1857, quoted by Finberg, *Life,* p. 437.

60 Thornbury, p. 359.

61 Finberg, *Life,* p. 438.

Chapter One

The Artist Emerges

Among the many stories that have come down to us concerning Turner's childhood is one which tells of his father, the barber of Maiden Lane, Covent Garden, boasting: 'My son, Sir, is going to be a painter.'[1] Unlike the fathers of so many famous artists who opposed their sons' vocations from the start, Turner's, we gather, understood and was proud of the ambition of his child. And if the story is to be believed, real ambition was involved: the whole tenor of the anecdote suggests determination, and the word 'painter', in Turner's youth, implied works of more significance than the water-colour views—'tinted drawings'—that the young man was to produce exclusively until 1795. It suggests that, at an early stage, he was set on making painting in oils his career. In 1796 that career began, and Turner went on to transform watercolour until it too attained the stature of 'painting'. But before that time he made a preliminary career for himself as a traditional topographical draughtsman—a career in which, within ten years, he had surpassed all his contemporaries.

In 1787 he signed two watercolours,[2] both probably copies from prints, which are of a proficiency that indicates a certain amount of previous experience. Four drawings of views in or near Margate[3] which, on stylistic grounds, would seem to have been done a little earlier, are apparently drawn direct from nature; one of them in particular, showing a view down a street, displays an understanding of perspective and an ability to convey both form and spatial recession which are very assured. Thornbury speaks of a drawing of 'Margate Church, executed by the artist when he was about nine years old';[4] if this is identifiable with the view of St. John's Church, Margate, in the same group, they may all perhaps belong to 1784. This is four years earlier than the date at which, according to Thornbury,[5] Turner was sent by his father to school at Margate. However, comparatively little development is observable between them and the print copies dated 1787, though there is a perceptible advance in the use of tone

Pl. 1

to suggest light and shade, which indicates that there may be indeed a difference of at least a year or so between them. We know that at about this time Turner was engaged also in colouring prints.[6]

There are allusions by Turner's biographers to a number of other early exercises, including an *Interior of Westminster Abbey* used by J. C. Crowle for his extra-illustrated copy of Pennant's *Tour of London,* now in the British Museum,[7] which is also said to include some copies by Turner after Paul Sandby.[8] These items have not been identified, but other copies exist which afford some evidence of the growth of Turner's response to pictorial problems.[9] Some of the more sophisticated of these, from William Gilpin's *Northern Tour,* have been assigned to the year 1787; they include additions and modifications of Gilpin's published designs, indicating an active interest in them as 'model' landscapes.[10]

Gilpin was one of the most influential theorists of the period: his formulation of the principle of the 'Picturesque' began by proposing as a general observation that the Picturesque is 'that particular quality, which makes objects chiefly pleasing in painting',[11] and went on to elaborate an ideal pictorial landscape preferring the 'rough' to the 'smooth', the variegated to the regular, ruins to new or intact buildings. It was a rationalization of well-established prefer-ences among topographers and antiquarian artists, and in its turn reaffirmed a certain type of rustic landscape as a desirable norm. Gilpin and his theory were a characteristic eighteenth-century phenomenon, produced by an age in which categorization was pursued universally, and a belief in absolute standards of conduct or thought was common to many fields of creativity. Turner's own origins in that period are constantly apparent in his work, and his lifelong reference to such 'standards' is explicable by his early background. Thus, he made a copy of part of an aquatint by Sandby after Fabris showing St. Vincent's Tower at Naples;[12] this too

1   St. John's Church, Margate   ?1784
Pen and black and grey ink and watercolour, 308 × 435
Private collection, U.K.   (Cat. No. 1)

2   A street in Margate, looking down to the harbour   ?1784
Pen and black ink and watercolour, 270 × 407
Private collection, U.K.   (Cat. No. 2)

illustrates his relationship to a contemporary preoccupation with the landscape of Italy, itself a kind of aesthetic standard which was to affect Turner's art profoundly.

In copying and emulating the work of other artists, Turner was not only teaching himself aspects of his profession; he was expressing a strong need to compete with others, setting himself the objective of bettering what they had done. This is the ambition implicit in his father's boast, and the ambition which was to shape, to a large extent, his whole achievement.

24

3   The Archbishop's palace, Lambeth R.A. 1790
Pencil and watercolour, 263 × 378
Indianapolis Museum of Art (gift in memory of Dr. and Mrs. Hugo
Pantzer by their children)   (Cat. No. 10)

The first phase of the rapid stylistic growth that begins to develop in 1789 is associated in particular with the architectural topographer, Thomas Malton,[13] in whose studio Turner was working by that year. He had already done work as an architectural draughtsman, for Thomas Hardwick of Brentford,[14] and, according to Thornbury, for William Porden (for whom, however, it is perhaps more likely that he worked in the later 1790s).[15] Malton, who was himself an artist, had a greater influence on Turner's practice than such architects could have: he provided a model of a fully formed and accomplished style for the kinds of views that Turner was beginning to settle into. He seems to have made a conscious decision to master that branch of art, even though, at almost the same time that he joined Malton, he became a student at the Schools of the Royal Academy, and was immediately engaged there in more elevated pursuits, such as making drawings from the Academy's fine collection of casts from the Antique; shortly afterwards he was admitted to the Life Class and drew from the nude model.[16] These disciplines were of great importance in his education; he clearly took them seriously, and figure studies of various kinds occur frequently among his early drawings. The sketchbook said to have been left behind by Turner at Bristol in 1791 contains, in addition to studies of buildings and trees, a number of more 'academic' drawings: there are copies from Gains-

4 Cottage interior by firelight *c.* 1790
Watercolour, 241 × 321
Trustees of the British Museum, London (T.B., XVII-L) (not in catalogue)

5 Study of ruins of Malmesbury Abbey 1791
Pencil and watercolour, with pen and brown ink, 187 × 265
Trustees of the British Museum, London (T.B., VI-12) (not in catalogue)

borough and Ruysdael, studies of an écorché figure, and imaginative subjects such as a cherub's head and a composition on the death of Ophelia.[17] The interests that governed the 'painter' in him are evident in work of this kind; but there can be no doubt that at this date he was concerned primarily with the problems of becoming an architectural view-maker. The large majority of his drawings are of specific buildings, evidently noted so that they could be used as subject-matter for watercolours.[18]

Pl.3 At the first opportunity after he had entered the Royal Academy Schools, Turner showed one of his drawings at the Academy's summer exhibition: in 1790 a view of *The Archbishop's palace, Lambeth* appeared in the catalogue. This is an intelligent imitation of Thomas Malton's style, which must have been what Turner intended. What is striking is that his figures are, if anything, more lively, more engagingly human, than those that people Malton's elegant designs; here Turner's real interests betray themselves, even while he is engaged in a consciously humble and objective task.

On the whole his early drawings do not support the view that Turner's first inspiration was the colourful confusion of Covent Garden Market. Ruskin, in an eloquent and imagi-

6 Thomas Malton (1748–1804)
St. Paul's: South Front (from Malton's *Picturesque Tour through London and Westminster,* 1792)
Etching and aquatint, 319 × 233
Trustees of the British Museum, London

7 Stoke House, Bristol, the seat of Lady Lippincote   1791
Watercolour, 299 × 412
Private collection   (Cat. No. 20)

native passage,[19] suggested that this was the case; but if Turner ever drew Covent Garden and its denizens, the drawings have not survived. Everything that we now have suggests that Turner was initially far more concerned, first, with grasping and reproducing the totality of already created works of art, and second, with absorbing the technique of his immediate masters, picturesque topographers who hardly ever drew the confusion of urban life for its own sake. When Turner was not copying prints, he drew country houses, churches, and stretches of parkland.[20]

It was an important step to move away from subjects centred on buildings to investigate scenery for its own pictorial value. The expansive view of Oxford that Turner produced from a sketch in 1789[21] cannot be counted as a serious attempt to render a broad landscape: it is essentially a topographical view of the city, in which nature is enlisted as decoration merely. The studies that Turner made of the Avon Gorge at Clifton in 1791[22] testify to a wholly new awareness of natural scenery. That is to say, it was an awareness that he had never before expressed in practice: the copies from Gilpin, which presumably predate the Bristol tour, show that Turner was alive to the theory; but in these drawings he responds to the actual presence of a landscape that was pictorially valuable on the principle Gilpin had enunciated. Several are compositions of considerable intricacy, taken

27

from unexpected viewpoints and packing much visual information into a small space. Turner seems anxious to involve a broad spectrum of implications in his designs: he is not content to single out one important feature, as in the usual topographical practice, but seeks to show the dramatic interrelationship of several ideas in one scene.

His exercises at the Royal Academy Schools will undoubtedly have led him to attach importance to grandeur of conception, whether or not it had an immediate bearing on

8 The rising squall – Hot Wells, from St. Vincent's rock, Bristol 1791–2 ? R.A. 1793
Watercolour, pen and brownish ink over pencil, 359 × 410
City Museum and Art Gallery, Bristol (Cat. No. 18)

his current practice. He no doubt heard with fascination the last of Sir Joshua Reynolds's Discourses, delivered to a large audience on 10 December 1790, which the President shaped as a panegyric of Michelangelo, identifying Michelangelo's peculiar greatness with his capacity for grandeur. 'The

9 The Pantheon, the morning after the fire   R.A. 1792
Watercolour over pencil, 395 × 515
Trustees of the British Museum, London (T.B., IX-A)   (Cat. No. 27)

sublime in painting', he said, 'as in poetry, so overpowers, and takes such possession of the whole mind, that no room is left for attention to minute criticism.'[23] The notion of 'overpowering' the spectator was emphatically a central one for the academic artists of the time: grandeur—usually in the context of human actions and emotions—was considered the keynote of serious and universal art. The term used by Reynolds, 'Sublime', had been current in art criticism since the beginning of the century, but had been freshly defined in 1757 by Edmund Burke[24] as denoting a quality in perceived objects appealing to the emotions of fear and astonishment, in contradistinction to beauty, which evokes feelings of love and pleasure. Burke applied it to all experience, but it came to have special significance in connection with the visual arts and, with the help of Gilpin and his theory of the Picturesque, the 'Sublime' was enrolled in the critical terminology of landscape appreciation. The 'Picturesque' was a more self-consciously 'aesthetic' theory, applicable mainly to painting; it was not so much an alternative to the 'Sublime' as a preliminary stage towards its stronger connotations of emotional significance, and its implication of a profound emotional response. In the arts this response might be

29

10 Edward Dayes (1763–1804)
Buckingham House, St. James's Park 1790
Watercolour, 395 × 648
Victoria and Albert Museum, London

represented directly by means of human figures, undergoing the Sublime experience on behalf of the spectator, or by means of heightened atmosphere: deep, sombre colours, violent contrasts of light and darkness, and design on a large scale are the features listed by Burke as being most conducive to the required effect.

These were all characteristics that Turner's work was to assume within the decade. But for the time being he did not attempt to show drawings that departed more than slightly from the central purpose of his practice. Two views of the Avon appeared in 1793—perhaps the fruit of his second visit to Bristol in 1792; but, if the work now identified as the exhibited *Rising squall—Hot Wells, from St. Vincent's rock Bristol* Pl.8 really was that shown in 1793, it seems likely that it and its companion were actually executed after the first visit, in 1791. The *Rising squall* is typical of his work of that year: the sinuous life of the figures in the *Archbishop's palace, Lambeth* now pervades the entire design.

In particular the trees are informed by a nervous, wriggling movement that demonstrates Turner's intense creative response to them, even while he handles them in terms of simple formulas. Similar movement is to be found in cloud formations, and the outlines of the cliffs. The buildings in the centre of the composition are given prominence by the clear contrasts of wash that Turner uses at this date to model his architecture in sunlight. What is important is that the life he infuses into the subject is one of *design:* he creates by bringing components together in an active and stimulating pattern, rather than by capturing faithfully the true appearance of things. The boat seen in silhouette at the right of the drawing is a formal convention, treated as such; yet its lines partake of the cheerful movement of the whole subject. These rhythms are Turner's own: it is here that we see his inclination to construct his scenes as works of art, not as reproductions of nature. The force of his picture is the force that his creative interpretation brings to a traditional scheme, not the penetrating accuracy of an artist seeing the subject unprejudiced by precedent.

11 Interior of the ruined refectory of St. Martin's Priory, Dover *c.* 1793
Watercolour, 249 × 174
Victoria and Albert Museum, London (Cat. No. 35)

12 St. Anselm's chapel, with part of Thomas-à-Becket's crown, Canterbury Cathedral R.A. 1794
Pencil and watercolour, 517 × 374
Whitworth Art Gallery, University of Manchester (Cat. No. 55)

31

13 Llanthony Abbey 1794
Pencil and watercolour, 327 × 424
Trustees of the British Museum, London (T.B., XXVII-R) (Cat. No. 65)

14 John Robert Cozens (1752–97)
The Pays de Valais c. 1780
Watercolour over pencil, 362 × 521
Yale Center for British Art, Paul Mellon Collection

By the close of 1792 this somewhat rococo style had almost vanished. Its bright colours—clear blues and yellows, with red frequently introduced in the figures—were renounced in favour of a more restricted palette of grey-greens, pale blue and black, which suggests that in the course of the year Turner had come decisively into contact with the drawings of Edward Dayes.[25] There is an indication that the large watercolour views of London that Dayes had been producing since the late 1780s had already made their mark on him in the view of *The Pantheon, the morning after the fire* that he showed at the Academy in 1792. Although the presence of Malton is still felt here, a larger comprehension, a greater breadth of idea is apparent than anything in Malton's work: the foreground contains numerous figures, large in scale, and of great importance in the design as as whole. They provide a human contrast to the architecture of the burnt-out building, which catches the pink glow of the morning sun and sparkles with the icicles that have formed after its drenching from the firemen's hoses. The watercolour is a complex production embodying many of Turner's enduring interests, and displaying both the sympathy with human life and the sensitivity to effects of light[26] that were to become the mainsprings of his art. He was already aware of the broader implications of the subjects with which topographers dealt, and could organize an elaborate composition to express them. Not only are there echoes of Dayes's London scenes—*Buckingham House,* of 1790,[27] for instance—but the vigour of the subject can

Pl. 9

Pl. 10

15 Thomas Hearne (1744–1817)
Wooded glen at Downton, Herefordshire
Pen and black ink and brown wash, 320 × 350
Victoria and Albert Museum, London (2933–1876)

16 Worcester Cathedral, west front c. 1794–5
Watercolour, with some pencil, 419 × 318
Trustees of the British Museum, London (Henderson Bequest)
(Cat. No. 67)

34

17 The interior of the ruins of Tintern Abbey 1794
Pencil and watercolour, 360 × 255
Trustees of the British Museum, London (T.B., XXIII-A) (not in catalogue)

18 Christ Church, Oxford *c.* 1794
Watercolour over pencil, 321 × 426
Trustees of the British Museum, London (Henderson Bequest) (Cat. No. 71)

19 Tewkesbury *c.* 1794
Watercolour over pencil, 307 × 415 (sight)
Private collection (Cat. No. 63)

perhaps be traced back to similar works by Thomas Rowlandson, and in particular to the famous *Vauxhall Gardens* that Rowlandson showed at the Academy in 1784.[28]

In June 1792 Turner made a journey to South Wales and the Wye valley, making pencil drawings[29] that display a tightness and precision that had not previously been apparent in his sketches; watercolours relating to the tour[30] are handled with a similar neatness and restraint. The sense of movement remains in the flicker of foliage or the rush of water, but these effects are achieved by short strokes of a brush dipped in muted greens and blues, and by a freer, rather calligraphic touching in of outline and foreground detail with pure black. The large drawings that he completed for commissions or for the Academy's walls share the mood of restraint, and demonstrate what the pencil studies corroborate—that Turner was still giving great attention to the drawing of architecture, in which he improved remarkably at this point. Two examples shown at the Academy in 1794, the *Inside of Tintern Abbey, Monmouthshire,*[31] and the view of *St. Anselm's chapel, with part of Thomas-à-Becket's crown, Canterbury* Pl.12 *Cathedral,* are both accomplished architectural studies, and splendidly dramatic compositions. They have the rather blue coloration of the smaller studies of the time, and Malton's influence survives most noticeably in the choice of viewpoint—a low one that ensures dramatic effects of soaring Pl.6 masonry and steep perspective.[32]

By 1793 Turner had become associated with Dr. Thomas Monro, and in the following year began to go to evening classes at Monro's domestic 'academy'[33] where he worked with his exact contemporary, Thomas Girtin.[34] Girtin's training had taken place partly in the studio of Dayes, whose influence on both artists was strong enough at this point to render their work very similar, a likeness no doubt increased by their association over the desks of Monro, where 'Girtin

20 Melincourt waterfall, near Abergarnedd 1795
Pencil, partially finished in watercolour, 262 × 198
Trustees of the British Museum, London (T.B., XXVI-8) (not in catalogue)

21 Extensive view from a hill, with an artist sketching 1795
Pencil and watercolour, 198 × 262
Trustees of the British Museum, London (T.B., XXIV-51) (not in catalogue)

22 Cathedral Church at Lincoln R.A. 1795
Watercolour over pencil, 450 × 350
Trustees of the British Museum, London (Henderson Bequest) (Cat. No. 124)

37

drew the outlines and Turner washed in the effects',[35] as they made copies from the work of Monro's favourite artists. Among these were Thomas Hearne[36] and John Robert Cozens,[37] who both favoured the muted palette used by Dayes; Hearne also practised a certain very recognizable mannerism when painting foliage, employing disjunct strokes of the brush to build up form almost as though it were made of bricks; this was a feature of Turner's style in 1793 and 1794. Cozens, far from making forms more solid, was renowned for dissolving them in a wide, airy atmosphere replete with his own idiosyncratic mood of melancholy; but he too applied his sombre grey-greens and browns with small, parallel strokes of the brush to construct solid masses; these contrasted with the pale washes that he applied to his distances, and so gave him a very wide range of atmospheric articulation previously unavailable to the watercolourist. Turner's copies after Cozens are usually executed in Dayes-like blue and grey washes, sometimes in a wider palette, including green and ochre. They do not imitate Cozens's method of applying colour, and are often handled very broadly. However, he evidently learned something of the intention behind Cozens's technique, since in 1794 he made a powerful watercolour of *Llanthony Abbey* which exploits the open, asymmetrical composition that Cozens often made the vehicle for his ideas. It is based on a strong diagonal which can perhaps be seen as a reinterpretation of the steep perspective lines of Turner's Maltonian architectural subjects, but which is more expressive of wildness and the romantic 'Sublime' that was to preoccupy Turner later in the decade. The restricted range of blues, greens and greys is derived directly from Cozens, and the atmospheric content of the whole design approaches his poetic wistfulness, though Turner's nascent romanticism buds more energetically and positively; indeed he never, even in his copies, set himself to imitate precisely the unique mood of Cozens's work.[38]

Yet another remarkable change came over his watercolour style in the ensuing year: one of the drawings shown at the Academy in 1795, the *Cathedral Church at Lincoln*, achieves a subtlety of lighting that is wholly unlike the bland cool light of, say, the *Christ Church, Oxford* of the preceding year: it makes use of a new palette of umbers and ochres, and is generally more warm in tone than the works of 1794. Once again, Turner's understanding of architecture seems to attain a new pitch of insight, marked not only by the firmness and precision of drawing, but by a fresh sense of artistic licence: the towers and spires of the cathedral are made to rise more slimly and elegantly above the surrounding buildings than

they do in his preparatory studies. The figures, too, are more richly invented, and more exquisitely realized, from the stage-coach entering the city to the fine still-life of the earthenware stall in the left foreground. All these elements are handled with a sensitivity that can best be explained by the fact that Turner had by now begun to experiment with oil-paint. Thornbury relates a tradition that his first picture in that medium was a view of Rochester Castle executed in 1793; but it is more likely that he did not seriously come to grips with oil until at least 1794 or possibly 1795.[39]

What distinguishes the 1795 view of Lincoln, however, is its total accomplishment. It is not, like most of its predecessors, an interesting experiment: it is a masterly topographical watercolour in which Turner surpasses the achievements of his masters. He had already successfully imitated Hearne, Dayes and the others. Here he is entirely himself; at this date not even his precocious associate, Girtin, made drawings which present their subject as such a coherent totality, perceived in so many aspects and bound together by such subtle lighting. The sketchbooks of this year provide further evidence of the advance in Turner's sensibility.[40] They contain drawings in pencil that reflect the methods imparted by his sustained work as architectural draughtsman, forceful, yet modulated, and articulated by punctuations of dots, similar to, though less coarse than, the pencil style of Girtin. This style had been evolving out of his early, tentative essays since about 1792, and it may have received some reinforcement from the lessons of Monro, and Monro's friend the equally enthusiastic tutor-patron John Henderson, who gave his pupils drawings by Canaletto to copy: Canaletto's firm, rhythmic style of outline drawing seems to be reflected in their work, though they may have learned it through the medium of topographical designs by Joseph Farington whose outline is a somewhat staid adaptation of Canaletto's.[41] But it should be said that the well-meaning lessons provided by Monro and Henderson could hardly advance the development of an artist as innately exploratory as Turner. Indeed, the large quantities of surviving studies, mostly copies, suggest that a great deal of his time was uselessly engrossed in repetitious and trivial exercises.

At this moment Turner's apprenticeship to other artists comes to an end: henceforward he could create works of art on his own terms. In his search for the means of expressing a larger significance he moved naturally from the example of his immediate colleagues and contemporaries to the precedents set by greater masters both of the present and of the past.

23 Woolverhampton, Staffordshire R.A., 1796
Watercolour, 318 × 419
Art Gallery and Museum, Wolverhampton (Cat. No. 139)

NOTES

1 Thornbury, p. 8. Mr. Turner's interlocutor is supposed to have been Thomas Stothard, R.A. (1755–1834).

2 Cat. Nos 5–6.

3 Cat. Nos 1–4.

4 Thornbury, p. 9.

5 Thornbury, p. 14.

6 There is a set of engravings in Henry Boswell's *Picturesque Views of the Antiquities of England and Wales,* said to have been coloured by Turner at a rate of twopence apiece, while he was staying with his uncle at Brentford in 1786–7, now in Brentford Public Library. See R.A. 1974–5, No. B 7, and Finberg, *Life,* p. 14.

7 See Cosmo Monkhouse, in *Dictionary of National Biography, LVII,* 1899.

8 Thornbury, p. 27. Paul Sandby, topographical watercolourist, 1725–1809.

9 The copies are in the Turner Bequest. For a discussion of them see Finberg, *Turner's Sketches and Drawings,* pp. 6–9.

10 T.B., I-D, H. The copies are derived from plates in William Gilpin's *Observations relative chiefly to Picturesque Beauty, made in the year 1772, on several parts of England; particularly the Mountains and Lakes of Cumberland, and Westmoreland,* 1786, vol. II, pp. 85, 227. It will be noted that this book was a very recent publication. Gilpin's illustrations were often, like the examples copied by Turner, oval, and they created a vogue for drawings of this shape which were reproduced in many of the 'Picturesque Tours' of the period. His early familiarity with these designs may have been recalled when, towards the end of his life, Turner painted several compositions making use of a circular format.

11 'Essay on Picturesque Beauty', in *Three Essays,* 2nd ed., 1794, p. 6.

12 T.B. I-E. Pietro Fabris (active *c.* 1768–78) worked in Naples but exhibited in London. Sandby aquatinted several of his views.

13 Thomas Malton, 1748–1804.

14 Thomas Hardwick, 1752–1829. Hardwick's son, Philip (1792–1870), became a Royal Academician and a good friend of Turner's; he was present at his funeral.

15 William Porden, 1755–1822. See Thornbury, p. 27, where the descriptions of drawings showing buildings with 'Grecian porches' and 'composite pediments' apply well to the architectural work that Turner was doing in the late 1790s (see Cat. section V(b) and Nos 328, 329). Finberg, *Life,* p. 16, note, correctly observes that Turner did not make these early architectural drawings in the capacity of a student of architecture: he was an architectural draughtsman then, as he was to remain for several years: his job was to make views, not elevations.

16 T.B., V is a collection of eighteen studies made at the 'Plaster Academy' between July 1790 and October 1793. For a list of the Academy's collection of casts see Joseph Baretti, *A Guide through the Royal Academy,* 1781. In 1791–2 Turner made some anatomical studies, T.B. X-A, B; he entered the Life Class in November 1792; eleven studies from the nude are in the Bequest, T.B., XVIII, but Finberg (*Inventory*) doubted whether more than four of these were actually by Turner.

17 The sketchbook is now in the Princeton Art Museum; it contains 81 leaves, of which many are blank. An inscription on the first page reads: 'The Sketch Book—of J. M. W. Turner—London as it was left at—Mr. Narraways—Bristol about 1790 or 1791'. Thomas Gainsborough, 1727–88; Jacob van Ruysdael, *c.* 1628–82.

18 See e.g. the *Oxford* sketchbook (T.B., II), *passim.*

19 John Ruskin, 'The Two Boyhoods', in *Modern Painters; Works,* VII, pp. 374–88. The passage asserts only that Turner 'not only could endure, but enjoyed and looked for *litter,* like Covent Garden wreck after the market'; and that he learned 'understanding of and regard for the poor'. As Ruskin saw, this might explain the pleasure that Turner always took in rendering the 'vulgar' aspects of humanity. He did not claim that Turner ever drew Covent Garden; but it would be reasonable to suppose that such an interest would have resulted in at least some preserved drawings. Similarly, the love of ships and the sea that pervaded Turner's work did not lead him to draw the activity on the nearby Thames; but see Lindsay, *J. M. W. Turner,* 1966, p. 15.

20 In the context of Turner's early attraction to natural as opposed to urban subjects, note Thornbury's report (p. 12) that 'old schoolfellows of Turner's used to say that his first attempts at art had been drawings of birds and flowers and trees from the schoolroom windows'. It would be rash to attach too much significance to these stock tales of an artist's early essays, however.

21 T.B., III-A.

22 T.B., VI-3 to 6; and Cat. No. 15.

23 Robert R. Wark, ed., *The Discourses of Sir Joshua Reynolds,* 1975, p. 276. Joshua Reynolds, 1723–92.

24 Edmund Burke, *A Philosophical Enquiry into the Origin of our Ideas of the Sublime and Beautiful,* 1757.

25 Edward Dayes, 1763–1804. Gage, 1969, p. 26, suggests that it was Turner's new interest in sketching in colour from nature that led to his using a more subdued palette; but the colouring of these works of late

1792 is itself artificially selective, suggesting that Turner was following a suggestion offered by another artist; this would be in keeping with his practice hitherto. It is not until the Midland tour of 1794 that we find strong evidence of Turner using colour to record what he found in nature.

26 An expressive colour study of the interior of the ruins is T.B., IX-B, repr. Gage, 1969, Pl. 1; and see comments there, p. 23.

27 The figures are unusually prominent in this drawing: Dayes's other London views employ staffage rather more on the scale of Malton's.

28 Thomas Rowlandson, 1756–1827. The drawing is in the Victoria and Albert Museum, London, P13-1967, repr. John Hayes, *Rowlandson: Watercolours and Drawings*, 1972, Pls. 16, 17. The influence of Rowlandson's characteristic swirling line is perhaps to be detected in Turner's energetic drawings of 1790–1—the *Rising squall*, discussed above, p. 30, for instance.

29 T.B., XII, XIII. These are all loose sheets, with pencil drawings occasionally touched with colour. It has been proposed that a Journal of a tour in North Wales, dated 1792, is evidence that Turner travelled in that region at this early date (see R.A. 1974, No. B8). The journal is in the Pierpont Morgan Library, New York. But it is clearly not the product of a young member of the lower middle class with an exceptionally intense visual receptivity; it can probably be discounted as a piece of 'Turneriana'.

30 E.g. Cat. Nos 43–7.

31 Cat. No. 57.

32 Typical examples of Malton's characteristic approach to his architectural subject-matter are to be found in the plates that he etched for his *Picturesque Tour through London and Westminster,* published in 1792, but with plates dated to several other years in the decade.

33 Dr. Thomas Monro, 1759–1833, medical adviser to George III and principal physician to Bethlem Hospital. For a brief but reliable biography of Monro see F. J. G. Jefferiss, Introduction to the exhibition catalogue *Dr. Monro and his Academy,* Victoria and Albert Museum, 1976. For a discussion of Monro's influence on Turner's early drawing style see Gage, 'Turner and the Picturesque', 1965, pp. 21–2.

34 See Girtin and Loshak, 1954, p. 28; and F. Hawcroft, *Thomas Girtin,* exhibition catalogue, 1975.

35 Joseph Farington, *Diary,* 11 November 1798.

36 Thomas Hearne, 1744–1817.

37 John Robert Cozens, 1752–97. See A. P. Oppé, *Alexander and John Robert Cozens,* 1952, and F. Hawcroft, *John Robert Cozens,* exhibition catalogue, 1971.

38 Finberg, *Life,* p. 38, points out that Turner's copies after Cozens are 'not even partial fulfilments of the pictorial ideas adumbrated in Cozens's sketches... They transpose Cozens's topographical material into an entirely different atmosphere of thought and feeling.'

39 P20 is a self-portrait dated in Butlin and Joll, *The Paintings of J. M. W. Turner,* 1977, to *c.* 1793; there is little internal evidence for its being a work by Turner, and we rely on the picture's provenance for its authentication. The view at Rochester to which Thornbury refers (p. 45) is untraced, but tentatively dated by Butlin and Joll (P. 21) to about 1794. It was described by Thomas Miller in *Turner and Girtin's Picturesque Views,* 1854, p. xxvii, as 'carefully but thinly painted, in just the manner one might suppose a water-colour artist would paint'. He nevertheless saw in it a strong similarity with the work of de Loutherbourg, whose style was not at all that of a 'water-colour artist'. Thornbury also, inconsistently, talks (p. 44) of Turner's 'first attempt in oil, from a sketch in crayon, of a sunset on the Thames, near the Red House, Battersea'. He dates this to 1795. Butlin and Joll (No. P2) suggest it is a misrecollection on the part of Thornbury's informant of the *Moonlight, a study at Millbank* shown at the Royal Academy in 1797. The change of Turner's style as a watercolourist in 1796 strongly suggests that it was not until that year or very shortly before that he took up painting in oil.

40 The *Isle of Wight,* the *Smaller South Wales,* and the *South Wales* sketchbooks (T.B., XXIV, XXV, XXVI). For a detailed study of the *South Wales* book see Finberg, Walpole Society, vols. III, pp. 87–97, and VI, pp. 95–103.

41 John Henderson, 1764–1834. Henderson owned a house close to Monro's in the Adelphi and organized copying activities similar to those of Monro's 'academy'. Joseph Farington, 1747–1821. Farington was a pupil of Richard Wilson, 1714–82. For Wilson see W. G. Constable, *Richard Wilson,* London, 1953. Antonio Canaletto, 1697–1768.

Chapter Two

Oil and Watercolour

The watercolours that Turner exhibited at the Academy in 1796 display a wider range of subject-matter and technical resource than his annual entries had ever done before. *Landaff*

Pl.24 *Cathedral* represents the perfection of the genre at which he had worked since 1790; other drawings break fresh ground.

Pl.25 The three interiors, *St. Erasmus in Bishop Islip's Chapel, Internal of a cottage, a study at Ely,* and *Trancept and Choir of Ely Minster,* mark a departure from the almost invariable open daylight of his previous work—though there are, of course, exceptions

Pl.11 to this, notably the *St. Martin's Priory, Dover* of 1793.[1] But whereas the rare earlier essays in interior lighting are limited in intention to record single effects, these exhibited works of 1796 reveal a new and more complex response. In terms of composition, the *St. Erasmus* (a view inside Westminster Abbey) is a development of the *Interior of Tintern* of 1794, making use of Malton's steep perspective.[2] The drama that Turner creates in this drawing, however, is conditioned by his use of chiaroscuro: the subtle control of light on masonry that distinguishes the *Lincoln* and the *Landaff* exteriors is extended to comprehend a continuum of light and shadow on everything that the viewer sees. The diagonals of the perspective are set off against opposing diagonals of light, so that the whole design is constructed on a soaring arch-shape that echoes the airy gothic structure it represents. The theme is repeated in two similar drawings shown at the Academy in successive years—the views of the interior of Ely Cathedral,[3] which are almost identical except that the light falls from opposite directions. That he should have repeated such a subject on commission is not surprising; that he exhibited the repetition indicates his strong interest in the theme that he explores differently in each.

In view of the great sophistication of his treatment of exterior lighting in the *Lincoln* and *Landaff* drawings, it is possible that Turner would have progressed naturally to this new stage of his development without prompting from

24   Landaff Cathedral, South Wales   R.A. 1796
Pencil and watercolour, 357 × 258
Trustees   of   the   British   Museum,   London   (T.B., XXVIII-A)
(Cat. No. 143)

43

PI.30 outside sources; but he had by this time probably had an opportunity to look at drawings by the Swiss artist Abraham-Louis Ducros, and etchings by the great Italian architectural engraver Giovanni Battista Piranesi:[4] the work of both was much admired and collected by Sir Richard Colt Hoare of Stourhead, Wiltshire, who became a patron of Turner in about 1795. It has been suggested that Turner first visited Stourhead in that year; this would certainly explain his sudden interest in architectural interiors, which are a recurrent and prominent theme of Ducros and Piranesi.[5] The *Internal of a cottage* is not explicable in this way. Both Piranesi and Ducros, in their distinctive ways, were topographical artists; whereas this drawing is treated simply as a domestic interior, with strong warm colouring and rich chiaroscuro set off by precisely rendered details. The mood here is Dutch,

and Turner's model would appear to be some Rembrandtesque genre painter such as Nicholas Maes.[6] An item in the Turner Bequest, probably dating from about 1790, which shows a *Cottage interior by firelight*, is an elaborate early PI.4 treatment of a similar theme, and indicates that Turner had been interested in such subjects from the beginning. It is, however, presented as a piece of sentimental genre, with children and a cat, based on the rustic cottage pieces of artists like Wheatley and William Redmore Bigg, or on the night scenes of Joseph Wright of Derby.[7] It is perhaps the most direct anticipation in his juvenile work of the theme and

26 Fishermen at sea ('The Cholmeley Sea Piece') R.A. 1796
Oil on canvas, 915 × 1224
Tate Gallery, London (Cat. No. P1)

inspiration of the first oil-painting that he exhibited, which
appeared on the Academy's walls in 1796.

The implications of these watercolour interiors were
pursued still further in the work submitted in 1797; reference
has already been made to Turner's repetition of his Ely

27 Rembrandt van Rijn (1606–69)
Holy Family resting on the Flight into Egypt 1647
Oil on canvas, 340 × 480
National Gallery of Ireland, Dublin

28 Trancept of Ewenny Priory, Glamorganshire R.A. 1797
Watercolour and scratching-out over pencil, 400 × 559
National Museum of Wales, Cardiff (Cat. No. 227)

29 Giovanni Battista Piranesi (1720–78)
The So-Called Villa of Maecenas at Tivoli. Interior 1764
(Hind 73)
Engraving, 470 × 620

30 Abraham-Louis-Rodolphe Ducros (1748–1810)
Ruins on the Forum Romanum with a view of the Colosseum
Watercolour with pen and black ink over pencil, 530 × 740
Yale Center for British Art, Paul Mellon Collection

31 Thomas Girtin (1775–1802)
Julian's Baths, Hotel de Cluny, Paris
Watercolour, 324 × 232
Messrs. Spink & Son Ltd., London

32 Copy after Vernet 1797
Watercolour with pen and ink and body-colour on grey paper prepared
with brown wash, 116 × 178
Trustees of the British Museum, London (T.B., XXXVII, 104–5) (not in
catalogue)

33 Claude-Joseph Vernet (1714–89)
A storm with a shipwreck 1754
Oil on canvas, 860 × 1360
Wallace Collection, London

47

34 Hubert's Tower, Fountains Abbey   1797
Pencil partly finished in watercolour, 371 × 261
Trustees of the British Museum, London (T.B., XXXV-80) (not in catalogue)

Cathedral subject. The first two of his long series of drawings of Salisbury Cathedral and town,[8] for Colt Hoare, appeared this year, and plainly took up the hint supplied by Hoare's Ducros and Piranesi collections: they are even grander in conception than the *St. Erasmus,* and prelude some of Turner's largest watercolours, which appeared later in the decade. The Rembrandtian suggestions of the *Internal of a cottage* were given fuller expression in a fourth subject, *Trancept of Ewenny Priory, Glamorganshire,* which does not appear to have been done on commission, and indeed bears all the signs of having been 'invented' specifically to enable Turner to explore the themes that interested him at the time. Its dark, enclosed space, arched over like a Roman tomb or temple such as Turner might have seen in Piranesi's work,[9] is shot through with limited shafts of light, taking a step further the dramatic contrast of the Westminster and Ely drawings by introducing two separate light sources, as he had done in his oil-painting of the year before.

Pl.28

Pl.29

The central themes of his watercolours at this time were then those that he took up in oil. But the necessity for the new medium was deeper and stronger than that of mere technical insufficiency: the decisive factors were the contemporary status of oil-painting versus that of watercolour, and Turner's fundamental ambition. Just as his early drawings were composed as 'pictures', and not simply as 'views', so, now, the crucial stimulus came from works of art rather than from the exigencies of practice. Another anecdote hints at this: Turner was looking over some prints with a friend, who reported: '"This," said Turner, with emotion, taking up a particular one, "made me a painter." It was a green *mezzotinto,* a Vandervelde—an upright; a single vessel running the wind and bearing up bravely against the waves.'[10] The print in question seems to have been one by Elisha Kirkall,[11] whose characteristic green-ink mezzotints after marine paintings were fairly common in eighteenth-century London. Turner's remark is significant. It suggests that there is a distinction to be made between the awakening of a visual interest in, say, sailing-ships such as he saw on the Thames in his youth, and the impulse to create works of art out of that material. The anecdote is undoubtedly corroborated by the fact that Turner's first exhibited oil-painting at the Royal Academy was a sea-piece, like a large proportion of his paintings over

35 Buttermere Lake with part of Cromackwater, Cumberland, a shower   R.A. 1798
Oil on canvas, 915 × 1220
Turner Bequest, Tate Gallery, London   (Cat. No. P7)

36 Dunstanborough Castle *c.* 1798
Pencil, brush and black ink, watercolour and body-colour on buff paper, 200 × 277
Trustees of the British Museum, London (T.B., XXXIII-S) (not in catalogue)

38 Dunstanburgh Castle, N.E. coast of Northumberland. Sun-rise after a squally night   R.A. 1798
Oil on canvas, 920 × 1230
National Gallery of Victoria, Melbourne, Australia   (Cat. No. P6)

37 Study of Kirkstall Refectory   1797
Pencil and some watercolour, 208 × 270
Trustees of the British Museum, London (T.B., XXXIV-10v) (not in catalogue)

39 Refectory of Kirkstall Abbey, Yorkshire   R.A. 1798
Watercolour over pencil, 448 × 651
Sir John Soane's Museum, London   (Cat. No. 234)

PI.26 the next five years.[12] We might even associate the pervasive dark green tonality of *Fishermen at sea* with the ink colour favoured by Kirkall. Turner had not previously shown any marine views, although several drawings among his earlier work indicate that ships, sailors, fishermen and coastal scenes had always interested him.[13]

But the oil-painting that appeared on the Academy's walls in 1796 was not by any means a translation into the new

medium of one of these subjects: it is a night scene, with a full moon appearing behind wind-torn clouds and casting a silvery glimmer on the heaving surface of the dark-green water. In the boat which is the focus of the composition a lantern is burning. The scheme of lighting is, in fact, closer to the strong chiaroscuro of the architectural interiors that Turner was beginning to produce in watercolours at the same date than to that in any of his previous outdoor subjects.

40 Harewood House, from the south-east   1798
Pencil and watercolour, 474 × 645
Coll.: The Earl of Harewood, Harewood House, Leeds (Cat. No. 217)

Like the interiors, *Fishermen at sea* is an intellectual exercise in which Turner is strongly conscious of precedents. It is not, perhaps, directly indebted to Rembrandt, although Rembrandt's use of light and shade must have been in his mind:[14] it is a *bravura* 'effect' piece in which examples by men such as Joseph Vernet, Philippe Jacques de Loutherbourg[15] and Joseph Wright suggest themselves. Wright was the foremost exponent in England of the vogue for 'Moonlights' and he came closer than any of his English contemporaries to the execution of the continental artists Vernet and de Loutherbourg. What is perhaps most striking about Turner's canvas is the professionalism of its technique, the smoothness and firmness with which the paint is handled, and a general lack of emphasis on the texture and expressive quality of the

medium itself. At about this time Turner began to study the work of the Welsh landscape painter Richard Wilson,[16] and shortly afterwards to imitate his *facture;* we must suppose that the use of a more 'continental' manner in his night-piece was a deliberate exercise, a conscious striving after polish. *Fishermen at sea* is extraordinarily free of the 'painterly' effects common to the work of most English painters in oil; but if Turner thought it desirable *en passant* to master the more disciplined style of Vernet, he evidently did not regard that

Pl.33

41   Aeneas and the Sibyl, Lake Avernus   *c.* 1798
Oil on canvas, 765 × 985
Turner Bequest, Tate Gallery, London   (Cat. No. P34)

style as the most suitable to his needs. We find it again—in a form closer to the idiom of Wright—in the painting shown at the Academy in 1797 under the title *Moonlight, a study at Millbank;*[17] but, thereafter, surviving works show what amounts to a rejection of careful, smooth finish for a bolder use of paint, a greater richness of impasto and increased compatibility of handling and mood.

42   Richard Wilson   (1714–82)
Apollo and the Seasons ? R.A. 1779
Oil on canvas, 1001 × 1257
Syndics of the Fitzwilliam Museum, Cambridge

43 Kilgarran castle on the Twyvey; hazy sunrise, previous to a sultry day R.A. 1799
Oil on canvas, 920 × 1220
National Trust (on loan to Wordsworth's house, Cockermouth) (Cat. No. P11)

45 Inside of the chapter house of Salisbury Cathedral
R.A. 1799
Pencil and watercolour, with scraping-out, 640 × 510
Whitworth Art Gallery, University of Manchester (Cat. No. 199)

44 Kilgarren Castle c. 1798
Watercolour, 267 × 365 (sight)
City Art Gallery, Manchester (Cat. No. 243)

46 Caernarvon Castle at sunset c. 1798
Pen and black ink, watercolour and body-colour on blue paper prepared with a reddish-brown wash, 138 × 215
Trustees of the British Museum, London (T.B., XLIII-39v) (not in catalogue)

47   Caernarvon castle   R.A. 1799
Watercolour over pencil, 570 × 825
Private collection   (Cat. No. 254)

Two pictures exhibited at the Academy in 1798 show that by that date Turner's manner had already absorbed the lessons of Richard Wilson. He had begun to make notes of pictures by Wilson and Vernet in a small sketchbook which probably belongs to the previous year, or even earlier:[18] it includes a series of studies of fishermen in their boats, made at Brighton, which may be connected with the *Fishermen at sea,* and drawings showing a wide variety of subjects—interiors,

snow scenes, sunsets, animal studies, landscapes. All the pages are washed over with a reddish-brown ground, and many of the sketches are made in a mixture of watercolour and body-colour (gouache). This book shows Turner revising his method of painting in watercolour in the light of his experience of oil, which taught him that greater tonal range and sonority can be obtained by working up towards highlights from a dark ground than by increasing the density of transparent pigments on white paper. The book also tells us that he was looking at the work of Vernet and Wilson at about the same time—an important point: in the painting of *Aeneas and the Sibyl,* which must have been executed about Pl.41 1798, he imitates not only the subject-matter of Wilson but Pl.42

also his handling of paint. The picture was based on a drawing provided by Sir Richard Colt Hoare, who seems to have requested a 'replacement' or pendant to his own Wilson, a view of *Lake Nemi*,[19] and it would have been quite in character for Turner deliberately to set himself to imitate Wilson's style. *Aeneas and the Sibyl* is his first deliberate attempt to speak that classical language in a finished picture, and foreshadows a major and lifelong preoccupation, but it does not find a natural place among the paintings of English landscapes that he showed at the Academy in 1798 and 1799, which pursue the 'Picturesque Sublime' of the northern counties, and avoid figures altogether. These, in their handling, depart from the manner of earlier pictures; they are rougher in finish, and the texture of the paint is employed in

48   Claude Lorrain   (1600–82)
Seaport: Embarkation of the Queen of Sheba   1648
Oil on canvas, 1486 × 1937
National Gallery, London

concert with resonant colour to evoke rugged scenery and the flickering play of light over wild country.

Most of the material for these pictures was gathered during a series of tours to the north of England and to North Wales. In 1796, presumably on account of his preoccupation with

49   Cader Idris: detail   *c.* 1799
Watercolour, 578 × 788
Private collection   (Cat. No. 259)

50 A canal tunnel near Leeds c. 1799
Watercolour, pen and brown ink, 241 × 400
Coll.: Richard Ivor, London   (Cat. No. 325)

oil-painting, Turner does not seem to have travelled far afield;[20] but in the following year he went to Yorkshire, Northumberland and the Lake District, and the journey yielded several important subjects, many of them chosen not for the sake of topographical or antiquarian connotations—although an appreciable number were evidently picked with the market for traditional watercolours in mind—but rather as offering scope for the expression of more personal feeling. Already the borderline between oil-painting and watercolour in Turner's work is not clearly defined: of the pictures that appeared in the Academy in 1798 four were in oil, six in watercolour, but the subject-matter of both groups was very similar. The watercolour of the *Refectory of Kirkstall Abbey, Yorkshire* is a development of the architectural chiaroscuro of *Ewenny Priory; Buttermere Lake with part of Cromackwater, Cumberland, a shower,* on the other hand, is an oil-painting which had been stated in its essentials as a watercolour study in one of the sketchbooks;[21] and *Dunstan-*

Pl.39

Pl.35

burgh Castle, N.E. coast of Northumberland. Sun-rise after a squally night, also an oil-painting, is associated with a group of vigorous experiments in wash and body-colour which make use of rough, toned paper and broad handling, so that they take on something of the character of oil sketches. This blending of intention and function is well illustrated by the *Academical* sketchbook,[22] of 1798, the year in which Turner first visited the country of Richard Wilson—North Wales.[23] Like the *Wilson* sketchbook, this one demonstrates a particular concern with medium and is of blue paper washed over with a red-brown tone. The drawings are in a variety of media: pen and ink, chalks, watercolour, body-colour, all used in combinations that are unexpected and highly original. A Wilson-like landscape[24] makes use of a rich body-colour,

Pl.38

Pl.36

51 Dolbadern Castle *c.* 1799
Pencil and watercolour, 677 × 972
Trustees of the British Museum, London (T.B., LXX-O) (not in catalogue)

heavily laid on in a brilliant chromatic scheme; and there is a series of studies of Caernarvon Castle[25] which cover an extraordinary gamut: from a subdued blue wash heightened with startling white body-colour to an elaborate co-ordina-tion of yellow, ochre and golden brown, in which the colours are applied thickly on their reddish-brown ground as if in deliberate imitation of the effect of oil. Just such an effect is tried out in an oil sketch on panel of the same subject and of the same size;[26] and Turner appears to be undecided as to whether the finished version of the design should be in the medium of watercolour or of oil. In fact, it appeared at the Academy in 1799 as a large watercolour, shot through with the hot glow of an orange sunset, the dark forms of castle and ships palpitating with partially reflected light to form a romantic vision of sunlight that transcends any previous attempts at this by Turner himself, or by Wilson, and which directly evokes the heroic sunset harbours of Claude Lorrain,

Pl.46

Pl.47

Pl.48

57

who had evolved a standard type of ideal landscape in Rome in the seventeenth century.[27]

Pl.43 Perhaps the most striking aspect of the identical nature of the intention of the paintings and watercolours at this time is their uncanny visual similarity. The painting of *Kilgarran castle on the Twyvey; hazy sunrise, previous to a sultry day,* which hung in the same exhibition as the *Caernarvon,* is handled with a characteristic use of rounded blobs of paint, somewhat flattened with the palette-knife so that they create linked patterns of rich lights across the principal masses. The effect is derived, evidently, from Wilson's handling of the medium, and is a mark of Turner's skill in manipulating paint both to inform and to express. What is curious is that he evolved a means of reproducing a precisely similar effect in watercolour. The exact method of producing these areas of highlight is described in a report by Farington, dated 1804: 'The lights are made out by drawing a pencil [brush] with water in it over the parts intended to be light (a general ground of dark colour having been laid where required) and

52 Caernarvon castle, North Wales R.A. 1800
Watercolour, 663 × 994
Trustees of the British Museum, London (T.B., LXX-M) (Cat. No. 263)

raising the colour so damped by the pencil by means of *blotting paper;* after which with crumbs of bread the parts are cleared. ...A rich draggy appearance may be obtained by passing a camel Hair pencil *nearly dry* over them, which only *flirts* the damp on the part so touched and by blotting paper the lights are shown partially.'[28]

The procedure can be observed in the watercolour that Turner made of the Kilgarren subject at about the same time Pl.44 as the painting, and in other finished watercolours. Although the effect is comparable with that of the oil-paintings, it was achieved by wholly different means—means appropriate to watercolour. It was in fact a brilliant technical invention, which enabled Turner to work in watercolour with the breadth and freedom of oil, but without sacrificing the

53 South view of the Gothic Abbey (Evening) now building at Fonthill, the seat of W. Beckford, Esq. R.A. 1800
Watercolour, 724 × 1060
Montreal Museum of Fine Arts, Quebec (Cat. No. 337)

Pl.51 integrity of the medium. A study such as that of Dolbadern Castle, in which the device is used very boldly, has something of the appearance of a free oil sketch, but retains its identity as a watercolour. It recalls Farington's remark that 'Turner has no settled process but drives the colours about till he has expressed the idea in his mind.'[29] These devices as such are of only minor importance; their significance lies in the fact that they point to Turner's determination, not to abandon watercolour in favour of the 'nobler' and more versatile medium of oil, but to forge a new way with watercolour which would make it equally noble and versatile and equally capable of bearing complex and weighty themes.

This is a more decisive development than it at first sight seems. The language of watercolour had been undergoing radical modifications at the hands of artists other than Turner during the decade. Colt Hoare claimed that his own favourite Ducros had decisively influenced the technical advances of English watercolour; he was able to point to Turner as an artist who had specifically benefited from Ducros's example.[30] But the problem that Turner confronted, that of forcing the medium to express the increasing emotional power that landscape commanded for his generation, was paralleled by the need felt by all practitioners of watercolour who exhibited at the Academy: not only was it necessary for them to render the medium as strong as possible in comparison with oil; they were tempted to adopt the subject-matter of oil-paintings as well. Artists as varied as Richard Westall[31] and Thomas Girtin used a range of Pl.31 subdued, harmonizing colour to create sonorous patterns conveying the grandeur of the 'Sublime'. It is worth recalling that Burke specified 'sad and fuscous colours, as black or

54 View over a valley 1801
Pencil, charcoal and white body-colour on white paper prepared with a grey wash, 305 × 479
Trustees of the British Museum, London (T.B., LVIII-6) (not in catalogue)

brown, or deep purple and the like' as those most readily associated with the 'Sublime'.[32] Turner followed a parallel path in the same years, although his 'Sublime' colour is much more varied than Girtin's: the large view of *Cader Idris*, for example, is based on a strong, dense blue, which dominates the whole design, and is enlivened with touches of bright red and yellow. The powerful harmonies of orange and brown in the Claudian *Caernarvon Castle*, already discussed, can also be seen as an exercise in the same mode. In addition to this wider and more inventive use of colour, Turner, in works like *Cader Idris*, presents a conception of the watercolour as a public work of art quite different from the still essentially intimate style of Girtin. It was his unique achievement to evolve what amounted to a new medium: watercolour true to itself that was capable of a scale and power comparable to those of oil.

The long-term effects of this achievement had little to do with the actual size of Turner's watercolours, even though he continued to execute at least a few large compositions until a fairly late date; it was the technical flexibility that was crucial, and which made it possible for him to employ watercolour as a medium equal and parallel to oil throughout his career. In due course, this technical flexibility was to be matched by a command of scale which rendered large watercolours superfluous: the smaller format appropriate to the medium could be made to contain subject-matter as varied or as grand as that usually reserved for paintings in oil. By 1800 he could already take material of full Claudian stature and render it in

watercolour with no sense of diminution or of strain: the large *Caernarvon castle, North Wales*, shown that year, is altogether more 'classical' than the golden view of the same ruin that appeared in 1799, and is a more elaborate conception. The extensive vista, with the distant sunlit castle between meadows, woods and sea, and the carefully devised foreground with its group of figures, are carried out on the full scale of an oil-painting; and yet the means by which Turner combines the elements of the composition into a unity are essentially those of watercolour; there is no passage that seems to be imitating oil, and much of the application of colour is in broad washes, used very boldly to control the tonal relationship of the parts. In the light areas of the distance, and in the beautifully stylized screen of trees on the left, the traditional interplay of delicately laid-on watercolour and white paper is exploited.

Turner, starting, as we have seen, with the assumption that serious art, as defined by the Academicians, was the object, could not have been content to use watercolour in the limited context of small-scale landscapes. It is significant that the first of his works to show the influence of Claude to a marked degree (*Aeneas and the Sibyl* must be regarded as pastiche of Wilson rather than as an attempt to adapt Claude) are the two watercolours of Caernarvon. The report of Turner's reaction to Claude's *Sacrifice to Apollo*, which he saw in the spring of 1799, would suggest that he might prefer to approach the master through the medium in which he was more thoroughly experienced: 'he was both pleased and unhappy while he viewed it, it seemed to be beyond the power of imitation'.[33]

The story again points to Turner's abiding sense of something to be achieved beyond what he had already accomplished. By 1799 he had proved sufficiently his ability as a watercolourist and as an oil-painter to attain election as Associate of the Academy;[34] this signal of his acceptance among the circle of the most highly regarded artists of the time seems to have had a palpable effect on the pattern of his output. It is as though he looked on it as a licence to create works of a character noticeably grander than he had hitherto produced. Up to this point his oil-paintings had been either of pure landscape, or of marine subjects with fishermen as their protagonists. The only exception to this was a picture of the *Battle of the Nile*, now lost. It appeared in the Academy's exhibition in 1799[35] and was his first attempt at a historical subject on canvas; but it dealt, of course, with very recent history (the battle took place in August 1798), and the inspiration must have been the sea-battles of Benjamin West

Pl.52

Pl.49

55 Kilchern castle, with the Cruchan Ben mountains, Scotland: Noon R.A. 1802
Watercolour, 533 × 772
City Museum and Art Gallery, Plymouth   (Cat. No. 344)

and, perhaps more seriously, of Philippe Jacques de Loutherbourg.[36] In 1800, the year immediately following Turner's election to the associateship, he exhibited a work of utterly Pl.59 new pretensions: *The fifth plague of Egypt,* illustrating a biblical theme and cast in the mould of the classic, heroic landscape tradition of Nicholas Poussin[37] and Wilson. The vigour of handling that distinguishes this canvas can be traced back to that in works such as *Kilgarran castle;* but no previous composition of his had been conceived on so grand a scale or had offered such opportunities for the virtuoso evocation of dramatic atmosphere. Turner heralded the new century with a further radical extension of the scope of his art.

56 Edinburgh, from Caulton-hill   R.A. 1804
Watercolour, 660 × 1004
Trustees of the British Museum, London (T.B., LX-H)   (Cat. No. 348)

NOTES

1 This drawing, though small in scale, anticipates much of the achievement of the interiors of 1796; compared with the evenly lit interior of *Eltham Palace* (Cat. No. 13), of about the same date, for instance, it is a concentrated essay in the rendering of strong chiaroscuro in a limited space, and not at all a predictable exercise for a watercolourist in England at that date.

2 See the comment on this drawing (Cat. No. 138) in Graham Reynolds, *Turner*, 1969, p. 22: 'the solitary figure and by sympathy the onlooker are dwarfed by the scale of the interior.' The principle of enlisting the spectator's sympathy by means of figures within the design was early grasped by Turner, and used as a mainspring of his dialogue with the viewer in much of his work. Note the vivid use of figures in the *Woolverhampton* of 1796 (Pl. 23).

3 Cat. Nos 194–5.

4 Ducros, 1748–1810; Piranesi, 1720–78.

5 See Gage, 'Turner and Stourhead', 1974, pp. 63–4, and Kenneth Woodbridge, *Landscape and Antiquity*, 1970, Pt. II, chap. 14. Sir Richard Colt Hoare, 1758–1838. Piranesi copies by Turner and Girtin exist, probably done for John Henderson in about 1795. The etching that Henderson used as a model is the *Carcere oscura con antenna pel suplizio de' malfatori*, Focillon 4. Turner's copy is in the Metropolitan Museum, New York; Girtin's in the British Museum, 1863–1–10–250. Turner developed an idea from the subject for some of his perspective lecture illustrations (T.B., CXCV -120, 121, 128).

6 Nicholas Maes, 1632-93. Maes was a pupil of Rembrandt who later established himself as a painter of domestic *genre*, to which he wrought something of the richness of Rembrandt's chiaroscuro. The colouring and subject-matter of the *Internal of a cottage* are reminiscent of those of Maes's *Kitchen with a woman at a pump* (Lord Swaythling collection).

7 Francis Wheatley, 1747–1801; William Redmore Bigg, 1755–1828; Joseph Wright of Derby, 1734–97. See Mary Webster, *Francis Wheatley*, 1970, and Benedict Nicolson, *Joseph Wright of Derby*, 1968.

8 Cat. Nos 196–214.

9 E.g. the two interior views of the 'Villa of Maecenas' in the *Vedute di Roma*, Hind 73 and 84. Gage, 1974, p. 64, suggests a likeness with the *Veduta interna dell'antico Tempio di Bacco*, Hind 81. Turner had also no doubt been impressed by Piranesi's *Carceri* series, Hind 1–16. He returned to the theme, colouring and layout of *Ewenny* in some of the Petworth paintings of the 1830s. For a Piranesian prototype for the *Ely* interiors, see the *Veduta di un Eliocamino*, Hind 133.

10 Thornbury, p. 8.

11 Elisha Kirkall, ?1682–1742. See A. G. H. Bachrach, 'J. M. W. Turner's "This made me a painter", a note on visual perception and representational accuracy' in *Light and Sight*, 1974.

12 The view of Rochester that is known to have preceded *Fishermen at sea* on his easel was less obviously inspired by Kirkall, however; though it featured a characteristic group of 'fishermen drawing their boats ashore in a gale'.

13 A particularly striking example of his youthful interest in stormy seas is the partly coloured drawing of about 1792, *A Storm off Dover* (T.B., XVI-G; repr. B.M., 1975, No. 2). See also B.M., 1975, Nos 3–4.

14 Rembrandt van Rijn, 1606–69. The effect of light from two sources, the moon and a fire, occurs in a Rembrandt composition which Turner could have seen at Stourhead: the *Holy Family resting on the flight* (Bredius 576), now in the National Gallery of Ireland, Dublin. See Gage, 1974, p. 64, where the picture (an outdoor subject) is associated with *Ewenny Priory*.

15 Claude Joseph Vernet, 1714–89; Philippe Jacques de Loutherbourg, 1740–1812; see Philip Conisbee, *Claude Joseph Vernet*, exhibition catalogue, Kenwood House, London, 1976, and Rudiger Joppien, *Philippe Jacques de Loutherbourg, R. A.*, exhibition catalogue, Kenwood House, 1973. For the painting technique of de Loutherbourg and his teacher François Casanova (who also taught Vernet) see Gage, 1969, pp. 29–30.

16 See note 18 below.

17 Cat. No. P2. Another painter of moonlight scenes, William Pether, ?1738–1821, may have been in Turner's mind when this was executed.

18 The *Wilson* sketchbook (T.B., XXXVII) was certainly in use by the end of 1797; it is labelled *Studies for Pictures. Copies of Wilson*. Copies and notes after pictures by Wilson are on pp. 86–7, 92–3. See also T.B., XXXIII-I, another copy from Wilson. A series of related drawings is T.B., XXXIII-L,N,P,Q, etc., and Cat. No. 149. Three of the series are reproduced in B.M., 1975, Nos 13–15. Another influence on the marine subjects of these years was no doubt the tradition of picturesque coastal scenes exemplified in works by Gainsborough (e.g. *Seashore with fishermen and boats setting out*, Mrs. Robert Mellon Bruce collection), and George Morland, 1763–1804.

19 For the genesis of Turner's picture see Gage, 1974, pp. 71–4.

20 See Finberg, *Life*, pp. 34–5.

21 T.B., XXXV-84; repr. Gerald Wilkinson, *Turner's Early Sketchbooks*, 1972, p. 46.

22 T.B., XLIII.

23 At the end of his life Turner spoke of his early visits to North Wales 'in search of Richard Wilson's birthplace' (letter to Hawksworth Fawkes

of 27 December 1847, quoted by Finberg, *Life,* p. 419): the association between the grand scenery of Snowdonia and the art of Wilson was clear in his mind.

24 On p. 46 verso.

25 Pp. 39 verso – 44 verso.

26 Cat. No. P28. For further comment on the relationship between this panel and the *Academical* sketchbook studies see Gage, 1969, p. 29.

27 John Julius Angerstein, who bought the drawing, was in fact the owner of a *Sea port* by Claude (1600–82) that impressed Turner profoundly: he was moved to tears 'because I shall never be able to paint anything like that picture' (M.S. *Recollections* of George Jones, Bodleian Library, Oxford). The picture in question was probably the *Embarkation of the Queen of Sheba* (Rothlisberger 114), but Angerstein owned another harbour scene by Claude shortly after this time: the *Embarkation of St. Ursula* (Rothlisberger 51). Angerstein's Claudes were all given to the National Gallery, London, as part of the foundation collection. For Angerstein see John Bunston, *John Julius Angerstein at Woodlands,* exhibition catalogue, London Borough of Greenwich, 1974, with introduction by Cyril Fry.

28 Farington, *Diary,* 28 March 1804. This process was only one of many by which Turner sought to extend the potential of watercolour in its own terms. Gage is correct in observing (1969, p. 27) that 'rather than seeing Turner's work in watercolours of the 1790s as aspiring towards the condition of oil, and oils in the 1830s and 1840s as aspiring to that of watercolour, we notice at any one moment that there are common expressive interests developing side by side in each medium.'

29 *Diary,* 16 November 1799.

30 Richard Colt Hoare, *History of Modern Wiltshire,* 1822, vol. I, p. 83. But Woodbridge, 1970, p. 179, suggests that Turner found Ducros's work uncongenial.

31 Richard Westall, 1765–1836. For Westall's contribution to watercolour practice see William Henry Pyne, *Somerset House Gazette,* vol. II, p. 46, and J. L. Roget, *History of the Old Water-Colour Society,* 1891, vol. I, p. 205: 'Westall's name is especially associated with a reform of figure-painting in water-colours corresponding to that which Turner and Girtin have the credit of effecting in landscape.'

32 Burke, 1757, Part II, section XVIII, p. 64.

33 Farington, *Diary,* 8 May 1799.

34 Finberg, *Life,* pp. 62–3.

35 Cat. No. P10. It was suggested by Lindsay (1966, p. 70) that a circular panorama of the blowing up of *L'Orient,* shown in London in 1799, might have been Turner's work; but it is now known that another artist named Turner, a coach-maker, perhaps William Turner of Walthamstow, was responsible (see Scott Wilcox, unpublished M. Litt. thesis, University of Edinburgh, 1976: 'The Panorama and Related Exhibitions in London').

36 Benjamin West, 1738–1820, succeeded Reynolds as President of the Royal Academy in 1792. Both West and de Loutherbourg contributed marine battle pieces to the Academy exhibitions; West's *Battle of La Hogue* appeared in 1780; de Loutherbourg produced *Lord Howe's Victory of the 1st of June 1794, The Battle of Camperdown,* 1796, and *The Battle of the Nile.*

37 Nicolas Poussin, 1594–1665, with Claude the greatest seventeenth-century exponent of classical landscape.

Chapter Three

High Art

The fifth plague of Egypt was hung in the same room at the Academy exhibition as an oil-painting of *Dolbadern Castle, North Wales;* this, although it followed the views of Coniston Fells, Kilgarran and Dunstanburgh in being a presentation of 'Sublime' natural scenery, placed a new emphasis on the historical, human connotations of the scene. Again this is done in conjunction with allusion to a master of the past: the banditti who stand under the precipitous cliff are borrowed from the imaginary, storm-racked landscapes of Salvator Rosa, the most romantic of the great seventeenth-century Italian painters;[1] but the verses that Turner had printed in the catalogue under the title refer to 'the tower Where hopeless OWEN, long imprison'd, pin'd, And wrung his hands for liberty, in vain'.[2] The contemplation of historical associations was an important aspect of 'Sublime' experience, if not one immediately germane to the purely visual problems that Turner seems to have confined himself to until now. Here the verses deliberately introduce the parallel intellectual theme; the historical allusion is made to suggest a contemporary political idea: 'Liberty' crowns the sequence of thoughts set in train by the view of Dolbadern Castle, and raises Turner's picture to a broader level of significance.

In these pictures Wilson's example bears fruit in ways more essential than the merely technical. The presentation of landscape as the setting for human drama portraying moral ideas, comparable with those of history-painting, had been established as a worthy activity of the painter when Wilson produced his highly successful *Niobe* in 1760.[3] It was based on seventeenth-century landscape types; but its integration of human and natural drama was altogether more theatrical: the landscape is conceived as a stage-set, fully endowed with dramatic 'effects' which enhance the emotional force of the subject. Wilson exactly parallels Reynolds's attempts at the same period to recast the portrait as heroic figure-painting, relying equally on the example of the old masters to provide models of generalized grandeur,[4] and on the contemporary stage to provide a language of gesture and expression sufficiently exaggerated to project dramatic ideas. Turner, as we have seen, was very much alive to the paintings of the past; he inherited, too, the theatricality of the serious art of his time. The Academy was dominated by artists who exploited histrionics, and the history-painter who carried most conviction to his contemporaries is the most explicitly theatrical of all: the Swiss-born Henry Fuseli.[5]

Turner could not directly make use of Fuseli's personal language of vivid and violent gesture; the structure and scale of his compositions were of another type altogether. But Fuseli could teach the young artist, in whatever field he worked, that exaggeration, to the point of utter fantasy, is a legitimate tool of expression.[6] Turner must have studied with care the means by which the influential Fuseli achieved his results, and their value in the creation of 'Sublime' effects must have been apparent to him. The appearance of *The fifth plague* at the Academy marks the beginning of a lifelong concern with scenes of cataclysm, cosmic disaster and elemental fury. Even if it is subjected to the careful organization of a composition modelled on Poussin, it derives much of its detail and atmosphere from *Niobe,* and contains an element of romantic theatricality that looks forward to the sensational apocalypses of John Martin.[7] This places the picture firmly in the imaginative world of which Fuseli was so significant a member. But, whereas Martin was to remain tied to the theatrical, Turner adapted and deflected Fuseli's lesson for his own subtler purposes and absorbed his histrionic manner into a far broader view of nature.

The theme was resumed in subsequent years: by a lost composition of *The army of the Medes destroyed in the desart by a whirlwind—foretold by Jeremiah, chap. XXV. ver. 32 and 33* in 1801,[8] followed in 1802 by *The tenth plague of Egypt* and, a few years later, by *The Destruction of Sodom* and *The Deluge,*[9]

65

57 Dolbadern Castle, North Wales R.A. 1800
Oil on canvas, 1195 × 902
Royal Academy of Arts, London (Cat. No. P12)

58 Salvator Rosa (1615–73)
Landscape with SS. Anthony Abbot and Paul the Hermit c. 1665–8
Oil on canvas, 673 × 495
Coll.: Denis Mahon

Pl.165 probably exhibited in 1805. The climax of the sequence was reached in 1812, when *Snow storm: Hannibal and his army crossing the Alps* appeared. But these history-paintings were not an isolated and distinct part of Turner's output. They only state, in a form particularly respected at the time, ideas that run through much of the rest of his work, which by 1801 was astonishingly diverse in type and conception. *The army of the Medes* was exhibited near a large marine, *Dutch boats in a gale: fishermen endeavouring to put their fish on board* ('The Bridgewater Sea Piece'), which is a picture of totally contrasting genre and inspiration. It was commissioned by the Duke of Bridgewater to hang as a companion to a painting by Willem van de Velde the younger,[10] a testimony to the esteem commanded by the three marines Turner had so far exhibited. But although the

Pl.62

Duke's picture was a companion for a van de Velde—it is in fact designed to form a very exact complement to van de Velde's composition—Turner needed to infuse it with greater significance than van de Velde's work ever implied. In its broad conception and bold, stormy chiaroscuro the picture parallels *The fifth plague;* but, where that work refers back to Poussin, the 'Bridgewater Sea Piece' invokes Rembrandt. It is a highly imaginative and rather 'learned' use of an unexpected source; but not so obscure that the

59 The fifth plague of Egypt: detail R.A. 1800
Oil on canvas, 1240 × 1830
Indianapolis Museum of Art, Indiana (gift in memory of Evan F. Lilly) (Cat. No. P13)

60   Richard Wilson   (1714–82)
The Destruction of Niobe's Children   1760
Oil on canvas, 1455 × 1898
Yale Center for British Art, Paul Mellon Collection

61   'Last Study to the Dutch Boats   D of B'   *c.* 1800
Pen and brown ink, and wash and white chalk on blue paper,
273 × 435
Trustees of the British Museum, London (T.B., LXXXI, 106–7)   (not in
catalogue)

62   Dutch boats in a gale: fishermen endeavouring to put their fish on board ('The Bridgewater Sea Piece')   R.A. 1801
Oil on canvas, 1625 × 2220
Private collection   (Cat. No. P 14)

reference was lost on the Academy's President, West, who said it was 'what Rembrandt thought of but could not do'.[11] He must have recognized in the groups of boats at the left of the design a quotation of Reynoldsian ingenuity from *Christ stilling the Tempest,* at that time in a private collection near London.[12]

At least one of the watercolours shown at the Royal Academy in 1801 was a work of a complexity similar to that of the 'Bridgewater Sea Piece'; although ostensibly a topographical work in Turner's advanced 'Sublime' manner of the later 1790s, *Pembroke castle, South Wales: thunder storm* Pl.64 *approaching* is in fact a fully worked-out landscape painting making prominent use of the activities of fishermen to express its subject, which is far from being strictly topographical, suggesting as it does that the castle overlooks a wide and violent sea rather than a well-protected bend of the river. This licence in treating reality shows that Turner had already seen the point of Fuseli's own expressionism, and was capable of using it in defiance of the strict principles of topography in which he had been nurtured. And yet, again in the 1801 exhibition, he showed that he was still a draughts-

man of picturesque antiquities: his watercolour of the
PI.45 *Chapter-house, Salisbury* was the latest of the series of views
that he had begun for Colt Hoare in 1795, and was to
continue to produce until 1805. It cannot be argued that his
work on this series was merely an irksome duty by this date,
for as recently as 1798 he had undertaken another set of
architectural views, of Oxford colleges for the *Oxford
Almanack,* on which he worked until 1804.[13]

Indeed, the *Chapter-house, Salisbury* is one of his largest and
grandest exercises in what may be termed the 'Architectural
Sublime'. And in 1800 he had also made the most imaginative
of all his 'house-portraits' in watercolour—the series of five
views of Fonthill, showing the new tower of William
PI.53 Beckford's gothic folly rising above the hills of its extensive
park at different times of the day. These five subjects,
morning, noon, afternoon, sunset and evening views, were
shown at the Academy.[14] They establish a new scale for the
watercolours: their treatment of open, rolling country is
altogether grander and more relaxed than the self-
consciously 'Sublime' landscapes of the preceding years, and
they are composed in the Claudian spaciousness employed
in the 1800 *Caernarvon castle,* but without its classicizing

overtones. Their breadth, and the understatement of their
compositions, make them important in the evolution of the
large-scale Swiss watercolours that were to emerge from the
continental tour of 1802.

Among the preparatory studies for these Fonthill subjects
occur some of the earliest of Turner's 'colour-structures', and
these show another aspect of the complex series of processes
that he had evolved for the creation of watercolours.[15] They
are large, often full-scale 'plans' of the broad, chromatic
relationships of a projected composition, and are concerned
not with the working out of the formal content but with the
establishment of colour harmonies and over-all atmosphere
as expressed in colour alone. They are, therefore, early
evidence that Turner was rendering not only the objective
facts of the natural world but his interpretation of them in
terms of colour, as opposed to form. Both now and

64 Pembroke castle, South Wales: thunder storm approaching
R.A. 1801
Watercolour, 508 × 991
Private collection   (Cat. No. 280)

throughout his life, however, Turner made colour studies for purposes other than that of planning compositions as colour systems. Usually such experiments, often called 'colour-beginnings', are preparatory to works in watercolour; but a notable series, on an unexpectedly small scale, is the group of chalk studies for the oil-painting of *Dolbadern Castle*, in the *Studies for Pictures* sketchbook.[16] The colour beginnings of this period, whether they are strictly concerned with the chromatic structure of projected works, or are exploring other pictorial problems, show Turner's extraordinary capacity to generalize, to realize the wider implications of any exercise and to explore them thoroughly.[17]

In 1801 he took a further step along the path of technical exploration when he made the group of sixty drawings in pencil, chalk and white body-colour of views taken during his tour of Scotland.[18] These were made on a grey-brown ground composed, we are told, of a wash of 'India Ink and tobacco water'.[19] Their intention is evidently not to charm the eye with either 'Picturesque' or 'Sublime' effects (these drawings have been castigated by some critics for their 'dulness');[20] they are exercises in the use of monochrome which parallel the early colour studies as attempts to obtain total mastery of the means of expression. They are concerned with the

Pl.54

65 Study for picture of 'The Deluge' *c*. 1804
Pen, brown ink and pencil on grey paper, 410 × 585
Trustees of the British Museum, London (T.B., CXX-X) (not in catalogue)

66 A coast scene with fishermen hauling a boat ashore ('The Iveagh Sea Piece') *c*. 1803–4
Oil on canvas, 914 × 1220
Iveagh Bequest, Kenwood, London (Cat. No. P144)

67 The tenth plague of Egypt R.A. 1802
Oil on canvas, 1420 × 2360
Turner Bequest, Tate Gallery, London (Cat. No. P17)

72

68　Ships bearing up for anchorage ('The Egremont Sea Piece')
R.A. 1802
Oil on canvas, 1195 × 1803
H.M. Treasury and the National Trust (Lord Egremont Collection),
Petworth House　(Cat. No. P18)

establishment in two dimensions, in grey and black only, of intricately modulated spaces: mountainsides, moorland, forest, rock and cloud are recorded in tones rather than outline, tones which are deliberately restricted so as to ensure the maximum precision in their relationships. The muted, somewhat monotonous results demonstrate a control of the pencil and of monochrome chalks far greater than had hitherto been apparent in Turner's drawing. That he felt the

value of the experiment is clear from the imaginative use to which he put the new discipline during the Swiss tour of the following year.[21]

These 'Scottish Pencils' show only one aspect of Turner's development as a draughtsman. His preoccupation with elaborate historical and marine paintings led him to make preparatory drawings in pen and ink, or in chalks, of a type quite different from the careful outlines that had served as the basis of his topographical subjects. They are different, too, from the colour studies in that their function is the more traditional one of determining subjects in terms of form: the essential elements are arranged and rearranged, groups of figures are planned, individual ones carefully posed, shipping, trees and other features of the designs are organized in

Pl.65

70 Nicolas Poussin (1594–1665)
Winter: The Deluge
Oil on canvas, 1180 × 1600
Musée du Louvre, Paris

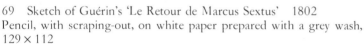

69 Sketch of Guérin's 'Le Retour de Marcus Sextus' 1802
Pencil, with scraping-out, on white paper prepared with a grey wash,
129 × 112
Trustees of the British Museum, London (T.B. LXXII-47) (not in
catalogue)

shifting relations, until a composition is arrived at from which work on the canvas itself can begin. Several sketchbooks dating from 1799 to 1806 contain trials of this kind; the most important is the large *Calais Pier* book,[22] in which PI. 62 the 'Bridgewater Sea Piece', *Fishermen upon a lee-shore, in squally weather*,[23] *The tenth plague of Egypt, Calais Pier, Macon*, the *Sun* PI. 81 *rising through vapour* and other subjects, including even one watercolour, can be seen in gestation. It is a book reserved specifically for Turner's most important undertakings. At no other period in his career was he to make such careful preparations for his canvases. He seems to have felt himself to be on trial, and this state of mind would have been unsurprising during the years immediately prior to his election as full member of the Royal Academy in February 1802.[24] The pictures that he showed in the exhibition of that year, oil and watercolour alike, were of impressive subjects covering a wide range of thematic material; but they were

followed up in the year after, and in 1804, by works just as ambitious. If Turner felt himself under some kind of constraint to produce works of 'High Art' it was not because he wished to become an Academician. The reverse is more probable: his interest in the Academy (which showed itself in his consistent involvement in its administrative affairs) was a concomitant of his respect for the tradition of serious art for which the Academy stood.

That tradition involved the study of European art, not only in English collections, but, as Reynolds had stated,[25] in the great continental galleries. Turner must have been anxious to begin his studies abroad, but the French war made travel impossible. Nevertheless, he began to teach himself the rudiments of French; the *Dolbadern* sketchbook contains grammatical notes which may have been made in 1799.[26] And he availed himself of the opportunity provided by the treaty of Amiens to cross the Channel in 1802. His principal goal was the Swiss Alps, but on his way home he stayed in Paris and spent much of his time in the Louvre, filling a small, square sketchbook[27] with drawings and notes recording his impressions of paintings in the collection, which at that moment was swelled with the plunder of Napoleon's Italian campaigns.[28] Some of the works that attracted his attention

74

71 Holy Family R.A. 1803
Oil on canvas, 1020 × 1415
Turner Bequest, Tate Gallery, London   (Cat. No. P49)

are noted simply as schemes of colours, the names of the colours being referred to by their initial letters and arranged as they lie on the canvases. These colour layouts suggest that Turner was looking in the works of the old masters for general patterns like the ones that he imposed on his own compositions with the aid of colour-structures; and many of the manuscript comments that he made at the same time are evidently concerned with the theme of chromatic organization.[29]

His analyses are not confined to such matters; he sees colour as an element in the overall purpose of each canvas, which is to represent a specific historical, human or religious subject. He notes, for instance, that Poussin's '"Baptism of Jesus" is red in the shadows owing to the ground, like the Nativity that Sir Joshua Reynolds mentioned, was an historical colour and ought always to be attended unto.'[30] He usually makes his technical observations alongside more

72 Sir Joshua Reynolds   (1723–92)
The Holy Family
Oil on canvas, 1956 × 1499
Huntington Library and Art Gallery, San Marino, California

73 The festival upon the opening of the vintage at Macon
R.A. 1803
Oil on canvas, 1460 × 2375
City Art Galleries, Sheffield   (Cat. No. P47)

general ones as to the mood and effect of the works he is
describing. His opening comment on Titian's *Entombment*
couples the two elements: 'This picture', he says, 'may be
ranked among the first of Titian's pictures as to colour and
pathos of effect,' and he devotes several pages to a discussion
in which they are treated concurrently as interdependent and
equal fields of interest.[31] Of the landscapes the one which
PL.70 earns his most concentrated attention is Poussin's *Deluge*, a
subject especially relevant to his own interest in cataclysms.

Although he found many faults in it, Turner could say: '...the
colour is sublime. It is natural—it is what a creative mind
must be imprest with by sympathy and horror.'[32] His sense of
the interrelationship of landscape with human subject is even
more explicit in the notes on Titian's *Death of St. Peter Martyr:* PL.78
'This picture is an instance of his great power as to
conception and sublimity of intelect [*sic*]—the characters are
finely contrasted, the composition is beyond all system, the
landscape tho' natural is heroic, the figure wonderfully

74 Claude Lorrain (1600–82)
Jacob with Laban and his daughters 1654 (or 1655)
Oil on canvas, 1422 × 1994
H.M. Treasury and National Trust (Lord Egremont Collection),
Petworth House

75 Ludolf Backhuizen (1631–1708)
Boats in a storm
Oil on canvas, 648 × 794
Governors of Dulwich College Picture Gallery

76 Calais Pier, with French poissards preparing for sea: an English
packet arriving   R.A. 1803
Oil on canvas, 1720 × 2400
Turner Bequest, National Gallery, London   (Cat. No. P48)

expressive of surprise and its concomitate [sic] fear... Surely
the sublimity of the whole lies in the simplicity of the parts
and not in the historical color...' [33]

He also studied works by Raphael, Correggio, Domeni-
chino, Rembrandt, Rubens and Ruysdael, in addition to the
PL.69 *Retour de Marcus Sextus* of Guérin, the only modern picture,
apparently, to find a place in the Louvre notebook. His

opinion of contemporary French painting is recorded by
Farington: 'he held it very low,—all made *up of Art*';
however, 'he thought Madame Gerard's little pictures very
ingenious' [34] and he went to David's studio to see the large
portrait of Napoleon on horseback that he was later to quote
in one of his vignette designs. [35] One name is conspicuously
absent from the Louvre sketchbook: that of Claude. There
were several Claudes to be seen there at that date and in other
Parisian collections such as that of Lucien Bonaparte, which
Turner may well have visited. [36]

Certainly, one of the most immediate and important
results of the visit to France was a large canvas, *The festival* PL.73

77 Venus and Adonis (Adonis departing for the Chase)   *c*. 1803–5
Oil on canvas, 1490 × 1194
Christopher Gibbs Ltd., London   (Cat. No. P150)

80

78 M. Rota (*c.* 1520–83)
Death of St. Peter Martyr (after Titian)
Engraving, 294 × 375
Trustees of the British Museum, London

79 François Boucher (1703–70)
The Visit of Venus to Vulcan 1754
Oil on canvas, 1640 × 830
Wallace Collection, London

80 Chryses R.A. 1811
Watercolour, 660 × 1004
Private collection, England (Cat. No. 492)

upon the opening of the vintage at Macon, which is the first of Turner's large-scale Claudian composition in oil. It is cool in colour, blues and greens predominating; but even these, according to early reports, were of unusual strength: 'when first painted it appeared of the most vivid greens and yellows', having been begun 'with size colour on an unprimed canvas'[37]—so that even while he was creating a work governed by many of the conventions of Classic landscape, he was tackling it in a novel way. The same can be said of the other large canvas that appeared in the 1803 Academy exhibition: *Calais Pier, with French poissards preparing for sea: an English packet arriving.* This is the most dramatic of the sequence of marines that Turner had been producing since 1796, and contrasts strikingly with the stately dignity of the sea-piece of the previous year, *Ships bearing up for anchorage*

PI. 76

PI. 68

('The Egremont Sea Piece'), which had achieved a grandeur that elevated it above the influence of Dutch realism, above even the Rembrandtesque drama of the 'Bridgewater Sea Piece'. *Calais Pier* reverts to the Dutch types that Turner had previously used as his models. In its realism it surpasses them: the incident it portrays had occurred on Turner's own arrival at Calais, when the 'Situation at Calais Bar' of the lighter bringing passengers ashore was perilous: 'Nearly swampt', as he noted against a study for the picture in the *Calais Pier* sketchbook.[38] He set great store by any personal experience

PI.75

81 Sun rising through vapour; fishermen cleaning and selling fish
R.A. 1807
Oil on canvas, 1345 × 1790
Turner Bequest, National Gallery, London   (Cat. No. P69)

of the 'Sublime'—indeed, it was only through such experience that the artist could hope to communicate grand ideas
to the public, as a critic had pointed out in 1796: Anthony
Pasquin, talking of Hoppner's *A Gale of Wind* exhibited in
that year, noted 'To be very estimable as a marine painter it is
incumbent on the professor to do what Backhuysen did, that

is to go to sea in a tempest, sketch the billows in the very
zenith of their convulsion, and embody and harmonize the
whole when the storm has ceased, and taste can regulate
reflection.'[39]

Both *Calais Pier* and *Macon* are examples of pictorial types
that recur often in Turner's work. In them the impact of the
Parisian collections is absorbed, along with other influences,
into his own originality. There are two other works derived
from the same experience which afford a clue to the full
extent of that impact. They seem to be a deliberate attempt to
expand the range of Turner's subject-matter, by his charac-

teristic method of imitating particular works by other artists. Both of them derive from the work of Titian: the *Venus and Adonis* announces what could be gathered from the *Louvre* notebook, that Turner admired Titian's *Death of St. Peter Martyr* enormously.[40] It is an unmistakable pastiche of that composition, differing from it most markedly in the comparative frivolity of its subject-matter. It is difficult to avoid the conclusion that, despite the evidence of the *Louvre* notebook, he had looked equally carefully at the work of France's own great masters of the immediate past: Boucher and Fragonard.[41] This delight in the lighter decorative aspects of the art of the old masters was to emerge again in the pictures influenced by Watteau of around 1820—a moment when Turner was reacting to the impact of another and even richer experience of Italian art.[42]

Pl. 77

Pl. 79

The sensuousness of the *Venus and Adonis* was contrasted by Turner with his other Titian 'pastiche', the *Holy Family,* an eminently solemn, not to say sombre work, which is none the less based on the same composition: an early sketch for it[43] shows that it was at first intended to be upright in format, with the group of putti above that figures in both the *St. Peter Martyr* and the *Venus and Adonis.* The change of plan may have been occasioned by Turner's wish to differentiate as sharply as possible between the two ideas, despite their common point of origin. Here again we have evidence that Turner had fully grasped the Reynoldsian principle of borrowing from the masters: combination and adaptation can be seen operating even in the most apparently direct imitations. It is a principle that pervades Turner's inspiration and creative processes throughout his career.

Pl. 71

NOTES

1 Salvator Rosa, 1615–73. Salvator was linked with Nicolas Poussin and Claude in the eighteenth-century mind as a supreme exponent of landscape; Reynolds praised him and Poussin together for 'the greatest uniformity of mind throughout their whole work'; he said Salvator's 'Rocks, Trees, Sky, even to his handling, have the same rude and wild character which animates his figures' (Fifth Discourse). Turner's 'Picturesque Sublime' landscapes of 1787–1800, of which *Dolbadern* is the historicizing culmination, evidently seek to emulate Salvator's unity of handling and mood.

2 It has been suggested (see R.A., 1974–5, No. 48) that these verses are by Turner himself—those accompanying the *Caernarvon castle, North Wales* shown in the same year appear to be his also; these, however, are in a somewhat different style. An interpretation of the picture in the light of the reference to 'Owen' is suggested by Holcomb, 'The Bridge in the Middle Distance: Symbolic Elements in Romantic Landscape', 1974, pp. 31–58. Owain Goch was released from Dolbadern after Edward I defeated the Welsh; the subject of the picture is therefore linked to that of Turner's other Welsh landscapes of the period by what he had read of Welsh history in guide-books to the region. For Turner's poetry see Lindsay, 1966, chap. 5 and elsewhere, especially p. 65: of all his versifying colleagues 'Turner was alone seriously and consistently trying to link verse and painting, and thus deepen his consciousness of aims'. See also Lindsay, *The Sunset Ship*, 1966.

3 Wilson executed at least three pictures with the subject of Niobe; they are Constable Nos 18–20. The most famous version, engraved by Woollett in 1761, is now in the Yale Center for British Art.

4 Reynolds's comments on the *Niobe* are interesting: he criticized the picture (in his Fourteenth Discourse, 1788) as showing a landscape 'too near common nature to admit supernatural objects'; Wilson, in fact, was accused of realism while pursuing the poetic, just as Turner was to be by Sir George Beaumont and others in the early years of the nineteenth century.

5 Thornbury's point (p.19) that Turner's father would have numbered many theatrical people among his customers should not be overlooked; and for the painter's interest in the theatre see Lindsay, *J. M. W. Turner*, 1966, p. 111.

6 Fuseli, in the fourth of his *Lectures on Painting*, 1801, p. 4, spoke of the 'delineation of character' in history-painting as 'properly speaking, the drama'. One of Fuseli's best-known and most powerfully fanciful renderings of an historical event was his *William Tell leaping from the boat*, made famous by an engraving of the 1780s by Charles Guttenberg (Schiff No. 719); the subject was particularly apt for treatment by Fuseli, himself a Swiss. In view of the arresting nature of the image and the Swiss theme, it seems likely that Turner had Fuseli in mind when he made a preliminary design for a picture of the same subject (in the *Calais Pier* sketchbook, T.B., LXXXI, p. 36; the sheet is inscribed 'Willm Tell escaping from the Boat'). The picture was not executed.

7 John Martin, 1789–1854.

8 Cat. No. P15. The exhibition catalogue misprints 'XXV' as 'XV'.

9 Cat. Nos P55, P56.

10 Willem van de Velde the younger, 1633–1707.

11 Faringdon, *Diary*, 18 April 1801.

12 Now in the Isabella Stewart Gardner Museum, Boston, Mass. (Bredius 547). Bachrach suggests (in a forthcoming publication) that a specific drama is being enacted in the group of boats at the left of the picture: one is putting about abruptly to avoid collision with another which rushes across her bows. This supplies the element of heightened human significance that, in the Rembrandt, is provided by the biblical subject.

13 Cat. section IV(c). For a full account of the genesis of this series see Luke Herrmann, *Ruskin and Turner*, 1968, pp. 55–8.

14 Faringdon (*Diary*, 10 July 1800) says the commission was originally for seven drawings; see Cat. Nos 335–9.

15 T.B., LXX-P is a large example; smaller ones appear in T.B., XLVII. See Gage, 1969, p. 31, and Pls. 7, 8; and below, chap. 7.

16 T.B., LXIX, pp. 103, etc. Some of the drawings listed by Finberg (*Inventory*, vol. I, p. 173) are actually offsets of the chalk studies on other pages.

17 This 'generalization' was no doubt a conscious and highly intelligent application of Reynolds's injunction: To give a general air of grandeur at first view, all trifling or artful play of little lights, or an attention to a variety of tints, is to be avoided; a quietness and simplicity must reign over the whole work; to which a breadth of uniform, and simple colour, will very much contribute'. Fourth Discourse, 1771.

18 T.B., LVIII. For a discussion of the 'Scottish Pencils' see B.M., 1975, No. 27. The term was coined by Ruskin when he sorted and labelled the contents of the Turner Bequest; it was adopted by Finberg in his *Inventory*.

19 Faringdon, *Diary*, 6 February 1802.

20 Ruskin, *Works*, VIII, p. 368. Finberg, *Life*, p. 74.

21 It was after the 'Scottish Pencil' experiment that Turner's manner of working in pencil moved decisively away from the 'Monro-Canaletto' tradition.

22 T.B., LXXXI.

23 Cat. No. P16.

24 See Finberg, *Life*, p. 76.

25 'I would chiefly recommend, that an implicit obedience to the *Rules of Art*, as established by the practice of the great Masters, should be exacted from the *young* Students. That those models, which have passed through the approbation of ages, should be considered by them as perfect and infallible guides; as subjects for their imitation, not their criticism.' First Discourse, 1769.

26 T.B., XLVI, inside front cover.

27 The *Studies in the Louvre* sketchbook, T.B., LXXII. For comments on this book see Finberg, *Life*, pp. 85–91, and Gage, 1969, pp. 61 ff., 100.

28 See Cecil Gould, *Trophy of Conquest*, 1965, and Paul Wescher, *Kunstraub unter Napoleon*, 1976.

29 Turner's approach to colour analysis was modelled on Reynolds's remarks on colour, in e.g. the Eighth Discourse, 1778 (Wark, ed., p. 159).

30 T.B., LXXII, p. 27. See Reynolds, 'Notes on the Art of Painting,' *Works*, ed. Edmund Malone, 1797, vol. II, pp. 249 etc.

31 T.B., LXXII, pp. 31 verso, 31 recto, 30 verso, 30 recto, 29d. Titian, *c.* 1490–1576. His *Entombment* is still in the Louvre.

32 Page 42. Poussin's picture is still in the Louvre.

33 Pp. 28 verso, 28 recto.

34 Farington, *Diary*, 4 October 1802. Pierre-Narcisse Guérin, 1774–1833; his *Marcus Sextus* had appeared at the Salon of 1799. Marguerite Gérard, 1761–1837, was a sister-in-law of Fragonard.

35 For Rogers's *Italy*: Cat. No. 1157, R.353. Jacques-Louis David, 1748–1825.

36 See Farington, *Diary*, 24 September 1802; the entry reports 'a beautiful Claude' in this collection, to which Farington and Hoppner 'had no introduction but upon applying to the Porter… were immediately admitted to see the pictures'.

37 See John Burnet, *Turner and His Works*, 1852, pp. 78–9.

38 T.B., LXXXI, pp. 58–9.

39 Anthony Pasquin (John Williams), *Memoirs of the Royal Academicians*, 1796, p. 31. Hoppner's picture is in the Tate Gallery (2765). It is a work which may well have had some influence on Turner's early sea-pieces. In the context of his concern for first-hand experience of storms note also the story of J. C. Vernet, who was 'so attached to his profession that he used to make voyages in bad weather on purpose to see the sky and ocean in picturesque perturbation. One day the storm was so violent that the ship's crew were in great consternation. Vernet desired a sailor to bind him to the mast. When every one was crying and praying, Vernet, with his eyes now upon the lightning, and now upon the mountainous waves, continued to exclaim, "How fine this is!"' (Joseph Sandell, *Memoranda of Art and Artists*, 1871, p. 154). Ludolf Backhuizen (1631–1708) was one of the foremost marine painters of seventeenth-century Holland.

40 His admiration was entirely consistent with contemporary enthusiasms: James Northcote, a self-consciously cynical commentator, once said that 'to find fault with the Peter Martyr is like speaking blasphemy' (*Conversations of James Northcote, R. A.*, ed. Ernest Fletcher, 1901, p. 58).

41 François Boucher, 1703–70. Jean-Honoré Fragonard, 1732–1806.

42 Antoine Watteau, 1684–1721. For works influenced by Watteau, see Cat. Nos P140, P229, P244, and chap. 9, pp. 206 f.

43 In the *Calais Pier* sketchbook, T.B., LXXXI, p. 63.

Chapter Four

Switzerland

The most complete document of Turner's attitude to his art in the first decade of the century is his *Liber Studiorum*. It is supposed that the idea of this work was suggested to him by his close friend, William Frederick Wells, a landscape painter of decidedly minor talent.[1] The scheme was, however, absolutely at one with Turner's own temperament, and reflects his mind on a number of levels.

It was, as its title implied, inspired by the *Liber Veritatis* of Claude Lorrain, who recorded all his finished pictures in monochrome drawings, which he kept together as a survey of his œuvre. In the eighteenth century this remarkable series of memoranda was in the possession of the Duke of Devonshire; two years after Turner's birth it was published as a set of near-facsimiles by Richard Earlom.[2] These were executed in a mixture of etching and mezzotint, and this was the medium in which Turner eventually produced his own series. He had initially considered using aquatint—barely introduced when Earlom's *Liber Veritatis* was in hand—but his final selection of mezzotint with etched outlines was evidently arrived at in the light of Earlom's precedent.[3] There was, nevertheless, a fundamental difference between the continuous record that Claude made concurrently with his paintings, and Turner's plan for the *Liber Studiorum*. These prints were not for his own information; they were to be public testimony to the range of his output. They incorporated many compositions that he had already executed, but they were amplified by many more which were produced solely with the purpose of filling out a sequence of issues designed to present his work as a landscape artist practising in several areas: the paper wrappers in which the parts appeared were entitled 'Liber Studiorum; Illustrative of Landscape Compositions, viz. Historical, Mountainous, Pastoral, Marine, and Architectural'.

This careful planning betrays Turner's strong academic bent: he, like the most theoretical of his predecessors, loved to categorize works of art, to label and define. Turner's love of the Academy and of Reynolds, of all the great theorists of the past, shows that such an approach was quite natural to him. Accordingly, he retrospectively divided his paintings into the types that he listed, and redrew them in pen and sepia wash, himself making an etched outline of the resulting drawing.[4] Pls. 82, 83, 84 This outline was farmed out to mezzotinters who added tone, under his close supervision; at first he relied almost entirely on his namesake Charles Turner,[5] but employed progres- Pl. 95 sively more engravers, towards the end of the series completing a number of the plates himself. The issues appeared between 1807 and 1819, constituting fourteen parts in all; each contained five plates, labelled with initial letters for each of the landscape types Turner specified in the title; in practice these were varied somewhat, and he

82 London from Greenwich (for the *Liber Studiorum*, R.26) 1810
Etching (proof), 178 × 265
Trustees of the British Museum, London (1920-7-1-1) (not in catalogue)

83 Shipping scene, with fishermen   *c.* 1810
Pen and brown wash, 217 × 291
Yale Center for British Art, Paul Mellon Collection (not in catalogue)

frequently used the designation 'EP' meaning, probably, 'Epic' or 'Elevated Pastoral' in place of one or other of the regular categories.[6]

The clear separation of subjects into differentiated landscape types was for Turner a demonstration of his versatility—his universality. As was already evident, he did not accept the limitations of any particular branch of art. So he made designs for the 'pastoral' category of the *Liber* which are oddly at variance with the tenor of his most characteristic work; and about the time the *Liber* was beginning to be published, he made not only paintings but watercolours too which reflect a desire to attempt every genre.[7]

One area of diversification which was to play an important part in the construction of the *Liber*, that of 'Mountainous landscape', was accorded close attention by Turner several years earlier than the date of its first issue. It was no doubt logically inevitable that he should progress from a study of the mountains of Wales and Scotland to those of Switzerland;

84 Devil's Bridge, St. Gothard (for the *Liber Studiorum*, unpubl., R.78)
c. 1819
Pen and brown ink and wash with some scratching-out, 215 × 253
Trustees of the British Museum, London (presented by Sir Joseph
Duveen, 1922) (not in catalogue)

but the Alps were absolutely essential to the stock-in-trade of
a landscape artist professing comprehensive interests and a
concern for the most serious aspects of nature. The 'Mountainous' category in the *Liber* could hardly have been
adequately filled without a knowledge of them.[8]

When he arrived in Paris after his tour, towards the end of
September 1802, he met Joseph Farington who, like many
Englishmen, was taking advantage of the Peace of Amiens.
Turner told him: 'The trees in Switzerland are bad for a
painter—fragments and precipices very romantic, and
strikingly grand. The country on the whole surpasses Wales;
and Scotland too...'[9] The categorizing, theorizing mentality

89

85 On the Lake of Brienz 1802
Pencil, with black and white chalk,
on grey paper, 211 × 284
Trustees of the British Museum,
London (T.B., LXXIV-43) (not in
catalogue)

86 Castle of Ringgenburg 1802
Pencil and black chalk and white
body-colour on grey paper, 215 ×
282
Trustees of the British Museum,
London (T.B., LXXOV-46) (not in
catalogue

90

87 Chateau de Rinkenberg, on the Lac de Brientz, Switzer-
land   1809
Watercolour, 281 × 394
Taft Museum, Cincinnati   (Cat. No. 388)

of the eighteenth century is apparent in these observations. In
fact the drawings that he made there demonstrate an
elaborate process of selection and reorganization which is far
removed from the straightforward topographical record-
making of the 1790s.

Considering the length of the Swiss tour, and the
exceptionally stimulating nature of the scenery that he

encountered, Turner made surprisingly few drawings of
what he saw. Two of the sketchbooks that he used are filled
with rapid notes, many of them made in France, while
another contains only a few studies, some in watercolour, of
figures in local costume. There are three others: the *Grenoble*
sketchbook, the *Lake Thun* sketchbook, and a larger one
containing views near Mont Blanc and in the Pass of
St. Gotthard.[10] Of these, the *Lake Thun* is the only one to
contain pencil sketches carried out in Turner's customary
way while travelling; the *Grenoble* book consists of sheets of
grey paper (all separated at an early date), on which he
worked in pencil with black and white chalks in a manner

89 Hospice of the Great St. Bernard ?1802
Watercolour over traces of pencil, 340 × 425
Trustees of the British Museum, London (T.B., CCLXIII-195) (not in catalogue)

88 The Great Fall of the Reichenbach 1802
Pencil, watercolour and body-colour on white paper prepared with a grey wash, 473 × 312
National Gallery of Ireland, Dublin (Cat. No. 361)

reminiscent of the experimental 'Scottish Pencils' of the preceding year. The subjects in this book are often, like the 'Scottish Pencils', elaborately worked up, and based on much slighter outline sketches made in pencil in one or other of the smaller books that he carried with him. It is, in fact, to some extent not so much a book in which records were made as a repository of ideas capable of completion as finished works.

This, indeed, was the function of most of his sketchbooks; but here the subjects are already taken, in many cases, beyond the stage of objective topography: they have been reconstructed as compositions in light and shade, with substantial modifications in detail. Later, completed watercolours of some of these subjects illustrate the purpose of the studies: a large view of the *Lake of Brienz* is peopled with rather Italianate figures whose presence is adumbrated in the *Grenoble* sketchbook sheet;[11] and a view of *Ringgenburg* is a more evolved chromatic expression of a design in strong chiaroscuro that Turner worked out here in broad masses of black chalk.

The larger book, *St. Gothard and Mont Blanc*, contains drawings of similar tonal elaboration; but here they are frequently already coloured in such a way as to present the broad atmosphere of the mountain subjects, and even drawn so that Turner had no need to reinterpret them when he used them for large-scale watercolours or paintings: the Pass of St. Gothard itself, of which he made an impressive watercolour in 1804, was transformed into a vertiginous, narrow ravine very different from the reality. Even the colouring of the subject is not essentially altered from what he put down in his study. The book is not simply an accumulation of 'raw material': it is a part of the creative process between observation and finished work of art.

Pl.85

Pls. 86, 8

Pl.93

90 Glacier and source of the Arveron, going up to the Mer de
Glace R.A. 1803
Watercolour, 685 × 1015
Yale Center for British Art, Paul Mellon Collection   (Cat. No. 365)

The most striking aspect of these drawings is their strongly
developed pictorial integration: the grey washed ground with
which Turner prepared all the leaves of the *St. Gothard and
Mont Blanc* book, continuing the exercise in tonal discipline of
the 'Scottish Pencils', seems to have been a premeditated
attempt to achieve 'ready-made' compositions, which he was
to use again on his first visit to Italy, though with very
different results.

The large number of finished Swiss views that appeared in
the years following rely closely on the material supplied by
this tour. They vary in size from sheets similar to those of the
St. Gothard and Mont Blanc book to huge drawings as large as
some of Turner's more sizeable paintings. The drawings
shown at the Academy and at Turner's newly-built gallery in
1803 and 1804 [12] are uncompromising essays in the 'Sublime' which take a stage further the theme of the large Welsh
landscapes of previous years, and combine it with the
Piranesian, architectural grandeur of the Salisbury interiors.
Turner's preoccupation with the enclosing formations of
rocks in these early Swiss subjects does indeed give his
designs a strongly architectural flavour—a sense of enclo-
sure, of claustrophobia that was, of course, essential to the

91 St. Huges denouncing vengeance on the shepherd of Cormayer, in the valley of d'Aoust   R.A. 1803
Watercolour, 673 × 1010
Sir John Soane's Museum, London   (Cat. No. 364)

eighteenth-century notion of the 'horror' of the mountains, the very opposite of his later exultation in open expanses of air and light between the peaks.

Pl. 97   This new, widened knowledge of mountain scenery was indirectly applied to the mythological and historical paintings that he was producing: it is evident in *The Goddess of Discord choosing the apple of contention in the garden of the Hesperides* where, as Ruskin pointed out,[13] carefully observed geological formations are transplanted into a fantasy landscape in which Pl. 101 they assume an unnatural but expressive scale. In *The fall of an Avalanche in the Grisons* and *Snow storm: Hannibal and his army crossing the Alps,* both dating from several years after the tour, precise details give way to more generalized evocation, but it

is clear that Turner relied heavily on his memory of Swiss scenery in conveying the scale of his subjects, even if, in one case at least, he transcribed particular features of the scene from observations made in England.[14] As far as his subject pictures were concerned, information might be gathered from any convenient source, and overall conviction was the goal, not the literal accuracy of, say, Holman Hunt, who

92   Chateaux de St. Michael, Bonneville, Savoy   R.A. 1803
Oil on canvas, 915 × 1220
Yale Center for British Art, Paul Mellon Collection   (Cat. No. P50)

painted his biblical subjects from the motif in the Holy Land.[15]

Pl. 101   In *The fall of an Avalanche* the presence of human beings is central to the picture's significance, since we must, to receive the full impact of the subject, believe that human beings are the victims of the disaster; yet the only sign of life—a most restrained hint—is the grey cat which clings terrified to the collapsing roof of the cottage. In the upright watercolour of *The passage of Mount St. Gothard* only a pair of laden mules, and the distant and diminutive figure of a supplicant at a shrine marking the place of death of some earlier traveller, complement the rigid austerity of the composition.

The majority of the finished drawings were acquired as the foundation of what was to become the largest contemporary collection of Turner's works: that of Walter Fawkes, of

93 The passage of Mount St. Gothard, taken from the centre of the Teufels Broch (Devil's Bridge), Switzerland 1804
Watercolour and scraping-out, 985 × 685
Abbot Hall Art Gallery, Kendal, Cumbria (Morse gift) (Cat. No. 366)

94 Fall of the Rhine at Schaffhausen R.A. 1806
Oil on canvas, 1447 × 2337
Museum of Fine Arts, Boston, Mass. (bequest of Alice Marian Curtis and special Picture Fund) (Cat. No. P61)

95 Charles Turner (1773–1857) (after J. M. W. Turner for the *Liber Studiorum*, R.15)
Lake of Thun, Swiss 1808
Mezzotint, 181 × 261
Trustees of the British Museum, London (1849–5–12–639)

Farnley, near Leeds, in Yorkshire. The first record of a connection between Fawkes and Turner is that of the purchase by Fawkes of one of the large watercolours that Turner showed at the Academy in 1803: the *Glacier and source* Pl.90 *of the Arveron, going up to the Mer de Glace.* In the following year he bought two more, the *St. Gothard* and *The great fall of the Reichenbach,*[16] from Turner's own gallery. It may be that Fawkes bought these drawings because he himself had been in Switzerland in 1802, and it is possible that he and Turner met as fellow-tourists there. He went on to acquire almost all the rest of the sequence of Swiss subjects that Turner produced, regularly until about 1810, then more rarely until 1820.[17]

These watercolours present Swiss scenery with directness and great power. Their grace and strength, and their imaginative use of the conventional devices of picturesque and mountain topography, achieve statements of a weight and grandeur without parallel in the canon of Alpine view-making. Yet they rely for their effect almost entirely on the depiction of the natural phenomena that had attracted tourists and artists throughout the preceding half-century. The subject-matter of each drawing is, for the most part, presented exactly as if it were a building of antiquarian interest: as grandly as possible, from a close point of view, with a clear delineation of all salient features, though with due stress on the sombre colour and brooding scale of the landscape. Technically, they exploit the full range of Turner's watercolour procedures, making use of broad washes blotted

96 The Lake of Thun, Switzerland ?1806
Watercolour, 280 × 390
Private collection (Cat. No. 373)

or sponged off to reveal under-layers of colour or the white of the paper; detail is added locally with strong, crisp delineation aided by scraping-out with a knife or finger-nail. Distances are articulated by loose but precise hatching with a dryish brush, which obtains the texture of rocks and forests, again assisted by scraping-out, sometimes with the wooden point of a brush. Colour-beginnings and unfinished drawings

from the series[18] show that Turner advanced quickly from the stage of blocking in the principal masses as simple washes of colour to an elaborate accumulation of detail, employing his fine hatching and blotting-out as soon as the paper was covered with colour. PI.89

The exact chronology of the Swiss watercolours is problematical. Some are dated; but those which are not present, at the moment, a somewhat ill-defined picture of Turner's technical progress. One of the earliest to be finished was the very large *St. Hugo denouncing vengeance on the shepherd of Cormayer,* shown at the Academy in 1803, and evidently Turner's first response to the Alps in terms of a major subject-picture: the two paintings of 1803[19] are essentially PI.91

97 The Goddess of Discord choosing the apple of contention in the garden of the Hesperides B.I. 1806
Oil on canvas, 1550 × 2185
Turner Bequest, Tate Gallery, London (Cat. No. P57)

topographical landscapes, though one of them, the *Chateaux* Pl.92 *de St. Michael, Bonneville,* bears traces of a vigorous organization in terms of classical compositional types, with a firm receding perspective giving palpable structure to the view of monumentally-conceived mountains.[20] Although the *St. Hugo* is a watercolour, it takes these motifs further: its main perspec-

98 Lake of Brienz, moonlight ?1806
Watercolour, 277 × 392
Private collection (Cat. No. 374)

99 Lake of Lucerne, from the landing place at Fluelen, looking towards
Bauen and Tell's chapel, Switzerland ?1807
R.A. 1815
Watercolour, 673 × 1003
Private collection (Cat. No. 378)

tive is central, instead of being at one side, and it is
emphasized by a stormy burst of light that anticipates the
vortex of *Hannibal crossing the Alps,* not painted until 1811–12.
In addition it takes as its subject an historical event (which
Turner must have found in a guide-book to the Val d'Aosta),
and unites the action of the figures with the manifestation of
supernatural anger in the electric storm above them, after the
example of Wilson.[21]

Fawkes did not acquire this elaborate essay in history; but
he may have bought a drawing which can date from very little

later, the view of *Lake Geneva and Mont Blanc,*[22] in which
classical precedent is treated very differently. This is, as far as
can be judged, the only one of all Turner's watercolours to
have been approached by means of the chalk studies that he
made when planning the large paintings of 1800: a sketch for
the composition appears in the *Calais Pier* book;[23] and the
finished work is indeed, in every respect but its medium, a
superb painting of classical landscape imbued with the lucid
tranquillity of Poussin. Instead of heroic figures taken from
history, however, Turner substitutes nude bathers, and a
group of cows and sheep that are treated entirely realistically.
The exquisite delicacy of the washes, and the shaping and
placing of the trees that act as repoussoir, are reminiscent of
the 1800 views of Caernarvon and Fonthill; it is tempting to
place this drawing among the first that Turner executed after
his return from the Continent, though its strong classical

flavour has prompted the suggestion that it belongs to about 1805.[24] In 1806 he exhibited one of the most direct of his
Pl.94 Swiss subjects, the *Fall of the Rhine at Schaffhausen,* a large painting in which no heroic drama provides a human parallel with the 'Sublime' scenery represented. Instead Turner invents an incident in which local people are momentarily stirred into frightened action, as two cart-horses begin to fight and a woman rushes to protect her child. The event is in no way related to the grand subject of the picture; yet it almost imperceptibly emphasizes the mood that Turner intends to convey: it contributes to a sense of awe—the traditional eighteenth-century response to the waterfall—by

100 The Castle of Chillon ?1809
Watercolour, with some scraping-out, 281 × 395
Trustees of the British Museum, London (Lloyd Bequest) (Cat. No. 390)

providing a more immediately local and tangible source of danger to human life. In addition it adds to the informative purpose of the work by telling us in what ways the local people of Schaffhausen were employed, how they dressed, and so on. This fine balance between informing and exciting is the motive of a great deal of Turner's art.

101   The fall of an Avalanche
in the Grisons ('Cottage des-
troyed by an avalanche')
Turner's gallery   1810
Oil on canvas, 900 × 1200
Turner Bequest, Tate Gallery,
London   (Cat. No. P109)

102   Philip James de Louther-
bourg   (1740–1812)
The Avalanche   1803
Oil on canvas, 1099 × 1600
Tate Gallery, London

103   Fortified pass, Val d'Aosta   1802
Watercolour and scratching-out on white paper prepared with a grey wash, 309 × 474
Syndics of the Fitzwilliam Museum, Cambridge   (Cat. No. 360)

The culminating watercolour of the Swiss series is a show-piece of 1815 that demonstrates all the resources of which he could by this date avail himself: *The Battle of Fort Rock, Val d'Aouste, Piedmont, 1796.* That he felt it to be a work of special importance is perhaps indicated by his choosing it for the Academy walls (since 1803 his watercolours had been shown almost exclusively at his own gallery); it hung there with three of the large Swiss views that Fawkes had already acquired. Once again, however, he did not buy Turner's history-piece: the *Fort Rock* remained in his studio and was found after his death blocking up an outhouse window, which may perhaps indicate that Turner, too, began to doubt its importance.[25]

Nevertheless it is one of the most illuminating of his works. Its genesis is well charted. Turner made a drawing of 'Fort Rock', in the Val d'Aosta, looking back towards Mont

Pl. 105

Pl. 103

104   Mont Blanc, from Fort Roch, in the Val d'Aosta   *c.*1804
Watercolour, 660 × 1000
Private collection, U.K.   (Cat. No. 369)

105 The Battle of Fort Rock, Val d'Aouste, Piedmont, 1796 R.A. 1815
Watercolour, 695 × 1010
Trustees of the British Museum, London (T.B., LXXX-G) (Cat. No. 399)

Blanc, in his *St. Gothard and Mont Blanc* sketchbook. It is precisely the kind of specific recording typical of that book—taking a single grand feature and presenting it sombrely, as it were in snapshot. The unadorned appearance of a narrow view, a mountain road and a valley between wooded slopes, is rendered in a restricted range of watercolour washes, with highlights scratched through the grey ground to the white paper. When Turner used this study for a large finished watercolour, which probably dates from about PL.104

1805−10, though it is not easy to place precisely, he followed his custom of inventing figures which give the view an immediate human relevance: three girls stare over the parapet at the left into the ravine, their gestures and expressions conveying astonishment at the spectacle of the gorge, which Turner makes more impressive by introducing a waterfall that drops vertically behind them. This emphasizes the height of the precipice, but does not reinforce the strong central perspective that is already present in the original study. It was not until the version of 1815 that all these elements were remoulded into a full-scale statement in terms of 'high art'. In the watercolour of that year the everyday figures are replaced by a scene of two armies meeting on the narrow bridge above the chasm, which from a lively waterfall is transformed into a black crevasse. The whole of the left side of the composition is devoted to a detailed account of this clash of forces—an incident from Napoleon's invasion of Italy in 1796 which may be said to embody the political and cultural differences of northern and southern Europe, and the natural division between them formed by the Alps. In the place of the admiring girls, a countrywoman with her child attends a wounded soldier; behind her, men tumble from the bridge, and the rocky fortress is involved in billows of smoke. Beyond, Mont Blanc is glimpsed in sunshine among turbulent clouds, and, down the centre of the design, the valley forms one of most complete and devastating punctuations in any of Turner's compositions, a plunging vertical that takes the eye endlessly downwards, and separates entirely the right half of the drawing, which consists simply of a bare, wild, rocky precipice, from the face of which tiny falls of water trickle into the gorge. The hostility of nature is opposed directly to the hostility of men towards each other; the mountains are presented as a grand and beautiful as well as a terrifying natural phenomenon, as a political and social as well as a geographical force.

The drawing combines many of Turner's recurrent themes in a single extraordinary statement, and it embodies as well the achieved climax of his technical evolution as a watercolourist.

By this date he generally treated paper itself as a completely malleable and adaptable medium; unlike Girtin and several of his contemporaries he did not use rough or tinted paper for finished drawings, preferring always to work on a smooth white wove Whatman paper or similar make. But he was by no means respectful of this fine-quality surface; and contemporary accounts suggest that he worked by blending paper and colour into one coherent entity. He was observed by a fellow-artist working on several drawings at the same time: he 'stretched the paper on boards and, after plunging them into water, he dropped the colours onto the paper whilst it was wet, making *marblings* and gradations throughout the work. His completing process was marvellously rapid, for he indicated his masses and incidents, took out half-lights, scraped out highlights and dragged, hatched and stippled until the design was finished.'[26] The speed of his method is testified to in another account, handed down at Farnley from Hawksworth Fawkes who, as a boy, was allowed to watch the creation of the *First-Rate, taking in stores*[27] in 1818: 'he began by pouring wet paint on to the paper until it was saturated, he tore, he scratched, he scrabbled at it in a kind of frenzy and the whole thing was chaos—but gradually and as if by magic the lovely ship, with all its exquisite minutia, came into being and

by luncheon time the drawing was taken down in triumph.'[28] Another account speaks of Turner 'tearing up the sea with his eagle-claw of a thumb-nail', and producing the drawing 'in three hours'.[29] It was also at Farnley that Turner had 'cords spread across the room as in that of a washer woman, and paper tinted with pink and blue and yellow hanging on them to dry'.[30]

The process of washing the paper with broad and subtly contrasted sweeps of colour was preliminary to, or even concurrent with, that of applying local detail 'exactly in the manner of William Hunt, of the Old Water-Colour Society... with clear, firm and unalterable touches one over another, or one into the interstices of another...'[31] Turner combines breadth with a persistent concern for minutely graded and modulated texture and local detail, applied with the most delicate strokes of the brush. But the minuteness of Turner's technique in no way impairs the dynamism of his watercolours: indeed, it was not until this elaborate process had been evolved, in the years about 1815–20, that he was able fully to match his style to the constantly changing world that he saw. It was only now that he could render not merely the forms and appearance of solid objects, but the very evanescence, the shift and flow of the air itself. The fine touches of his brush could convey in watercolour a wider expanse of open air, of space filled with light, than he could depict in any other medium. It was therefore possible for him, when he returned to Switzerland, to draw not so much the mountains themselves as the spaces between them.

A watercolour of a Swiss subject executed in the early 'thirties, a view of *Schaffhausen* derived from an outline taken in 1802,[32] provides a valuable contrast with the great painting of 1806: the viewpoint is much further from the fall, and the presentation of the scene oddly more literal; Turner relies for his effect entirely on the splendour of atmosphere that he can now achieve by means of his mature watercolour technique. The sublime horror of the waterfall seen from immediately below is replaced by a sublimity more subtly perceived: that of light in air, modified by countless constantly changing conditions. The more open and expansive view is essential to the portrayal of this aspect of nature; hence the importance of Switzerland in Turner's late works. In these circumstances the simple evidences of human life that he introduces as information and animation can be allowed to exist for themselves, in the vividly created air of their own environment. By their very nature as inhabitants of the real Switzerland, they become participants in Turner's personal drama.

Pl. 206

NOTES

1 William Frederick Wells, 1762–1836. See the letter from Clara Wheeler (née Wells) to a Mr. Elliot, 27 July 1853: 'The world are almost as much indebted to my father as to Turner for the exquisite Liber Studiorum, for without him I am sure it never would have existed—he was constantly urging Turner to undertake a work on the plan of Liber Veritatis. I remember over and over again hearing him say—"For your own credit's sake Turner you ought to give a work to the public which will do you justice..." Turner placed implicit confidence in my father's judgement, but he required much and long continued spurring before he could be urged to undertake Liber Studiorum.' Quoted by Rawlinson, *Liber Studiorum,* 2nd ed. 1906, pp. xii–xiii. See also J. L. Roget, *Liber Studiorum,* 1879, p. 20: 'it was first thought of at the house of his friend, Mr. Wells... the first drawing was made for it in his parlour (at Addiscombe).' For Turner with Wells at Knockholt, see Thornbury, pp. 234–6. A full account of the *Liber* and its plates is given in Finberg, *Liber Studiorum,* 1924.

2 Richard Earlom, engraver, 1743–1822. The publisher was Boydell. The work appeared between 1777 and 1819. Claude's original is now in the British Museum; see Michael Kitson, *Claude Lorrain, Liber Veritatis,* 1978.

3 One plate, the *Bridge and Goats* (R. 43), was executed in aquatint, but Turner could not agree with the engraver, F. C. Lewis, over the price for the work, and their partnership was discontinued.

4 The majority of the sepia designs for the series, and Turner's many preparatory studies, are in the Turner Bequest, CXV, CXVI, CXVII, CXVIII.

5 Charles Turner, 1773–1857.

6 Turner had originally envisaged 100 plates in all. A frontispiece was issued as an extra plate in the tenth part, 1812. For the signification of the initials 'E.P' see the long discussion in J. L. Roget, 1879, pp. 26 ff.

7 See below, chap. 5, p. 123.

8 There is no reason why Wells should not have suggested the *Liber* as early as 1800, before Turner went to Switzerland. The two men are said to have been introduced in 1792; see Roget, 1879. There are records of Turner staying with Wells on several occasions around 1800 (see Finberg, *Life,* p. 69).

9 Farington, *Diary,* 1 October 1802.

10 The sketchbooks used on the tour are: *Small Calais Pier* (T.B., LXXI), *Studies in the Louvre* (T.B., LXXII), *France, Savoy, Piedmont* (T.B., LXXIII), *Grenoble* (T.B., LXXIV), *St. Gothard and Mont Blanc* (T.B., LXXV), *Lake Thun* (T.B., LXXVI), *Rhine Strassburg and Oxford* (T.B., LXXVII) and *Swiss Figures* (T.B., LXXVIII). There are also nineteen large sheets with drawings made on the spot, T.B., LXXIX. The itinerary took him to Chalon, Mâcon, Geneva, Bonneville, Chamonix, Courmayeur, Aosta, St. Bernard, Marti-gny, Vevey, Thun, Interlaken, Lauterbrunnen, Grindelwald, Meiringen, Lucerne, St. Gotthard, Zurich, Schaffhausen, and along the Rhine.

11 The finished view of the *Lake of Brienz* is Cat. No. 386.

12 At the R.A. in 1803 *St. Huges* (sic) *denouncing vengeance on the shepherd of Cormayer* (sic), *in the valley of d'Aoust* (384), and *Glacier and source of the Arveron, going up to the Mer de Glace* (396); at Turner's gallery in 1804 *The passage of Mount St. Gothard, taken from the centre of the Teufels Broch (Devils Bridge), Switzerland,* and *The great fall of the Riechenbach* (sic), *in the valley of Hasle, Switzerland.*

13 See Ruskin, *Works,* XIII, pp. 113–19.

14 See Thornbury, p. 239.

15 Holman Hunt, 1827–1910. See Hunt's MS. *Account of a Second Journey to the Dead Sea* (John Rylands Library, Manchester) for details of his attempt to complete *The Scapegoat* on the spot (quoted in Mary Bennett, *William Holman Hunt,* exhibition catalogue, 1969, No. 33).

16 Cat. No. 367.

17 For Fawkes, see Lindsay, 1966, p. 112. Thornbury (p. 237) says Turner and Fawkes met 'in the course of an early topographical tour in the district, when he was visiting Richmond for Whitaker, or sketching for Lord Harewood'. If these circumstances are correct, the date would have been *c.* 1798–9.

18 For example, T.B., CCLXIII-195 (Pl. 89) and T.B., LXXX-D (Cat. No. 363).

19 Cat. Nos P46, P50.

20 Butlin and Joll (No. 50) relate the composition of this picture to Poussin's *Landscape with a Roman Road* (Blunt 210) at Dulwich.

21 See comments on *St. Hugo* and its relation to the composition of the *Splügen Pass* of 1842 (Cat. No. 1523) in Russell and Wilton, 1976, p. 27.

22 Cat. No. 370.

23 T.B., LXXXI, p. 20.

24 See Nicholas Serota, 'J. M. W. Turner's Alpine Tours', unpublished thesis, 1970, and Russell and Wilton, 1976, p. 40.

25 Reported by the Revd. W. Kingsley; see Ruskin, *Works,* XIII, p. 534.

26 B. Webber, *James Orrock, R. I.,* 1903, vol. I, pp. 60–1.

27 Cat. No. 499.

28 Typescript by Edith Mary Fawkes, National Gallery Library, London.

29 See Thornbury, p. 239.

30 W. L. Leitch, 'The Early History of Turner's Yorkshire Drawings', *Athenaeum,* 1894, p. 327.

31 Ruskin, *Works,* XIII, p. 247.

32 Cat. No. 406. The watercolour is based on T.B., LXXIX-E.

Chapter Five

Turner and Nature

For Turner, the Royal Academy was not simply the place to which he personally felt himself to belong: it was the proper and natural point of reference for anyone who professed to be an artist. When he took up his duties as Professor of Perspective in 1811 (he had assumed the office in 1807) he was touchingly conscious of the weight other instructors had given to his position, and modelled his approach and style on those of Reynolds himself: 'I cannot look back,' he began his first lecture, 'but with pride and pleasure to that time the Halcyon perhaps of my days when I received instruction within these walls, and listened, I hope I did, with a just sense and respect towards the institution and its then President, whose Discourses must be yet warm in many a recollection.'[1] He tried, as Reynolds had done, to guide the Academy's students by constant reference to the masters of the past: his reading in preparation for the lectures was extensive and careful, and so wide-ranging in his concern for the whole theory of art that it was complained that he spoke 'for the Professors of Painting and Architecture, the word Perspective hardly mentioned.'[2] But although he larded his talks with references to the works of Poussin, Salvator, Claude and Titian, with all of whom, as we have seen, he was intelligently familiar, he laid a proper emphasis on the necessity of studying 'Nature and her effects', which the painter is enabled to imitate by means of the 'science of art' that he (and the Academy as a whole) strove to inculcate.

He admitted that certain natural phenomena, such as reflections, 'evade every attempt to reduce them to anything like rule or practicality. What seems one day to be governed by one cause is destroyed the next by a different atmosphere. In our variable climate', he went on, 'where [all] the seasons are recognizable in one day, where all the vapoury turbulence involves the face of things, where nature seems to sport in all her dignity and dispensing incidents for the artist's study... how happily is the landscape painter situated, how roused by

every change of nature in every moment, that allows no langour even in her effects which she places before him, and demands most peremptorily every moment his admiration and investigation, to store his mind with every change of time and place.'[3]

The sentiment anticipates John Constable's delight in climatic variation, as recorded in his Introduction and notes to the *English Landscape Scenery* of 1833.[4] Constable's whole output, indeed, testifies to an absorbing interest in the business of recording that variation, and his habit of working out of doors in oil gives vividness to the idea of him as a 'natural' painter—one between whom and the observed world no membrane of artifice supervenes. Turner, by contrast, worked in oil out of doors only on rare occasions, and even his watercolour studies were probably executed indoors more commonly than otherwise. For all their technical spontaneity they frequently give the impression of being evolved and elaborately ordered images, far removed from the immediate records that the new Romantic love of informal 'sketching' most characteristically produced.[5]

Turner's work out of doors, in fact, was governed by two needs that were in origin traditional and, perhaps, 'Academic'. On the one hand he required a full reference library of topographical subjects: as his career had begun as a topographer, so he continued to base his art as a landscape painter on a professional capacity to make views of recognizable places, and his sketchbooks are largely taken up with the recording of specific scenes for future use. On the other hand his art as a painter of the 'Sublime' demanded a mastery of natural 'effect'. There is an intimate link between the notion of sketching on the spot and the theory of the 'Sublime'; for it is only by convincingly suggesting scale and the variation of light that the grandeur of a landscape can be conveyed. It was his mastery of the vast scale of the mountains that contributed so largely to the achievement of John Robert

106 Chevening Park, Kent *c.* 1800
Oil and watercolour (?) and size on paper, 278 × 378
Trustees of the British Museum, London (T.B., XCV(a)-B) (Cat. No. P157)

Cozens; and it was central to Turner's ambition that he should study to evoke scale. Hence, when he draws from nature he does not study small objects: he attempts to capture whole landscapes. So his studies out of doors, when they are not concerned simply to record, are frequently essays in scale: he developed washes of colour that express, above all, the distance, breadth and atmospheric variety of a view. His pencil notes themselves evolved towards a comparable expressiveness: the already flexible outline style that he had derived from Canaletto and Cozens became looser and quicker, and by 1801 was flexible enough to capture the sweep of a range of hills as readily as the detail of a city roofscape. At the height of his interest in the grand scenery of Wales and northern England, he made a number of large colour studies which show wide sweeps of mountain countryside.[6] They are sufficiently complete, in many cases, and sufficiently weighty in their handling of impressive natural phenomena, to seem almost like finished works from the studio; yet they appear, on the evidence of their treatment, to have been coloured out of doors. Even on the small scale of a pocket sketchbook, the colour studies seek to preserve broad atmospheric effects, not the minutiae of rustic detail: the misty panoramas of Edinburgh that Turner noted on his journey to Scotland in 1801[7] are examples of the process. The same interests dominate his patterns of note-taking during the Swiss journey of the following year.

The mass of studies of cloud, of storms and sunsets, of tranquil seas, that he made all through his career testify to his compelling need to express *space*—the medium through which alone his landscapes could come to life. Incidental detail, such as the growth of plants or the movement of water, were things that Turner understood from observation without making elaborate records. There are accounts of him spending hours together, even at the end of his life, studying such minutiae;[8] the *Skies* sketchbook[9] contains a series of careful transcripts of particular cloud effects, very different from the generalized studies of skies that abound among the

Pl. 154

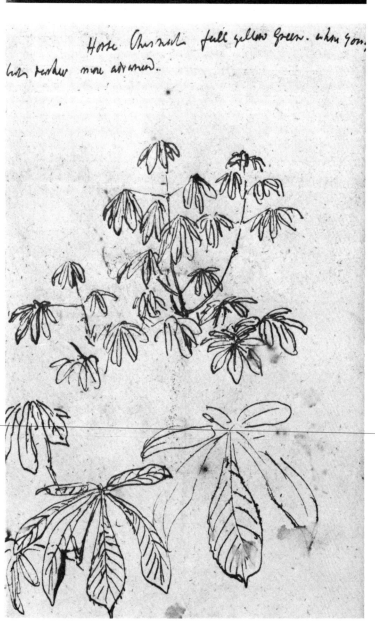

107 Study of the leaves of a horse chestnut *c.* 1801
Pen and ink, 207 × 130
Trustees of the British Museum, London (T.B., LXI-63) (not in catalogue)

108 Windsor Castle from the Thames *c*. 1804–6
Oil on canvas, 889 × 1194
H.M. Treasury and National Trust (Lord Egremont Collection),
Petworth House (Cat. No. P149)

loose sheets of the Bequest, which in all probability must be regarded as inventions rather than direct records. He did not always need to put down what he learned. The process of drawing in colour was a process of rendering *into art*—a step towards the creation of a public statement. For this reason

nearly all Turner's coloured sketches bear marks of organization and reinterpretation that make them quite different from the characteristic open-air studies of his contemporaries. We have only to look at exceptions to this generalization to grasp its accuracy: in 1813 Turner made a number of studies in oil on paper during a tour of Devon and Cornwall, Pl. 124 which are of uncharacteristic immediacy and directness.[10] In this case, we have evidence that he was actively encouraged to work in this elaborate medium out of doors: 'After he returned to Plymouth, in the neighbourhood of which he

109 Bensor or Bensington, near Wallingford
1806-7
Watercolour, 257 × 370
Trustees of the British Museum, London (T.B., XCV-13) (not in catalogue)

110 The ford *c.* 1806-7
Watercolour (unfinished), 533 × 756
Trustees of the British Museum, London (T.B., LXX-K) (not in catalogue)

111 Washing sheep *c.* 1806-7
Oil on canvas, 845 × 1165
Turner Bequest, Tate Gallery, London (Cat. No. P.173)

110

112 Pope's Villa, at Twickenham 1808
Oil on canvas, 915 × 1206
Trustees of the Walter Morrison Picture Settlement   (Cat. No. P72)

remained some weeks, Mr. John [Ambrose Johns, a painter and a friend of Turner's at Plymouth] fitted up a small portable painting-box, containing some prepared paper for oil sketches, as well as the other necessary materials. When Turner halted at a scene and seemed inclined to sketch it, Johns produced the inviting box, and the great artist, finding everything ready to his hand, immediately began to work...'[11]

But Turner did not make it his regular practice to use that medium in the open air, even watercolour being too time-consuming while he was travelling. There are repeated affirmations among early sources to the effect that he added colour to outline sketches only when he had reached his lodging.[12] Nevertheless, for a short time about 1800 when he was staying with his friend William Wells at Knockholt in Kent, he does seem to have experimented with using oil as a sketching medium.[13] A more impressive essay along these   Pl.106

111

113   The unpaid bill, or the Dentist reproving his son's prodigality
R.A.1808
Oil on panel, 594 × 800
Coll.: Dennis Lennox   (Cat. No. P81)

114   Charles Turner (1774–1837) (after J M W Turner for the *Liber Studiorum*, R. 17)
Farmyard with cock, 1809
Mezzotint, 174 × 254
Trustees of the British Museum, London   (1869–11–9–35)

115 Ploughing up Turnips, near Slough 1809
Oil on canvas, 1020 × 1300
Turner Bequest, Tate Gallery, London (Cat. No. P89)

lines is embodied in the series of panels and canvases that he worked at later in the first decade of the century, often, according to one account, from a boat which he took down the Thames and its tributary, the Wey.[14] This expansive method of open-air sketching is quite different from the hurried note-taking in pocketbooks that was Turner's usual practice. It denotes a new relationship with the country-side—one, perhaps, more analogous to that of the country-bred Constable than any Turner had hitherto enjoyed. At a time shortly before the presumed date of these oil studies, he had acquired a *pied-à-terre* by the Thames, Sion Ferry House at Isleworth near Richmond; this was probably in 1804, the date of the completion of his gallery in Harley Street, and

soon after the death of his mother.[15] The move was a direct consequence of his professional success and established him, in his own modest and industrious way, as a 'country gentleman'. It brought him into contact with a new landscape, which was to be a potent and lasting source of inspiration: the Thames, between London and Windsor, became the subject of many pictures, and the scenery of the river at Isleworth in particular was transformed in his imagination into a Classical landscape out of which some of his noblest Carthaginian motifs were to grow.[16]

116   Tabley, the seat of Sir J. F. Leicester, Bart.: Windy day
R.A. 1809
Oil on canvas, 915 × 1206
Victoria University of Manchester   (Cat. No. P98)

117   Cottage Steps, Children feeding Chickens   1809
(R.A. 1811)
Watercolour, 611 × 463
Private collection, Japan   (Cat. No. 490)

118   The garreteer's petition   *c.* 1808
Pen and brown ink and wash with a little watercolour, 184 × 302
Trustees of the British Museum, London (T.B., CXXI-A)   (not in catalogue)

120   Woodland scene, *c.* 1810–15
Watercolour, 280 × 229
Coll.: Lady Monk Bretton   (Cat. No. 419)

119   Harvest Dinner, Kingston Bank   1809
Oil on canvas, 1020 × 1300
Turner Bequest, Tate Gallery, London   (Cat. No. P90)

121   Somer-Hill, near Tunbridge, the seat of W. F. Woodgate, Esq.
R.A. 1811
Oil on canvas, 915 × 1223
National Galleries of Scotland, Edinburgh   (Cat. No. P116)

122 Scarborough Town and Castle: Morning: Boys catching crabs
R.A. 1811
Watercolour, 687 × 1016
Private collection (Cat. No. 528)

Pl. 111 The canvases and panels that Turner painted in his boat on the water are notes of glimpses, trees and sky, or the undergrowth at the river's edge; sometimes they are incomplete rustic subjects, cows watering, with groups of buildings and trees disposed according to a more or less formal plan. All of them are on a white ground, which begins to occur in his finished paintings at this period, and which seems to owe something to his practice in watercolour as, perhaps, does the general thinness of paint and looseness of handling. There are in fact watercolour studies made along the Thames at much the same date which share the fresh, informal atmosphere of the oil sketches;[17] they are of great beauty and assurance, and the watercolour is applied with a limpid grace and firmness that seems to mark a new departure in his development. The studies vary from unplanned notes of trees and plant-life by the water to more carefully composed scenes in which boats or trees play an ordained part in the design of the sheet. The more spontaneous are, in this case, the more impressive: they Pl. 109 have a freshness and strength that make them among the finest of all romantic open-air watercolours. There are other watercolours apparently of Thames-side scenes, evidently Pl. 110 executed around 1805, which seem to be studio works—half-finished studies and compositional schemes which are even closer to the oil sketches in mood and colouring than the watercolours in his sketchbooks.

123 Frosty Morning R.A. 1813
Oil on canvas, 1135 × 1745
Turner Bequest, Tate Gallery, London (Cat. No. P127)

These may well have been preparatory exercises for more elaborate works; and the hours that Turner spent in sketching beside the Thames did bear fruit of a more formal nature. Amongst the splendid continental subjects that he exhibited in these years there appeared also pictures like the two views of *Walton Bridges* of 1806,[18] the *Thames near Windsor: Evening—men dragging nets on shore* and *Cliveden on Thames* of 1807, and the *View of Richmond Hill and Bridge*[19] which, with several others in the same vein, hung in the 1808 exhibition. These pictures breathe an air of tranquil poetry far removed from the 'Sublime' histrionics of, say, *The Goddess of*

124 A river valley 1813
Oil on prepared paper, 235 × 298
Trustees of the British Museum, London (T.B. CXXX-E)
(Cat. No. P217)

125 Crossing the brook R.A. 1815
Oil on canvas, 1930 × 1650
Turner Bequest, Tate Gallery, London (Cat. No. P130)

119

Discord choosing the apple of contention in the garden of the Hesperides. But they are clearly works of a different class from the open-air studies that have been discussed. Some, like the *Richmond Hill and Bridge,* are constructed on overtly Claudian principles; others, it is true, seem composed in a less orthodox way, but they all differ from the open-air sketches in one important respect: they are lit in an altogether more theatrical manner. In the sketches blue sky and clouds are allowed to dispose themselves as they will across the design, to give a spontaneous and 'natural' effect. In the exhibited paintings there is nearly always a rich golden glow that transforms reality into a vision tinted with grandeur. The expansive

126 The Vale of Ashburnham   1816
Watercolour, 379 × 563
Trustees of the British Museum, London (Salting Bequest)
(Cat. No. 425)

127 Crook of Lune, looking towards Hornby Castle   1816–18
Watercolour, 280 × 417
Courtauld Institute of Art, University of London (Sir Stephen Courtauld Bequest)   (Cat. No. 575)

128 Kirby Lonsdale Churchyard   *c.* 1818
Watercolour, 286 × 415
Private collection   (Cat. No. 578)

mood of calm that runs through this series is also the keynote of a more obviously 'academic' picture of the same time—*Sun rising through vapour: fishermen cleaning and selling fish* of 1807.[20] Here the evocation of cool morning light diffused through mist is applied to a large marine painted in emulation of the Dutch school. The picture demonstrates that we cannot regard the glowing skies of the English scenes simply as renderings of nature for her own sake. The golden haze that envelops the distance in *Ploughing up Turnips, near Slough,* is

Pl.115

also a pictorial effect that deliberately suggests the old masters; especially, in this case, the Dutchman Cuyp,[21] though associations of Claude are also present. Even in a direct and apparently topographical house-portrait like *Somer-Hill, near Tonbridge,* which has been compared with Pl.121 work by Constable,[22] the sheer breadth of the design and the spell-binding stillness of the scene betray a self-consciousness alien to Constable's art, and hint at grand effects. We have only to compare the glimmering water in the foreground of *Somer-Hill* with that of the much later dawn views of the Rigi Pl.248 to realize the painting belongs to an extended sequence of contemplative morning subjects in which, throughout his life, Turner expressed some of his most personal responses to nature on the grandest scale.

129 The Avenue, Farnley *c.* 1818
Black chalk, watercolour
and body-colour on a grey
ground, 311 × 419 (sight)
Coll.: Mrs. Cecil Keith
(Cat. No. 600)

130 Roman Tower at
Andernach 1817
Body-colour on white
paper prepared with a
grey wash, 197 × 311
Isabella Stewart Gardner
Museum, Boston, Mass.
(Cat. No. 663)

131 Raby Castle, the seat of the Earl of Darlington R.A. 1818
Oil on canvas, 1190 × 1806
Walters Art Gallery, Baltimore, Maryland (Cat. No. P136)

It is nevertheless true that a more informal note was creeping into Turner's paintings at this date. The genre scenes which appeared in 1807 and 1808, *A country blacksmith*[23] and *The unpaid bill,* reflect not so much nature as a more 'naturalistic' art: that of the young Scot David Wilkie, whose *Blind Fiddler,*[24] in the seventeenth-century Netherlandish manner of Teniers and Ostade, had attracted much attention in 1806.[25] It was typical of Turner to have chosen for imitation a contemporary who was himself strongly indebted to an artist of the past. Even here, however, a more

general movement was at work than the mere copying of a new fashion, for in 1809 Turner again showed a genre piece, this time based on an idea that he had found in the satires of William Hogarth: *The garreteer's petition* alludes to Hogarth's engraving of *The Distress'd Poet,* and some of the verses that Turner composed to accompany the subject echo the lines from the *Dunciad* that Hogarth appended to his plate.[26]

There is apparent, therefore, a real determination on Turner's part to broaden the basis of his achievement; this is made clear, too, in the importance that he attached to the 'Pastoral' plates of his *Liber Studiorum,* designs that concentrate on 'low' subjects, often with humorous incident. Two watercolours that treat this class of theme, *November: Flounder-fishing*[27] and *May: Chickens,* show that he regarded any developments that he made as applicable to all media.

Pl.113

Pl.118

Pl.114

Pl.117

The juxtaposition of circumstantial rustic detail and poetically heightened atmospheric effect which creates the mood of oil-paintings like *Ploughing up Turnips, near Slough,* is the signal of an emerging pattern. Turner's sketchbooks, as well as his finished drawings, bear witness to a continuous preoccupation with the kind of human activity that the title of this picture makes so specific, and in the next decade he established the flawless blend of rural genre with heroic landscape that was to be characteristic of his watercolour views, at least, for the rest of his life. It was developed in the *Picturesque Views on the Southern Coast of England,* begun in 1810 when Turner was commissioned by the engraver and print-publisher, George Cooke, to make views of the coastal scenery of southern England, from Kent to Devon and Cornwall.[28] The project occupied him until the early 1820s, by which time he had undertaken many other such commissions. Although small in size these views are full-scale landscapes, often dealing with subjects chosen for their complexity, with varied perspectives of interrelated sea and land. The *Southern Coast* views cannot often be reconciled with preconceived Claudian or other compositional schemes: they are organized according to a grandiose logic of geographical reality, and the tension between topography and art which results is an important element in their success.

The *Southern Coast* tours that he made in about 1815 were combined with work for another commission. This was a set of thirteen watercolour views in the neighbourhood of Hastings for John Fuller, of Rosehill Park, Sussex.[29] For these drawings Turner worked on a larger size of sheet; in them there is almost no hint of the self-consciousness with which Turner generally translated reality into art. Yet all the Fuller subjects are sweeping vistas that demand great compositional subtlety, and are integrated by the most delicate interplay of colours. The splendid panorama of *The Vale of Ashburnham* Pl. 126

132 Study of plants *c.* 1820
Pen and brown ink with scraping-out on white paper prepared with a wash of dark grey-brown, 111 × 161
Trustees of the British Museum, London (T.B., CXLII-8) (not in catalogue)

133 The Thames from Richmond Hill *c.* 1815
Pencil and watercolour, 188 × 271
Trustees of the British Museum, London (T.B., CXCVII-B) (not in catalogue)

134 England: Richmond Hill, on the Prince Regent's Birthday
R.A. 1819
Oil on canvas, 1800 × 3345
Turner Bequest, Tate Gallery, London (Cat. No. P140)

135 Richmond Hill *c.* 1820-5
Watercolour and body-colour, 297 × 489
The Lady Lever Collection, Port Sunlight, Cheshire (Cat. No. 518)

136 W. B. Cooke (1788–1855) (after J.M.W. Turner for *Picturesque Views on the Southern Coast of England*, R. 109)
Entrance of Fowey Harbour, Cornwall 1820
Engraving, 156 × 239
Trustees of the British Museum, London (1850–10–14–117) (not in catalogue)

shows how Turner, in making his initial notes from nature, already organized what he saw to take on the format of a picture. His pencil drawing of the subject contains fore-ground detail that corresponds almost exactly with that in the finished work:[30] but it must be observed that in translating nature into the universal language of his art Turner almost always generalized such features as the isolated trees that figure in his foregrounds: the studies of pines that Ruskin

Pl.125   suggested were the foundation for the trees in *Crossing the brook* are rare in their particularization.[31] In about 1810 Turner made an oil-painting of Rose Hill which has the same expansive simplicity as the Fuller watercolours;[32] later, in 1817, he infused the same characteristic with 'Sublime' power in the most splendid of all his house-portraits, that of

Pl.131   *Raby Castle,* with its panoramic setting of North-country hills.

Even these ostensibly topographical works nearly always, therefore, have the overtones of art rather than of simple

nature. This is also true of the famous *Frosty Morning* of 1813, Pl.123 perhaps the least theatrical of Turner's major works, but nevertheless lit by a low incipient sunrise, handled so as to enhance the expectant mood of the scene in a way that is not strictly 'realistic'; and with a road running directly into the distance that creates a perspective of classical firmness.

Frosty Morning was the outcome of one of the journeys to Farnley Hall in Yorkshire that Turner made regularly between about 1810 and 1825. At Farnley Turner was able to relax in an atmosphere as familiar and informal as that of the Thames at Twickenham. He went shooting on the moors

137 What you will! R.A. 1822
Oil on canvas, 482 × 520
Coll.: Sir Michael Sobell (Cat. No. P229)

with his host and made drawings of the game that he bagged. Fawkes's brother wrote a book on the plumage of birds for which Turner supplied a series of illustrations, drawn in watercolour from life.[33] He made careful studies of the house, recording its interiors with graceful precision, its surrounding landscape with a soft informality that occurs sometimes

127

in his private sketches of this time, but in no other works made for a patron. The most inventive of his drawings for Fawkes, however, are the series of 'Fairfaxiana' evolved round the family collection of Civil War relics, kept in an oak cupboard of which he made a neat study, with pasted-on 'doors' that could be opened and shut. The mood of historical curiosity that pervades these designs is no doubt Fawkes's rather than Turner's own; but the spirit in which they are composed, with witty assemblages of armour, weapons, piles of documents, and period details of all kinds, is one of slightly

138 View from the Terrace of a Villa at Niton, Isle of Wight, from sketches by a lady R.A. 1826
Oil on canvas, 455 × 610
Coll.: Mr. William A. Coolidge, Boston, Mass. (Cat. No. P234)

139 Mortlake Terrace, the seat of William Moffatt, Esq. Summer's evening: detail R.A. 1827
Oil on canvas, 920 × 1220
National Gallery of Art, Washington, D.C. (Cat. No. P239)

140 East Cowes Castle, the seat of J. Nash, Esq.; the Regatta beating to windward R.A. 1828
Oil on canvas, 902 × 1207
Indianapolis Museum of Art, Indiana (Cat. No. P242)

Pl. 129 pedantic jocularity which may well have epitomized the personal bond that tied Fawkes to Turner.[34]

The Farnley drawings[35] are by no means consistent in their execution or finish. Some are chalk sketches, roughly coloured, on a grey ground; others—especially the interiors—are superbly precise, elegant views which recall that Turner had been an architect's draughtsman in his youth. None, however, was actually noted down in this form; they are all, more or less, worked up from preliminary pencil Pl. 130 drawings. The same is true of the fifty-one Rhine views of

1817, which Fawkes acquired as a complete set from Turner.[36] Here too there is great variety in the degree of finish, but no single item can be said to have been 'finished' in the sense that Turner would have exhibited it publicly in that state. It is significant that the Rhine drawings do not appear

141 Virginia Water   *c.* 1829
Watercolour, 290 × 443
Private collection   (Cat. No. 519)

in the printed catalogue of Fawkes's exhibition of 1819. He was to make fully finished watercolours from some of the Rhine subjects a year or two later.[37] It seems fairly clear that Fawkes was allowed to buy the set because of his close personal friendship with Turner, who did not, as far as can be judged, favour any other patron with such a mark of intimacy, until the young Ruskin began to badger him for sheets from his sketchbooks; that was a somewhat different sort of relationship.

With their relative freedom and 'spontaneity', the Farnley

views and the Rhine drawings belong only in part to the world of the Thames studies of the previous decade. Their freshness is genuine enough; but it is not unpremeditated. The Rhine drawings are almost all carefully composed, and their grey grounds exploited to give a sombre splendour to each vista. The Farnley subjects are less studied, and some are among the least contrived of Turner's works; the topographer's desire to record is blended with a personal affection for the scenes which once again brings Turner close to Constable. In his later colour studies Turner often drew with as much freedom, and with as strong a sense of the immediate presence of his motif; but he never again, except in a few of the Petworth interiors which follow naturally from the Farnley sequence, pursued an intimate personal need at the expense of formal and public values: the great colour experiments that he was to make in the 1820s made it all but impossible for him ever again to create a watercolour study with the simplicity and directness that he achieved in the drawings of these years.[38]

Pl.134 The work which crowns his output of English subjects in this decade is the enormous *England: Richmond Hill, on the Prince Regent's Birthday,* exhibited in 1819. As in *Crossing the brook,* rural England is here presented in terms of Claude; but the classical overtones are unexpectedly muted: the predominant mood of the picture is one of sunny informality, of naturalness, and a refined, elegant homeliness. This may be in part because Turner had already treated the view in a fully classical vein in his large picture of *Thomson's Aeolian Harp* of 1809.[39] The ineradicable influence of art is present, however, in more unexpected ways: the figures which form the colourful foreground are a conscious emulation of Watteau,[40] and foreshadow one of Turner's great enthusiasms of the next decade. Further, the whole picture probably owes its conception to another painting: its exceptional size may have been inspired by the appearance at the British Institution, shortly before, of an enormous view from Richmond Hill by Thomas Hofland, the rival who had taken the Institution's premium from Turner's *Apullia in search of Appullus* in 1814.[41]

Pl.135 But if in the large picture Turner could not avoid overtones of art, he made, a few years later, a watercolour of the same view which is remarkably free of such connotations. The elegantly poised trees and Watteauesque figures have been replaced by a very simple open composition. Although the view itself is grand, Turner's presentation of it is understated and direct, and in this it reflects the mood of several of his works in the mid-1820s. Both this drawing and the very large canvas of 1819 may rely at least partly on the Pl.133 study in watercolour that he must have made in about 1815, in which the scene is approached entirely naturalistically, and

with no attempt to impose a 'composition' on what is simply an expansive stretch of flat country divided by a curving river. This direct vision is elaborately recreated in the large picture; but in the finished watercolour only the cheerful and informal figures intervene to 'place' the scenery in a social context.[42]

This watercolour, to judge from the costumes of the figures, belongs to the early or mid-1820s. In the year in which it was engraved, 1826,[43] Turner showed the first of two other views on the Thames in that district, the pair of portraits of *Mortlake Terrace, the seat of William Moffatt, Esq.*[44] Pl.139 *Richmond Hill* shares with these exquisite canvases a pale golden sunlight and an easy informality which bespeak Turner's especial affection for those stretches of the Thames; and we may observe a similar freshness and freedom from bombast in the two views of *Virginia Water,* watercolours Pl.141 made for George IV but not purchased by him.[45] The two pictures of *Mortlake Terrace* are small in size, and charmingly intimate in mood; in none of Turner's works does his idyllic sunlight strike so gently through the trees; yet the times of day chosen for these views are calculated to afford the most brilliant effect of direct low sun: one is 'Early (Summer's) Morning', the other 'Summer's Evening', and the screen of trees along the embankment provides a delicate foil to the bright light beyond. The way in which the brilliance of the sun dissolves the form of the parapet in the second picture is a wonderfully literal rendering of the phenomenon of dazzling light; yet the effect is wholly realistic: Turner takes Burke's pronouncement that 'such a light as that of the sun, immediately exerted on the eye as it overpowers the sense, is a very great idea'[46]—a pronouncement that he had long ago taken to heart—and adopts it in a context quite other than that of 'Sublime' landscape. By doing so he brings home even more powerfully the inherent grandeur of natural phenomena as they present themselves to us continually.

NOTES

1   The majority of Turner's lecture notes are in the British Library, Add. MSS. 46151. For a transcription of one lecture see Ziff, 'Backgrounds', 1963, pp. 124–47.

2   W. T. Whitley, 'Turner as a Lecturer', *Burlington Magazine*, vol. XXII, 1913, p. 206. See also Gage, 1969, pp. 106 ff.

3   Lecture note, Add. MSS. 46151 CC; transcribed in Gage, 1969, p. 213.

4   *Various Subjects of Landscape, Characteristic of English Scenery, From Pictures Painted by John Constable, R. A.* first appeared in 1830. By the time of the appearance of the second edition, in 1833, Constable had composed a full verbal account of his intention 'to mark the influence of light and shadow upon Landscape, not only in its general impression, and as a means of rendering a proper emphasis on the parts, but also to show its use and power as a medium of expression, so as to note "the day, the hour, the sunshine, and the shade"'. Constable goes on to contrast his own approach, seeking 'perfection at its PRIMITIVE SOURCE, NATURE' with that of 'the Artist, intent only on the study of departed excellence', who 'produces, either "imitative," "scholastic," or that which has been termed "Eclectic Art" '. It is difficult to believe that he did not include Turner in this second category; though we know from Leslie (quoted by Thornbury, p. 407) that Constable once asked 'Did you ever see a picture by Turner, and not wish to possess it?'

5   For a study of the Romantic penchant for painting out of doors see Gage, *A Decade of English Naturalism, 1810–1820,* exhibition catalogue, 1969–70.

6   T.B., LX(a).

7   T.B., LV, pp. 5, 6, 10. See Herrmann, *Turner,* 1975, Pl. 25.

8   For instance, in Sir Walter Armstrong, *Turner,* 1902, pp. 130–1: Stopford Brooke described Turner 'squatting on his heels at the river's edge, and looking down intently into the water... half an hour later, the figure was still there and still intent in the same way... the object of his curiosity was the pattern made by the ripples at the edge of the tide.' See also Thornbury, p. 121: F. E. Trimmer 'was told by Howard [Henry Howard, R.A.] he [Turner] would spend hours sketching a stone'. Few drawings of this sort have survived.

9   T.B., CLVIII. See Pl. 154.

10   Cat. Nos P213–P225.

11   Thornbury, p. 153.

12   See for example the letter to John Soane from his son in Naples, 1819, quoted on p. 143 below; and Ruskin in *Works,* VI, p. 37: 'These

pencil scratches he put a few blots of colour on (I suppose... the same evening, certainly *not* upon the spot)'; and Thornbury, p. 93: 'He generally preferred the pencil-point, writing in here and there the colours and effects.'

13   Cat. Nos P154–P158. Butlin and Joll, 1977, follow Finberg in dating these to 1805–6, but they seem to belong stylistically to the years 1799–1801 (see B.M., 1975, No. 24).

14   Cat. Nos P177–P194. See Thornbury, pp. 120–1.

15   Turner's mother died probably at Bethlem Hospital on 15 April 1804. See Introduction, p. 12.

16   See, in particular, the *Studies for Pictures, Isleworth,* sketchbook, T.B., XC, in which views on the Thames alternate with Classical compositions that derive from them (for reproductions see Wilkinson, 1974, pp. 106–9).

17   In the *Thames from Reading to Walton* sketchbook, T.B., XCV.

18   Cat. Nos P60 and P63.

19   Cat. Nos P64, P66 and P73.

20   The hazy sun that is so superbly made the central motif of this picture, and which plays an important part in the English subjects of these years, was a theme that had been treated in the 1790s by one of Turner's most diverse and surprising colleagues in landscape, George Arnald, 1763–1841. In 1797 Arnald had shown (R.A. 596) a picture entitled *Sun breaking through a fog,* in the spirit of Turner's own climatic studies of the following year. In 1796 he had shown *A Country Churchyard—moonlight* (9) and *A farrier's shop* (310); this was the kind of variety that Turner himself aimed at. Arnald began to exhibit in 1788, but was not made A.R.A. until 1810.

21   Aelbert Cuyp, 1620–91.

22   Compare Constable's *Wivenhoe Park,* National Gallery, Washington, exhibited R.A. 1817 (85).

23   Cat. No. P68.

24   David Wilkie, 1785–1841. Tate Gallery, 99.

25   David Teniers the younger, 1610–90; Adriaen van Ostade, 1610–84. For comment on *The unpaid bill* as an exercise in imitating Rembrandt see Gage, *Rain, Steam and Speed,* 1972, p. 49.

26   Turner's painting is Cat. No. P100; William Hogarth, 1697–1764: his print is Paulson 145, Pl. 156. Among the lines of verse that Turner scribbled on his drawing for *The garreteer's petition* (Pl. 118) occurs one, 'Sinking from thought to thought a vast profound', engraved below Hogarth's subject; it was quoted from Pope's *Dunciad,* Book I, line 118.

27   Cat. No. 491.

28 Cat. section VIII(b). For a full account of the project see Finberg, *Turner's Southern Coast*, 1929.

29 Cat. Nos 423–35.

30 The sketch is T.B., CXXXVII, pp. 68v–69.

31 These studies are in the *Plymouth, Hamoaze* sketchbook, T.B., CXXXI, pp. 117 verso, 118, and in the *Devon Rivers No. 2* sketchbook, T.B., CXXXIII, p. 37. There are several drawings of individual plants in the *Walmer Ferry* sketchbook of about 1815 (T.B., CXLII); they are annotated 'Plantain, Nettle, Cat's tail, Daisy, Lilock, Grass', 'Hop and Willow', 'Thistle, Nettle, Convolvulus,' etc. (see Pl. 132). Other such studies occasionally occur, e.g. the group of weeds on p. 2 of the *River* sketchbook (T.B., XCVI), which appears in the foreground of the view of More Park in the *Rivers of England* series (Cat. No. 734).

32 Cat. No. P211.

33 See Finberg, *Life*, p. 431; also Finberg, *Turner's Watercolours at Farnley Hall*, 1912, pp. 89–96, and R.A. 1974, No. B127.

34 The 'Fairfaxiana' drawings are still at Farnley; one other, a 'frontispiece', is Cat. No. 582.

35 The main series of views of the house and its grounds, and the countryside in the vicinity (the 'Wharfedales' as Fawkes called them) are Cat. section X(d).

36 Cat. section XI(a).

37 Cat. Nos 690–3, Add. 689(a).

38 See chap. 7, especially pp. 161–2.

39 Cat. No. P86.

40 See Ziff, *Art Bulletin*, 1971, p. 126. Ziff points out that Turner made use in this picture of figures that he had copied from Watteau's *L'Isle Enchantée* in the *Hints River* sketchbook (T.B., CXLI, pp. 26 verso, 27), repr. Wilkinson, *The Sketches of Turner R.A., 1802–20*, 1974, p. 174.

41 *Apullia in search of Appullus* is Cat. No. P128. Thomas Hofland, 1777–1843, showed at the Academy in 1815 (374) a *View from Richmond Hill, evening* which was entered in the British Institution catalogue, when it appeared at that exhibition in 1816, with dimensions (presumably, according to the British Institution practice, including frame) 6'9" × 9'3" (2057 × 2819). Turner's *Richmond Hill* is 5'10" × 10'11" (1778 × 3227)—less square, but altogether rather larger. Further comment on the picture and its genesis is offered by Stuckey, *Turner—His Birthday and Related Matters*.

42 Compare Turner's later version of the subject, for *England and Wales* (Cat. No. 879), which preserves the same atmosphere but is a more artificial composition.

43 For the *Literary Souvenir*, R. 314.

44 Cat. Nos P235 and P239.

45 Cat. Nos 519–20. These were also engraved for an annual—*The Keepsake*, 1830 (R. 322, 323).

46 Burke, 1757, p. 62.

Chapter Six

Italy 1819

Turner's interest in Italy can be traced from his earliest drawings: it must have been implanted when he made his copy after Fabris, showing ruins at Naples, in about 1787,[1] and is revealed in the studies that he made from Wilson and Vernet when he was first exploring the language of oil. As we have seen, the dominant roles played by both Wilson and Claude in forming Turner's approach to the Academy picture carried with them an explicit reference to Italian landscape. His experimental essay in Wilson's manner, *Aeneas and the Sibyl, Lake Avernus,*[2] actually sets out to represent a specific Italian location, with the aid of a drawing made on the spot by Colt Hoare; and, among the numerous Claudian subjects painted in the early years of the new century, the attempt to create a recognizable Mediterranean mood occurs often: in Pl.142 *Mercury and Hersé,* for instance, of 1811; in *Dido and Aeneas,* of 1814;[3] and in the two Greek subjects of 1816, after drawings Pl.144 made on the spot by H. Gally Knight, of *The Temple of Jupiter Panellenius restored,*[4] and in ruins. In addition to these there are English subjects that seem to make a compromise with Italian features—for example, *Crossing the brook,* of 1815, in which light, trees, even architecture take on something of the character that would fit them to appear in a classical scene. When the defeat of Napoleon at Waterloo left Europe open again to travellers, Turner must have responded at once to the promise of the renewed accessibility of the south: the Pl.168 *Landscape: Composition of Tivoli* of 1817 is a full-blown classical landscape in watercolour which seems to express the mounting excitement of anticipation, touchingly restrained in its admission that it cannot claim to be topographically authoritative, for *Tivoli* makes it plain that Turner is flirting with an imagined scene and not offering (what he was accustomed to offer in his watercolours) a record which, in spite of any creative freedom, would take its starting-point from the need for information.[5]

By this time, however, he was becoming well equipped with accurate knowledge of Italy. The *Eruption of Vesuvius,* Pl.145 from the same year as the *Tivoli,* is evidently based on a drawing carefully made on the spot, and two smaller views, showing the volcano active and in repose respectively, were also made about the same time.[6] They recall the fact that Turner had imbibed a great deal of information about the appearance of Italy from the drawings of John Robert Cozens which he had copied for Dr. Monro in the mid-1790s. And in 1818 he was commissioned to make watercolours from pencil drawings taken on the spot by James Hakewill for a book of a *Picturesque Tour of Italy,* published in 1820.[7] These watercolours are complete realizations of eighteen views in Florence, Rome, Naples and elsewhere. In the main, relying as they do on the more prosaic vision of an amateur, they are somewhat stiff in presentation; but they include much lively invention in the matter of detail, especially in the introduction of figures suggesting Italian life. Thus Italy was a constant and vivid presence in Turner's imagination throughout the years prior to his visit.

The journey was inevitable, not only for himself but for his interested fellow-artists; for example, the portrait painter Thomas Lawrence, in Rome in 1819, found Turner's landscapes constantly coming to mind (a remarkable tribute to the latter's imaginative realization of a land he had not yet seen): 'Turner should come to Rome. His genius would here be supplied with materials, and entirely congenial with it... It is a fact, that the country and scenes around me *do* thus impress themselves upon me; and that Turner is always associated with them; Claude, though frequently, not so often; and Gaspard Poussin still less.'[8] Pl.143

Turner's association with James Hakewill over the *Picturesque Tour of Italy* provided him not only with the informative task of rendering actual Italian scenes, but also with a

142 Mercury and Hersé R.A. 1811
Oil on canvas, 1905 × 1600
Private collection (Cat. No. P114)

143 Gaspard Poussin (1613–75)
The Falls of Tivoli
Oil on canvas, 990 × 810
Wallace Collection, London

144 View of the Temple of Jupiter Panel-
lenius in the island of AEgina, with the Greek
national dance of the Romaika: Acropolis of
Athens in the distance. Painted from a sketch
taken by H. Gally Knight, Esq. in 1810
R.A. 1816
Oil on canvas, 1182 × 1781
Coll.: The Duke of Northumberland, K.G.
(Cat. No. P134)

145 Eruption of Vesuvius 1817
Watercolour, 286 × 397
Yale Center for British Art, Paul Mellon Collection (Cat. No. 697)

personal guide to the places he was about to visit. In a sketchbook labelled by Turner *Route to Rome*[9] Hakewill carefully wrote out a full account of where to go and what to see, which we may assume Turner used as the basis for arranging his tour. Such notes, of course, give Hakewill's own idea of a recommendable route; but we may imagine that Turner prompted him to mention where the 'best view of Geneva' was to be had; the search for fine vantage-points was an important part of his journeying and he would naturally ask about well-known views. The care with which he prepared for this tour parallels his approach to the sketching expeditions of the 1790s, for another book, *Italian Guide*,[10] is inscribed '*98 Foreign Hint*', and contains numerous thumb-nail copies of Italian views from another published guide;[11] this is a particularly illuminating example of the way in which Turner prepared himself visually for a tour which, he must have felt, would bring him into contact with more than he could hope to absorb. In fact he absorbed an astonishing amount, and in the four months of his trip filled some twenty

146 Rome from the Monte Mario *c.* 1818
Watercolour, 137 × 213
Yale Center for British Art, Paul Mellon Collection   (Cat. No. 708)

sketchbooks, nearly all of which, it seems, he had stocked up
with before leaving England.

His urgent sense of the need to retain a mass of new
information apparently led him, at the outset of the journey,
to begin a journal; its only entry appears at the front of the
sketchbook labelled *Paris, Cross France, R[ou]ṭ[e] to Italy*. It
refers to a day early in August 1819, when he 'Left Dover at
10. Arr. at Calais at 3 in a boat from the Packet Boat...'[12] After

147 Venice: San Giorgio Maggiore from the Dogana   1819
Watercolour, 224 × 287
Trustees of the British Museum, London (T.B., CLXXXI–4)   (not in
catalogue)

138

149 Richard Wilson (1714–82)
Ponte Molle, Monte Mario 1754
Black chalk and stump heightened with white on grey paper,
282 × 413
Henry E. Huntington Library and Art Gallery, San Marino, California

148 The Temple of the Sibyl seen from below 1819
Pencil and scraping-out on white paper prepared with a grey wash,
252 × 195
Trustees of the British Museum, London (T.B., CLXXXIII-47) (not in
catalogue)

150 View from Naples looking towards Vesuvius 1819
Pencil, partly finished in watercolour, 254 × 405
Trustees of the British Museum, London (T.B., CLXXXVII-18) (not in
catalogue)

a few lines the journal ends; but Turner maintained his
vigilance of observation in sketches which show his progress
through France, over the pass of Mont Cenis and down to
Turin, his first important stopping-place in Italy. Here he
began to draw with new intensity, and filled a book[13] with
sketches of that city and of Como, Lugano and Lake
Maggiore. In another book[14] he proceeds from Milan to
Venice where, according to Finberg's estimate, he must have
stayed about a fortnight. He then moved on, via Bologna,
Rimini, Ancona, Macerata and Foligno, to Rome, which he
reached some time in October. Hakewill had advised him to
'take some mode of travelling gently to Rome, as Perugia,
Spoleto, Terni, Narni, Civita Castellana should all be stopped
at'. Turner visited most of these places.

In Rome his activity was even more intense than hitherto:
he used his sketchbooks not only for the usual noting of
buildings and scenery but also to record a very large number
of the antiquities in the Vatican Museum and for his
comments on paintings, such as the *Aurora* of Guido Reni in
the Palazzo Rospigliosi.[15] In addition he avoided letting
anyone know where he was staying, and Hakewill's notes
give us no clue about this. Nevertheless, he seems to have

taken some part in the social life of the English artists who always formed a sizeable colony at Rome. We know that two Academicians with whom he was on close terms, Sir Francis Chantrey and John Jackson,[16] were in the city at the same time; and there is an account in the diary of Tom Moore, the poet, of a visit to the Accademia Veneziana with Canova, Lawrence, Chantrey, Jackson and Turner, and they 'all dined together except Canova, who has not dined from home these twelve years.'[17] But Turner's preoccupations were not social, and he spent much time outside the city, drawing at Tivoli, Albano, Nemi and Naples.

The immediate attraction of Naples was Vesuvius, which began to be active in October 1819 and produced a minor eruption in December. It seems that Turner left Rome specifically to observe the volcano late in October; whether he returned later is not clear. He also followed Hakewill's

advice and drew at Herculaneum, Pozzuoli, the Bay of Baiae and all over Naples. Before returning to Rome he went still further south to make sketches of the Greek temples at Paestum.

Of the nineteen books of drawings devoted to Turner's experiences in Italy four contain work in watercolour: another, the *Skies* book,[18] may also have been filled on this tour; all the rest are full of pencil sketches.[19] Most are of a standard 11 × 18 cm format, which Turner often used during the middle part of his career, and they are carefully inscribed

152 Rome: The Forum with a rainbow 1819
Pencil, watercolour and body-colour on white paper prepared with a
wash of grey, 229 × 367
Trustees of the British Museum, London (T.B., CLXXXIX-46) (not in
catalogue)

on their covers with the names of the principal places
recorded in them; they form a readily accessible library of
reference material, filed, as it were, under subject. The
drawings in them are all in the rapid, outline style that Turner
used on his travels. Often, when he finds himself in an
important city, Milan or Venice, for instance, he makes
particularly careful notes of the architecture, and, as in Rome,
of the antiquities; many of the drawings in the *Tivoli and Rome*
book are of sculpture and paintings in the Vatican; and the
book labelled *Vatican fragments* contains, almost exclusively,

studies of classical works; while the *St. Peter's* book is largely
concerned with some of the major monuments. All these
details are stored away as valuable information, just as are the
records of the costumes of 'Venetian Merchants' or of north
Italian peasants in the *Return from Italy* book.[20] On the whole,
though, it is noteworthy that Turner spent less time on this
tour drawing the local people and their activities than was his
usual practice—in France and Holland, for example.

We should not expect to find anything other than sketches
dating from the period of the tour itself; but some of the
drawings are in watercolour, and several of them are taken to
a considerable degree of elaboration. Within the limits of the
sketch, in fact, Turner employed a very wide range of
techniques to convey what he saw in Italy. The *Tivoli*
sketchbook has a grey ground washed on to one side of all its
leaves, and the pencil drawing is amplified by wiping out the

153 Rome: view of a garden 1819
Watercolour and body-colour with scraping-out on white paper prepared with a grey wash, 132 × 255
Trustees of the British Museum, London (T.B., CXC-64) (not in catalogue)

154 Study of sky ?1819
Watercolour, 124 × 246
Trustees of the British Museum, London (T.B., CLVIII-42) (not in catalogue)

PI. 148 white lights from this ground. The drawings are, in fact, chiaroscuro studies in black and white on grey. The use of a grey ground in this way goes back, of course, to the Swiss tour of 1802; which practice, as we have seen, grew naturally out of experiments made in Scotland and elsewhere. The Rhine views of 1817 were also done on grey-prepared grounds, and it should come as no surprise that Turner once again employs this device. But there is, nevertheless, something unexpected about the appearance of a dark ground-tone in the studies which he made of Italian landscape. It cannot have been mere force of habit—Turner was independent of habits that served no useful purpose.

His initial colour experiments in Italy show that he was able at once to respond freshly to what he found: they are two views on Lake Como, the first pages in the *Como and Venice* sketchbook, which uses no grey ground. These watercolours have a delicacy in the rendering of detail, and possess a brilliance in the suggestion of light, that convince us that Turner knew precisely how to manage the new scenery with which he was confronted. In the same book there is an extraordinary view across roofs towards a campanile and a dome in some town on his route out, which is equally assured;[21] and on the next page the breathtaking vision of
PI. 147 *S. Giorgio Maggiore from the Dogana,* at Venice, is one of the most memorable of all the Italian watercolours. In all, this book contains four Venetian subjects, each of great breadth and simplicity:[22] they seem to indicate that Turner was happy to discard, as it were, all the technical accretions of his career hitherto, in order to approach a new landscape as innocently as possible. The directness of such studies is the more

remarkable when we remember how much greater cause Turner had, even than Lawrence, to see Italy through Claude's eyes. But there is nothing of Claude in the views of the Campagna that occur in the *Rome: C[olour?] Studies* book; even the two watercolours of the cascades at Tivoli[23] seem to be independent of precedents, for they show us what is there in a language reminiscent of the freshness of expression found in the series of Thames watercolours of about 1806. This is perhaps the last sequence of watercolours that can be compared with that earlier group, and it occupies a similar place in Turner's progress; both series are notable for a casting off of formulas and an intensification of the unaffected observation of nature.

There are also pencil drawings without colour, and these, when they occur on pages washed with Turner's grey ground (*Tivoli* and other larger notebooks), often suggest the warm, atmospheric compositions in black chalk on grey paper that Richard Wilson made for the Earl of Dartmouth in Rome in PI. 149 the 1750s.[24] It cannot have been a coincidence that he should recall Wilson's work in the city where Wilson first established himself as a landscape artist, and there may have been an element of conscious 'homage' in such a combination of subject and medium. But Turner had his own purposes in working as he did, and in any case he was fascinated by the broad vistas of buildings, and the views of the Campagna and distant hills that he found in Rome. They presented him with a new range of atmospheric effects, as well as with new topography; and his essays in colour must have played an essential part in the process of absorbing them. We find elaborate studies involving both watercolour and body-

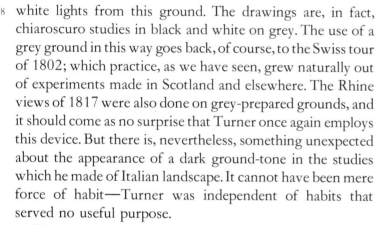

142

155 Bay of Naples, with Vesuvius—morning   1820
Watercolour, 265 × 387
Private collection   (Cat. No. 722)

colour on the grey ground, depicting complicated effects of
Pl. 152 light, with sunsets, moonlight, rainbows; sometimes a pen is
used in the rendering of detail. Although many of these are as
subtle, soft and evanescent as the pure watercolours, others
use the opaque body-colour to produce a bold, almost
strident effect of ochre masonry against blue sky, which
recalls the work of the Italian *vedutisti*—Labruzzi, Zucchi and
Clérisseau, for instance.[25]

The preoccupation with climatic conditions is even more
Pl. 154 evident in the *Skies* sketchbook, until now not associated with
the Italian tour, but almost certainly used in Rome or Naples,
since it contains at least one sheet (p. 42) very close in feeling

and treatment to, for instance, page 64 of the *Small Roman
C[olour?] Studies* book.[26] This sheet shows a sunset sky with a
line of stone pines on the horizon, strongly suggesting Italy.
The book is almost filled with a series of sky studies, executed
in fluid and pearly washes of colour. It seems most likely that
the more elaborate studies in other books were made at
Turner's lodgings; he would probably not have equipped
himself in the field with all the tools necessary for their
execution. While at Naples, we are told, he made 'pencil
sketches to the astonishment of the Fashionables, who
wonder of what use these rough draughts can be...' Turner
had said that 'it would take up too much time to colour in the
open air—he could make 15 or 16 pencil sketches to one
coloured.'[27] However, there is every reason to believe that
some at least of the more spontaneous and immediate pure
watercolour sketches were noted on the spot. An account

143

156   The Rialto, Venice   *c.* 1820
Watercolour, 286 × 413
Indianapolis   Museum   of   Art,   Indiana   (Pantzer   Collection)
(Cat. No. 718)

exists of Turner sketching in Italy with an amateur artist, R. J. Graves: 'At times... when they had fixed upon a point of view, to which they returned day after day, Turner would content himself with making one careful outline of the scene, and then, while Graves worked on, Turner would remain apparently doing nothing, till at some particular moment, perhaps on the third day, he would exclaim "there it is" and seizing his colours, work rapidly until he had noted down the peculiar effect he wished to fix in his memory.'[28]

The visit to Italy did not give rise to an immediate spate of paintings; Turner seems rather to have concentrated his efforts on a few works, but these were of more than usual importance for him. The first-hand experience of the masterpieces of Italian art apparently gave him fresh cause to review the status of landscape painting, and what it was capable of achieving; for the greatest productions of Italy (despite Claude and Poussin) were those figure-subjects which had been the inspiration for all that was considered vital to the serious art of modern England. In other words, Turner once again, as at the beginning of his academic career, was brought face to face with the problem of how to reconcile the essentially 'secondary' genre of landscape painting with his intentions as an artist on the highest plane of creative activity. The dilemma was accentuated, perhaps, by the scope of the work of other painters active in Rome when Turner was there; that he was conscious of them is shown by the list he made of many of their names in a

157 Rome: the Colosseum   1820
Watercolour, 277 × 293
Trustees of the British Museum, London (Lloyd Bequest)
(Cat. No. 723)

notebook,[29] including those of members of the flourishing movement of younger artists, mostly German or French, who admired Dürer and Raphael and were attempting in their paintings to imitate the clarity of colour and purity of line, as well as the solemnity of subject-matter, for which those masters were celebrated. It is possible that the lucidity and freshness of some of Turner's own watercolours made during the Italian trip owe something to his awareness of this school; but it is much more likely that, as we have already noted, these qualities were inherent in his attitude of deliberate openness, of unprejudiced receptivity, to everything that was new.

On his arrival in London, Turner must have very quickly begun to tackle a painting that would reassure him of his own place in the creative scheme of things. Two enormous canvases seem to have been worked on, and one of them was ready for submission to the Academy's Exhibition in the summer of 1820. The other was never completed: it is a view on the Grand Canal at Venice, taken from close to the water-line, the composition spanned by the arch of the Rialto Bridge. Whether it was begun first or not, it remained

145

158 Venice, from Fusina 1821
Watercolour, 286 × 406
Private collection (Cat. No. 721)

incomplete; even the picture that he did succeed in finishing bears signs of struggle—hardly surprising in view of its size and the speed with which it must have been executed (a reason for supposing that the *Rialto* was *not* started first). Pl.161 *Rome from the Vatican. Raffaelle accompanied by La Fornarina, preparing his pictures for the decoration of the Loggia* measures 177 × 335.5 cm, and, next to the *Rialto* and *England: Richmond Hill on the Prince Regent's Birthday,* was his largest work to date.[30] But it was not only size that the Italian masters had impressed on Turner; their humanistic subject-matter was even more important. Turner was, of course, an artist for whom humanity was always of central significance; but Italy challenged him to state more explicitly his own relationship with the tradition of humanist art. In *Rome from the Vatican* he seems to have done this by presenting a view of the universal artist surrounded by the fruits of his genius — sculpture, architectural designs, and paintings, including portraits, reli-

gious subjects and landscape. Certainly, however, the majority of those who saw it when it was first shown in public will have taken it as a piece of the fashionable 'historical genre', perhaps even as a commemoration of the death of Raphael exactly three hundred years before.[31]

In his concern to convey a complex message about the Renaissance *Uomo universale,* Turner tries to make his composition bear more weight than it will support: the perspective of the all-important still-life and figures in the foreground is based on an optical illusion that produces some odd proportions and impossible juxtapositions. This does serve an altogether grander end, though, for it creates a broad

159   Interior of St. Peter's, Rome   1821
Watercolour, 292 × 413
Private collection   (Cat. No. 724)

space under the arch of the loggia through which the panorama of Rome can be viewed, and it is in this, the landscape, that the picture is a total success. The city lies in shimmering heat, with golden stucco and pink roofs, and with the snow-capped mountains beyond; and this is the theme of many of the watercolour studies in the *Rome: C[olour?] Studies* book. Here it is translated into the medium of oil, and on to a much larger scale, so that we are almost in the world of the great Panoramas which Robert Barker had made so popular in London.[32] The cultural importance of the Vatican in the life of Rome as a whole is conveyed both by the parts of it that we see through the arch, especially Bernini's

piazza—an anachronism, of course, if we think of the picture as a historical piece—and by the perspective of the arcade to the right, which suggests the great treasures of art that Rome possesses: it is a very carefully rendered interior, for which Turner used some of the copious pencil notes which he had made on the spot.[33]

Turner may have worked on this view over Rome concurrently with two watercolours, *Rome from Monte Mario* and *Rome from the Pincian*,[34] both of which were probably executed some time in 1820 and so must have preceded his next Italian oil-painting. The view from Monte Mario had been one of the subjects that Hakewill asked him to interpret, and it is one of the liveliest of that series, with a vigorously conceived group of figures in peasant costume in the foreground. The version that followed Turner's visit is more elaborate, making use of a screen of slender tree-trunks, which stands between us and the shimmering city. The

Pl. 146

160   Venice: the Rialto   *c.* 1820
Watercolour, 287 × 407
National Gallery of Ireland, Dublin   (Cat. No. 725)

161   Rome from the Vatican. Raffaelle accompanied by La Fornarina,
preparing his pictures for the decoration of the Loggia   R.A. 1820
Oil on canvas, 1770 × 3355
Turner Bequest, Tate Gallery, London   (Cat. No. P228)

breadth of the scene suggests, as did that of some of the other views made in Rome, that Turner was thinking of Richard Wilson; but here he employs the full range of his formal watercolour technique to convey the atmosphere of the place. *Rome from the Pincian* approaches more closely to the type of roofscape that occurs in *Rome from the Vatican:* the pink and orange buildings, half obscured by haze, stretch away before us towards the distant hills; in the foreground women tend olives and melon plants.

These two watercolours are roughly uniform in size, about 343 × 445 mm, and belong to a group of seven Italian drawings made for Walter Fawkes immediately after Turner's return to England. Among them are two other Roman subjects, *The Colosseum,* dated 1820, and an *Interior of St. Peter's,* Pls. 157 recalling, in its scale and in the directness of its recording, the grand ecclesiastical interiors of the 1790s. This watercolour is dated 1821, and may well have been the last of the group to be executed. In the course of producing this set of Italian subjects, Turner drew, again for Fawkes, another souvenir of his journey: the *Snowstorm, Mont Cenis,* very different in mood from the rest, and indeed a kind of foil, with its swirling snow-clouds and sombre colours, to the congenial warmth of the southern subjects. It is as though Turner, in making up the

162   The Bay of Baiae, with Apollo and the Sybil   R.A. 1823
Oil on canvas, 1455 × 2390
Turner Bequest, Tate Gallery, London   (Cat. No. P230)

Pl.162

record of his travels, had once more to recall the unavoidable barrier of the Alps and all that those mountains meant in terms of distance and contrast to Italy.[35]

The next oil-painting to result from the tour was *The Bay of Baiae, with Apollo and the Sybil,* exhibited at the Academy in 1823. Like *Rome from the Vatican* in 1820, it was Turner's only Academy entry of that year. The picture is a sequel to *Crossing the brook,* of 1815; it belongs to the long succession of compositions based on the Claudian system, and like *Crossing the brook,* is a strangely reticent, contemplative work, painted with a delicacy of touch and of colouring, especially in the background, that reveals much of Turner's personal response to the beauty of the particular landscape. It is perhaps not surprising that both pictures have been interpreted as having an allegorical meaning particularly close to his private life

and psychology.[36] The line of verse that Turner added to the title of the 1823 picture in the catalogue does not, for once, suggest any hidden meanings; it says merely, 'Waft me to sunny Baiae's shore', and on the painting are inscribed the words '*Liquidae Placuere Baiae*', from Horace's *Ode to Calliope* (Book III, No. 4, 1. 24). The quotation is entirely appropriate: it reminds us of the 'literary landscape' of Italy, which Englishmen knew through the poets, and suggests that it is such a vision that Turner presents. After the circumstantial recording of the view of Rome in *Rome from the Vatican*, he returns here to his favourite theme, but equipped now with a sounder basis in fact for the fantasy that he creates. The critics who acclaimed the picture must have been aware of the classical story which it illustrates: Apollo offers the Sibyl as many years as she holds grains of sand in her hand; she accepts the dispensation, without asking for eternal youth, and lives on only to waste away to nothing but a disembodied voice. It was a subject typical of heroic classical landscapes since Wilson, and need not have been taken as an allegory of the decline of civilization—the wasting away of Roman

163 Forum Romanum, for Mr. Soane's Museum R.A. 1826
Oil on canvas, 1455 × 2375
Turner Bequest, Tate Gallery, London (Cat. No. P233)

power under the influence of corruption. Turner, however, includes a snake and a white rabbit (symbolizing Venus) in the scene, and it would be in keeping with his heightened sense of the seriousness of landscape painting to imply a universal theme. But if we attach too much importance to this aspect of the picture's meaning, we are bound to find a certain discrepancy between the theme and its statement. Contemporary critics, at any rate, admired it principally for displaying 'the rich, the glowing and the splendid' in nature.[37]

PL. 163 The last of the paintings to result from the 1819 visit to Italy is a view of the *Forum Romanum, for Mr. Soane's Museum,* a very appropriate subject to hang among the archaeological curiosities that Turner's long-standing associate, the architect Sir John Soane,[38] had accumulated and packed into his narrow terrace-house in Lincoln's Inn Fields. It must, however, have been too big for that very economically planned interior, and Turner never parted with it. Its grand

scale is once more suggestive of the constraint under which Turner felt himself labouring: its design contrasts with that of both *Rome from the Vatican* and *The Bay of Baiae* in being constructed very solidly out of architectural forms: the blocks of masonry which divide the composition give it a feeling of volume very different from the airy void around which the buildings gyrate in *Rome from the Vatican,* or from the open oval curves of *The Bay of Baiae.* This picture did not appear until 1826, and was one of four oil-paintings which Turner showed at the Royal Academy in that year; none of the others alluded to the south or to classical landscape. The next pictures of Italian subjects that he was to produce were painted in Rome itself, when he returned there in 1828.

150

NOTES

1 See chap. 1, p. 23.

2 See chap. 2, p. 53.

3 Cat. No. P129.

4 Cat. No. P133.

5 See chap. 7, pp. 157–9. A contemporary use of the term 'composition' in this sense is George Arnald's picture, *A Composition—Paestum*, exhibited at the Royal Academy in 1811 (209) under that title, but shown again apparently at the British Institution in 1812 (133) as *A composition from a description of Paestum*. Turner meant to imply exactly the same lack of first-hand knowledge in the title he gave his view of Tivoli.

6 Cat. Nos 698–9.

7 Cat. Nos 700–17.

8 Quoted in Finberg, *Life*, p. 260. Gaspar Dughet 1615–75, brother-in-law of Nicolas Poussin and known by that surname, was almost as celebrated a landscape painter, and much imitated in the eighteenth century.

9 T.B., CLXXI.

10 T.B., CLXXII.

11 *Select Views in Italy, with Topographical and Historical Descriptions in English and French*, 1792–6.

12 T.B., CLXXIII, p. 1 verso.

13 T.B., CLXXIV.

14 T.B., CLXXV.

15 In the *Remarks (Italy)* sketchbook, T.B., CXCIII, p. 3.

16 Chantrey, 1781–1841; Jackson, 1778–1831.

17 Tom Moore, *Memoirs, Journal and Correspondence*, ed. Russell, 1853–6, vol. III, p. 74.

18 T.B., CLVIII.

19 The sketchbooks used in Italy are: *Paris, France, Savoy 2* (T.B., CLXXIII), *Turin, Como, Lugano, Maggiore* (T.B., CLXXIV), *Milan to Venice* (T.B., CLXXV), *Venice to Ancona* (T.B., CLXXVI), *Ancona to Rome* (T.B., CLXXVII), *Tivoli and Rome* (T.B., CLXXIX), *Vatican fragments* (T.B., CLXXX), *Como and Venice* (T.B., CLXXXI), *Albano, Nemi, Rome* (T.B., CLXXXII), *Tivoli* (T.B., CLXXXIII), *Gandolfo to Naples* (T.B., CLXXXIV), *Pompeii, Amalfi, Sorrento and Herculaneum* (T.B., CLXXXV), *Naples, Paestum and Rome* (T.B., CLXXXVI), *Naples, Rome C. Studies* (T.B., CLXXXVII), *St. Peter's* (T.B., CLXXXVIII), *Rome: C. Studies* (T.B., CLXXXIX), *Small Roman C. Studies* (T.B., CXC), *Rome and Florence* (T.B., CXCI), *Return from Italy* (T.B., CXCII), and *Remarks (Italy)* (T.B., CXCIII). Turner may also have used the *Skies* sketchbook (T.B., CLVIII) and the *Passage of the Simplon* (T.B., CXCIV). The initial 'C.' which distinguishes three of the Roman sketchbooks is thought to stand for 'Colour' or, possibly, 'Chiaroscuro'. The former seems the more likely interpretation.

20 The 'Venetian Merchants' are noted on p. 44 verso of the *Milan to Venice* sketchbook (T.B., CLXXV); the *Return from Italy* book (T.B., CXCII) contains numerous studies inscribed 'Men shovelling away snow for the carriage'; 'Brown shawls, white caps, striped Gaiters'; 'People going to Market', etc.

21 T.B., CLXXXI-3, repr. Wilkinson, 1974, p. 186.

22 Pp. 4, 5, 6 and 7.

23 T.B., CLXXXVII-28, 32.

24 At least twenty of these drawings were known to Farington as late as 1811, though they subsequently disappeared for many years. See Brinsley Ford, 'The Dartmouth Collection of Drawings by Richard Wilson', *Burlington Magazine*, 1948, vol. XC, pp. 337–45.

25 Carlo Labruzzi, 1748–1817, Antonio Zucchi, 1726–95, Charles-Louis Clérisseau, 1722–1820. A view of the dome of St. Peter's beyond an archway in the style of the *vedutisti* of the period belonged to Turner (T.B., CCCLXXX-18); I have suggested (B.M., 1975, No. 62) that although this is probably by another hand than Turner's, as Finberg believed, it has much in common with the drawings for the perspective lectures (T.B., CXCV) and may have been a deliberate pastiche of the work of the Italian 'souvenir' painters, executed before Turner went to Italy.

26 Wilkinson, *Turner's Colour Sketches, 1820–34*, 1975, p. 20, has already questioned Finberg's dating (followed by Martin Butlin, 1962, *Turner Watercolours*, p. 34) of *c*. 1818, suggesting *c*. 1820 as a more likely period.

27 Letter to John Soane from his son, 15 November 1819; see Arthur T. Bolton, ed., *The Portrait of Sir John Soane, R.A.*, 1927, pp. 284–5.

28 Quoted by Armstrong, 1902, p. 96, from a biographical note by William Stokes, in Robert James Graves, *Studies in Physiology and Medicine*, 1863, p. xi.

29 T.B., CXCIII, p. 99. See Gage, 1969, p. 101.

30 A full and illuminating discussion of this picture is in Gage, 1969, pp. 93-5. An even larger canvas was the *Battle of Trafalgar* (P 252), comissioned by George IV in 1822. This measures 259 x 365.8 cm.

31 An anecdote familiar to Turner's generation was that 'When Raffaelle was engaged in painting the gallery of his friend Agostino Ghighi [sic] he was so much in love with a beautiful Roman lady that his passion interfered with his genius and his fame. Agostino persuaded the lady to pass her mornings in the gallery, and thus induced Raffaelle to continue his work' (James Elmes, *The Arts and Artists, or Anecdotes & Relics, of the schools of Painting, Sculpture & Architecture*, vol. II, 1825, p. 96). The association with Raphael's tercentenary was made by Ron Parkinson.

32 Robert Barker, 1739–1806. See Roget, 1891, vol. I, pp. 104 ff.; Lindsay, 1966, pp. 70–1; and see chap. 2, note 35 above.

33 Drawings of the Loggie occur in the *Tivoli and Rome* sketchbook, T.B., CLXXIX, pp. 13 verso − 21. One of these (on p. 18) shows subjects from the decorations relating to the story of the Flood; for an elaborate interpretation of the significance of these scenes in the final picture see Mordechai Omer, *Burlington Magazine*, 1975, pp. 694–702.

34 Cat. Nos 719–20.

35 Cat. No. 402. For Turner's attitude to the Alps as barrier between north and south see chap. 4, p. 104 above.

36 E.g. by Lindsay, 1966, pp. 72–3; and by Gage, 1974, pp. 45–6.

37 *European Magazine*, May 1823.

38 Sir John Soane, 1753–1837.

Chapter Seven

Turner's Change of Colour: Hannibal to Ulysses

No picture better illustrates the difficulty of providing a simple description of Turner's stylistic development than the great *Snow storm: Hannibal and his army crossing the Alps* which appeared in 1812. The hanging committee of the Royal Academy had great difficulty in finding a suitable place to show this canvas:[1] that in itself is an indication of its great difference from the other works there, and from Turner's previous submissions. It had been foreshadowed, nevertheless, by a brilliantly eccentric Alpine subject exhibited at his own gallery in 1810, the *Avalanche in the Grisons,* in which a large proportion of the picture-space is filled by a nebulous patch of grey colour, applied with a very freely used palette knife. Even so, compared with that work, the subject-matter of *Hannibal* seems eroded into vagueness by the atmospheric conditions it represents; the *Avalanche,* in spite of its boldly irregular composition, is crisp, its principal focus a very solid chunk of rock.[2] The focus of *Hannibal* is a 'sun... low, broad, and wan',[3] bleared by a swirl of thick snow; the solid foreground detail, chosen to convey as aphoristically as possible the ideas of rape and looting, is confined to a small area close to the lower edge of the picture. Its construction, too, compared with earlier canvases of similar large size, seems eroded. In its turbulence and compositional irregularity it can perhaps be seen as a logical successor to *The wreck of a transport ship,* painted in about 1810; but there an accumulation of detail is of vital importance in conveying the picture's meaning. The landscapes modelled on Claude provide other antecedents: for they, seeking ideal generalization, point the way to the total suppression of detail in the interest of overall effect; and they have, of course, the same light-centred vortex scheme on which *Hannibal* is based. But such works are rare before *Hannibal:* the *Macon* and *Sun rising through vapour* are the only important examples, and it is only in the chalk sketches for the latter that the sun is shown as a dimmed circle, as it appears in *Hannibal.*[4] In fact it is to the

Pl.165

Pl.164

164 The wreck of a transport ship   *c.* 1810
Oil on canvas, 1272 × 2412
Fundação Calouste Gulbenkian, Lisbon   (Cat. No. P210)

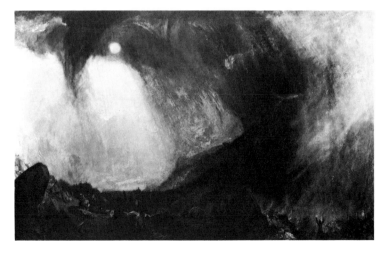

165 Snow storm: Hannibal and his army crossing the Alps R.A. 1812
Oil on canvas, 1460 × 2375
Turner Bequest, Tate Gallery, London   (Cat. No. P126)

153

166 Dido building Carthage; or the rise of the Carthaginian Empire.—1st book of Virgil's Æneid   R.A. 1815
Oil on canvas, 1555 × 2320
Turner Bequest, Tate Gallery, London   (Cat. No. P131)

167 The decline of the Carthaginian Empire—Rome being determined on the overthrow of her hated rival, demanded from her such terms as might either force her into war or ruin her by compliance: the enervated Carthaginians, in their anxiety for peace, consented to give up even their arms and their children   R.A. 1817
Oil on canvas, 1700 × 2385
Turner Bequest, Tate Gallery, London   (Cat. No. P135)

168 Landscape: Composition of Tivoli 1817
Watercolour, 676 × 1020
Private collection (Cat. No. 495)

seascapes rather than to the landscapes of Turner's later work
that *Hannibal* looks forward. In particular, the 'indistinctness'
Pl.213 of *Staffa* (1832) is created out of the same black and grey, with
the same dull-orange sun, the same livid opening of white
light in the sky as are found in the earlier work. The late *Snow
228, 231 storm,* of 1842, and the *Evening of the Deluge,* of 1843, are also
works in this line of descent.[5]

These are all pictures from which strong colour is absent;
yet they use the range of greys, from white to black, with the
expressive purpose of full colour. *Hannibal* is perhaps the first

of Turner's pictures to treat black as an expressive element in
the colour gamut rather than merely as a necessary agent of
chiaroscuro. In this it anticipates the changes that were to
take place in Turner's use of colour over the next two
decades.[6]

What *Hannibal* most vividly shows us is Turner's attraction
to subjects that could be composed by resolution into areas of
colour or tone independent of traditional formal considera-
tions. Its interest as the work which announces the genre that
was to be exploited by John Martin and Francis Danby[7] is far
outweighed by the fact that it operates on an infinitely subtler
level, going beyond their work in the evocation of atmosphere just as it does in its real moral purpose. Here, Turner is
not concerned, as they are, simply to provide a Sublime thrill;
the serious preoccupation in this picture with philosophical

169   Colour-beginning: Tivoli   *c.* 1817
Pencil and watercolour, 664 × 1001
Trustees of the British Museum, London (T.B., CXCVII-A) (not in catalogue)

problems especially topical during the war with France (1812 was the year of Napoleon's retreat from Moscow)[8] is clear not only from the catalogue entry[9] but also from the very restraint with which he suggests the struggle and misery of the army's progress: Turner's understanding of what climatic conditions can do to the human mind and body is far deeper than that of an 'apocalypse painter'.

PL.166   In the same way, in his next great statement on the Carthaginian theme, *Dido building Carthage; or the rise of the Carthaginian Empire*, the Claudian formula that underlies it is also balanced between human preciseness and atmospheric generality. The queen, surrounded by her commanders and architects, stands in front of a richly invented scene of activity—a heroic, mythical harbour in which great visions are being brought to reality by the exertions of a vigorous labour force. As in *Hannibal,* Turner's choice of detail is not random: each figure has a task to perform in conveying the total meaning of the picture. In the foreground two girls watch a group of small boys pushing out toy boats onto the water, an image which brings the picture vividly into the world of known experience, embodies the human purpose of Dido's plan and symbolizes the ultimate futility of it. But this mass of detail—all significant and invented with clear and exact purpose on Turner's part—is subsumed under the grand pictorial point made by the colour of the painting. The Claudian motif is emphasized—the tree at the right bears up lustrously dark against the light; but, to a much greater extent than in Claude's seaport subjects, the colour of the picture as a whole is pervaded with the gold of the rising sun. Just as

156

170   Dort, or Dordrecht: The Dort packet-boat from Rotterdam becalmed   R.A. 1818
Oil on canvas, 1575 × 2330
Yale Center for British Art, Paul Mellon Collection   (Cat. No. P137)

Ploughing up Turnips, near Slough took grandeur from its golden mist, so *Dido* is generalized as a symphony in gold. That such a scheme was not a mere Claudian cliché is shown by the muted, cool palette of *Crossing the brook,* exhibited in the same year, equally Claudian in inspiration but quite different in intention. The generalized golden scheme was, of course, to be used frequently in subsequent pictures, particularly in the

Pl.167 sequel to *Dido building Carthage, The decline of the Carthaginian*
Pl.170 *Empire,* exhibited in 1817, and in the *Dort,* of 1818.

These two pictures reflect the Claudian and the Cuypian poles from which Turner's love of diffused sunlight drew its models; each has its successors—the Mediterranean, idealized scenes that recur so frequently, and the northern, specific landscapes and townscapes; but in both classes of work the overriding importance of a unified scheme of colour becomes more and more evident. Turner's compositional organization cannot yet, at this period, be traced in terms of the sketches in oils that he seems to have begun to make regularly after about 1827;[10] but the finished pictures can be analysed in much the same way as the watercolours.

There is a convenient parallel to the composition of *Dido building Carthage* in the large watercolour of *Tivoli,* exhibited in 1817, although the philosophical significance of the

171 Aelbert Cuyp (1620–91)
River scene with view of Dordrecht
Oil on canvas, 1000 × 1360
Wallace Collection, London

172 Cologne, from the river 1820
Watercolour, 308 × 463
Seattle Art Museum, Washington (gift of Mr. and Mrs. Louis Breche-min) (Cat. No. 690)

173 The Bass Rock (for *The Provincial Antiquities of Scotland*) *c.* 1824
Watercolour, 159 × 254
The Lady Lever Collection, Port Sunlight, Cheshire   (Cat. No. 1069)

landscape is not elaborated with figures as it is in *Dido:* a few countrywomen suffice to set off the deliberately 'antique' flavour of the scenery. (The watercolour points up sharply the modernity and rigour of Turner's thinking in *Dido.*) It is, nevertheless, a highly evolved, elaborate design, and a colour-beginning survives which shows Turner working out the composition as a balance of abstract forms and restricted colour forces. The composition is founded on a contrast between pinkish-ochre or yellow, and pale blue. It is punctuated by a strong dark green accent, confined to a single sector of the design and reinforcing the pattern of vertical bands on which the whole is organized. In the finished watercolour the clarity of this scheme is confused by Turner's introduction of echoing notes—warm colour among the cool and *vice versa;* but the final arrangement of the components is different from that in the sketch precisely in that it makes the essential structure clearer: the right-hand block of tone is given a firm vertical boundary in the temple wall; and the central view of towers is reversed to bring about a carefully modulated recession, articulated by further, distant verticals.

Pl. 169

174 Harbour of Dieppe (changement de domicile)   R.A. 1825
Oil on canvas, 1737 × 2254
Frick Collection, New York   (Cat. No. P231)

An even earlier example of this process can be seen in the large preparatory study for *Scarborough* of 1811,[11] which is already simply a pale, sandy-gold wash over a very large area of paper, expressing the basic idea of the *Scarborough* that appeared in the Academy exhibition that year. It was possible in watercolour to wash the entire surface of a sheet with a single hue and to allow that to create and sustain the mood of the whole work; from *Hannibal* onwards, Turner seems to

Pl. 122

have applied the same principle to his largest canvases. It is as though they were conceived initially in watercolour, even if, in all probability, Turner hardly ever used that medium when

160

175 Norham Castle, on the Tweed (for *Rivers of England*) *c.* 1823
Watercolour, 156 × 216
Trustees of the British Museum, London (T.B., CCVIII-O) (Cat. No. 736)

he was preparing his oil-paintings. The lessons learned in one context were easily applicable in the other.[12]

As this principle became established, Turner was liberated more and more from the classic chiaroscuro opposition of light and dark on which oil-paintings were traditionally founded. Where in *Dido building Carthage* we are aware of a dark tree against a bright sky, in the *Tivoli* colour-beginning we are more conscious of a colour contrast than a tonal one: pale yellow with pale blue. In the two fine successors to the *Dort* which Turner produced in 1825 and 1826, *Dieppe* and

Pl.174

Cologne, the whole drama of the subject is in each case realized in the framework of a colour opposition: blue and pink in *Dieppe,* blue and orange in *Cologne.* A similar scheme is even more apparent in a watercolour of *Cologne* (1820), where intersecting wedges of ochre and blue form a composition of pure colour contrasts (without tonal variation) that do not correspond to the various physical divisions in the subject: water, buildings, boats, etc. These elements are absorbed into the broader chromatic scheme, which is a purely pictorial invention.

Pl.176
Pl.172

The principle of dividing the sheet of paper on which a watercolour was to be painted into bold, primary areas of broad colour was well established as a part of the process of working in that medium. Manuals such as John Laporte's *The Progress of a Water-Colour Drawing* published examples of

161

176 Cologne, the arrival of a packet boat. Evening   R.A. 1826
Oil and possibly watercolour on canvas, 1686 × 2241
Frick Collection, New York   (Cat. No. P232)

landscape design initially coloured in blue, pink and yellow strips rather like the most primitive of Turner's colour-beginnings.[13] There can be no doubt that Turner, in making his colour-structures, consciously developed this method of working. But the conventional procedure adhered, if only roughly, to the basic divisions of sky, distance and foreground, while Turner used his 'blocking-out' process as a deliberate counterpoint to the literal subject-matter. He also abandoned the conventional colour schemes for his own more subtle and flexible ones; and, at an early moment, he learned to apply the same principle to his oil-paintings. In doing so, he earned the opprobrium of those who upheld

tradition: Sir George Beaumont, a regular and prominent litanist of the defects of Turner's art, stated in 1812 that 'Much harm... has been done by endeavouring to make painting in oil appear like watercolours, by which, in attempting to give lightness and clearness, the force of oil painting has been lost.'[14] In oil-paintings like *Dieppe* and *Cologne* Turner can be seen establishing the concreteness and

162

177 Shields Lighthouse *c.* 1825
Mezzotint (R.801, trial proof *a*), 151 × 212
Trustees of the British Museum, London (1912–10–14–4)   (not in catalogue)

178   View of Orvieto, painted in Rome   1828
Oil on canvas, 915 × 1230
Turner Bequest, Tate Gallery, London   (Cat. No. P292)

163

power of colour masses independent of tonal contrast. Within each formal colour area light and shade are allowed to play freely; however, they no longer control the principal masses, which exist on a broader plane; all incidental contrasts are comprehended in generalized oppositions of warm and cool colour. The development was noticed as early as 1810 by a somewhat hostile critic of *Petworth, Sussex, the seat of the Earl of Egremont: Dewy morning*, shown in that year: 'it was manifestly Mr. Turner's design', he wrote, 'to express the peculiar hue and pellucidness of objects seen through a medium of air, in other words to express the clearness of atmosphere. To effect this purpose it was necessary to select those dark material objects which serve as a foil to aerial lights and to produce atmosphere by their contrast. Mr Turner has neglected to use these necessary foils and has thus made a confusion between aerial lights and the appropriate gloom of objects.'[15]

Having reached this point Turner was in a position to paint pictures without the conventional reference to black as denoting the absence of light: he could use black as a colour,

180　The Lake, Petworth: sunset, fighting bucks　*c.* 1829
Oil on canvas, 622 × 1460
H. M. Treasury and National Trust (Lord Egremont Collection).
Petworth House　(Cat. No. P288)

symbolically if he chose; at the same time, colour could be infused with a new expressive force by being used in brighter, purer keys than had been possible before. The full effect of this change began to make itself felt in the paintings that Turner was producing about the time of his second visit to Italy: the *Orvieto,* of 1828, and the Petworth subjects, especially *Sunset, fighting bucks* and *Petworth Park, Tillington Church in the Distance,*[16] which were done perhaps in the same year, all speak a new language of saturated colour diffused through a rich broken paint surface.

Pl.178
Pl.180

The significance of this moment in Turner's development was acknowledged by the critic of *Ulysses deriding Polyphemus,* exhibited in 1829, who spoke of the picture as a 'violent departure from his former style'; another reviewer called it 'colouring run mad—positive vermilion, positive indigo, and all the most glaring tints of green, yellow and purple'.[17] Exactly the same uncompromising colour occurs in the watercolour work of the period; indeed, the new status of colour is even more clearly marked in the studies made at Petworth in about 1827 or 1828,[18] and in similar ones of

Pl.181

scenes on European rivers made for the projected series, *The Rivers of Europe.*[19] These are all on sheets of blue paper, a support that Turner had generally in the past avoided, except for pen or chalk studies done with the old masters looking over his shoulder, as it were. The first closely datable examples of work on these small sheets of blue paper are those in pen and brown ink that he made at East Cowes Castle in the summer of 1827;[20] these must have been followed fairly closely by the Petworth ones, which are in colour alone, with very little use of outline; and it is possible that they were even preceded by the first of the many coloured drawings for the *Rivers of Europe,* which Turner began work on in 1825.[21] Throughout these sequences, whatever their exact dating, there runs an attitude to colour unlike that in any of Turner's other works. The blue paper seems to have been chosen specifically to promote a vivid and intense use of body-colour; it has an effect utterly different from that of the grey- or brown-washed grounds that he had hitherto employed. Upon it vermilion, lime green, purple, opaque white, orange and blue have a brilliance which could only be achieved in pure watercolour by the application of an elaborate and minuscule technique. At the same date, from 1826 onwards, Turner was in fact occupied with the vignette illustrations to Rogers,[22] in which he pushed that watercolour technique as far as it could go towards a comparable intensity and brilliance of colour; but with body-colour on

Pls. 183, 184

Pl.179

165

blue paper he could achieve the desired effect immediately in a rapid sketch, and in the case of those designs for the *Rivers of Europe* that were finished—for the Loire and the Seine—Turner even submitted his work to the engravers in this medium, the only finished work on tinted paper that he did.[23]

There seems to have been some direct connection between the heightened colour of these designs—both those in watercolour for Rogers and those in body-colour for the *French Rivers*—and their function as models for the engraver. They were begun at the moment when Turner had just explored the possibilities of print-making in some depth, and the whole progress of his approach to colour in the 1820s may be seen as a paradoxical corollary to his activities in black and white. His first direct experience of print-making

181 Ulysses deriding Polyphemus—Homer's Odyssey   R.A. 1829
Oil on canvas, 1325 × 2030
Turner Bequest, National Gallery, London   (Cat. No. P330)

seems to have been the etching of outlines for the mezzo-tinters of his *Liber Studiorum;* gradually, as the series progressed, Turner became more and more interested in the medium of mezzotint, and in its later stages he invented subjects that exploited fully its characteristic dramatic contrasts of velvety blackness with white paper. He actually mezzotinted some of these himself, and they are of a grandeur and expressive force that show how personally and fully he was responding to the medium.[24] So excited did he become with the idea of mezzotint that when the *Liber* came to an end

166

182 On the Moselle *c.* 1825–34
Body-colour, with pen, on blue paper, 137 × 184
Private collection   (Cat. No. 1029)

in 1819 he embarked on two new series of designs to be mezzotinted on the newly introduced steel plates, the *Rivers of England* and the *Ports of England* (on which he was at work during the first half of the 1820s, and which appeared between 1823 and 1828).[25] The drawings for these plates are in a small format like those of the *Southern Coast* series, and though they are not so complex, generally, in composition, they are significantly more elaborate in terms of colour. They are executed on white paper, and hence exhibit the tendency towards minute handling that was brought to an extreme in the vignettes. Even though many of them have now faded, they are still among the most colourful of Turner's finished watercolours, and show a preoccupation with effects of light that is not to be found in the *Southern Coast* or in other previous series. The first of them, *Shields on the River Tyne,*[26] is a night-piece obviously conceived to exploit mezzotint effects, but nevertheless presenting a rich contrast of inky blue, orange and silver. Another, *Arundel Castle,*[27] has a very large and prominent rainbow, which sheds a prismatic radiance over the whole subject and seems to crystallize Turner's interest here in rendering colours as brilliantly and

183 Huy on the Meuse *c.* 1825–34
Watercolour and body-colour, with some pen on blue paper, 140 × 194
Syndics of the Fitzwilliam Museum, Cambridge (Ruskin gift 1861)
(Cat. No. 1024)

delicately as possible. It has been suggested that yet another, PL.175 the *Norham Castle,* represents Turner's first fully-fledged application of colour strictly according to the optical principles of prismatic fragmentation. Whether this is true or not, the idea reflects the novel impact of colour in these drawings.[28]

Once again, Turner made some mezzotints on his own account;[29] they cannot be directly connected with the two series, but there are clear points of contact. They are nearly all, like the *Shields,* night or twilight scenes, with beautiful and iridescent effects of cloud and moonlight; the studies are in rich shimmering colour; the prints of a tenebrous blackness unparalleled in any of Turner's other work. Twelve of these designs have been traced, but no formal project has been discovered to explain them, and they have been called the 'Little Liber Studiorum' for want of a more exact description. They seem to have been a necessary exercise for Turner. It is possible that he received the impulse to make them partly from the publication in mezzotint of a subject by Francis Danby, the *Sunset at Sea* of 1826, which bears a strong

184   View over a town at sunset: a cemetery in the foreground
c. 1832
Body-colour on blue paper, 140 × 190
Trustees of the British Museum, London (T.B., CCLIX–192)   (not in
catalogue)

Pl. 177 resemblance to the *Shields Lighthouse* in Turner's set.[30] More
important, these prints follow through the implications of
mezzotint which enabled him thereafter to come to grips
with the problem of translating colour into black and white,
and especially to the black and white of the line-engraver. It
gave him the insight to exploit the process by forcing the
engravers really to 'translate', to find wholly new equivalents

in a different language, rather than to copy on steel a design
that lent itself easily to restatement in line. He was compelling
engravers to think of line as a mere medium through which
non-linear effects had to be conveyed. Hence his almost
exaggerated stress on colour in the *Rivers of Europe* and
vignette designs.[31]

It is, therefore, perhaps no coincidence that *Ulysses* should
have been painted at just the time when these schemes were
in progress. Its strong colour does not seem to reflect the
broadening influence of the colour-plans for the finished
watercolours; it is indeed one of the most confusing of
Turner's works when viewed as a composition in colour; but
it does echo the vividness of the drawings for the engravers in

185 Rhodes (for *Lord Byron's Works*) *c.* 1823–4
Watercolour and body-colour, with scraping-out, 133 × 226
Yale Center for British Art, Paul Mellon Collection   (Cat. No. 1215)

which Turner deliberately recasts form as colour and uses black, not as shadow, but as an expressive factor equal to other colours employed expressionistically rather than naturalistically.[32] The interrelationship at this period of his work in oil, watercolour and engraving cannot easily be analysed; each has an important, fruitful bearing on the other two sections of his output, and it was perhaps because he was engaged simultaneously on work in all three media that his attitude to colour evolved as it did: it was intimately connected with his progressing response to the technical means by which his ideas were expressed.

NOTES

1 See Finberg, *Life*, pp. 188–9.

2 The picture is at least in part an allusion to the work of an artist whose style was the reverse of imprecise or allusive: de Loutherbourg, whose own canvas of *An Avalanche, or ice-fall, in the Alps, near the Scheideck, in the Valley of Lauterbrunnen* had been shown at the Academy in 1804 (Pl. 102). It was bought by Sir John Leicester, in whose gallery Turner is known often to have studied it. See Joppien, 1973, No. 46.

3 From Turner's verses, printed with the entry in the R.A. catalogue; see Cat. No. P126.

4 T.B., LXXXI, pp. 24, 26, 34, 56.

5 See Gage, 'The Distinctness of Turner', 1975. 'Indistinctness' was the charge levelled against Turner's *Staffa* by its purchaser in 1845, James Lenox of New York; to which Turner asked Leslie to reply: 'You should tell Mr. Lenox that indistinctness is my fault.' Until recently the last word of this quotation was read as 'forte'. Gage argues correctly that Turner was always concerned to present his images as concretely as possible, but overlooks the traditional ascription of special emotional and expressive power to 'indistinctness' in eighteenth-century aesthetic theory: Gilpin, for example, says 'Many images owe their sublimity to their *indistinctness;* and frequently what we call sublime is the effect of that heat and fermentation, which ensues in the imagination from it's [*sic*] ineffectual efforts to conceive some dark, obtuse idea beyond it's grasp. Bring the same within the compass of it's comprehension, and it may continue *great;* but it will cease to be *sublime*... In general, the poet has great advantages over the painter, in the process of *sublimication,* if the term may be allowed. The business of the former is only to *excite ideas;* that of the latter, to *represent* them' (*Remarks on Forest Scenery,* 1791, vol. I, p. 252).

6 As late as 1835 George Field, in his *Chromatography,* p. 174, discussed the pictorial significance of black in Burkean, not scientific terms: 'it is the instrument of solemnity, obscurity, breadth and boundlessness, the terrible, the sublime, and the profound'; and it should be noted that these are all effectively symbolic uses of black *as a colour:* the use of black as an instrument of chiaroscuro is mentioned 'by contrast' to these. The effectiveness of Turner's use of colour depends on its traditional connotations. It is only remarkable that artists had in general failed to exploit these direct 'meanings' of colours since the Renaissance.

7 Francis Danby, 1793–1861.

8 Gage (Paris, 1972, No. 262) suggests that Turner saw a parallel between the struggle of Rome and Carthage and the Anglo-French wars of his own day.

9 See note 3 above.

10 Earlier oil sketches do of course exist: the *Sketch for 'Harvest Dinner, Kingston Bank'* (Cat. No. P160), for instance, and the preparatory studies for the *Battle of Trafalgar* (Cat. Nos P250, P251); and the pictures connected with George IV's visit to Edinburgh in 1822 (Cat. Nos P247–P249) should perhaps be placed in the same category; but the studies that Turner made in connection with the Cowes regatta in 1827, some on large pieces of canvas divided up only after his death, and others dating from the Roman stay of 1828, mark an apparent change towards greater emphasis on such sketches; stylistically, it is appropriate to date most of those that survive to the 1830s or '40s (see chap. 9, p. 224).

11 T.B., CXCVI-C.

12 It was on account of Turner's use of pale grounds in his pictures from this date (*c.* 1811–13), and the consequent lightening of the whole canvas, that Beaumont particularly objected to his abandonment of established principles in the painting of landscape. See Finberg, *Life,* pp. 194–5.

13 For example, a leaf of the *Como and Venice* sketchbook, T.B., CLXXXI, p. 10, repr. Gage, 1969, Pl. 38. See comments on Turner's emphatic horizontals and verticals in Lawrence Gowing, *Imagination and Reality,* 1966, p. 27, where they are compared with 'Compositions to be avoided' from Frank Howard's *The Sketcher's Manual,* 1837. In the course of his career Turner allowed the fundamental colour-partitions of his compositions to become more and more apparent; but he never permitted them to stand baldly as they appear in the 'colour-structures', invariably alleviating their starkness with carefully placed points of focus and 'echoes' of colour from different sectors of the design. John Laporte, 1761–1839. His manual was published, apparently in a second edition, in 1812.

14 Sir George Beaumont, 1753–1827. Farington, *Diary,* 12 October 1812.

15 *La Belle Assemblée,* 1810, vol. I, p. 250, quoted by Finberg, *Life,* p. 169. *Petworth... Dewy morning* is Cat. No. P113.

16 Cat. No. P283.

17 The *Morning Herald,* quoted in W. T. Whitley, *Art in England, 1821–1837,* 1930, p. 164.

18 T.B., CCXLIV, Pl. 179, and Cat. Nos 906–12.

19 For the genesis of the 'Rivers of Europe' project see section XV.

20 T.B., CCXXVII(a) and CCXXVIII. See Reynolds, 'Turner at East Cowes Castle', 1966.

21 T.B., CCXIV-CCXXIV, CCXXIX, CCXXX, CCXLVII-CCXLIX, CCLIII-CCLV, CCLVII-CCLX.

22   See Cat. section XVI(d).

23   For Turner's choice of paper in connection with work in water-colour see above, chap. 4, p. 104.

24   For the *Liber Studiorum* see above, chap. 4, p. 87. The plates that Turner mezzotinted himself are probably: R. 28, R. 35, R. 39, R. 44, R. 50, R. 55, R. 58, R. 60, R. 66 and R. 70. He also worked on some of the late unpublished plates: *Stonehenge at Daybreak* R. 81, and *The Deluge* R. 88.

25   Cat. sections XIII(a), XIII(b).

26   Cat. No. 732.

27   Cat. No. 748.

28   The claim for *Norham Castle* as Turner's first 'prismastic' work is made by Gerald Finley, 'Turner's Colour and Optics', 1973, pp. 386 ff. where the development is associated with Turner's visit to Edinburgh of 1822. See also Finley, 'An Early Experiment with Colour Theory', 1967, pp. 357–66. Gage, 1969, p. 124 sees a colour-beginning for *Crichton Castle* of 1818 (T.B., CLXX, p. 4) as 'the first work... to be wholly based on a structure of red, yellow and blue'; this was made after Turner's visit to Edinburgh in that year, when he may have encountered Sir David Brewster, whose *Treatise on Optics* interested him when it was published in 1831. However, Gage also observes (pp. 111, 250, note 189) prismatic treatment in a study of *Raby Castle* (T.B., CLVI, pp. 23 verso, 24) which was certainly made before Turner's visit to Edinburgh. In my view the observations of both writers are inaccurate: Turner did not generally in his watercolours employ primary colours in this way; though Hazlitt, in the *Examiner,* mentioned 'the quackery of painting trees blue and yellow to produce the effect of green at a distance' in some of the oil paintings (see Finberg, *Life,* pp. 246–7). James Skene in his article for the *Edinburgh Encyclopaedia* spoke of Turner's 'singular mixture of prismatic colours, with which he represents sky and water': see Finley, 1973, *loc. cit.* Turner certainly broke down the colour-components of his compositions into elementary masses or blocks of colour, but he generally used secondary not primary colours for this purpose, adding primary colours locally afterwards. Some of the vignettes are exceptional in beginning with primary colours (e.g. T.B., CCLXXX-77, 82, repr. Wilton, *Turner Watercolors,* 1977, Nos 55, 56).

29   R. 799–809a; and see Cat. section XIII(c).

30   Danby's picture was shown at the Academy in 1824; it was mezzotinted in 1826 by F.C. Lewis; repr. Eric Adams, *Francis Danby,* 1973, p. 134. The 'Little Liber' was associated with 'the Martinesque' by Sidney Colvin, 'Turner's Evening Gun', 1872, p. 76. Turner's design for *Shields Lighthouse* is T.B., CCLXII-308 (Cat. No. 771).

31   The process of 'translation' was not necessarily regarded as a mere technical necessity by other artists: Constable's *English Landscape Scenery* of 1829–33 is an exercise as serious as Turner's, and Constable exerted a similar control over his engraver (David Lucas). Field, *loc. cit.,* praised this work, however, for its use of black and white as chiaroscuro—as a mode of 'exhibiting the powers of the pencil in light and shade', and it seems clear that Constable did not conceive the mezzotint medium as one of 'colour'; Danby, on the other hand, and Martin, who engraved his own mezzotint plates after his pictures, both exploited black in Field's alternative 'Sublime' sense, i.e., as a colour with an emotional force and significance in its own right.

32   For further comment on *Ulysses* see chap. 9, pp. 194 ff.

Chapter Eight

England and Wales

One of the most striking manifestations of Turner's eighteenth-century upbringing was his lifelong preference for producing works in sequences. The idea is rooted deeply in his working method, and there is hardly a drawing in the Turner Bequest that cannot be said to belong to a more or less extended series of related studies. Even among the paintings, where it was natural for him to produce single works, his propensity to link his ideas from one work to the next, to form implicit series, is noticeable.[1] In the finished watercolours the notion can be seen to spring from the eighteenth-century topographer's need to make drawings for publication so that they could all be rendered by the engraver in a uniform 'set'. The *Copper-Plate Magazine,* Turner's first commission for work of this kind, demanded sixteen small views,[2] which he took care to make uniform, even though the rather simplified topography involved was already alien to his sophisticated style.

With his next series of any length, the views for the *Oxford Almanack,*[3] he must have at once sensed that he was working within the carefully defined limits of a well-established publication: the *Almanack's* engraved head-pieces had taken on a standardized format many years previously and artists like Michael 'Angelo' Rooker[4] and Edward Dayes had provided clear precedents for the kind of work required. Turner seems gladly to have adopted their mode; even though once again, by the time he came to accept the commission his own style had outstripped the type of work he was imitating. Several other projects, however, gave him an opportunity to create watercolours outside the restricting bounds of architectural topography, and in the views that he made for Whitaker's *History of the Parish of Whalley* of about 1800 he began to establish his personal style in book illustration, reflecting something of the 'grand manner' of his largest watercolours.[5] Even these were occasionally made in sets: the Fonthill subjects exhibited at the Academy in 1800

form a classic example of unusual coherence, and the Salisbury drawings for Colt Hoare exhibit a strong sense of underlying unity. The Swiss drawings acquired by Fawkes are independent works, but by the time that Turner was engaged on them the habit was established, and they too can be seen as a loosely related sequence. The two series that Fawkes acquired towards 1820, the 1817 Rhine drawings and the views of Farnley and its neighbourhood, illustrate Turner's quite gratuitous use of the series form in his maturity.[6]

But these two groups are essentially private, intimate in mood; it was proper that Turner's closest friend should become their owner. By that date he had for some time been engaged on a project more significant for the development of his art as a watercolourist: the forty *Picturesque Views on the Southern Coast of England.*[7] In this series he came to grips, for the first time in his full maturity, with an extensive project involving a large number of subjects composed within very small dimensions. He had, by 1810 or thereabouts, fixed on a regular or standard size for those of his finished watercolours that were not especially large: about 300×420 mm. The *Southern Coast* drawings are much smaller—smaller than most of the sketchbooks in which he normally used colour; and the designs themselves are of considerably greater complexity than most of his colour studies. They frequently make prominent use of the human figure; in fact it is in this series that Turner's meticulous and loving observation of human activity as a constant referent for landscape first comes fully into its own. It was the great achievement of his technical maturity that he could, by this time, express so much with such precision in so small a format. But even while this remarkable group of drawings was going forward, he was reaffirming the slightly larger, 300×420 mm format as a norm in his work for another of Whitaker's projects, the *History of Richmondshire,*[8] of which only one volume was published, containing twenty of Turner's designs. The

186 Louth, Lincolnshire (for *England and Wales*) *c.* 1827
Watercolour and scraping-out, 285 × 420
Trustees of the British Museum, London (Salting Bequest)
(Cat. No. 809)

engravings in this volume were very little bigger than those for the *Southern Coast* (about 265 × 190 mm), but the original watercolours are on sheets that offer greater room for expansion. It is an historical and antiquarian work, and the plates perform a primarily informative function. The combination of literal accuracy in these designs with great formal sophistication is an impressive mark of the maturity Turner's topographical art had now achieved. Views like the *Crook of Lune* or *Kirby Lonsdale Churchyard* are richly and expressively invented throughout; but the little sheets of the *Southern Coast* served for equally complex ideas. Size was not, as it had been with the great 'Sublime' watercolours of the North-country, Welsh or Swiss subjects, a feature essential to Turner's meaning. Indeed, the shift of his attention from the walls of

Pl. 127
Pl. 128

the Academy or of his own gallery to the published engraving more or less dictated a change of scale; but that change of scale was rendered possible by his more subtle and flexible technique. Since watercolour was such an essential means of expression to him, he was bound to seek ways of promoting that expression publicly; he made the businesslike calculation that engraving was the best publicity, and accordingly devoted much of this time to what has been thought of as a lesser occupation.

174

187 Prudhoe Castle, Northumberland (for *England and Wales*)
c. 1826
Watercolour, 292 × 408
Trustees of the British Museum, London (Lloyd Bequest)
(Cat. No. 798)

The series of *Picturesque Views in England and Wales* demonstrates beyond doubt that Turner thought of watercolour as a principal occupation: it was intended to comprise 120 subjects, although in the event only 96 were engraved, and they are conceived in the most ambitious terms.[9] By comparison with what he produced in oil during the first five years of the enterprise—1825 to 1830—the forty *England and Wales* drawings published in that period represent an astonishing range of landscape types, each worked out in great detail, rather as the *Richmondshire* series had been, but with considerably greater concern for variety within the series, and comprehensiveness in each view.

The terms of reference for the publication were those of other picturesque topographical works of the early nineteenth century; though they did not include the specifically antiquarian connotations of Whitaker's book. Charles Heath,[10] the promoter of the enterprise, was himself by profession an engraver and had, in 1826, turned his attention

to popular 'souvenirs' and 'annuals' as means of promoting engravers' work. He was, indeed, largely responsible for the vogue for anthologies of sentimental prose, poetry and painting which subsisted throughout the 1830s and '40s, and himself published some of the best known—*The Keepsake* and the *Amulet* among them. Several of Turner's watercolours were engraved for these 'annuals', and it is possible that

188 'The Bivalve Courtship' *c.* 1831
Pencil, 85 × 110
Trustees of the British Museum, London (T.B., CCLXXIX(a)–7) (not in catalogue)

189 Stamford, Lincolnshire (for *England and Wales*) *c.* 1828
Watercolour, 293 × 420
Lincolnshire Museums Service, Usher Gallery, Lincoln (Cat. No. 817)

Heath actually had an agreement with Turner to use some of his subjects, for whose existence there is often no other obvious reason.[11] Heath's intention, then, was primarily to publish decorative topographical views; in choosing Turner as his artist he acknowledged too that he sought a wider market through Turner's fame; just as Samuel Rogers did when, in 1826, he asked Turner to illustrate his poem *Italy*, for a new edition.[12]

190 Richmond Hill and Bridge, Surrey (for *England and Wales*) *c.* 1831
Watercolour with some body-colour, 291 × 435
Trustees of the British Museum, London (Lloyd Bequest)
(Cat. No. 833)

191 Ely Cathedral, Cambridgeshire (for *England and Wales*)   *c.* 1831
Watercolour, 302 × 410
Private collection   (Cat. No. 845)

177

192 Llanberis Lake, Wales (for *England and Wales*) *c.* 1832
Watercolour with some body-colour, 314 × 470
National Galleries of Scotland, Edinburgh   (Cat. No. 855)

In these circumstances it is to be supposed that Heath made few stipulations as to the content of Turner's drawings. The work was to be issued in paper-covered parts, four plates in each, and its success depended on the beauty and richness of Turner's invention, together with the quality of the engravers' interpretations. On these two aspects of the problem Turner brought all his powers to bear. The drawings were planned with an analytical rigour that can be associated with few other works, of any period in his life,[13] and the engravings were supervised, checked and corrected with the meticulousness that Turner had brought to all reproductions of his works since the establishment of his fruitful relationship with William Bernard and George Cooke over the *Southern Coast* series in 1814.

Unlike the other sequences of views that he had been commissioned to make, the *England and Wales* subjects were not related in any way to a clear theme. They therefore represent Turner's own choice of views, picked from sketches made during his tours of England since the beginning of his career. There are subjects based on drawings made in 1792; others were collected on a tour made specially for the work, in 1830. Others again are derived from existing finished works, in watercolour or oil; and many more were planned, some even finished, that never reached the engraver's desk. There is no evident 'plan' in the sequence; but it is difficult to refrain from classifying the various subjects rather as Turner had done when organizing the *Liber Studiorum,* and finding groups of contrasting or complementary views—coastal, mountainous, pastoral, urban, etc.[14]

The intricate compositions of so many of the *Southern Coast* subjects are replaced by broader, simpler designs in which the elements are manipulated with greater force and directness to produce impressive descriptions of atmosphere, often focussing on some single human event. The struggle to achieve unity in diversity that characterizes Turner's work in watercolour throughout his life can be seen resolved in scores of ways in these drawings, and generalizations will not adequately describe them; it might be argued that they have no unity beyond their format and the fact that they all depict scenes in, or off the coasts of, England and Wales. Some of them, it is evident, are views that Turner might have made for any context; the *Longships Lighthouse* which appeared in 1836, for example,[15] is essentially similar to the small watercolour of a *Shipwreck off Hastings* now in Dublin;[16] and the two views of Richmond, Yorkshire might have taken their place in Whitaker's *Richmondshire*, as also might the *Chain Bridge over the River Tees*.[17] In its entirety the *England and Wales* series presents more than a sequence of views: it is a compendium

193 Colour-beginning: Blenheim *c.* 1832
Watercolour, 360 × 587
Trustees of the British Museum, London (T.B., CCLXIII-365) (not in catalogue)

194 Blenheim House and Park, Oxford (for *England and Wales*) *c.* 1832
Watercolour with some scraping-out, 296 × 468
City Museums and Art Gallery, Birmingham (Cat. No. 846)

of all aspects of English life, and the scenery of which it treats is seen through the eyes of English people whose world that scenery makes up. The characteristic note is set by the view of Pl. 189 *Stamford* in which, as a fierce storm breaks over the town, travellers dismount from the recently arrived stage-coach and run for shelter through the rain. Beside the coach, waiting while a companion unloads luggage, a tiny, hunched and crippled old woman stands patiently, unable to look up and help or to see the grandeur of the stormy light on the old buildings of Stamford. Her presence in the design is not advertised; it makes no sentimental point; it is simply an element in what Turner knew and observed of life. Nevertheless, it goes some way to placing the drawing in a class of landscape rather different from that of picturesque topography. It draws our attention to all Turner's figures, as tokens of his concern for human life, and we are obliged to interpret the whole series—and indeed all his mature

195 Dudley, Worcestershire (for *England and Wales*) *c.* 1832
Watercolour and body-colour, 288 × 430
The Lady Lever Collection, Port Sunlight, Cheshire   (Cat. No. 858)

watercolours—as balanced works of art in which the total significance of landscape, of climate and architecture and rural scenery, brought together in a fusion of the academic and topographical traditions, is measured invariably in terms of its significance for human beings.

The sketchbooks are full of notes that show this concern: Pl. 188 studies of people engaged in their daily occupations, with detailed records of their costume and the paraphernalia of their trades and pastimes. The books connected with the journey that Turner made specifically to look for *England and Wales* material, perhaps oddly, contain no such observations;[18] but it is evident that he did not rely on these

196 Caernarvon Castle, Wales (for *England and Wales*)   *c.* 1833
Watercolour over traces of pencil, 278 × 418
Trustees of the British Museum, London (Lloyd Bequest)
(Cat. No. 857)

197 Ullswater, Cumberland (for *England and Wales*)   *c.* 1833
Watercolour, 330 × 426
Coll.: Brian Pilkington, London   (Cat. No. 860)

198   Llanthony Abbey, Monmouthshire (for *England and Wales*)
c. 1835
Watercolour with some body-colour, 298 × 426
Indianapolis Museum of Art (gift in memory of Dr. and Mrs. Hugo
O. Pantzer by their children)   (Cat. No. 863)

memoranda for his information: they merely bear witness to his all-embracing sympathy for human detail. That sympathy was maintained throughout his life: in spite of the very perfunctory and haphazard nature of many of the small notebooks that he used in the late part of his career, we find similar observations in them.[19] The ordinary occupations that figure in these records are constantly introduced into his work, paintings and watercolours alike; and he prided himself on the accuracy with which he understood and conveyed the specific nature of all employments: in a letter of

199   The High Street, Oxford 1830
Pencil, 112 × 190
Trustees of the British Museum, London (T.B., CCXXXVIII-1v)   (not in catalogue)
The drawing on which the colour-beginning (Pl. 200) was based.

200 The High Street, Oxford 1830–5
Watercolour, 352 × 514
Trustees of the British Museum, London (T.B., CCLXIII-106) (not in catalogue)

1810 to a patron, James Wyatt, about his painting of *Oxford High Street*,[20] he wrote: 'The figures introduced are as follows—two Clericals, one in black with a master of arts gown, the other with lawn sleeves for the Bishop (being in want of a little white and purple scarf) preceded by and follow'd by a Beadle. Hence arise some questions—first, is it right or wrong to introduce the Bishop crossing the street in conversation with his robes, whether he should wear a cap?

what kind of a staff the Beadles use, and if they wear caps?—in short, these are the principal figures, and if you will favour me with answers to the foregoing questions and likewise describe to me the particulars of each dress, I should be much obliged to you, for I could wish to be right.'[21] And writing to John Britton in 1811 about the engraving of *Pope's Villa*, he pointed out that 'Baskets to entrap eels is not technical—being called Eel pots'.[22]   Pl.112

Ruskin fully appreciated the value of the *England and Wales* drawings as records of English weather; he enumerated in *Modern Painters* the different climatic conditions they describe; and he was alive to the fact that landscape is interesting as art only in so far as it reflects 'the physical

201 Merton College, Oxford c. 1830
Watercolour, 295 × 433
Trustees of the British Museum, London (T.B., CCLXIII-349)
(Cat. No. 887)

202 W. R. Smith (after J. M. W. Turner for *England and Wales*, R. 225)
Entrance to Fowey Harbour, Cornwall 1829
Engraving, 163 × 230
Trustees of the British Museum, London (1850—10—14—117)

conditions appointed for human existence';[23] yet he was capable of missing entirely the central strength of the *England and Wales* designs, as he did when, discussing the *Louth* of 1829, he called the teeming and exquisitely observed life of the market-place 'what he [Turner] clearly felt to be objectionable', though he admitted that he painted it 'first as a part, and a very principal part, of the English scenery he had undertaken to illustrate'. So Ruskin sees Turner dwelling '(I think ironically) on the elaborate carving of the church spire, with which the foreground interests are so distantly and vaguely connected'.[24] There is indeed an irony in this wonderful drawing: Turner extracted the detail of the church spire from the *North of England* sketchbook that he had used in 1797, and which he drew on very heavily for material for *England and Wales;* and there is a rather perfunctory quality in his handling of the architecture which is emphatically not the case with the lively scene in the foreground, with its horse-dealers, stall-holders, and admiring country-folk. But Ruskin did have a sense, if somewhat confused, of the sheer comprehensiveness of Turner's sympathy: of the superb *Devonport* he wrote that it revealed 'the especial forte of England in "vulgarity".' This 'manifested itself to him, either in Richmond picnics, barrack domestic life, jockey commerce, or here, finally, in the general relationships of Jack ashore. With all this, nevertheless, he had in himself no small sympathy; he liked it at once and was disgusted by it; and while he lived, in imagination, in ancient Carthage, lived,

practically, in modern Margate.'[25] But Ruskin is hardly justified in attributing his own disgust to Turner. The artist's love of crowds, the variety and vitality of the market-place or the fairground, animates *St. Catherine's Hill, Saltash, Plymouth*[26] and numerous others; it can be traced back to drawings of the 1790s like, for example, *Woolverhampton;*[27] and it was to reach great heights of expression in the swarming crowds of the late paintings and Swiss watercolours, where humanity becomes a force of nature as vigorous and immeasurable as that of the sea or the mountains. These scenes of common life betray enormous delight in detail, and delicate insight into the differences brought about by region, or by class—the middle-class refinement of the picnickers in *Richmond Hill and Bridge,* beautifully set off by a restrained and understated Claudian composition, is an example of this penetration. The genre elements here are entirely Turner's own, and his art is inconceivable without them. They owe little or nothing to the sentimental genre subjects of Wilkie that Turner imitated early in the century, and rise far above any subsequent attempts in the same vein; indeed, there is almost nothing in English art to compare with them for universality and compassion. To the extent that the *England and Wales* series,

Pl.23

Pl.190

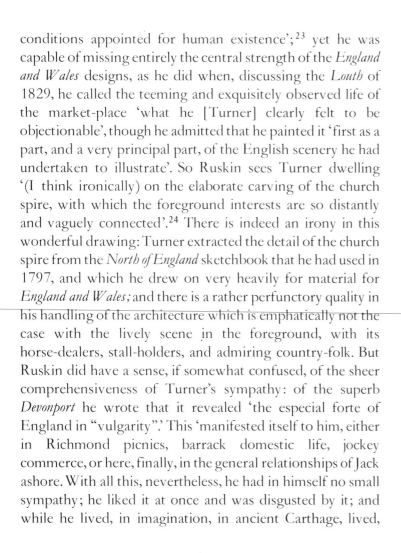

203 Arona: detail c. 1828
Watercolour, 292 × 422
Coll.: Brian Pilkington, London (Cat. No. 730)

204 St. Germain-en-Laye *c.* 1830
Watercolour, 299 × 457
Musée du Louvre, Paris   (Cat. No. 1045)

taken as a whole, exhibits Turner's humanity at its broadest and subtlest, it is the central document of his art, and the most complete expression of a profound theme in the history of landscape.

But Turner allows his concern to emerge incidentally, because it is really there, and not because he feels the need to proclaim a message or to weld individual subjects together by some overriding theme. In *Bolton Abbey,* published in 1827,[28] he records his own delight in a stretch of water that he noted for its 'beautiful refl[ectio]ns', and depicts his favourite pastime, angling, as one appropriate to the serene and isolated calm of the scene with a single figure and his tackle in an informal composition and narrow, intimate view. By contrast, *Prudhoe Castle* is stiltedly Italianate in its lighting and in the disposition of its elements. It was not Turner's habit to present what he saw totally free from such aesthetic 'preconceptions'; but in general the *England and Wales* subjects achieve pictorial grandeur by entirely original means, and rarely rely on any model, unless it is a work

Pl. 187

already produced by Turner himself. The view of *Ely,* issued in 1833, is a remarkable illustration of the new vocabulary of the 'Sublime' that he had evolved. It is based on a drawing of 1794, from which he had made a view for Colt Hoare that depends for its effect on a Girtinian stress on the quality of ancient masonry, and on the characteristic steep perspective and interrupted vision of Malton.[29] Just as with the drawing of *Schaffhausen* that he made at this date, he adopts a distant viewpoint which includes more of the whole subject, and for the 'Sublime' effect of a towering and enclosing structure substitutes a presentation which more perfectly conveys its real scale in a free and limitless ambiance of air. The cottages that cluster round the cathedral contribute to this; the finely conceived figures characteristically do so, by suggesting the mundane activity of the life of the town; the splendidly

Pl. 191

Pl. 206

simple but subtle play of light across the whole scene provides the clinching element, which both unifies and enlarges the entire view.

Another subject that derives from a very early drawing is PI.198 the *Llanthony Abbey,* published in 1836. The watercolour of 1794 is itself highly atmospheric, and its dominant diagonal stresses marked a step toward greater compositional expressiveness; Turner, in reinterpreting the design, seized on these diagonals and embodied them in the very light itself that strikes down through the mist billowing across the scene: great parallels of black-blue, or blackish-green, divide the sheet so that forms are perceived partially in and partially through them, a series of overlapping and translucent bands of contrasted tone to which all details of the subject are subdued. Something of the same division of space by light can be seen in *Ely,* but whereas there the process simply emphasizes the openness and expanse of the view, in *Llanthony* Turner's early original exercise in diagonals is transformed into a vast abstract pattern that moulds the whole image. The transference of form from solid objects to space itself is most clearly to be seen here; it is, of course, a result of Turner's system of organization in terms of colour masses, and seems to presuppose some preliminary study in which the diagonal bands of contrasted colour are adumbrated without their attendant topography. No such study for *Llanthony* has come to light, though some sheets in the Turner Bequest embody the feature of strong, slanting shafts of colour.[30]

In fact it is apparent that a very large number of the colour studies in the Turner Bequest, especially those on sheets of paper measuring approximately 254 × 178 mm or larger, are connected with the *England and Wales* project, which Turner tackled particularly from the standpoint of complex colour organization. Many of the colour-beginnings supply evidence of subjects that were not developed; many are too generalized or primitive as colour layouts to afford clues as to their subjects; but some are clearly preparatory for identifiable designs, and they establish a type of loose, broadly-washed study, using soft secondary or tertiary colours, which may be regarded as characteristic of those related to the *England and Wales* project. Occasionally, sequences of such studies show Turner working towards a composition through several experimental schemes.[31] Rarely, a colour-beginning like that 93, 194 for *Blenheim* dwells on isolated effects of detail rather than on the interrelationship of basic blocks of colour.

As we have seen, Turner was working in this way on compositions for the *Rivers of England* and other projects in

205 Marly *c.* 1831
Watercolour and some body-colour, 286 × 426
Trustees of the British Museum, London (Lloyd Bequest)
(Cat. No. 1047)

the early 1820s, but the colour-layout study seems to have been most important to his procedure in connection with the *England and Wales* subjects on which he was engaged in the early 1830s. Many of them can be connected with scenes noted on his tour of the Midlands in 1830, and the effects of this kind of colour analysis are most evident in the finished drawings of the next few years. *Dudley* is palpably a PI.195 composition built out of contrasted segments of blocked colour; but in working out his design Turner masks his carefully laid foundation by an intricate overlay of echoing colours, reverberating from one area to another, so that the ground plan is barely perceptible. In some cases a spatial architecture is imposed on the landscape arbitrarily in order to create compositional solidity. The view of *Llanberis Lake* is PI.192 an odd example of this: the grand spectacle of mountains with clouds, trees, and dark lake, is unified by a series of horizontal shafts of light and shadow which have no natural justification, and exist purely to impose comprehensive and binding dynamism on the diversity of the scene. Another instance of this process of unification occurs in the splendidly diverse *St. Germain-en-Laye,* from the group of French subjects PI.204 Turner executed at this period; here the basic structure of horizontal bands of pink, blue and ochre is reinforced by an extraordinary blue shadow, cast by no possible object, which strengthens the central blue zone and binds the design more rigorously together.[32]

Artificialities of this kind seem to be peculiar to the years around 1830, when Turner was incorporating more and

187

206 Falls of the Rhine at Schaffhausen 1831–2
Watercolour and body-colour, 309 × 457
City Museums and Art Gallery, Birmingham (Cat. No. 406)

more natural and human content into his watercolours; he felt the need to force coherence on his conceptions as they became richer and more intricate. But the colour-beginning was not indispensable; many of these subjects seem to have been drawn direct on to the final sheet without preliminary notes beyond the initial pencil record on which Turner relied for his topographical 'germ'. In the next decade equally complex subjects were worked out on the basis of a very different type of preparation.[33]

The engravers whom Heath employed to render these astonishing ideas in black and white line were among the most accomplished of their day; several of them had collaborated with Turner in the past on work for the *History of Richmondshire* and Scott's *Antiquities*. They were involved, during the decade of the *England and Wales* venture, in other projects—the *French Rivers* and the vignette illustrations—to which Turner brought his usual critical and creative assiduity.

They were alive to his requirements, and had evolved, with the aid of his sharp comments on their proof impressions, a language that was a remarkable and very beautiful equivalent in monochrome of his elaborate conceptions.[34] Heath made a point of advertising that the *England and Wales* plates were to be 'printed uniformly with the Southern Coast' but in fact they were slightly larger and, as has been observed, 'more elaborate and more skilful.'[35] The engravers received about £100 for each plate; while Turner probably got only about half that sum for each drawing that he made. Work proceeded briskly, and plates were completed within a year or so of the drawings being delivered.[36] In 1832 the first sixty plates were

207 Melrose (for Scott's *Poetical Works*) *c.* 1832
Watercolour, 101 × 155
National Galleries of Scotland, Edinburgh (Vaughan Bequest)
(Cat. No. 1080)

published together in a volume, but the second half of the work was never completed: despite the high quality of the engraving, and the supreme art of the designs themselves, the *Picturesque Views in England and Wales* failed to sell. Only thirty-six of the projected sixty remaining plates were published, and the stock of prints, together with the engraved plates, was offered to Henry Bohn, the print-seller who was later to reprint Constable's *English Landscape Scenery*. Bohn however would not meet Heath's price, and the plates and prints were put up for auction by Southgate & Co. in 1839. 'Just at the moment the auctioneer was about to mount the rostrum, Mr Turner stepped in, and bought it [the stock] privately, at the reserved price of three thousand pounds, much to the vexation of many who had come prepared to buy

portions of it. Immediately after the purchase, Mr Turner walked up to Mr Bohn, with whom he was very well acquainted, and said to him, "So, Sir, you were going to buy my England and Wales, to sell cheap, I suppose—make umbrella prints of them, eh?—but I have taken care of that. No more of my plates shall be worn to shadows." Upon Mr Bohn's replying, that his object was the printed stock (which was very large) rather than the copper-plates, he said "O! very well, I don't want the stock. I only want to keep the coppers out of your clutches".'[37] Bohn would not, however, give Turner the £3,000 he asked for the prints. A complete edition of the series in two volumes, with 'Descriptive and Historical Illustrations' by H. E. Lloyd, Esq. had been published in 1838, prior to the sale.

The drawings themselves were not allowed to remain as a set; Heath exhibited some of them in 1829 at the Egyptian Hall in Piccadilly, and sixty-six subjects were shown at the gallery of Messrs. Moon, Boys and Graves in 1833. By that date Heath had disposed of those that had been engraved to various regular patrons of Turner, notably Godfrey Windus, Samuel Rogers and J. H. Maw. Turner made no attempt, as he did with the *Rivers* and *Ports* drawings, or the *French Rivers* series, to keep the watercolours together in his own possession. To that extent it is legitimate to see each work as an individual production, independent of a larger context. But just as Turner was temperamentally inclined to work in series, so his watercolours gain from being assessed in groups, and the rich contrasts of the *England and Wales* subjects shed a lustre over the sequence that enhances the powerful impact of so many and varied aspects of English life.

When Heath exhibited the earlier drawings of the *England and Wales* series at the Egyptian Hall in 1829, he advertised 'a projected work ... on Italy', which was to be 'of a similar kind' to the current undertaking.[38] One of the drawings at the Egyptian Gallery was the *Lake Albano*[39] which Heath published in *The Keepsake* in 1829, and it seems reasonable to suppose that this may have been intended for the Italian publication, and that other Italian scenes engraved for *The Keepsake* were also destined for that work: certainly, Turner made several such views between about 1826 and his departure for Rome in 1828, and they preserve the general proportions and approach of the *England and Wales* drawings.[40] The project was never carried out, but the existence of the proposal suggests that there may have been a further scheme, for views in France, on which Turner worked after his tour through France in 1829. Even more French views appeared in *The Keepsake* than Italian ones: *Saumur, Nantes,*

St. Germain-en-Laye, and *Marly* were all published, and others exist—the *Grandville,* for instance—which were not.[14] All these drawings exhibit features characteristic of the rather free, opulent watercolour style that Turner adopted about 1830, a style that is typical of these years, and which gave way to a tighter and more meticulous manner towards the mid-1830s.[42]

If, as seems possible, a third series was planned, the fact adds weight to the conviction implanted by the *England and Wales* series that Turner felt himself especially at ease with the form of expression that he had evolved for these works. It was a type that he perpetuated in the much smaller but equally detailed plates designed as book illustrations in the 1830s: there, although confined to a tiny space, only about 102×127 mm, Turner created some of his most expansive and densely populated views—particularly those that he made for Cadell's edition of Scott, which appeared between 1834 and 1836.[43] The *Melrose,* for example, which Turner designed for the 'Lay of the Last Minstrel', illustrates his ability to establish irresistibly a vast and poetically charged aerial expanse by means of a mass of detail, rendered (both in the original watercolour and in the engraving from it) with the exquisite precision of a miniaturist, yet never losing that softness and gentleness of modulation on which these subtle atmospheric effects rely. The foreground figures of the *Melrose* are apparently Turner, Cadell and their companions picnicking; they inform us poignantly and wittily that the splendour of nature is inseparable from the ordinary human perception—our own—by which it is seen and felt.

Pl.205

Pl.207

NOTES

1 Some of these sequences of paintings are discussed in chap. 9. See Ruskin, *Works*, XIII, p. 9: Ruskin notes Turner's 'earnest desire to arrange his works in connected groups, and his evident intention with respect to each drawing, that it should be considered as expressing part of a continuous system of thought. The practical result of this feeling was that he commenced many series of drawings ... under titles representing rather the relation which the executed designs bore to the materials accumulated in his own mind, than the position which they could justifiably claim when contemplated by others.' In the context of the series of the *Liber Studiorum*, Ruskin, *Works*, VII, p. 434, quotes Turner as saying, 'What is the use of them but together?' The comment applies to many other series in Turner's output.

2 Cat. section 1(b).

3 See above, chap. 3, note 13, and Cat. Nos 295–304.

4 Michael 'Angelo' Rooker, engraver and topographical watercolourist, 1743 or 1746–1801.

5 Cat. section IV(b).

6 See chap. 5, pp. 130–1. In connection with Fawkes's Swiss drawings, note Turner's comment to W. B. Cooke: 'the Swiss drawings are either bound together or cannot be lent.' See Thornbury, p. 189.

7 See chap. 5, p. 124.

8 Cat. section X(c).

9 Cat. section XIV(a).

10 Charles Heath, 1785–1848.

11 The engravings after Turner that appeared in 'annuals' are R. 313–47; for a suggestion as to the purpose of some of these drawings see p. 190.

12 See Holcomb, 'A Neglected Classical Phase of Turner's Art: his Vignettes to Rogers's "Italy"', 1969.

13 Comparably elaborate preparations were made for the pictures exhibited at the Academy in 1800–5 (in the *Calais Pier* sketchbook, etc.); but there Turner's concern was to solve compositional problems in terms of the grouping and balancing of parts of the subject. The *England and Wales* drawings were planned both compositionally and chromatically, often at great length (see p. 187).

14 For instance, in the first issue (1827) the subjects can be categorized as 'Mountainous' (*Rivaulx Abbey*); 'Urban' or 'Industrial' (*Lancaster from the Aqueduct*); 'Classical' (*Dartmouth Cove*); and 'Pastoral' (*Bolton Abbey*). There is no consistency, however, in the way the subjects are grouped, and it may be that Turner chose views at random, and that they were engraved and published as they were drawn.

15 Cat. No. 864.

16 Cat. No. 511.

17 Cat. Nos 791, 808, 878.

18 The sketchbooks are *Kenilworth* (T.B., CCXXXVIII), *Worcester and Shrewsbury* (T.B., CCXXXIX) and *Birmingham and Coventry* (T.B., CCXL).

19 E.g. in the *Lake of Zug and Goldau* sketchbook (T.B., CCCXXXI) of *c*. 1843: 'Figures on Bridge watching the dragging up of Salmon nets' (p. 20). Lindsay, *J. M. W. Turner*, 1966, p. 17, lists some of Turner's comments on the activities of children, in the context of the interest in childhood displayed in his work.

20 Cat. No. P102.

21 Turner to Wyatt, 28 February 1810; quoted by Finberg, *Life*, pp. 164–5.

22 Quoted by Finberg, *Life*, p. 184.

23 Ruskin, *Works*, XXII, p. 12.

24 Ruskin, *Works*, XIII, p. 438.

25 *Ibid.*, pp. 438–9. *Devonport* is Cat. No. 813.

26 Cat. Nos 837, 794, 835.

27 See Cat. No. 139 for a further comment.

28 Cat. No. 788.

29 The original study is T.B., XXI-Y; the watercolour is Cat. No. 193.

30 E.g. T.B., CCLXIII-14; repr. Wilkinson, 1975, p. 102.

31 The sequence of studies of a view in *Oxford High Street*, for example, is T.B., CCLXIII-3, 4, 5, 106, 362; see Pl. 200, and R.A. 1974, Nos 443–7.

32 This apparently arbitrary use of a colour structure has in fact highly respectable precedents: in his Eighth Discourse Reynolds says: 'Those painters who have best understood the art of producing a good effect, have adopted one principle that seems perfectly conformable to reason; that a part may be sacrificed for the good of the whole. Thus, whether the masses consist of light or shadow, it is necessary that they should be compact and of pleasing shape: to this end some parts may be darker and some lighter, and reflexions stronger than nature would warrant. Paul Veronese took great liberties of this kind. It is said, that being once asked, why certain figures were painted in shade, as no cause was seen in the picture itself; he turned off the enquiry by answering, "*una nuevola che passa*," a cloud is passing which has overshadowed them.'

33 See chap. 10, pp. 194 ff.

34 See Gage, 1969, chap. 2, pp. 42–52; and Omer, *Turner and the Poets*, exhibition catalogue, 1975.

35 Finberg, *Life*, p. 301.

36 Ruskin in *Modern Painters* stated that 'Turner certainly made none of the drawings for that series [i.e. *England and Wales*] long before they were wanted; and if, therefore, we suppose the drawing to have been made so much as three years before the publication of the plate, it will be setting the date as far back as is in the slightest degree probable' (*Works*, VI, p. 43). In the Catalogue *England and Wales* drawings have generally been given a date within one or two years of publication; but it remains possible that some drawings, like the *Saltash* (Cat. No. 794), were ready considerably earlier.

37 Alaric Watts, Biographical Sketch of Turner, in Ritchie, *Liber Fluviorum*, 1853, p. xxi, note.

38 See Finberg, *Life*, p. 488, note, and B.M. 1975, No. 145.

39 Cat. No. 731.

40 Cat. Nos 726–31.

41 Cat. section XV(d). A series of Rhine subjects may also have been in hand in the 1830s; see Addenda to the Watercolour Catalogue, No. 1378a.

42 The free hatching of the drawings of this period is seen by Gage (1969, p. 96 and note 89) as revealing 'a strong interest in the tempera and fresco work of the Trecento and Quattrocento'. This seems to find an obscure cause for an effect characteristic of watercolour technique in the early nineteenth century, especially that of miniaturists such as W. H. Hunt and John Linnell. Linnell did imitate fresco painting in watercolour, but the result is very different from his usual hatched manner of drawing portraits (see the *Mrs. Wilberforce and her child* in the Yale Center for British Art, dated 1824 and inscribed *Water Colors;* it is painted on a prepared millboard to resemble a work in fresco by Perugino or Ghirlandaio). Compare also the very pronounced and brightly coloured hatching in Turner's vignette of *Lake Leman* in the Boston Museum of Fine Arts (Cat. No. 1313).

43 Cat. section XVI(c).

Chapter Nine

The Subject-Matter of Turner's Late Paintings

In the years from 1821 to 1825 Turner exhibited only three oil-paintings: the little Watteau pastiche, *What you will!*, *The Bay of Baiae*, and *Harbour of Dieppe*.[1] In 1821 he showed nothing. The last picture that he produced before this hiatus was his enormous *Rome from the Vatican*. In its complexity it had no precedent in his art; it is a grand, public statement of private feeling and philosophy.[2] After his return to full production in 1826—and especially after 1830—we find many subjects that seem to partake of the same abstruseness, and to demand, if anything, more ingenuity in penetrating their meaning. There are times when it is as if his natural and instinctive bent for the visual had been overtaken by the more obscure and literary meditations that he was accustomed to express in poetry; as though he had set new objectives for his pictures—the objectives of a temperamental recluse who no longer cared to communicate easily with his public. The inward significance of these works has been much debated and questioned. The problems increase in the 1840s, and culminate in the impermeable mystery of *Undine giving the ring to Masaniello, fisherman of Naples* and its pair, *The Angel standing in the sun*, of 1846.

In his watercolours, nevertheless, however formal or public their intention, Turner confined his meaning to the simply visual, to what is readily assimilable by looking at the image, without reference to literary, historical or other associations. Obliquity of allusion was reserved for the oil-paintings—and only for some of these. There is perhaps only one watercolour that hints at what may be a hidden personal meaning: the *Chryses* of 1811. This is, possibly, no more than a historical subject-piece; as such, it is unusual enough. The verses from Pope's translation of the *Iliad*, with which it was accompanied in the Royal Academy catalogue, provide the reference necessary to understand the illustration; and yet we may wonder why Turner chose this subject. It shows Chryses, having sued in vain of the Greeks for the

release of his daughter Chryseis, praying to Apollo for vengeance. Turner had contemplated painting the subject of Ulysses offering Chryseis to her Father a few years earlier, but set in a large-scale classical harbour scene.[3] Here there are none of the customary elements of a classical landscape; only a rocky shore and a burning sky. Pope's lines emphasize what the drawing clearly enacts:

'Silent he wander'd by the sounding main;
Till safe at distance to his God he prays;
The God who darts around the world his rays.'[4]

If, as some have claimed, the sunsets of Turner's late pictures have a personal symbolic meaning, *Chryses* may be an early

208 Messieurs les voyageurs on their return from Italy (par la diligence) in a snow drift upon Mount Tarrar, 22nd of January, 1829 R.A. 1829
Watercolour and body-colour, 545 × 747
Trustees of the British Museum, London (Lloyd Bequest) (Cat. No. 405)

209   Vision of Medea   1828
Oil on canvas, 1735 × 2410
Turner Bequest, Tate Gallery, London   (Cat. No. P293)

statement of Turner's apprehension of the sun as God, as a force with some intense private significance for him.[5]

There is no explicit anticipation of this idea in the earlier pictures. In the exhibition at which *Chryses* was shown, another subject involving Apollo, the *Apollo and Python*,[6] makes no allusion to the god's association with the sun. The golden sunlight of *Dido building Carthage* and *The decline of the Carthaginian Empire* cannot be said to express a personal symbolic idea: its derivation from the paintings of Claude is clear, and the simple opposition of sunrise to sunset is an entirely 'open' use of imagery. Not until *Ulysses deriding Polyphemus* is the symbolical potential explored further. There Turner portrays the sunrise with a literal application of mythology: Apollo's horses leap over the horizon in a burst of light, borrowing a motif used by Flaxman in his illustrations to Pope's Homer.[7] Even here, however, there is direct

thematic justification for such a motif: the whole *Ulysses* canvas is a recreation of the golden landscape of the enchanted past. It is vividly real: the shadowy giant, the crowded ship, and the water sparkling with nereids firmly establish the mood of the picture, just as the dream-like rocks (which, perhaps significantly, echo those of *Chryses*), the ships with sculptured prows and billowing sails penetrate into a reality unlike our own, yet equally compelling. It has been seen to embody a comment on the natural phenomena of earth, air and water as understood by contemporary scientific investigation and hypothesis;[8] but it seems superfluous to

Pl. 181

210 Fort Vimieux R.A. 1831
Oil on canvas, 711 × 1067
Private collection (Cat. No. P341)

the richness of the work as a whole to read quasi-didactic meanings into it. We may, however, consider it to present natural forces as primeval elements in a gloriously pristine world, rather as Ruskin saw another of Turner's Apollo pictures, the *Apollo and Daphne* of 1837,[9] which he interpreted as a celebration of the union of water and earth—Daphne being the child of a River God and Terra.[10] The suggestion that, to contemporary eyes, mythological personifications of natural forces and elements might thus be made to extend and reinforce the meaning of a landscape is pertinent to an interpretation of *Ulysses*. Such personifications were common in academic painting of the early nineteenth century. In particular, Henry Howard, who had become an Associate of the Royal Academy at almost the same time as Turner—in 1800—and followed him to full membership in 1807, had made a speciality of such pictures.[11] His *Hylas and the Naiads*, of 1797, had been bought by Lord Egremont and may well have influenced Turner's taking up of similar themes in the late 1820s and 1830s. He was particularly fond of painting nymphs personifying the stars and planets, adorned, just as the nereids in *Ulysses* are, with diaphanous shifts, and gemlike points of light on their foreheads.

211 Lucy, Countess of Carlisle and Dorothy Percy's visit to their father, Lord Percy, when under attainder upon the supposition of his being concerned in the gunpowder plot R.A. 1831
Oil on oak panel, 405 × 700
Turner Bequest, Tate Gallery, London (Cat. No. P338)

The recreation of legends with their full complement of fantastic characters was to recur in Turner's later work; *Ulysses* marks the beginning of the phase. In his earlier pictures mythological subjects did not penetrate the realm of faery. There is one odd exception to this: the repainting of *Rispah watching the bodies of her sons* that Turner showed in his own gallery in 1808, which was described by a reviewer as a subject 'taken from the Runic superstitions'—a work possibly intended to evoke the atmosphere of magic and witchery sometimes attempted by West and Fuseli.[12] In the later period there are several examples of this genre. Another picture with origins, like *Ulysses,* in the Roman stay of 1828 is Pl.209 also a fantasy based on Greek legend: the *Vision of Medea* in which the atmosphere of the 'Runic superstitions' picture is recast in an Italian, perhaps Venetian vein (possibly suggested by Reynold's great *Macbeth and the Witches* at Petworth).[13]

212 Charles Robert Leslie (1794–1859)
Lucy Percy, Countess of Carlisle, bringing the Pardon to her Father
Oil on canvas, 508 × 1092
Petworth Collection

Here the figures take an important role, and the spirits are given palpable physical presence. The more numinous phenomena of *Ulysses* reappear in the canvas of *The parting of Hero* Pl.219 *and Leander,* begun *c.* 1836; a 'subsidiary perspective' of classical architecture on the left contrasts strangely with a nebulous wall of water and spray on the right, peopled with sea-sprites.

196

213 Staffa, Fingal's cave R.A. 1832
Oil on canvas, 915 × 1220
Yale Center for British Art, Paul Mellon Collection (Cat. No. P347)

The presence of these nereids confirms the impression given by *Ulysses* and *Medea* that Turner was absorbing into his repertoire the type of fantastic subject favoured not only by his contemporary Howard, but, perhaps more significantly, by younger artists like Francis Danby and William Etty.[14] The rich, brilliantly coloured canvases that Etty was submit-

ting to the Academy in the 1820s, signalling a renewed interest in Titian—one critic in 1825 had 'little doubt that the works of Titian were on their first appearance what Mr. Etty's are now'[15]—may have prompted Turner's use of brilliant red and blue in *Ulysses,* as well as his choice of a theme in which the alluring spirits of the sea are given so striking a part. Etty had exhibited a picture of *The Parting of Hero and Leander* in 1827, and Turner's treatment of that subject may well have been a response to this. Such oblique relations with other Academicians and their work are latent throughout Turner's career; the life and activity of the

Academy could not but be of primary interest to him, devoted to it as he was. As late as 1846 he painted a 'faery' picture that alluded to another artist. *Queen Mab's Cave,* shown in that year, is generally seen as a direct reference to Danby's picture *The Enchanted Island,* which had been issued as a mezzotint in 1841.[16]

The nereids or 'Undines' of *Ulysses* were mentioned scathingly by the vitriolic critic of *Blackwood's Magazine,* the Rev. John Eagles, who provoked Ruskin's first defence of

214 Van Goyen, looking out for a subject   R.A. 1833
Oil on canvas, 918 × 1229
Frick Collection, New York   (Cat. No. P350)

Turner; and it has been suggested[17] that a much later 'faery' picture, *Undine giving the ring to Masaniello, fisherman of Naples* of 1846 is a jibe at this hostile criticism. Its pendant, *The Angel standing in the sun,* is a balancing reference to Ruskin, Turner's

215   The Burning of the House of Lords and Commons, 16th October, 1834   B.I. 1835
Oil on canvas, 920 × 1230
Philadelphia Museum of Art (John H. McFadden Collection) (Cat. No. P359)

most enthusiastic supporter, who had written of Turner in *Modern Painters* as 'standing like the great angel of the Apocalypse, clothed with a cloud, and with a rainbow upon his head, and with the sun and stars given into his hand.'[18] While in the one picture the artist presents himself as Ruskin's angel, asssociated with the sun, in the other he is a fisherman associated with Turner's favourite pastime, angling. Although this interpretation is 'private' and abstruse, it seems to be really necessary as an explanation of the two works, and of the connection between them (though we should not overlook the fact that Danby had exhibited two pictures entitled *Subject from the Revelations* at the Royal

Academy exhibition of 1829; Turner would have been aware of them). His two canvases were not hung or catalogued together at the exhibition, but were evidently conceived as a pair in the square format and opposing hot and cold colour schemes that characterize two other pairs of the 1840s, *Peace—burial at sea* and *War. The exile and the rock limpet* of 1842; and *Shade and darkness—the evening of the Deluge* and *Light and colour—the morning after the Deluge* of 1843.[19]

Pls. 230, 229
Pl. 231
Pl. 232

Each of these pairs has its own distinct significance, though each can be found to have some immediate, if superficial, meaning simply in terms of antithetical subject-

216   The bright stone of honour (Ehrenbrietstein [*sic*]) and the tomb of Marceau, from Byron's *Childe Harold*   R.A. 1835
Oil on canvas, 930 × 1230
Private collection   (Cat. No. P361)

217   Keelmen heaving in coals by night: detail   R.A. 1835
Oil on canvas, 902 × 1219
National Gallery of Art, Washington, D.C. (Widener Collection)
(Cat. No. P360)

matter. But this is not true of the pair of 1846, and the explanation that has just been summarized, or something similar to it, must be adduced if we are to make sense of the pairing at all.[20]

In the context of his art such explanations seem out of place; but in the context of Turner's character the solution to the *Undine* riddle rings true. It is suggested that his preoccupation with so trifling a matter as the attitudes of critics in *Undine* and the *Angel* was occasioned by his sense of approaching death.[21] Turner was severely ill in 1845, and it is possible that he felt that these might be among his last works.

218   Rome from Mount Aventine   R.A. 1836
Oil on canvas, 916 × 1246
Coll.: The Earl of Rosebery   (Cat. No. P366)

In fact the attitudes of critics were of crucial importance to him, precisely because of the weight he attached to public communication. It would have been wholly fitting if these pictures had constituted his final statement. The anxious sense of his own achievement and its neglect or recognition can be traced throughout his life: it forms much of the burden

219   The parting of Hero and Leander—from the Greek of Musæus
R.A. 1837
Oil on canvas, 1460 × 2360
Turner Bequest, National Gallery, London   (Cat. No. P370)

of Turner's meaning in *Rome from the Vatican*. It is a corollary of the ambition that initially shaped his career, and which kept him in rivalry with other artists both past and present.

This sense of insecurity, bred of ambition, almost panic-stricken at times, inspired Turner's 'manuscript poem' *Fallacies of Hope,* first quoted with *Hannibal and his army crossing the Alps* in 1812 (see P 126).[22] The relevance of the lines to the painting is clear enough. Their relevance in broader terms to Turner's theme is subtler: they very poignantly express an insight into Hannibal's situation, not conveyed by the picture itself: 'Capua's joys beware!' is not the most obvious of glosses on the unsuccessful Carthaginian invasion.[23]

The next subject to which lines from the *Fallacies of Hope* were added was the only watercolour ever so signalled, *The*

Battle of Fort Rock of 1815. This deals, as we have noted, with Napoleon's invasion of Italy in 1796 (see No. 399).[24] Turner's verses here, as in *Hannibal,* are not a mere lament on the futility of war, even if the *Fort Rock* lines do conclude on an image of 'plundering hordes' strewing Italy's 'plains with woe'. But whereas the watercolour treats of the action and fate of the common man, as Turner's watercolours so often do (Napoleon's name does not appear in title or verse), *Hannibal* is about a specific man, his personal action and his personal fate. Turner's earliest understanding of the 'Sublime' had led him, as we have seen, to focus the emotional content of his pictures on individual heroes—like the 'hopeless Owen' of *Dolbadern Castle.*[25] Throughout his mature career he gave many of his major canvases significance in this way. It was not until the end of his life that the full purpose of these references began to be manifest, and even then it was obscure. The pair of 1842, *Peace* and *War,* makes the matter clearer. Once again the opposition of colour—blue and black in *Peace,* yellow and red in *War*—gives a superficial clarity to the coupling. The real contrast, or pairing, is that of, on the

220 Regulus 1828 B.I. 1837
Oil on canvas, 910 × 1240
Turner Bequest, Tate Gallery, London   (Cat. No. P294)

222 Interior at Petworth *c.* 1837
Oil on canvas, 910 × 1220
Turner Bequest, Tate Gallery, London   (Cat. No. P449)

221 A vaulted hall *c.* 1835
Oil on mahogany, 750 × 915
Turner Bequest, Tate Gallery, London   (Cat. No. P450)

one hand, David Wilkie, an artist, and on the other, Napoleon, a military hero, like Hannibal. There is a direct precedent for this use of Napoleon as a motif for a meditation on the hero's destiny: Benjamin Robert Haydon, in his journal for 22 May 1831, noted: 'Had a magnificent conception of the three musings of Napoleon: musing on St. Helena,

sun set; musing at Fontainebleau, sun meridian; musing in Egypt, break of day'.[26] He finished the *Napoleon on St. Helena* in 1831; if Turner did not see it, he might have read a clear description of it in Wordsworth's sonnet on the picture, published in 1832. Both Haydon and Turner would have been familiar with Byron's *Ode to Napoleon*,[27] which pivots on the contrast of material power and moral baseness, on the futility of glory without honour: 'Who would soar the solar height / To set in such a starless night?' The intensity of *War*, with its red glare, is carried through into the lines from the *Fallacies of Hope* that go with it; Turner apostrophizes the 'rock limpet':

> 'Ah! thy tent-formed shell is like
> A soldier's nightly bivouac, alone
> Amidst a sea of blood—
> —but you can join your comrades.'

Picture and verses alike express the concentrated loneliness of a great man: both loneliness and greatness Turner felt that he shared. An artist—and he knew that he was a great artist: the knowledge was part and parcel of his ambition—is a hero. That also is the message of *Peace,* where Wilkie, first Turner's rival and later his friend, is given a hero's burial.[28]

It is for its connection with this theme that *Rome from the Vatican* is the key picture that it is. In it are combined Turner's conception of himself as an artist and his sense of membership in the brotherhood of great artists past and present.

223 Ancient Italy—Ovid banished from Rome   R.A. 1838
Oil on canvas, 946 × 1250
Private collection   (Cat. No. P375)

There is an abundance of other works in which he makes a 'hero' of a brother artist. His view of Venice of 1833, which shows 'Canaletti painting',[29] places the *vedutista* in one of his own views, just as Rembrandt bursts into the shadowy Rembrandtesque interior of *Rembrandt's daughter*,[30] exhibited in 1827, or Van Goyen, in *Van Goyen, looking out for a subject*, of

1833, is afloat in a seventeenth-century Dutch seascape. In fact, Van Goyen is not obviously visible in the design; his place in the title suffices to make the point, just as Ruysdael's does in the more allusive *Port Ruysdael* of 1827, a fictitious Dutch port used again in a title of 1844.[31] There are other, more devious approaches to the same theme, which show that the artist as a person, or his works, may equally be taken as subjects: *Depositing of John Bellini's three pictures in la Chiesa Redentore, Venice* (1841)[32] is a joyous celebration of the triumph of art. *Watteau study by Fresnoy's rules* (1831) places

Pl.214

224 The Fighting 'Temeraire' tugged to her last berth to be broken up
1838 (R.A. 1839)
Oil on canvas, 910 × 1220
Turner Bequest, National Gallery, London (Cat. No. P377)

Watteau in his own studio, surrounded by his canvases—a complex commentary on the man, his art, and the theory (Du Fresnoy's) on which his art was supposed to rest, or of which it was a demonstration.[33] The subject may be seen as a communication, if not to the general public, then to Turner's fellow-painters in the Academy, with whom, as I have suggested in the case of Etty, he seems to have had pleasure in conducting little 'dialogues'—some of which led to acrimony when he deliberately modified his own pictures on varnishing days to the detriment of his neighbours'.[34]

Yet the *Watteau Study* is not simply an imitation of Watteau. Another small picture on panel, similar in scale and date, is a more unexpected 'homage': this is the scene of *Lucy, Countess of Carlisle and Dorothy Percy's visit to their father*, which Pl.211 makes sly use of figures from Van Dyck portraits at

225   Slavers throwing overboard the dead and dying—Typhon coming
on ('The Slave Ship')   R.A. 1840
Oil on canvas, 910 × 1380
Museum of Fine Arts, Boston, Mass.   (Cat. No. P385)

Petworth. In format and conception it bears little relation to
Van Dyck's typical work, though it does come close in style
and genre to a small picture of *Lucy Percy, Countess of Carlisle,*
bringing the Pardon to her Father, painted by the rising young
artist Charles Robert Leslie for Lord Egremont, with whom

he too stayed.[35] It is effectively a sequel to the scene Turner
painted. Perhaps the two artists co-ordinated their works,
intending to produce matching panels for the decoration of a
room at Petworth; in the event only Leslie's was hung there,
with another by him, *Charles II and Lady Margaret Bellenden.*[36]
As he had done when Wilkie rose to favour in 1806, Turner
embarked on a type of painting unusual for him, and
subordinated his own manner to that of a younger man. The
Watteau Study, couched as it is in the same small format with
figures in costume, is in fact another essay in the Leslian

207

226 Giudecca, la Donna della Salute and San Georgio ('The Guidecca from the Canale di Fusina') R.A. 1841
Oil on canvas, 610×915
Coll.: Mr. William Wood Prince, Chicago (Cat. No. P391)

mode of historical genre; Watteau seen through Leslie's eyes, perhaps,[37] as much as Turner's, just as the *Boccaccio* picture of 1828 summons up Watteau through the eyes of Stothard, whose illustrations to Pickering's edition of the *Decameron* had appeared in 1825.[38]

Turner's visits to Petworth, which seem to have become a regular event from about 1827, evidently acted as a catalyst to his competitive nature. A number of the subjects that are now thought to have been painted either at Petworth or under the influence of what he had seen there,[39] reflect the renewed impact on his imagination of Rembrandt's resonant chiaroscuro; but whereas his youthful understanding of the example was applied to architecture and to landscape, now Turner brought it to bear on history pictures, genre scenes

and portraits. More than ever he seems to have felt the need to demonstrate the range and diversity of his art—especially in the field of history. It is remarkable that those of the group that he chose for exhibition were the pictures most obviously painted in imitation of other artists; the *Watteau Study*, the Leslie pastiche, and the two most overtly Rembrandtian, *Pilate washing his hands* and *Jessica*, which both appeared in 1830.[40] The first of these two, a crowded scene in which, characteristically, the principal (eponymous) character is not

227 Antonio Canal, il Canaletto (1697–1768)
Venice: The Basin of San Marco, on Ascension Day
Oil on canvas, 1219 × 1828
National Gallery, London (4453)

228 Snow storm—steam-boat off a harbour's mouth making signals in
shallow water, and going by the lead. The author was in this storm on the
night the Ariel left Harwich R.A. 1842
Oil on canvas, 915 × 1220
Turner Bequest, Tate Gallery, London (Cat. No. P398)

at once identifiable, is unequivocally an attempt to imitate the style of Rembrandt's religious subjects: not only are lighting and colour tuned to the Rembrandtian gamut, but the costumes and general mood of the work clearly set Rembrandt as the measure by which everything is to be judged. We have ample confirmation that such 'borrowings' were considered by Turner wholly legitimate extensions of his own practice in the story of his painting *The Burning Fiery Furnace* for the Academy exhibition of 1832 in direct rivalry with his friend, George Jones, who had expressed his intention of submitting a picture of that subject.[41] Turner's version is not an ostentatiously virtuoso performance in his own most familiar style, an attempt to dazzle and annihilate competition as his colleagues sometimes accused him of doing; it is another elaborate Rembrandt-style invention, in which even the drama of the fire itself is subordinated to a group of figures in the foreground, just as the lamenting women at the centre of the composition of *Pilate washing his hands* eclipse the main action.[42] The context of good-humoured rivalry in which the picture was created may explain why it is not as extravagantly conceived as some of the other works on the theme of fire that Turner produced in the 1830s; but *The Burning Fiery Furnace* fits in stylistically with the evidently serious statement of *Pilate,* and with another, unfinished, biblical subject in the same vein, *Christ driving the Traders from the Temple.*[43] His exhibition of works like these is a measure of the seriousness with which he undertook them.

Pl.222   One of these canvases, known simply as *Interior at Petworth,* which is among the works of this group that were not exhibited, has none of the figures that enliven the Petworth subjects as a rule, and seems (it is very broadly and allusively painted) to show an empty, shuttered room with an open, baroque sarcophagus with a coat of arms, and beyond, a burst of white light in an open well. It is difficult to decipher, although considerable detail is suggested—overturned furniture, dogs playing, and scattered papers. This odd sketch has been thought to express Turner's grief at the death of Lord Egremont in 1837.[44]

But the high semicircular arch with the burst of light beyond it is unlike anything at Petworth. It suggests rather the dramatic vaults, imitating Roman *thermae,* that figure in the buildings of Soane, especially as interpreted by Soane's draughtsman J. M. Gandy.[45] The Soanesque quality of several Pl.221   of the so-called 'Petworth' interiors is striking—*A vaulted hall,* for instance, suggests the old Colonial Office of Soane's Bank of England, as well as recalling the Piranesian

inspiration behind Turner's *Ewenny Priory* of 1797.[46] We do not know exactly when these pictures were executed, and it is hazardous to associate them with any single event; but Soane died at the beginning of the same year as Egremont, and if Turner was working on these subjects at that time, the work of Soane, a fellow-academician, may well have been in his mind. Furthermore, although the sarcophagus in the *Interior at Petworth* is indisputably a baroque one, the atmosphere of the picture is oddly evocative of the scene that Haydon described in his diary, when, on 28 March 1825, he noted 'I was at Soane's last night to see his [Egyptian] sarcophagus by lamp-light... Soane's house is a perfect Cretan labyrinth: curious narrow staircases, landing places, balconies, spring doors, and little rooms with fragments up to the ceiling.' Turner was present at this occasion, which must have been an oddly impressive one that he might well have remembered.[47]

Death on a Pale Horse, one of the least 'Turnerian' of the Petworth series, possibly suggested by Egremont's sketch by West for *The Triumph of Death,* has been seen as a response to the death of Turner's own father in 1829.[48] We know that the succession of deaths of his patrons, fellow-artists and relatives between 1825, when Fawkes died, and 1837, produced a deep-rooted melancholy in Turner, which may well have intensified those personal feelings which became the motivation for many of his pictures. His increasing isolation is foreshadowed by the remarks he made on the death of Lawrence in 1830: 'Alas, only two short months Sir Thomas followed the coffin of Dawe to the same place. We were then his pallbearers. Who will do the like for me, or when, God only knows how soon; my poor father's death proved a heavy blow upon me, and has been followed by others of the same dark kind.' He continued significantly: 'However, it is something to feel that gifted talent can be acknowledged by the many...'[49] For Turner, recognition was the only valid compensation for the miseries of a lonely old age.

The evasive symbolism of the empty, windswept *Interior at Petworth* was not displayed in public; Turner was giving vent to purely private feeling, and he did not generally place such a burden of obscure meaning on a work intended for the Academy. The symbolism of *Peace* and *War,* for example, is a conventional language; what is personal about it is its intensity. The funeral black of the sails of Wilkie's ship serves a perfectly clear descriptive function, even if Clarkson Stanfield did complain that it was not true to life.[50] Turner's reply, 'I only wish I had any colour to make them blacker'

229   War. The exile and the rock limpet   R.A. 1842
Oil on canvas, 795 × 795
Turner Bequest, Tate Gallery, London   (Cat. No. P400)

230   Peace—burial at sea   R.A. 1842
Oil on canvas, 870 × 865
Turner Bequest, Tate Gallery, London   (Cat. No. P399)

gives us an insight into the depth of his feeling; but his use of black in that context is not at all difficult to understand. The suggestion that black is also an allusion to Wilkie's fondness for that colour in his later works would also be consistent with Turner's attitude to other artists, though there is not enough of Wilkie's spirit in Turner's use of it to substantiate the hypothesis; the symbolism of black is obvious and unavoidable. It has been proposed that *The Pifferari* was a response to Wilkie's use of that title in a picture exhibited in 1829.[51]

Like the black of *Peace,* the red of *War* has a symbolic function that we do not feel to be abstruse. The idea of blood was associated in Turner's mind not only with death and disaster but with more gradual termination—the decay of empires, the falling of a hero's star. The lines of verse that accompanied *The decline of the Carthaginian Empire* in the Academy's 1817 catalogue emphasized the symbolic sunset that illumines the scene:

'...o'er the western wave th' ensanguin'd sun,
In gathering haze a stormy signal spread,
And set portentous.'[52]

231   Shade and darkness—the evening of the Deluge   R.A. 1843
Oil on canvas, 785 × 780
Turner Bequest, Tate Gallery, London   (Cat. No. P404)

The setting of Napoleon's power is even more emphatically 'ensanguin'd'. Turner used the imagery of a red sky in a comparably emotive fashion to provide the atmosphere of Pl. 225 *Slavers throwing overboard the dead and dying,* of 1840, and (most Pl. 252 unusually) of the watercolour of *Goldau,* of 1843. Ruskin's comment on the latter is applicable equally to the *Slavers*: 'He [Turner] was very definitely in the habit of indicating the association of any subject with circumstances of death, especially the death of multitudes, by placing it under one of his most deeply *crimsoned* sunset skies.'[53] In the *Goldau* the scarlet sky is Turner's only hint that he is depicting a view famous for a disastrous avalanche. In *Slavers* death is in the very title of the work: the red sky requires no apology or explanation.

Pl. 224 Another symbolic sunset is that of *The Fighting 'Temeraire' tugged to her last berth to be broken up,*[54] a picture shown in 1839. As in *War,* or *The decline of Carthage,* a snuffing-out of heroic strength is the subject. The old ship, a veteran of Trafalgar, itself a symbol of glory and heroism, provides a substitute for the human protagonist whom Turner so often makes the focus of his idea, if not of his composition. It has been supposed that, like Napoleon, and like the Angel in the Sun, the *Temeraire* is an image of Turner himself—here contemplating his own old age and death, while claiming for himself a heroic past.[55] He called the work his 'darling', a fact which reinforces an intuitive sense that the subject had some such meaning for him: though the sheer beauty of the image it presents would be enough to explain his fondness for it.[56]

Pl. 234 A personal symbolism has also been invoked to explain *The Sun of Venice going to sea,* of 1843. It is a fresh, open composition, on the white ground that Turner employed for most of his late Venetian subjects, well described by the opening lines of Turner's verse in the catalogue:

'Far shines the morn, and soft the zephyrs blow,
Venezia's fisher spreads her painted sail so gay...'

but the answering lines contradict it:

'Nor heeds the demon that in grim repose
Expects his evening prey.'

There is no evidence of any 'demon' in the picture; no brewing storm, as in the *Slavers,* no foreknown historical failure, as in *Hannibal* or *The decline of Carthage.* It has therefore been proposed that the *Sun of Venice* is another vessel acting as an image of the artist.[57] Again, his own impending death provides a clue to his state of mind: he himself is the 'evening prey' of the grim demon. However, the symbolism of the Sun here closely parallels that in the Carthage and Napoleon pictures; as a Victorian critic pointed out, the image painted on the sail 'represents Venice herself, with the sun rising gloriously just above the horizon'. The city, however glorious, must like ancient Carthage—or modern Britain—eventually sink in decline. Nevertheless, Venice still vigorously 'lived' in her artistic heritage: she was a symbol not of past glory, but of present vitality—and hence a parallel with a living man like Turner himself.[58]

One of the Venetian watercolour studies of about 1840 Pl. 233 shows the *Sun of Venice,* somewhat as Turner painted her.[59] Turner rarely made direct preparations in watercolour for his works in oil; though another Venice study, *Looking towards Fusina,* was said by Ruskin to be the 'original sketch' for a picture exhibited in 1843: *St. Benedetto, looking towards Fusina.*[60] The technical resemblances between the Venetian oil-paintings of the 1840s and the watercolour studies are not perhaps as great as has sometimes been suggested; but Turner's white ground, over which local detail is scattered as isolated touches of sharp colour (usually added on the varnishing days) produces an effect akin to that of the watercolours: namely, one of brilliant light disintegrating and absorbing forms in an overall blondness of atmosphere. This can be said of many other late paintings. In some instances, probably of very late date, watercolour has been found on the surface of paintings, Turner having apparently used both media together; this has interest as an insight into his ideas on technique in this period, but it is not immediately clear why such touches, delicate to the point of imperceptibility, were functionally necessary.[61]

But it was not only the technique of watercolour that Turner transferred to his paintings. His habit of making drawings in sequences affected his output in oil, and he seems to have regarded the themes of his paintings as extensible through many individual works, even more deliberately and homogeneously, if anything, than those of his watercolours. And, as with them, he kept several 'sets' on hand simultaneously.

In about 1830 he launched on the long sequence of Dutch subjects, dominated by a uniform pale tonality, though greyer and more 'northern' than the whiteness of the Venice pictures, and not, like them, associated with any corresponding group of watercolours. A later and less extensive set is

232 Light and colour (Goethe's Theory)—the morning after the Deluge—Moses writing the book of Genesis   R.A. 1843
Oil on canvas, 785 × 785
Turner Bequest, Tate Gallery, London   (Cat. No. P405)

233 The Sun of Venice 1840
Watercolour, with pen, 219 × 317
National Galleries of Scotland, Edinburgh (Vaughan Bequest)
(Cat. No. 1374)

that of the Whaling scenes exhibited in 1845–6; these, again, are related to a set of drawings, though there is no direct functional connection between the works in the different media.[62] The Carthage pictures, which appeared frequently from 1814 until the end of Turner's life, may also be thought of as a coherent group, as I shall discuss later. There are in addition several pairs produced either together or sequentially: for instance, the views of *The Temple of Jupiter Panellenius, restored* and *The Temple of Jupiter Panellenius in the island of Aegina, with the Greek national dance of the Romaika,* exhibited in 1816.[63] It was not uncommon for artists to reconstruct ancient buildings according to the speculations of archaeologists; nor for them to make views of ruins after 'sketches on the spot' by travellers—Turner was to do this for several Middle Eastern subjects in the illustrations to Byron and the Bible in the 1830s. These two large paintings

are presented without comment—the lines of verse under the title of the first are purely descriptive and do not invite us to contemplate the grandeur of a civilization now in decay; though in the very next year, 1817, *The decline of the Carthaginian Empire* openly did so. *Modern Italy—the Pifferari* and *Ancient Italy—Ovid banished from Rome,* both shown in 1838, equally leave their message to be guessed at; though the implied contrast between the ancient poet and his simple peasant successors among the Abruzzi presumably reflects a decline in splendour and sophistication analogous to that suggested by the Aegina pictures.[64] A parallel point, about

Pl.223

234   The Sun of Venice going to sea   R.A. 1843
Oil on canvas, 615 × 920
Turner Bequest, Tate Gallery, London   (Cat. No. P402)

politics as well as the arts, emerges from *Ancient Rome: Agrippina landing with the ashes of Germanicus. The Triumphal Bridge and Palace of the Caesars restored* and *Modern Rome—Campo Vaccino* which appeared in the next exhibition, that of 1839.[65] Here Turner's theme is that of Thomson in Part III of his poem *Liberty* (1735), the establishment of the principle of liberty in the Republic, and its later subversion. The ruined forum, certainly, is a readily grasped symbol of ancient political freedoms now destroyed; the accompanying verses are misquoted from the fourth canto of Byron's *Childe Harold's Pilgrimage,* and the artist has painted the scene in the atmospheric conditions they describe:

'The moon is up, and yet it is not night,
The sun as yet divides the day with her.'

These lines immediately follow a well-known description of Italy in ruins:

'The commonwealth of kings, the men of Rome!
And even since, and now, fair Italy!
Thou art the garden of the world, the home
Of all art yields, and Nature can decree;
Even in thy desert, what is like to thee?
Thy very weeds are beautiful, thy waste
More rich than other climes' fertility:
Thy wreck a glory, and thy ruin graced
With an immaculate charm which cannot be
defaced.'[66]

215

The decay of civilizations is not necessarily complete, nor entirely to be deplored. Turner used these very lines to expand the title of another Italian subject, called simply *Childe Harold's pilgrimage—Italy,* exhibited in 1832.[67]

Other coupled pictures—*War* and *Peace, Shade and darkness* and *Light and colour (Goethe's Theory),* and *Undine* and the *Angel*—have already been mentioned. These ought perhaps to be thought of not simply as individual pairs but as a loosely connected series: their common exploration of the red-blue, warm-cool colour contrast is enough to justify such a suggestion. Charles Lock Eastlake's translation of Goethe's *Farbenlehre,* which proposed the theory that warm colours and cool colours carry with them opposing emotional associations, appeared in 1840,[68] and the first of the series must have been begun soon afterwards, probably in 1841. It was only in one of the second pair that Turner specified Goethe as their source; but the point could hardly have been made with less than two pictures. A further common feature of these canvases is their circular format (their frames are square, but some of them originally had circular or octagonal slips). This is the most extreme form of Turner's 'vortex', an expression of the dynamism of light derived from, but almost the opposite of, the placid diffusion of light from a central source that forms Claude's pictorial structures.[69] In *Shade and darkness—the evening of the Deluge* a deep spiral of shadow takes the eye into a brightly illuminated distance; through the whole depth of the design long lines of animals file towards the shadowy ark. In the foreground, obscured by darkness, the human race awaits its destruction in the ignorance of sleep. Turner must have borne in mind the apocalyptic pictures of Danby, and the *Eve of the Deluge* that John Martin exhibited at the Academy in 1841 with a pair, *The Assuagement.* Though his own *Deluge* paintings in no way imitate Martin, they should probably be regarded, like so many of his canvases, as tacit 'answers' or responses to a challenge that he felt had been thrown down by another artist.

The morning after the Deluge is plainly the pair of *Shade and darkness;* but it is in many ways wholly different in conception. Its full title is *Light and colour (Goethe's Theory)—the morning after the Deluge—Moses writing the book of Genesis.* This tells us several things: first, that it is conceived in a conscious opposition to *Shade and darkness;* second, that the work is about a theory, just as the *Watteau Study* had discussed the rules laid down by Du Fresnoy. No artist is referred to as an exponent of the rules in question (Goethe himself intended his observations to be taken as a matter of physics, not as a guide for painters merely). But in fact the picture does

vividly suggest other works of art. Its composition is not a vortex based on a lengthy spiral; it is a much shallower concavity, like a dish, or the dome of a church on which a vision of a Theophany has been painted. In the centre, as the figure of Christ, the Virgin, or the Pantocrator appears in light on a cupola, so Moses sits enthroned in brilliantly-lit clouds, above the brazen serpent, symbol of the salvation of mankind through God's Covenant after the Flood. In the ebbing waters, shot through with rainbow light, swarm the nereids and sea-sprites of *Ulysses* and *Hero and Leander;* they parallel the crowded saints and angels of an Italian *Gloria.* It is hard to say whether Turner intended to celebrate a particular fellow-artist in this conceit: he had probably never seen Correggio's dome at Parma,[70] but in both Rome and Venice he had ample opportunity to see painted cupolas by Baroque masters from Lanfranco to Tiepolo.[71] We may note that the Brocklesby Mausoleum, which he had drawn in about 1798, contained a painted cupola of this type.[72] The juxtaposition of an art-historical model with a hero figure (this time Moses) follows the pattern of the earlier *War* and *Peace,* while much of the imagery foreshadows that of *Undine* and the *Angel,* works in which the art-historical reference is slyly turned to critics, and the artist himself disguised as the hero.

Such groupings of the paintings in series or sequences may not correspond to a definite thematic intention in Turner's mind. The author of the *Liber Studiorum* should never be supposed to have wanted to limit himself, in whatever group of his works, to a single statement. But on the whole the sequences of oil-paintings are fairly coherent; they tend to take up and rework ideas common to each set, and they fall into definite and distinct colour patterns. The series of subjects taken from the Anglo-Dutch wars, for instance—*Admiral Van Tromp's barge at the entrance of the Texel, Van Tromp returning after the battle off the Dogger Bank,* and so on—do not necessarily ask to be read as episodes of a single progressive statement; but as seascapes they are sufficiently homogeneous in colour, scale, and general conception to link the Van Tromp scenes with the *Rotterdam ferry-boat* or *Van Goyen, looking out for a subject.*[73] The historical group derives its pictorial motivation from the same sources as the rest; but Turner's keen sense that a picture requires a human referent, and that, in painting as opposed to watercolour drawing, that referent may profitably be one of Aristotelian weight and universality, prompted him to choose subjects—or titles at least—that both justified and enlarged the significance of the mode in which he chose to cast these works. In one case, the *Ostend,* of 1844, it is difficult to avoid reading a figure in one

235 Rain, Steam, and Speed—The Great Western Railway
R.A. 1844
Oil on canvas, 910 × 1220
Turner Bequest, National Gallery, London   (Cat. No. P409)

of the small boats as Christ: the subject is a 'Seascape with Christ stilling the tempest' analogous to the traditional landscape focused upon a historical or mythological motif.[74] It was not necessary for Turner in the 1840s to press such an allusion—there is no reference to it in the catalogue; but his eighteenth-century upbringing and his reverence for Reynolds had instilled deep in him the notion that art requires large and universal motives. No one was more able than he to sidestep such a demand; but he obeyed it on occasion simply because he always accepted its validity. The same is probably true of the Van Tromp pictures. Turner certainly does not appear to have looked on Van Tromp as a hero with whom he might identify himself; the scene of *Van Tromp, going about to please his masters* (the last of the set)[75] has the effect of adding a mildly mocking touch to the whole

217

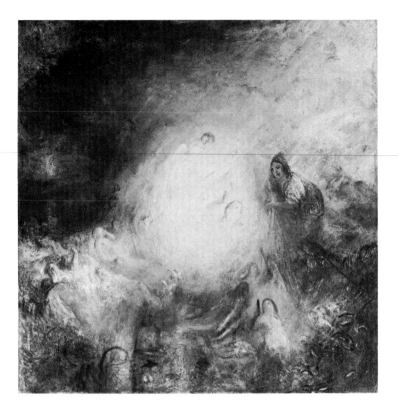

236 Undine giving the ring to Masaniello, fisherman of Naples   R.A. 1846
Oil on canvas, 790 × 790
Turner Bequest, Tate Gallery, London   (Cat. No. P424)

of expressive watercolour studies.[79] As depictions of fire the pictures belong to a rather diffuse 'set' of their own, to which other paintings of the same period, such as *Fire at Sea*[80] and *The Burning Fiery Furnace* and even one or two watercolours, can be added.

Similarly, the political overtones of *Slavers throwing overboard the dead and dying* ought not to be discounted, but must be allowed to take second place to the study of a human tragedy in a setting which expresses it in natural and elemental terms that are primarily visual. We cannot fail to be impressed by the picture's message of disaster, though the lines from the *Fallacies of Hope* that go with the title do not allude to the inhumanity of the action recorded: the victim of 'fallacious hope' is the slaver himself, for whom the impending typhoon means a loss of profits and a threat to his ship: Turner ironically condoles with the profiteer whom he is able to present objectively as the protagonist of a high moral drama:

'throw overboard
The dead and dying—ne'er heed their chains.
Hope, Hope, fallacious Hope!
Where is thy market now?'

The horror of the scene is the more impressive in that it is almost glossed over: only the gathering sea-beasts round the half-submerged limbs, and a few helpless hands above the water, make specific what the red sky symbolically announces. It is a more particularized and ironic 'Deluge' picture. While the *Slavers* was on the walls of the Academy, on 1 June 1840, Prince Albert gave his first public address as Consort at a meeting of the Anti-Slave League; the coincidence may well have suggested to Turner a possible new patron.[81] At any rate he made a more explicit bid for the Consort's favour in the following year, when he painted *Schloss Rosenau, seat of H. R. H. Prince Albert of Coburg,* for the Academy exhibition.[82] But none of his works was ever bought by the royal family (unless we consider as an acquisition the *Battle of Trafalgar,* commissioned by George IV in 1823 but quickly banished from St. James's to Greenwich Hospital).[83]

The other 'political' canvases, at any rate, cannot be accused of pessimism. The historical parallel of the invasion of William of Orange and the 'stormy passage' of the Reform Bill suggests the success, not the failure of the enterprise; and, if they are symbolic, the 'Burning of the Houses of Parliament' pictures must likewise be seen as the two strophes of a hymn of political triumph. One of the dangers

group, as if, retrospectively, Turner were asking us to see it as a satirical sequence, almost in the manner of Hogarth. The scene that appeared at the Academy in 1832, *The Prince of Orange ... landed at Torbay, November 4th, 1688, after a stormy passage* has been interpreted as a purposeful comment on the Reform Bill, passed in the same year, and thus a consciously topical choice of subject.[76] This is a reasonable supposition; what is in question is whether Turner intended to make a political comment of a more than general nature. He presumably supported reform, if he shared his friend Walter Fawkes's progressive opinions;[77] the subject was therefore agreeably pertinent to a current question; but the *matter* of the picture is that of the other Dutch works: its colouring, composition and mood tally with them. Equally, the two pictures of the burning of the Houses of Parliament that Turner showed in 1835[78] may be thought of as a symbolic record of the destruction by reform of the old, corrupt parliamentary system. But these canvases are very evidently concerned with the striking visual phenomenon of the fire itself, watched by Turner with avidity and noted (either on the spot or immediately afterwards, from memory) in a series

Pl. 215

that have beset recent criticism of Turner's later paintings has been the assumption that his art was essentially one of despair. The apparently gratuitous note of doom so often sounded by the *Fallacies of Hope* has encouraged commentators to search for hidden pessimism everywhere. Let us take a more positive approach.

The Prince of Orange, after a stormy night, landed at Torbay and successfully conducted the Glorious Revolution that initiated British democracy. Turner probably derived as much interest from the fact that William landed after a rough voyage as from any political parallel that may have prompted his choice of subject. He was himself immensely stimulated by travel and the experiences it generates.[84] He could identify himself with anyone who had undergone a difficult journey—even if there is nothing in the *William of Orange* picture to make us feel that William is a hero of personal significance for Turner, despite the identity of their names. He often used his own adventures on the road or at sea as subject-matter for statements about the endurance of men and their perpetual intercourse with elemental nature. One of the earliest of his works to impress the public as a vividly personal utterance from his brush was *Calais Pier,* a picture that translated an autobiographical event into the universal in the form of a huge imitation of a painting by a Dutch master. The artist's own experience of danger when 'nearly swampt' at the Calais harbour bar is the impulse behind the generalized expression of a scene that is, in the full eighteenth-century sense, 'Sublime'.

There are two watercolours which commemorate the same sense of achievement in having endured the extreme Pl.208 dangers of travel: *Snowstorm: Mont Cenis* of 1820 and *Messieurs les voyageurs on their return from Italy (par la diligence) in a snow drift upon mount Tarrar,* of 1829. The first of these records an incident that Turner could recall clearly several years later;[85] the second is an important document of Turner's attitude to travel and its place in his art. Its long and specific title is evidently a humorous reference to a shared adversity. There is every reason to believe that the top-hatted figure silhouetted against the firelight in the foreground is Turner himself—a possibly unique case of his taking a visible role in one of his own dramas.[86] The point of the picture is precisely this: that the artist was there, one of a group of 'voyageurs' who would all remember the incident. Its contrast with the earlier *Mont Cenis* is striking: instead of being a study of natural sublimities in which human beings are almost lost, it focuses on the plight of the travellers, and its use of Rembrandtian chiaroscuro brings echoes of Rembrandt's

237   The Angel standing in the sun   R.A. 1846
Oil on canvas, 785 × 785
Turner Bequest, Tate Gallery, London   (Cat. No. P425)

own concern for human suffering: the storm is only an accessory to the human action. It is no accident that this watercolour was executed at the time of Turner's renewed interest in Rembrandt's figure subjects: it is the most complete of all Turner's translations of Rembrandt's themes into the language of his own art.

Given his understanding of nature as comprising the conditions in which human beings live, we can understand why Turner entitled a much later representation of a snowstorm as he did: the painting shown at the Academy in 1842 is called *Snow storm—steam-boat off a harbour's mouth* Pl.228 *making signals in shallow water, and going by the lead. The author was in this storm on the night the Ariel left Harwich.* Turner makes a point of informing us that the picture represents a real and personal experience, just as it was important to his meaning that he himself had been in the overturned diligence on Mont Tarare. With its confusion of forms and chaotic whirl of dim colour, the painting was in need of defence against the critics who were all too ready to pounce on it as an extreme case of Turner's scorn for truth or comprehensibility. In fact, he was deeply hurt by the accusation that he had produced a 'mass of soap-suds and whitewash.'[87] The statement in the title that he had experienced weather conditions like those he painted was an assertion that he was not exaggerating. Those predisposed to sympathize with him—Ruskin and the Revd. William Kingsley, for example—sought for an inner meaning in the confusion; but Turner was emphatic that the 'meaning' of the picture was in its truth to nature—that is, in its accessibility to everyone as a mimetic 'reminder' of the experienced world. Therein lies its universality. 'I did not paint it to be understood,' Turner said, and we feel the scornful inverted commas round 'understood'; 'but I wished to show what such a scene was like; I got the sailors to lash me to the mast to observe it; I was lashed for four hours and I did not expect to escape but I felt bound to record it if I did.'[88] He underwent this 'Sublime' experience in order to pursue the old need for natural grandeur to a new peak of sensation—a peak which he now felt his technical powers fully capable of attaining.

Pl.235   The supreme example of Turner's recreation of the 'Sublime' in the terms of his fully matured vision and technique is *Rain, Steam and Speed—The Great Western Railway,* exhibited in 1844. This is another celebration of travel; no one can have been more alive than Turner to the fact that railways represented a fresh departure for the old tradition of landscape, offering a new vocabulary with which to describe that heightening of emotional tension associated with impressive natural phenomena which is the essence of 'Sublime' experience. Speed especially was a very novel factor of life, with the power to alter our apprehension of nature; while the steam of railway locomotives was a new ingredient in the atmosphere that Turner loved to render. He had already repeatedly made pictorial capital out of the smoke of chimneys and industrial towns—especially in his water-colours; and in the pictures of steamships, from *Staffa, Fingal's cave* of 1832 onwards. The particular blend of the white, volatile vapour of the engine, and the velocity of its motion, carried the drama of experiencing nature through travel to new heights. Even a mundane element like rain, never referred to in the literature of the 'Sublime' unless in the extreme manifestation of a deluge or violent storm, is transmuted by speed into a grandly exhilarating experience.

If Turner was able to add phenomena of the mechanical and industrial age to his vocabulary of the 'Sublime', without feeling that the old term had lost its validity either as a category of human experience or as a vehicle for aesthetic communication,[89] he was likewise capable of giving fresh life to the visual conventions of painting: the very structure of *Rain, Steam and Speed,* for all its starkness, its apparent 'laxity of form and licence of effect', as a contemporary found,[90] is in fact classic. Its receding perspective is at once more solidly delineated than the late 'vortex' compositions, and more dynamically free than they; the principal formal element, the sharply receding viaduct, is derived from the perspectives of roads, rivers and arcades reminiscent of Poussin that can be found in works like the 1803 *Bonneville,* the *Frosty Morning,* or *Rome from the Vatican.* The *Burning of the Houses of Parliament*   Cf. Pl. (Philadelphia version) prefigures the composition of *Rain, Steam and Speed* very closely. The stabilizing feature of the second bridge at the left of the canvas performs a function analogous to that of the bridge in *Apullia and Appullus* of 1814, which is taken almost literally from Claude; though, as if by the centrifugal energy of the whole design, both principal structural elements have been pushed to the edges of the canvas. As with the *Snow storm—steam-boat off a harbour's mouth* the crucial novelty is not the plan of the picture but Turner's insistence on the vivid reality of natural elements hitherto unknown, ignored or considered unpaintable.

An equally successful exercise of the same type is *Keelmen*   Pl.217 *heaving in coals by night,* shown at the Royal Academy in 1835. In this case Turner is almost self-consciously classical, not only in the superb balance of the composition round its central axis of light, but in the very quality of his paint-surface: it is of a smoothness and refinement of finish rare in his work by that time. With grand assurance, Turner, as in *Rain, Steam and Speed,* makes an entirely contemporary picture about the visual splendour of his own world. The breadth of its atmosphere, the brilliance of its concentrated lights—the ethereal shimmer of the full moon and the intermittent bursts of energetic flame—are as majestic as anything he ever uttered on the subject of the ancient gods and heroes; and there is nothing in the picture to suggest that the artist's intention was 'to be understood': it is, like perhaps all his greatest paintings, self-explanatory.[91]

Another picture which is probably more straightforward than it is allowed to be is the work that Turner showed in 1837 at the British Institution under the unusually brief title of *Regulus.*[92] The story of Regulus is part of the history of   Pl.220 Carthage, and the picture belongs to the sequence of paintings that the idea of Carthage inspired, from *Hannibal* and *Dido and Aeneas* in 1812 and 1814 to the four subjects that Turner exhibited in 1850. Some of the subjects he chose are fictitious, taken from the *Aeneid;* others are historical; the distinction is unimportant, just as the distinction between the 'historical' Dutch pictures and those showing imaginary incidents is secondary to the main fact of 'Dutchness' with its art-historical associations. With the notable exception of *Hannibal,* all the Carthage pictures are cast as brilliantly golden harbour scenes inspired by the Claude seaports at sunset, of which the Angerstein collection in London boasted some splendid examples. Turner cannot but have remembered also the later Claude subject of the *Landing of Aeneas,* which, when he saw it in 1799, had made him 'both pleased and unhappy while he viewed it, it seemed to be beyond the power of imitation.'[93] He may also have seen the *Aeneas at Delos* in Henry Hope's collection, sold by Christie's in June 1816. The whole series is an expression of his continuing need to respond to a challenge that he had fixed on as a key test of his own stature.

The repeated reference to the Angerstein Claudes, open and deliberate as it is, at least in the principal works of the series, unites what might otherwise seem a fairly arbitrary selection of titles. As with the other 'sequences' we should probably regard their serial nature as a very loose one. We are directed to find in these works the imagery of greatness doomed to decay: Turner mentioned 'Hope's delusive smile' in his lines for the 1817 picture, and other paintings with Roman themes are still more explicit: *Palestrina—composition,* of 1830,[94] refers to Hannibal 'misdeeming of his strength' as he 'marked with eagle-eye Rome as his victim'; and *Caligula's palace and bridge* shown in the following year has lines that ask:

> 'What now remains of all the mighty bridge...
> Caligula, but mighty fragments left,
> Monuments of doubt and ruined hopes...'[95]

Regulus was first shown in Rome while Turner was there in 1828; it never appeared on the walls of the Academy, and when it was exhibited at the British Institution, in 1837, Turner modified it considerably: his work on it, when it had already been hung, was remarked on and carefully noted by artists who were present. Turner was 'scumbling a lot of white into his picture—nearly all over it... The picture was a mass of red and yellow of all varieties. Every object was in this fiery state ... The sun ... was in the centre; from it were drawn—ruled—lines to mark the rays; these lines were rather strongly marked, I suppose to guide his eye. The picture gradually became wonderfully effective, just the effect of brilliant sunlight absorbing everything and throwing a misty haze over every object.'[96] A critic remarked that 'the sun absolutely dazzles the eyes.'[97] Turner's ruled lines indicating the irradiation of the sunlight remind us of the

lines of perspective in *Rain, Steam and Speed,* and the achievement of a unified effect of light, which overwhelms all other features of the picture and comprehends all detail, is comparable to the universal mist of the later work, or to the enveloping snowstorm of *Steam-boat off a harbour's mouth.* Once again we cannot help conceiving Turner's own character as the central and motive force in the work. The sun here is just the same all-powerful god to whom Chryses prays; *Regulus* enacts more forcibly than any other of Turner's paintings the sentiment of his famous, if apocryphal 'the Sun is God'.[98]

The identification of Turner with the protagonists of his pictures gains further strength from the reminder that Regulus was punished for his betrayal of the Carthaginians by having his eyelids cut off, and being blinded by the glare of the sun, before being shut up in a barrel stuck with spikes. That suggestion may well lie behind the 'revised version' of the picture.[99] But it does not represent the scene in which Regulus undergoes this torture, though the barrel rolled forward by a man at the left of the composition may perhaps be a reference to his later suffering. The mise-en-scène is unmistakably that of a classic 'embarkation', and, in spite of Turner's very unspecific title, the picture reads unambiguously as such. It was published in Turner's lifetime as *Ancient Carthage—The Embarcation of Regulus,*[100] and the mood, both of the original and of the engravings made from it, is one of ceremonial and public splendour, consonant with the departure of an important embassy and not with the shame and degradation of torture. We may compare *Ovid banished from Rome,* where an almost equally brilliant effect of sunlight is achieved (without any biographical justification); just as Ovid is a type of the artist alienated from society, so Regulus in a similar composition is the military hero doomed to failure and disgrace. Regulus has been thought to be altogether absent from the scene, and he has therefore been identified with the spectator, staring into the blinding sun.[101] This misinterprets the embarkation subject, and presupposes a use of quasi-cinematic techniques hardly congruent with early nineteenth-century attitudes to the way a picture works. In fact the engravers of the subject found Regulus as a relatively prominent figure, very brightly lit, at the top of the flight of steps leading down to the water at the right; he is hardly more unobtrusive than, say, Pilate or Van Goyen in the pictures named after them, or, indeed, than the protagonists of some of the other Carthage subjects.[102] We may argue simply that Regulus is both present in the picture, and made to dictate the psychological mood of the scene; this is analogous to saying that the *Snow storm* shows us through

Turner's eyes the storm and the steam-boat to whose mast Turner is tied.

In all the pictures we have discussed the balance of aesthetic and art-historical principle against observed and experienced reality is, as it had been from the beginning of Turner's career, the working framework of his communication. The question to be asked about these late works is, wherein lies the essential difference between them and their predecessors of his earlier years? Is it simply (or 'complexly') a matter of their more liberated and expressive use of colour and in the rendering of effects of light? Is it in their disintegration of the clarity of apprehended reality, in order to recreate a more scientifically or more emotionally accurate view of nature? Or are these works really preoccupied with private and cryptic statements that Turner knew no one would understand, and hardly wished anyone to? Ruskin, passionately concerned with understanding what Turner had to say, sometimes found an unwillingness on Turner's part to explain:

'...the want of appreciation touched him sorely, chiefly the not understanding his meaning. He tried hard one day, for a quarter of an hour, to make me guess what he was doing in the picture of 'Napoleon' before it had been exhibited, giving me hint after hint in a rough way; but I could not guess, and he would not tell.'[103]

In the case of that particular picture Turner's desire to impart the secret of his meaning was inhibited by reticence over a private and personal theme—the description of his behaviour in this instance bespeaks that of a shy man wanting, but unable, to bring himself to a full explanation. Ruskin may well have sought help with *War. The exile and the rock limpet;* but sometimes he mistook the level at which Turner's work was intended to operate: 'He knows a great deal more about my paintings than I do,' Turner is supposed to have said; 'he puts things into my head, and points out meanings in them I never intended.'[104] It seems reasonable, and just to Turner, to stress that he was interested above all in the visual world and in visible effects. Those of his pictures which cry loudest for elucidation—*Rome from the Vatican, War,* and *Undine* and the *Angel* especially—are not among his most satisfactory productions: they carry with them the evidence of the strain with which they were created, and lack the total conviction and spontaneity of invention that is typical of those pictures in which Turner is speaking directly as an artist about human experience in general. It is clear from the list of his final contributions to the Academy exhibitions that that capacity to generalize remained with him to the end,

despite the occasional intrusion of a coarser personal note.

At the same exhibition to which he sent the enigmatic *Angel standing in the sun* and *Undine,* Turner showed two Venetian subjects (his last),[105] of sufficient perspicuity to be bought by Windus, and two whaling pictures, which, like two others shown the previous year, explore the same motifs—shipping and firelight—that had generated *Keelmen heaving in coals by night* in 1835, and, indeed, his first exhibited picture, the *Fishermen at sea* of 1796. But the seascape of ice and snow is a new setting, if anticipated, perhaps, by some of the bleaker of his Swiss mountain passes. The visual novelty of such a scene seems to have impressed him as much as did the speed and steam of the railway, and he went to considerable lengths to glean, from Thomas Beale's *The Natural History of the Sperm Whale* and other sources, detailed accounts of whaling and whalers. One of the canvases is identified in the catalogue by a description of a human activity as elaborate as any that occurs in his titles: *Whalers (boiling blubber) entangled in flaw ice, endeavouring to extricate themselves.*[106] He presents not a romantic fiction, but an aspect of the human condition. If these whaling canvases are indistinct, they are sufficiently precise to convey the Arctic light and the biting cold in which the boilers' fires provide such welcome warmth. There is, even at the period of *Undine* and the *Angel,* a hearty and well-defined realism in Turner's work; not, it is true, the realism practised by his contemporaries, but a truth to nature and a human compassion that we can recognize as the mainsprings of his greatest art.

In the two following years Turner exhibited in London only two new works, and these were earlier canvases partially repainted. One of them, *The Wreck buoy,* celebrates the wild atmosphere of a sea storm that had inspired him all his life; the other, *The hero of a hundred fights,* is a tribute to the Duke of Wellington that is unambiguously triumphant.[107] It is a burst of brilliant light painted on to a shadowy interior of the 1790s—a complete image of the revolution in Turner's vision, the substitution of light for darkness in the canon of the 'Sublime', and of his commensurate alteration of technique, from the precise and polished execution of his earliest pictures to the expressionistic splashes of colour with which he dazzled and puzzled the public of the 1830s and 1840s. He may have shown such a work to draw attention to that great change; but equally he may have done so in the conviction that his retouching was all of a piece with what was beneath it; that each style was a natural and proper way of expressing a different aspect of the world. In the same year as *The Wreck*

238   A wreck, with fishing-boats *c.* 1840–5
Oil on canvas, 915 × 1220
Turner Bequest, Tate Gallery, London   (Cat. No. P470)

buoy he showed some untouched early works, among them his Titian pastiche of about 1803, *Venus and Adonis,* and if we are in any doubt as to whether that was intended to be seen as a contrast with present achievements or a reminder that he had from the beginning worked as a 'history painter' of the highest seriousness, we have only to look at the list of his exhibits in 1850, the last that he sent to the Academy.[108]

Every one of them is a new work, painted perhaps, as has been suggested, 'to make his farewell with becoming dignity'.[109] Every one of them is a further contribution to the suite of his Dido and Aeneas pictures, each captioned with a line from the *Fallacies of Hope.* Once again Turner's view of the story as a parable of 'the vanity of human wishes' is expounded in his verses. The pictures themselves are further variants on the golden perspectives of the earlier Carthage subjects; in them the golden light that was a common feature of the series becomes the all-enveloping medium in which the scene is dissolved, as the Snowstorm absorbs the Steam-boat, as the white light of Venice disintegrates its architecture.

Was the elaborate historical or contemporary subject-matter that Turner chose for his paintings no more than an excuse for the presentation of 'general effects'? We have seen how in his later pictures elemental forces—fire, wind, the sea, light—are isolated and expressed with a new power. He devoted much energy to the rendering of such effects in the mass of oil studies that crowded his studio by the time of his death. Many of these studies treat almost solely of the most

Pl.238

general effects: the surface of a rough sea; a mass of cloud; or a burst of light across water or mountains. They are to be distinguished from other studies, such as *Venice: the Piazzetta with the Ceremony of the Doge marrying the Sea* or the large *Harbour with town and fortress* [110] which, whether intentionally 'unfinished' or not, are clearly workings-out of detailed compositions of an exhibitable type. The oil sketches that concentrate on the rendering of a single effect, shorn of human or any other detail, are usually remarkable for the absence of any formal structure; though sometimes, as in the *Norham Castle, sunrise*, [111] a composition that Turner had used many times before is revived and subjected to a radical reinterpretation in terms of pure colour and light. It is analogous, in this respect, to other 'revisions' or 'revivals' of Turner's later years. Early examples of these studies, dating from the 1820s—before that period the oil sketch has a wholly different place in his output [112]—are explorations for some particular envisaged painting: the studies of rocks connected with *Ulysses,* or of yachts for the *Cowes regatta* pictures. All these types either borrow or anticipate the structure or incident of completed compositions. The studies of waves, of clouds, of bursts of light that seem to exist for their own sake, apart, are not in any way reliant on compositional protocols; they are free, often chaotic, responses to the amorphous truth of nature, and in them paint is used with a comparable freedom, flung, piled, or smeared on to the canvas as if under the impact of a fierce and uncooled emotion.

Such techniques occur as often in the finished canvases; but, however generalized the effect of the finished works, however freely the paint is applied, their structure is always emphatically more formal. Turner might have painted a study of rain and steam in which a whole canvas was covered with the mingled greys, blues and ochres of his great painting, a formless evocation of pure atmosphere; but the finished work is built upon the rigid structural foundation I have already described. Even the *Snow storm* which Turner intended should recommend itself for its verisimilitude is in fact cunningly imposed on a pattern of quite strongly marked divisions: the turbulent chaos that we apprehend is a product of skilfully regulated art—not the randomness that we seem to find in some of the studies.

There are then two factors that principally distinguish Turner's finished works from the preparatory or exploratory studies he made incidentally to their production. The first is a clearly recognizable, if often masterfully disguised, formal structure; the other is a repeated insistence on the 'Sublime' not merely as a theory of grandeur in nature or art but as the principle of human response to and involvement in that grandeur. The interplay of nature with human emotion is constant in Turner's work: it was not enough for him to sit quietly before tranquil nature and record it fervently, as Constable did: art of the highest order demanded a more explicit and more public statement of the interrelationship. One of the verses from the *Fallacies of Hope* that appeared in the 1850 catalogue sums up the point: *The visit to the tomb* is captioned with the line:

'The sun went down in wrath at such deceit.'

The grandeur of the sunset is not simply a portrayal of a splendid natural phenomenon: it is linked with a human emotion directly connected with the events treated of in the picture—the betrayal of Dido by Aeneas and the 'wrath' felt not only by people involved, but by the whole of nature, and so by ourselves as we contemplate the story: there is a direct reciprocity between human and natural drama.

NOTES

1   Cat. Nos P229, P230, P231.

2   See chap. 6, pp. 146–7.

3   T.B., XC, p. 50. Turner may have been thinking of Claude's *Ulysses restituting Chryseis* (Rothlisberger 80), which he might have seen in Paris in 1802.

4   Pope, *The Iliad*, Book I, ll. 50–2.

5   Early writers give *Chryses* the title 'Chryses worshipping the setting sun' which makes explicit the theme of the drawing. See Redgrave, 1866, vol. II, p. 126.

6   Cat. No. P115. Gage, 1969, p. 139, argues that the picture represents a 'struggle of the elements' of light and shade; but it is closer to a conventional allegory of (moral) light and darkness.

7   John Flaxman, 1755–1826. See his illustration, *Neptune rising from the Sea*, to Pope's *Iliad*, Book XIII, ll. 67 ff. Gage, 1969, p. 131, states that Turner's horses of Apollo were 'adapted directly from Stuart and Revett's presentation of the east pediment of the Parthenon, in the *Antiquities of Athens*'; but the adaptation is a fairly thorough-going one, and Flaxman's use of the motif is closer to Turner's image. Compare also the central group in Flaxman's *Achilles Shield*, in the collection of Her Majesty the Queen.

8   See Gage, 1969, pp. 128–32 for an elaborate and fascinating interpretation of the picture in these terms.

9   Cat. No. P369.

10   Ruskin, *Works*, XIII, p. 150: 'Turner has put his whole strength into the expression of the roundings of the hills, under the influence of the torrents; has insisted on the loveliest features of mountain scenery when full of rivers.'

11   Henry Howard, 1769–1847. For accounts of Howard, a friend of Trimmer's, and his contact with Turner see Thornbury, pp. 122–4, 258–60.

12   Cat. No. P79.

13   Turner drew Reynolds's vast history picture in position in the Drawing Room at Petworth, T.B., CCXLIV-108. Egremont acquired the work in 1807 or shortly after. It remains at Petworth (Collins Baker No. 61), but is in poor condition.

14   William Etty, 1787–1849.

15   *The Literary Gazette*, quoted by W. T. Whitley, 1930, p. 87.

16   Danby had first exhibited his picture in 1825, but as Gage suggests, R.A. 1974, Nos B41, 42, the mezzotint of 1841 by George Henry Phillips is the more likely source for Turner's picture. For a possible connection between Turner and another mezzotint after Danby, see p. 168. *Queen Mab's Cave* is P420.

17   By Stuckey in 'Turner, Masaniello and the Angel', *Jahrbuch der Berliner Museen*, vol. XVIII, 1976, pp. 156–75. Eagles's article appeared in *Blackwood's Magazine* for October 1836. Eagles wrote of *Ulysses:* 'There are modern pictures that would make you long for a parasol, and put you in fear of the yellow fever, ... scenes pretending to be a Fairy Land that are as hot as capsicum; terribly tropical, "sub curru nimium propinque solis"—where an Undine would be dried and withered...'

18   Ruskin, *Works*, III, p. 254, note. The quotation was omitted from later editions of *Modern Painters* as blasphemous; see Lindsay, 1966, p. 213. In connection with the derivation of the subject of *Undine giving the ring to Masaniello* it may be observed that Ruskin had used the imagery of a magic ring being conferred by one person on another at the beginning of his reply to the *Blackwood's* article, which Turner read, though it was not published: 'What sort of critic he may be, to whom Maga [i.e. *Blackwood's Magazine*] has presented the magic ring of her authority appears to me very difficult to determine...' (*Works*, III, p. 635).

19   Another version of *Shade and darkness* is P443.

20   Turner's enjoyment of private jokes incomprehensible to other people was often remarked on; see for example S. Redgrave, *A Dictionary of Artists*, 1878, p. 437: 'Taciturn and reserved, he was no less a jovial associate at the occasional meetings of his professional brethren, and full of jokes which it was difficult to comprehend.' Reynolds, 1969, pp. 202–3, suggests a reminiscence of 'one of Martin's angels'; this is probably present, but it cannot explain the subject-matter of the picture in relation to *Undine*.

21   Stuckey, 1976, pp. 169–70.

22   See Introduction, pp. 14–15.

23   It might almost be interpreted as a gloss on the more familiar moment of Hannibal showing his armies the 'fertile plains of Italy', as J. R. Cozens entitled his version of the subject in 1776. Turner is known to have admired Cozens's picture, which is now lost.

24   See chap. 4, pp. 102–4.

25   See chap. 3, p. 65.

26   Benjamin Robert Haydon, 1786–1846. See Pope, ed., *Haydon's Diary*, 1963, vol. III, p. 518. The picture was in the collection of Sir Robert Peel. Wordsworth's poem, written on 11 June 1831, is explicit:

> Sky without cloud—ocean without a wave;
> And the one Man that laboured to enslave
> The World, sole-standing high on the bare hill—
> Back turned, arms folded, the unapparent face
> Tinged, we may fancy, in this dreary place
> With light reflected from the invisible sun
> Set, like his fortunes; but not set for aye
> Like them. The unguilty Power pursues his way,
> And before *him* doth dawn perpetual run.

Haydon's work often centres on the hero motif: his *Portrait of the Duke of*

Wellington upon the Field of Waterloo (Liverpool) was also celebrated by Wordsworth, and Haydon's portrait of *Wordsworth on Helvellyn* (National Portrait Gallery, London) belongs to the same class of romantic statement.

27 Published in 1814.

28 See Lindsay,... *J. M. W. Turner,* 1966, p. 203: 'The limpet... in its innocence, is still an integrated part of nature. Wilkie as the artist who has fulfilled himself becomes a living part of that nature in the consecrated moment of death; Napoleon is condemned to be alone and for ever alienated'; and Ruskin's summary of Turner to Thornbury: 'He knew his own power, and felt himself utterly alone in the world from its not being understood' (Thornbury, Preface p. xi). For Turner's rivalry with Wilkie see Redgrave, 1866, vol. II, pp. 103–9.

29 Cat. No. P349.

30 Cat. No. P238. See Gage, 1972, pp. 50–2.

31 Cat. No. P237. The 1844 picture is *Fishing boats bringing a disabled ship into Port Ruysdael* (Cat. No. P408).

32 Cat. No. P393.

33 Cat. No. P340. See Gage, 1969, p. 92. Du Fresnoy's *De Arte Graphica,* which was translated many times in the eighteenth century, was a standard manual for artists with which Turner, like all his colleagues, was familiar as a matter of course.

34 Stories of such incidents are numerous; see Redgrave, 1866, loc. cit., for an anecdote involving Wilkie. Gage, 1969, chap. 10, discusses Turner's use of the Varnishing Days at length, postulating that he consciously 'taught' his colleagues by means of his 'performances'. See Introduction, p. 19.

35 Charles Robert Leslie, 1794–1859. The picture is Collins Baker No. 224.

36 Collins Baker No. 221. A drawing by Turner shows Leslie's paintings installed together in the white and gold room at Petworth: T.B., CCXLIV-14; repr. B.M. 1975, No. 128.

37 Leslie's pictures often display the influence of Watteau; e.g. the *Bourgeois Gentilhomme,* in the Victoria and Albert Museum.

38 *Boccaccio relating the tale of the bird-cage,* Cat. No. P244. The allusions were immediately recognized: the *Literary Gazette,* 17 May 1828, wrote: 'Watteau and Stothard, be quiet! Here is much more than you could match.' Thornbury (p. 222) asserts Turner's admiration for Stothard, whom 'he frequently praised... It is true that he painted his Boccaccio picture in distinct rivalry of Stothard; but he openly expressed his desire that Stothard, above all men, should like his pictures.'

39 See R.A. 1974, Nos 325–39.

40 Cat. Nos P332 and P333.

41 Cat. No. P346. George Jones, 1786–1869. See Finberg, *Life,* p. 335.

42 It is also possible that Turner's picture is actually an attempt to paint in the style of Jones himself.

43 Cat. No. P436.

44 The interpretation was made by David Thomas, in an unpublished lecture. See Butlin and Joll, 1977, No. 449.

45 Joseph Michael Gandy, 1771–1843. He began his career as assistant to Wyatt; his association with Soane dated from about 1811. Many of his impressively fanciful watercolours of Soane's designs are in Sir John Soane's Museum.

46 See Dorothy Stroud, *The Architecture of Sir John Soane,* 1961, Pl. 86. For the profound effect of Soane's death on Turner see Bernard Falk, *Turner the Painter: his Hidden Life,* 1938, p. 191. Soane, Gandy and Turner seem all alike to be influenced by Piranesi; it is remarkable that that youthful interest of Turner's should be revived, along with others, at this date. Note, in this context, Clara Wheeler's remark: 'I have often heard Turner say that, if he could begin life again, he would rather be an architect than a painter' (Thornbury, p. 236).

47 Clarke Olney, *Benjamin Robert Haydon, Historical Painter,* 1952, pp. 161–2. The Belzoni sarcophagus of Seti I was discovered in 1817; Soane gave a three-day reception to celebrate its acquisition in April 1825. See Bolton, 1927, pp. 371 ff.

48 Turner's picture is Cat. No. P259; West's is Collins Baker No. 219. See Gowing, 1966, p. 27.

49 Letter to George Jones, 22 January 1830; see Thornbury, pp. 331–2.

50 Clarkson Stanfield, 1793–1867, marine painter and watercolourist. The anecdote is recorded in George Jones, *Recollections.* Ruskin too found the black sails unsatisfactory.

51 See Herrmann, 1975, p. 45. Wilkie had begun to paint in a new style, dominated by rich blacks imitative of Velazquez, Ribera and other masters, after a visit to Spain and Italy; his first works in this manner appeared in 1829, when Turner's *Ulysses* provided a striking illustration of an opposing system. See Finberg, *Life,* p. 314. *The Pifferari* is Cat. No. P374.

52 See comments on this picture in chap. 7, p. 157.

53 Ruskin, *Works,* VI, p. 381. For *Goldau,* see chap. 10, p. 238.

54 Pl. 224. This picture is the subject of extensive discussion in Louis Hawes, 'Turner's Fighting Temeraire', *Art Quarterly,* vol. XXXV, 1972, pp. 22–48.

55 Hawes, 1972, pp. 34–8.

56 See Finberg, *Life,* p. 417.

57 Hawes, 1972, p. 42, and Stuckey, 1976, p. 168.

58 See Colvin, 'The Sun of Venice going to Sea', 1874, pp. 161–2, and Michael Kitson, *Turner,* 1964, p. 81. Gage, 1969, p. 146, traces the source of Turner's idea in Shelley's *Lines written among the Euganean Hills,* part of which had been published in 1838 under the title *Venice.*

59 Cat. No. 1374.

60 The drawing is T.B., CCCXV-13, B.M. 1975, No. 239; the painting is Cat. No. P406. Ruskin's comment is in *Works,* XIII, p. 215.

61 Watercolour was used on some of the late reworkings of early themes that 'escaped' the Turner Bequest, Cat. Nos P509–P520; for their date, see chap. 10, p. 247 and note.

62 The whaling pictures are Cat. Nos P414, P415, P423, and P426. Drawings of whaling subjects are Cat. Nos 1411, 1412, and in T.B., CCLIII, CCCLVII.

63 Cat. Nos P133 and P134.

64 Gage, 'Turner's Academic Friendships: C. L. Eastlake', *Burlington Magazine,* CX, 1968, p. 682 note, suggests that the *Italy* pair (Cat. Nos P374 and P375) are concerned with superstition ancient and modern; the punishment of Ovid's 'blasphemy' parallels the Italian peasants' use of music in their primitive religious ceremonies. See also Gage, 1974, pp. 77–8.

65 Cat. Nos P378 and P379.

66 *Childe Harold's Pilgrimage,* Canto IV, stanzas xxvi, xxvii.

67 Cat. No. P342.

68 The *Farbenlehre* was published in German in 1810. Turner read and annotated the book; see Gage, 1969, chap. 11. Eastlake, 1793–1865, was

a friend of Turner's; see Gage, 1968, pp. 677–85.

69 These 'circular' compositions have been seen as deriving from the characteristic shape of the vignettes that Turner had worked on for Rogers and others (see Holcomb, 'The Vignette and Vertical Composition in Turner's Œuvre', *Art Quarterly*, XXXII, 1970, pp. 16–29). It is noteworthy that the brilliant contrasts of primary colours common to the late circular pictures are foreshadowed only in some of the more brilliantly coloured vignettes; see above, chap. 7, note 28. Gowing, 1966, p. 23, suggests that Turner's interest in such shapes first emerges in his studies of spheres for use in the Perspective lectures. This observation might well apply to the 'humid bubbles' which 'emulous of light, Reflected [Earth's] lost forms, each in prismatic guise' of *Light and Colour*. The first composition in circular form to be exhibited was the *Bacchus and Ariadne* of 1840 (Cat. No. P382).

70 Hakewill drew Turner's attention to Correggio (1494–1534) at Parma in a note on a loose sheet in the Turner Bequest, T.B., CCCLXVIII-B; there are also indications that Parma was on Turner's route in the *Route to Rome* sketchbook, T.B., CLXXI, pp. 1, 21 and in the *Italian Guide* book, T.B., CLXXII, p. 4.

71 Giovanni Lanfranco, 1582–1647; G. B. Tiepolo, 1696–1770. A modello for the decoration of a dome by Carlo Carlone (1686–1775) with a *Glorification of the Cross*, now in the Indianapolis Art Museum, exemplifies the compositional type that is followed in Turner's picture.

72 See Cat. No. 330, and the colour study of the interior of the Mausoleum, T.B., CXCV 130, repr. Gage, 1969, Pl. 57.

73 See C. Cunningham, 'Turner's Van Tromp Paintings', *Art Quarterly*, XV, 1952, pp. 323 ff. *Admiral van Tromp's barge* is Cat. No. P339, *Van Tromp returning* P351, the *Rotterdam ferry-boat* P348.

74 Cat. No. P407. The picture is discussed by C. H. Heilmann, *Pantheon*, 1976. Werner Hoffmann drew my attention to the apparent presence of the 'Christ stilling the Tempest' motif.

75 Cat. No. P410. The full title is: *Van Tromp, going about to please his masters, ships a sea, getting a good wetting.—Vide Lives of Dutch Painters.*

76 Cat. No. P343. Butlin and Joll, 1977, point out that another picture shown in 1832, *Helvoetsluys* (P345), may be regarded as a companion, since William sailed from that port in 1688. Professor Bachrach suggested the connection with the Reform Bill.

77 See Lindsay, *J. M. W. Turner*, 1966, pp. 138–9. Lindsay's account of Turner tends to exaggerate Turner's radicalism; Thornbury believed 'he was a Tory' (p. 282).

78 Cat. Nos P359 and P364.

79 See Butlin, 1962, p. 54; Gowing, 1966, p. 33, and R.A. 1974, No. 456, where I disagree with the current view that the studies (T.B., CCLXXXIII) were made out of doors.

80 *Fire at sea* is Cat. No. P460. Watercolours are *Fire at Fenning's Wharf* (Cat. No. 523) and some colour-beginnings e.g. T.B., CCLXHI-89, (B.M. 1975, No. 204); and the finished watercolour of the *Burning of the Houses of Parliament* in the Turner Bequest (Cat. No. 522).

81 The picture may rely on Thomson's account of a Typhoon in Summer, from the *Seasons*, and T. Clarkson's *History of the Rise, Progress and Accomplishment of the Abolition of the Slave Trade*, 1808, 2nd ed., 1839, in which year Wilberforce's biography was published.

82 Cat. No. P392. Monkhouse (*DNB*) suggests that the picture was intended 'as a compliment to the Queen'; Turner may have expected her to acknowledge it.

83 Cat. No. P252.

84 For Turner's unexpected eloquence on the subject of his travels, see the report of Mr. Rose of Jersey (Thornbury, pp. 243–4). His love of travel is poignantly illustrated by his promise to Bartlett, who first attended him as doctor in his final illness, 'should he recover to take me on the continent and shew me all the places he had visited' (Finberg, *Life*, p. 437).

85 In a letter to James Holworthy of 7 January 1826, British Library, Add. MSS. 50118, ff. 72–3. See Russell and Wilton, 1976, p. 70. Turner described the circumstances of the second accident in a letter to Eastlake; see Gage, 1972, pp. 38–40, where it is quoted in the context of a discussion of Turner and travel.

86 Compare Turner's 'self-portrait' in the tranquil landscape of *Melrose*, Pl. 207.

87 See Ruskin, *Works*, XIII, p. 161.

88 See Ruskin, *Works*, VII, p. 445 note.

89 There was indeed no reason why he should, since many of the early 'Sublime' landscapes, by himself as well as by de Loutherbourg, Wright and others, had depended on modern industrial phenomena; see Francis Klingender, *Art and the Industrial Revolution*, 1947, rev. eds. 1968 and 1972.

90 *Spectator*, 11 May 1844.

91 It was painted as a companion to the *Venice* (Cat. No. P356), executed for Henry McConnell and shown at the Academy in 1834. Butlin and Joll suggest that Turner drew a deliberate parallel between the decaying power of Venice and the economic prosperity of England; but see comments on p. 212, on Venice as an image of political decay.

92 Cat. No. P294.

93 Farington, *Diary*, 8 May 1799. For the Angerstein Claudes see chap. 2, note 27.

94 Cat. No. P295.

95 Cat. No. P337. See Gage, *Art Quarterly*, 1974, p. 47.

96 Lionel Cust, 'The Portraits of J. M. W. Turner', *Magazine of Art*, 1895, pp. 248–9, quoted by Gage, 1969, p. 169.

97 *Literary Gazette*, 4 February 1837.

98 See Ruskin, *Works*, XXXVI, p. 543. The remark seems to underline the most obvious aspect of Turner's work too neatly to be credible.

99 See Gage, 1969, p. 143.

100 A large plate with this title was engraved in 1840 by D. Wilson (R. 649). See also R. N. Wornum, *Turner Gallery* (R. 723). Another plate was entitled '*Regulus leaving home in order to return to Carthage*'; see Henry Ottley, *Biographical and Critical Dictionary of Recent and Living Painters and Engravers...*, 1877, p. 165.

101 See R.A. 1974, No. 474.

102 There is an exact analogy in the vignette of Napoleon at Fontainebleau, Cat. No. 1115.

103 Ruskin, *Works*, VII, p. 435, note.

104 Ruskin, *Works*, VI, pp. 274–5, note.

105 Cat. Nos P421 and P422.

106 These pictures have been discussed in an unpublished paper by John McCoubrey.

107 *The Wreck buoy* is Cat. No. P428; *The hero of a hundred fights* Cat. No. P427. This last is usually described as a scene at the casting of Matthew Cotes Wyatt's equestrian statue of Wellington in 1846. Once in position at Hyde Park Corner, the work aroused a storm of disapproval, and it seems rather unlikely that Turner would have drawn attention to a fellow-artist's embarrassment by alluding to it in a picture. But his dear

friend Chantrey had been responsible for another equestrian figure of Wellington, which was completed after his death by an assistant, Henry Weekes, cast at Chantrey's own foundry in Eccleston Place, and erected in 1840 in front of the Royal Exchange (see Gunnis, *Dictionary of British Sculptors, 1660–1851,* 1953, pp. 93, 447). There is every reason to suppose that Turner might have been invited to see the casting of Chantrey's work, and that he would have painted a tribute to his dead friend and colleague while at the same time honouring another 'hero'.

108 Cat. Nos P429, P430, P431, P432.
109 Finberg, *Life,* p. 427.
110 Cat. Nos P501 and P527.
111 Cat. No. P512.
112 See chap. 7, p. 157, and note 10.

Chapter Ten

The Late Watercolours

We have seen to what extent an abstruse personal element entered into some major pictures of the 1840s, which may diminish their satisfactoriness as works of art; we have also noticed that in other paintings of the same period Turner was able to achieve new heights of expressive power, concentrating on natural phenomena of especial grandeur or emotional force and rendering them with a broad freedom that has been likened to his use of watercolour wash. When we come to examine the watercolours of this period, a very different state of affairs presents itself.

There exists a mass of work in watercolours that is extremely difficult to date, but which for various reasons—often on the evidence of watermarks—can be confidently assigned to the last decade or so of Turner's life. Many are very slight; they are brief jottings of effects, either seen or imagined, and seem to relate to no ultimate project, even though they were evidently executed in groups or series, perhaps dozens at a time. The slightest of them appear to belong to the years after 1845 when, as Ruskin testifies, Turner became ill and suffered a noticeable decay of his powers:[1] they are sometimes mere splashes and daubs of ill-defined colour, smeared on to the paper as if with a finger or a stick. But it is only the coarseness of these studies that betrays their lateness: as far as economy or slightness are concerned, there are drawings of all periods that are as allusive and imprecise. What is strangest about the last watercolour studies is a new and unexpected note of 'literariness' in them: they are frequently annotated by Turner with oddly poignant remarks, scribbled on them in pencil. One of the most interesting of these enigmatic PI.239 captions is that on a drawing of a foundering hulk: 'Lost to all Hope she lies/each sea breaks over a derelict/on an unknown shore/the sea folk [?] only sharing [?] the triumph'—which seems to be a snatch of Turner's gloomy versification. The subject of the sketch, however, despite its

rough quality and general slightness, is closely connected with a series of oil-paintings that Turner produced at various times during his career. The composition can be traced back to *A Ship aground* of about 1828,[2] and to *Fort Vimieux* of 1831, PI.210 and the whole mood of the drawing is that of one of the more 'pessimistic' late paintings.[3] Altogether it is not perhaps inappropriate to see a connection between the loose washes of some of these watercolour studies and the broad effects of light, cloud or storm that so often form the subject-matter of the oil-paintings.[4]

The main element that brings these studies close to the spirit of the paintings is, however, the 'literariness' of their inscriptions. In general, the distinguishing characteristic of the watercolours is their freedom from the philosophical associations that imbue the paintings with sombre meaning. We are almost never prompted to enquire into hidden meanings in the watercolours: they speak for themselves with such freshness, and yet with such intensity and complexity, that no ulterior significance need be presumed.

As we have seen, the most far-reaching and wide-ranging of his exercises in watercolour were conducted within a ready-made literary context: the picturesque and topographical tour. In the 1840s he no longer worked for publishers like Cooke and Heath; but he did not give up working in sequences, and he certainly did not abandon his practice of bringing watercolour drawings to a state of elaborate completion.

In the large watercolours that he made immediately after the end of his work on the *Picturesque Views in England and Wales* in about 1837–8, there is a noticeable return to the most formal and 'historical' of his compositional schemes. These drawings group themselves logically round the view of *Oberwesel*, dated 1840. Some may belong to the year or so PI.243 immediately before that date. The subjects vary: they are all continental views, culled from tours made at different times

239 'Lost to all Hope...' *c.* 1845–50
Watercolour and pencil, 229 × 324
Yale Center for British Art, Paul Mellon Collection (Cat. No. 1425)

in the preceding ten or even twenty years; apart from two,
Pl.244 the *Oberwesel* and *Nemi*, which were published together
among subjects from the oil-paintings in 'Finden's Royal
Gallery of British Art', 1842, we have no evidence that
Turner conceived the group as a 'set'; he would presumably
have had all the subjects engraved if that had been the case.
One subject, Heidelberg seen from the opposite bank of the
Neckar, was in fact treated three times; once, as I shall
demonstrate, probably much later;[5] the two other versions
Pl.245 seem to belong to the years about 1840.[6] The design that was
engraved by T. A. Pryor was said by Pryor to have been
executed at his suggestion in 1840 from a sketch of his own.[7]
This may seem unlikely in view of the frequency with which
Turner repeated the subject, but the story is possibly
Pl.246 confirmed by the existence of a rather unusual working

drawing for the composition, partially coloured and annotated, in the Turner Bequest. It is carefully plotted out with
considerable detail, especially in the figures, as though Turner
were feeling his way with an alien theme; though by this time
he had often enough 'translated' other artists' sketches: in the
Landscape Illustrations for the Bible and *Views in India* that both
appeared in 1836, he had had quite recent experience of the
process.[8]

The second of the two Heidelberg views of about 1840,
that in the Manchester City Art Gallery, must, if Pryor's story

230

is true, be a reworking of the other version, since it adopts similar figures as well as a similar viewpoint. The large dignity of its composition is typical of these watercolours; it marks a moment of pause between the experimental mixture of classical and topographical forms in the *England and Wales* series, and the expansive vortex that characterizes the later drawings. *Oberwesel,* with its long axis of reflecting water and Claudian tree at the right, is a restatement of the compositional theme of *Prudhoe Castle* of 1826; and *Tancarville on the Seine* pursues the same motif.[9] The classicism of the *Nemi* is self-evident: it is perhaps Turner's last and conscious tribute to the memory of Wilson.[10] The atmospheric effects achieved by these drawings are most intricately wrought; delicate touches of pure colour mingle with a filigree of scratching-out that renders the air alive with quivering light. Turner's technical powers are here at their most apparent; and indeed there is something deliberately artificial, self-consciously grand about the series, evoking the paintings of Claude as his work in watercolour had not done since the early part of his career. But in spite of the vivid presence here of the old masters, it seems at least possible that Turner had also in mind the scumbled white impasto of Constable, in whose later pictures the device had become a mannerism. Constable died in 1837, and though he and Turner were not close friends, the event cannot but have contributed to Turner's mounting sense of isolation and bereavement at that period. His instinctive desire to adopt the viewpoint, or the subject-matter, or the manner of a contemporary may have expressed itself in this instance in such a way.

Pl.241 It was perhaps to escape his accumulating and gloomy emotions that Turner visited Switzerland in 1841. His stay in Venice in 1840 had already, as far as we can tell, prompted an outpouring of meditative colour studies that betokens an exceptional sense of identification with that city; but despite the quantity of the studies, and several paintings, he made no finished drawings of Venice. This is one of the oddest aspects of the list of his late watercolours. Switzerland, on the other hand, had just the opposite effect on him. He returned there in 1842 and in the two following years, and might well have continued to take his summer holidays by Lake Lucerne if he had not become ill in 1845. The tenacity with which he pursued his intention of making finished drawings of subjects gleaned in Switzerland is illuminating. He made, as at Venice, huge quantities of colour sketches,[11] which would certainly have satisfied him if he was by this time, as has been claimed, concerned only with inward and personal expression and impatient of the formulas and formalities of 'public' art. It is

240   Venice   ?*c.* 1835–40
Pencil and watercolour, approx. 145 × 140, vignette
Private collection   (Cat. No. 1314)

true that he made no attempt to exhibit his Swiss drawings; nor were they, for the most part, engraved.[12] But he nevertheless tried to recreate the conditions under which he had produced his best work in watercolour in the past: lacking a regular publisher for a book of picturesque views, he provoked his friends and patrons to commission a set of drawings by choosing subjects from a bundle of 'samples' that he worked up specially from his sketches. Four of the subjects had already been completed to give customers some idea of what to expect, and how to interpret the 'samples'. Turner wanted ten commissions but got only nine; he went ahead with the project nevertheless, and, what is more, repeated the proposal in the following year. On this occasion, only six drawings were commissioned; Turner was still determined to work by this method, and in 1845 another full set of ten appeared.[13]

This is a remarkable story; it is told by Ruskin with much circumstantial detail, and can hardly be rejected as essentially inaccurate. It consorts hardly at all with the accepted view of Turner at this date, but shows him still profoundly dependent

241 Venice: The Grand Canal, with S. Simeone Piccolo: dusk 1840
Watercolour, 221 × 318
Trustees of the British Museum, London (T.B., CCCXV-8) (not in catalogue)

upon old professional habits of working, and, more signifi-cant, upon a traditional relationship with his public, who were no longer accessible as they had been through engravings or exhibitions. His patrons were reduced to a very small band—Ruskin and Munro of Novar between them bought twenty of the twenty-six watercolours of 1842, 1843 and 1845: there was no evident encouragement from a wider public.

But the process of communication at the level of the 'finished work' was essential to Turner. We have only to compare the studies and 'samples' of Swiss subjects with his worked-out drawings to realize that he could not, in fact, say all that he had to say within the confines of the sketch alone. His work on the *England and Wales* series, and on the continental views of around 1840, shows his apprehension of landscape broadening and his technique expanding to

comprehend it; and just as he had found a channel of expression for newly-developed technique and landscape vision in the Switzerland of 1802, so again in the 1840s he turned to the scenery of that country to provide the fullest reciprocity with his ideas.

The 'sample' studies belong, on the whole, to the same class of drawings as the Venetian colour studies. It is by no means certain that Turner had made all the Venetian sequence before he embarked for Switzerland in August 1841: many of them may have been reminiscences rather than direct records, and the series as a whole has the air of a developing

232

242   Ehrenbreitstein and Coblenz   *c.* 1840
Watercolour, 229 × 280
Private collection   (Cat. No. 1321)

fantasy on Venetian themes which could as well have been evolved in England as in Italy. Even so, there are several drawings that clearly record particular moments; and in looking at the whole series we receive a strong impression of their having been done together, or at least within a relatively short time.[14] The Swiss studies seem to reflect a similar gamut of conditions. A large number of them are apparently notes made either directly from the subject or immediately after the experience, and they often incorporate quite detailed particulars of topography or architecture. Others are more broadly

243 Oberwesel 1840
Watercolour and body-colour with scraping-out, 345 × 530
Private collection (Cat. No. 1380)

244 Lake Nemi *c.* 1840
Watercolour and scraping-out, 347 × 515
Trustees of the British Museum, London (Lloyd Bequest)
(Cat. No. 1381)

organized, apparently as evocations in pure colour of certain well-known motifs—the Dent d'Oche, for instance, or the castle of La Bâtiaz at Martigny—in their setting of airy perspectives.[15]

There is a third category, however, of which relatively few of the Venetian drawings are examples: that of the worked up study for sale or presentation as a 'sample'. We know that Turner did make such studies of Venetian subjects: the view of *The Grand Canal with the Salute*,[16] which was in the hands of his agent Thomas Griffith, is very highly wrought, even making use of body-colour—extremely rare in such works—and must have been intended either for sale or as a gift to Griffith for services rendered. It alone constitutes

234

245 Heidelberg, with a rainbow *c*. 1841
Watercolour, 311 × 521
Private collection   (Cat. No. 1377)

proof that Turner was prepared to extract such drawings
from his notebooks and let them out of his hands to become
the property of other people. It is not clear, however, that he
made a regular practice of selling such pieces to the general
public; it may be that only personal friends and associates
were allowed to become the possessors of intimate works of
the type—as Fawkes had been allowed to buy the essentially
private Rhine series of 1817. The mass of similar studies that
are now in scattered collections may have been acquired from
the artist's studio after his death, besides those that Ruskin
certainly persuaded Turner to let him have.

But Ruskin was not in full sympathy with the studies of the
'sample' type. He found that they fell between two functional

246   Colour-beginning: Heidelberg 1840–1
Pencil and watercolour, 484 × 693
Trustees of the British Museum, London (T.B., CCCLXV–34)   (not in
catalogue)

235

stools: 'it is not easy to see the use of carrying them so far, unless these views were to be ultimately completed.'[17] But he himself supplied the answer to the dilemma, in his description of Turner's plan to use studies as guides to prospective patrons. They had a quite specific function, distinct, apparently, from that of any of Turner's other studies. They were intended to show what each subject might comprehend in the way of detail, without necessarily elaborating all of it. They were studies conceived as complete, if unfinished, compositions. It is interesting that with one exception[18] none of them left Turner's hands; he had no wish to present them as completed works. Those colour studies of Swiss scenes that

247   The first steamer on Lake Lucerne   ? 1841
Watercolour, with some scraping-out, over traces of pencil, 231 × 289
University College, London   (Cat. No. 1482)

are not in the Bequest are, nevertheless, often as fully wrought, and belong to much the same category technically. But they are not 'composed' as finishable designs; their function, in Turner's eyes, was essentially different.

The history of the Swiss watercolours and the anomaly of the 'sample' studies points to the fact that Turner attached great importance to his finished drawings of the 1840s. It will be helpful, perhaps, to view them against the background of

236

248 The Blue Rigi: Lake of Lucerne—sunrise 1842
Watercolour, 297 × 450
Private collection (Cat. No. 1524)

the paintings, which, as we have seen, often at this date present a single aspect of nature as an isolated phenomenon of the 'Sublime': sunlight through evening haze; rain and steam mingled; a blizzard. The subject-matter of such paintings is contrived to point the human significance of those phenomena, and their technique is designed to convey them as boldly as possible. The watercolours, by contrast, persist in the tradition of Turner's expanded topographical mode, presenting a complete and intricately woven account of all aspects of each chosen scene; but at the same time they unmistakably reflect his increased concern for single, unified effects of atmosphere in a new and very concise compositional plan. His earlier elaborate variations on traditional models seem to have synthesized into a remarkable simplicity of structure, adapted to the needs of his new themes. The principal of these is the dynamic of light in the context of a vast open space, which allows for the minutest inflections of tone and colour over a huge area of landscape. Intimations of such subtleties of articulation abound in the *England and Wales* set, and a drawing like the *Tancarville* of about 1840 is a supreme example of such manipulation of watercolour; but it was not until he applied himself to depicting a landscape on the scale of Switzerland that Turner could fully exploit the potential of his latest technical explorations.[19] It was in

237

watercolour, not in oil that he could distinguish by colour one tiny stroke from the next, and give that distinction its full weight in a design. A few late paintings bear witness to his attempts to mould oil in the same way. Some, as has been noted, retain touches added by the artist in watercolour; a circumstance which suggests that Turner was conscious of the relative coarseness of his late style of painting in oil compared with what he could achieve in watercolour.[20]

This increased concern for subtle modulation of colour takes very different forms in the watercolours and the oil-paintings. The symbolic colour of the late paintings, especially the use of primaries—following, perhaps, as has been proposed, the clue given by Sir David Brewster in his *Treatise on Optics*[21]—is not the same thing as the dynamic colour of the drawings. There is nothing symbolic about the Swiss watercolours, with the clear and illuminating exception Pl.252 of the *Goldau* of 1843. *Goldau* is so decisively different from its companions that, although it comes half-way through the Swiss series and not at the beginning, it forms a convenient point of entry for a discussion of the group as a whole.

The symbolic red of its sky brings *Goldau,* as I have suggested, close to the mood and intention of some of the late paintings. It is a watercolour unusually preoccupied with a grand 'public' effect of the 'Sublime', related, like the *Slaver* and other pictures of catastrophe, to human fate. What is particularly surprising about it in this context is its technique: its odd look of having been laid in with a palette knife, especially in the flat splashes of yellow and red in the upper sky. But the most unexpected feature of all is the perfunctory use of figures in the foreground, which suggests that Turner is here concerned not with his familiar complete topography, but with a statement of the single isolated phenomenon of the sunset. We know that the emotional weight of the drawing lies in what the blood-red sunset stands for: just as the Alpine cottage destroyed by an avalanche was understood to contain human lives although they appear nowhere in the picture, so here the heavy boulders of the foreground tell the story of the avalanche of 1806 in which 457 people died.[22] Much of the delicacy of Turner's complex involutions of colour is sacrificed here for a single bold effect. The marvellous precision with which he indicates Arth church spire, 'a point of fire at the edge of the distant lake', as Ruskin observed, serves to make that spire a focus in an otherwise very sweeping statement.[23]

A view of the same spire from the opposite direction, in which a rich blue dominates so that we might suspect it of being a kind of companion piece to *Goldau,* has none of its

obsessive concentration on a single idea.[24] The light changes over the mountains and hills with marvellous softness, and the foreground figures, although not numerous, are calculated to express the mood of a hot sunny morning that Turner intends to convey. Perhaps the *Faido,* also of 1843, Pl.253 approaches nearer to being a 'monothematic' work; we might certainly adduce an absence of figures as confirmation that Turner is more concerned to present a single dramatic image than to portray a changing sequence of conditions. The texture of the composition is consistently broken and rough, allowing the eye little of that calm which Turner loved to include in his broadest views. Rocks and water are bound up together in a stormy frenzy that seems to exclude, to threaten the very existence of man. Ruskin devoted much space in *Modern Painters* to demonstrating that this is one of the most firmly human-oriented of Turner's works, and that the minuscule post-chaise that is barely noticeable in the fury of the surrounding elements in fact makes the point of the subject: 'in reality, the place is approached through one of the most sublime ravines in the Alps... in no other wise could we have come than by the coach road... the full essence and soul of the scene, and consummation of all the wonderfulness of the torrents and Alps, lay in a postchaise with small ponies and postboys, which accordingly [Turner inserted]... at the turn of the road.'[25]

Many of the watercolours that had resulted from Turner's visit to the Alps in 1802 were invented to suggest how insignificant man is beside the vastness and wonder of wild nature. Ruskin's interpretation of the *Faido* suggests that such a 'Sublime' response was alien to the sympathies of the mature Turner. We should perhaps allow for Ruskin's enthusiasm for his own doctrine that landscape is rendered significant only by its relation to human affairs; but the other Swiss drawings reinforce the notion that Turner himself was of the same opinion. The attitude was, indeed, a logical extension of the 'Sublime' principle, as we have seen with the *England and Wales* drawings: in making man the touchstone of landscape he obeyed a rule with which he had grown up.[26]

We might be justified in taking an opposite view if all the Swiss drawings of this late period were like the three views of Pls. 248, the Rigi that Turner included in his 1842 set. They show the mountain at dawn, conveying a mood of silent and almost

249   The Red Rigi: detail   1842
Watercolour, 305 × 458
National Gallery of Victoria, Melbourne   (Cat. No. 1525)

adoring wonder before purely natural beauty:[27] the expansive calm of the *Rigi* drawings is among Turner's profoundest achievements and his numerous studies of the mountain confirm that he found it an irresistible subject of contemplation. His way of isolating it as a single phenomenon, his choice of it as a worthy subject of a drawing in its own right, says much for his sense of its immutable and remote beauty; but the fact that he chose in these studies, and in the three finished watercolours that he made of the Rigi, to express a contemplative and inward mood does not mean that in his old age he had renounced men and the 'human landscape'. It should be noted that even in these drawings human activities are suggested: indeed the early morning industry of the

250 Lake Lucerne: Bay of Uri from above Brunnen 1842
Watercolour over pencil, 292 × 457
Private collection (Cat. No. 1526)

251 Lucerne from the Walls 1842
Watercolour with scraping-out, 295 × 455
The Lady Lever Collection, Port Sunlight, Cheshire (Cat. No. 1529)

252 Goldau 1843
Watercolour, 305 × 470
Private collection   (Cat. No. 1537)

lake—the fishermen, the log rafts, travellers waiting for a
ferry—is carefully exploited to show not simply the artist's
response to the scene, but the scene as experienced by those
for whose daily lives it forms the setting.

It is therefore perhaps a false distinction to make between
those subjects which suggest Turner's rapt, Wordsworthian
ecstasy before natural beauty and those which present the
bustle of a more social scene. The view of *Zurich* in the 1842
set is surely an ecstatic work—its brilliant white light and
immense distances are among Turner's most exhilarating and
moving visions; and yet it is at least partly so effective

because of the urban panorama that it comprehends: the
clustered houses, the distant spires, and the thronging life of
the foreground streets, which seems to be a specific
representation of the activity prior to Zurich's annual vintage
festival,[28] all contribute to a kind of topography that Turner
had practised from his early years. The view of *Leeds* of 1816
is a comparable drawing from the first half of his career.[29]
Here, however, Turner has deliberately distorted topographical fact to produce his rapturous account of the city: his
widening of the narrow Fröschengraben moat to create a
broad and scintillating waterway is an extreme example of his
lifelong readiness to be poetically rather than geographically
accurate.

The 1842 *Zurich* is a particularly striking blend of the
ecstatic personal response with more objective discussion of
a human habitat. The view of *Lucerne from the Walls* of the Pl.251

241

same year, by contrast, is one of the most thoroughgoing and complete topographical statements that Turner ever made; and although he has altered certain details in the relations of different parts of the scene, the subject as a whole is recorded as it can still be seen today (despite Ruskin's lament that Lucerne had already, in his time, been sadly changed from the old city that Turner drew).[30] The sunny, summery atmosphere in which the city is bathed is nevertheless expressed with magical poetry; the picturesque town, distant shimmering lake and Rigi, the strolling townspeople and marksmen practising at the butts, are all involved in a statement as precise and informative as any of the *England and Wales* subjects. The bright colour of the drawing reinforces its mood—clear yellow and blue create a scheme of summery freshness that is itself an embodiment of Turner's theme.

Pl. 254 Both the *Lucerne* and the *Zurich* of 1842 have parallels among the drawings of 1845. *Schaffhausen: the town and castle* is a clear and comprehensive record like the *Lucerne*, though its atmosphere is less sunny and its technique, like that of all the 1845 drawings, is broader and coarser. The *Zurich: fête* seems at first sight to be almost a repeat of the earlier *Zurich,* but is if anything more crowded with figures, more concerned with the 'social' aspects of the subject, and at the same time more expressive of the dazzling and dissolving effect of the low sunlight. Both these drawings have faded, and so cannot be fully and fairly compared with their predecessors; but Ruskin denied that Turner's drawings of this year were of the quality of the earlier ones, and there is undeniably a loss of precision and delicacy of touch in them. Yet their preoccupations are unchanged; the range of subject-matter in the late set is very much the same as in that of 1842: it is the 1843 group of six that exhibits a differentiation of subject-matter, and that is only in its tendency to take up rather more specific and isolated topics—the sunset of *Goldau;* the moonlight of *Lucerne;* the rocks of *Faido.* Only the *Lake of Zug: early morning* and the view of *Bellinzona from the road to Locarno* partake of the customary breadth and expansiveness of vista.

But it is misleading to try to group these Swiss drawings too precisely according to type. Their variety is typical of Turner at all periods of his life, and it is only surprising that, with the exception of the *Coblenz* in the 1842 set, all the subjects were found in Switzerland. We have no certain evidence that the 'sample' studies were similarly exclusive, but it seems likely that they were, especially since Ruskin's account implies that. What the unused 'samples' may have been can only be conjectured. From its high degree of finish

in some areas, and the indication of figures in the foreground, I am inclined to think that the splendid *Lausanne: Sunset* was one.[31] A drawing of *Bellinzona from the North* also shows many figures apparently in some kind of religious procession, but is not worked up to the pitch of most of the 'samples', and bears little sign of being conceived as a finishable composition: it is perhaps too direct a record.[32] In the same way the series of drawings that Turner made in Fribourg in 1841,[33] dramatic as they are, and full of detail as they frequently are, seem to be essentially notes. They make great use of a pen dipped in colour—red, blue, green or yellow—to outline forms and sometimes indicate the colour scheme of a view without any wash. This was a device that Turner exploited in several late studies to achieve rapidly that combination of precision, overall colour patterns, and a sense of reflected light, that his complicated watercolour technique was designed to produce. It is to be seen at its loveliest in the Heidelberg drawings of 1844, when he made his last Swiss journey, and added three books full of views on the Neckar and Rhine.[34] Although he used a pen frequently in his Swiss studies—notably on the tour to Bellinzona of 1843, when he often touched up a sketch with red ink—he did not usually record the scenery of Switzerland in the coloured ink outlines that he employed in Fribourg and later in Heidelberg, forming a whole subject out of light touches of the pen subordinated to broad areas of general colour. It is a shorthand that can be seen developing parallel with the loosening technique of the finished watercolours in about 1843–5.

By the time he had completed his set of ten drawings in 1845, Turner was ill and evidence of this can be observed in his work. The change makes all the more remarkable the steadily maintained exactness and miniature precision of execution in all the watercolours up to this moment. According to Ruskin, from now on Turner's work decayed into the fumblings of old age and infirmity. But Turner did not stop drawing, and neither did Ruskin stop acquiring. Early in 1848, presumably after a period during which the artist's health had improved, Ruskin bought two more Swiss subjects; the *Brunig Pass* and the *Descent of the St. Gothard.*[35] Pl. 257 Both follow the pattern of the Swiss drawings of the first half of the decade, and are executed with a minute touch; they treat of large misty mountain valleys, dotted as always with humanity. They are nevertheless still coarser than the examples of 1845, and despite the grandeur of their content do not quite achieve the magnificence of their precursors. The *Descent of the St. Gothard* passed from Ruskin to Munro of Novar, who lent it to the Manchester Art Treasures

253   The Pass of Faido   1843
Watercolour and scraping-out over pencil, 305 × 470
Private collection   (Cat. No. 1538)

Exhibition of 1857, with the note that it was 'His last drawing'. Ruskin may well have believed it to be Turner's final finished work in watercolour, though, knowing the man as he did, he can hardly have thought that Turner had laid down his pencil for ever. Even though his health was rapidly deteriorating, Turner could no more have given up the habit of drawing than that of breathing. It is very likely, however, that, recognizing Ruskin's opinion, Turner took care not to let him see his work.

After 1848, then, in the secrecy of his own house, Turner continued to make watercolours just as he had insisted on doing hitherto. He made them now regardless of purchasers; but he made them in the same spirit as before: as a series, a loosely linked group of subjects, of his own choosing, that may have been intended to comprise a set of ten like those he had already completed. There are, however, several differences, and the existence of such a group has to be projected from somewhat scattered evidence. The drawings do not concentrate on Swiss subjects, though Swiss scenes occur among them; and they are rather larger in size than the earlier sets, most of the sheets being about 370 × 545 mm. There is a noticeable change in Turner's handling of watercolour, towards looser washes and sparser hatchings. One of the drawings is on a sheet watermarked 1846, which sets a *terminus post quem;* it is unlikely, on that evidence alone, that they are earlier than 1847, in which case they might have been done at about the same time as the *Brunig Pass* and

254   Zurich: fête, early morning   1845
Watercolour, some pencil, with scraping-out, 293 × 475
Kunsthaus, Zurich   (Cat. No. 1548)

Descent of the St. Gothard. But the loose handling of some examples marks them as belonging to a still later date. These drawings also appear to be connected with a series of colour-beginnings, on sheets of paper roughly the size of the finished works. They are distinctive in their mood, sombre browns and blues filling the paper with subdued colour, reinforced occasionally with somewhat untidy penwork. The finished watercolours can be put into an order which demonstrates a plain stylistic development within the set—a development from the manner of the 1845 drawings to a style that is, effectively, entirely 'new'.[36]

Pl.255   The first of the set, stylistically, is perhaps the *Heidelberg* in the National Gallery of Scotland. Its haze of sunlight, bursting from behind the hill to cover the view of the city in a net of filigree pink and gold, is achieved by rather the same process of fine scraping-out that we see in, say, the *Descent of the St. Gothard,* while the generalized handling of the crowded figures in the foreground is close to that of 1845 drawings such as the *Zurich* or *Fluelen from the Lake.* It is a wholly successful work, and, indeed, one of the great masterpieces of

Turner's late years; the perfection with which the all-enveloping atmosphere is rendered, and the glorious colouring, suggest total mastery and control—and yet the technique is quite incompatible with any date before 1844 or 1845. It should not be forgotten that Turner visited Heidelberg for the last time in 1844; it seems likely that the large painting of the city in the Turner Bequest dates from this time, too.[37] But in fact the design of the watercolour is derived from that of the 1840 views mentioned above. The layout and evocation of atmosphere in the watercolour are not unlike the painting of *The visit to the tomb,* which Turner showed at the Academy in 1850. There is a leaf from a roll sketchbook, now in the Victoria and Albert Museum, and known as *Lyons*[38] which, Pl.256 although only a study, is very close in colouring and compositional type both to this *Heidelberg* and to the 1845

255 Heidelberg, *c.* 1846
Watercolour, 372 × 557
National Galleries of Scotland, Edinburgh (Cat. No. 1554)

Zurich: fête; all three drawings are distinguished by an arched
formation of clouds, and by thronging crowds of figures,
with a long many-arched bridge as a central focus.

Although it bears many signs of belonging to the same
phase of Turner's output as the 1845 *Zurich, Heidelberg* is
characterized by a general looseness of touch and blurring of
detail that brings it close to the style and mood of two other
drawings of roughly the same size: one is known as *Pallanza,
Lake Maggiore,* the other as *Lake Geneva.* Both these titles seem
to be inaccurate, though it is probable that both are Swiss
subjects. They seem to have been executed at very much the
same time, for each is carried out in a similar range of
orange-browns and prussian blue, and in each the usual

process of hatching to model details of the landscape has been
carried out in a limited area of the design. In each case, the
foreground with groups of figures seems unfinished; though
the so-called *Lake Geneva* (which actually shows Oberhofen
on Lake Thun) is perhaps a finished work. The treatment of
the figures is close to that in the *Heidelberg,* with which this
pair also shares a very similar approach to composition, as
well as the almost identical sheet size.

One curious feature of the *Oberhofen* is Turner's use in it of
a stepped platform on which the foreground figures stand. It
is a device that appears from time to time in earlier
drawings—the *Arona, Lake Maggiore* of about 1828 might be   Pl.203
cited as an example—but in these cases it is carefully
integrated into the topographical as well as the compositional
structure of the design; that is, Turner presents some
recognizable and specific architectural feature as the foreground where his figures are placed. In the *Oberhofen* the
platform in the foreground has a factitious appearance, as if it

245

Pl. 258

had been invented simply to provide a stage for his figures. If this effect is only marginally obtrusive, it is pronounced in another drawing, the Taft Museum's *Lake of Thun*. Here the parapet on which various figures are sitting or standing is reminiscent of the riverside wall in the *Marly-sur-Seine* of about 1829; but while in the *Marly* Turner makes natural use of an easily understood feature of the scene, in *Lake Thun* he seems to have evolved an elaborate platform to occupy the foreground of the design. (There is no such feature in the *Pallanza,* which may in any case be incomplete.) A similar device occurs in a view of *Florence* which is very like the *Lake Thun* in layout, though it is not on the usual large sheet of

256 Lyons ?*c.* 1846
Watercolour, with some body-colour, 241 × 305
Victoria and Albert Museum, London   (Cat. No. 1555)

paper; and the foreground 'stage' again appears in the *Genoa* at Manchester. *Genoa* and *Lake Thun* seem to form a pair as much as *Pallanza* and *Oberhofen* do; apart from the development of the pronounced 'platform' or stage in the foregrounds of these subjects, it would perhaps be difficult to link all of them together very firmly. *Genoa, Florence* and *Lake Thun* have figures on a larger scale than the others, and are in many

Pl.259

257　The Brunig Pass, from Meiringen　1847–8
Watercolour, 318 × 527
Private collection　(Cat. No. 1550)

respects executed in a very similar manner: the looseness of handling characteristic of all these watercolours reaches an extreme of generalization here, and indeed it is more in total conception than in particular details of execution that we recognize Turner's hand. There may be points of comparison with some of the late 'restatements' of earlier themes among the oil-paintings—*Woman with a Tambourine,* for instance. These are usually dated to the late 1830s, but they have sufficient points of similarity with the watercolours under

discussion to suggest that they too are products of Turner's last years.[39] There is little possibility of these drawings being fitted in to Turner's output at any earlier date; and their size, exactly conformable with that of *Oberhofen* and *Pallanza,* suggests that they belong at the end of the last series of his finished watercolours.

Another sheet, known as *Sion, near the Simplon Pass,* which may have been done shortly after the two drawings bought by Ruskin in 1848, brings the set to seven. The group of colour-beginnings related to the set may supply further subjects that Turner intended for it: one is known as *Lake Nemi,* but is probably of a Swiss scene; it is developed from a roll sketchbook sheet that we might legitimately call a 'sample' study, if Turner had still been referring to patrons for the

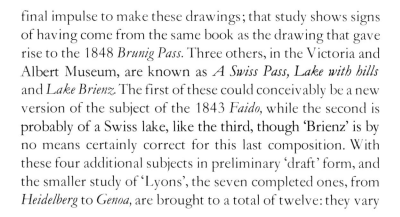

258   Lake of Thun   *c.* 1850–1
Watercolour, 369 × 541
Taft Museum, Cincinnati, Ohio   (Cat. No. 1567)

259   Genoa   *c.* 1850–1
Pencil and watercolour, with blotting-out, 370 × 543
City Art Gallery, Manchester   (Cat. No. 1569)

final impulse to make these drawings; that study shows signs of having come from the same book as the drawing that gave rise to the 1848 *Brunig Pass.* Three others, in the Victoria and Albert Museum, are known as *A Swiss Pass, Lake with hills* and *Lake Brienz.* The first of these could conceivably be a new version of the subject of the 1843 *Faido,* while the second is probably of a Swiss lake, like the third, though 'Brienz' is by no means certainly correct for this last composition. With these four additional subjects in preliminary 'draft' form, and the smaller study of 'Lyons', the seven completed ones, from *Heidelberg* to *Genoa,* are brought to a total of twelve: they vary considerably in technique, implying a steady and fairly rapid movement towards the open, loose manner of *Genoa* and the so-called *Lake Thun;* Turner perhaps was occupied over a longer period than previously in producing so many drawings—they are, it is true, rather larger than usual. But it is difficult to restrain the belief that he was working on a further 'set' of ten when he died. This would be in keeping with his attitude to his work throughout his life, and reaffirms his constant concern with the finished watercolour that can be seen as the most consistent and central medium of communication for him in his entire life's work.

NOTES

1 See Ruskin, *Works*, XIII, p. 99: 'In 1845 his health gave way, and his mind and sight partially failed. The pictures painted in the last five years of his life are of wholly inferior value.' The majority of the drawings discussed here are in the Turner Bequest (CCCLXIV, CCCLXV, and elsewhere).

2 Cat. No. P287.

3 See also the related drawing, with further lines of verse, *Wreck on the Goodwin Sands*, Cat. No. 1426.

4 See chap. 9, p. 224. *Lost to all Hope...* seems to use a motif from one of the oil studies, Cat. No. P459.

5 See, p. 244.

6 Cat. Nos 1376–7.

7 See Rawlinson, No. 663. Turner 'at first discouraged him [Pryor], as his large engravings had not latterly been selling well, but on reflection he yielded and promptly made the *Heidelberg* drawing from a sketch of Pryor's, charging the latter a hundred guineas for it.'

8 See Cat. sections XVI (f), (i).

9 Cat. No. 1379.

10 The sculptured stones in the foreground repeat a motif characteristic of Wilson's Italian views, and used by Turner in his Wilson pastiche, *Aeneas and the Sibyl*, of *c.* 1798.

11 Sketchbooks used on these journeys are probably 1841: *Rhine and Switzerland* (T.B., CCCXXV), *Lucerne and Berne* (T.B., CCCXXVIII), *Between Lucerne and Thun* (T.B., CCCXXIX), *Rhine, Flushing and Lausanne* (T.B., CCCXXX); others, now dismembered, are: *Fribourg, Lausanne and Geneva* (T. B., CCCXXXII), *Fluelen, Berne and Fribourg* (T.B., CCCXXXIII), *Lausanne* (T.B., CCCXXXIV) and *Fribourg* (T.B., CCCXXXV); 1842: roll sketchbooks now apparently broken up and confused, probably including sheets from the series listed in the *Inventory* as T.B., CCCXLI and CCCXLIV; 1843: *Lake of Zug and Goldau* (T.B., CCCXXXI), *Bellinzona* (T.B., CCCXXXVI), *Como and Splügen* (T.B., CCCXXXVIII) and *Mountain Fortress* (T.B., CCCXXXIX); 1844: *Berne, Heidelberg, and Rhine* (T.B., CCCXXVI), *Ostend, Rhine and Berne* (T.B., CCCXXVII), *Lucerne* (T.B., CCCXLV), *Thun, Interlaken, Lauterbrunnen and Grindelwald* (T.B., CCCXLVI), *Meiringen and Grindelwald* (T.B., CCCXLVII), *Grindelwald* (T.B., CCCXLVIII), *Between Olten and Basle* (T.B., CCCL), *Heidelberg* (T.B., CCCLII), *Rheinfelden* (T.B., CCCXLIX), and *Rhine and Rhine Castles* (T.B., CCCLI).

12 Only two of these subjects appeared: *Lake of Lucerne* and *Zurich* (R. 671, 672); Cat. Nos 1547, 1548, both published after Turner's death.

13 Ruskin, *Works*, XIII, pp. 477–84. This account varies slightly from information given elsewhere by Ruskin; the complete list of the finished Swiss watercolours is given here, Cat. section XX, Cat. Nos 1523–49.

14 See R.A. 1974, pp. 154–5.

15 E.g. T.B., CCCXXXIV-10, repr. Wilton, 1977, No. 65, and T.B., CCCXXXII-23, repr. B.M., 1975, No. 274.

16 Cat. No. 1368. Repr. R.A. 1974, p. 148.

17 Ruskin, *Works*, XIII, p. 200. See also Russell and Wilton, 1976, pp. 80, 122.

18 Cat. No. 1528.

19 See above chap. 4, p. 104.

20 See chap. 9, pp. 212–3, and below, note 39.

21 See Gage, 1969, pp. 124–5.

22 See Russell and Wilton, 1976, p. 106.

23 Ruskin, *Works*, XIII, p. 456.

24 Cat. No. 1535.

25 Ruskin, *Works*, VI, pp. 37 ff. See also Russell and Wilton, 1976, p. 110.

26 Another major Romantic artist, Samuel Palmer (1805–81) held exactly the same view; see Foreword and Palmer, *Letters,* ed. Raymond Lister, 1974, vol. I, p. 516.

27 See Finberg, 1910, pp. 134–5.

28 See Russell and Wilton, 1976, p. 122.

29 Cat. No. 544.

30 Ruskin, *Works*, XIII, p. 200.

31 T.B., CCCLXIV-350; repr. Russell and Wilton, 1976, p. 80.

32 T.B., CCCLXIV-343; repr. Russell and Wilton, 1976, p. 112.

33 In the *Fribourg* sketchbook, T.B., CCCXXXV. See Russell and Wilton, 1976, pp. 81–4.

34 See note 11 above, and B.M. 1975, Nos 293–299.

35 See Ruskin, *Works*, XIII, p. 194, and Finberg, *Life,* p. 420. Ruskin's date of 1850 is almost certainly a mistake for 1848. The two drawings are Cat. Nos 1550, 1552.

36 The watercolours of this final group, together with related studies, are Cat. section XX(b), Cat. Nos 1553–69. The sheet watermarked 1846 is *Oberhofen, on Lake Thun*, previously known as 'Lake Geneva', Cat. No. 1557.

37 Cat. No. P440. It was engraved for the *Turner Gallery* as *Heidelberg Castle in the Olden Time* (R. 732). Its swarming crowds of figures seem to belong with those of the second *Zurich* view, and the two *Venice* pairs

shown at the Academy in 1845 and 1846; though such crowds, rather differently handled, occur in pictures of the 1830s as well; e.g. *The Burning of the House of Lords and Commons,* of 1835 (P359; Pl. 215).

38 A colour reproduction is in Butlin, 1962, Pl. 28.

39 The series of 'restatements' (see chap. 9, p. 224) is usually dated to *c.* 1835–40: see Butlin and Joll, Nos 509–522. They are canvases, executed generally in hazy orange-brown and creamy yellow, which reinterpret subjects such as *The fall of the Clyde* of 1802 (Cat. No. 343), probably using as a basis the *Liber Studiorum* plate published in 1809 (R. 18). Other subjects from the *Liber* which appear in the series are *Woman and Tambourine* (R. 3), *Bridge in the Middle Distance* (R. 13), *Solitude* (R. 53), and *The Rape of Europa* (R. 1) after a design Turner sketched as the central motif for the *Liber* frontispiece. Apart from their use of old subjects, and extremely generalized treatment, these canvases have in common with the late set of watercolours under discussion a somewhat mysterious provenance: Ruskin makes no reference to either group, and although all these works are unlike the finished drawings and paintings that Turner usually sold, they did not remain in his studio (see Kitson, 'Un Nouveau Turner au Musée du Louvre', *La Revue du Louvre,* XIX, 1969, pp. 247–56). The implication is that they were among the works that Turner 'suppressed' after he came to feel that Ruskin sensed his powers diminishing, and that after his death they were appropriated by Mrs. Booth or her son, John Pound, who certainly owned two of the oil-paintings. Another of the reinterpretations of *Liber* subjects, however, remained to become part of the Bequest—*Norham Castle, sunrise.* But this is executed in a wider range of colours than the rest, and may perhaps be regarded as being 'outside' the set.

Catalogues of
Paintings and Watercolours

Catalogue of paintings

The following catalogue of Turner's oil-paintings adheres to the numbering in Martin Butlin and Evelyn Joll, *The Paintings of J. M. W. Turner,* 1977, to which work I am indebted for almost all the information here, and to which the reader should refer for full entries on all the paintings. I have restricted the apparatus to notes of the date and place of original exhibition (if any), and references to the 1974-5 Bicentenary exhibitions, where relevant; together with support, dimensions, provenance and present collection. Titles are quoted from the original catalogues when possible. The medium is taken to be oil unless otherwise specified, and measurements are given in millimetres, height before width. Instances of engraving are taken direct from Butlin and Joll, including their references to plates for the *Liber Studiorum,* which, however, are not direct reproductions of pictures; they invariably derive from monochrome drawings adapted by Turner from his painted compositions. These drawings, mostly in the Turner Bequest, are cited. Works illustrated in the main text are indicated by an asterisk placed after the title. Exhibitions at the Royal Academy and the British Institution are denoted by the abbreviations R.A. and B.I. respectively.

The numbering is differentiated from that of the catalogue of watercolours by the prefixed letter P. Where my opinion as to the authenticity or date of a work is at variance with that of Butlin and Joll I have added a note to that effect. I have omitted only the final section of their catalogue, Nos 542–563: Works no longer attributed to Turner; this includes some copies. The catalogue is arranged under the following headings:

1 Early works 1793–1802 (Nos P1–P45)

| Nos P1–P19 | Exhibited pictures | 1796–1802 |
| P20–P45 | Unexhibited works | 1793–1800 |

| | Nos P20–P42 | Miscellaneous |
| | P43–P45 | Copies after other artists |

2 From 1803 to Turner's first visit to Italy 1819 (Nos P46–P227)

| Nos P46–P140 | Exhibited pictures | 1803–1819 |
| P141–P227 | Unexhibited works | 1803–1819 |

	Nos P141–P153	Miscellaneous 1803–1805
	P154–P159	Knockholt sketches c. 1805–1806
	P160–P176	Large Thames sketches c. 1806–1807
	P177–P194	Small Thames sketches c. 1807
	P195–P212	Miscellaneous 1805–1815
	P213–P225	Devon oil sketches c. 1813 (T.B. & Leeds P225)
	P226	Mellon *Lake Avernus*
	P227	Tate *Richmond Hill* c. 1819

3 From Turner's first visit to Italy to his second i.e. 1819–1828 (Nos P228–P291)

| Nos P228–P244 | Exhibited pictures | 1820–1828 |
| P245–P291 | Unexhibited works | 1820–1829 |

	Nos P245–P259	Miscellaneous c. 1820–1825
	P260–P268	Cowes sketches 1827
	P269–P281	Miscellaneous c. 1825–1830
	P282–P291	Petworth landscapes c. 1828–1830

4 Works painted in Rome 1828–1829 (Nos P292–P328)

| Nos P292–P295 | Exhibited pictures | 1828 |
| P296–P328 | Unexhibited works | |

	Nos P296–P301	Miscellaneous
	P302–P317	Roman sketches ?1828
	P318–P327	Small Italian sketches ?1828
	P328	Miscellaneous c. 1825–1830

5 Later works 1829–1851 (Nos P329–P532)

| Nos P329–P432 | Exhibited pictures | |
| P433–P532 | Unexhibited works | 1829-1851 |

	Nos P433–P486	Miscellaneous
	P487–P500	Sketches of Coast and other scenes ?c. 1840–1845
	P501–P508	Venice c. 1835–1845
	P509–P532	Miscellaneous

6 Untraced works of unknown date (Nos P533–P541)

1 Early Works 1793–1802 (Nos P1-P45)

Nos P1–P19
Exhibited pictures 1796–1802

P1 Fishermen at sea ('The Cholmeley Sea Piece')* R.A. 1796 (305)

Canvas, 915 x 1224
Engr.: in mezzotint by Turner for his *Liber Studiorum,* unpubl. (R. 85)
Exh.: R.A. 1974(19)
Prov.: purchased by General Stewart 1796; ...by descent to F. W. A. Fairfax-Cholmeley; sold through Agnew to the Tate Gallery 1972
Coll.: Tate Gallery, London (1585)

P2 Moonlight, a study at Millbank R.A. 1797 (136)

Mahogany, 315 x 405
Exh.: R.A. 1974 (20)
Coll.: Turner Bequest, Tate Gallery, London (459)

P3 Fishermen coming ashore at sun set, previous to a gale ('The Mildmay Sea Piece') R.A. 1797 (344)

Canvas, 915 x 1220
Engr.: in mezzotint by W. Annis and I. C. Easling for the *Liber Studiorum,* publ. 11 February 1812 (R. 40)
Prov.: perhaps painted for Sir John Mildmay, Bt.; G. R. Burnett; sale Christie 24 March 1860 (82, as 'Autumnal sunset at sea'), bt. Shepherd
Coll.: untraced

P4 Winesdale, Yorkshire, an Autumnal morning R.A. 1798 (118)

Size unknown
The title probably refers to Wensleydale, visited by Turner during his sketching tour in the summer of 1797
Coll.: untraced

P5 Morning amongst the Coniston Fells, Cumberland R.A. 1798 (196)

Canvas, 1230 x 897
Coll.: Turner Bequest, Tate Gallery, London (461)

The following verses appeared with the title in the catalogue:

> "Ye mists and exhalations that now rise
> From hill or streaming [*sic*] lake, dusky or gray,
> Till the sun paints your fleecy skirts with gold,
> In honour to the world's great Author, rise."
> Milton Par. Lost, Book V.

P6 Dunstanburgh Castle, N.E. coast of Northumberland. Sun-rise after a squally night* R.A. 1798 (322)

Canvas, 920 x 1230
Engr.: in mezzotint by Charles Turner for the *Liber Studiorum,* publ. 10 June 1808 (R.14).
Prov.: W. Penn, of Stoke Poges, by 1808; almost certainly Granville Penn, of Stoke Poges Court; sale Christie 10 July 1851 (69, as 'Corfe Castle from the sea'), bt. Gambart; M. T. Birchall by 1857, from whom bt. by Agnew, 1870, and sold to John Heugh, sale Christie 24 April 1874 (184), bt. Mayne (for the Duke of Westminster), sale Christie 10 May 1884 (99), bt. in; presented to the National Gallery of Victoria by the first duke, 1888
Coll.: National Gallery of Victoria, Melbourne, Australia (313/1)

The following verses appeared with the title in the catalogue:

> "The precipice abrupt,
> Breaking horror on the blacken'd flood,
> Softens at thy return. —The desert joys,
> Wildly thro' all his melancholy bounds,
> Rude ruins glitter; and the briny deep,
> Seen from some pointed promontory's top,
> Far from the blue horizon's utmost verge,
> Restless reflects a floating gleam."
> Vide Thompson's Seasons.

P7 Buttermere Lake with part of Cromackwater, Cumberland, a shower* R.A. 1798 (527)

Canvas, 915 x 1220
Exh.: R.A. 1974 (30)
Coll.: Turner Bequest, Tate Gallery, London (460)

The following verses appeared with the title in the catalogue:

> "Till in the western sky the downward sun
> Looks out effulgent — The rapid radiance instantaneous strikes
> The illumin'd mountains —in a yellow mist
> Bestriding earth —the grand ethereal bow
> Shoots up immense, and every hue unfolds."
> Vide Thompson's Seasons.

P8 Fishermen becalmed previous to a storm, twilight R.A. 1799 (55)

Size unknown
Provenance and whereabouts unknown

P9 Harlech Castle, from Twgwyn ferry, summer's evening twilight R.A. 1799 (192)

Canvas, 870 x 1195
Prov.: acquired from the artist by the fifth Earl Cowper; the Hon. H. Finch-Hatton by 1903; Sir Donald Currie; by descent to Mrs. M. D. Fergusson, from whom bt. Agnew 1961 and sold to present collection the same year
Coll.: Yale Center for British Art, Paul Mellon Collection

The following verses appeared with the title in the catalogue:

> "Now came still evening on, and twilight grey,
> Had in her sober livery all things clad."
> "— Hesperus that led
> The starry host rode brightest till the moon
> Rising in clouded majesty unveiled her peerless light."
> Milton's Par. Lost, Book 4.

P10 Battle of the Nile, at 10 o'clock when the L'Orient blew up, from the station of the gun boats between the battery and castle of Aboukir R.A. 1799 (275)

Size unknown
Provenance and whereabouts unknown

P11 Kilgarran castle on the Twyvey; hazy sunrise, previous to a sultry day* R.A. 1799 (305)

Canvas, 920 x 1220
Engr.: by J. Young in the *Leicester Gallery* 1821 (27)
Exh.: R.A. 1974 (47)
Prov.: probably William Delamotte, the painter (1775–1863); Sir John Leicester (later Lord de Tabley), sale Christie 7 July 1827 (17), bt. Butter-

worth; William Cave; sale, Christie 29 June 1854 (61), bt. Wallis; anon. sale Foster 3 February 1858 (106), bt. in; Joseph Gillott, sale Christie 27 April 1872 (305), bt. H. L. Bischoffsheim; bequeathed to his daughter Lady Fitzgerald; by descent to Lady Mildred Fitzgerald, who bequeathed the picture to the National Trust, 1970
Coll.: National Trust (on loan to Wordsworth's House, Cockermouth)

P12   Dolbadern Castle, North Wales*
R.A. 1800 (200)

Canvas, 1195 x 902
Exh.: R.A. 1974 (48)
Prov.: Turner's Diploma Work deposited by the artist after his election as an Academician on 12 February 1802.
Coll.: Royal Academy of Arts, Burlington House.

The following verses appeared with the title in the catalogue:

> How awful is the silence of the waste,
> Where nature lifts her mountains to the sky.
> Majestic solitude, behold the tower
> Where hopeless OWEN, long imprison'd, pin'd,
> And wrung his hands for liberty, in vain.

P13   The fifth plague of Egypt*   R.A. 1800 (206)

Canvas, 1240 x 1830
Engr.: in mezzotint by C. Turner for the *Liber Studiorum*, publ. 10 June 1808 (R. 16)
Exh.: R.A. 1974 (206)
Prov.: William Beckford, of Fonthill, sale at Fonthill 24 August 1807 (581), bt. Jeffrey; George Young by 1853; sale Christie 19 May 1866 (26), bt. Lord Grosvenor, later Marquess of Westminster; Sir J. R. Robinson; bt. from him by Sir Francis Cook, Bt., in 1876; bt. by Agnew from the Cook Collection in 1852 and sold to Sir Alexander Korda, 1953, who sold it through E. Speelman Ltd. in 1955 to the John Herron Art Museum, Indianapolis; since 1970 the Indianapolis Museum of Art
Coll.: Indianapolis Museum of Art, Indiana (gift in memory of Evan F. Lilly)

In the R.A. catalogue, the title was accompanied by a quotation from Exodus, chap. IX, ver. 23, referring to the plague of hail and fire.

P14   Dutch boats in a gale: fishermen endeavouring to put their fish on board ('The Bridgewater Sea Piece')*   R.A. 1801 (157)

Canvas, 1625 x 2220
Engr.: by J. Fittler for the *British Gallery of Pictures — Stafford Gallery*, 1812;

by J. Young for the *Stafford Gallery*, 1825; by J. C. Armytage in *The Turner Gallery*, 1859
Exh.: R.A. 1974 (71)
Prov.: painted for Francis Egerton, third and last Duke of Bridgewater; bequeathed with a life interest to his nephew, first Marquess of Stafford, with reversion to his nephew's second son, Lord Francis Leveson Gower, later first Earl of Ellesmere; by descent, then sold by the Trustees of the Ellesmere 1939 Settlement, Christie 18 June 1976 (121), bt. Hazlitt, Gooden and Fox for present owner
Private collection, England

P15   The army of the Medes destroyed in the desart by a whirlwind — foretold by Jeremiah, chap. xv, ver. 32 and 33   R.A. 1801 (281)

Size unknown
Provenance and whereabouts unknown

P16   Fishermen upon a lee-shore, in squally weather   R.A. 1802 (110)

Canvas, 914 x 1220
Engr.: by J. Cousen in *The Turner Gallery*, 1859, as 'Fishing Boats; a Coast Scene'
Prov.: bt. from the artist by Samuel Dobree; by descent to his son, H. H. Dobree; sale Christie 17 June 1842 (11, as 'A fishing boat pulling off from the shore, among the breakers, near a wooden pier, which another boat is approaching, under a grand stormy sky in a fresh breeze'), bt. E. S. Ellis, sale Christie 16 April 1853 (84, as 'A seashore with a fishing boat pushing off and a lugger making for the mouth of a harbour, a fine gleam of sunshine breaking through the clouds above'), bt. Gambart; Charles Birch; Francis T. Rufford by 1857; T. Horrocks Miller by 1889; by descent to Thomas Pitt Miller, sale Christie 26 April 1946 (111), bt. Agnew; D. V. Shaw-Kennedy, sold for his executors by Agnew to the Gallery, 1951
Coll.: Southampton Art Gallery

One of two pictures acquired by Dobree; the other, P144, was until recently known by the title of this, the exhibited work.

P17   The tenth plague of Egypt*   R.A. 1802 (153)

Canvas, 1420 x 2360
Engr.: in mezzotint by W. Say for the *Liber Studiorum*, publ. 1 January 1816 (R. 61)
Coll.: Turner Bequest, Tate Gallery, London (470)

P18   Ships bearing up for anchorage ('The Egremont Sea Piece')*   R.A. 1802 (227)

Canvas, 1195 x 1803
Sig. lower right: *J M W Turner pinx*
Engr.: in mezzotint by Charles Turner for the *Liber Studiorum*, publ. 20 February 1808 (entitled 'Ships in a breeze', R. 10). The composition of the print is considerably more concentrated than that of the oil-painting; the sepia drawing for the print is T.B., CXVI-M
Exh.: R.A. 1974 (72)
Prov.: bought from the artist by George, third Earl of Egremont, possibly in 1802, but in his collection by 1805; by descent to the third Lord Leconfield, who in 1947 conveyed Petworth to the

National Trust; in 1957 the contents of the State Rooms accepted by the Treasury in part payment of death duties
Coll.: H. M. Treasury and the National Trust (Lord Egremont Collection), Petworth House (33)

P19   Jason   R.A. 1802 (519)

Canvas, 900 x 1195
Engr.: in mezzotint by Charles Turner for the *Liber Studiorum*, publ. 11 June 1807 (R. 6). The pen and sepia drawing for the print is T.B., CXVI-E
Exh.: R.A. 1974 (73)
Coll.: Turner Bequest, Tate Gallery, London (471)

Nos P20–P45
Unexhibited works 1793–1800

Nos P20–P42 Miscellaneous

P20   Self-portrait   c. 1793

Canvas, 520 x 420
Inscr. on the frame: *J M W TURNER SUA MANU LUSTRO ETATIS QUARTO*
Prov.: said to have been given by Turner to his housekeeper, Hannah Danby, and bequeathed by her in 1854 to John Ruskin; bequeathed by Ruskin to Arthur and Joan Severn; at Brantwood until Severn's death in 1931; sale Sotheby 20 May 1931 (132), bt. Sir Arthur Russell, Bt.; Marjorie, Lady Russell; Christie 21 March 1969 (76), bt. Agnew for Kurt Pantzer, and given to Indianapolis Museum, 1972
Coll.: Indianapolis Museum of Art, Indiana (gift in memory of Dr. and Mrs. Hugo O. Pantzer by their children)

P21   Rochester Castle, with fishermen drawing boats ashore in a gale   c. 1794

Size unknown
Prov.: Dr. Nixon, Bishop of Tasmania, in 1854 (according to Thornbury the picture was finished at Foot's Cray parsonage, 'the residence of the father of Dr. Nixon').
Coll.: untraced

P22   Limekiln at Coalbrookdale   c. 1797

Panel, 290 x 377
Engr.: by F. C. Lewis, 1825
Prov.: J. J. Chalon, R.A. by 1825; perhaps John Clow; sale Winstanley 3 December 1852 (89, as

'''Lime Kilns by night'' drawing, engraved'), bt. in; Wallis; sale Christie 16 April 1853 (108), bt. in; C. G. Potter sale Christie 6 March 1886 (167), bt. in; C. V. Bagot sale Christie 1 July 1905 (112), bt. in; P. Potter; bt. from Mrs. Potter by Agnew, 1909; Christie 18 March 1911 (93), bt. in; W. Lockett Agnew, sale Christie 8 June 1918 (70), bt. Walford; D. F. Ward, sale Sotheby 23 November 1966 (86), bt. Patch; bt. by present owners from Agnew, 1967
Coll.: Yale Center for British Art, Paul Mellon Collection

P23 Interior of a Romanesque church c. 1795–1800

Mahogany, 610 x 500
Coll.: Turner Bequest, Tate Gallery, London (5529)

P24 Interior of a Gothic church c. 1797

Mahogany, 280 x 405
Engr.: in mezzotint by the artist for the *Liber Studiorum*, publ. 1 January 1819 (R. 70)
Coll.: Turner Bequest, Tate Gallery, London (5536)

P25 Self-portrait c. 1798

Canvas, 745 x 585
Exh.: R.A. 1974 (B1)
Coll.: Turner Bequest, Tate Gallery, London (458)

P26,
P27 Two views of Plompton Rocks c. 1798

Canvas, each 1220 x 1375
Exh.: R.A. 1974 (31,32)
Prov.: painted c. 1798 for Edward Lascelles, first Earl of Harewood, or possibly for his son Edward, later Viscount Lascelles, for the Library at Harewood, where they remain
Coll.: The Earl of Harewood

P28 Caernarvon castle c. 1798

Pine, 155 x 230
Exh.: R.A. 1974 (45)
Coll.: Turner Bequest, Tate Gallery, London (1867)

P29 View in Wales: mountain scene with village and castle — evening c. 1798

Coll.: Turner Bequest, Tate Gallery, London (466)

P30 Mountain scene with castle c. 1798

Canvas, 440 x 540
Exh.: R.A. 1974 (35)
Coll.: Turner Bequest, Tate Gallery, London (465)

P31 View of a town c. 1798

Canvas, 240 x 325
Exh.: R.A. 1974 (34)
Coll.: Turner Bequest, Tate Gallery, London (475)

P32 Dunstanborough Castle c. 1798

Canvas, 470 x 690
Prov.: Simms; A. Andrews (not included in his sale at Christie 14 April 1888); Messrs. Dowdeswell; A. G. Temple, from whom bt. Agnew, 1899, and sold to E. F. Milliken, New York; anon. (Milliken) sales Christie 3 May 1902 (43) and 23 May 1903 (79), bt. in on both occasions; Mrs. C. M. de Graff; sale Christie 21 February 1930 (75), bt. Meatyard, from whom bt. Leggatt, and sold to Dunedin, 1931
Coll.: Dunedin Public Art Gallery, New Zealand

P33 Shipping by a breakwater c. 1798

Mahogany, 303 x 194
Exh.: R.A. 1794 (33)
Coll.: Turner Bequest, Tate Gallery, London (469)

P34 Aeneas and the Sibyl, Lake Avernus* c. 1798

Canvas, 765 x 985
Exh.: R.A. 1974 (46)
Coll.: Turner Bequest, Tate Gallery, London (463)

P35 Wild landscape, with figures, sunset c. 1799–1800

Oil and ink on paper, 261 x 388
Coll.: Trustees of the British Museum (T.B., XCV (a)-G)

P36 Kilgarran Castle c. 1799

Canvas, 558 x 685
Prov.: Wynn Ellis; sale Christie 6 May 1876 (117), bt. Beaumont; Wentworth B. Beaumont; sale Christie 30 May 1891 (86), bt. in; by descent to the present owner
Coll.: The Viscount Allendale

P37 Kilgarran Castle c. 1799–1800

Canvas, 603 x 742
Engr.: by Gustave Greux for the J. W. Wilson Exhibition Catalogue, 1873
Prov.: Joseph Gillott, who bt. it from the artist; sale Christie 27 April 1872 (303), bt. Leon Gauchez, dealer in Brussels; John W. Wilson, Brussels; sale, Hôtel Drouot, Paris, 27–8 April 1874 (13), bt. M. Outran; anon. (L. Gauchez) sale Christie 10 May 1879 (58), bt. Levy; executors of Albert Levy, sale Christie 3 May 1884 (14), bt. in; Martin H. Colnaghi; Arthur Sanderson, Edinburgh; sale Christie 3 July 1908 (46), bt. in; G. Beatson Blair, Manchester; R. B. Beckett, from whom purchased by the Leicester Museum, 1955
Coll.: Leicester Museum and Art Gallery (71A 1955)

P38 Mountain landscape with a lake ('In the Trossachs') c. 1799–1800

Canvas, 641 x 988
Prov.: H. A. J. Munro of Novar by 1857; anon. sale Christie 15 June 1861 (96, as 'Loch Katrine'), bt. in; Munro sale, Christie 11 May 1867 (180, as 'Loch Katrine or the Trossachs'), bt. White; bt. from White by Agnew, 1869, as 'Loch Katrine' and sold in 1870 to K. D. Hodgson; bt. back by

Agnew in 1893 and sold to James Orrock, sale Christie 27 April 1895 (308), bt. in; bt. from Orrock by Agnew 1901 and sold same year to Humphrey Roberts, sale Christie 21 May 1908 (102), bt. Agnew, who sold it to W. B. Paterson (dealer); bt. from the Marlay Fund by the Fitzwilliam Museum in 1925 through Paterson from an anonymous owner
Coll.: Fitzwilliam Museum, Cambridge (Marlay Additions 17)

P39 Landscape with lake and fallen tree c. 1800?

Canvas, 390 x 605
Coll.: Turner Bequest, Tate Gallery, London (3557)

P40 A storm in the mountains c. 1801–2

Canvas, 240 x 305
Prov.: Wynn Ellis; sale Christie 6 May 1876 (110), bt. Agnew; H. Crossley; H. Darrell-Brown by 1899; sale Christie 23 May 1924 (43) bt. Agnew; Miss A. G. Bickham; sale Christie 25 November 1927 (49), bt. Agnew; H. L. Fison, 1927; sale Christie 6 November 1959 (28), bt. Agnew for Mrs. E. A. Leavett-Shenley; sale Christie 17 March 1967 (67), bt. Agnew for the present owner
Coll.: Lady Kleinwort

P41 Tummel Bridge, Perthshire c. 1802–3

Panel, 280 x 465
Engr.: by J. Barnard, 1852
Prov.: R. Nicholson, of York, sale Christie 13 July 1849 (207, as 'Dummel Bridge'), bt. Wallis; anon. sale Christie 1 April 1852 (84, as 'Dummel Bridge'), bt. Gambart; John Miller, of Liverpool, sale Christie 22 May 1858 (244), bt. Gambart; bt. Agnew, 1858, from Rought and sold to R. P. Grey; bt. back by Agnew, 1863, and sold to James Fenton, sale Christie 28 February 1880 (405), bt. Wertheimer; Sigismund Rucker (sold before 1902); Mrs. Tempest Hicks; sale Christie 26 November 1926 (116), bt. in; bt. Pawsey and Payne, from whom bt. Agnew and sold to R. W. Lloyd, 1927; bt. by present owners from Oscar and Peter Johnson Ltd., 1963
Coll.: Yale Center for British Art, Paul Mellon Collection

P42 View on Clapham Common c. 1800–5

Mahogany, 320 x 445
Coll.: Turner Bequest, Tate Gallery, London (468)

Apparently a work of the same date as the Knockholt sketches; see note to Nos P154– P159.

Nos P43–P45 Copies after other artists

P43 Diana and Callisto c. 1796

Canvas, 565 x 915
Coll.: Turner Bequest, Tate Gallery, London (5490)

A copy or variant of Richard Wilson's composition of this subject.

P44 Tivoli: Temple of the Sibyl and the Roman Campagna *c.* 1798

Canvas, 735 x 965
Exh.: R.A. 1974 (B36)
Coll.: Turner Bequest, Tate Gallery, London (5512)

Based on a composition by Richard Wilson that exists in a number of versions.

P45 Landscape with windmill and rainbow *c.* 1795–1800

Canvas, 705 x 900
Coll.: Turner Bequest, Tate Gallery, London (5489)

Based on a composition by Gainsborough, now lost, but known from an engraving and an old sale catalogue reproduction.

2 From 1803 to Turner's first visit to Italy 1819 (Nos P46–P227)

Nos P46–P140
Exhibited pictures 1803–1819

P46 Bonneville Savoy, with Mont Blanc R.A. 1803 (24)

Canvas, 915 x 1220
Prov.: John Green, sale Christie (at Green's house in Blackheath) 26 April 1830 (72, as 'A view in Switzerland with Mont Blanc in the distance'), bt. Munro of Novar; Henry Webb, from whom bt. Agnew, 1861; John Heugh, from whom bt. Agnew, 1863, and sold to Thomas Miller; by descent to Thomas Pitt Miller of Singleton Park, near Blackpool, sale Christie 26 April 1946 (109), bt. Agnew for the father of the present owner
Private collection, Scotland

P47 The festival upon the opening of the vintage at Macon* R.A. 1803 (110)

Canvas, 1460 × 2375
Exh.: B.I. 1849 (43); R.A. 1974 (76)
Prov.: bought from the artist by the Earl of Yarborough, 1804; by descent until Yarborough sale, Christie 12 July 1929 (106), bt. Agnew; sold in 1938 to Gooden and Fox on behalf of E. E. Cook; bequeathed to Sheffield through the National Art-Collections Fund by E. E. Cook, 1955
Coll.: City Art Galleries, Sheffield

P48 Calais Pier, with French poissards preparing for sea: an English packet arriving* R.A. 1803 (146)

Canvas, 1720 × 2400
Engr.: in mezzotint by T. Lupton, unpubl., 1827
Exh.: R.A. 1974 (75)
Coll.: Turner Bequest, Tate Gallery, London (472)

P49 Holy Family* R.A. 1803 (156)

Canvas, 1020 × 1415
Exh.: R.A. 1974 (77)
Coll.: Turner Bequest, Tate Gallery, London (473)

P50 Chateaux de St. Michael, Bonneville, Savoy* R.A. 1803 (237)

Canvas, 915 × 1220
Exh.: R.A. 1974 (74)
Prov.: bought from the artist by Samuel Dobree, 1804; William Young Ottley, from whom bt. by the first Earl of Camperdown, sale Christie 21 February 1919 (159), bt. Agnew; Capt. R. A. Tatton, sale Christie 14 December 1928 (59), bt. Agnew for S. L. (later Sir Stephen) Courtauld, sale Sotheby 27 June 1973 (55), bt. Agnew, by whom sold to the present owners, 1977
Coll.: Yale Center for British Art, Paul Mellon Collection

P51 Old Margate Pier ? Turner's gallery 1804

Panel, 275 × 407
Prov.: given by the artist to Samuel Dobree, 1804; by descent to his son, H. H. Dobree, sale Christie 17 June 1842 (10), bt. Bonamy Dobree; Holbrook Gaskell, sale 11 June 1920 (41), bt. in; inherited from Sir Holbrook Gaskell's estate by present owner, 1951
Coll.: Ernest Gaskell, Wolverhampton

P52 Boats carrying out anchors and cables to Dutch men of war, in 1665 R.A. 1804 (183)

Canvas, 1015 × 1305
Exh.: R.A. 1974 (79)
Prov.: bought from the artist by Samuel Dobree, 1804; Thomas, Lord Delamere; anon. (executors of Lord Delamere) sale Christie 24 May 1856 (128), bt. in; acquired after sale by W. Benoni White, sale Christie 24 May 1879 (280), bt. White (? member of the family), W. Houldsworth, sale Christie 23 May 1891 (57), bt. in; sale Christie 11 May 1896, bt. McLean; Sir Horatio Davies, Bt., M.P., by

1899; Sir George Donaldson by 1903; bt. from him by W. A. Clark, Senator for Montana, 1907, and bequeathed with his collection to the Corcoran Gallery, 1926
Coll.: Corcoran Gallery of Art (W. A. Clark Collection), Washington, D. C.

P53 Narcissus and Echo R.A. 1804 (207)

Canvas, 863 × 1168
Engr.: in soft ground etching by the artist for the *Liber Studiorum*, unpubl. (R.90)
Prov.: bought from the artist by the third Earl of Egremont between 1810 and 1819; by descent to the third Lord Leconfield, who in 1947 conveyed Petworth to the National Trust; 1957, the contents of the State Rooms accepted by the Treasury in part payment of death duties.
Coll.: H. M. Treasury and the National Trust (Lord Egremont Collection), Petworth House (46)

The following verses appeared with the title in the catalogue:

"So melts the youth, and languishes away;
His beauty withers, and his limbs decay;
And none of those attractive charms remain
To which the slighted Echo su'd in vain.
She saw him in his present misery
Whom spite of all her wrongs, she griev'd to see:
She answer'd sadly to the lover's moan,
Sigh'd back his sighs, and groan'd to every groan:
'Ah youth, belov'd in vain!' Narcissus cries;
'Ah youth, belov'd in vain!' the nymph replies.
'Farewell!' says he: the parting sound scarce fell
From his faint lips, but she rèply'd 'farewell!'''

P54   The Shipwreck   Turner's gallery   1805

Canvas, 1705 × 2415
Engr.: in mezzotint by Charles Turner, 1806, publ.
1 January 1807 (R. 751)
in aquatint by T. Fielding, 1825 (R. 828)
Exh.: R.A. 1974 (82)
Prov.: bought 1806 by Sir John Leicester;
exchanged 1807 for *Fall of the Rhine at Schaff-hausen* (No. P61)
Coll.: Turner Bequest, Tate Gallery, London (476)

P55   The Deluge   ? Turner's gallery   1805

Canvas, 1430 × 2350
Engr.: by J. P. Quilley, 1828
Exh.: R.A. 1974 (81)
Coll.: Turner Bequest, Tate Gallery, London (493)

P56   The Destruction of Sodom   ? Turner's gallery   1805

Canvas, 1460 × 2375
Coll.: Turner Bequest, Tate Gallery, London (474)

P57   The Goddess of Discord choosing the apple of contention in the garden of the Hesperides*   B.I. 1806 (55)

Canvas, 1550 × 2185
Coll.: Turner Bequest, Tate Gallery, London (477)

P58   Battle of Trafalgar, as seen from the mizen starboard shrouds of the Victory   Turner's gallery   1806

Canvas, 1710 × 2390
Sig. on bulwark lower centre: *JMW Turner*
Exh.: R.A. 1974 (84)
Coll.: Turner Bequest, Tate Gallery, London (480)

P59   The Victory returning from Trafalgar   ? Turner's gallery   1806

Canvas, 670 × 750
Engr.: a drawing in the British Museum (CXVIII-C, Vaughan Bequest) is listed to be engraved for the *Liber Studiorum* (R. 99), but unpubl.
Prov.: bought by Walter Fawkes from the artist; by descent to Revd. Ayscough Fawkes, sale Christie 27 June 1890 (61), bt. Agnew for Sir Donald Currie; by descent to his grand-daughter, Mrs. L. B. Murray, from whom bt. Agnew 1960 and sold to Paul Mellon
Coll.: Yale Center for British Art, Paul Mellon Collection

P60   Walton Bridges   ? Turner's gallery 1806

Canvas, 927 × 1238
Sig. lower right: *JMW Turner RA*
Exh.: Birmingham Society of Artists, 1847 (129); R.A. 1974 (131)
Prov.: bought from the artist by Sir John Leicester by 1807, and either exchanged or sold by him before 1819; Thomas Wright of Upton, sale Christie 7 June 1845 (58), bt. Pennell; Joseph Gillott by 1847, sale Christie 27 April 1872 (307), bt. Agnew

for H. W. F. Bolchow, sale Christie 2 May 1891 (105), bt. Agnew, from whom bt. Lord Wantage; by descent to the present owner
Coll.: Loyd Collection

P61   Fall of the Rhine at Schaffhausen*   R.A. 1806 (182)

Canvas, 1447 × 2337
Prov.: bought from the artist by Sir John Leicester in 1807 in part exchange for *The Shipwreck* (No. P54); remained in the Tabley collection until 1912, when bt. from Lady Leicester Warren by Agnew and Sulley, and sold by Sulley to the Boston Museum, 1913
Coll.: Museum of Fine Arts, Boston, Mass. (13.2723; bequest of Alice Marian Curtis and special picture Fund)

P62   Sheerness and the Isle of Sheppey, with the Junction of the Thames and the Medway from the Nore ('The junction of the Thames and the Medway')   ? Turner's gallery   1807

Canvas, 1086 × 1435
Engr.: by J. Fisher (R. 168a), plate unfinished
Prov.: bought by Thomas Lister Parker in 1807, probably from Turner's gallery; Parker sale Christie 9 March 1811 (29), bt. in; John Newington Hughes, of Winchester; sale Christie 15 April 1848 (147), bt. Thomas Rought, from whom bt. by Joseph Gillott, 3 May 1848, sale Christie 28 April 1872 (306), bt. Agnew; Richard Hemming; bt. Agnew from Mrs. Hemming 1892 and sold 1893 to Wallis and Co., who sold it to P. A. B. Widener, of Philadelphia; passed to the National Gallery with the Widener Collection 1942
Coll.: National Gallery of Art, Widener Collection, Washington, D. C.

P63 Walton Bridges ? Turner's gallery 1807
Canvas, 922 × 1224
Engr.: by A. Boulard, 1895, publ. by A. Tooth and Sons
Exh.: R.A. 1974 (132)
Prov.: bought by the Earl of Essex possibly from Turner's gallery in 1807; sale 'Modern Pictures from Cassiobury Park collected early in the century by George, 5th Earl of Essex' Christie 22 July 1893 (47), bt. in; James Orrock before winter of 1899–1900; sale Christie 4 June 1904 (139), bt. Agnew; bt. back by Orrock 1905; Sir Joseph Beecham by 1910, sale Christie 3 May 1917 (75), bt. Duncan; acquired by Frank Rinder in 1919–1920 for the Felton Bequest
Coll.: National Gallery of Victoria, Melbourne (Felton Bequest)

P64 The Thames near Windsor ? Turner's gallery 1807

Canvas, 890 × 1194
Prov.: bought by Lord Egremont, possibly 1807; by descent to the third Lord Leconfield, who in 1947 conveyed Petworth to the National Trust; in 1957 the contents of the State Rooms accepted by the Treasury in part payment of death duties
Coll.: H. M. Treasury and the National Trust (Lord Egremont Collection), Petworth House (21)

P65 Newark Abbey on the Wey ? Turner's gallery 1807

Canvas, 915 × 1230
Prov.: Sir John Leicester (later Lord de Tabley), sale Christie (at 24 Hill Street) 7 July 1827 (19, as 'Thames Lighter at Teddington'), bt. Sir Thomas Lawrence, sale Christie 15 May 1830 (117, as

'Canal scene with barges'), bt. Penney; Pall Mall Gallery; sale Christie 20 March 1838 (214, as '"The Lock–glowing effect of sunlight'. From Lord de Tabley's Collection"), bt. in; John Allnutt; Charles Macdonald of Cressbrook, sale Christie 29 May 1855 (77, as 'Newark Castle'), bt. in; Christie 5 June 1858 (51), bt. Gregory; anon. sale Christie 22 May 1868 (86), bt. Agnew and sold to Thomas Woolner, R.A.; Kirkman Hodgson, M. P., from whom bt. back by Agnew in 1893 and sold to James Orrock; bt. back by Agnew in 1901 and sold to Sir Charles Tennant, Bt.; by descent to the Hon. Colin Tennant, from whom bt. Agnew in 1961 and sold to Paul Mellon
Coll.: Yale Center for British Art, Paul Mellon Collection

P66 Cliveden on Thames ? Turner's gallery 1807

Canvas, 385 × 585
Prov.: Mrs. E. Vaughan, bequeathed 1885 to the National Gallery; transferred to the Tate Gallery 1912.
Coll.: Tate Gallery, London (1180)

P67 The Mouth of the Thames ? Turner's gallery 1807

Canvas, 308 × 457
Engr.: in mezzotint by Frank Short, R.A.
Prov.: bought by Agnew from Pennell in February 1864 and sold to William Holmes in September; L. Flatow; sale Christie 9 June 1865 (53), bt. Colnaghi; Hugh Lupus Grosvenor, first Duke of Westminster, by 1868; by descent in Grosvenor family; Trustees of the Grosvenor Estate; destroyed by enemy action during Second World War

P68 A country blacksmith disputing upon the price of iron, and the price charged to the butcher for shoeing his poney R.A. 1807 (135)

Oil (550 × 780) on pine (575 × 805)
Sig. lower left: *JMW Turner RA*
Exh.: R.A. 1974 (133)
Prov.: bought 1808 by Sir John Leicester (later first Lord de Tabley), sale Christie 7 July 1827 (14), bt. by the artist
Coll.: Turner Bequest, Tate Gallery, London (478)

P69 Sun rising through vapour; fishermen cleaning and selling fish* R.A. 1807
Canvas, 1345 × 1790
Prov.: bought 1818 by Sir John Leicester (later Lord de Tabley), sale Christie 7 July 1827 (46), bt. by the artist
Coll.: Turner Bequest, National Gallery, London (479)

P70 Union of the Thames and Isis Turner's gallery 1808

Canvas, 910 × 1215
Inscr. lower left: *J M W Turner RA*
Coll.: Turner Bequest, Tate Gallery, London (462)

P71 The Thames at Eton Turner's gallery 1808

Canvas, 595 × 900
Prov.: bought by Lord Egremont, perhaps from the 1808 exhibition at Turner's gallery; by descent to the third Lord Leconfield, who in 1947 conveyed Petworth to the National Trust; 1957 the contents of the State Rooms accepted by the Treasury in part payment of death duties

Coll.: H. M. Treasury and the National Trust (Lord Egremont Collection), Petworth House (108)

P72   Pope's Villa at Twickenham* Turner's gallery   1808

Canvas, 915 × 1206
Sig. lower left: *JMW   Turner RA PP*
Exh.: R.A. 1974 (148)
Engr.: by John Pye (figures by J. Heath) for Britton's *Fine Arts of the English School,* 1811
Prov.: bought by Sir John Leicester (created Lord de Tabley 1826) from Turner's gallery in 1808; sale Christie (at 24 Hill Street, London) 7 July 1827 (24), bt. James Morrison; by descent to the present owners
Coll.: Trustees of the Walter Morrison Picture Settlement

P73   View of Richmond Hill and Bridge Turner's gallery   1808

Canvas, 815 × 1220
Coll.: Turner Bequest, Tate Gallery, London (557)

P74   Purfleet and the Essex Shore as seen from Long Reach Turner's gallery   1808

Canvas, 914 × 1220
Sig. and dated lower right: *JMW Turner RA PP 1808*
Prov.: bought by the Earl of Essex from Turner's gallery in 1808; sale 'Modern Pictures from Cassiobury Park collected early in the century by George, 5th Earl of Essex', Christie 22 July 1893 (48), bt. in; John H. McFadden, Philadelphia, by 1899; George J. Gould, Lakewood, New Jersey by 1900; Alister McDonal, sale Christie 1 June 1945

(65), bt. Goris; Baron C. E. Janssen, Brussels, from whom purchased by the present owner
Private collection, Belgium

P75   The Confluence of the Thames and the Medway Turner's gallery   1808

Canvas, 890 × 1194
Sig. lower right: *JMW Turner RA fe*
Prov.: bought by the third Earl of Egremont, probably from Turner's gallery in 1808; by descent to the third Lord Leconfield, who in 1947 conveyed Petworth to the National Trust; in 1957 the contents of the State Rooms accepted by the Treasury in part payment of death duties
Coll.: H. M. Treasury and the National Trust (Lord Egremont Collection), Petworth House (665)

P76   Sheerness as seen from the Nore Turner's gallery   1808

Canvas, 1054 × 1498
Prov.: ? Samuel Dobree: H. H. Dobree, sale Christie 17 June 1842 (12) bt. Crockford, who sold it to Bryant, from whom bt. by Sir Thomas Baring, sale Christie 2 June 1848 (61), bt. William Wells, of Redleaf; sale Christie 10 May 1890 (72), bt. Agnew, from whom bt. by Lord Wantage; by descent to the present owner
Coll.: Loyd Collection

P77   The Forest of Bere Turner's gallery   1808

Canvas, 889 × 1194
Sig. lower right centre: *...Turner RA*
Exh.: R.A. 1974 (149)
Prov.: bought by Lord Egremont from Turner's gallery in 1808; by descent to the third Lord

Leconfield, who conveyed Petworth to the National Trust in 1947; in 1957 the contents of the State Rooms accepted by the Treasury in part payment of death duties
Coll.: H. M. Treasury and the National Trust (Lord Egremont Collection), Petworth House (39)

P78   Margate Turner's gallery   1808

Canvas, 901 × 1206
Prov.: bought by Lord Egremont, perhaps from Turner's gallery in 1808; by descent to the third Lord Leconfield, who in 1947 conveyed Petworth to the National Trust; in 1957 the contents of the State Rooms accepted by the Treasury in part payment of death duties
Coll.: H. M. Treasury and the National Trust (Lord Egremont Collection), Petworth House (672)

P79   A subject from the Runic superstitions (?); reworking of 'Rispah watching the Bodies of her Sons' Turner's gallery   1808

Canvas, 915 × 1220
Engr.: in mezzotint by R. Dunkarton for the *Liber Studiorum*, publ. 23 April 1812 (R. 46); the preliminary pen and sepia drawing from the Vaughan Bequest, British Museum, catalogued with the Turner Bequest as CXVII-U
Exh.: R.A. 1974 (85)
Coll.: Turner Bequest, Tate Gallery, London (464)

P80　Spithead: Boat's crew recovering an Anchor　Turner's gallery　1808

Canvas, 1715 × 2350
Coll.: Turner Bequest, Tate Gallery, London (481)
Exhibited under the above title at the R.A. 1809 (22). When it appeared in Turner's gallery in 1808 it was noted as being unfinished, and showing 'two of the Danish Ships which were seized at Copenhagen entering Portsmouth harbour'.

P81　The unpaid bill, or the Dentist reproving his son's prodigality *　R.A. 1808 (167)

Panel, 594 × 800
Prov.: painted for Richard Payne Knight as a pendant to his Rembrandt of *The Cradle* (also on panel and of identical size), and at Downton ever since in the possession of Payne Knight's heirs
Coll.: Dennis Lennox, Esq.

P82　Sketch of a Bank with Gipsies　Turner's gallery　1809 (1)

Canvas, 615 × 840
Coll.: Turner Bequest, Tate Gallery, London (467)

P83　The Quiet Ruin, Cattle in Water : a Sketch, Evening　? Turner's gallery　1809 (2, as 'Sketch of Cows, &c.')

Mahogany, 610 × 765
Coll.: Turner Bequest, Tate Gallery, London (487)

P84　River Scene, with Cattle　? Turner's gallery 1809 (2, as 'Sketch of Cows &c.')

Canvas, 1285 × 1740
Coll.: Turner Bequest, Tate Gallery, London (1857)

P85　Shoeburyness Fisherman hailing a Whitstable Hoy ('The Pilot boat and the Red Cap')　Turner's gallery　1809 (4)

Canvas, 915 × 1220
Sig. lower right: *JMW Turner RA*

Prov.: bought from Turner by Walter Fawkes; in the Farnley collection until 1912, when bt. Agnew and Knoedler; sold by the latter in 1916 to J. Horace Harding; bt. by the Gallery, 1939
Coll.: National Gallery of Canada, Ottawa (4423)

P86　Thomson's Æolian Harp　Turner's gallery 1809 (6)

Canvas, 1676 × 3020
Prov.: probably bt. by James Morrison in the 1820s; first documented in the Morrison Collection by Waagen, 1857; by descent; Walter Morrison Picture Settlement; acquired by the gallery, 1979
Coll.: City Art Gallery, Manchester

The title in the catalogue was accompanied by thirty-two lines of verse, headed: 'To a gentleman at Putney, requesting him to place one [i.e. an Æolian harp] in his grounds'; and beginning:

'On Thomson's tomb the dewy drops distil,
Soft tears of Pity shed for Pope's lost fame
[*sc.* 'fane']...'

P87　Fishing upon the Blythe-sand, tide setting in　Turner's gallery　1809 (7)

Canvas, 890 × 1195
Exh.: R.A. 1974 (155)
Coll.: Turner Bequest, Tate Gallery, London (496)

P88　Near the Thames' Lock, Windsor　Turner's gallery　1809 (8)

Canvas, 889 × 1180
Sig. lower right: *JMW Turner RA*
Prov.: bought by the third Earl of Egremont, perhaps from Turner's gallery in 1809; by descent to the third Lord Leconfield, who in 1947 conveyed Petworth to the National Trust; in 1957 the

contents of the State Rooms accepted by the Treasury in part payment of death duties
Coll.: H. M. Treasury and the National Trust (Lord Egremont Collection), Petworth House (649)

The following verses appeared with the title in the catalogue:

> Say, Father Thames, for thou hast seen
> Full many a sprightly race,
> Disporting on thy margin green,
> The paths of pleasure trace,
> Who foremost now delight to cleave
> With pliant arms thy glassy wave.
>
> — Gray.

P89   Ploughing up Turnips, near Slough*
Turner's gallery   1809 (9)

Canvas, 1020 × 1300
Exh.: R.A. 1974 (156)
Coll.: Turner Bequest, Tate Gallery, London (486)

P90   Harvest Dinner, Kingston Bank*
Turner's gallery   1809 (10)

Canvas, 1020 × 1300
Engr.: in mezzotint by the artist for the *Liber Studiorum* (R. 87) but not publ.; the preliminary pen and sepia drawing from the Vaughan Bequest, British Museum, and catalogued as T.B., CXVIII-W
Coll.: Turner Bequest, Tate Gallery, London (491)

P91   Guardship at the Great Nore, Sheerness, &c.   Turner's gallery   1809 (11)

Canvas, 914 × 1245
Sig. lower right: *JMW Turner RA*
Engr.: by J. and G. P. Nichols in the *Art Journal*, 1 October 1856, p. 297
Exh.: R.A. 1974 (153)
Prov.: James Wadmore by 1834; sale Christie 5 May 1854 (186) bt. Rought acting for W. O. Foster, of Stourbridge; by descent to Major A. W. Foster of Apley Park, Bridgnorth, from whom passed to the present owner
Coll.: Major-General E. H. Goulburn, D.S.O.

P92   Trout Fishing in the Dee, Corwen Bridge and Cottage   Turner's gallery 1809 (13)

Canvas, 915 × 1220
Sig. lower right: *JMW T...* (if the picture were

cleaned the signature 'JMW Turner RA' would probably reappear)
Prov.: bought by George, fifth Earl of Essex, presumably Turner's gallery in 1809; sale, 'Modern Pictures from Cassiobury Park', Christie 22 July 1893 (46), bt. A. Nattali for Abel Buckley; Arthur Sanderson by 1902; bt. by Agnew and sold to Scott and Fowles, New York, from whom bt. by C. P. Taft, Cincinnati, in 1905; given with the rest of the Taft Collection to the citizens of Cincinnati, 1931
Coll.: Taft Museum, Cincinnati, Ohio (459)

P93, P94   Fishing-boats in a Calm (two pictures of this title)   Turner's gallery   1809 (14,17)

Sizes unknown
Provenance and whereabouts unknown

P95   Sun rising through vapour ? Turner's gallery 1809

Canvas, 690 × 1020
Sig. lower right: *JMW Turner RA*
Prov.: bought from Turner by Walter Fawkes; by descent to Revd. Ayscough Fawkes, sale Christie 27 June 1890 (62), bt. McLean, from whom bt. Mrs. Johnstone Foster; Dowager Lady Inchiquin (Mrs. Johnstone's daughter); sale Christie 23 July 1937 (142), bt. Alexander; bt. by the Barber Institute from the Leicester Galleries 1938
Coll.: Barber Institute of Fine Arts, Birmingham

P96   Bilsen Brook Turner's gallery 1809 (15)

Size unknown
Provenance and whereabouts unknown

P97   London   Turner's gallery   1809 (16)

Canvas, 900 × 1200
Inscr. lower left centre: *1809* and *JMW Turner RA PP* (?)
Engr.: in mezzotint by Charles Turner for the *Liber Studiorum*, publ. 1 January 1811 (R. 26). The preliminary sepia drawing is T.B., CXVII-D
Exh.: R.A. 1974 (152)
Prov.: bt. by Walter Fawkes, 1811; returned to artist by exchange at unknown date
Coll.: Turner Bequest, Tate Gallery, London (483)

The following verses appeared with the title in the catalogue:

> Where burthen'd Thames reflects the crowded sail,
> Commercial care and busy toils prevail,
> Whose murky veil, aspiring to the skies,
> Obscures thy beauty, and thy form denies,
> Save where thy spires pierce the doubtful air,
> As gleams of hope amidst a world of care.

P98   Tabley, the seat of Sir J. F. Leicester, Bart.: Windy day*   R.A. 1809 (105)

Canvas, 915 × 1206
Sig. lower right: *JMW Turner RA*
Engr.: by J. Young for the *Leicester Gallery*, 1821 (68)
Exh.: R.A. 1974 (150)
Prov.: painted in 1808 for Sir John Leicester, created Lord de Tabley, 1826; by descent to Lieut.-Col. J. L. B. Leicester-Warren, by whom bequested to the university, 1975
Coll.: Victoria University of Manchester

P99   Tabley, Cheshire, the seat of Sir J. F. Leicester, Bart.: Calm Morning   R.A. 1809 (146)

Canvas, 915 × 1168
Sig. lower right: *JMW Turner RA*
Engr.: by J. Young for the *Leicester Gallery,* 1821 (43)
Exh.: R.A. 1974 (151)
Prov.: painted in 1808 for Sir John Leicester, later Lord de Tabley, sale Christie (at 24 Hill Street) 7 July 1827'(34), bt. by the third Earl of Egremont; by descent to the third Lord Leconfield, who in 1947 conveyed Petworth to the National Trust; in 1957 the contents of the State Rooms accepted by the Treasury in part payment of death duties
Coll.: H. M. Treasury and the National Trust (Lord Egremont Collection), Petworth House (8)

P100   The garreteer's petition R.A. 1809 (175)
Mahogany, 550 × 790
Exh.: R.A. 1974 (184)
Coll.: Turner Bequest, Tate Gallery, London (482)

The following verses appeared with the title in the catalogue:

> "Aid me, ye Powers! O bid my thoughts to roll
> In quick succession, animate my soul;
> Descend my Muse, and every thought refine,
> And finish well my long, my *long-sought* line."

P101   Grand Junction Canal at Southall Mill ('Windmill and Lock') Turner's gallery 1810 (2)

Canvas, 920 × 1220
Engr.: in mezzotint by W. Say for the *Liber Studiorum,* publ. 1 June 1811 (R.27)
Prov.: J. Hogarth (print-seller); sale Christie 14 June 1851 (89, as 'The Lock, Evening'), bt. Bicknell; Charles Birch of Edgbaston; sale Foster

15 February 1855 (16), bt. Leo Redpath; sale Christie 23 May 1857 (354), bt. Gant or Gaut; Thomas Birchall by 1862, from whom bt. Agnew in 1870 and sold to John Heugh, sale 5 April 1874 (185), bt. Cox; Sir Francis Cook, Richmond, by 1899; by descent to his great-grandson; Trustees of the Cook Collection, sale Christie 19 March 1965 (102), bt. Agnew, from whom bt. by the father of the present owner
Private collection, England

P102   High Street, Oxford Turner's gallery 1810 (3)

Canvas, 685 × 1003
Sig. lower right: *IMW Turner RA*
Engr.: by J. Pye and S. Middiman, with figures by C. Heath, publ. by James Wyatt 14 March 1812 (R. 79); by W. E. Albutt (a small replica, R. 79a), 1828
Exh.: R.A. 1974 (159)
Prov.: commissioned by the Oxford picture-dealer and frame-maker, James Wyatt, to be engraved; a copy of the picture was apparently in the Wyatt sale, Christie 2-6 July 1853 (546); Jesse Watts Russell; sale Christie 3 July 1875 (30), bt. Agnew, from whom bt. by Lord Overstone; by descent to the present owner
Coll.: Loyd Collection

P103   The Lake of Geneva from Montreux, Chillion, etc. Turner's gallery 1810 (6)

Canvas, 1054 × 1650
Prov.: bought by Walter Fawkes, perhaps from Turner's gallery in 1810; by descent to the Revd. Ayscough Fawkes, sale Christie 27 June 1890 (59), bt. in; bt. by Sir Donald Currie 1891; by descent to his grand-daughter, Mrs. L. B. Murray, from whom bt. Agnew 1950; Mrs. Mildred Browning Green 1951; presented by her and her

husband, Judge Lucius P. Green, to the Museum, 1956
Coll.: Los Angeles County Museum, California

P104   Linlithgow Palace, Scotland Turner's gallery   1810 (8)

Canvas, 914 × 1220
Prov.: painted for Sir George Phillips; by descent to Sir George's eldest daughter, Juliana, who married the second Earl of Camperdown, 1839; Camperdown sale Christie 2 February 1919 (158), bt. Agnew; F. J. Nettlefold, who presented it to the Gallery, 1948
Coll.: Walker Art Gallery, Liverpool

P105   Hastings: Fishmarket on the Sands Turner's gallery 1810 (9, as 'Fish Market')

Canvas, 910 × 1206
Signed and dated lower left: *JMW Turner RA 1810*
Prov.: bought by John Fuller, M. P., of Rosehill Park, Sussex, probably in 1810; by descent to Sir Alexander Acland-Hood, sale Christie 4 April 1908 (98), bt. Agnew; Pandeli Ralli; bt. by Kansas Museum through Sulley, 1933
Coll.: William Rockhill Nelson Gallery and Atkins Museum of Fine Arts, Kansas City, Missouri

P106   Calder Bridge, Cumberland Turner's gallery   1810 (10)

Canvas, 915 × 1220
Prov.: bought from Turner by Elhanan Bicknell, probably among a group of six Turner oils

Canvas, 603 × 902
Prov.: painted for the third Earl of Egremont; by descent to the third Lord Leconfield, who in 1947 conveyed Petworth to the National Trust; in 1957 the contents of the State Rooms accepted by the Treasury in part payment of death duties
Coll.: H. M. Treasury and the National Trust (Lord Egremont Collection), Petworth House (653)

P109   The fall of an Avalanche in the Grisons ('Cottage destroyed by an Avalanche')*   Turner's gallery 1810 (14)

Canvas, 900 × 1200
Exh.: R.A. 1974 (87)
Coll.: Turner Bequest, Tate Gallery, London (489)

P110   Rosllyn   Turner's gallery   1810 (15)

Size unknown
Provenance and whereabouts unknown

Canvas, 902 × 1220
Prov.: painted for William, first Earl of Lonsdale, by descent to the present owner
Private collection, England

P113   Petworth, Sussex, the seat of the Earl of Egremont: Dewy morning   R.A. 1810 (158)

Canvas, 914 × 1206
Signed and dated lower left: *JMW Turner RA 1810*
Prov.: painted for the third Earl of Egremont in 1810 by descent to the third Lord Leconfield, who in 1947 conveyed Petworth to the National Trust; in 1957 the contents of the State Rooms accepted by the Treasury in part payment of death duties
Coll.: H.M. Treasury and the National Trust (Lord Egremont Collection), Petworth House (636)

purchased in March 1844; sale Christie 25 April 1863 (110), bt. H. Bicknell; bt. Agnew from Smith in 1868 and sold to Thomas Ashton; bt. Agnew jointly with Knoedler and Sulley 1917; Sulley sale Christie 1 June 1934 (36), bt. Agnew; sold to R. V. B. Emmons 1937; by descent to the present owner
Coll.: Professor Hamilton Emmons

P111   Lowther Castle, Westmoreland, the seat of the Earl of Lonsdale: North-west view from Ulleswater lane: Evening R.A. 1810 (85)

Canvas, 902 × 1220
Prov.: painted for William, first Earl of Lonsdale; by descent to the present owner
Private collection, England

P114   Mercury and Hersé*   R.A. 1811

Canvas, 1905 × 1600
Sig. lower centre: *JMW Turner   RA PP*
Engr.: by J. Cousen, 1842 (R. 655)
Prov.: Sir John Swinburne, who bt. the picture from Turner early in 1813; remained in the Swinburne family until after 1862; Sir John Pender by 1872; sale Christie 29 May 1897 (82), bt. Tooth; Sir Samuel Montagu, Bt., created Lord Swaythling in 1907, by 1899; sale Christie 12 July 1946 (38), bt. in; sale Christie 16 June 1961 (65), bt. Betts; sold by Leggatt to the present owner 1962
Private collection, England

P107   Dorchester Mead, Oxfordshire   Turner's gallery   1810 (12)

Canvas, 1015 × 1300
Exh.: R.A. 1974 (157)
Prov.: George Hibbert, sale Christie 13 June 1829 (24), bt. by the artist
Coll.: Turner Bequest, Tate Gallery, London (485)

Until recently this picture was mistitled 'Abingdon'.

P108   Cockermouth Castle   Turner's gallery   1810 (13)

P112   Lowther Castle, Westmoreland, the seat of the Earl of Lonsdale (the north front), with the River Lowther; Mid-day   R.A. 1810 (115)

P115   Apollo and Python   R.A. 1811 (81)

Canvas, 1455 × 2375
Coll.: Turner Bequest, Tate Gallery, London (488)

The following verses appeared with the title in the catalogue:

"Envenom'd by thy darts, the monster coil'd
Portentous horrible, and vast his snake-like
  form:
Rent the huge portal of the rocky den,
And in the throes of death he tore,
His many wounds in one, while earth
Absorbing, blacken'd with his gore."

Hymn of Callimachus.

P116   Somer-Hill, near Tunbridge, the seat of W. F. Woodgate, Esq.* R.A. 1811 (177)

Canvas, 915 × 1223
Exh.: R.A. 1974 (158)
Prov.: James Alexander, sale Christie 24 May 1851 (38), bt. in; Wynn Ellis, sale Christie 6 May 1876 (120), bt. Agnew; sold to Ralph Brocklebank 1878; sale Christie 7 July 1922 (71), bt. Agnew for the National Gallery of Scotland (with funds from the Cowan Smith Bequest)
Coll.: National Galleries of Scotland, Edinburgh (1614)

P117   Whalley Bridge and Abbey, Lancashire: Dyers washing and drying cloth R.A. 1811 (244)

Canvas, 612 × 920
Prov.: J. Newington Hughes, sale Christie 15 April 1848 (145) bt. Brown; Wynn Ellis by 1850-1, sale 6 May 1876 (118), bt. Agnew, from whom bt. Lord Overstone; by descent to the present owner
Coll.: Loyd Collection

P118   The River Plym   Turner's gallery 1812

Size probably 915 × 1218
Provenance and whereabouts unknown

P119   Hulks on the Tamar   ? Turner's gallery 1812

Canvas, 902 × 1206
Sig. lower right: *JMW Turner RA*
Prov.: bought by the third Earl of Egremont, perhaps from Turner's gallery in 1812; by descent to the third Lord Leconfield, who in 1947 conveyed Petworth to the National Trust; in 1957 the contents of the State Rooms accepted by the Treasury in part payment of death duties

Coll.: H. M. Treasury and the National Trust (Lord Egremont Collection), Petworth House (656)

P120   Teignmouth   Turner's gallery   1812

Canvas, 902 × 1207
Sig. lower left: *J WM Turn...*
Prov.: bought by the third Earl of Egremont, probably from Turner's gallery in 1812: by descent to the third Lord Leconfield, who in 1947 conveyed Petworth to the National Trust; in 1957 the contents of the State Rooms accepted by the Treasury in part payment of death duties
Coll.: H. M. Treasury and the National Trust (Lord Egremont Collection), Petworth House (658)

P121   Saltash with the Water Ferry   Turner's gallery   1812

Canvas, 893 × 1206
Exh.: Royal Hibernian Academy, 1846 (106)

Prov.: J. Hogarth (print-seller), sale Christie 13 June 1851 (50a), bt. Bicknell; John Miller, of Liverpool, by 1853; sale Christie 22 May 1858 (249), bt. Gambart; Miss Maria C. Miller by 1868 and until after 1885; Henry G. Marquand, who gave it to the Metropolitan Museum in 1889
Coll.: Metropolitan Museum of Art, New York (89.15.9)

P122   Ivy Bridge Mill, Devonshire   Turner's gallery   1812

Canvas, 890 × 1194
Prov.: Elhanan Bicknell, who bt. it probably in the spring of 1844 as one among five others which he got from Turner at the same time that he bt. *Palestrina* (No. P295); sale Christie 25 April 1863 (104), bt. in; H. S. Bicknell; sale Christie 9 April 1881 (462), bt. Vokins; William Hollins by 1888; bt. from Mrs. Hollins by Agnew, 1897, and sold to Pandeli Ralli in 1899; with Sulley 1928; Lt.-Col. Innes by 1935, from whom it passed to the present owner
Private collection, England

P123   St. Mawes at the Pilchard Season   Turner's gallery   1812

Canvas, 910 × 1205
Coll.: Turner Bequest, Tate Gallery, London (484)

P124   A view of the Castle of St. Michael, near Bonneville, Savoy R.A. 1812 (149)

Canvas, 920 × 1232

Engr.: in mezzotint by H. Dawe for the *Liber Studiorum* publ. 1 January 1816 (R.64). The pen and sepia drawing for the engraving is T.B., CXVIII-J
Prov.: John Gibbons; Revd. B. Gibbons, sale Christie 26 May 1894 (61), bt. Agnew; sold 1894 to John G. Johnson of Philadelphia, by whom bequeathed to the City of Philadelphia in 1917, with his collection, which has been installed in the Philadelphia Museum since the early 1930s
Coll.: John G. Johnson Collection, Philadelphia, Pennsylvania

Cf. No. P50, from which this subject derives.

P125 View of Oxford, from the Abingdon Road R.A. 1812 (169)

Canvas, 660 × 977
Engr.: by J. Pye, with figures by C. Heath, 1818 (R.80)
Exh.: R.A. 1974 (160)
Prov.: commissioned by James Wyatt (print-seller of Oxford) as a companion to *High Street, Oxford* (No. P102) and painted between Christmas 1811 and April 1812; J. Watts Russell; sale Christie 3 July 1875 (31), bt. Agnew; John (later Sir John) Fowler; sale Christie 6 May 1899 (80), bt. Tooth; bt. by Agnew from Tooth, 1915; Victor Reinaecker, 1922; C. Morland Agnew, 1924; bt. by Agnew from executors of C. M. Agnew, 1949; H. P. F. Borthwick Norton; bt. from his widow by Agnew 1953, and sold to Leggatt who sold it to the present owner
Private collection, England

P126 Snow storm: Hannibal and his army crossing the Alps* R.A. 1812 (258)

Canvas, 1460 × 2375
Exh.: R.A. 1974 (88)
Coll.: Turner Bequest, Tate Gallery, London (490)

The following verses appeared with the title in the catalogue:

"Craft, treachery, and fraud—Salassian force,
Hung on the fainting rear! then Plunder seiz'd
The victor and the captive,—Saguntum's spoil,
Alike became their prey; still the chief advanc'd,
Look'd on the sun with hope;—low, broad, and wan;
While the fierce archer of the downward year
Stains Italy's blanch'd barrier with storms.
In vain each pass, ensanguin'd deep with dead,
Or rocky fragments, wide destruction roll'd.
Still on Campania's fertile plains—he thought,
But the loud breeze sob'd, 'Capua's joys beware!'"

M. S. P. Fallacies of Hope.

P127 Frosty Morning* R.A. 1813 (15)

Canvas, 1135 × 1745
Exh.: R.A. 1974 (161)
Coll.: Turner Bequest, Tate Gallery, London (492)

P128 Apullia in search of Appullus Vide Ovid B.I. 1814 (168)

Canvas, 1460 × 2385
Inscr. lower left: *Apullia in Search of Appulus learns from the Swain the Cause of his Metamorphosis* on tree lower left: *Appulus*
Exh.: R.A. 1974 (162)
Coll.: Turner Bequest, Tate Gallery, London (495)

P129 Dido and Æneas R.A. 1814 (177)

Canvas, 1460 × 2370
Engr.: by W. R. Smith 1842 (R.652)
Coll.: Turner Bequest, Tate Gallery, London (494)

The following verses appeared with the title in the catalogue:

"When next the sun his rising light displays,
And gilds the world below with purple rays,
The Queen, Æneas, and the Tyrian Court,
Shall to the shady woods for sylvan games resort."

4th Book of Dryden's Æneis.

P130 Crossing the brook* R.A. 1815 (94)

Canvas, 1930 × 1650
Engr.: by R. Brandard 1842 (R.656)
Exh.: R.A. 1974 (164)
Coll.: Turner Bequest, Tate Gallery, London (497)

P131 Dido building Carthage; or the rise of the Carthaginian Empire.—1st book of Virgil's Æneid* R.A. 1815 (158)

Canvas, 1555 × 2320
Signed and dated on wall at left: *JMW Turner 1815*
Inscr. on tomb right: *SICHAEO;* and left, with title

Coll.: Turner Bequest, National Gallery, London (498)

P132 The eruption of the Souffrier Mountains, in the island of St. Vincent, at midnight, on the 30th of April, 1812, from a sketch taken at the time by Hugh P. Keane, Esq. R.A. 1815 (258)

Canvas, 794 × 1048
Engr.: in mezzotint by Charles Turner, publ. 6 November 1815 (R. 792)
Exh.: R.A. 1974 (163)
Prov.: no history known until bt. from S. T. Gooden by Agnew, 1902, and sold to Pandeli Ralli, 1904; A. J. Sulley; sale Christie 1 June 1934 (26), bt. in; R. L. Lowy sale Christie 8 May 1942 (118), bt. Richards; entered the present collection 1948
Coll.: University of Liverpool

The following verses appeared with the title in the catalogue:

Then in stupendous horror grew
The red Volcano to the view,
And shook in thunders of its own,
While the blaz'd hill in lightnings shone,
Scattering their arrows round.
As down its sides of liquid flame
The devastating cataract came,
With melting rocks, and crackling woods,
And mingled roar of boiling floods,
And roll'd along the ground!

P133 The Temple of Jupiter Panellenius restored R.A. 1816 (55)

Canvas, 1168 × 1778
Engr.: by John Pye, 1828 (R.208)
Prov.: Wynn Ellis, sale Christie 6 May 1876 (121), since when it has disappeared, or possibly since the anon. sale at Phillips, 30 April 1884, bt. Gambart
Coll.: untraced

The following verses appeared with the title in the catalogue:

"'Twas now the earliest morning; soon the sun,
Rising above Ægina, poured his light
Amid the forest, and with ray aslant,
Entering its depth, illumed the branching pines,
Brightened their bark, tinged with a redder hue
Its rusty stains, and cast along the ground
Long lines of shadow, where they rose erect
Like pillars of the temple."

P134 View of the Temple of Jupiter Panellenius, in the island of Ægina, with the Greek national dance of the Romaika: the Acropolis of Athens in the distance. Painted from a sketch taken by H. Gally Knight, Esq. in 1810* R.A. 1816 (71)

Canvas, 1182 × 1781
Signed and dated on rock in left foreground: *JMW Turner RA 1814* (the last figure is uncertain)
Engr.: in mezzotint by H. Dawe for the *Liber Studiorum* unpubl. (R.77). Two sepia drawings connected with the print exist: T.B., CXVII-S, incorporated into the Turner Bequest from the Vaughan Bequest to the British Museum; another sold at Sotheby's, 15 July 1964 (43), bt. Leggatt
Prov.: bought from George Pennell by Joseph Gillott in June 1843 (the first recorded purchase of a Turner by Gillott); Adam Fairrie sale, 1856; bt. by Algernon, fourth Duke of Northumberland from Colnaghi; by descent to the present owner
Coll.: The Duke of Northumberland, K.G.

P135 The decline of the Carthaginian Empire—Rome being determined on the overthrow of her hated rival, demanded from her such terms as might either force her into war, or ruin her by compliance: the enervated Carthaginians, in their anxiety for peace, consented to give up even their arms and their children* R.A. 1817 (195)

Canvas, 1700 × 2385
Exh.: R.A. 1974 (165)
Coll.: Turner Bequest, Tate Gallery, London (499)

The following verses appeared with the title in the catalogue:

"...At Hope's delusive smile,
The chieftain's safety and the mother's pride,
Were to th' insidious conqu'ror's grasp resign'd;
While o'er the western wave th' ensanguin'd sun,
In gathering haze a stormy signal spread,
And set portentous."

P136 Raby Castle, the seat of the Earl of Darlington* R.A. 1818 (129)

Canvas, 1190 × 1806
Prov.: painted 1817–8 for the third Earl of Darlington, created first Duke of Cleveland 1833; by descent to the fourth duke, on whose death, 1891, the title became extinct; his widow presumably sold the picture in 1901; with Messrs. Wallis, 1899, and later in the year with W. Scott and Son, Montreal; bt. Henry Walters, of Baltimore before 1902; the Walters Collection willed to the City of Baltimore, 1931
Coll.: Walters Art Gallery, Baltimore, Maryland (37.41)

P137 Dort or Dordrecht: The Dort packet-boat from Rotterdam becalmed* R.A. 1818 (166)

Canvas, 1575 × 2330
Signed and dated on a log lower right: *JMW Turner RA 1818 Dort*

Engr.: in P.G. Hamerton, *Les Artistes Célèbres—Turner* and in the *Magazine of Art* 1887
Prov.: Walter Fawkes, who bt. it at the R.A. 1818; Fawkes sale Christie 2 July 1937 (61), bt. in; sold by Agnew to Paul Mellon 1966 on behalf of Major le G. G. W. Horton-Fawkes
Coll.: Yale Center for British Art, Paul Mellon Collection

P138 The Field of Waterloo R.A. 1818 (263)

Canvas, 1475 × 2390
Engr.: in mezzotint by F. C. Lewis 1830, unpubl. (R. 795)
Coll.: Turner Bequest, Tate Gallery, London (500)

The following verses appeared with the title in the catalogue:

"Last noon beheld them full of lusty life;
Last eve in Beauty's circle proudly gay;
The midnight brought the signal—sound of strife;
The morn the marshalling of arms—the day,
Battle's magnificently stern array!
The thunder clouds close o'er it, which when rent,
The earth is covered thick with other clay
Which her own clay shall cover, heaped and pent,
Rider and horse—friend, foe, in one red burial blent!"

[Byron's *Childe Harold*, III, 28]

P139 Entrance of the Meuse: Orange-merchant on the Bar, going to pieces; Brill Church bearing S. E. by S. Masensluys E. by S. R.A. 1819 (136)

Canvas, 1755 × 2465
Exh.: R.A. 1974 (166)
Coll.: Turner Bequest, Tate Gallery, London (501)

P140 England: Richmond Hill, on the Prince Regent's Birthday* R.A. 1819 (206)

Canvas, 1800 × 3345
Exh.: R.A. 1974 (167)
Coll.: Turner Bequest, Tate Gallery, London (502)

The following verses appeared with the title in the catalogue:

"Which way, Amanda, shall we bend our course?
The choice perplexes. Wherefore should we chuse?
All is the same with thee. Say, shall we wind
Along the streams? or walk the smiling mead?
Or court the forest-glades? or wander wild
Among the waving harvests? or ascend,
While radiant Summer opens all its pride,
Thy Hill, delightful Shene?"

Thomson.

Nos P141–P227
Unexhibited works   1803–1819

Nos P141–P153 Miscellaneous 1803–1805

P141 Conway Castle *c.* 1803

Canvas, 1035 × 1397
Prov.: William Leader, who either ordered or bt. it direct from Turner; J. T. Leader (son), sale Christie 28 June 1840 (62), bt. Brown; Wynn Ellis by 1855, sale 6 May 1876 (119), bt. the Duke of Westminster; by descent to the present owners
Coll.: Trustees of the Grosvenor Estate

P142 Fishing-boats entering Calais Harbour *c.* 1803

Canvas, 737 × 984
Engr.: in mezzotint by the artist for the *Liber Studiorum* publ. January 1816 (R. 55); no drawing is known for this plate
Prov.: no early history of this picture is known, but presumably still in Turner's possession in 1816; the provenance from 1884 to 1902 can be deduced from loan exhibitions and from Armstrong; Henry Drake by 1884 and until 1892; bt. by Henry Clay Frick from Knoedler in 1904; Archibald Coats by 1893 and until at least 1902
Coll.: Frick Collection, New York (04.1.120)

P143 Seascape with a squall coming up *c.* 1803-4

Canvas, 457 × 610
Prov.: Jack Bannister, a famous comedian, who seems to have bought it from the artist 1803-4; Bannister's Executors' sale Foster 28 March 1849 (89), bt. Farrer; John Gibbons (d. 1851); Revd. B. Gibbons; sale Christie 26 May 1894 (62), bt. Agnew; Sir Julian Goldsmid, Bt.; sale Christie 13 June 1896 (53), bt. Agnew; Pandeli Ralli until 1929; Howard Young Galleries, New York; acquired by the Malden Public Library in 1930 from the Vose Galleries of Boston, with funds provided by Elisha S. Converse and Mary D. Converse
Coll.: Malden Public Library, Malden, Mass.

P144   A coast scene with fishermen hauling a boat ashore ('The Iveagh Sea Piece')* c. 1803-4

Canvas, 914 × 1220
Engr.: by A. L. Brunet-Debaines
Prov.: bought from Turner by Samuel Dobree; Thomas, first Lord Delamere; anon. (executors of Lord Delamere) sale Christie 24 May 1856 (129), bt. in; after sale acquired by W. Benoni White, dealer; sale Christie 24 May 1870 (279), bt. Agnew; sold to Sir E. C. Guinness (created first Earl of Iveagh 1919) 1888, who bequeathed it as part of the Iveagh Bequest to Kenwood House, Hampstead
Coll.: Iveagh Bequest, Kenwood

See note to P16.

P145   Fishmarket on the beach c. 1802-4

Canvas, 445 × 590
Prov.: ? Day, Hinton House, probably before 1813; bequeathed by Mrs. Day to the Foxcroft family and then by inheritance to Mrs. R. W. Robertson-Glasgow; sale Sotheby 30 November 1960 (127), bt. in; by descent to the present owner
Coll.: R. F. Robertson-Glasgow, Hinton House, Hinton Charterhouse

P146   The Pass of St. Gotthard c. 1803-4

Canvas, 806 × 642
Prov.: John Allnutt, for whom this and No. P147 were said to have been painted; G. R. Burnett; sale Christie 13 February 1875 (137), bt. Coleman; F. Beresford Wright, from whom bt. Agnew 1909; Hon. A. J. Balfour 1910; bt. back by Agnew 1916; C. Morland Agnew, from whose executors bt. by Birmingham Art Gallery in 1935 through the Trustees of the Public Picture Gallery Fund (198/35)
Coll.: City Museums and Art Gallery, Birmingham

P147   The Devil's Bridge, St. Gotthard c. 1803-4

Canvas, 768 × 628
Prov.: John Allnutt (see No. P146); G. R. Burnett; sale Christie 13 February 1875 (136), bt. Agnew; sold in May to Holbrook Gaskell; sale Christie 24 June 1909 (98), bt. Sulley; J. R. Thomas; sale Christie 19 November 1920 (151), bt. Sampson; E. R. Bacon, New York; by descent; 1976 Agnew, by whom sold to present owner
Private collection

P148   Bonneville, Savoy c. 1803-5

Panel, 335 × 489
Prov.: Walter Fawkes, who bt. it from Turner; by descent to Revd. Ayscough Fawkes, sale Christie 27 June 1890 (60, as 'Peasants driving Sheep in Apennines'), bt. Vokins; E. Louis Raphael by 1893; Leggatt, who sold it to the Hon. Mrs. Whitelaw Reid 1927; Reid sale, American Art Association, New York, 14-18 May 1935 (1178, as 'A scene in the Apennines'), bt. E. and A. Silberman
Coll.: untraced

P149   Windsor Castle from the Thames* c. 1804-6

Canvas, 889 × 1194

Sig. lower right: *JMW Turner RA Isleworth*
Exh.: R.A. 1974 (80)
Prov.: bought from Turner by the third Earl of Egremont; by descent to the third Lord Leconfield, who in 1947 conveyed Petworth to the National Trust; in 1957 the contents of the State Rooms accepted by the Treasury in part payment of death duties
Coll.: H. M. Treasury and the National Trust (Lord Egremont Collection), Petworth House (4)

P150   Venus and Adonis (Adonis departing for the Chase)* c. 1803-5

Canvas, 1490 × 1194
Sig. lower right: *JMW Turner*
Exh.: R.A. 1849 (206); R.A. 1974 (78)
Prov.: John Green, of Blackheath; sale Christie 26 April 1830 (82), bt. Munro of Novar; Munro sale Christie 6 April 1878 (103), bt. E. Benjamin; C. Becket-Denison; sale Christie 13 June 1885 (892), bt. Agnew; Sir W. Cuthbert Quilter, Bt.; sale Christie 9 July 1909 (82), bt. in; by descent to Sir Raymond Quilter, Bt.; with Leggatt 1960, who sold it to Huntington Hartford, New York, sale Sotheby 17 March 1971 (56), bt. in; acquired the following year by the present owners
Coll.: Christopher Gibbs Ltd., London

P151   Venus and the dead Adonis ? c. 1805

Canvas, 315 × 450
Coll.: Turner Bequest, Tate Gallery, London (5493)

P152   The procuress (?) ? c. 1805

Canvas, 1215 × 915
Coll.: Turner Bequest, Tate Gallery, London (5500)

P153   The Finding of Moses c. 1805

Canvas, 1505 × 1115
Coll.: Turner Bequest, Tate Gallery, London (5497)

Nos P154–P159   Knockholt sketches c. 1805– 1806

The above dating is given by Butlin, but the style of these studies is more consistent with Turner's work both in oil and watercolour of c. 1799–1800; cf. No. P42 and the watercolour Cat. No. 292; and see Farington's report of 30 October 1799, that Turner 'had been in Kent painting from Beech trees'. This may well refer to the studies of trees in Chevening Park (Nos P156–P158).

P154   The kitchen of Wells's cottage, Knockholt

Oil and watercolour (?) and ink on paper, 274 × 375
Inscr. on back: *101 Wells Kitchen Knockholt*
Exh.: B.M. 1975 (24)
Coll.: Trustees of the British Museum (T.B., XCV (a)–A)

P155   Interior of a cottage

Oil and watercolour (?) and ink on paper, 275 × 370
Inscr. on back: *103 Interior of a cottage Kent*
Coll.: Trustees of the British Museum (T.B., XCV (a)–C)

P156   Chevening Park

Oil and watercolour (?) and size on paper, 273 × 376
Inscr. on back: *104 Chevening Park*
Exh.: B.M. 1975 (25)
Coll.: Trustees of the British Museum (T.B., XCV (a)–D)

P157   Chevening Park, Kent*

Oil and watercolour (?) and size on paper, 278 × 378
Inscr. on back: *102 Chevening Park Kent*
Coll.: Trustees of the British Museum (T.B., XCV (a)–B)

P158   'An evening effect'; trees at Knockholt

Oil, size and watercolour on paper, 240 × 165
Inscr. on back: *106 Knockholt Kent*
Coll.: Trustees of the British Museum (T.B., XCV (a)–E)

The title 'An evening effect' is Finberg's.

P159   An armchair

Oil on sized paper, 279 × 227
Coll.: Trustees of the British Museum (T.B., XCV (a)–F)

Nos P160–P176   Large Thames sketches c. 1806–1807

P160   Sketch of 'Harvest Dinner, Kingston Bank' c. 1806-7

Canvas, 610 × 915
Coll.: Turner Bequest, Tate Gallery, London (2696)

P161   Goring Mill and Church c. 1806-7

Canvas, 855 × 1160
Exh.: R.A. 1974 (145, as 'Cleeve Mill (?)')
Coll.: Turner Bequest, Tate Gallery, London (2704)

P162 Caversham Bridge with cattle in the water c. 1806–7

Canvas, 855 × 1160
Coll.: Turner Bequest, Tate Gallery, London (2697)

P163 A Thames backwater, with Windsor Castle in the distance c. 1806–7

Canvas, 865 × 1210
Coll.: Turner Bequest, Tate Gallery, London (2691)

P164 Hampton Court, from the Thames c. 1806–7

Canvas, 860 × 1200
Exh.: R.A. 1974 (143)
Coll.: Turner Bequest, Tate Gallery, London (2693)

P165 The Thames glimpsed between trees, possibly at Kew Bridge c. 1806–7

Canvas, 910 × 1215
Coll.: Turner Bequest, Tate Gallery, London (5519)

P166 House beside the river, with trees and sheep c. 1806–7

Canvas, 905 × 1165
Coll.: Turner Bequest, Tate Gallery, London (2694)

P167 Weir and cattle c. 1806–7

Canvas, 880 × 1200
Coll.: Turner Bequest, Tate Gallery, London (2705)

P168 Barge on the river—sunset c. 1806–7

Canvas, 850 × 1160
Coll.: Turner Bequest, Tate Gallery, London (2707)

P169 Trees beside the river, with bridge in the middle distance c. 1806–7

Canvas, 880 × 1205
Coll.: Turner Bequest, Tate Gallery, London (2692)

P170 Men with horses crossing a river c. 1806–7

Oil over pencil on canvas, 880 × 1185
Coll.: Turner Bequest, Tate Gallery, London (2695)

P171 River scene with weir in the middle distance c. 1806–7

Canvas, 855 × 1155
Coll.: Turner Bequest, Tate Gallery, London (2703)

P172 Willows beside a stream c. 1806–7

Canvas, 860 × 1165
Exh.: R.A. 1974 (146)
Coll.: Turner Bequest, Tate Gallery, London (2706)

P173 Washing sheep* c. 1806–7

Canvas, 845 × 1165
Exh.: R.A. 1974 (144)
Coll.: Turner Bequest, Tate Gallery, London (2699)

P174 Harbour scene, probably Margate c. 1806–7

Canvas, 855 × 1160
Coll.: Turner Bequest, Tate Gallery, London (2700)

P175 Shipping at the mouth of the Thames c. 1806–7

Canvas, 860 × 1170
Exh.: R.A. 1974 (154)
Coll.: Turner Bequest, Tate Gallery, London (2702)

P176 Coast scene with fishermen and boats c. 1806–7

Canvas, 855 × 1160
Coll.: Turner Bequest, Tate Gallery, London (2698)

Nos P177–P194 Small Thames sketches c. 1807

P177 Windsor Castle from Salt Hill c. 1807

Mahogany veneer, 270 × 735
Exh.: R.A. 1974 (139)
Coll.: Turner Bequest, Tate Gallery, London (2312)

P178 Windsor from Lower Hope c. 1807

Mahogany veneer, 320 × 735
Coll.: Turner Bequest, Tate Gallery, London (2678)

P179 Windsor Castle from the meadows c. 1807

Mahogany veneer, 220 × 555
Coll.: Turner Bequest, Tate Gallery, London (2308)

P180 Windsor Castle from the river c. 1807

Mahogany veneer, 200 × 365
Coll.: Turner Bequest, Tate Gallery, London (2306)

P181 Eton from the river c. 1807

Mahogany veneer, 370 × 665
Exh.: R.A. 1974 (140)
Coll.: Turner Bequest, Tate Gallery, London (2313)

P182 The ford c. 1807

Mahogany veneer, 370 × 735
Coll.: Turner Bequest, Tate Gallery, London (2679)

P183 The Thames near Windsor c. 1807

Mahogany veneer, 175 × 265
Coll.: Turner Bequest, Tate Gallery, London (2305)

P184 The Thames near Walton Bridges c. 1807

Mahogany veneer, 370 × 735
Exh.: R.A. 1974 (138)
Coll.: Turner Bequest, Tate Gallery, London (2680)

P185 Walton Reach c. 1807

Mahogany veneer, 370 × 735
Coll.: Turner Bequest, Tate Gallery, London (2681)

P186 Tree tops and sky, Guildford Castle (?): evening c. 1807

Mahogany veneer, 275 × 735
Exh.: R.A. 1974 (141)
Coll.: Turner Bequest, Tate Gallery, London (2309)

P187 St. Catherine's Hill, Guildford c. 1807

Mahogany veneer, 365 × 735
Coll.: Turner Bequest, Tate Gallery, London (2676)

P188 Guildford from the banks of the Wey c. 1807

Mahogany veneer, 250 × 200
Exh.: R.A. 1974 (135)
Coll.: Turner Bequest, Tate Gallery, London (2310)

P189 A narrow valley c. 1807

Mahogany veneer, 215 × 165
Coll.: Turner Bequest, Tate Gallery, London (2303)

P190 Godalming from the south c. 1807

Mahogany veneer, 200 × 350
Exh.: R.A. 1974 (136)
Coll.: Turner Bequest, Tate Gallery, London (2304)

P191 Newark Abbey *c*.1807

Mahogany veneer, 295 × 350
Coll.: Turner Bequest, Tate Gallery, London
(2302)

P192 Newark Abbey on the Wey *c*.1807

Mahogany veneer, 370 × 735
Coll.: Turner Bequest, Tate Gallery, London
(2677)

P193 On the Thames (?) *c*.1807

Mahogany veneer, 295 × 350
Coll.: Turner Bequest, Tate Gallery, London
(2307)

P194 Sunset on the river *c*.1807

Mahogany veneer, 295 × 350
Exh.: R.A. 1974 (137)
Coll.: Turner Bequest, Tate Gallery, London
(2311)

Nos P195–P212 Miscellaneous 1805–1815

P195 Windsor Park: cows in a woody landscape *c*.1805–7

Canvas mounted on pine, 475 × 715
Coll.: Turner Bequest, Tate Gallery, London
(5541)

P196 Cows in a landscape, with a footbridge *c*.1805–7

Canvas, 480 × 710
Coll.: Turner Bequest, Tate Gallery, London
(4657)

P197 Hurley House on the Thames *c*.1807–9

Canvas, 394 × 685
Engr.: by R. Wallis in the *Art Journal,* 1854 (R. 701)
and in *The Turner Gallery* (1875 ed.) as 'On the
Thames' (R. 701)
in lithograph by unknown engraver *c*. 1852 as 'On
the Thames' (R. 840a)
Prov.: painted for Thomas Wright of Upton; John
Miller, of Liverpool; sale Christie 22 May 1858
(241), bt. Robertson; Sir Donald Currie by 1888; by
descent to the present owners; sale Sotheby 17
July 1974 (37), property of Major F. D. Mirrielees's
will—bt. in
Coll.: Mrs. M. V. Gairdner and others

P198 On the River Brent *c*.1807–9

Canvas, 375 × 686
Prov.: Thomas Griffith, Turner's dealer; 'Mr.
Brooks' of the St. James's Gallery, Regent Street,
sale Christie 29 April 1871 (121), bt. Cox; Adam-
son (according to Armstrong); A. M. Wilson; sale
Christie 3 April 1914 (26), bt. Agnew and sold to
Major (later Sir) Stephen Courtauld; bequeathed by
Lady Courtauld to the present owners
Private collection

P199 A valley between hills *c*.1807

Paper, 160 × 230
Prov.: John Edward Taylor, sale Christie 5 July
1912 (99, as 'A valley scene'), bt. Wallis; bt. from
Knoedler by Agnew in 1939 and sold to the present
owner in 1941
Coll.: Ian Greenlees, Esq.

P200 Cattle in a stream under a bridge *c*.1805–7

Mahogany, 315 × 400
Coll.: Turner Bequest, Tate Gallery, London
(5534)

P201 Newark Abbey *c*.1807–8

Panel, 279 × 457
Prov.: Revd. Dr. Thomas Lancaster, Perpetual
Curate of Merton, Surrey; John Pye, engraver; sale
Christie 20 May 1874 (39), bt. Agnew, from whom
bt. by Lord Overstone; by descent to the present
owner
Coll.: Loyd Collection

P202 Windsor Forest: reaping *c*.1807

Oak, 900 × 1220
Exh.: R.A. 1974 (147)
Coll.: Turner Bequest, Tate Gallery, London
(4663)

P203 Gipsy camp *c*.1807

Oak, 1220 × 915
Coll.: Turner Bequest, Tate Gallery, London
(3048)

P204 The Thames at Weybridge *c*.1807–10

Canvas, 880 × 1194
Engr.: in mezzotint by W. Say for the *Liber Studio-
rum* (under title 'Isis'), publ. 1 January 1819
(R. 68). The drawing is in the British Museum,
Vaughan Bequest, incorporated into the Turner
Bequest (T.B., CXVIII-N)
Prov.: bought by the third Earl of Egremont, possi-
bly from Turner's gallery, *c*. 1807, but certainly he
owned it by 1819; by descent to the third Lord
Leconfield, who in 1947 conveyed Petworth to the
National Trust; in 1957 the contents of the State
Rooms accepted by the Treasury in part payment of
death duties
Coll.: H. M. Treasury and the National Trust (Lord
Egremont Collection), Petworth House (5)

P205 'The Leader Sea Piece' *c*.1807–9

Size unknown
Engr.: in mezzotint by Charles Turner for the *Liber
Studiorum* publ. 29 March 1809 (R. 20). The draw-
ing is T.B., CXVI-X
Prov.: William Leader by 1809, when the *Liber
Studiorum* engraving was published; otherwise no
record of this picture
Coll.: untraced

P206 Gravesend? *c*.1807–10

Canvas, 1143 × 1524
Prov.: in Turner's studio, December 1810; ? in the
collection of Charles Borrett in 1862
Coll.: untraced

P207 An artists' colourman's workshop *c*.1807

Oil on pine, 620 × 915
Inscr. on book above door, centre right: *OLD
MASTERS;* and illegibly on vat, lower left
Coll.: Turner Bequest, Tate Gallery, London
(5503)

P208 Tabley House 1808

Oil and gum arabic on paper, 227 × 296
Coll.: Turner Bequest, Trustees of the British
Museum (T.B., CIII–18)

P209 Harvest Home *c*.1809

Pine, 905 × 1205
Coll.: Turner Bequest, Tate Gallery, London (562)

P210 The wreck of a transport ship* *c*.1810

Canvas, 1272 × 2412
Exh.: B.I. 1849 (38); R.A. 1974 (83)
Engr.: by T. O. Barlow, R.A.
Prov.: bought in 1810 by the Hon. Charles Pelham,
who succeeded his father as Lord Yarborough in
1823, and was created first Earl Yarborough in
1837; bt. by C. S. Gulbenkian from the Yarborough
Collection in 1920, through A. Ruck
Coll.: Fundação Calouste Gulbenkian, Lisbon

P211 Rosehill Park, Sussex *c*.1810

Canvas, 889 × 1195
Sig. lower left: *JMW Turner RA*(?) *PP*
Exh.: R.A. 1974 (142)
Prov.: almost certainly painted for the owner of
Rosehill, John Fuller, M.P. for Sussex; by descent to
the present owner
Coll.: Major Sir George Meyrick, Bt., Bodorgan,
Anglesey

P212 Mountain stream *c*.1810–15

Oil over pencil on paper, 445 × 590
Coll.: Turner Bequest, Tate Gallery, London
(561a)

Nos P213–P225 Devon oil sketches *c.*1813

P213   A village in a hollow   1813

Oil over black chalk on prepared paper,
150 × 235
Coll.: Trustees of the British Museum (T.B.,
CXXX–A)

P214   Landscape with a bridge and a church tower beyond   1813

Oil over black chalk on prepared paper,
140 × 235
verso: **Landscape study** 1813
Oil on unprepared side of paper, 165 × 140
Inscr.: *8* and $\frac{1}{a}$
Coll.: Trustees of the British Museum (T.B.,
CXXX–B)

P215   Falmouth Harbour   1813

Oil on prepared paper, 160 × 235
Exh.: R.A. 1974 (124)
Coll.: Trustees of the British Museum (T.B.,
CXXX–C)

P216   A quarry   1813

Oil on prepared paper, 135 × 235
Exh.: R.A. 1974 (125)
Coll.: Trustees of the British Museum (T.B.,
CXXX–D)

P217   A river valley*   1813

Oil on prepared paper, 235 × 298
Exh.: R.A. 1974 (126)
Coll.: Trustees of the British Museum (T.B., CXXX–E)

P218   A bridge with a cottage and trees beyond   1813

Oil over black chalk on prepared paper,
150 × 235
Coll.: Trustees of the British Museum (T.B., CXXX–F)

P219   A river with distant town   1813

Oil on prepared paper, 145 × 235
Coll.: Trustees of the British Museum (T.B.,
CXXX–G)

P220   A distant town, perhaps Exeter   1813

Oil on paper, 100 × 235
Coll.: Trustees of the British Museum (T.B.,
CXXX–H)

P221   Bed of a torrent with bridge in the distance   1813

Oil on prepared paper, 159 × 267
Coll.: Trustees of the British Museum (T.B., CXXX–I)

P222   Barges   1813

Oil over black chalk on prepared paper,
150 × 235
Coll.: Trustees of the British Museum (T.B., CXXX–J)

P223   Devonshire bridge with cottage   1813

Oil over black chalk on prepared paper,
150 × 235
Coll.: Trustees of the British Museum (T.B.,
CXXX–K)

P224   A road leading down into a valley   1813

Oil on prepared paper, 145 × 235
Coll.: Trustees of the British Museum (T.B.,
CXXX–Add. L)

P225   A valley in Devonshire   1813

Millboard, 194 × 263
Prov.: John Edward Taylor; sale Christie 5 July
1912 (103), bt. Wallis; bt. from Messrs. Meatyard
by Agnes and Norman Lupton, who bequeathed it
to Leeds in 1952 (entitled 'Landscape, possibly
near Plymouth', but so far the view is unidentified)
Coll.: Leeds City Art Galleries (No. 13.278/53)

Nos P226, P227

P226   Lake Avernus: Æneas and the Cumaean Sibyl   1814–15

Canvas, 720 × 970
Prov.: painted for Sir Richard Colt Hoare; by
descent to Sir Henry Colt Hoare, sale Christie
2 June 1883 (17), bt. McLean; Capt. C. G. Reid-
Walker; bt. in 1963 by Paul Mellon from Gooden
and Fox Ltd.
Coll.: Yale Center for British Art, Paul Mellon
Collection

P227   Richmond Hill with girls carrying corn   *c.*1819

Canvas, 1470 × 2380
Coll.: Turner Bequest, Tate Gallery, London
(5546)

3   From Turner's first visit to Italy to his second i.e. 1819–1828 (Nos P228–P291)

Nos P228–P244
Exhibited pictures   1820–1828

P228   Rome from the Vatican. Raffaelle accompanied by La Fornarina, preparing his pictures for the decoration of the Loggia*   R.A. 1820 (206)

Canvas, 1770 × 3355
Inscr. on plan lower centre: *Pianta del Vaticano*
Exh.: R.A. 1974 (236)
Coll.: Turner Bequest, Tate Gallery, London (503)

P229   What you will!*   R.A. 1822 (114)

Canvas, 482 × 520
Exh.: R.A. 1974 (307)
Prov.: Sir Francis Chantrey, R.A., who bt. the
picture at the R.A. exhibition of 1822; Lady Chan-
trey, sale Christie 15 June 1861 (91), bt. Agnew; R.
Newsham; J. H. Nettlefold, sale Christie 12
February 1910 (68), bt. Vicars, from whom bt.
Agnew and sold to H. Darell-Brown; sale Christie
22 May 1924 (42), bt. in; sold on behalf of
Darell-Brown's executors by Agnew in 1927 to
Albert Rofé; bt. back from the Rofé collection by
Agnew in 1959 and sold to the present owner
Coll.: Sir Michael Sobell

P230   The Bay of Baiae, with Apollo and the Sybil*   R.A. 1823 (77)

Canvas, 1455 × 2390
Inscr. on stone lower left: *Liquidae Placuere Baiae*
Exh.: R.A. 1974 (237)
Coll.: Turner Bequest, Tate Gallery, London (505)

P231   Harbour of Dieppe (changement de domi-cile)*   R.A. 1825 (152)

Canvas, 1737 × 2254
Dated on the logs chained together in the right
foreground: *182(5 ?)*
Prov.: James Wadmore; sale Christie 5–6 May
1854 (185), bt. Grundy, the Liverpool dealer, on
behalf of John Naylor, of Leighton Hall, Welshpool;
bt. from J. M. Naylor in 1910, together with
Cologne (No. P232) by Agnew and Sulley, through
Dyer and Sons; Knoedler by 1911, who sold it to
H. C. Frick in 1914
Coll.: Frick Collection, New York (14.1.122)

P232   Cologne, the arrival of a packet boat. Evening*   R.A. 1826 (72)

Oil and possibly watercolour on canvas,
1686 × 2241
Prov.: Broadhurst; James Wadmore; sale Christie
5–6 May 1854 (184), bt. Grundy (see No. P231)
acting on behalf of John Naylor of Leighton Hall,
Welshpool, bt. from J. M. Naylor in 1910, together
with *Dieppe* (see No. P231) by Agnew and Sulley
through Dyer and Sons; Knoedler by 1911 from
whom bt. by H. C. Frick in 1914
Coll.: Frick Collection, New York (14.1.119)

P233   Forum Romanum, for Mr. Soane's Museum*   R.A. 1826 (132)

Canvas, 1455 × 2375
Exh.: R.A. 1974 (238)
Coll.: Turner Bequest, Tate Gallery, London (504)

P234   View from the Terrace of a Villa at Niton, Isle of Wight, from sketches by a lady*   R.A. 1826 (297)

Canvas, 455 × 610
Exh.: R.A. 1974 (309)
Prov.: painted for Lady Willoughby Gordon; by
descent to her grand-daughter, Mrs. Disney Leith,
and then to her son, the seventh Lord Burgh; sale
Christie 26 July 1926 (27), bt. Sampson; with
Tooth 1929, from whom bt. by the present owner
in 1933
Coll.: Mr. William A. Coolidge, Boston, Mass.

P235   The seat of William Moffatt, Esq., at Mortlake. Early (Summer's) Morning R.A. 1826 (324)

Canvas, 930 × 1232
Prov.: painted for William Moffatt; Harriott sale Christie 23 June 1838 (111), bt. Allnutt; E. I. Fripp; sale Christie 9 July 1864 (126, as 'Barnes Terrace on the Thames'), bt. G. E. Fripp, therefore probably bt. in; Sam Mendel, from whom bt. by Agnew in 1873; then sold to James Price, 1874; sale Christie 18 June 1895 (64), bt. Agnew for Stephen Holland; sale Christie 25 June 1908 (111), bt. Knoedler; Andrew Mellon (?); H. C. Frick 1909
Coll.: Frick Collection, New York, (09.1.121)

Christie 11 March 1899 (40), bt. Tooth; Hon. (later Sir) George Drummond, Montreal, by 1901; sale Christie 27 June 1919 (158), bt. Knoedler; sold in 1946 to John J. Astor, New York; sale Parke Bernet 19 October 1961 (44), bt. Newhouse and Agnew; bt. by Paul Mellon from Agnew in 1962
Coll.: Yale Center for British Art, Paul Mellon Collection

P236   'Now for the Painter,' (rope) Passengers going on board ('Pas de Calais') R.A. 1827 (74)

Canvas, 1702 × 2235
Engr.: by W. Davison, 1830
by J. Cousen in the *Turner Gallery*, 1859
Prov.: bought by John Naylor, of Leighton Hall, Welshpool, from Turner in 1851; bt. from J. M. Naylor by Agnew through Dyer and Sons in 1910; sold in 1928 to F. J. Nettlefold, who presented it to the Gallery in 1947
Coll.: City Art Gallery, Manchester

P237   Port Ruysdael R.A. 1827 (147)

Canvas, 920 × 1225
Prov.: bought from Turner in March 1844 by Elhanan Bicknell (together with five other Turner oils); Bicknell sale Christie 25 April 1863 (120), bt. Agnew for John Heugh; bt. back by Agnew in 1864 and sold to John (afterwards Sir John) Kelk; sale

P238   Rembrandt's daughter R.A. 1827 (166)

Canvas, 1220 × 863
Prov.: bought at the R.A. in 1827 by Francis Hawksworth Fawkes, the only work by Turner to be added to the Farnley collection after the death of Walter Fawkes in 1825; bt. from F. H. Fawkes in 1912 by Agnew and Knoedler, and sold to Edward Forbes, by whom given to the Museum in 1917
Coll.: Fogg Art Museum, Harvard, Cambridge, Mass. (1917.214)

P239   Mortlake Terrace, the seat of William Moffatt, Esq. Summer's evening* R.A. 1827 (300)

Canvas: 920 × 1220
Exh.: R.A. 1974 (310)
Engr.: by G. Cooke in the *Book of Gems*, 1836 (R. 644)
Prov.: painted for William Moffatt (d. 1831); Harriott sale Christie 23 June 1838 (112), bt. Allnutt; Revd. E. T. Daniell; sale Christie 17 March 1843 (160), bt. M. E. Creswick; bt. by Agnew in 1851 from Creswick and sold to Samuel Ashton;

by descent to Capt. Ashton, from whom bt. Agnew 1920; Knoedler, who sold it to Andrew Mellon, December 1920; given by him to the National Gallery, 1937
Coll.: National Gallery of Art, Washington, D.C. (109)

P240   Scene in Derbyshire R.A. 1827 (319)

Size unknown
Provenance and whereabouts unknown

The following verse appeared with the title in the catalogue:

"When first the sun with beacon red."

See note to No. P270.

P241   Dido directing the equipment of the fleet, or the morning of the Carthaginian Empire R.A. 1828 (70)

Plywood, transferred from canvas, 1500 × 2260
Coll.: Turner Bequest, Tate Gallery, London (506)

P242   East Cowes Castle, the seat of J. Nash, Esq.; the Regatta beating to windward* R.A. 1828 (113)

Canvas, 902 × 1207
Exh.: R.A. 1974 (321)
Prov.: painted for John Nash, together with No. P243; Nash sale Christie 11 July 1835 (88), bt. Tiffin; E. W. Parker; sale Christie 2 July 1909 (100), bt. Agnew jointly with Knoedler; W. G. Warden, Philadelphia; M. C. D. Borden; sale New York, 13–14 February 1913 (29), bt. W. W. Seaman for Col. Ambrose Monell; Mrs. Harrison Williams; Newhouse Galleries, New York, from whom bt. N. G. Noyes; presented to the Museum by Mrs. Noyes, 1971
Coll.: Indianapolis Museum of Art, Indiana (71.32)

P243   East Cowes Castle, the seat of J. Nash, Esq.; the Regatta starting for their moorings R.A. 1828 (152)

Canvas, 914 × 1232
Prov.: painted for John Nash; Nash sale Christie 11 July 1835 (87), bt. Tiffin, agent for John Sheepshanks, who gave it to the Museum, 1857.

Coll.: Victoria and Albert Museum, London (210).

P244   Boccaccio relating the tale of the Bird-cage   R.A. 1828 (262)

Canvas, 1220 × 905
Engr.: in mezzotint by J. P. Quilley 1830 (R.797) unpubl.; by C. H. Jeens for *The Turner Gallery,* 1859 (R.720)
Exh.: R.A. 1974 (322)
Coll.: Turner Bequest, Tate Gallery, London (507)

Nos P245–P291
Unexhibited Pictures
1820–1829

Nos P245–P259   Miscellaneous
c. 1820–1825

P245   The Rialto, Venice   *c.* 1820

Canvas, 1775 × 3355
Coll.: Turner Bequest, Tate Gallery, London (5543)

P246   An avenue of trees   ?*c.* 1822

Canvas, 495 × 535
Coll.: Turner Bequest, Tate Gallery, London (5483)

P247   George IV at St. Giles's, Edinburgh   *c.* 1822

Mahogany, 760 × 915
Coll.: Turner Bequest, Tate Gallery, London (2857)

P248   George IV at the Provost's Banquet in the Parliament House, Edinburgh   *c.* 1822

Mahogany, 685 × 918
Exh.: R.A. 1974 (308)
Coll.: Turner Bequest, Tate Gallery, London (2858)

P249   Scene in a church or vaulted hall   *c.* 1820–30

Canvas, 750 × 990
Coll.: Turner Bequest, Tate Gallery, London (5492)

P250   First sketch for 'The Battle of Trafalgar'   *c.* 1823

Canvas, 910 × 1205
Coll.: Turner Bequest, Tate Gallery, London (5480)

P251   Second sketch for 'The Battle of Trafalgar'   *c.* 1823

Canvas, 900 × 1210
Coll.: Turner Bequest, Tate Gallery, London (556)

P252   The Battle of Trafalgar   1823–4

Canvas, 2590 × 3658
Engr.: by W. Miller in *The Turner Gallery,* 1859 (R. 698)
Prov.: commissioned by George IV in the latter part of 1823 as a pendant to de Loutherbourg's *Glorious First of June;* both pictures were intended as part of a series to commemorate British victories to hang in St. James's Palace—a project to which George

273

Jones had already contributed two large paintings of *Vittoria* and *Waterloo;* but the Government were not satisfied with Turner's picture (finished in February 1824) and the king gave it to Greenwich Hospital in 1829 to hang in the Picture Gallery there
Coll.: National Maritime Museum, Greenwich

P253 Tynemouth Priory *c.* 1820–5

Canvas, 320 × 610
Coll.: Turner Bequest, Tate Gallery, London (3133)

P254 View on the Avon *c.* 1825

Canvas, 380 × 530
Prov.: unknown; purchased by the present owner 1955
Private collection, England

P255 River scene, North Italy *? c.* 1820–30

Canvas, 360 × 640
Coll.: Turner Bequest, Tate Gallery, London (2988)

P256 Valley with a distant bridge and tower *c.* 1825

Canvas, 910 × 1220
Coll.: Turner Bequest, Tate Gallery, London (5505)

P257 Landscape composition *c.* 1820–30

Canvas, 550 × 750
Coll.: Turner Bequest, Tate Gallery, London (5523)

P258 The cobbler's home *c.* 1825

Mahogany, 595 × 800
Coll.: Turner Bequest, Tate Gallery, London (2055)

P259 Death on a Pale Horse? *c.* 1825–30

Canvas, 600 × 755
Exh.: R.A. 1974 (335)
Coll.: Turner Bequest, Tate Gallery, London (5504)

Nos P260-P268 Cowes sketches 1827

P260 Sketch for 'East Cowes Castle, the Regatta beating to windward' No. 1 1827

Canvas, 300 × 490
Exh.: R.A. 1974 (311)
Coll.: Turner Bequest, Tate Gallery, London (1995)

P261 Sketch for 'East Cowes Castle, the Regatta Beating to windward' No. 2 1827

Canvas, 450 × 605
Exh.: R.A. 1974 (312)
Coll.: Turner Bequest, Tate Gallery, London (1994)

P262 Sketch for 'East Cowes Castle, the Regatta beating to windward' No. 3 1827

Canvas, 465 × 720
Exh.: R.A. 1974 (313)
Coll.: Turner Bequest, Tate Gallery, London (1993)

P263 Sketch for 'East Cowes Castle, the Regatta starting for their moorings' No. 1 1827

Canvas, 460 × 605
Exh.: R.A. 1974 (314)
Coll.: Turner Bequest, Tate Gallery, London (1998)

P264 Sketch for 'East Cowes Castle, the Regatta starting for their moorings' No. 2 1827

Canvas, 445 × 735
Exh.: R.A. 1974 (315)
Coll.: Turner Bequest, Tate Gallery, London (2000)

P265 Sketch for 'East Cowes Castle, the Regatta starting for their moorings' No. 3 1827

Canvas, 450 × 610
Exh.: R.A. 1974 (316)
Coll.: Turner Bequest, Tate Gallery, London (1997)

P266   Between Decks   1827

Canvas, 305 × 485
Exh.: R.A. 1974 (318)
Coll.: Turner Bequest, Tate Gallery, London
(1996)

P267   Shipping off East Cowes Headland 1827

Canvas, 460 × 600
Exh.: R.A. 1974 (317)
Coll.: Turner Bequest, Tate Gallery, London
(1999)

P268   Study of sea and sky, Isle of Wight 1827

Canvas, 305 × 485
Exh.: R.A. 1974 (319)
Coll.: Turner Bequest, Tate Gallery, London
(2001)

Nos P269–P281 Miscellaneous   c. 1825–1830

P269   Near Northcourt in the Isle of Wight c. 1827

Canvas, 437 × 613
Sig. lower left: *J M W Turner RA*
Prov.: Sir Willoughby Gordon, whose wife had been
a pupil of Turner's; 1818 Lady Gordon inherited
Northcourt, jointly with her sister Lady Swinburne;
by descent to Mrs. Disney Leith, and then to
seventh Lord Burgh; sale Christie 9 July 1926 (28),
bt. Sampson; John Levy Galleries, New York;
Marsden J. Perry; sale Parke Bernet, New York,
7 May 1948 (79), bt. The Renaissance Galleries;
Maurice du Plessis (Prime Minister of the Province
of Quebec), who gave it to the Quebec Museum in
1959 (No. G-59, 579P)
Coll.: Musée du Québec

P270   A view overlooking a lake   c. 1827

Canvas, 710 × 532
Prov.: Sir James and Lady Willoughby Gordon, who
probably acquired it from the artist c. 1827; by
descent to their grand-daughter, Mrs. Disney Leith,
and then to her son, the seventh Lord Burgh; sale
Christie 9 July 1926 (26), bt. Langton Douglas;
Theodore T. Ellis by November 1927; bequeathed
to the Worcester Art Museum by his widow, Mary
G. Ellis, in 1940 (No. 1940.59).
Coll.: Worcester Art Museum, Worcester, Mass.
(Theodore T. Ellis and Mary G. Ellis Collection)

Finberg identified this picture, apparently incorrect-
ly, with the *Scene in Derbyshire* exhibited in 1827
(No. P240).

P271   Three seascapes   c. 1827

Canvas, 910 × 605
Exh.: R.A. 1974 (320)
Coll.: Turner Bequest, Tate Gallery, London
(5491)

P272   A sandy beach   c. 1825–30

Canvas, 600 × 915
Coll.: Turner Bequest, Tate Gallery, London
(5521)

P273   Rocky coast   c. 1825–30

Canvas, 500 × 655
Coll.: Turner Bequest, Tate Gallery, London
(5499)

P274   Seascape with a yacht?   c. 1825–30

Canvas, 500 × 660
Coll.: Turner Bequest, Tate Gallery, London
(5485)

P275   Seascape with a sailing-boat and a ship c. 1825–30

Canvas, 470 × 610
Coll.: Turner Bequest, Tate Gallery, London
(5520)

P276   Lake or river, with trees on the right c. 1825–30

Millboard, 410 × 595
Coll.: Turner Bequest, Tate Gallery, London
(5525)

P277   Shipping   ? c. 1825–30

Mahogany, 680 × 915
Coll.: Turner Bequest, Tate Gallery, London
(2879)

P278   Shipping with a flag   ? c. 1825–30

Mahogany, 750 × 920
Coll.: Turner Bequest, Tate Gallery, London
(2880)

P279   Steamer and lightship   c. 1825–30

Canvas, 915 × 1215
Coll.: Turner Bequest, Tate Gallery, London
(5478)

P280   Two compositions: a Claudian seaport and an open landscape   c. 1825–30

Canvas, 335 × 605
Coll.: Turner Bequest, Tate Gallery, London
(5533)

P281   Landscape with a castle on a promontory ? c. 1820–30

Canvas, 490 × 405
Coll.: Turner Bequest, Tate Gallery, London
(5484)

Nos P282–P291   Petworth landscapes c. 1828–1830

P282   Evening landscape, probably Chichester Canal   c. 1828

Canvas, 650 × 1260

Exh.: R.A. 1974 (330)
Prov.: presumably by descent from the artist to
Miss M. H. Turner, by whom presented to the
Gallery, 1944
Coll.: Tate Gallery, London (5563)

P283   Petworth Park: Tillington Church in the distance   c. 1828

Canvas, 645 × 1455
Exh.: R.A. 1974 (325)
Coll.: Turner Bequest, Tate Gallery, London (559)

P284   The Lake, Petworth, sunset   c. 1828

Canvas, 650 × 1410
Exh.: R.A. 1974 (326)
Coll.: Turner Bequest, Tate Gallery, London
(2701)

P285   Chichester Canal   c. 1828

Canvas, 655 × 1345
Exh.: R.A. 1974 (327)
Coll.: Turner Bequest, Tate Gallery, London (560)

P286   The Chain Pier, Brighton, *c.* 1828

Canvas, 710 × 1365
Exh.: R.A. 1974 (328)
Coll.: Turner Bequest, Tate Gallery, London (2064)

P287   A ship aground *c.* 1828

Canvas, 700 × 1360
Exh.: R.A. 1974 (329)
Coll.: Turner Bequest, Tate Gallery, London (2065)

P288   The Lake, Petworth: sunset, fighting bucks* *c.* 1829

Canvas, 622 × 1460
Engr.: by J. Cousen for *The Turner Gallery* as 'Petworth Park', 1859 (R. 718)
Prov.: painted for the third Earl of Egremont for the dining-room at Petworth; by descent to the third Lord Leconfield who in 1947 conveyed Petworth to the National Trust; in 1957 the contents of the State Rooms accepted by the Treasury in part payment of death duties
Coll.: H. M. Treasury and the National Trust, (Lord Egremont Collection), Petworth House (132)

P289   The Lake, Petworth: sunset, a stag drinking *c.* 1829

Canvas, 635 × 1321
Prov.: painted for the third Earl of Egremont for the dining-room at Petworth; by descent to the third Lord Leconfield who in 1947 conveyed Petworth to the National Trust; in 1957 the contents of the State Rooms accepted by the Treasury in part payment of death duties

Coll.: H. M. Treasury and the National Trust (Lord Egremont Collection), Petworth House (142)

P290   Chichester Canal *c.* 1829

Canvas, 635 × 1321
Prov.: painted for the third Earl of Egremont for the dining-room at Petworth; by descent to the third Lord Leconfield, who in 1947 conveyed Petworth to the National Trust; in 1957 the contents of the State Rooms accepted by the Treasury in part payment of death duties
Coll.: H. M. Treasury and the National Trust (Lord Egremont Collection), Petworth House (130)

P291   Brighton from the sea *c.* 1829

Canvas, 635 × 1321
Engr.: by R. Wallis in *The Turner Gallery* as 'The Chain Pier, Brighton', 1859 (R. 719)
Prov.: painted for the third Earl of Egremont for the dining-room at Petworth; by descent to the third Lord Leconfield, who in 1947 conveyed Petworth to the National Trust; in 1957 the contents of the State Rooms accepted in part payment of death duties.
Coll.: H. M. Treasury and the National Trust (Lord Egremont Collection), Petworth House (140)

4 Works painted in Rome (1828-1829 Nos P292-P328)

Nos P292-P295 Exhibited pictures 1828

P292   View of Orvieto, painted in Rome* 1828, exhibited Rome 1828-9   R.A. 1830 (30)

Canvas, 915 × 1230
Exh.: R.A. 1974 (472)
Coll.: Turner Bequest, Tate Gallery, London (511)

P293   Vision of Medea* 1828, exhibited Rome 1828-9   R.A. 1831 (178)

Canvas, 1735 × 2410
Exh.: R.A. 1974 (473)
Coll.: Turner Bequest, Tate Gallery, London (513)

The following verses appeared with the title in the R.A. catalogue:

> "Or Medea, who in the full tide of witchery
> Had lured the dragon, gained her Jason's love,
> Had filled the spell-bound bowl with Æson's life,
> Yet dashed it to the ground and raised the poisonous snake
> High in the jaundiced sky to writhe its murderous coil,
> Infuriate in the wreck of hope, withdrew
> And in the fired palace her twin offspring threw."
>
> *MS. Fallacies of Hope.*

P294   Regulus* 1828, reworked 1837, exhibited Rome 1828-9   B.I. 1837 (120)

Canvas, 910 × 1240
Engr.: by D. Wilson 1840 as 'Ancient Carthage —The Embarcation of Regulus' (R. 649) by S. Bradshaw for *The Turner Gallery*, 1859 (R. 723)
Exh.: R.A. 1974 (474)
Coll.: Turner Bequest, Tate Gallery, London (519)

P295   Palestrina—composition ?1828   R.A. 1830 (181)

Canvas, 1405 × 2490
Exh.: Royal Scottish Academy, 1845
Prov.: sold March 1844 to Elhanan Bicknell, sale Christie 25 April 1863 (122), bt. (in) Henry Bicknell, sale Christie 25 March 1865 (206), bt. (in) Miller, and sale Christie 9 April 1881 (463), bt. Agnew for James Dyson Perrins; Charles William Dyson Perrins by 1939, bequeathed 1958 to the National Gallery, London; transferred to the Tate Gallery, 1961
Coll.: Tate Gallery, London (6283)

The following verses appeared with the title in the catalogue:

> "Or from yon mural rock, high-crowned Praeneste,
> Where, misdeeming of his strength, the Carthaginian stood,
> And marked with eagle-eye, Rome as his victim."
>
> *MS. Fallacies of Hope.*

Nos P296–P328 Unexhibited works

Nos P296–P301 Miscellaneous

P296 Reclining Venus 1828

Canvas, 1750 × 2490
Coll.: Turner Bequest, Tate Gallery, London
(5498)

P297 Two recumbent nude figures 1828

Canvas, 1745 × 2490
Coll.: Turner Bequest, Tate Gallery, London
(5517)

P298 Outline of the Venus Pudica 1828

Canvas, 1355 × 980
Coll.: Turner Bequest, Tate Gallery, London
(5509)

P299 Southern landscape 1828

Canvas, 1765 × 2520
Coll.: Turner Bequest, Tate Gallery, London
(5510)

P300 Southern landscape, with an aqueduct and waterfall ?1828

Canvas, 1500 × 2490
Coll.: Turner Bequest, Tate Gallery, London
(5506)

P301 Italian landscape, probably Civita di Bagnoreggio ?1828

Canvas, 1500 × 2495
Coll.: Turner Bequest, Tate Gallery, London
(5473)

Nos P302–P317 Roman sketches ?1828

P302 Sketch for 'Ulysses deriding Polyphemus' ?1828

Canvas, 600 × 890
Exh.: R.A. 1974 (475)
Coll.: Turner Bequest, Tate Gallery, London
(2958)

P303 Italian bay ?1828

Canvas, 605 × 1020
Coll.: Turner Bequest, Tate Gallery, London
(2959)

P304 Lake Nemi ?1828

Canvas, 605 × 995
Exh.: R.A. 1974 (476)
Coll.: Turner Bequest, Tate Gallery, London
(3027)

P305 Ariccia (?): sunset ?1828

Canvas, 605 × 795
Coll.: Turner Bequest, Tate Gallery, London
(2990)

P306 Overlooking the coast, with classical building ?1828

Canvas, 605 × 845
Coll.: Turner Bequest, Tate Gallery, London
(2991)

P307 Italian landscape, with tower, trees and figures ?1828

Canvas, 600 × 885
Coll.: Turner Bequest, Tate Gallery, London
(2992)

P308 Classical harbour scene ?1828

Canvas, 605 × 1020
Coll.: Turner Bequest, Tate Gallery, London
(3026)

P309 Rocky bay ?1828

Canvas, 605 × 920
Coll.: Turner Bequest, Tate Gallery, London
(3380)

P310 Archway, with trees by the sea ?1828

Canvas, 600 × 875
Exh.: R.A. 1974 (478)
Coll.: Turner Bequest, Tate Gallery, London
(3381)

P311 Tivoli, the Cascatelle ?1828

Canvas, 605 × 780
Exh.: R.A. 1974 (477)
Coll.: Turner Bequest, Tate Gallery, London
(3388)

P312 Italian landscape with bridge and tower ?1828

Canvas, 605 × 980
Coll.: Turner Bequest, Tate Gallery, London
(3387)

P313 Claudian harbour scene ?1828

Canvas, 600 × 925
Exh.: R.A. 1974 (479)
Coll.: Turner Bequest, Tate Gallery, London
(3382)

P314 Stack and fire? ?1828

Canvas, 600 × 845
Coll.: Turner Bequest, Tate Gallery, London
(3383)

P315 A park ?1828

Canvas, 605 × 985
Coll.: Turner Bequest, Tate Gallery, London
(3384)

P316 Scene on the banks of a river ?1828

Canvas, 605 × 890
Exh.: R.A. 1974 (480)
Coll.: Turner Bequest, Tate Gallery, London
(3385)

P317 Fishing-boat in a mist ?1828

Canvas, 600 × 910
Coll.: Turner Bequest, Tate Gallery, London
(3386)

Nos P318–P327 Small Italian sketches ?1828

P318 Hilltown on the edge of the Campagna ?1828

Millboard, 410 × 595
Exh.: R.A. 1974 (471)
Coll.: Turner Bequest, Tate Gallery, London
(5526)

P319 Seacoast with ruin, probably the Bay of Baiae ?1828

Muslin mounted on millboard, 410 × 600
Coll.: Turner Bequest, Tate Gallery, London
(5530)

P320 Coast scene near Naples ?1828

Millboard, 410 × 595
Exh.: R.A. 1974 (470)
Coll.: Turner Bequest, Tate Gallery, London
(5527)

P321 Landscape with trees and a castle ?1828

Millboard, 415 × 600
Coll.: Turner Bequest, Tate Gallery, London
(5528)

P322   Mountainous landscape   ?1828

Muslin mounted on millboard, 410 × 595
Coll.: Turner Bequest, Tate Gallery, London
(5531)

P323   Hilly landscape with tower (?)   ?1828

Muslin mounted on millboard, 420 × 525
Coll.: Turner Bequest, Tate Gallery, London
(5532)

P324   Landscape with a tree on the right
?1828

Millboard, 280 × 415
Coll.: Turner Bequest, Tate Gallery, London
(5545)

P325   Seascape with burning hulk   ?1828

Muslin mounted on millboard, 240 × 415
Coll.: Turner Bequest, Tate Gallery, London
(5535)

P326   A seashore   ?1828

Muslin mounted on millboard, 415 × 520
Coll.: Turner Bequest, Tate Gallery, London
(5524)

P327   Seascape   ?1828

Millboard, 420 × 520
Coll.: Turner Bequest, Tate Gallery, London
(5481)

No. P328   Miscellaneous   c. 1825–1830

P328   Italian landscape with a tower
c. 1825–1830

Canvas, 585 × 760
Coll.: Turner Bequest, Tate Gallery, London
(5540)

5   Later works   1829–1851
(Nos P329–532)

Nos P329–P432   Exhibited pictures

P329   The Banks of the Loire   R.A. 1829 (19)

Size unknown
Provenance and whereabouts unknown

**P330   Ulysses deriding Polyphemus—Homer's
Odyssey***   R.A. 1829 (42)

Canvas, 1325 × 2030
Inscr. on flag of ship upper centre: ΟΔΥΣΣΕ
Exh.: R.A. 1974 (482)
Coll.: Turner Bequest, National Gallery, London
(508)

P331   The Loretto necklace   R.A. 1829 (337)

Canvas, 1310 × 1750
Coll.: Turner Bequest, Tate Gallery, London (509)

P332   Pilate washing his hands   R.A. 1830 (7)

Canvas, 915 × 1220
Exh.: R.A. 1974 (332)
Coll.: Turner Bequest, Tate Gallery, London (510)

Exhibited with text from Matthew, chap. XXVII,
ver. 24, appended to the title.

P333   Jessica   R.A. 1830 (226)

Canvas, 1220 × 917
Exh.: R.A. 1974 (331)
Prov.: bought from Turner by the third Earl of
Egremont, by April 1831; by descent to the third
Lord Leconfield, who in 1947 conveyed Petworth
to the National Trust; in 1957 the contents of the
State Rooms accepted by the Treasury in part
payment of death duties
Coll.: H. M. Treasury and the National Trust (Lord
Egremont Collection), Petworth House (91)

The following quotation was appended to the title
in the R.A. catalogue:

"*Shylock—Jessica, shut the window, I say.*"
Merchant of Venice.

**P334   Calais sands, low water, Poissards
collecting bait**   R.A. 1830 (304)

Canvas, 730 × 1070
Exh.: R.A. 1974 (508)
Prov.: Joseph Gillott, reputedly acquired from the
artist among a group of eight Turner paintings,
c. 1844; bt. from Gillott by Thomas Rought in
December 1846; apparently re-entered the Gillott
collection and in his sale, Christie 20 April 1872
(161), bt. Agnew for Thomas Wrigley, who gave it
to Bury Art Gallery, 1897
Coll.: Public Library and Art Gallery, Bury, Lancashire

**P335   Fish-market on the sands—the sun
rising through a vapour**   R.A. 1830
(432)

Canvas, 863 × 1118
Prov.: William Wells, of Redleaf; probably sold by
Wells, Christie 28 May 1852 (50), bt. Graves; John
Chapman, M. P., by 1857; by descent to his youn-
ger son, George John Chapman; sold c. 1936 to an
American dealer; Jones sale Parke-Bernet, New
York, 4–5 December 1941 (74), bt. Billy Rose, New
York, who owned it at the time it was destroyed in a
fire, 1956.

P336 Life-boat and Manby apparatus going off to a stranded vessel making signal (blue lights) of distress R.A. 1831 (73)

Canvas, 914 × 1220
Engr.: by R. Brandard in *The Turner Gallery*, 1859, as 'Vessel in distress off Yarmouth' (R. 726) and in the *Art Journal*, 1863
Exh.: R.A. 1974 (509)
Prov.: painted for the architect, John Nash, or perhaps bought by him at the R.A. in 1831; sale Christie 11 July 1835 (89, as 'Blue Lights off Yarmouth'), bt. Tiffin, probably acting on behalf of John Sheepshanks, by whom given to the Museum, 1827
Coll.: Victoria and Albert Museum, London (211)

P337 Caligula's palace and bridge R.A. 1831 (162)

Canvas, 1370 × 2465
Engr.: by E. Goodall 1842 (R. 653)
Exh.: R.A. 1974 (485)
Coll.: Turner Bequest, Tate Gallery, London (512)

The following verses appeared with the title in the catalogue:

"What now remains of all the mighty bridge
Which made the Lacrine lake an inner pool,
Caligula, but mighty fragments left,
Monuments of doubt and ruined hopes
Yet gleaming in the morning's ray, that tell
How Baia's shore was loved in times gone by?"

MS. Fallacies of Hope.

P338 Lucy, Countess of Carlisle and Dorothy Percy's visit to their father, Lord Percy, when under attainder upon the supposition of his being concerned in the gunpowder plot* R.A. 1831 (263)

Oak panel, 405 × 700

Exh.: R.A. 1974 (333)
Coll.: Turner Bequest, Tate Gallery, London (515)

P339 Admiral Van Tromp's barge at the entrance of the Texel, 1645 R.A. 1831 (228)

Canvas, 902 × 1219
Prov.: bought by Sir John Soane from the R.A. exhibition 1831; presented, with the collection at his house in Lincoln's Inn Fields, by Sir John Soane to the nation in 1833
Coll.: Sir John Soane's Museum, London

P340 Watteau study by Fresnoy's rules R.A. 1831 (298)

Oak panel, 405 × 700
Exh.: R.A. 1974 (334)
Coll.: Turner Bequest, Tate Gallery, London (514)

The following verses appeared with the title in the catalogue:

"White, when it shines with unstained lustre clear,
May bear an object back or bring it near;"

Fresnoy's Art of Painting, 496.

P341 Fort Vimieux* R.A. 1831 (406)

Canvas, 711 × 1067
Exh.: R.A. 1974 (510)
Prov.: bought from Turner *c.* 1845 by Charles Meigh, of Shelton, Staffordshire; sale Christie 21 June 1850 (154), bt. Col. James Lenox, who gave it to the Lenox Library, New York (now the New York Public Library); sale Parke Bernet 17 October 1956 (43), bt. Agnew on behalf of Arthur Tooth and Sons, who sold it to the present owner
Private collection, England

Turner's full title for this work was a quotation from 'Naval Anecdotes':

"In this arduous service (of reconnaissance) on the French coast, 1805, one of our cruisers took the ground, and had to sustain the attack of the flying artillery along shore, the batteries and the fort of Vimieux, which fired heated shot, until she could warp off at the rising tide, which set in with all the appearance of a stormy night."

Naval Anecdotes.

P342 Childe Harold's pilgrimage—Italy R.A. 1832 (70)

Canvas, 1420 × 2480
Coll.: Turner Bequest, Tate Gallery, London (516)

The following verses appeared with the title in the catalogue:

"... and now, fair Italy!
Thou art the garden of the world.
Even in thy desert what is like to thee?
Thy very weeds are beautiful, thy waste
More rich than other climes' fertility:
Thy wreck a glory and thy ruin graced
With an immaculate charm which cannot be defaced."

Lord Byron, Canto IV.

P343 The Prince of Orange, William III, embarked from Holland, landed at Torbay, November 4th, 1688, after a stormy passage R.A. 1832 (153)

Canvas, 905 × 1200
Prov.: Robert Vernon, presumably purchased at the R.A. 1832; by whom given to the National Gallery, 1847; transferred to the Tate Gallery 1912
Coll.: Tate Gallery, London (369)

P344 Van Tromp's shallop, at the entrance of the Scheldt R.A. 1832 (206)

Canvas, 890 × 1195

Prov.: John Miller, of Liverpool, who bought it from the artist; by descent to T. Horrocks Miller and then to Thomas Pitt Miller, of Singleton Park, Blackpool; sale Christie 26 April 1946 (108), bt. Fine Art Society; consigned by them in 1951 to the Vose Galleries of Boston, from whom bt. by the Wadsworth Atheneum (Summer Collection: No. 1951-233)
Coll.: Wadsworth Atheneum, Hartford, Connecticut

P345 Helvoetsluys;—the City of Utrecht, 64, going to sea R.A. 1832 (284)

Canvas, 914 × 1220
Prov.: bought from Turner early in 1844 by Elhanan Bicknell, of Herne Hill; Bicknell sale Christie 25 April 1863 (102), bt. Agnew for John Heugh; bt. back by Agnew in 1864 and sold to Miss Woods; bt. back by Agnew in 1883 and sold to James Price; sale Christie 15 June 1895 (65), bt. Agnew; A. J. Forbes-Leith; bt. back by Agnew 1895 and sold to James Ross, of Montreal; sale Christie 23 July 1954 (56), bt. Col. S. J. L. Hardie; his executors' sale Sotheby 19 November 1969 (125), bt. Agnew; bt. by the University of Indiana in 1971 (gift of Mrs. Nicholas H. Noyes)
Coll.: Middle Western University Collection, Indiana.

P346 Shadrach, Meshach and Abednego in the Burning Fiery Furnace R.A. 1832 (355)

Mahogany, 915 × 710
Exh.: R.A. 1974 (B39)

Coll.: Turner Bequest, Tate Gallery, London (517)

Titled in the R.A. catalogue with a quotation from Daniel, chap III, 26.

P347 Staffa, Fingal's cave* R.A. 1832 (453)

Canvas, 915 × 1220
Sig. lower right: *J M W Turner RA*
Exh.: R.A. 1974 (490)
Prov.: bought from Turner in 1845 by Col. James Lenox, of New York; given by Col. Lenox to the Lenox Library (later the New York Public Library); sale Parke Bernet, New York, 17 October 1956 (39), bt. Agnew; Lord Astor of Hever, from whom acquired by Paul Mellon, 1978
Coll.: Yale Center for British Art, Paul Mellon Collection

Exhibited in 1832 with the following quotation:
'... nor of a theme less solemn tells
That mighty surge that ebbs and swells,
And still, between each awful pause,
From the high vault an answer draws.'
Sir Walter Scott's Lord of the Isles, Canto IV.

P348 Rotterdam ferry-boat R.A. 1833 (8)

Canvas, 927 × 1232
Prov.: H. A. J. Munro of Novar, who bt. it from the R.A. exhibition; sale Christie 6 April 1878 (101), bt. Agnew; Kirkman D. Hodgson, M. P.; bt. back by Agnew in 1893 and sold to Sir Charles Tennant; by descent to his grandson, the second Lord Glenconner, from whom bt. Knoedler in 1923 and sold the same year to Andrew Mellon; given to his daughter, Mrs. Ailsa Mellon Bruce, who bequeathed it to the National Gallery, 1970
Coll.: National Gallery of Art, Washington D.C.

P349 Bridge of Sighs, Ducal Palace and Custom-house, Venice: Canaletti painting R.A. 1833 (109)

Mahogany, 510 × 825
Exh.: R.A. 1974 (529)
Prov.: Robert Vernon, by whom purchased at the R.A. 1833, and given to the National Gallery 1847; transferred to the Tate Gallery 1912
Coll.: Tate Gallery, London (370)

P350 Van Goyen, looking out for a subject* R.A. 1833 (125)

Canvas, 918 × 1229
Prov.: bought from Turner in 1844 by Elhanan Bicknell; sale Christie 25 April 1863 (97), bt. Agnew for John Heugh; bt. back by Agnew in 1864 and sold to John Graham; sale Christie 30 April 1887 (92), bt. Agnew; F. B. Henson; bt. in 1900 from Mrs. Guthrie by Agnew; Knoedler, who sold it to H. C. Frick in 1901
Coll.: Frick Collection, New York (01.1.118)

P351 Van Tromp returning after the battle off the Dogger Bank R.A. 1833 (146)

Canvas, 905 × 1210
Coll.: Turner Bequest, Tate Gallery, London (537)

P352 Ducal Palace, Venice R.A. 1833 (169)

Size unknown
Engr.: by W. Miller, 1854, as 'The Piazzetta, Venice' (R. 674)
Provenance and whereabouts unknown

P353 Mouth of the Seine, Quille-bœuf R.A. 1833 (462)

Canvas, 915 × 1232

Exh.: R.A. 1974 (491)
Prov.: Charles Birch, of Harborne, near Birmingham, by 1849; T. Horrocks Miller by 1889; by descent to his nephew T. Pitt Miller; sale Christie 26 April 1946 (110), bt. Knoedler for C. S. Gulbenkian
Coll.: Fundaçao Calouste Gulbenkian, Lisbon

Exhibited with the following note in the catalogue: 'This estuary is so dangerous from its quicksands, that any vessel taking the ground is liable to be stranded and overwhelmed by the rising tide, which rushes in in one wave.'

P354 The fountain of Indolence R.A. 1834 (52)

Canvas, 1065 × 1664
Prov.: H. Lumley, from whom bt. in 1882 by Agnew and sold to W. H. Vanderbilt; by descent in the Vanderbilt family until 1958, when acquired by Lord Beaverbrook
Coll.: Beaverbrook Foundations, on loan to the Beaverbrook Art Gallery, Fredericton, New Brunswick (59.259)

P355 The golden bough, (MS. 'Fallacies of Hope') R.A. 1834 (75)

Canvas, 1040 × 1635
Prov.: Robert Vernon, who purchased it before the R.A. 1834 exhibition, and by him given to the National Gallery in 1847; transferred to the Tate Gallery, 1929
Coll.: Tate Gallery, London (371)

P356 Venice R.A. 1834 (175)

Canvas, 902 × 1219
Prov.: painted for Henry McConnell; bt. from him by John Naylor; bt. from Mrs. Naylor by Agnew in 1910 through Dyer and Sons; sold through Sulley to P. A. B. Widener, of Philadelphia, who bequeathed it to the National Gallery, 1942
Coll.: National Gallery of Art, Washington, D. C. (681)

P357 Wreckers,—coast of Northumberland, with a steam-boat assisting a ship off shore R.A. 1834 (199)

Canvas, 914 × 1219
Prov.: bought from Turner by Elhanan Bicknell in 1844, with five other oils; Bicknell sale Christie 25 April 1863 (108), bt. Agnew; John (later Sir John) Pender; sale Christie 29 May 1897 (83), bt. Wallis; A. M. Byers, of Pittsburgh, by 1901; by descent to Mrs. Lyon Slater
Coll.: Yale Center for British Art, Paul Mellon Collection

P358 St. Michael's Mount, Cornwall R.A. 1834 (317)

Canvas, 610 × 774

Engr.: by J. Cousen in the *Art Journal* and in *The Turner Gallery* 1859 (R. 727a)
by W. Miller 1866 (R. 684)
Prov.: bought by John Sheepshanks, probably at the R.A. exhibition, or perhaps commissioned by him and given to the Museum, 1857
Coll.: Victoria and Albert Museum, London (209)

P359 The Burning of the House of Lords and Commons, 16th of October, 1834* B.I. 1835 (58)

Canvas, 920 × 1230
Exh.: R.A. 1974 (512)
Prov.: bought at the B. I. exhibition by Chambers Hall, sold by him to Mr. Colls, according to Burnet; Charles Birch by 1852; Lloyd Bros; sale Foster 13 June 1855 (59), bt. Wallis; H. Wallis; sale Christie 16 November 1860 (209), bt. White; C. J. Palmer; his executors' sale Christie 16 May 1868 (133), bt. Agnew; John Graham; bt. back from him by Agnew in 1873 and sold to Holbrook Gaskell; sale Christie 24 June 1909 (97), bt. Agnew; sold to J. H. McFadden, of Philadelphia, by whom it was bequeathed to the Museum, 1921
Coll.: Philadelphia Museum of Art (John H. McFadden Collection)

P360 Keelmen heaving in coals by night* R.A. 1835 (24)

Canvas, 902 × 1219
Sig. on the buoy on left: *JMWT*
Exh.: R.A. 1974 (513)
Prov.: painted for Henry McConnell; bt. in 1849 from him by John Naylor; bt. by Agnew from Mrs. Naylor in 1910 through Dyer and Sons; Sulley and Co.; P. A. B. Widener, of Philadelphia, who bequeathed it to the National Gallery, 1942
Coll.: National Gallery of Art, Washington, D. C. (682)

P361 The bright stone of honour (Ehrenbrietstein) and the tomb of Marceau, from Byron's *Childe Harold** R.A. 1835 (74)

Canvas, 930 × 1230
Engr.: by John Pye 1845 (R. 662)
by J. Cousen for *The Turner Gallery,* 1859 (R. 729a)
Exh.: R.A. 1974 (514)
Prov.: painted for John Pye, the engraver (for the purpose of making a plate); in Turner's studio by 1844, when it was bt. by Elhanan Bicknell with five other oils; Bicknell sale Christie 25 April 1863

(118), bt. Agnew for Ralph Brocklebank; sold 1942, for the trustees of Capt H. C. R. Brocklebank, by Agnew to the second Viscount Allendale; sale Sotheby 7 July 1965 (90), bt. Agnew for the father of the present owners
Private collection, London

P362 Venice, from the porch of Madonna della Salute R.A. 1835 (155)

Canvas, 914 × 1220
Engr.: by W. Miller, publ. 1 June 1838 (as 'The Grand Canal, Venice', R. 648)
by R. Brandard for *The Turner Gallery*, 1875 (as 'The Grand Canal, Venice', R. 729)
Prov.: H. A. J. Munro of Novar; sale, Christie 26 March 1860 (150), bt. Gambart; John Heugh, from whom bt. by Agnew, 1862, and sold to Sam Mendel, of Manchester; sale Christie 24 April 1875 (445), bt. Agnew; bt. from Agnew by Lord Dudley after the sale; sold by Lord Dudley c. 1890; Cornelius Vanderbilt, who presented it to the Museum, 1899
Coll.: Metropolitan Museum, New York (99.31)

P363 Line-fishing off Hastings R.A. 1835 (234)

Canvas, 584 × 762
Engr.: by W. Miller for *The Turner Gallery*, 1859 (R. 728)
Prov.: bought at the R.A. exhibition 1835 by John Sheepshanks (or possibly commissioned by him); given by him to the Museum, 1857)
Coll.: Victoria and Albert Museum, London (207)

P364 The burning of the Houses of Lords and Commons, October 16, 1834 R.A. 1835 (294)

Canvas, 925 × 1230
Prov.: bought from Turner by J. G. Marshall, of Headingly, Leeds; sale Christie 28 April 1888 (32), bt. in under name of 'Ponsford', and by descent to James Marshall; for sale at the Leicester Galleries, London, but returned to the owner; acquired by John L. Severance from Knoedler in 1922, and by him bequeathed to Cleveland in 1936
Coll.: Cleveland Museum of Art, Ohio (bequest of John L. Severance)

P365 Juliet and her nurse R.A. 1836 (73)

Canvas, 890 × 1206
Engr.: by G. Hollis 1842 (as 'St. Mark's Place, Venice–Juliet and her Nurse', R. 654)
Prov.: bought by H. A. J. Munro of Novar at the R.A. 1836 exhibition; sale Christie 6 April 1878 (100), bt. Agnew; Kirkman Hodgson, M. P., from whom bt. back by Agnew, 1893, and sold to James Price; not included in Price sale of 1895, but sold during that year to Messrs. Wallis; Col. O. H. Payne, New York, by 1901; by descent to the present owner
Coll.: Mrs. Flora Whitney Miller, New York

P366 Rome from Mount Aventine * R.A. 1836 (144)

Canvas, 916 × 1246
Exh.: R.A. 1974 (515)
Prov.: bought by H. A. J. Munro of Novar from the R.A. 1836 exhibition; sale Christie 6 April 1878 (98), bt. Davis; probably bt. for or by Lord Rosebery at the 1878 sale; by descent to the present owner
Coll.: The Earl of Rosebery

P367 Mercury and Argus R.A. 1836 (182)

Canvas, 1500 × 1092
Engr.: by J. T. Willmore, 1841 (R. 650); and for *The Turner Gallery*, 1859 (R. 733)
Prov.: Joseph Gillott by 1845; sold to Charles Birch in June 1845; bt. by John Naylor, certainly by 1854; bt. Agnew 1863 and sold to John Graham; sale Christie 30 April 1887 (93), bt. Laurie; Sir Donald Alexander Smith by November 1888 (created Lord Strathcona and Mount Royal in 1897); sold by the third Baron Strathcona and Mount Royal to the Gallery, 1951, through Agnew

Coll.: National Gallery of Canada, Ottawa

P368 The Grand Canal, Venice R.A. 1837 (31)

Canvas, 1480 × 1105
Prov.: Joseph Gillott in March 1845 ('in the care of George Pennell, Berners Street, London'); bt. by Charles Birch in December 1845; bt. by John James Ruskin on 27 April 1847 through Thomas Rought; Ruskin sale Christie 8 June 1872 (68), bt. Agnew; Baron A. Grant, 1873, for whom Agnew resold to Ralph Brocklebank, 1874; sold by R. Brocklebank's executors through Agnew to Duveen in October 1922; acquired by Henry Huntington on 23 November 1922
Coll.: Henry E. Huntington Library and Art Gallery, San Marino, California

The following verses appeared with the title in the catalogue:

> "*Antonio.* Hear me yet, good Shylock.
> *Shylock.* I'll have my bond."
>
> *Merchant of Venice, Act III, Sc. 3.*

P369 Apollo and Daphne. — *Ovid's Metamorphoses* R.A. 1837 (130)

Mahogany, 1100 × 1990
Coll.: Turner Bequest, Tate Gallery, London (520)

The following verses appeared with the title in the catalogue:

> "Sure is my bow, unerring is my dart;
> But, ah! more deadley his who pierced my heart.

* * * * * * * * * * * * * * * * * * * *

> As when th' impatient greyhound, slipt from far,
> Bounds o'er the glebe to course the fearful hare,
> She, in her speed, does all her safety lay;
> And he, with double speed, pursues the prey."

P370   The parting of Hero and Leander — from the Greek of Musæus* R.A. 1837 (274)

Canvas, 1460 × 2360
Coll.: Turner Bequest, National Gallery, London (521)

The following verses appeared with the title in the catalogue:

> "The morning came too soon, with crimsoned blush
> Chiding the tardy night and Cynthia's warning beam;
> But love yet lingers on the terraced steep,
> Upheld young Hymen's torch and failing lamp,
> The token of departure never to return.
> Wild dashed the Hellespont its straited surge.
> And on the raised spray appeared Leander's fall."

P371   Snow-storm, avalanche and inundation —a scene in the upper part of Val d'Aout, Piedmont R.A. 1837 (480)

Canvas, 915 × 1225
Exh.: R.A. 1974 (567)

Prov.: Joseph Gillott in March 1854 (with the dealer George Pennell, for sale); H. A. J. Munro of Novar, sale Christie 6 April 1878 (102), bt. Lord Wharncliffe, who still owned it in 1889; James Price; sale Christie 15 June 1895 (66), bt. Agnew for Sir Donald Currie; by descent to his grand-daughter, Mrs. Craven from whom bt. by Agnew, 1947; sold to the Art Institute (Frederick T. Haskell Collection), December 1947, through Roland, Browse and Delbanco
Coll.: Art Institute of Chicago, Illinois

P372   Fishing Boats, with Hucksters bargaining for Fish ('Dutch Fishing Boats') B.I. 1838 (134)

Canvas, 1743 × 2241
Sig. on topmost flag of the large fishing-boat: *J M W Turner*
Prov.: bought from Turner in 1851 by John Naylor; bt. from Mrs. Naylor in 1910 by Agnew through Dyer and Sons and sold the same year to Mrs. W. W. Kimball; presented to the Art Institute from the collection of Mr. and Mrs. W. W. Kimball, 1922
Coll.: Art Institute of Chicago, Illinois (No. 4472)

P373   Phryne going to the public bath as Venus—Demosthenes taunted by Æschines R.A. 1838 (31)

Canvas, 1805 × 1650
Coll.: Turner Bequest, Tate Gallery, London (522)

P374   Modern Italy—the Pifferari R.A. 1838 (57)

Canvas, 925 × 1230
Engr.: by W. Miller 1842 (R. 658) and for *The Turner Gallery*, 1859 (R. 736)
Prov.: H. A. J. Munro of Novar, who bt. it from the artist; sale Christie 11 May 1867 (176), bt. Johnstone; James Fallows; sale Christie 23 May 1868 (145), bt. Johnstone; Butler Johnstone; Munro of Novar sale Christie 6 April 1878 (97), bt. Price; David Price sale Christie 2 April 1892 (110), bt. Laurie; Kirkman Hodgson; James Reid of Auchterarder; presented by his sons to the Art Gallery, 1896
Coll.: Art Gallery and Museum, Glasgow

P375   Ancient Italy—Ovid banished from Rome* R.A. 1838 (192)

Canvas, 946 × 1250
Engr.: by J. T. Willmore 1842 (R. 657) and for *The Turner Gallery*, 1859 (R. 735)
Prov.: bought by H. A. J. Munro of Novar at the 1838 exhibition; sale Christie 6 April 1878 (96), bt. Agnew; Kirkman Hodgson; bt. back by Agnew in 1893 and sold to Messrs. Sedelmeyer, Paris, who sold it to Camille Groult; by descent to his grandson M. Pierre Bordeaux Groult, from whom bt. by Wildenstein and Agnew 1971; bt. from the latter by Dr. Correa da Silva, Lisbon, 1973; resold through Agnew to the present owner in 1975
Private collection

P376   Fountain of Fallacy B.I. 1839 (58)

Canvas, 1015 × 1625 (including the frame)
Prov.: William Marshall of Eaton Square (?)
Coll.: Beaverbrook Art Gallery, Fredericton, New Brunswick (?)

Joll discusses a possible provenance for this picture at length, but favours the view that the work is identical with the *Fountain of Indolence* (P354). The 1839 catalogue entry included the following verses:

> Its rainbow—dew diffused fell on each anxious lip
> Working wild fantasy, imagining;
> First, Science in the immeasurable abyss of thought,
> Measured her orbits slumbering.

MS. Poem, Fallacies of Hope.

P377 **The Fighting 'Temeraire' tugged to her last berth to be broken up, 1838***
R.A. 1839 (43)

Canvas, 910 × 1220
Coll.: Turner Bequest, National Gallery, London (524)

The following verses appeared with the title in the catalogue:

"The flag which braved the battle and the breeze,
No longer owns her."

P378 **Ancient Rome; Agrippina landing with the ashes of Germanicus. The Triumphal Bridge and Palace of the Cæsars restored** R.A. 1839 (66)

Canvas, 915 × 1220
Exh.: R.A. 1974 (516)
Coll.: Turner Bequest, Tate Gallery, London (523)

The following verses appeared with the title in the catalogue:

———"The clear stream,
Aye,—the yellow Tiber glimmers to her beam,
Even while the sun is setting."

P379 **Modern Rome—Campo Vaccino**
R.A. 1839 (70)

Canvas, 902 × 1220
Exh.: R.A. 1974 (517)
Prov.: H. A. J. Munro of Novar, who probably bt. it at the R.A. 1839 exhibition; sale Christie 6 April 1878 (99), bt. Davis, probably a *nom de vente* for

the fifth Earl of Rosebery, or an agent acting for him; by descent to the present owner
Coll.: The Earl of Rosebery

The following lines were appended to the title in the catalogue:

"The moon is up, and yet it is not night,
The sun as yet divides the day with her."

—*Lord Byron.*

P380 **Pluto carrying off Proserpine**—*Ovid's Metam.* R.A. 1839 (360)

Canvas, 924 × 1236
Prov.: ? John Wethered; John Chapman, M.P., by 1852 or certainly by 1857; by descent to his son Edward Chapman M.P.; bt. 1911 from Sulley by Knoedler and sold to Watson B. Dickerman in 1912; given to the National Gallery, 1951 by Mrs. Dickerman in memory of her husband.
Coll.: National Gallery of Art, Washington, D.C. (1080)

P381 **Cicero at his villa** R.A. 1839 (463)

Canvas, 927 × 1232
Prov.: Joseph Gillott by March 1845; John Miller, of Liverpool, by 1848; H. A. J. Munro of Novar after 1848; sale Christie 11 May 1867 (179), bt. Lord Powerscourt; bt. from him by Agnew in 1872 and sold to Edward Hermon; sale Christie 13 May 1882 (81) bt. in; Sir Charles Seely; Sir Hugh Seely, from whom bt. by Knoedler in 1928 and sold in October 1928 to Anthony de Rothschild; by descent to the present owner
Coll.: Evelyn de Rothschild, Esq., Ascott, Bucks.

P382 **Bacchus and Ariadne** R.A. 1840 (27)

Canvas, 790 × 790
Coll.: Turner Bequest, Tate Gallery, London (525)

P383 **Venice, the Bridge of Sighs** R.A. 1840 (55)

Canvas, 610 × 915
Exh.: R.A. 1974 (530)
Coll.: Turner Bequest, Tate Gallery, London (527)

The following verse appeared with the title in the catalogue:

"I stood upon a bridge, a palace and a prison on each hand."

—*Byron.*

P384 **Venice, from the Canale della Giudecca, chiesa di S. Maria della Salute, &c.**
R.A. 1840 (71)

Canvas, 610 × 914
Prov.: painted for John Sheepshanks, who gave it to the Museum, 1857
Coll.: Victoria and Albert Museum, London (208)

P385 Slavers throwing overboard the dead and dying—Typhon coming on ('The Slave Ship')* R.A. 1840 (203)

Canvas, 910 × 1380
Exh.: R.A. 1974 (518)
Prov.: with Turner's dealer, Thomas Griffith, for sale in December 1843; bt. by John James Ruskin and given to his son John Ruskin as a New Year's present, 1844; Ruskin sale Christie 15 April 1869 (50), bt. in; sold by Ruskin to America, 1872; J. T. Johnston, New York, 1873; Miss A. Hooper, Boston; W. H. S. Lothrop, Boston; acquired by the Museum, 1899 (Henry Lillie Pierce Fund)
Coll.: Museum of Fine Arts, Boston, Mass. (99.22)

The following verses appeared with the title in the catalogue:

"Aloft all hands, strike the top-masts and belay;
Yon angry setting sun and fierce-edged clouds
Declare the Typhon's coming.
Before it sweep your decks, throw overbroad
The dead and dying—ne'er heed their chains.
Hope, Hope, fallacious Hope!
Where is thy market now?"

—*MS. Fallacies of Hope.*

P386 The new moon; or, 'I've lost my boat, you shan't have your hoop' R.A. 1840 (243)

Mahogany, 655 × 815
Coll.: Turner Bequest, Tate Gallery, London (526)

P387 Rockets and blue lights (close at hand) to warn steam-boats of shoal water R.A. 1840 (419)

Canvas, 902 × 1194
Engr.: in chromolithography by Robert Carrick 1852 (R. 850)
Prov.: with Turner's dealer, Thomas Griffith, for sale in December 1843; Charles Birch by 1850; bt. from him by John Naylor; bt. Agnew from Naylor in 1863; John Graham 1863-4 and then repur-

chased by Agnew; Henry McConnell 1864; sale Christie 27 March 1886 (77), bt. Agnew; Sir Julian Goldsmid; sale Christie 13 June 1896 (54), bt. Agnew; James Orrock 1901; Charles T. Yerkes, New York by 1902; sale American Art Galleries, New York, 5 April 1910 (75), bt. Duveen; bt. Knoedler from Duveen in 1914 and sold to G. Eastman; returned by him in 1916 and sold to C. M. Schwab; sold by him after 1928 to Knoedler from whom bt. by Robert Sterling Clark, 1932
Coll.: Sterling and Francine Clark Art Institute, Williamstown, Mass.

P388 Neapolitan fisher-girls surprised bathing by moonlight ? R.A. 1840 (461)

Canvas, 651 × 803
Exh.: Royal Scottish Academy, 1845
Prov.: Robert Vernon, who bt. it at the R.A. 1840 exhibition; sale Christie 6 May 1842 (107), bt. Fuller; John Miller by 1845; bt. from Lloyd Bros. in 1856 by Agnew and sold to the dealer William Cox; anon. sale at Foster's, London, 29 January 1857 (193), bt. in; C. E. Flavell sale Christie 26 March 1860 (151a), bt. Flatow; Munro of Novar; Phyllis Woolner; sale Christie 23 April 1954 (118), bt. Appleby, from whom bt. by the present owner; sale Sotheby 23 October 1974 (23) as 'Turner (after)', withdrawn
Private collection, London

It is uncertain whether this or No. P389 is the work exhibited at the R.A. in 1840.

P389 Neapolitan fisher-girls surprised bathing by moonlight ? R.A. 1840 (461)

Panel, 635 × 787
Prov.: Thomas Woolner, R.A.; sale Christie

12 June 1875 (133), bt. Ellis; Henry McConnell; sale Christie 27 March 1886 (75), bt. W. B. Dennison; George Coats, Glasgow by 1901; by descent to the present owner.
Private collection, Scotland

See note to No. P388.

P390 Ducal Palace, Dogano, with part of San Georgio, Venice R.A. 1841 (53)

Canvas, 635 × 930
Prov.: bought on Varnishing Day at the 1841 R.A. exhibition by Turner's friend, the sculptor, Sir Francis Chantrey, R.A.; W. J. Broderip; sale Christie 18 June 1853 (89), bt. Egg; T. Horrocks Miller by 1889; bt. from Mrs. Horrocks Miller in 1925 by Agnew jointly with Duveen and sold by the latter in November 1925 to Mrs. F. F. Prentiss, of Cleveland; bequeathed by her to Oberlin, 1944
Coll.: Dudley Peter Allen Memorial Art Museum, Oberlin, Ohio (44:54)

P391 Giudecca, la Donna della Salute and San Georgio ('The Giudecca from the Canale di Fusina')* R.A. 1841 (66)

Canvas, 610 × 915
Exh.: R.A. 1974 (531)
Prov.: bought by Elhanan Bicknell at the R.A. in 1841; sale Christie 25 April 1863 (116), bt. Agnew for Sir John Pender; sale Christie 29 May 1897 (85), bt. Agnew for Sir Donald Currie; by descent to his grandson, Major G. L. K. Wisely, for whom Agnew sold the picture to the present owner in 1959.
Coll.: Mr. William Wood Prince, Chicago

P392   Schloss Rosenau, seat of H. R. H. Prince Albert of Coburg, near Coburg, Germany R.A. 1841 (176)

Canvas, 970 × 1248
Prov.: Joseph Gillott by 1845, and almost certainly one of a group of eight pictures purchased by him from Turner, c. 1844; Gillott sale Christie 20 April 1872 (162), bt. Agnew and sold to C. Skipper; sale Christie 24 May 1884 (100), bt. Agnew and sold to George Holt 1886; by descent to his daughter, Emma Holt, who bequeathed it to the City of Liverpool, 1944
Coll.: Walker Art Gallery, Liverpool

A replica is No. P442.

P393   Depositing of John Bellini's three pictures in la Chiesa Redentore, Venice R.A. 1841 (277)

Canvas, 736 × 1155
Engr.: by J. T. Willmore for the *Art Union,* 1858, and in the *Magazine of Art,* 1897 (R. 677a)
Prov.: bought from Charles Birch in December 1847 by Joseph Gillott and resold by him to Thomas Rought in January 1849; Lloyd Brothers; sale Foster 13 June 1855 (60), bt. in; bt. by Agnew from Lloyd in 1857 and sold to Richard Hemming of Bentley Manor, Bromsgrove; bt. back from Mrs. Hemming in 1892 by Agnew and sold to Sir John Pender; his sale Christie 29 May 1897 (84), bt. Agnew for J. Pierpont Morgan; in the Morgan collection until c. 1947, when bt. by Myron Taylor, the U.S. Ambassador to the Vatican; acquired from him in 1961 by Wildenstein and Agnew and sold in the same year by the latter to the Hon. Colin Tennant, from whom bt. by the present owner, 1969
Private collection

P394   Dawn of Christianity (Flight into Egypt) R.A. 1841 (532)

Canvas, circular, diameter 785
Exh.: R.A. 1974 (519)
Prov.: B. G. Windus, who bt. it at the R.A. 1841 exhibition; sale Christie 20 June 1853 (3), bt. in; sale Christie 26 March 1859 (49), bt. in; sale Christie 19 July 1862 (57), bt. Rought; Louis Huth, sale Christie 2 March 1872 (74), bt. Agnew; R. K. Hodgson, M. P., from whom bt. back by Agnew in 1891; sold to Sir Donald Currie; presented to the Belfast Art Gallery by Lady Currie, 1913
Coll.: Ulster Museum, Belfast (276:1913)

The following quotation appeared with the title in the catalogue:

"That star has risen."

—*Rev. T. Gisborne's Walks in a Forest.*

P395   Glaucus and Scylla R.A. 1841 (542)

Panel, 790 × 775
Prov.: bought by B. G. Windus at the R.A. 1841 exhibition; sale Christie 20 June 1853 (40), bt. in; sale Christie 26 March 1859 (50), bt. in; sale Christie 19 July 1862 (58), bt. Rought; Louis Huth, sale Christie 2 March 1872 (73), bt. Tooth; José de Murrieta, Marquis de Santurce, sale Christie 7 April 1883 (171), bt. in; Sir Horatio Davis, 1901; Sedelmeyer Gallery, Paris, 1902; John Jaffe, Nice, 1903–43; bt. by Agnew from Emile Leitz, Paris, 1956; Howard Young Galleries, New York, 1957; Mrs. Chamberlain until 1966, when acquired by the Kimbell Art Foundation
Coll.: Kimbell Art Foundation, Fort Worth, Texas (No. AP 66.11)

P396   The Dogano, San Giorgio, Citella, from the steps of the Europa R.A. 1842 (52)

Canvas, 620 × 925
Exh.: R.A. 1974 (532)
Prov.: Robert Vernon, purchased at the R.A. 1842 exhibition and given to the National Gallery, 1847; transferred to the Tate Gallery 1949

Coll.: Tate Gallery, London (372)

P397   Campo Santo, Venice R.A. 1842 (73)

Canvas, 622 × 927
Engr.: in the *Art Journal,* 1899
by J. C. Armytage, an etching of the cirrus in the sky published in *Modern Painters* (1860, v. Pl. 67)
Prov.: bought at the R.A. 1842 exhibition by Elhanan Bicknell or perhaps painted for him; sale Christie 25 April 1863 (112), bt. Agnew for Henry McConnell; sale Christie 27 March 1886 (76), bt. S. White for Mrs. J. M. Keiller, of Dundee; acquired from her in 1916 through Henry Reinhardt and Son by Edward Drummond Libbey and presented by him to the Museum, 1926
Coll.: Toledo Museum of Art, Ohio

P398   Snow storm—steam-boat off a harbour's mouth making signals in shallow water, and going by the lead. The author was in this storm on the night the Ariel left Harwich* R.A. 1842 (182)

Canvas, 915 × 1220
Exh.: R.A. 1974 (504)
Coll.: Turner Bequest, Tate Gallery, London (530)

P399   Peace—burial at sea* R.A. 1842 (338)

Canvas, 870 × 865
Exh.: R.A. 1974 (521)
Coll.: Turner Bequest, Tate Gallery, London (528)

The following verses appeared with the title in the catalogue:

"The midnight torch gleamed o'er the steamer's side,
And Merit's corse was yielded to the tide."

—*Fallacies of Hope.*

P400 War. The exile and the rock limpet*
R.A. 1842 (353)

Canvas, 795 × 795
Coll.: Turner Bequest, Tate Gallery, London (529)

The following verses appeared with the title in the catalogue:

> "Ah! thy tent-formed shell is like
> A soldier's nightly bivouac, alone
> Amidst a sea of blood———
> —but you can join your comrades."
>
> —*Fallacies of Hope.*

P401 The opening of the Wallhalla, 1842
R.A. 1843 (14)

Mahogany, 1125 × 2005
Coll.: Turner Bequest, Tate Gallery, London (533)

The following verses appeared with the title in the catalogue:

> "*L'honneur au Roi de Bavière.*"
> "Who rode on thy relentless car fallacious
>   Hope?
> He, though scathed at Ratisbon, poured on
> The tide of war o'er all thy plain, Bavare,
> Like the swollen Danube to the gates of
>   Wien.
> But peace returns—the morning ray
> Beams on the Wallhalla, reared to science and
>   the arts,
> For men renowned, of German fatherland."
>
> *Fallacies of Hope, MS.*

P402 The Sun of Venice going to sea*
R.A. 1843 (129)

Canvas, 615 × 920
Inscr. on sail: *Sol de VENEZA MI RAI.I...*
Exh.: R.A. 1974 (534)
Coll.: Turner Bequest, Tate Gallery, London (535)

The following verses appeared with the title in the catalogue:

> "Fair shines the morn, and soft the zephyrs
>   blow,
> Venezia's fisher spreads his painted sail so
>   gay,
> Nor heeds the demon that in grim repose
> Expects his evening prey."
>
> —*Fallacies of Hope, MS.*

(The text varies in different editions of the catalogue)

P403 Dogana, and Madonna della Salute, Venice R.A. 1843 (144)

Canvas, 630 × 930
Sig. on wall in lower right corner: *J M W T*
Exh.: R.A. 1974 (533)

Prov.: Edwin Bullock, who bt. it at the R.A. 1843 exhibition, Bullock sale Christie 21 May 1870 (143), bt. Agnew; sold to John Fowler; sale Christie 6 May 1899 (79), bt. Agnew for James Ross, of Montreal; sale Christie 8 July 1927 (28), bt. Agnew for Alvan T. Fuller, of Boston, Mass.; given to Washington in memory of Governor Alvan T. Fuller by the Fuller Foundation 1961
Coll.: National Gallery of Art, Washington, D.C. (1604)

P404 Shade and darkness—the evening of the Deluge* R.A. 1843 (363)

Canvas, 785 × 780
Exh.: R.A. 1974 (522)
Coll.: Turner Bequest, Tate Gallery, London (531)

The following verses appeared with the title in the catalogue:

> "The moon put forth her sign of woe
>   unheeded;
> But disobedience slept; the dark'ning Deluge
>   closed around,
> And the last token came: the giant framework
>   floated,
> The roused birds forsook their nightly shelters
>   screaming,
> And the beasts waded to the ark."
>
> —*Fallacies of Hope, MS.*

Another version of the subject is No. P443.

P405 Light and colour (Goethe's Theory)—the morning after the Deluge—Moses writing the book of Genesis* R.A. 1843 (385)

Canvas, 785 × 785
Exh.: R.A. 1974 (523)
Coll.: Turner Bequest, Tate Gallery, London (532)

The following verses appeared with the title in the catalogue:

> "The ark stood firm on Ararat; th' returning
>   sun
> Exhaled earth's humid bubbles, and emulous
>   of light,
> Reflected her lost forms, each in prismatic
>   guise
> Hope's harbinger, ephemeral as the summer
>   fly
> Which rises, flits, expands, and dies."
>
> —*Fallacies of Hope, MS.*

P406 St. Benedetto, looking towards Fusina
R.A. 1843 (554)

Canvas, 615 × 920

Exh.: R.A. 1974 (535)
Coll.: Turner Bequest, Tate Gallery, London (534)

P407 Ostend R.A. 1844 (11)

Canvas, 929 × 1232
Exh.: R.A. 1974 (506)
Prov.: H. A. J. Munro of Novar, who may have bt. it at the R.A. 1844 exhibition, but owned it by 1847; sale Christie 24 March 1860 (151), bt. Gambart; T. C. Farrer (?); Cornelius Vanderbilt II; by descent to his daughter, Countess Szechenyi, from whose heirs it was acquired by Agnew; bt. by the Munich Gallery, 1975
Coll.: Bayerische Staatsgemäldesammlungen, Neue Pinakothek, Munich (14435)

P408 Fishing boats bringing a disabled ship into Port Ruysdael R.A. 1844 (21)

Canvas, 915 × 1230
Coll.: Turner Bequest, Tate Gallery, London (536)

P409 Rain, Steam, and Speed—The Great Western Railway* R.A. 1844 (62)

Canvas, 910 × 1220
Coll.: Turner Bequest, National Gallery, London (538)

P410 Van Tromp, going about to please his masters, ships a sea, getting a good wetting—Vide Lives of Dutch Painters R.A. 1844 (253)

Canvas, 914 × 1219
Engr.: in the *Magazine of Art,* 1899
Prov.: Charles Birch by 1845 (probably through George Pennell, who may have had it on consignment from Joseph Gillott); John Miller, of Liverpool, by 1850; sale Christie 22 May 1858 (248), bt. Gambart; bt. 1867 by Agnew from Miller, who had probably bt. it back from Gambart between 1858 and 1867, and sold to Henry Woods, J. P.; sale Christie 5 May 1883 (147), bt. Martin, a *nom de vente* for Thomas Holloway; passed with the rest of the Holloway collection to Holloway College
Coll.: Royal Holloway College, Englefield Green

P411 Venice—Maria della Salute R.A. 1844 (345)

Canvas, 615 × 920
Coll.: Turner Bequest, Tate Gallery, London (539)

P412 Approach to Venice R.A. 1844 (356)

Canvas, 620 × 940
Prov.: B. G. Windus; sale Christie 20 June 1853 (5), bt. Gambart; Charles Birch; sale Foster 28 February 1856 (57), bt. Wells (?); Joseph Gillott by 1860; bt. 1863 from Gambart by Agnew and sold to James Fallows; later in 1863 exchanged by Fallows with Agnew and sold to J. Smith; bt. back

from his executors in 1870 by Agnew and sold to W. Moir; bt. from Mrs. Moir in 1899 by Agnew; Sir Charles Tennant; bt. by Knoedler from the second Lord Glenconner in 1923 and sold to Andrew Mellon, who gave it to the National Gallery, 1937
Coll.: National Gallery of Art, Washington, D.C. (110)

The following verses appeared with the title in the catalogue:

"The path lies o'er the sea invisible,
And from the land we went
As to a floating city, steering in,
And gliding up her streets as in a dream,
So smoothly, silently."—*Roger's Italy.*
"The moon is up, and yet it is not night,
The sun as yet disputes the day with her."

—*Byron*

P413 Venice Quay, Ducal Palace R.A. 1844 (430)

Canvas, 620 × 925
Coll.: Turner Bequest, Tate Gallery, London (540)

P414 Whalers—Vide Beale's Voyage, p. 163 R.A. 1845 (50)

Canvas, 910 × 1220
Coll.: Turner Bequest, Tate Gallery, London (545)

P415 Whalers—Vide Beale's Voyage, p. 175 ('The Whale Ship') R.A. 1845 (77)

Canvas, 917 × 1225
Prov.: Elhanan Bicknell (?), who may have commissioned it, but seems to have returned it to the artist soon after the R.A. 1845 exhibition; H. A. J. Munro of Novar (?); Joseph Hogarth, sale Christie 13 June

1851 (48), bt. Gambart; John Miller of Liverpool, sale Christie 22 May 1858 (247), bt. Gambart; bt. by Agnew from Miller in 1867 and sold to F. R. Leyland; sale Christie 13 June 1874 (115), bt. in; Thomas Woolner, R.A., sale Christie 12 June 1875 (132) bt. in; Charles Cooper, sale Christie 21 April 1883 (151), bt. Vokins; Francis Seymour Haden, sale Christie 23 May 1891 (110), bt. in; bt. by the Metropolitan Museum, 1896 (Wolfe Fund)
Coll.: Metropolitan Museum, New York (96:26)

P416 Venice, evening, going to the ball—MS. Fallacies of Hope R.A. 1845 (117)

Canvas, 615 × 925
Prov.: painted for William Wethered, junior, of King's Lynn, who must have returned it to Turner before the artist's death
Coll.: Turner Bequest, Tate Gallery, London (543)

P417 Morning, returning from the ball, St. Martino—MS. Fallacies of Hope R.A. 1845 (162)

Canvas, 620 × 925
Prov.: painted for Francis McCracken, of Belfast, but returned to the artist almost certainly by the autumn of 1846
Coll.: Turner Bequest, Tate Gallery, London (544)

P418   Venice—noon. MS. Fallacies of Hope R.A. 1845 (396)

Canvas, 610 × 915
Coll.: Turner Bequest, Tate Gallery, London (541)

P419   Venice—sunset, a fisher. MS. Fallacies of Hope R.A. 1845 (433)

Canvas, 610 × 542
Coll.: Turner Bequest, Tate Gallery, London (542)

P420   Queen Mab's Cave B.I. 1846 (57)

Canvas, 920 × 1225
Exh.: R.A. 1974 (B42)
Coll.: Turner Bequest, Tate Gallery, London (548)

Two verses appeared in the catalogue:

"Frisk it, frisk it, by the Moonlight beam."
Midsummer Night's Dream.

"Thy Orgies, Mab, are manifold."
MSS. Fallacies of Hope.

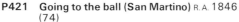

P421   Going to the ball (San Martino) R.A. 1846 (74)
P422   Returning from the ball (St. Martha) R.A. 1846 (59)

Canvas, each 610 × 914
Prov.: B. G. Windus, sale Christie 20 June 1853 (1), bt. Gambart and (2), bt. Wallis; both pictures bt. by Joseph Gillott from Henry Wallis 23 March 1854; Gillott sale Christie 20 April 1872 (159) and (160), both bt. by the Earl of Bective; sale Christie 4 May 1878 (62) and (63), bt. in; James Price by 1887, sale Christie 15 June 1895 (62) and (63), both bt. Agnew; Sir Donald Currie; by descent to his grandson, Major F. D. Mirrielees, for whom sold by Agnew in 1937 to Knoedler, who sold them to the present owner
Private collection, U.S.A.

P423   "Hurrah! for the whaler Erebus! another fish!"—Beale's Voyage. R.A. 1846 (237)

Canvas, 900 × 1210
Coll.: Turner Bequest, Tate Gallery, London (546)

P424   Undine giving the ring to Masaniello, fisherman of Naples* R.A. 1846 (384)

Canvas, 790 × 790
Coll.: Turner Bequest, Tate Gallery, London (549)

P425   The Angel standing in the sun* R.A. 1846 (411)

Canvas, 785 × 785
Exh.: R.A. 1974 (526)
Coll.: Turner Bequest, Tate Gallery, London (550)

The title appeared in the R.A. catalogue with a quotation from Revelation, chap XIX, 17, 18, and the following verses:

"The morning march that flashes to the sun;
The feast of vultures when the day is done."
—*Rogers.*

P426   Whalers (boiling blubber) entangled in flaw ice, endeavouring to extricate themselves R.A. 1846 (494)

Canvas, 900 × 1200
Exh.: R.A. 1974 (524)
Coll.: Turner Bequest, Tate Gallery, London (547)

P427   The hero of a hundred fights c. 1800-10; reworked and exhibited R.A. 1847 (180)

Canvas, 910 × 1210
Exh.: R.A. 1974 (527)
Coll.: Turner Bequest, Tate Gallery, London (551)

The following note appeared in the catalogue:

An idea suggested by the German invocation upon casting the bell: In England called tapping the furnace.

MS. Fallacies of Hope.

P428   The Wreck buoy c. 1807; reworked and exhibited R.A. 1849 (81)

Canvas, 927 × 1232
Prov.: H. A. J. Munro of Novar; sale Christie 11 May 1867, (177), bt. Agnew for John Graham; sale Christie 30 April 1887 (91), bt. Agnew; sold to George Holt, of Liverpool, 1888; bequeathed by his daughter, Miss Emma Holt, 1944
Coll.: Walker Art Gallery, Liverpool (Holt Bequest)

Canvas, 915 × 1220
Coll.: Turner Bequest, Tate Gallery, London (555)

The following verse appeared with the title in the catalogue:

"The sun went down in wrath at such deceit."

—*MS. Fallacies of Hope.*

P436 Christ driving the Traders from the Temple *c.* 1832

Mahogany, 920 × 705
Coll.: Turner Bequest, Tate Gallery, London (5474)

P429 Mercury sent to admonish Æneas R.A. 1850 (174)

Canvas, 905 × 1210
Exh.: R.A. 1974 (528)
Coll.: Turner Bequest, Tate Gallery, London (553)

The following verses appeared with the title in the catalogue:

"Beneath the morning mist,
    Mercury waited to tell him of his neglected
    fleet."

—*MS. Fallacies of Hope.*

P432 The departure of the fleet R.A. 1850 (482)

Canvas, 915 × 1220
Coll.: Turner Bequest, Tate Gallery, London (554)

The following verses appeared with the title in the catalogue:

"The orient moon shone on the departing
    fleet,
Nemesis invoked, the priest held the poisoned
    cup."

—*MS. Fallacies of Hope.*

P437 Tivoli: Tobias and the Angel *c.* 1835

Canvas, 905 × 1210
Exh.: R.A. 1974 (488)
Coll.: Turner Bequest, Tate Gallery, London (2067)

P438 The Arch of Constantine, Rome *c.* 1835

Canvas, 910 × 1220
Exh.: R.A. 1974 (487)
Coll.: Turner Bequest, Tate Gallery, London (2066)

P430 Æneas relating his story to Dido R.A. 1850 (192)

Canvas, approx. 915 × 1220
Prov.: Turner Bequest, Tate Gallery, London (552); destroyed

The following verses appeared with the title in the catalogue:

"Fallacious Hope beneath the moon's pale
    crescent shone,
Dido listened to Troy being lost and won."

—*MS. Fallacies of Hope.*

Nos P433–P532 Unexhibited Works 1829–1851

Nos P433–P486 Miscellaneous

P433 Landscape: Christ and the Woman of Samaria *c.* 1830

Canvas, 1455 × 2375
Exh.: R.A. 1974 (486)
Coll.: Turner Bequest, Tate Gallery, London (1875)

P439 Mountain glen, perhaps with Diana and Actaeon *c.* 1835–40

Canvas, 1490 × 1110
Coll.: Turner Bequest, Tate Gallery, London (561)

P434 Rocky bay, with figures *c.* 1830

Canvas, 915 × 1245
Exh.: R.A. 1974 (483)
Coll.: Turner Bequest, Tate Gallery, London (1989)

P435 The Vision of Jacob's Ladder *?c.* 1830

Canvas, 1230 × 1880
Exh.: R.A. 1974 (484)
Coll.: Turner Bequest, Tate Gallery, London (5507)

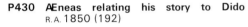

P431 The visit to the tomb R.A. 1850 (373)

P440 Heidelberg *c.* 1840–5

Canvas, 1320 × 2010
Exh.: R.A. 1974 (574)
Coll.: Turner Bequest, Tate Gallery, London (518)

P441 Studies for 'Dawn of Christianity' *c.* 1841

Canvas, 1335 × 650
Coll.: Turner Bequest, Tate Gallery, London
(5508)

See No. P394.

P442 Rosenau *c.* 1841–4

Canvas, 965 × 1245
Sig. lower left: *JMW Turner*
Prov.: Col. E. F. W. Barker; G. Barker-Harland; bt. in
1965 from Oscar and Peter Johnson Ltd. by Paul
Mellon
Coll.: Yale Center for British Art, Paul Mellon
Collection

A replica of No. P392, perhaps by another hand.

P443 The Evening of the Deluge *c.* 1843

Canvas, 760 × 760
Prov.: Revd. T. J. Judkin; Mrs. Judkin, sale Christie
13 January 1872 (35, as 'The Animals going into
the ark—circle'), bt. White; William Houldsworth
by 1878; Christie 23 May 1891 (59), bt. in; sale
Christie 11 May 1896 (54), bt. Shepherd; Maurice
Kahn from whom bt. by Agnew in 1900 and sold to
H. Darell-Brown, 1901; sale Christie 23 May 1924
(41), bt. Carroll; with Howard Young Galleries,
New York, 1928; Mrs. Lilian Timken by 1933;
bequeathed by her to Washington, 1959
Coll.: National Gallery of Art, Washington, D.C.
(1592)

A version of No. P404.

P444 A lady in Van Dyck costume *c.* 1830–5

Canvas, 1210 × 910
Coll.: Turner Bequest, Tate Gallery, London
(5511)

P445 Dinner in a great room with figures in costume *c.* 1830–5

Canvas, 910 × 1220
Exh.: R.A. 1974 (338)
Coll.: Turner Bequest, Tate Gallery, London
(5502)

P446 Figures in a building *c.* 1830–5

Canvas, 915 × 1220
Coll.: Turner Bequest, Tate Gallery, London
(5496)

P447 Music party, Petworth *c.* 1835

Canvas, 1210 × 905
Exh.: R.A. 1974 (336)
Coll.: Turner Bequest, Tate Gallery, London
(3550)

P448 Two women with a letter *c.* 1835

Canvas, 1220 × 915

Coll.: Turner Bequest, Tate Gallery, London
(5501)

P449 Interior at Petworth* *c.* 1837

Canvas, 910 × 1220
Exh.: R.A. 1974 (339)
Coll.: Turner Bequest, Tate Gallery, London
(1988)

P450 A vaulted hall* *c.* 1835

Mahogany, 750 × 915
Coll.: Turner Bequest, Tate Gallery, London
(5539)

P451 The Cave of Despair, from Spenser's 'Faery Queene' (?) *c.* 1835

Mahogany, 510 × 810
Coll.: Turner Bequest, Tate Gallery, London
(5522)

P452 Head of a person asleep *c.* 1835

Canvas, 245 × 300
Coll.: Turner Bequest, Tate Gallery, London
(5494)

P453 The Evening Star *c.* 1830

Canvas, 925 × 1230
Coll.: Turner Bequest, National Gallery, London
(1991)

P454 Hastings *c.* 1830–5

Canvas, 910 × 1220
Exh.: R.A. 1974 (493)
Coll.: Turner Bequest, Tate Gallery, London
(1986)

P455 Rough sea with wreckage *c.* 1830–5

Canvas, 920 × 1225
Exh.: R.A. 1974 (492)
Coll.: Turner Bequest, Tate Gallery, London
(1980)

P456 Breakers with a flat beach *c.* 1830–5

Canvas, 900 × 1210
Coll.: Turner Bequest, Tate Gallery, London
(1987)

P457 Waves breaking against the wind *c.* 1835

Canvas, 585 × 890
Coll.: Turner Bequest, Tate Gallery, London
(2881)

P458 Waves breaking on a lee shore *c.* 1835

Canvas, 600 × 950
Coll.: Turner Bequest, Tate Gallery, London
(2882)

P459   Waves breaking on a shore *c.* 1835

Canvas, 465 × 605
Coll.: Turner Bequest, Tate Gallery, London
(5495)

P460   Fire at sea *c.* 1835

Canvas, 1715 × 1205
Exh.: R.A. 1974 (496)
Coll.: Turner Bequest, Tate Gallery, London (558)

P461   Yacht approaching the coast
  c. 1835–40

Canvas, 1020 × 1420
Exh.: R.A. 1974 (494)
Coll.: Turner Bequest, Tate Gallery, London
(4662)

P462   Stormy   sea   with   blazing   wreck
  c. 1835–40

Canvas, 995 × 1415
Exh.: R.A. 1974 (495)
Coll.: Turner Bequest, Tate Gallery, London
(4658)

P463   Stormy sea with dolphins *c.* 1835–40

Canvas, 910 × 1020
Exh.: R.A. 1974 (501)
Coll.: Turner Bequest, Tate Gallery, London
(4664)

P464   Margate (?) from the sea *c.* 1835–40

Canvas, 915 × 1225
Coll.: Turner Bequest, Tate Gallery, London
(1984)

P465   Seascape *c.* 1835–40

Canvas, 900 × 1210
Coll.: Turner Bequest, Tate Gallery, London
(5515)

P466   Seascape   with   storm   coming   on
  c. 1840

Canvas, 915 × 1215
Exh.: R.A. 1974 (502)
Coll.: Turner Bequest, Tate Gallery, London
(4445)

P467   Seascape with distant coast *c.* 1840

Canvas, 915 × 1220
Inscr. upper right: $\frac{M}{C}$ M N Ns T Ts
Exh.: R.A. 1974 (503)
Coll.: Turner Bequest, Tate Gallery, London
(5516)

P468   Seascape with buoy *c.* 1840

Canvas, 915 × 1220
Coll.: Turner Bequest, Tate Gallery, London
(5477)

P469   Sun setting over a lake *c.* 1840

Canvas, 910 × 1225
Coll.: Turner Bequest, Tate Gallery, London
(4665)

P470   A wreck, with fishing-boats* *c.* 1840–5

Canvas, 915 × 1220
Coll.: Turner Bequest, Tate Gallery, London
(2425)

P471   Rough sea *c.* 1840–5

Canvas, 915 × 1220
Coll.: Turner Bequest, Tate Gallery, London
(5479)

P472   Seascape: Folkestone *c.* 1845

Canvas, 883 × 1175
Prov.: Sir Donald Currie by 1894; by descent to his
grandson, D. J. Molteno, from whom bt. by Agnew
in 1950 and sold to the present owner in 1951
Coll.: Lord Clark of Saltwood, O. M., C. H.

P473   Sunrise with sea monsters *c.* 1845

Canvas, 915 × 1220
Exh.: R.A. 1974 (507)
Coll.: Turner Bequest, Tate Gallery, London
(1990)

P474   The beacon light *c.* 1835–40

Canvas, 597 × 927
Prov.: Mrs. Booth; to her son, John Pound; sale
Christie 25 March 1865 (197), bt. Agnew; sold to
Abel Buckley; bt. back from him by Agnew in 1868
and sold to R. Brocklebank; sale Christie 7 July
1922 (72), bt. Blaker for Miss Gwendoline Davies,
who bequeathed it to Cardiff in 1952
Coll.: National Museum of Wales, Cardiff (807)

P475   Margate Harbour *c.* 1835–40

Canvas, 458 × 610
Exh.: R.A. 1974 (497)
Prov.: possibly lot 198 in John Pound sale, Christie
25 March 1865 as 'Off Margate Pier', bt. Agnew;
H. T. Broadhurst; F. R. Leyland, sale Christie
9 March 1872 (72) bt. in; James Polak, dealer,
from whom bt. by George Holt, March 1872; by
descent to his daughter Miss Emma Holt, who
bequeathed it with the rest of her collection to the
City of Liverpool, December 1944
Coll.: Walker Art Gallery, Liverpool (Sudley Hall)

P476   Off the Nore: wind and water *c.* 1840

Canvas, 305 × 460
Prov.: possibly to be identified with lot 201 in the
Pound sale, Christie 24 March 1865 as 'Squally
Weather', bt. Bicknell; H. S. Bicknell, sale Christie
9 April 1881 (460, as 'Squally Weather'), bt.
Johnston; anon. sale (Christie's catalogue identi-
fies the vendor as Johnston) 12 December 1898
(137), bt. Leggatt; bt. from Leggatt by Agnew in
1899 and sold to P. Westmacott, from whom
repurchased by Agnew in 1901; James Orrock;
sale Christie 4 June 1904 (141), bt. R. Smith; John
Barrett, Connecticut
Coll.: Yale Center for British Art, Paul Mellon
Collection

P477   Wreckers   on   the   coast: sun   rising
  through mist *c.* 1835–40

Canvas, 355 × 522
Prov.: Mrs. Booth; her son, John Pound, sale
Christie 24 March 1865 (202, as 'Wreckers
—early morning'), bt. Vokins; Sir Donald Currie; by
descent to his grand-daughter, Mrs. M. D. Fergus-
son, from whom bt. by Agnew, 1971; Mr. and
Mrs. Patrick Gibson 1972; sold on their behalf by
Agnew to the present owner, 1974
Private collection

P478   Morning after the wreck *c.* 1835–40

Canvas, 380 × 610
Exh.: R.A. 1974 (323)
Prov.: Mrs. Booth; her son, John Pound, ? sale
Christie 24 March 1865 (204, as 'Off Mar-
gate—Hazy Morning'); M. T. Shaw; sale Christie
20 March 1880 (102), bt. Vokins; bt. from Messrs.
Dowdeswell in 1910 by Miss Gwendoline Davies
and bequeathed by her to the Museum, 1952
Coll.: National Museum of Wales, Cardiff (806)

P479   Off Ramsgate (?) *c.* 1840

Canvas, 311 × 483
Prov.: Mrs. Booth; her son, John Pound, sale
Christie 25 March 1865 (205, as 'View off

Margate—Evening'), bt. Agnew; sold to W.J. Houldsworth in 1866; bt. back by Agnew in January 1881 and sold to Dr. Jex Blake, who became headmaster of Rugby in 1874 and founded the Rugby School of Art Museum in 1878; probably gave the picture to the School, 1887
Coll.: Rugby School

P480 The storm c. 1840–5

Canvas, 324 × 545
Prov.: a label on the back states that this and the companion picture (No. P481) were given by the artist to Mrs. Pounds (sic) i.e. Mrs. Booth, and that it was bt. from her daughter by Agnew for S. G. Holland; sale Christie 25 June 1908 (112), bt. Knoedler, presumably jointly with Colnaghi, who sold it to Miss Margaret Davies in November 1908; bequeathed by her to the Museum, 1963
Coll.: National Museum of Wales, Cardiff (972)

P481 The day after the storm 1840–5

Canvas, 305 × 533
Prov.: as for No. P480, until 1908, when it was sold by S. G. Holland at Christie 25 June (113), bt. Colnaghi, who sold it the same year to Miss Gwendoline Davies, who bequeathed it to the Museum, 1952
Coll.: National Museum of Wales, Cardiff (810)

P482 Waves breaking on the shore c. 1840

Canvas, 445 × 635
Prov.: Mr. and Mrs. Franklin MacVeagh, of Chicago, who bt. the picture in England in 1889; bt. from Mrs. MacVeagh's daughter-in-law in Washington in 1961 by Agnew; sold to Paul Mellon, 1962
Coll.: Yale Center for British Art, Paul Mellon Collection

P483 Off Deal c. 1835

Millboard, 215 × 298
Prov.: said to have been given by Turner to Mrs. Booth; her son, John Pound, and given by him to Mrs. M. A. Pound, who in turn gave it to A. Austin; sent by him anon. sale Christie 11 June 1909 (190), bt. Dowdeswell, from whom bt. by Miss Margaret Davies, sale Sotheby 24 February 1960 (93) bt. Mathiessen Gallery, from whom bt. by the Nationalmuseum 1960
Coll.: Nationalmuseum, Stockholm (5526)

P484 A sailing-boat off Deal c. 1835

Millboard, 230 × 305
Exh.: R.A. 1974 (324)
Prov.: as for No. P483, until sold at Christie 11 June 1909 (191), bt. Dowdeswell, from whom bt. by Miss Gwendoline Davies, 1910; bequeathed by her to the Museum, 1952
Coll.: National Museum of Wales, Cardiff (811)

P485 Riders on a beach c. 1835

Millboard, 230 × 305
Coll.: Turner Bequest, Trustees of the British Museum (1972.U.745)

P486 Shore scene with waves and break-water c. 1835

Millboard, 230 × 305
Coll.: Turner Bequest, Trustees of the British Museum (1974.U.850)

Nos P487–P500 Sketches of coast and other scenes ?c. 1840–1845

P487 Coast scene, with buildings ?c. 1840–5

Millboard, 305 × 475
Exh.: R.A. 1974 (469)
Coll.: Turner Bequest, Trustees of the British Museum (1972.U.738)

P488 Red sky over a beach ?c. 1840–5

Millboard, 305 × 480
Coll.: Turner Bequest, Trustees of the British Museum (1972.U.746)

P489 Ship in a storm ?c. 1840–5

Millboard, 300 × 475
Exh.: R.A. 1974 (498)
Coll.: Turner Bequest, Trustees of the British Museum (1972.U.739)

P490 Calm sea with distant grey clouds ?c. 1840–5

Millboard, 300 × 480
Coll.: Turner Bequest, Trustees of the British Museum, (1972.U.743)

P491 Coast scene with breaking waves ?c. 1840–5

Millboard, 295 × 485
Coll.: Turner Bequest, Trustees of the British Museum (1972.U.741)

P492 Sea and sky? ?c. 1840–5

Millboard, 300 × 460
Coll.: Turner Bequest, Trustees of the British Museum (1972.U.740)

P493 Sand and sky? ?c. 1840–5

Millboard, 300 × 480
Coll.: Turner Bequest, Trustees of the British Museum (1972.U.742)

P494 Yellow sky? ?c. 1840–5

Millboard, 300 × 475
Coll.: Turner Bequest, Trustees of the British Museum (1972.U.744)

P495 Coast scene ?c. 1840–5

Millboard, 270 × 305
Coll.: Turner Bequest, Trustees of the British Museum (1974.U.851)

P496 Figures on a beach ?c. 1840–5

Millboard, 260 × 300
Coll.: Turner Bequest, Trustees of the British Museum (1974.U.852)

P497 Sunset seen from a beach with break-water ?c. 1840–5

Millboard, 258 × 300
Exh.: R.A. 1974 (500)
Coll.: Turner Bequest, Trustees of the British Museum (1974.U.848)

P498 Sailing-boat in a rough sea ?c. 1840–5

Millboard, 265 × 305
Coll.: Turner Bequest, Trustees of the British Museum (1972.U.748)

P499 Two figures on a beach with a boat ?c. 1840–5

Millboard, 245 × 345
Exh.: R.A. 1974 (499)
Coll.: Turner Bequest, Trustees of the British Museum (1972.U.747)

P500 Waves breaking on a beach ?c. 1840–5

Millboard, 250 × 345
Coll.: Turner Bequest, Trustees of the British Museum (1974.U.849)

Nos P501–P508 Venice c. 1835–1845

P501 Venice, the Piazzetta with the Ceremony of the Doge marrying the Sea c. 1835

Canvas, 915 × 1220
Coll.: Turner Bequest, Tate Gallery, London (4446)

P502 Venice with the Salute c. 1840–5

Canvas, 620 × 925
Exh.: R.A. 1974 (536)
Coll.: Turner Bequest, Tate Gallery, London (5487)

P503-P515

P503 Scene in Venice *c.* 1840–5

Canvas, 620 × 925
Exh.: R.A. 1974 (537)
Coll.: Turner Bequest, Tate Gallery, London
(5488)

P504 Venetian scene *c.* 1840–5

Canvas, 795 × 790
Coll.: Turner Bequest, Tate Gallery, London
(5482)

P505 Procession of boats with distant smoke, Venice *c.* 1845

Canvas, 900 × 1205
Coll.: Turner Bequest, Tate Gallery, London
(2068)

P506 Festive Lagoon scene, Venice? *c.* 1845

Canvas, 910 × 1210
Exh.: R.A. 1974 (538)
Coll.: Turner Bequest, Tate Gallery, London
(4660)

P507 Riva degli Schiavone, Venice: water fête *c.* 1841–5

Canvas, 720 × 1125
Coll.: Turner Bequest, Tate Gallery, London
(4661)

P508 Venetian Festival *c.* 1845

Canvas, 725 × 1135
Coll.: Turner Bequest, Tate Gallery, London
(4659)

Nos P509–P532 Miscellaneous

P509 Landscape with a river and a bay in the distance *c.* 1835–40

Canvas, 940 × 1230
Exh.: R.A. 1974 (620)
Prov.: Camille Groult, Paris by 1890; by descent to

his grandson, M. Pierre Bordeaux-Groult, from whom purchased by the Louvre in 1967 (No. R.F. 1967–2)
Coll.: Musée du Louvre, Paris

For a different view of the dating of Nos P509–P521 see chap. 10, note 39.

P510 The Fall of the Clyde *c.* 1835–40

Canvas, 890 × 1195
Exh.: R.A. 1974 (621)
Prov.: Revd. Thomas Prater; sale Christie 6 May 1871 (128), bt. Campbell; Sir Hugh H. Campbell, sale Christie 2 May 1874 (125), bt. Agnew from whom bt. by W. J. Houldsworth; Sir William Houldsworth sale Christie 25 May 1891 (58), bt. Agnew for Sir Joseph Robinson; sale Christie 6 July 1923 (29), bt. Tooth from whom bt. by Lord Leverhulme, September 1923
Coll.: Lady Lever Art Gallery, Port Sunlight, Cheshire

P511 Landscape with Walton Bridges *c.* 1835–40

Canvas, 863 × 1175
Prov.: Mrs. Booth; her son, John Pound, sale Christie 25 March 1865 (195), bt. Agnew; John Smith; bt. back from Smith's executors in 1870 by Agnew and sold in 1871 to John Graham; sale Christie 30 April 1887 (90), bt. Agnew; sold in May 1887 to J. S. Morgan; by descent to his great-grandson, the present owner
Coll.: Mr. H. S. Morgan, New York

P512 Norham Castle, sunrise *c.* 1835–40

Canvas, 910 × 1220
Exh.: R.A. 1974 (650)
Coll.: Turner Bequest, Tate Gallery, London
(1981)

P513 Landscape: woman with tambourine *c.* 1835–40

Canvas, 885 × 1180
Exh.: R.A. 1974 (623)
Prov.: Mrs. Booth; her son, John Pound, sale Christie 25 March 1865 (196), bt. Agnew; John Smith; bt. back from Smith's executors by Agnew in 1870 and sold in 1871 to James Price; sale Christie 18 June 1895 (61), bt. Agnew; Sir Donald Currie; by descent to the present owner
Coll.: Mrs. M. D. Fergusson

P514 Europa and the Bull *c.* 1835–40

Canvas, 908 × 1216
Prov.: Revd. Thomas Prater; sale Christie 6 May 1871 (127) bt. Cassels; W. R. Cassels, sale Christie 30 June 1906 (63), bt. Colnaghi; C. P. Taft, Cincinnati, 1907; bequeathed by him to Cincinnati 1931
Coll.: Taft Museum, Cincinnati, Ohio (1931: 422)

P515 Sunrise, a castle on a bay: 'Solitude' *c.* 1835–40

Canvas, 910 × 1220
Exh.: R.A. 1974 (622)
Coll.: Turner Bequest, Tate Gallery, London
(1985)

P516 Sunrise, with a boat between headlands *c.* 1835–40

Canvas, 915 × 1220
Exh.: R.A. 1974 (625)
Coll.: Turner Bequest, Tate Gallery, London (2002)

P517 Landscape with river and distant mountains *c.* 1835–40

Canvas, 920 × 1225
Exh.: R.A. 1974 (624)
Prov.: Robert Durning Holt, who acquired it 'perhaps not long after 1876'; given by Lady Holt (his daughter) to the Walker Art Gallery, 1945
Coll.: Walker Art Gallery, Liverpool

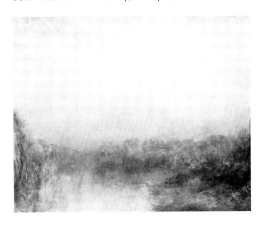

P518 The Ponte delle Torri, Spoleto *c.* 1835–40

Canvas, 910 × 1220
Coll.: Turner Bequest, Tate Gallery, London (2424)

P519 Monte Rosa *c.* 1835–40

Canvas, 915 × 1220
Exh.: R.A. 1974 (619)
Prov.: Sir Donald Currie by 1894; by descent to his grand-daughter, Mrs. L. B. Murray, from whom bt. by Agnew in 1960 and sold to Paul Mellon
Coll.: Yale Center for British Art, Paul Mellon Collection

P520 The Val d'Aosta *c.* 1835–40

Canvas, 914 × 1219
Exh.: R.A. 1974 (568)

Prov.: Camille Groult, Paris, by 1894; by descent to his grandson, M. Pierre Bordeaux-Groult, from whom bt. Agnew and Wildenstein in 1971; bt. by the Gallery from Agnew, 1973
Coll.: National Gallery of Victoria, Melbourne

P521 Mountain scene with lake and hut *c.* 1835–40

Oil and pencil on canvas, 710 × 965
Exh.: R.A. 1974 (569)
Coll.: Turner Bequest, Tate Gallery, London (5476)

P522 Mountain landscape *c.* 1835–40

Canvas, 710 × 965
Exh.: R.A. 1974 (570)
Coll.: Turner Bequest, Tate Gallery, London (5486)

P523 The Thames above Waterloo Bridge *c.* 1830–35

Canvas, 905 × 1210
Exh.: R.A. 1974 (435)
Coll.: Turner Bequest, Tate Gallery, London (1992)

P524 Abbotsford 1834–6

Japanned metal tray, oval 508 × 635
Prov.: presented by Turner to Sir Walter Scott's daughter Sophia Lockhart; ? bequeathed by her to Scott's butler, William Dalgleish; Henry Wright, who on leaving Edinburgh, *c.* 1856, presented it to John Renton, from whose family it was bt. in 1896 by Thomas Craig-Brown; Trustees of E. T. Craig-Brown deceased, sale Sotheby 1 December 1954 (151), bt. Mitchell for Mrs. Katherine Conroy, who presented it to the John Herron Art Museum in memory of Evan F. Lilly
Coll.: Indianapolis Museum of Art, Indiana (55.22)

This item is undoubtedly not by Turner. It derives from the watercolour illustration, Cat. No. 1142.

P525 Sunset ? *c.* 1830–5

Canvas, 670 × 820
Coll.: Turner Bequest, Tate Gallery, London (1876)

P526 A mountain lake at sunset *c.* 1830–5

Panel (painted on the lid of a box), 235 × 155
Prov.: the Earl of Arran, whose ancestor, the fourth Earl, was certainly acquainted with Turner; bt. from Leggatt by Agnew in 1960 and sold to the present owner
Coll.: Mr. William Wood Prince, Chicago

P527 Harbour with town and fortress ? *c.* 1830

Canvas, 1725 × 2235

Coll.: Turner Bequest, Tate Gallery, London (5514)

P528 Estuary, with rocks and buildings *c.* 1830-40

Canvas, 1730 × 2435
Coll.: Turner Bequest, Tate Gallery, London (5518)

P529 Seaport in the Grand Style *? c.* 1830-40

Canvas, 1725 × 2435
Coll.: Turner Bequest, Tate Gallery, London (5544)

P530 Extensive landscape, with river or estuary and a distant mountain *? c.* 1830-40

Canvas, original size approx. 1410 × 2515
Coll.: Turner Bequest, Tate Gallery, London (5542)

P531 Landscape with water *c.* 1835-40

Canvas, 1220 × 1820
Coll.: Turner Bequest, Tate Gallery, London (5513)

P532 A river seen from a hill *c.* 1840-5

Canvas, 790 × 795
Coll.: Turner Bequest, Tate Gallery, London (5475)

6 Untraced works of unknown date (Nos P533-P541)

P533 Fishing-boats in a stiff breeze

Size unknown
Prov.: painted for Turner's close friend and executor, Henry S. Trimmer, whom Turner met *c.* 1805-6; Trimmer sale Christie 17 March 1860 (42), bt. Hooper; bt. in September 1860 by Agnew from Holmes and sold to John Heugh; no subsequent history is known (it seems probable that the picture was later known by another title, e.g. *The Mouth of the Thames* (No. P67)

P534 Coast Scene

Size unknown but possibly 317 × 444
Prov.: ? Joseph Gillott sale Christie 27 April 1872 (299, as 'Coast Scene—stranded Boat and Old Capstan'), bt. Betts; ? Thomas and Betteridge sale, Birmingham 8 April 1892 (120), bt. Wigzell; no subsequent history known

P535 Distant view of Margate Cliffs, from the sea

Size unknown
Prov.: J. Carpenter by 1833

P536 View in Savoy

Size unknown
Prov.: Oakley by 1834

P537 Landscape

Size unknown
Exh.: Birmingham Society of Artists 1834 (9)

P538 Landscape

Size unknown
Prov.: J. Allnutt by 1835
Exh.: Birmingham Society of Artists 1835 (17)

P539 A storm

Size unknown
Prov.: Sarah Rogers, the sister of Samuel and Henry Rogers; her collection was viewed by Waagen in 1854; no subsequent trace

P540 Seapiece, with fishing-boats off a wooden pier, a gale coming on

Size unknown
Prov.: Samuel Rogers, the poet; Rogers sale Christie 2 May 1856 (528), bt. Ratcliffe; no subsequent history known

P541 Kilgarran Castle *? c.* 1799

Panel: 240 × 342
Prov.: John Miller, of Liverpool; sale Christie 22 May 1858 (250), bt. Agnew; sold 24 May to Colnaghi; Sidney Castle by 1899 and until at least 1902; no further history known

Catalogue of watercolours

This catalogue of Turner's watercolours cannot be complete: the enormous quantity of his work in the medium, and the large number of drawings still untraced, make such an undertaking almost impossible. I list here, with some exceptions, those watercolours which have been located, or which belong to, or are associated with, important series of published work, or which are recorded in the catalogues of exhibitions held in Turner's lifetime. Items from the Turner Bequest have only been included when they are exhibited, engraved, or otherwise finished works, though frequent reference is made to sketches and studies in the Bequest which are directly related to finished watercolours. The Bequest is always referred to by the initials T.B., followed by a number from Finberg's *Inventory* (see Bibliography). Drawings in pencil alone, or with only slight washes, have generally been omitted, since they would have swelled the catalogue to unmanageable size; and the copies after J. R. Cozens and others which Turner made in the 1790s have also been omitted, partly, again, for reasons of space, and partly because this is an area where attribution presents as yet insoluble problems.

The works on which I have drawn are few, for few have previously attempted a catalogue of this scope. A handful of published catalogues of individual collections are referred to in the relevant entries: Luke Herrmann's *Ruskin and Turner,* 1968, which catalogues the drawings in the Ashmolean Museum, Oxford, is denoted by the abbreviation 'Herrmann' followed by a number. 'Cormack' likewise denotes Malcolm Cormack's *Catalogue of [Turner's] Drawings and Watercolours in the Fitzwilliam Museum, Cambridge,* 1975. Michael Kitson's catalogue of *Turner Watercolours from the Collection of Sir Stephen Courtauld,* 1974, is referred to as 'Kitson'. The only published list of all Turner's major works in watercolour is that of Sir Walter Armstrong's *Turner,* 1902, pp. 238–86. This is unnumbered and incomplete, but must form the basis of any new catalogue. The most extensive research on the whole œuvre is contained in Alexander and Hilda Finberg's manuscript card index in the Print Room of the British Museum (referred to here as 'Index'); to this too I am enormously indebted.

To save space, I have omitted references to literature in the individual entries, and have listed only those exhibitions which took place in Turner's lifetime, with the exception of the two large bicentenary exhibitions held in London in 1974–5: that at the Royal Academy and that at the British Museum, referred to here as R.A. 1974 and B.M. 1975 respectively. C.G. indicates the two exhibitions held at W. B. Cooke's Gallery, 9 Soho Square, in 1822 and 1823; E.H. is Heath's exhibition at the Egyptian Hall, Piccadilly in 1829; and M.G.B. refers to the two exhibitions of 1832 and 1833, held at the gallery of Messrs. Moon, Boys & Graves, Pall Mall East. 'Grosvenor Place' and 'Leeds' stand for the two places at which Fawkes's collection was shown publicly.

Medium is described as fully as possible, given that in some cases I have been unable to examine the originals. Support is taken to be white paper (usually wove, and often made by Whatman) unless otherwise specified. Measurements are in millimetres, height before width. An asterisk following the title indicates that the work is illustrated in the main text.
The catalogue is arranged under the following headings:

SECTION I
Nos 1–122   Early work

SECTION II
Nos 123–181   Drawings of *c.* 1795–1796

SECTION III
Nos 182–226   The Essex, Hoare and Lascelles commissions, *c.* 1794–1807

SECTION IV
Nos 227–313 Work for exhibition and engraving, *c.* 1797–1810

SECTION I
Nos 1–122   Early work

I(a)   Nos 1–86
Watercolours, 1784–1794

Nos 1–4 are survivors of a series of six drawings given by Turner's mother to Jane Hunt, of London, who married James Taylor, of Bakewell, Derbyshire. The subjects are all of Margate or its neighbourhood.

Turner is traditionally supposed to have visited Margate in his boyhood, though Thornbury's account has been discredited by Finberg (*Life*, p. 17). Thornbury states (pp. 14–5) that he was there in 1788, but elsewhere he states that a drawing of Margate Church was executed when Turner was nine years old, that is, in 1784. He refers to this drawing also (p. 9) as 'one of the boy's earliest works that I have yet heard of'.

1   St. John's Church, Margate*   ?1784

Pen and black and grey ink and watercolour, 308 × 435
Prov.: Mary Turner (the artist's mother) by whom given to Jane Taylor (née Hunt), of Bakewell, Derbyshire; by descent to present owner
Private collection, U.K.

This may be the drawing referred to as having been made when Turner was nine years old, though it is not unlike a drawing dated 1787 in the Turner Bequest of *Clifton, Nuneham Harcourt, near Abingdon* (T.B., I-B; No. 6).

2   A street in Margate, looking down to the harbour*   ?1784

Pen and black ink and watercolour, 270 × 407
Prov.: Mary Turner (the artist's mother), by whom given to Jane Taylor (née Hunt), of Bakewell, Derbyshire; by descent to present owner
Private collection, U.K.

There can be little doubt that this drawing shows Margate, looking down towards the harbour, and the cliffs of Birchington, with the twin towers of Reculver on the distant headland. It was presumably executed at the same date as No. 1.

3   Minster Church, Isle of Thanet   ?1784

Pen and black ink and watercolour, 305 × 426

Prov.: Mary Turner (the artist's mother), by whom given to Jane Taylor (née Hunt), of Bakewell, Derbyshire; by descent to present owner
Private collection, U.K.

This church is identifiable with that drawn from the same viewpoint by Benjamin Thomas Pouncy and engraved in 1794. It probably dates from the same time as the two Margate drawings (Nos 1, 2). Minster in Thanet is a village about eight miles south-west of Margate.

4   View of Minster, Isle of Thanet   ?1784

Pen and black ink and watercolour: 276 × 378
Prov.: Mary Turner (the artist's mother), by whom given to Jane Taylor (née Hunt), of Bakewell, Derbyshire; by descent to present owner
Private collection, U.K.

The scene is identifiable on account of the exact similarity of the church in this drawing to that in No 3.

5   Folly Bridge and Bacon's Tower, Oxford
1787

Pen and black ink and wash with watercolour, 308 × 432
Signed and dated lower right: *W Turner 1787*
Coll.: Trustees of the British Museum (T.B., I-A)

This composition is copied from an engraving by James Basire, after a drawing probably by Edward Dayes, published in the Oxford *Almanack*, 1780, as 'North-West View of Friar Bacon's Study, &c' (see Finberg, 1910, p. 9). This and No. 6 are catalogued here as Turner's earliest dated works. Another copy of the print is now with the Turner Bequest, although it was not inventoried by Finberg.

6   Clifton, Nuneham Harcourt, near Abingdon
1787

Pen and ink and watercolour, 298 × 426
Signed and dated lower left: *W Turner 1787*
Inscr. verso: *D.º House from grounds*
Coll.: Trustees of the British Museum (T.B., I-B)

Finberg (*Inventory*) suggests that this, like No. 5, is a copy from a print, though such drawings of houses are common among Turner's early studies on the spot, worked up as finished designs. Drawings of Clifton, Nuneham Harcourt occur in the *Oxford* sketchbook (T.B., II-6, 10, 15, 16).

7   All Souls' Church, Maidstone   ?c. 1787

Watercolour, pen and brown ink, 332 × 464
Prov.: W. G. Rawlinson; Miss Alice Walker, by whom bequeathed to the museum, 1932
Coll.: Victoria and Albert Museum, London (21–1932)

Stylistically rather unlike the drawings of this period in the Turner Bequest, but probably by Turner, who may have visited Maidstone on his journeys through Kent. The composition might, however, be taken from a print (cf. T.B., I-A, No. 5). Another version of the subject is in the Fine Arts Center, Colorado Springs, Ralph O. Giddings Bequest. This seems less like Turner's work, but was considered to be authentic by Ruskin when he was shown it in 1886 by its owner, Dr. Pocock of Brighton.

8   Radley Hall from the south-east*   1789

Pencil and watercolour, with some pen and brown ink, 294 × 438
Sig. lower right: *Wm Turner pinxit*
Exh.: R.A. 1974 (1)
Coll.: Trustees of the British Museum (T.B., III-D)

This and the following drawing were enclosed by the artist in grey and yellow washline borders, still extant. Both reflect the influence of Thomas Malton (1748–1804). Turner made studies of Radley Hall in the *Oxford* sketchbook (T.B., II-2v, 9, 14).

9 Radley Hall from the north-west 1789

Pencil and watercolour, with some pen and brown ink, 294 × 438
Coll.: Trustees of the British Museum (T.B., III-C)

See No. 8.

10 The Archbishop's palace, Lambeth*
R.A. 1790 (644)

Pencil and watercolour, 263 × 378
Exh.: R.A. 1974 (2)
Prov.: John Narraway, Bristol; Miss Dart; W. G. Rawlinson; Mrs. Courtauld; F. Stevenson, 1902; R.A. Tatton, sale Christie 14 December 1928 (2), bt. Permain; Christie 5 July 1946 (40); Waters; Agnew 1967; Kurt Pantzer 1968, by whom given to the museum
Coll.: Indianapolis Museum of Art

This is Turner's first exhibited work at the Royal Academy. Malton's style of architectural topography is interpreted here in a far more sophisticated way than in the views of Radley Hall (Nos 8, 9). The watercolour is probably based on sketches the artist made of this subject in his earliest known notebook, of *c.* 1789, the *Oxford* sketchbook (T.B., II); another watercolour of the subject was made for Thomas Hardwick, the architect. A sketch in this notebook of Isleworth church was the basis for a watercolour made for Hardwick, who also owned a view made by Turner of the old church at Wanstead, which was replaced by a new one built from Hardwick's designs. These are untraced.

11 Self-portrait *c.* 1790

Watercolour, touched with white, 95 × 70 (oval)
Exh.: R.A. 1974 (B9)
Prov.: John Narraway; Ann Dart; Ruskin (1860); Mrs. Booth; Daniel Pound; C. Monkhouse
Coll.: Trustees of the National Portrait Gallery, London

This unusual study has been dated to the early 1790s. In it the artist seems younger than he appears in George Dance's profile portrait of him dated 1792, and the technique and bright colouring correspond with features of Turner's work in about

1790 to 1791. It is perhaps unlikely to date from any later time.

12 King John's Palace, Eltham R.A. 1791 (494)

Watercolour, 356 × 267
Prov.: Sir William Drake's sale, 1891; Mrs. E. Crawshay-Bailey (1953)
Private collection

13 Interior of King John's Palace, Eltham *c.* 1793

Watercolour, 332 × 270
Prov.: H. Ferrar; Sotheby 20 April 1972 (65); Cyril and Shirley Fry, from whom purchased 1972
Coll.: Yale Center for British Art, Paul Mellon Collection

Although grouped here for convenience with the exterior view of the palace (No. 12), this is unlikely to have been executed as a companion to that drawing. It seems to belong to a slightly later phase of Turner's development.
See Addenda, No. 13 a.

14 Sweakley, near Uxbridge, the seat of the Rev. Mr. Clarke R.A. 1791 (560)

Watercolour, size unknown
Provenance and whereabouts unknown

Nos 15–26 (with the exceptions of Nos 22, 23) are drawings made as a result of Turner's visits to Bristol and Malmesbury in 1791 and 1792.

15 River Avon: Wallis's Wall *c.* 1791

Watercolour, 178 × 254
Prov.: William Ward; O. E. Spicer, sale Sotheby 22 November 1961 (46), bt. G. D. Lockett, Clonterbrook House
Coll.: The Clonterbrook Trustees, Clonterbrook House, Congleton, Cheshire

One of a series of studies of scenes on the Avon, usually of Clifton Gorge, which Turner made in 1791. Several occur in the *Bristol and Malmesbury* sketchbook (T.B. VI) and elsewhere (e.g. T.B. VII, B and G). This sheet may come from the sketchbook, as may another recorded drawing, *River Avon seen from near Hot Wells*, formerly in Sir Charles Robinson's collection (Armstrong, p. 244). The series culminated in the two finished watercolours of the Avon near Bristol (exh. R.A. 1793; Nos 17, 18).

16 South porch of St. Mary Redcliffe Church, Bristol 1791–2

Pen, brown ink and watercolour, 356 × 298
Engr.: by J. Pye for *The Lady and Gentleman's Annual Pocket Ledger*, 1814 (R. 81)
Prov.: Narraway family; Mr. Short
Coll.: City Museum and Art Gallery, Bristol (K347)

17 View of the River Avon, near St. Vincent's Rock, Bristol ?1791–2 R.A. 1793 (263)

Watercolour and scraping-out with pen and ? brown ink, 172 × 245
Inscr. (on rock): *W Turner fe*
Prov.: anon. sale Christie 27 April 1864 (90); T. A. Tatton, sale Christie 14 December 1928 (7, as 'Mouth of the Avon'); ?Cotswold Gallery 1930; anon. sale Sotheby 6 June 1951 (120, as 'Mouth of the Avon, near Bristol, seen from cliffs below Clifton')
Coll.: untraced

The exhibited drawing may perhaps be identified with the *River Avon seen from cliffs below Clifton*, described by Armstrong (p. 244) as showing 'topsails of vessels seen from above mouth of cave; boys climbing among rocks'. This, according to Finberg (Index) was in the collections of T. A. Tatton and Rawlinson (repr. *Studio*, 1909, pl. II; see No. 18).

18 The rising squall—Hot Wells, from St. Vincent's rock, Bristol* 1791–2 ?R.A. 1793 (323)

Watercolour, pen and brown ink over pencil, 359 × 410
Inscr. lower right: *Wᵐ Turner Delinᵗ*
Prov.: ?Rev. J. Nixon, for whom drawn; Dr. Nixon; anon. sale Christie 9 July 1864 (152), bt. in Reynolds; Mrs. H. S. Fussey, Hull, from whom bt. 1925
Coll.: City Museum and Art Gallery, Bristol (K816)

This drawing and the version catalogued below (No. 19) have been the subject of some confusion. Finberg seems to have considered that the subject was that shown at the Academy in 1793 as 'The rising squall...', but in neither version is there any sign of bad weather. The provenance as given here as far as Reynolds may refer rather to a drawing called *Hotwells Bristol—storm coming on*, which is untraced, but very possibly the exhibited subject. It is perhaps unlikely that a drawing in the style of this one, which by 1793 Turner had outdated, would have been shown publicly in that year; but see No. 17 above.

19 Old Hot Wells House, Bristol 1791–2

Pencil, watercolour, pen and brown ink, 273 × 340
Inscr. on transom of dinghy: *William/TURNER* and on a rock: *W Turner* (partially obliterated)

Prov.: John Narraway; Miss Ann Dart, until 1860; presented to the Bristol Fine Arts Academy, later known as the Royal West of England Academy, from whom purchased by the City Art Gallery, Bristol, 1931 (K1091); deaccessioned 1958; Miss K. Gotch Robinson, sale Osmond, Tricks and Son, Clifton, 16 November 1978 (92), bt. Baskett & Day; Agnew, 1979
Coll.: with Messrs. Thos. Agnew & Sons

A slightly weaker variant of No. 18 above.

20 Stoke House, Bristol, the seat of Lady Lippincote* 1791

Watercolour, 299 × 412
Sig. lower right: *William Turner Delin*
Prov.: Narraway family; Herbert Thomas; Mrs. Annie Thomas; Sir Patrick Thomas; Leger Galleries, 1976
Private collection

Two studies of Stoke House occur in the *Bristol and Malmesbury* sketchbook (T.B., VI, 16r and 16v). The second of these was used in making this finished drawing.

21 Cote House, near Bristol *c*. 1791

Watercolour, 292 × 254
Prov.: T. W. R. Woodman; purchased by the gallery in 1957
Coll.: Cecil Higgins Art Gallery, Bedford (P173)

Turner made a drawing of Cote House in 1791 (T.B., VI-17v; see E. Croft-Murray, 'An unpublished early watercolour by J. M. W. Turner, Cote House, Bristol', *The Burlington Magazine*, April 1948 pp. 107–9). The drawing in the *Bristol and Malmesbury* sketchbook is inscribed on the back: *Mr. Fowler's on Durdum* [i.e. Durdham] *Downs, near Bristol*. Captain Fowler may have been the first owner of the finished drawing. In his article Croft-Murray dates the drawing to 1792–5, but it was probably executed soon after Turner's visit to Bristol in the summer of 1791.

22 Windy day, Lullingstone Park, Kent *c*. 1791

Watercolour, 184 × 260
Inscr. in pencil upper right: *John Dyke Lullingston*
Prov.: Price Turner; A. Keiley; the Palser Gallery,

London; Mrs. T. W. Lamont, by whose children given to the museum, 1953
Coll.: Smith College Museum of Art, Northampton, Mass. (1953:23)

23 Dent de Lion, Margate *c*. 1791

Pen and dark brown/black ink and watercolour over pencil, 257 × 346
Prov.: Miss Dart; W. G. Rawlinson; T. A. Tatton, sale Christie 14 December 1928 (3); A. Finberg; H. Finberg; Fine Art Society, London, 1942; R. J. Minney; Christie 16 June 1970 (121) bt. Baskett and Day; bt. by Paul Mellon from John Baskett, 1970
Coll.: Yale Center for British Art, Paul Mellon Collection

24 Malmesbury Abbey *c*. 1791

Pen and brown ink and watercolour, 191 × 262

Prov.: Sir Hickman Bacon, Bt.; by descent to present owner
Private collection

This is perhaps a leaf from the *Bristol and Malmesbury* sketchbook (T.B., VI), in which a number of views of Malmesbury Abbey are noted, some in full colour. Others appear on separate sheets (T.B., VII, C, D and E).

25 Malmsbury Abbey R.A. 1792 (436)

Watercolour, 546 × 387
Sig. lower right: *W Turner delint*
Prov.: Mrs. Cooper 1857; Herbert A. Day, by whom presented to the museum
Coll.: Castle Museum, Norwich

A drawing worked up from Turner's studies at Malmesbury in 1791; Finberg *(Inventory)* notes that it combines elements of the two sheets T.B., VII, C and D, both of which show the ruined west tower of the abbey.

26 Malmesbury Abbey *c.* 1792–3

Watercolour, 190 × 267
Sig. lower left: *W Turner*
Prov.: ? Alexander Monro
Coll.: Art Gallery and Museum, Bury, Lancashire

Based on a drawing in the *Bristol and Malmesbury* sketchbook (T.B., VI-12,13, inscr.: *South East View of Malmsbury Abbey 1791*).

27 The Pantheon, the morning after the fire*
R.A. 1792 (472)

Watercolour over pencil, 395 × 515
Sig. lower left: *W Turner Del*
Exh.: R.A. 1974 (7)
Coll.: Trustees of the British Museum (T.B., IX-A)

Two studies of the ruins of the burnt-out Pantheon, a London assembly hall with interior based on the Pantheon in Rome, are T.B., IX, B and C; a third study was recorded by Finberg *(Inventory,* I, p. 13); for another view of the subject see No. 28. The fire occurred on 14th February 1792.

28 The Pantheon, the morning after the fire
1792

Watercolour, 295 × 239
Prov.: Thomas Hardwick; C. Hardwick; D. C. Thomson; Messrs. W. & A. Gilbey Ltd. (until 1963)
Coll.: Marks & Spencer Ltd., London

This drawing was acquired by Thomas Hardwick, an architect for whom Turner worked around 1790. It was at one time thought to be the drawing shown in 1792 (472), but No. 27 seems more likely to have been the exhibited work. Turner's study for the subject of No. 28 is T.B., IX-B.

29 Craig-y-foel, Radnorshire 1792

Watercolour over pencil, touched with reed pen, 167 × 209

Sig. lower right: *W Turner*
Inscr. on verso in contemporary hand: *Drawing by Turner/at his 1st Visit to Hereford/on his way to Rayder &/.../24 June 1792/a present* (in ink)
1 Originale Sketch/W. M. Turner (in ink)
near Rhaidder (in pencil, perhaps by the artist)
Engr.: in aquatint by T. H. Fielding, 1820 (as 'View near Plynlimon', R. 826)
Prov.: Revd. Robert Finch, by whom bequeathed to the Taylor Institution, 1830; transferred to the museum, 1913
Coll.: Visitors of the Ashmolean Museum, Oxford (Herrmann 88)

There is no reason to doubt the inscription on the back of this drawing, which provides interesting evidence of a radical change in Turner's treatment of landscape, probably as a result of the influence of Edward Dayes (see Finberg, *Life,* pp. 21–2, and Herrmann, 1968, No. 88).

30 Glastonbury Abbey 1792

Watercolour over pencil, 190 × 250
Signed and dated lower left: *WT* (monogram) *1792*
Prov.: Dr. T. S. Matthews, sale Sotheby 20 July 1978 (100), bt. Nichimen
Private collection

31 Gate of St. Augustine's monastery, Canterbury R.A. 1793 (316)

Watercolour, 521 × 407
Sig.: *W. Turner*
Prov.: Sir W. Tite, sale Christie 4 April 1874 (3), bt. Durlacher
Coll.: untraced

This may be a larger version of the composition of Nos 32, 33. The dimensions given in the International Exhibition catalogue of 1862 (992— $20\frac{1}{2} × 16''$, 514 × 406), suggest that it is an upright sheet, but this may not be so. The provenance is dubious and may have been confused with that given here for No. 32.

32 St. Augustine's Gate, Canterbury 1792–3

Pencil and watercolour, 211 × 270
Sig. lower right: *W Turner Delin* (in pencil)
Prov.: ? W. L. Leitch, sale Christie 17 March 1884 (304, as 'Old Gate of Canterbury'), bt. 'W. W.';

Mrs. E. L. Berthon, sale Christie 15 May 1891 (121), bt. Nathan; Agnew, from whom purchased 1971
Coll.: Yale Center for British Art, Paul Mellon Collection

The uncertain identification of No. 31 suggests that this drawing may, in fact, be that exhibited in 1793. The composition is almost identical to that of No. 33 of which this is a small replica.

33 St. Augustine's Gate, Canterbury 1793–4

Watercolour over pencil, 343 × 493
Sig. lower right: *W. Turner*
Prov.: purchased from Agnew's 1962
Coll.: Yale Center for British Art, Paul Mellon Collection

See No. 32.

34 Christ Church Gate, Canterbury *c.* 1793

Watercolour over pencil, 266 × 260
Sig. lower right, in ink: *Wm Turner* [? *del*]
Prov.: Charles Stokes, by descent to Hannah Cooper(?); John Ruskin; by whom given to the museum, 1861
Coll.: Syndics of the Fitzwilliam Museum, Cambridge (Cormack 1)

This is a smaller version of the subject which was exhibited at the R.A. 1794 (No. 53). Compare the two drawings of *St. Augustine's Gate, Canterbury* (Nos 32, 33). A pencil drawing of this subject, but from a different viewpoint, is T.B. XV-A.

35 Interior of the ruined refectory of St. Martin's Priory, Dover* *c.* 1793

Watercolour, 249 × 174
Sig. lower right: *Turner*
Prov.: ? Dr. Thomas Monro; Lady Powell, by whom bequeathed to the museum, 1934
Coll.: Victoria and Albert Museum, London (P.25.1934)

A pencil study of the exterior of St. Martin's Priory, probably of 1792, is in the Philadelphia Art Museum.

36 Malmesbury Abbey *c.* 1793

Watercolour, 356 × 267
Sig. lower centre: *W Turner Pinx*^t
Prov: Thomas Woolner; Charles Kurtz, sale Christie 12 March 1880 (34), bt. Grindley; Mrs. John A. James; Lewis Molteno; by descent to present owner
Private collection, Scotland

This drawing was referred to by Finberg as 'Canterbury: ruins of St. Augustine's Abbey', and has also been called 'The One Tun Inn'.

37 Malmesbury Abbey *c.* 1793

Watercolour, 241 × 202
Prov.: purchased 1926
Coll.: Smith College Museum of Art, Northampton, Mass. (1926: 2-1)

This is an inferior version (with no figures) of No. 36.

38 Tom Tower, Christ Church, Oxford *c.* 1793

Pencil and watercolour, 315 × 240
Sig. lower right: *W Turner*
Prov.: Agnew, 1977
Private collection

Compare the slightly smaller version of the subject in the Turner Bequest (T.B., XIV-B). Turner's pencil study is T.B. XIV-A.

39 The Remains of Abingdon Abbey now called Starve Castle Abingdon *c.* 1793

Watercolour, with pen and black ink, 270 × 207
Sig. lower right: *W Turner delin*
Inscr. on the cart, left: with the title

Prov.: A. E. Preston, F.S.A., by whom bequeathed to the museum, 1942
Coll.: Visitors of the Ashmolean Museum, Oxford (Herrmann 90)

40 St. Mary's Church, Monken Hadley 1793

Watercolour, 267 × 356
Signed and dated on tombstone lower centre: *W Turner 1793*
Exh.: R.A. 1974 (B.20)
Prov.: Dr. Thomas Monro; by descent to the present owner
Coll.: Monro family collection

The house in the left-hand background was owned by Dr. Thomas Monro's brother, James. This is the first known dated document of Turner's contact with Dr. Thomas Monro as a collector of his work.
See also Addenda No. 40a.

41 Great Bookham Church c. 1793

Watercolour, 230 × 343
Sig. lower right (on gravestone): *Turner*
Prov.: ? Dr. Monro, sale Christie 26 June 1833 (124), bt. Sargeant; ? Grundy & Smith, sale Christie 29 June 1883 (8), bt. Permain; Revd. E. C. Dewick, by whom presented to the gallery, 1919

Coll.: Walker Art Gallery, Liverpool (1165)

42 Corfe Castle c. 1793

Pencil and watercolour, 212 × 285
Prov.: William Smith, by whom given to the museum, 1876
Coll.: Victoria and Albert Museum, London (2961–1876)

Nos 43–72 include a large number of drawings made as a result of Turner's tours to Rhayader, in central Wales, 1792, and to Monmouthshire in 1793.

43 Llanvihangel, Crucorney, Monmouthshire c. 1793

Watercolour, 156 × 219
Inscr. (on label attached to backing): *Llange angle, Criccornel Monmouthshire*
Prov.: Anon. sale Christie 1 March 1977 (115)
Coll.: Norman E. Ellott, Vancouver, Canada

44 Arch of the old abbey, Evesham 1793

Blue and grey washes, watercolour and black ink over pencil, 211 × 279
Signed and dated lower left: *W Turner 1793*
Prov.: Mrs. Worthington; Montague Guest, 1910; G. Morland Agnew; C. Gerald Agnew; Thos. Agnew & Sons, from whom purchased by an anon. donor to the museum
Coll.: Museum of Art, Rhode Island School of Design, Providence, R. I.

Turner's original pencil outline drawing for this subject, probably done in 1792, is now in the William Hayes Ackland Memorial Art Center, Chapel Hill, North Carolina (68.9.1). Another pencil drawing of Evesham is in the British Museum, Lloyd Bequest (1958-7-12-397). See also No. 45.

45 Old archway at Evesham c. 1793–4

Watercolour over pencil, 212 × 276
Sig. lower left: *W. Turner*
Prov.: Christie 5 June 1973 (124), bt. Randall
Coll.: T. M. Randall, Bedford, England

46　Hereford Cathedral　*c.*1793

Watercolour, 309 × 419
Prov.: given by the Friends of the Art Gallery, 1932
Coll.: Hereford City Museum and Art Galleries

A pencil study of the cathedral, from a different viewpoint, is in the same collection.

Sig. lower right: *W Turner*
Prov.: R. Chambers; J. Smith; W. Leaf; Earl Beauchamp; Mrs. Mary Worthington, by whom bequeathed, 1904
Coll.: Whitworth Art Gallery, University of Manchester (D.10.1904)

G. Agnew; Mrs. Desmond Whitaker; Agnew, from whom bt. by present owner, 1964
Private collection, England

47　The Preaching Cross, Hereford　*c.*1793-4

Watercolour, 203 × 260
Prov.: E. J. Taylor; William Wood; John Radford Norcop, Brand Hall (Salop) sale, 4 October 1951, bt. by Stoke-on-Trent
Coll.: City Museum and Art Gallery, Stoke-on-Trent

48　Second Fall of the river Monach, Devil's Bridge, Cardiganshire　R.A. 1794 (333)

Watercolour, size unknown
Provenance and whereabouts unknown

Drawings of waterfalls on the River Mynach occur in T.B., XII, H, I.

49　Porch of Great Malvern Abbey, Worcestershire　R.A. 1794 (336)

Pencil, watercolour and gouache, 321 × 429

50　Malvern Abbey　1794

Watercolour, 318 × 419
Signed and dated: *W Turner 1794*
Prov.: Mrs. Ashton; Mrs. P. W. Kessler; Sotheby 19 November 1970 (107), bt. Agnew
Private collection

Turner used this view as the basis of his design for the *England and Wales* series (R. 258; No. 834). The structure on the right is the Abbey Gate, the top of which can be seen above the trees at the extreme right of No. 49.

51　Great Malvern Abbey　*c.*1794

Watercolour, 318 × 407
Prov.: George Tite; Palser Gallery, London 1914; Sir Thomas Barlow
Coll.: untraced

52　Evesham: the Church of St. Lawrence, as seen through Abbot Lichfield's Tower　*c.*1794

Watercolour over pencil, 210 × 266
Sig. lower right: *W Turner*
Prov.: Montague Guest; C. Morland Agnew; Alan

53　Christ Church Gate, Canterbury　R.A. 1794 (388)

Watercolour, with pen and brown ink, 512 × 400
Sig. lower right: *W Turner*
Prov.: Sir W. Tite, sale Christie 4 July 1874 (3), bt. Durlacher; Mrs. Berthon, sale Christie 15 May 1891 (121), bt. Nathan
Private collection, Scotland

Finberg's suggestion (*Life,,,,* p. 457) that this drawing can be identified with the smaller watercolour in the Fitzwilliam Museum (No. 34) is clearly unsatisfactory.

54　Christ Church Gate, Canterbury　*c.*1794

Pencil and watercolour, 228 × 274
Sig. lower right: *Turner* (erased)
Prov.: Sotheby 24 March 1977 (150); Paul Mellon
Coll.: Yale Center for British Art, Paul Mellon Collection

The basis for this drawing is the watercolour T.B., XVII-A, which Finberg (*Inventory*) tentatively titled 'A gateway to the Priory, Bridlington, Yorks (?)'.

55 St. Anselm's chapel, with part of Thomas-à-Becket's crown, Canterbury Cathedral*
R.A. 1794 (408)

Pencil and watercolour, 517 × 374
Signed and dated lower right: *Turner 179* (date cut)
Exh.: R.A. 1974 (10)
Prov.: Dr. Thomas Monro; sale Christie 26 June 1833 (122), bt. J. M. W. Turner; J. E. Taylor, by whom given to the Whitworth Institute, 1892.
Coll.: Whitworth Art Gallery, University of Manchester (D.113.1892)

56 The West Gate, Canterbury *c.* 1794

Watercolour, 280 × 203
Sig. lower left: *Turner*
Prov.: Henry Vaughan, by whom given to the gallery, 1900
Coll.: National Gallery of Ireland, Dublin (2408)

57 Inside of Tintern Abbey, Monmouthshire
R.A. 1794 (402)

Watercolour, 321 × 251
Exh.: R.A. 1974 (B16)
Prov.: W. Smith, by whom given to the museum 1871

Coll.: Victoria and Albert Museum, London (1683–1871)

A view towards the east window. A preparatory study is T.B., XXIII-A (B.M. 1975 (5)), and the pencil drawing made on the spot is T.B., XII-E. Nos 58 and 59 show a different view.

58 Transept of Tintern Abbey, Monmouthshire *c.* 1794   ? R.A. 1795 (589)

Watercolour over pencil, with pen and ink, 355 × 260
Sig. lower right: *Turner*
Prov.: James Moore; Miss Miller; purchased from the Magdalen College Fund in 1917
Coll.: Visitors of the Ashmolean Museum, Oxford (Herrmann 91)

For another version of this subject see No. 59. It is not certain which of the two watercolours is to be identified with that shown at the R.A. in 1795. The outline pencil drawing made on the spot, probably in 1792, is now in the Wellesley College Museum, Mass.

59 Tintern Abbey: the transept *c.* 1794

Watercolour, 345 × 254
Prov.: J. E. Taylor, sale Christie 5 July 1912 (59), bt. Agnew; J. F. Haworth, sale Christie 25 June

1926 (151), bt. Agnew; R. W. Lloyd, by whom bequeathed to the museum 1958
Coll.: Trustees of the British Museum (1958-7-12-400)

See No. 58.

60 Tintern Abbey, west front *c.* 1794

Watercolour over pencil, 419 × 316
Sig. lower right: *Turner*
Prov.: John Henderson; by descent to his son, who bequeathed it to the museum, 1878
Coll.: Trustees of the British Museum (1878-12-28-41)

This view is based on a pencil drawing T.B., XII-D.

61 Ruins of west front, Tintern Abbey *c.* 1794–5

Watercolour over pencil, 325 × 235
Prov.: Hon. Mrs. Rowley; anon. sale, Christie 30 June 1916 (60 A), bt. Agnew
Coll.: Fundaçao Calouste Gulbenkian, Lisbon

A repetition of No. 60.

62 Part of a gothic building (St. Albans Cathedral) *c.* 1794

Pencil and watercolour, 235 × 210

Inscr. lower right: *Turner*
Prov.: William Smith, by whom given to the museum, 1871
Coll.: Victoria and Albert Museum, London (1684–1871)

The pencil study for this is in the Victoria and Albert Museum (P.105-1922). An inferior version, almost certainly a copy by another hand, is in the National Gallery of Ireland (Vaughan Bequest 2283).

63 Tewkesbury* *c.* 1794

Watercolour over pencil, 307 × 415 (sight)
Sig. lower centre: *Turner*
Prov.: anon. sale Christie 25 February 1929 (47), bt. George Healing; by descent to the present owner
Private collection

64 Malmesbury 1794

Pencil and watercolour, 356 × 254
Signed and dated lower left: *Turner 1794*
Prov.: J. E. Taylor, sale Christie 5 July 1912 (61), bt. Agnew; C. M. Mason; A. M. Mason, sale Sotheby 21 March 1974 (101), bt. Albany Gallery
Private collection

65 Llanthony Abbey* 1794

Pencil and watercolour, 327 × 424
Inscr. lower left: *1794* and *W Turner* (name partly scratched out)
Exh.: R.A. 1974 (11)
Coll.: Trustees of the British Museum (T.B., XXVII-R)

Turner's pencil outline drawing of the subject is T.B., XII-F. For other versions see No. 66. The view was used as the basis for the *England and Wales* drawing of Llanthony (No. 863). No. 66 is a smaller version of the subject, with modifications in the figures.

66 Llanthony Abbey *c.* 1794

Pencil and watercolour, 208 × 282
Sig. lower right: *Turner*
Engr.: in aquatint by G. Hunt for *Scenery in S. Wales*, 1823 (R. 827)

Prov.: R. Chambers, sale Christie 29 March 1859 (176), bt. Gregory; C. S. Bale, sale Christie 14 May 1881 (189), bt. Agnew; Dr. John Percy, sale Christie 23 April 1890 (1262), bt. Agnew; J. E. Taylor, sale Christie 5 July 1912 (76), bt. Agnew; Walter Stoye; by descent to the present owner
Private collection

A drawing of this subject in the Pantzer Collection, Indianapolis (Berkeley 1975, No. 7), is falsely signed and dated 1802. It appears to be a copy, perhaps made by a pupil under Turner's supervision. Finberg (*Inventory,* I, p. 55) refers to another small drawing of the subject, signed and dated 1795, in the possession of T. E. Watson, of Newport, Monmouthshire.

67 Worcester Cathedral, west front* *c.* 1794–5

Watercolour, with some pencil, 419 × 318
Signed and dated lower right: *W Turner 1794 [? or 5]*, and lower right centre: *Turner*
Prov.: John Henderson; by descent to his son, by whom bequeathed to the museum 1878
Coll.: Trustees of the British Museum (1878-12-28-43)

A pencil drawing inscribed *West Window of Worcester Cathedral,* signed and dated July 9 (? 1792) is in the Pantzer Collection, Indianapolis.

68 Magdalen College, Oxford *c.* 1794

Watercolour over pencil, 357 × 263

Sig. lower right: *W. Turner*
Prov.: George Salting, by whom bequeathed to the museum, 1910
Coll.: Trustees of the British Museum (1910-2-12-286)

Finberg (Index) records a smaller watercolour of this subject (*The Founder's Tower*) 265 × 205, sold Christie 8 June 1917. It was probably drawn a little earlier.

69 Magdalen Tower and Bridge, Oxford ? 1794

Watercolour over pencil, 286 × 222
Signed and dated: *Turner 1794*
Prov.: Dr. Thomas Monro, sale Christie 26 June 1833; Broderip; A. G. Kurtz, sale Christie 11 May 1891 (193), bt. Agnew; presented by the Guarantors of the Royal Jubilee Exhibition, 1887
Coll.: Whitworth Art Gallery, University of Manchester (D.6.1887)

A replica of No. 70 below.

70 Magdalen Tower and Bridge, Oxford ? 1794

Watercolour and pencil, 285 × 224

Prov.: John Henderson; by descent to his son, by whom bequeathed to the museum, 1878
Coll.: Trustees of the British Museum (1878-12-28-39)

The original version of No. 69 above.

---

71 Christ Church, Oxford* *c.* 1794

Watercolour over pencil, 321 × 426
Sig. lower right: *Turner*
Exh.: B.M. 1975 (6)
Prov.: John Henderson; by descent to his son, by whom bequeathed to the museum, 1878
Coll.: Trustees of the British Museum (1878-12-28-42)

72 Christ Church, Oxford 1794

Pencil and watercolour, 395 × 320
Signed and dated lower right: *Turner 1794*
Prov.: with Messrs. Thomas McLean, Haymarket; Revd. E. S. Dewick, given by Mrs. E. S. Dewick, 1918
Coll.: Syndics of the Fitzwilliam Museum, Cambridge (Cormack 4)

73 The ruined abbey at Haddington *c.* 1794

Watercolour over pencil, 175 × 203
Prov.: John Ruskin, by whom given to the Ruskin, School, Oxford, 1875; transferred to the museum, 1938

Coll.: Visitors of the Ashmolean Museum, Oxford (Herrmann 60)

Copied from an engraving by W. Byrne after Thomas Hearne (dated 25 March 1786) in *Antiquities of Great Britain,* vol. I. Haddington is in East Lothian, near Edinburgh, and Turner did not visit it until 1801.

74 Edinburgh Castle *c.* 1794

Pencil and watercolour, 180 × 247
Prov.: John Henderson; by descent to his son, by whom bequeathed to the museum, 1878
Coll.: Trustees of the British Museum (1878-12-28-49)

Copied from a print after Thomas Hearne dated 1780.

Nos 75–82 are subjects derived from Turner's tour in 1794 to the Midland counties, as far as Denbighshire and Derbyshire.

75 Cambridge: Clare Hall *c.* 1794

Watercolour, 210 × 267
Engr.: in aquatint by H. Reeve, 1807
Prov.: Alfred de Pass; Capt. the Hon. W. R. Wyndham; Mrs. Phyllis Brooks; Mirander Greenwood, Albemarle, Virginia
Coll.: untraced

76 King's College Chapel, Cambridge: ? the Choir *c.* 1794

Watercolour, 311 × 235
Prov.: Murrieta, sale Christie 23 May 1873 (142), bt. Agnew
Coll.: untraced

See No. 77.

---

77 Choir in King's College Chapel, Cambridge ?1794 R.A. 1795 (616)

Watercolour, size unknown
Provenance and whereabouts unknown

This is possibly identical with the Murrieta drawing (No. 76), which, though its precise subject is not known, may have been a view of the choir executed as a companion to the *West End* (No. 78), which has similar measurements. One of these drawings, or a later view of the chapel (interior or exterior?), was in Turner's gallery in 1809, and another, or the

same, in John Naylor's collection. There is no positive evidence that more than two views were made: one of the west end and one of the choir. A pencil drawing of the choir is T.B., XXII Aa (not in the *Inventory*). Drawings of the exterior are T.B., XXI-Z and T.B., XXII-A.

78 West End of King's College Chapel, Cambridge *c.* 1794

Watercolour, 329 × 229
Prov.: Charles Stokes; T. Hughes; Mrs. Hughes, sale Sotheby 28 November 1922, bt. Ellis & Smith
Coll.: King's College, Cambridge

See No. 77.

79 Warwick Castle and Bridge 1794

Watercolour and pencil, with gum, 425 × 527
Prov.: ?Dr. Thomas Monro; W. Leech; T.W. Wright; presented to the Whitworth Institute by the Guarantors of the Royal Jubilee Exhibition, 1887
Coll.: Whitworth Art Gallery, University of Manchester (D.11.1887)

---

80 Lichfield Cathedral *c.* 1794

Watercolour, 308 × 225
Prov.: Mrs. John Turner; George Goyder, sale Christie 5 June 1973 (131), bt. Randall

Coll.: T. M. Randall, Bedford, England

A pencil drawing of Lichfield Cathedral from the south-east is T.B., XXII-M.

81 Rhaiado Gwy Bridge, over the River Wye ?1794

Pencil and watercolour, 190 × 255
Inscr. lower left: *Turner RA*
Prov.: ? Administrators of Mrs. Simkins dec'd, sale Christie 25 November 1882 (82); purchased 1952
Coll.: National Museum of Wales, Cardiff (3217)

82 Old Bridge, Shrewsbury 1794 R.A. 1795 (593) as 'Welsh Bridge at Shrewsbury'

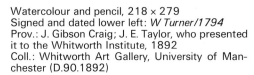

Watercolour and pencil, 218 × 279
Signed and dated lower left: *W Turner/1794*
Prov.: J. Gibson Craig; J. E. Taylor, who presented it to the Whitworth Institute, 1892
Coll.: Whitworth Art Gallery, University of Manchester (D.90.1892)

The pencil drawing on which this watercolour is based is T.B., XXI-D.

83 The old watermill *c*. 1794

Watercolour over pencil, 251 × 187
Sig. lower right: *Turner*
Prov.: J. E. Taylor, who presented it to the Institute, 1892
Coll.: Whitworth Art Gallery, University of Manchester (D.87.1892)

Based on a pencil drawing in the *Marford Mill* sketchbook (T.B., XX, 18v-19); Finberg *(Inventory)* mistakenly identified this subject as the *Marford Mill* shown at the R.A. in 1795 (No. 125).

84 A watermill 1794

Pencil and watercolour, 211 × 148
Prov.: Colnaghi, 1971
Coll.: Dr. Charles Warren

85 The Angler 1794

Pen and watercolour, 229 × 154
Signed and dated on verso: *Turner 1794*
Prov.: Andrew Caldwell; Mrs. M. Reub-ten Cate sale, Sotheby 29 November 1973 (89), bt. Agnew
Coll.: Yale Center for British Art, Paul Mellon Collection

86 Near Winchmore Hill *c*. 1794

Watercolour over pencil, 300 × 224
Inscr. on verso: *near Winchmore Hill* (not in Turner's hand)
Prov.: Gilbert Davis
Coll.: Henry E. Huntington Library and Art Gallery, San Marino, California (59.55.1287)

I(b) Nos 87–122
Drawings for the *Copper-Plate Magazine,* **1794–1798, and for miscellaneous minor publications to 1800**

Nos 87–122 are drawings engraved for the *Copper-Plate Magazine,* a joint venture of John Walker, engraver, and Messrs. Harrison & Co. Turner's Midland tour of 1794 was planned so that he could collect material for this work; in all sixteen subjects were engraved between 1794 and 1798. All the plates bear the name of the *Copper-Plate Magazine,* although the title of the publication was changed at some point to *The Itinerant.* The plates were reprinted in 1853, when they were published by Hogarth in *Turner and Girtin's Picturesque Views 60 years since,* and again in 1873, when Bentley revived the collection as *Turner and Girtin's Picturesque Views a 100 years ago.*

87   Rochester   *c.* 1793

Watercolour, size unknown
Engr.: by J. Walker and J. Storer for John Walker's *Copper-Plate Magazine,* 1 May 1794 (R. 1)
Provenance and whereabouts unknown

Turner's pencil drawing of this subject is T.B., XV-B.

88   Chepstow Castle   *c.* 1793

Watercolour, 203 × 297
Sig. lower left: *Turner*
Engr.: by J. Storer for Walker's *Copper-Plate Magazine,* 1 November 1794 (R. 2)
Prov.: ?R. Chambers, sale Christie 29 March 1859 (7, as 'Chepstow Castle and Bridge'), bt. Gambart; ?anon, sale, Foster 19 November 1860 (88, as 'Chepstow Castle and Bridge'), bt. in; ?Sir Joseph Heron, sale Christie 9 June 1890 (75), bt. Walford; Cotswold Gallery; Sir Stephen Courtauld; presented to the Institute by his family in his memory, 1974
Coll.: Courtauld Institute of Art, University of London (1.74; Kitson 1)

Finberg (Index) gives a drawing of this subject, 12 × 16 $\frac{1}{4}$'' (300 × 412) to Monro, Leaf and Heron; but the drawing in the anon. sale of 1860 looks more like the subject for engraving.

89   Nottingham   *c.* 1794

Watercolour, size unknown
Engr.: by J. Walker for Walker's *Copper-Plate Magazine,* 28 February 1795 (R. 3); the plate was also used for *The Gentleman's Magazine,* 1831, Provenance and whereabouts unknown

Ruskin illustrated this composition in *Modern Painters,* pointing out that Turner used the same view for his *England and Wales* 'Nottingham' (No. 850).

90   Bridgnorth   *c.* 1794

Watercolour, size unknown
Engr.: by J. Walker for Walker's *Copper-Plate Magazine,* 1 August 1795 (R. 4)
Provenance and whereabouts unknown

See the pencil drawing in the *Matlock* sketchbook (T.B., XIX–20).

91   Matlock   1794

Pencil and watercolour, 105 × 164 (sight)
Engr.: by J. Widnell for Walker's *Copper-Plate Magazine,* 1 October 1795 (R. 5)
Prov.: R. Chambers; C. J. Skipper; Kurt Pantzer, by whom given to the museum
Coll.: Indianapolis Museum of Art

92   Birmingham   *c.* 1794

Watercolour, size unknown
Engr.: by J. Storer for Walker's *Copper-Plate Magazine,* 2 November 1795 (R. 6)
Prov.: W. Wood
Coll.: untraced

93   Chester   *c.* 1794

Watercolour, size unknown
Engr.: by J. Walker for Walker's *Copper-Plate Magazine,* 1 January 1796 (R. 7)
Provenance and whereabouts unknown

94   Peterborough Cathedral from the north   *c.* 1795

Watercolour, 114 × 178
Engr.: by J. Walker for Walker's *Copper-Plate Magazine,* 1 May 1796 (R. 8)
Prov.: W. G. Rawlinson; purchased through the National Art-Collections Fund, 1939

Coll.: City Museum and Art Gallery, Peterborough

The pencil drawing for this composition is T.B., XXI-V.

95   Ely, from the south   *c.* 1796

Watercolour over pencil, 105 × 170
Engr.: by J. Walker for Walker's *Copper-Plate Magazine,* 1 March 1796 (R. 9)
Prov.: Revd. W. MacGregor, sale Christie 23 April 1937 (18), bt. Borenius; Oscar and Peter Johnson, 1966
Coll.: Mr. and Mrs. Paul Mellon, Upperville, Virginia

96   Westminster Bridge   ?1796

Pencil, pen and indian ink, watercolour and white body-colour, 127 × 213
Inscr. verso: *Westminster Bridge/JMW Turner RA* (in an early-nineteenth-century hand)
Engr.: by J. Walker for Walker's *Copper-Plate Magazine,* 1 August 1797 (R. 10)
Exh.: ?C.G. 1822 (271)
Prov.: ?John Britton; G. E. J. Powell, by whom bequeathed to the college
Coll.: University College of Wales, Aberystwyth

This drawing seems to be Turner's design for the *Copper-Plate Magazine* subject, though different in detail; it is slightly more elaborate than the surviving drawings from this series, both in its use of body-colour and in its delicate effects of light. A preliminary drawing is T.B., XXXIII-W; this differs from the plate in exactly the same respects. Changes may have been made in the course of engraving. Rawlinson (I, No. 10) and Finberg (*Life,* p. 483) identified the study as the drawing of *Westminster Bridge, from the Surrey Side, looking towards Westminster* exhibited at Cooke's gallery in 1822 as 'an early Drawing of the Artist', but if this is indeed the exhibited subject, the finished version at Aberystwyth would certainly have been that shown.

97 Flint, from Park-Gate *c.*1796

Watercolour, size unknown
Engr.: by J. Walker for Walker's *Copper-Plate Magazine,* 1 August 1797 (R. 11)
Prov.: Nancy, Princess Imeretinsky, sale Sotheby, 21 March 1974 (103), bt. Mrs. Gerda Newman
Private collection

A pencil drawing of this subject is in the National Museum of Wales, Cardiff (Miss A. B. Watson gift 1935, No. 1986).

98 Hampton Court, Herefordshire *c.*1796

Watercolour, size unknown
Engr.: by J. Walker for Walker's *Copper-Plate Magazine,* 1 September 1797 (R. 12)
Provenance and whereabouts unknown

Turner's pencil drawing for this view of the house from the south-east is in the *South Wales* sketch-book (T.B., XXVI-51), which is also the basis for the watercolour made in *c.*1806 for Sir Richard Colt Hoare (Cat. No. 216).

99 Elgin Cathedral *c.*1796

Watercolour, size unknown
Engr.: by J. Walker for Walker's *Copper-Plate Magazine,* 1 July 1797 (R. 15a)
Provenance and whereabouts unknown

Turner did not visit Scotland until 1801; for this subject he used a drawing by the amateur antiquarian James Moore (1762–99).

100 Carlisle *c.*1797

Watercolour, 130 × 191
Engr.: by J. Walker for Walker's *Copper-Plate Magazine,* 2 October 1797 (R. 13)
Prov.: Fairfax Murray; Rush Cheney; Nelson C. White
Coll.: untraced

101 Wakefield *c.*1797

Watercolour, size unknown
Engr.: by J. Walker for Walker's *Copper-Plate Magazine,* 1 June 1798 (R 14)
Provenance and whereabouts unknown

102 Sheffield, from Derbyshire Lane
*c.*1797

Watercolour, 114 × 165
Engr.: by J. Walker for Walker's *Copper-Plate Magazine,* 1 August 1798 (R. 15)

Prov.: John Ruskin; Ruskin Museum, Sheffield
Coll.: Guild of St. George, Ruskin Collection, University of Reading

103 Tower of London *c.*1794

Watercolour, size unknown
Engr.: by T. Tagg for the *Lady's Pocket Magazine,* 1 January 1795 (R. 16); the plate was also used for *England Delineated,* 1804

This is one of the sixteen subjects engraved for the *Pocket Magazine,* the *Lady's Pocket Magazine* and the *Pocket Print Magazine,* issued by the same publishers as the *Copper-Plate Magazine* in 1795 and 1796. The series of plates was used again for *England Delineated,* 1804.

The other subjects are:

104 Chelsea Hospital *c.*1794

Engr.: by J. Storer, publ. 2 March 1795 (R. 17)

105 Oxford *c.*1794

Engr.: by T. Tagg, publ. 1 June 1795 (R. 18)

106 Cambridge, with King's College Chapel
*c.*1794

Engr.: by T. Tagg, publ. 1 June 1795 (R. 19)
See pencil drawing, T.B., XXI-Z.

107 Windsor *c.*1794

Engr.: by Rothwell, publ. 1 June 1795 (R. 20)

108 Flint *c.*1794

Engr.: by T. Tagg, publ. 1 July 1795 (R. 21)

109 Bath *c.*1794

Engr.: by G. Murray, publ. 1 August 1795 (R. 22)

110 Worcester *c.*1794

Engr.: by Rothwell, publ. 1 August 1795 (R. 23)

111 Wallingford *c.*1794

Engr.: by T. Tagg, publ. 1 September 1795 (R. 24)

112 Tonbridge Castle *c.*1794

Engr.: by G. Murray, publ. 1 September 1795 (R. 25)

A different view of Tonbridge Castle in the Fitz-william Museum (Cormack 3) is a 'Monro School' type drawing; its attribution to Turner has been questioned, but it may well be authentic, of about 1795–6.

113 Swansea *c.*1794

Engr.: by Rothwell, publ. 1 September 1795 (R. 26)

114 Guildford *c.*1794

Engr.: by Rothwell, publ. 1 October 1795 (R. 27)

115 Neath *c.*1794

Engr.: by G. Murray, publ. 1 October 1795 (R. 28)

116 Staines *c.*1794

Engr.: by G. Murray, publ. 1 November 1795 (R. 29)

117 Bristol *c.*1795

Watercolour over pencil, 65 × 113
Engr.: by T. Tagg, publ. 1 January 1796 (R. 30)
Prov.: bought 1902
Coll.: City Museum and Art Gallery, Bristol (K51)

118 Northampton *c.*1794

Engr.: by T. Tagg, no date reference in Rawlinson (R. 31)

The pencil drawing for this subject is in the *Matlock* sketchbook (T.B., XIX-12).

Two engravings by Samuel Rawle, dated 1800, of Dunster Castle, Somerset, record a pair of drawings which were the first of Turner's works to be issued independently of letterpress, as separate plates. Neither drawing has been traced, and it may be that they were executed some time before the date of the engravings. Another plate of Dunster Castle by Rawle, after Turner, appeared in 1798. J. Greig's *Windsor from the Forest,* like the plates in *England Delineated,* made use of work nearly a decade old, if the print gives any clue as to the appearance of Turner's drawing. These four untraced items are Nos 119–122 below.

119 Dunster Castle, Somersetshire,
North-east view *c.*1800

Watercolour, 241 × 356
Engr.: by S. Rawle, 1 May 1800, and dedicated to Mr. J. Fownes Luttrell, M.P. (R. 48)
Prov.: Col. Hibbert, sale Christie 1886; E. B. Lees, sale Christie 12 June 1912

---

120 Dunster Castle, Somersetshire, South-west view *c.* 1800

Watercolour, 241 × 368
Engr.: by S. Rawle, 1 May 1800, and dedicated to Mr. J. Fownes Luttrell, M. P. (R. 49)
Prov.: Col. Hibbert, sale Christie 1886 (as 'Dunster Castle from the park')

121 Dunster Castle *c.* 1797

Watercolour, size unknown
Engr.: by S. Rawle and publ. by J. Sewell, Cornhill, 1 March 1798 (R. 50)

Rawlinson says he knows of only one impression: 'It bears no date or publication line.' The British Museum possesses an impression bearing title, publication date (as above) and, above the print: *EUROPEAN MAGAZINE.*

122 Windsor from the forest *?c.* 1795

Watercolour, 211 × 317
Engr.: by J. Greig for *Views of London and its Environs,* 1804 (R. 72)
Prov.: unknown

SECTION II
Nos 123–181 Drawings of *c.* 1795–1796

123 St. Hughe's the Burgundian's porch at Lincoln Cathedral R.A. 1795 (411)

Watercolour, size unknown
Exh.: C.G. 1824 (136)
Prov.: Robert Clutterbuck 1874
Coll.: untraced

124 Cathedral Church at Lincoln* R.A. 1795 (621)

Watercolour over pencil, 450 × 350
Signed and dated lower right: *W Turner 1795*
Exh.: B.M. 1975 (7)
Prov.: John Henderson, sen.; John Henderson, jun., by whom bequeathed to the museum, 1878
Coll.: Trustees of the British Museum (1878–12–28–48)

The subject was drawn by Turner in pencil (T.B., XXI-O); it shows the towers of the cathedral rising above Exchequer Gate, seen from Bailgate.

125 Marford Mill, Wrexham, Denbighshire R.A. 1795 (581)

Watercolour over pencil, 280 × 197
Sig. lower right: *Turner*
Prov.: given to the museum by a group of subscribers, 1923
Coll.: National Museum of Wales, Cardiff (No. 3216)

T.B., XXI-L is a pencil drawing of the subject, inscribed by Turner: *Marford Mill Denbighshire.*

126 West entrance of Peterborough Cathedral R.A. 1795 (585)

Watercolour, 311 × 229
Sig. lower right: *W Turner*
Prov.: Dr. Thomas Monro; Dr. Claude Ponsonby; W. G. Rawlinson; T. A. Tatton, Christie sale 14 December 1928 (9), bt. Agnew; Walter Jones, sale Christie 3 July 1942 (52); Agnew
Coll.: City Museum and Art Gallery, Peterborough

A pencil drawing of the West front of Peterborough Cathedral is T.B., XXI-T.

127 West entrance of Peterborough Cathedral 1795

Watercolour over pencil, 313 × 230
Signed and dated lower right: *W Turner 1795*
Prov.: Messrs. Hodgson, from whom bt. by present owner
Private collection, U.K.

A replica of No. 126 above.

128 View near the Devil's bridge, with the river Ryddol, Cardiganshire R.A. 1795 (609)

Watercolour, size unknown
Provenance and whereabouts unknown

129 Rochester 1795

Watercolour over pencil, 228 × 303
Signed and dated lower right: *W Turner 1795*
Prov.: ? Adam Fairrie, sale Christie 16 March 1861; Wallis & Son, from whom purchased by James Blair, 1912, who bequeathed it to the museum, 1917
Coll.: City Art Gallery, Manchester (1917.97)

130 Pembury Mill, near Tunbridge Wells *c.* 1795–6

Pencil and watercolour, 203 × 277
Sig. lower right: *W Turner*
Coll.: Victoria and Albert Museum, London (1160–1901)

See No. 169.

131 Saltwood Castle, Kent *c.* 1795

Watercolour and pencil, 144 × 203
Prov.: Weldon; bequeathed by Mrs. W. F. R. Weldon to the museum, 1937
Coll.: Visitors of the Ashmolean Museum, Oxford (Herrmann 99)

This drawing is not accepted by Herrmann, but there seems to be no reason to doubt its authenticity, although it is a slight example of Turner's work at this period.

132 Folly Bridge, Oxford *c.* 1795

Watercolour over pencil, 203 × 267
Inscr. (not in Turner's hand) lower left: *JMW Turner;* verso: *Folly Bridge Oxford/1800*
Prov.: G. E. J. Powell, by whom bequeathed to the college
Coll.: University College of Wales, Aberystwyth

133 Christ Church Cathedral, from the Fellow's Garden *c.* 1795

Watercolour, 205 × 275
Prov.: Sir Henry Stucley Theobald, K. C.; Robert Tronson, sale Christie 2 March 1976 (123, as 'The Cathedral, Christ Church, Oxford, from the Dean's garden', bt. Christ Church
Coll.: The Governing Body of Christ Church, Oxford

Turner drew Christ Church Cathedral from a similar viewpoint and in a similar composition, but from further away in the grounds of Corpus Christi College, for the *Oxford Almanack* in about 1803 (No. 304).

134 West front of Wells Cathedral *c.* 1795

Watercolour, 413 × 540
Sig. lower right: *W. Turner*
Prov.: ?John Allnutt, sale Christie 18 June 1863 (25); Abel Buckley; anon. sale Christie 27 May 1910 (47), bt. Wallis; Agnew 1912; Lord Leverhulme
Coll.: The Lady Lever Collection, Port Sunlight, Cheshire (327)

A drawing of the west front of Wells Cathedral is in the *Smaller South Wales* sketchbook (T.B., XXV-4). Armstrong (p. 284) records a watercolour of the same subject, formerly in Windus's collection (sale Christie 1868). He also associates this with the

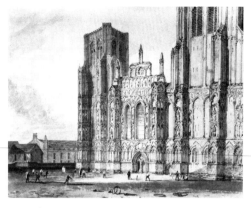

Wells Cathedral shown at Cooke's gallery in 1822 (95).

135 Edgar Tower (King Edgar's Gate), Worcester *c.* 1795

Pencil and watercolour, 298 × 413
Prov.: J. R. Fordham; A. R. Fordham, sale Christie 12 July 1918 (104), bt. Eccles; Agnew 1955; given to the museum in memory of Evan F. Lilly
Coll.: Indianapolis Museum of Art

The pencil drawing of this subject is in the Fogg Art Museum, Harvard University.

136 The English Bridge, Shrewsbury *c.* 1795

Watercolour, 247 × 295
Sig. lower right: *Turner*
Prov.: Earl of Essex, by whom given to R.F., 1826;

James Gibson Craig; Christie 23 April 1887 (5); Watson; London art market 1976
Private collection, U.K.

A pencil drawing of this subject is T.B., XXI-E. An inscription verso reads: 'This drawing was brought to Lord Malden (now Lord Essex) by Turner's father when he lived in Maiden Lane. Turner was then about 16 years old. The drawing was given me by Lord E. who related this anecdote. R.F. 1826.'

137 A ruined farmhouse *c.* 1795

Pencil and watercolour, 197 × 260
Sig. lower left: *W. Turner*
Prov.: J. Pyke Thompson, by whom bequeathed to the museum, 1898
Coll.: National Museum of Wales, Cardiff (3219)

Possibly a leaf from the *South Wales* sketchbook (T.B. XXVI).

138 St. Erasmus in Bishop Islip's Chapel R.A. 1796 (395)

Pencil and watercolour, 546 × 398
Inscr.: *WILLIAM TURNER NATUS 1775*
Exh.: B.M. 1975 (9)
Prov.: Lord Harewood; sale Christie 1 May 1858 (36); John Dillon; sale Christie 17 April 1869 (47); John Heugh; sale 17 March 1877 (35); J. Morris; D. S. Thompson, 1912; Christie, 1917, bt. Boswell; Agnew; R. W. Lloyd, by whom bequeathed to the museum 1958
Coll.: Trustees of the British Museum (1958–7-12–402)

139 Woolverhampton, Staffordshire*
R.A. 1796 (651)

Watercolour, 318 × 419
Prov.: Lord Sudeley, sale Christie 21 June 1884 (114), bt. Colnaghi; Somerset Beaumont, sale Christie 11 May 1917 (130), bt. King; Mrs. King; F. Gaskell, by whom bequeathed to the gallery, 1933
Coll.: Art Gallery and Museum, Wolverhampton (W 102)

Armstrong (p. 285) suggests that the figures are 'perhaps not by Turner'; but the foreground activity is typical and this is, in fact, one of Turner's first crowd scenes, foreshadowing many *England and Wales* subjects.

140 Llandilo Bridge and Dinevor Castle
R.A. 1796 (656)

Watercolour, 356 × 502
Sig. lower left: *W Turner*
Prov.: anon. sale Sotheby 27 July 1938 (25), bt. Palser; purchased by the museum, 1938
Coll.: National Museum of Wales, Cardiff (498a)

The rich colouring of this drawing is an early indication of Turner's experiments in oil, and foreshadows by two or three years the palette of full-scale 'Sublime' subjects, such as *Cader Idris* (No. 259).

141 Internal of a cottage, a study at Ely*
R.A. 1796 (686)

Watercolour over pencil, 198 × 271
Sig. lower centre right (pen): *W Turner*; above this (point of brush): *W Turner*; left-hand side (point of brush): *W Turner*
Exh.: R.A. 1974 (14)
Coll.: Trustees of the British Museum (T.B., XXIX-X)

The identification of the drawing in the Turner Bequest as the 'Internal of a cottage' exhibited in 1796 is tentative; Finberg proposed it in his *Inventory*. It is supported by the careful finish and meticulous detail of the drawing, as well as by the signature. The use of the word 'study' is unusual in Turner's exhibited titles; cf. No. 239.

142 Chale Farm, Isle of Wight R.A. 1796 (699)

Watercolour, ?215 × 165
Prov.: ?John Landseer
Coll.: untraced

In the *Isle of Wight* sketchbook (T.B., XXIV) Turner noted a list of 'order'd drawings' including several for 'Mr. Landseer'—the engraver of the five views in the Isle of Wight, now untraced, (R. 34–37a). The title's are 'Godshill' (deleted), 'Colwell Bay', 'Brading Harbour' (deleted), 'Carrisbrook Castle', and 'Totnell Bay', all indicated as 10 × 7½'' (254 × 190.5). Landseer also ordered some drawings of a 'Second size', which is apparently 8½ × 6½'' (216 × 165); 'Chale Farm' is one of these, together with 'Mottestone Mill'. Various other Isle of Wight subjects are also mentioned, including 'Steephill Cove' and 'Appuldurcomb and Newport', which were to be of a large size, 12 × 8'' (305 × 203). None of these subjects is now traced.
See also Nos 176–181.

143 Landaff Cathedral, South Wales* R.A. 1796 (701)

Pencil and watercolour, 357 × 258
Exh.: B.M. 1975 (10)
Coll.: Trustees of the British Museum (T.B., XXVIII-A).

Based on a pencil drawing in the *South Wales* sketchbook (T.B., XXVI-4), inscribed: *Dr. Mathews*; presumably indicating a commission. No other version of the subject is known.

144 Remains of Waltham Abbey, Essex
R.A. 1796 (702)

Watercolour, 330 × 432
Prov.: ?Huskisson, sale Christie 1864, bt. in (Bell); M. B. Huish (R.A. 1887); F. Stevenson; Cotswold Gallery, 1924
Coll.: untraced

145 West front of Bath Abbey R.A. 1796 (715)

Watercolour, 235 × 280
Sig.: *W Turner*
Prov.: ?Hurrell; sale Christie 8 July 1893 (7, as 'Abbey Church, Bath'), bt. Ash; sale Christie 18 April 1894 (59), bt. Mayo; Agnew 1901; James Gresham
Coll.: untraced

146 Old Blackfriars Bridge *c.* 1796

Pencil and watercolour, with scraping-out, 260 × 172
Prov.: J. E. Taylor, by whom presented to the Whitworth Institute, 1892
Coll.: Whitworth Art Gallery, University of Manchester (D.89.1892)

Another version of this subject, probably made at the same time, is in a private collection.

147 Brighthelmstone *c.* 1796

Pencil and watercolour, 407 × 541
Inscr. on transom of boat: *HOPE of Brighton*
Prov.: John Heugh
Coll.: Victoria and Albert Museum, London (135–1878)

This drawing is close in style and colouring to the so-called 'Rottingdean' at the Fitzwilliam (No. 148). Turner made many drawings along the coast near Brighton at about this time, including the series of small studies on coarse paper, T.B., XXXIII, K, L, N, P, Q, R, and some pages of the *Wilson* sketchbook, T.B., XXXVII; see also the *Studies near Brighton* sketchbook (T.B., XXX). Another example of the small Brighton studies, which is now in private hands, is No. 149; No. 150 may come from the same group.

148 View on the Sussex coast (Rottingdean)
c. 1796

Pencil and watercolour, 395 × 505
Prov.: Christie 1907 (as 'Rottingdean'), bt. Palser; bt. for the Friends of the Fitzwilliam, by whom given 1913
Coll.: Syndics of the Fitzwilliam Museum, Cambridge (751; Cormack 6)

See No. 147.

149   A fishing-boat in a choppy sea*   *c.*1796

Watercolour and body-colour on coarse grey paper,
135 × 208
Inscr. on verso in early-nineteenth-century hand:
*Drawn by JMW Turner/when giving a lesson to Wm
Blake (probably at the end of the 18th century)*
Exh.: R.A. 1974 (36)
Prov.: unknown
Private collection

William Blake, of Newhouse, took regular lessons
from Turner in the 1970s and commissioned a
number of drawings from him.

150   Crest of the wave   *c.*1796

Watercolour and body-colour, with pen and brown
ink on buff paper, 201 × 275
Prov.: Gilbert Davis
Coll.: Henry E. Huntington Library and Art Gallery,
San Marino, California (59.55.1285)

**151   Fishermen hauling a boat ashore at the
edge of a lake**   *c.*1796

Watercolour, 180 × 230
Prov.: Sotheby 17 June 1974 (132), bt.
D. Guerett
Coll.: untraced

This relates to drawings in the Turner Bequest: see
No. 147 above.

Nos 152–163 are executed in a uniform style, finer
and more delicate than that of most of Turner's
work hitherto; in particular, the foliage of trees is
rendered with a feathery, almost feminine touch.
Such delicacy is characteristic of several works of
about 1796, e.g. the figures in *Landaff Cathedral*
(No. 143), but it is especially so of this group of rural
subjects. Many of them show the estate of the
scholar and collector William Lock, at Norbury,
Surrey.
It is known that Turner visited Norbury about this
time in order to draw William Lock's fernhouse
(No. 239).

152   A view in Kent   *c.*1796

Watercolour over pencil, 222 × 359
Prov.: ?W. F. Wells; C.S. Bale, sale Christie 14 May
1881 (191), bt. Agnew; J. E. Taylor, by whom
presented to the Whitworth Institute, 1892
Coll.: Whitworth Art Gallery, University of Manchester (D.95.1892)

153   Norbury Park, Surrey   *c.*1796

Watercolour, 254 × 381
Prov.: Dr. Thomas Monro; W. G. Rawlinson; Sir
Charles Robinson
Coll.: untraced

154   Norbury Park   *c.*1796

Pencil and blue and grey washes, 141 × 258
Inscr. foreground (perhaps by Turner): *bright light.*
on verso: *with Girtin* (in a modern hand)
Prov.: ?Dr. Thomas Monro; Burney; by descent
to David Rolt, sale Christie 9 November 1976 (37),
bt. Shelton
Coll.: Queensland Art Gallery, Brisbane

155   Beech trees, Norbury Park, Leatherhead
*c.*1796

Watercolour, 430 × 425
Prov.: Dr. Monro; Henry Vaughan, by whom
bequeathed to the gallery, 1900
Coll.: National Gallery of Ireland, Dublin (2409)

A drawing in pencil and grey wash of *Beech Trees,*
possibly of the same time, is in the Indianapolis
Museum of Art (13.442).

156   Norbury Park, Leatherhead   *c.*1796

Watercolour, 216 × 356
Prov.: F. Burton, 1867; Frank C. Parker
Private collection

157   A great tree   *c.*1796

Pencil and watercolour, 252 × 386 (a thin strip of
paper added along lower edge)
Prov.: W. Parker; by descent to Capt. Parker, sale
Sotheby 12 December 1928 (59), bt. L. G. Duke,
from whom bt. by Paul Mellon, 1961
Coll.: Yale Center for British Art, Paul Mellon
Collection

**158   Landscape, with trees, figures, bridge and
stream**   *c.*1796

Pencil and watercolour, 253 × 348
Prov.: Edith, Lady Powell, by whom bequeathed to
the museum, 1934
Coll.: Victoria and Albert Museum, London
(P42–1934)

**159   A   horse   and   cattle   by   a   tree   in
watermeadows**   *c.*1796

Pencil and watercolour, 310 × 230
Prov.: anon. sale Christie 9 November 1976 (42),
bt. Van Haeften
Private collection

**160   The pack waggon, going through Bagley
          Wood,   looking   towards   Abingdon,
          Oxfordshire**   *c.* 1796

Watercolour, 254 × 352
Prov.: Phillips Son & Neale, 19 July 1966 (6), bt.
Maas, by whom sold to present owner
Private collection

161   Hilly landscape with a large tree   *c.* 1796

Watercolour over pencil, 198 × 273
Sig. lower left: *W Turner*
Prov.: unknown
Coll.: National Gallery of Canada, Ottawa (6229)

The view is apparently of Box Hill, Surrey, close to
William Lock's estate.

162   View in Sussex   *c.* 1796

Watercolour over pencil, 248 × 343
Prov.: Miss P. Woolner; Agnew, 1926; Miss
Deakin; Agnew, 1928, from whom purchased by
T. N. Brown; by descent to present owner
Private collection

163   Box Hill, Surrey (?)   *c.* 1796

Pencil and watercolour, 226 × 300
Prov.: Edith, Lady Powell, by whom bequeathed to
the museum 1934
Coll.: Victoria and Albert Museum, London
(P. 29–1934)

164   Winchester Cross, Hampshire   *c.* 1796

Watercolour, 222 × 175
Inscr.: *made by Mr Turner for Mr Alexan... in
1796*
Engr.: by J. Powell, 1800 (R.51)
Prov.: ? William Alexander, for whom drawn;
J. E. Taylor, by whom presented to the Whitworth
Institute, 1892
Coll.: Whitworth Art Gallery, University of Man-
chester (D.84.1892)

A drawing of this subject is on p. 4 of the *Isle of
Wight* sketchbook (T.B., XXIV). It is inscribed *Winchester Cross*.
William Alexander (1767–1816) was an associate
of Dr. Monro, and his simple, direct style of picturesque architectural topography may possibly have
influenced Turner in works like this and other
drawings of the same date.

165   Christ Church, Oxford, from near Carfax
          c. 1796

Watercolour over pencil, 247 × 331
Sig. lower centre: *W Turner*
Prov.: Lord Mansfield
Coll.: National Gallery of Canada, Ottawa (3124)

Based on a partially coloured drawing in the *South
Wales* sketchbook (T.B., XXVI–97). There is another
version of this subject in a private collection, U.S.A.
It is possible that No. 165 is a pair with No. 306;
Lord Mansfield was a graduate of Christ Church,
Oxford.

166   A Wiltshire cottage   *?c.* 1796

Pencil and watercolour, 184 × 250
Prov.: Walter Stoye; by descent to present
owner
Private collection

167   Newport Castle   *c.* 1796

Watercolour, 230 × 302

Sig. lower right: *W Turner*
Prov.: Sir Joseph Heron, sale Christie 9 June 1890 (79), bt. Agnew; Mrs. Kershaw; George Salting, by whom bequeathed to the museum, 1910
Coll.: Trustees of the British Museum (1910–2–12–289)

A drawing of the castle is in the *South Wales* sketchbook (T.B., XXVI–3).

168 Newark upon Trent Castle *c.* 1796

Watercolour, 303 × 421
Inscr. verso in pencil: *Newark-upon-Trent/J.M.W. Turner*
Prov.: P. R. Bennett; bt. Agnew 1971
Coll.: Yale Center for British Art, Paul Mellon Collection

169 A watermill *c.* 1796

Watercolour over pencil, 347 × 493
Prov.: C. P. Manuk and Miss G. M. Coles, by whom bequeathed to the museum through the National Art-Collections Fund, 1948
Coll.: Trustees of the British Museum (1948-10-9-9).

A more elaborate treatment of the subject of No. 130, Pembury Mill.

170 On the coast near Tenby 1796

Watercolour, 261 × 383
Sig. lower left: *W Turner 1796*
Prov.: ? Australian collection; Hurlbutt; J. Leslie Wright by 1949; by descent to the present owner
Private collection

171 Welsh coast scene 1795–6

Watercolour, with pen and ink, 160 × 232
Sig. lower left: *W Turner*
Prov.: anon. sale Sotheby 16 March 1978 (76), bt. Agnew
Coll.: with Thos. Agnew & Sons Ltd., London

172 Ploughing *c.* 1796

Watercolour, pen and brown ink, 255 × 356
Prov.: Gilbert Davis
Coll.: Henry E. Huntington Library and Art Gallery, San Marino, California (59.55.1282)

Despite a slight difference in the sizes, it is possible that this design was intended as a pair to that of No. 173; the latter, however, bears the marks of being a finished drawing, while this remains a sketch which was not engraved.

173 Autumn—sowing grain *c.* 1796

Pencil and watercolour, 217 × 325

Engr.: in aquatint by John Hassell, 1813 (R.817)
Prov.: Charles Stokes; Mrs. J. Hugues (of Reigate); Mrs. S. V. Carey (Surrey), from whom purchased 1970
Coll.: Yale Center for British Art, Paul Mellon Collection

See No. 172.

174 Windsor Castle and Park, with deer *c.* 1796

Pencil and watercolour, 206 × 288
Prov.: L. G. Duke
Coll.: Mr. and Mrs. Paul Mellon, Upperville, Virginia

175 A river in spate *c.* 1796

Watercolour over pencil 355 × 495
Prov.: J. E. Taylor, sale Christie 5 July 1912 (94), bt. Agnew; Dr. D. Lloyd Roberts (1912), by whom bequeathed to the gallery, 1920
Coll.: City Art Gallery, Manchester (1920.623)

Nos 176–181 are six drawings, now untraced, the compositions of which are recorded in a set of unfinished engravings by John Landseer for an unpublished work of about 1799. The dimensions as given here, and their probable date, are derived from Armstrong (p. 285), who cites a sale catalogue, ? Christie 1873, where they were described as 'six early drawings in the style of Morland'. The vendor was given as 'Miss James'. See note to No. 142 above.

176 Cowes, Isle of Wight *c.*1796

Watercolour, 190 × 254 (no Rawlinson No.)

---

177 Orchard Bay, Isle of Wight *c.*1796

Watercolour, 190 × 254 (R. 34)
Prov.: Thomas Woolner, sale Christie 12 June 1875 (94), bt. Agnew

---

178 Freshwater Bay, Isle of Wight *c.*1796

Watercolour, 190 × 254 (R. 35)

---

179 Alum Bay, Isle of Wight *c.*1796

Watercolour, 190 × 254 (R. 36)

---

180 Alum Bay, with the Needles *c.*1796

Watercolour, 190 × 254 (R. 37)

---

181 Shanklin Castle, Isle of Wight *c.*1796

Watercolour, 190 × 254 (R. 37a)

SECTION III
Nos 182–226 The Essex, Hoare and Lascelles commissions, *c.*1794–1807

III (a)   Nos 182–192
Drawings commissioned by Viscount Malden (fifth Earl of Essex), *c.*1794–1807

Turner's *South Wales* sketchbook (T.B, XXVI), in use in 1795, records (p. 5) among 'other order'd drawings' five for 'Lord Viscount Malden, Hampton Court in Herefordshire'. The titles are 'Cascade', 'Oak', 'Chaple', 'N Front', 'S Front'. The first four of these subjects were executed in that year or shortly afterwards. The *South Front,* if it was completed, is apparently missing, but it may have been used as the design for the subject engraved for the *Copper-Plate Magazine* in 1797 (R. 12; Cat. No. 98). Turner was commissioned to make two more views of Hampton Court by Sir Richard Colt Hoare; these were also noted in the sketchbook (T.B., XXVI–5), but were not executed until later (see Nos 215, 216), when Turner repeated the *North Front* design he had made for Malden; the *South Front* may also be a repetition of the missing earlier drawing. Confusion has arisen because of the existence of a further view of the *North Front* (No. 182), engraved for Britton and Brayley's *Beauties of England and Wales* (R. 63); this has been thought to be the missing *South Front.* Viscount Malden became the fifth Earl of Essex in 1799.
Turner made two drawings in the grounds of Cassiobury, Essex's seat in Hertfordshire, in the 1790s; and later, probably about 1807, was commissioned to make four large drawings of Cassiobury, which were published as aquatints in a *History and Description of Cassiobury Park,* which appeared in 1816. These four drawings seem to have belonged originally to Essex, and Finberg (*Life,* p. 149) suggests they may have been exhibited in Turner's gallery in 1808.

182 View of Hampton Court, Herefordshire, from the north-east *c.*1796

Pencil and watercolour, with some body-colour, 356 × 470
Engr.: by J. Storer, 1801, for Britton and Brayley's *Beauties of England and Wales* (R. 63)
Prov.: ?Viscount Malden, later fifth Earl of Essex; Mrs. Mary Worthington, by whom bequeathed to the Whitworth Institute, 1904
Coll.: Whitworth Art Gallery, University of Manchester (D.13.1904)

The subject has been known as 'The South Front'.

183 View of Hampton Court, Herefordshire, from the north-west *c.*1796

Pencil and watercolour, with some body-colour, 320 × 425
Prov.: Viscount Malden, later fifth Earl of Essex; J. E. Taylor, by whom given to the Whitworth Institute, 1892
Coll.: Whitworth Art Gallery, University of Manchester (D.96.1892)

A drawing of this subject is in the *South Wales* sketchbook (T.B., XXVI–53). Turner repeated this composition for Colt Hoare in 1806 (No. 215).

---

184 Oak tree, Hampton Court, Herefordshire *c.*1796

Pencil and watercolour, with some body-colour, 305 × 413
Prov.: Viscount Malden, later fifth Earl of Essex; Mrs. Mary Worthington, by whom bequeathed to the Whitworth Institute, 1904
Coll.: Whitworth Art Gallery, University of Manchester (D.12.1904)

Turner's pencil drawing of this subject is in the *South Wales* sketchbook (T.B., XXVI–49).

185 The Chapel, Hampton Court, Herefordshire *c.*1795

Pencil and watercolour, with some body-colour, 312 × 411
Sig. lower right: *W Turner*
Prov.: Viscount Malden, later fifth Earl of Essex; Mrs. Mary Worthington, by whom bequeathed to the Whitworth Institute, 1904
Coll.: Whitworth Art Gallery, University of Manchester (D.11.1904)

The pencil drawing for this is in the *South Wales* sketchbook (T.B. XXVI–52).

186 The Cascades, Hampton Court, Herefordshire 1795

Pencil and watercolour, with some body-colour, 314 × 411

Signed and dated lower right: *W Turner 1795;* sig. also lower left
Prov.: Viscount Malden, later fifth Earl of Essex; William Smith, by whom given to the museum, 1871
Coll.: Victoria and Albert Museum, London (1682–1871)

The pencil drawing for this is in the *South Wales* sketchbook (T.B. XXVI–50).

187 Cottages in the park at Cassiobury *c.* 1794–5

Watercolour, 181 × 254
Prov.: Gerald Agnew; Capt. R. H. Peters
Private collection

188 Cassiobury Park (the Deer House) *c.* 1796–7

Pencil and watercolour, 360 × 470
Prov.: J. Leslie Wright; anon. sale Sotheby, 23 June 1948 (43), bt. Agnew; James R. Page (1952); estate of Mrs. Kate van Nuy Page; acquired by the gallery 1966
Coll.: Henry E. Huntington Library and Art Gallery, San Marino, California (66.54)

189 Cassiobury, Herts *c.* 1807

Watercolour and scraping-out over pencil, 472 × 589
Engr.: in aquatint by J. Hill for *History and Description of Cassiobury Park,* 1816 (R. 818)
Prov.: ? the fifth Earl of Essex
Coll.: Museum of Fine Arts, Boston, Mass. (gift of the Estate of James Jackson Higginson)

A study for this subject is in the Whitworth Art Gallery, University of Manchester.

190 West Front, Cassiobury *c.* 1807

Watercolour, size unknown (upright)
Engr.: in aquatint by J. Hill for *History and Description of Cassiobury Park,* 1816 (R. 819)
Prov.: ? the fifth Earl of Essex
Coll.: untraced

191 North-west Front, Cassiobury (with hounds and huntsmen) *c.* 1807

Watercolour and scraping-out, 280 × 394
Engr.: in aquatint by J. Hill for *History and Description of Cassiobury Park,* 1816 (R. 820)
Prov.: ? fifth Earl of Essex; William Quilter, sale Christie 9 April 1875 (244), bt. Agnew; H. W. F. Bolckow, sale Christie 18 June 1892 (143), bt. Agnew; C. Morland Agnew, 1894, by whom bequeathed to Major Kenneth Agnew, by whom bequeathed to Vice-Admiral Sir William Agnew; Agnew, 1979
Private collection, U.S.A.

192 The Great Cloister, Cassiobury *c.* 1807

Watercolour, size unknown
Engr.: in aquatint by J. Hill for *History and Description of Cassiobury Park,* 1816 (R. 821)
Prov.: ? the fifth Earl of Essex; ? B. G. Windus; Davidson
Coll.: untraced

III(b) Nos 193–216
Drawings commissioned by Sir Richard Colt Hoare, *c.* 1796–1806

The name of 'Sir Richard Hoare' appears in Turner's *Isle of Wight* sketchbook (T.B. XXIV), of 1795, against two titles: 'Salisbury Porch' and 'Front of Salisbury'. The entry is annotated 'Size of Ely', presumably refering to the large interior of Ely Cathedral which Turner was preparing to show at the Academy in the following year (No. 194). Turner's note that Colt Hoare wanted drawings of Salisbury the size of his exhibited *Ely* suggests that Hoare himself purchased that drawing. The transaction is not recorded; but Hoare did acquire another view of Ely which Turner made in about 1796 (No. 193). The large interior was repeated, with minor modifications, for the Bishop of Ely; this version was exhibited in 1797 (No. 195). Colt Hoare appears again as the commissioner of a 'N Front of Hampton Court' and a companion South Front in the listed 'order'd drawings' in the *South Wales* sketchbook (T.B., XXVI). Turner made a visit to Hampton Court, Herefordshire, in 1798, making drawings in the *Hereford Court* sketchbook (T.B., XXXVIII) of the

house and of Malmesbury Abbey. Studies of the latter are annotated 'Sir Richard Colt Hoare, Bart', but the drawings of Hampton Court are inscribed 'Earl of Essex' (see note to Nos 182–192). A loose sheet in the Turner Bequest (CCCLXVIII–A) contains a list outlining an extensive commission from Colt Hoare for views of Salisbury town and cathedral, on which Turner was engaged between about 1795 and 1805. Two series were undertaken; a set of ten small drawings of buildings in and around Salisbury, and another set of ten larger sheets showings views of the cathedral. The titles as given by Turner are:

No. 1 Bishop's Palace
2 St. Thomas's Church
3 Ancient Arch in Mr. Wyndham's Garden
4 Close Gate
5 Ancient Market Place
6 New Council Room
7 St. Ed Church, by the Market Place
8 Wilton House
9 St. Edmunds Church
10 Poultry Cross

1 Chapter House
2 Do
3 Cloisters
4 General View of Church from Bishop's Garden
5 East Front
6 West Do
7 North Do
8 Transept
9 Choir—Audley Chapel
10 Entrance from West Door

(Finberg, *Inventory,* II, p. 1218)

The surviving drawings do not account for the whole of this list, and it may be assumed that Turner did not execute all the subjects. Completed cathedral subjects are Nos 196–203, and these correspond to another list made by Turner (T.B., CCCLXXX–20v): '2 Chapter. 2 inside. 1 Cloyster; 2 outside. 1 general.' These were dispersed at the sale of the Stourhead Heirlooms in 1883. The nine drawings of the smaller set, bound in an album, remained together until 1927 (Nos 204–208, 211–214).
Colt Hoare's two Hampton Court drawings were executed towards the end of Turner's work on the Salisbury commission, about 1806 (Nos 215, 216), for Hoare's copy of *An Account of the Manor of Marden in Hertfordshire,* privately published by Thomas, Earl of Coningsby.

193 Ely from the south-east *c.* 1796

Pencil and watercolour, 242 × 330
Prov.: Sir Richard Colt Hoare; Kelsey Heirlooms

sale, Bearnes & Waycotts, Torquay, June 1974; Sotheby, 1 April 1976 (126), bt. Hunter
Coll.: Colin Hunter

A complete pencil study of the cathedral seen from this angle (slightly further away) is in a private collection. It was used again for the *England and Wales* drawing (No. 845). Turner made it on his Midland tour of 1794, when he also produced a study of the west tower (T.B., XXI–Y) from this angle, partially coloured.

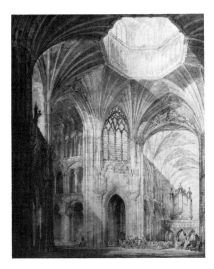

194 Trancept and Choir of Ely Minster ?R.A. 1796 (711)

Pencil and watercolour, 660 × 508
Prov.: ? Sir Richard Colt Hoare; R. Chambers; R. Durning Holt, of Liverpool; by descent to present owner
Coll.: The Lord Methuen, Corsham

A large pencil drawing of the crossing of Ely Cathedral, made in 1794, is T.B., XXII–P. (See also No. 195.)

195 Ely Cathedral, South Trancept ?R.A. 1797 (464)

Watercolour, 629 × 489
Exh.: R.A. 1974 (13)

Prov.: Dr. Yorke, Bishop of Ely (for whom drawn), and heirs; Stephen Winkworth, sale Sotheby 29 May 1946 (10), bt. Agnew; H. F. P. Borthwick-Norton; purchased for the gallery through the Lyon Bequest, 1954
Coll.: Aberdeen Art Gallery (54.2)

See No. 194. The principal difference between these two drawings is that in No. 194 the light falls from the left, and in No. 195 from the right. There is some doubt as to which drawing belongs to which year.

196 North porch of Salisbury Cathedral R.A. 1797 (517)

Watercolour, 650 × 500
Prov.: Sir Richard Colt Hoare; by descent, Sir Henry Hoare, sale Christie 2 June 1883 (20), bt. Gibbs
Coll.: untraced

197 Choir of Salisbury Cathedral (with Lady Chapel) R.A. 1797 (450)

Pencil and watercolour, 648 × 508
Inscr. lower right: *Turner/SARUM* and lower centre: *ΣIOV*; and dated lower left: *1797*
Prov.: Sir Richard Colt Hoare; by descent to Sir Henry Hoare, sale Christie 2 June 1883 (23), bt. Agnew; Fothergill Watson 1884; Agnew 1924; C. Morland Agnew; by descent to Miss E. M. Agnew, who bequeathed it to Vice-Admiral Sir William Agnew, by whom bequeathed to the museum after leaving a life interest to his widow, who died 1977
Coll.: Salisbury and South Wiltshire Museum, Salisbury

198 West front of Salisbury Cathedral R.A. 1799 (335)

Watercolour over pencil, 485 × 660
Prov.: Sir Richard Colt Hoare; by descent, Sir Henry Hoare, sale Christie 2 June 1883 (18), bt. Gibbs; Mrs. Cash; Revd. John Park Haslam, by whom bequeathed to the museum in memory of his father
Coll.: Harris Museum and Art Gallery, Preston (1257)

A drawing of the west front of the cathedral is on p. 16 of the *Isle of Wight* sketchbook (T.B. XXIV).

199 Inside of the chapter house of Salisbury Cathedral * R.A. 1799 (327)

Pencil and watercolour, with scraping-out, 640 × 510
Prov.: Sir Richard Colt Hoare; by descent, Sir Henry Hoare, sale Christie 2 June 1883 (25), bt. Gibbs; Mrs. von Mumm; Sir William Agnew, presented by him to the Whitworth Institute, 1889
Coll.: Whitworth Art Gallery, University of Manchester (D.3.1889)

200 View of Salisbury Cathedral, from the Bishop's garden 1797–8

Pencil and watercolour, 513 × 678
Prov.: Sir Richard Colt Hoare; by descent, Sir Henry Hoare, sale Christie 2 June 1883 (19), bt. Gibbs; F. Flint 1888; J. Penders 1897
Coll.: City Museums and Art Gallery, Birmingham (9'97)

201 Chapter-house, Salisbury R.A. 1801 (415)

Pencil and watercolour, 660 × 508
Prov.: Sir Richard Colt Hoare; by descent, Sir Henry Hoare, sale Christie 2 June 1883 (24), bt. Agnew
Coll.: Victoria and Albert Museum, London (503–1883)

202　South view from the cloisters, Salisbury Cathedral *c.* 1802

Pencil and watercolour, 680 × 496
Sig. lower left: *JMW Turner RA*
Prov.: Sir Richard Colt Hoare; by descent, Sir Henry Hoare, sale Christie 2 June 1883 (21), bt. Agnew
Coll.: Victoria and Albert Museum, London (502–1883)

203　Interior of Salisbury Cathedral, looking towards the North Transept 1802–5

Pencil and watercolour, 660 × 508
Inscr. lower centre: *TURNER RA* and lower left: *EPISCOP...SARUM*
Exh.: R.A. 1974 (15)
Prov.: Sir Richard Colt Hoare; by descent to Sir Henry Hoare, sale Christie 2 June 1883 (22), bt. Agnew; Mrs. von Mumm; R. J. Munn, sale Christie 6 May 1921 (7), bt. Agnew; C. Morland Agnew; by descent to Vice-Admiral Sir William Agnew, who bequeathed it to the museum after leaving a life interest to his widow, who died 1977
Coll.: Salisbury and South Wiltshire Museum, Salisbury

204　Bishop's Palace, Salisbury *c.* 1795

Pencil and watercolour, 284 × 389
Sig. lower right: *W Turner*
Prov.: Sir Richard Colt Hoare; Sir Henry Hoare, sale Christie 30 July and 4 and 7 August 1883 (in a volume), bt. Revd. J. H. Ellis; H. A. Steward, sale Christie 28 July 1927 (6), bt. Agnew; Dr. A. W. Young; Spink, from whom purchased, 1952
Coll.: Cecil Higgins Art Gallery, Bedford (P.97)

205　St. Edmund's Church, Salisbury *c.* 1800–2

Pencil and watercolour, 384 × 270
Sig. lower right: *W. Turner*
Exh.: BM 1975 (23)
Prov.: Sir Richard Colt Hoare; Sir Henry Hoare, sale Christie 30 July and 4 and 7 August 1883 (in a volume), bt. Revd. J. H. Ellis; H. A. Steward, sale Christie 28 July 1927 (9); bt. Agnew; R. W. Lloyd, by whom bequeathed to the museum, 1958
Coll.: Trustees of the British Museum (1958–7–12–403)

206　A gothic arch in a garden at Salisbury *c.* 1800

Pencil and watercolour, 379 × 293
Sig. lower right: *W Turner*
Exh.: B.M. 1975 (22)
Prov.: Sir Richard Colt Hoare; Sir Henry Hoare, sale Christie 30 July and 4 and 7 August 1883 (in a volume), bt. Revd. J. H. Ellis; H. A. Steward, sale Christie 28 July 1927 (7), bt. Agnew; R. W. Lloyd,

by whom bequeathed to the museum, 1958
Coll.: Trustees of the British Museum (1958–7–12–404)

A watercolour study of this subject is T.B., L–I.

207　St. Martin's Church, Salisbury *c.* 1800

Pencil and watercolour, 321 × 435
Sig. lower right: *JMW Turner*
Prov.: Sir Richard Colt Hoare; Sir Henry Hoare, sale Christie 30 July and 4 and 7 August 1883 (in a volume), bt. Revd. J. H. Ellis; H. A. Steward, sale Christie 28 July 1927 (3), bt. Permain; P. C. Manuk and Miss G. M. Coles, by whom bequeathed to the museum through the National Arts-Collection Fund, 1948
Coll.: Trustees of the British Museum (1948–10–9–8)

Another watercolour drawing of St. Martin's Church is in the Turner Bequest (T.B., XXVII–B).

208　Gateway to the Close, Salisbury 1802–5

Pencil and watercolour, 456 × 315
Sig. lower right: *JMW Turner RA*
Inscr. verso in pencil (?Turner's hand): *Sʳ R Hoare Bart/Salisbury* (?) *& Hampton*
Prov.: Sir Richard Colt Hoare; Sir Henry Hoare, sale Christie 30 July and 4 and 7 August 1883 (in a volume), bt. Revd. J. H. Ellis; H. A. Steward, sale Christie 28 July 1927 (2), bt. Leggatt; P. C. Manuk and Miss G. M. Coles, by whom bequeathed to the museum through the National Art-Collections Fund, 1948

211 Poultry Cross, Salisbury *c.* 1800–2

Pencil and watercolour, 362 × 480
Sig. lower right (brown ink): *JMW Turner*
Prov.: Sir Richard Colt Hoare; Sir Henry Hoare, sale Christie 30 July and 4 and 7 August 1883 (in a volume), bt. Revd. J. H. Ellis; H. A. Steward, sale Christie 28 July 1927 (5), bt. Leggatt; Mrs. Esther Slater Kerrigen; Parke Bernet, 1942; Scott & Fowles; John Regina, by whom given to Patrick Sardoni; French & Co., New York, 1977
Private collection

A drawing of the Poultry Cross is in the *Isle of Wight* sketchbook (TB XXIV–18).

215 Hampton Court, Herefordshire, seen from the north-west *c.* 1806

Watercolour and scratching-out, 202 × 305
Prov.: Sir Richard Colt Hoare; by descent to Sir Henry Hoare, sale Sotheby 30 July 1883 (450); Coningsby Disraeli; Colnaghi, from whom purchased, 1971
Coll.: Yale Center for British Art, Paul Mellon Collection

A repetition of the earlier design (No. 183).

Coll.: Syndics of the Fitzwilliam Museum, Cambridge (PD 38–1948; Cormack 11)

A watercolour of this subject was exhibited at the R.A. in 1796 (see Nos 209, 210).

---

209 Gateway to the Close, Salisbury
?R.A. 1796 (369)

Pencil and watercolour, size unknown
Prov.: Augustus Walker's gallery, 1930; J. Leslie Wright; Fine Art Society, London; Sir Adrian and Lady Holman
Coll.: untraced

This is an earlier version of the subject of No. 208. See No. 210.

---

212 Ancient Market Place, Salisbury *c.* 1805

Pencil and watercolour, 280 × 385
Sig. lower right: *JMW Turner*
Prov.: Sir Richard Colt Hoare; Sir Henry Hoare, sale Christie 30 July and 4 and 7 August 1883 (in a volume), bt. Revd. J. H. Ellis; H. A. Steward, sale Christie 28 July 1927 (8), bt. Agnew; Roland Addy; Mrs. Joan Thirsk, by whom bequeathed to the gallery, 1978
Coll.: South Yorkshire County Council, Cooper Art Gallery, Barnsley, Yorkshire.

---

213 New Council Room, Salisbury *c.* 1805

Watercolour, 305 × 390
Sig.: *JMWT*
Prov.: Sir Richard Colt Hoare; Sir Henry Hoare, sale Christie 30 July and 4 and 7 August 1883 (in a volume), bt. Revd. J. H. Ellis; H. A. Steward, sale Christie 28 July 1927 (4), bt. Agnew; Roland Addy; Mrs. Joan Thirsk, by whom bequeathed to the gallery, 1978
Coll.: South Yorkshire County Council, Cooper Art Gallery, Barnsley, Yorkshire

Drawings of the exterior of the Council House at Salisbury are T.B., L-O, P.

210 Gateway to the Close, Salisbury *c.* 1796

Pencil and watercolour, 381 × 508 (sight)
Prov.: given to the college by Mrs. Porcelli and Miss Mayo 1914
Coll.: Newnham College, Cambridge

Possibly the drawing shown at the R.A. 1796 (see No. 209). Turner repeated the composition for Colt Hoare's Salisbury series (see No. 208). The 'Close Gate, Sarum' was noted by Turner on p. 19 of the *Isle of Wight* sketchbook (T.B. XXIV).

214 Wilton House, near Salisbury *c.* 1800–5

Pencil and watercolour, 305 × 455
Sig. lower right: *JMWT*
Prov.: Sir Richard Colt Hoare; Sir Henry Hoare, sale Christie 30 July and 4 and 7 August 1883 (in a volume), bt. Revd. J. H. Ellis; H. A. Steward, sale Christie 28 July 1927 (1), bt. Leggatt; Herbert, 1932
Private collection

In 1801 Lord Pembroke employed Wyatt to make alterations to the house. This view is of the east front before the alterations.

216 Hampton Court, Herefordshire, seen from the south-east *c.* 1806

Watercolour and scratching-out, 202 × 305
Prov.: Sir Richard Colt Hoare; by descent to Sir Henry Hoare, sale Sotheby 30 July 1883 (450); Coningsby Disraeli; Colnaghi, from whom purchased, 1971
Coll.: Yale Center for British Art, Paul Mellon Collection

Turner's pencil drawing for this view of the house from the south-east is in the *South Wales* sketchbook (T.B., XXVI–51), which is also the basis for the watercolour made in *c.* 1796 (No. 98).

III(c) Nos 217–226
Drawings commissioned by the Lascelles family, *c.* 1797–1798

The *North of England* sketchbook (T.B., XXXIV) contains evidence of Turner's first visit to the seat of Edward Lascelles, first Earl of Harewood, in 1797. In addition to several drawings made in the neighbourhood, there is a list of commissions inside the front cover, which includes 'Mr. Lacelles, Harwood Castle. L. Mr. Lacelles, Harwood Castle. L.' and 'Hon. Mr. Lacelles. Kirkstall. L' (L stands for 'large'). If Turner meant to distinguish between 'Mr. Lacelles' and the 'Hon. Mr. Lacelles' he presumably meant Henry Lascelles, later second Earl of Harewood, and Edward Lascelles, the first earl's elder son, who took the courtesy title of Viscount Lascelles in 1812, but predeceased his father. It is still uncertain which of the sons commissioned which drawings. The two views of Harewood Castle, one of them still at Harewood, are Nos 221, 222; the view of Kirkstall is No. 224. Turner also made four large views of Harewood House, one of which was engraved in 1816 (No. 219). A further subject, apparently executed at the same time as the others, in 1797–8, was *Norham Castle*, of which Turner made a second version a little later. It is not clear which of these was commissioned by the Lascelles (see Nos 225, 226).

the fourth Earl, who gave it to his sister, Lady Florence Cust, by whom it was presented to the fifth Earl, 1880; by descent to present owner
Coll.: The Earl of Harewood, Harewood House, Leeds, Yorkshire

The drawing on which this subject is based is T.B., XXXIV–76. For *Loidis and Elmete* see Nos 584–586.

217 Harewood House, from the south-east * 1798

Pencil and watercolour, 474 × 645
Signed and dated: *W Turner 98*
Exh.: R.A. 1974 (27)
Prov.: first Earl of Harewood or Edward (or Henry) Lascelles, for whom drawn; by descent to the fourth Earl, who gave it to his sister, the Countess of Wharncliffe, by whom presented as a wedding gift to the sixth Earl, 1922; by descent to present owner
Coll.: The Earl of Harewood, Harewood House, Leeds, Yorkshire

218 Harewood House, from the north-east 1798

Pencil and watercolour, 495 × 645
Sig.: *W. Turner*
Prov.: first Earl of Harewood or Edward (or Henry) Lascelles, for whom drawn; by descent to the fourth Earl, who gave it to his sister, Lady Mary Meade, from whom it passed to the fifth Earl; by descent to present owner
Coll.: The Earl of Harewood, Harewood House, Leeds, Yorkshire

219 Harewood House, from the south-west 1798

Pencil and watercolour, 510 × 654
Sig.: *W Turner*
Engr.: by J. Scott for Whitaker's *Loidis and Elmete*, 1816 (R. 83)
Prov.: the first Earl of Harewood or Edward (or Henry) Lascelles, for whom drawn; by descent to

220 Harewood House, from the south 1798

Pencil and watercolour, 470 × 661
Signed and dated: 1798
Prov.: the first Earl of Harewood or Edward (or Henry) Lascelles, for whom drawn; ?Jackson Smith, of Sheffield (see Ruskin, *Works*, III, p. 580); Lord Joicey; Benyon, 1946
Coll.: untraced

221 Harewood Castle, from the north 1798

Pencil and watercolour, 457 × 652
Sig. lower centre: *W Turner*
Exh.: R.A. 1974 (28)
Prov.: Edward or Henry Lascelles, for whom drawn; ?(this or No. 222) sale Christie 1 May 1858 (58), bt. Beaumont; by 1902 Mrs. Newall, sale 8 May 1923 (153), bt. sixth Earl of Harewood; by descent to present owner
Coll.: The Earl of Harewood, Harewood House, Leeds, Yorkshire

Turner made several drawings of Harewood Castle: T.B., XXXIV, 67–74. This or the following drawing seems to have left Harewood at some period and was recovered by the sixth Earl in 1923 (Cormack, p. 32, n. 5); it may be identifiable with a drawing noted by Finberg as having been in the collection of Mrs. Newall.

222 Harewood Castle, from the south 1798

Watercolour, size unknown
Prov.: Edward or Henry Lascelles, for whom drawn; ?(this or No. 221) sale Christie 1 May 1858 (58), bt. Beaumont
Coll.: untraced

See No. 221.

223 Harewood Castle *c*. 1798

Watercolour, 222 × 305
Prov.: William Blake of Newhouse, for whom drawn; Holbrook Gaskell
Coll.: untraced

A drawing associated by Finberg with this composition is T.B., XXXIV–67; it is inscribed verso: *Wm Blake*. Blake (not the poet) was a pupil of Turner's (see No. 149). Finberg (*Life*, p. 45) refers to a 'smaller, and later, drawing' (i.e. than the Harewood set) 'signed "J.M.W. Turner" ... in the collection of the Princess Royal'. This may be identifiable with the Gaskell drawing.

224 Kirkstall Abbey, Yorkshire 1797

Watercolour, 514 × 749
Sig. left centre: *W Turner*
Prov.: Edward or Henry Lascelles; by descent to the fourth Earl of Harewood, sale Christie 1 May 1858 (47), bt. Townend; Mrs. Townend, sale Christie 2 July 1887 (76), bt. Polak; Revd. E. S. Dewick, given by Mrs. E. S. Dewick to the museum, 1918
Coll.: Syndics of the Fitzwilliam Museum, Cambridge (918; Cormack 7)

The drawing for this view is T.B., XXXIV–16.

225 Norham Castle on the Tweed, Summer's morn ?R.A. 1798 (353)

Pencil and watercolour, 509 × 735
Sig. lower left: *Turner*
Exh.: R.A. 1974 (640)
Prov.: Mrs. Thwaites
Private collection

See note to No. 226.

226 Norham Castle *c*. 1798

Watercolour, 501 × 705
Prov.: Edward Lascelles; by descent to the fourth Earl of Harewood, sale Christie 1 May 1858 (55), bt. Colnaghi; John Dillon, sale Christie 17 April 1869 (48), bt. Agnew; W. Moir; Laundy Walters; by descent to the present owners
Private collection

Turner's pencil drawing of Norham Castle is T.B., XXXIV–57. He went on to make two elaborate 'colour beginnings' of the composition (T.B., L-B, C), which were presumably preparatory to the work shown at the R.A. in 1798. It is not clear which of the two finished versions was exhibited. Finberg (*Life*, p. 460) suggests that it was the Lascelles/Laundy Walters drawing, but he also says that the Walters drawing is 'apparently later in date than the Thwaites drawing' (Index). If so, it seems likely that the Thwaites drawing is the exhibited work, which appeared in the R.A. catalogue accompanied by four lines from Thomson's *Seasons*:

> 'But yonder comes the powerful King of Day,
> Rejoicing in the East: the lessening cloud,
> The kindling azure, and the mountain's brow
> Illumin'd—his near approach betoken glad'.

The drawing 'in the possession of the late Lord Lascells' was used as the subject of a *Liber Studiorum* plate (R. 57) for which Turner made a sepia drawing (T.B., CXVIII-D).

SECTION IV
Nos 227–313 Work for exhibition and engraving, *c.* 1797– 1810

IV(a) Nos 227–284
Exhibited and other drawings, 1797–1801

These reflect Turner's experience of working in oil, and the tours that he made to the North of England and North Wales in 1797 and 1798.

227 Trancept of Ewenny Priory, Glamorganshire* R.A. 1797 (427)

Watercolour and scratching-out over pencil, 400 × 559
Exh.: R.A. 1974 (16)
Prov.: 'Property of a Trust', sale Christie 29 April 1869 (122), bt. Agnew; T. Woolner; Sir Joseph Heron, sale Christie 9 June 1890 (84), bt. Palser for J. Pyke Thompson, who bequeathed it to the museum, 1897
Coll.: National Museum of Wales, Cardiff (497a)

The pencil drawing of this subject is in the *Smaller South Wales* sketchbook (T.B., XXV–11), in use in 1795.

228 Ullswater, with Patterdale Old Hall 1797

Watercolour over traces of pencil, 258 × 371
Inscr. by Turner on verso in ink: *Patterdale Grange (?) of Patterdale ... (?)*
Prov.: Cotswold Gallery, 1926, Sir Sydney Cockerell; given by the Friends of the Fitzwilliam, 1926
Coll.: Syndics of the Fitzwilliam Museum, Cambridge (1171; Cormack 8)

This sheet is closely related to the group of drawings in the Turner Bequest (XXXVI) associated with Turner's visit to the Lake District in 1797. Draw-

ings of Patterdale occur in the *Tweed and Lakes* sketchbook (T.B., XXXV–44, 45). It is possible that this sheet once formed a part of that book.

229 Patterdale *c.* 1797

Watercolour, size unknown
Engr.: by J. Heath for Mawman's *Excursion to the Highlands and English Lakes*, 1805 (R. 75)
Provenance and whereabouts unknown

For Turner's drawings of Patterdale see No. 228. Two other drawings engraved for Mawman's *Excursion* are Nos 352, 353.

230 Mountain stream, Coniston *c.* 1797

Watercolour, 254 × 362
Prov.: Horatio Micholls; Harold E. Blaiberg, sale Sotheby 19 April 1961 (34), bt. G. D. Lockett, Clonterbrook House
Coll.: Clonterbrook Trustees, Congleton, Cheshire

231 Landscape with mill, Durham Cathedral in the background *c.* 1797

Pencil and watercolour, 175 × 250
Prov.: Benjamin Barnard (a pupil of Turner's) died 1848 ; sale Foster 8 December 1920 (84) ; William Spooner
Coll.: Mrs. M. Spooner

232 North-east view of Grantham Church, Lincolnshire *c.* 1797

Watercolour over pencil, 133 × 178 (after a sketch by R. B. Schnebbelie)
Sig. lower left: *W Turner*
Inscr. on early mount : *NE VIEW of Grantham CHURCH, Lincolnshire*
Engr.: by B. Howlett for *Selection of Views in the County of Lincoln*, 1797–1801, publ. 1 March 1797 (R. 32)
Prov.: John Baskett, from whom bt. by Paul Mellon, 1974
Coll.: Yale Center for British Art, Paul Mellon Collection

Another subject engraved for the same work is No. 240.

233 Great Malvern Churchyard, with Malvern Beacon *c.* 1797

Watercolour, 254 × 356
Prov.: Sir Charles Robinson
Coll.: untraced

234 Refectory of Kirkstall Abbey, Yorkshire* R.A. 1798 (346)

Watercolour over pencil, 448 × 651
Sig. lower right: *JMW Turner*
Engr.: by J. Scott for Britton's *Architectural Antiquities*, 1814 (R. 82)
Prov.: Sir John Soane
Coll.: Sir John Soane's Museum, London

The drawing on which this watercolour is based is in the *North of England* sketchbook (T.B., XXXIV– 10v). A further drawing of the refectory (the crypt) is on p. 11 (see also No. 235). Turner's design for the *Liber Studiorum* plate (R. 39) is T.B., CXVII-O.

235 Kirkstall Abbey Refectory *c.* 1798

Watercolour and body-colour, with pen (? brown ink), 416 × 546
Prov.: J. E. Taylor, sale Christie 5 July 1912 (52), bt. Agnew; Sir J. E. Johnson-Ferguson, Bt., sale

bt. Leggatt; Sotheby 10 December 1958 (101);
Fine Art Society, London, from whom purchased by
donor, 1959, and given to museum anonymously
Coll.: Museum of Art, Rhode Island School of
Design, Providence, R.I. (71.153.3)

Based on a drawing in the *North of England*
sketchbook (T.B., XXXIV–83).
See No. 232.

Christie 30 May 1930 (36); J. S. M. Pearson, sale
Christie 4 November 1975 (58), bt. Ahern.
Private collection

See also No. 234.

236   Holy Island cathedral, Northumberland
R.A. 1798 (404)

Watercolour, size unknown
Prov.: Mrs. Moss sale, 1873
Coll.: untraced

Perhaps the composition on which Turner based
his *Liber Studiorum* plate (R. 11). The drawing for
this subject is T.B., XXXIV–54. A different view, *Off
Holy Island,* was in the collection of Mrs. Sara
Austen, sale Christie, 11 April (cat. printed as for
10 April) 1889 (199), bt. Vokins. It may be the
drawing recorded as being in the J. Vavasseur
collection (Finberg, Index). Both measured
approximately 166 × 242.

**238   The dormitory and transcept of Fountain's
Abbey—Evening**   R.A. 1798 (435)

Watercolour, 456 × 610
Sig.: *W Turner*
Engr.: by J. Basire for Whitaker's *History and Anti-
quities of Craven in the County of York,* 1812
(R. 77)
Prov.: William Ward, 1899; anon. collection
U.S.A.
Private collection, U.K.

This drawing appeared in the R.A. catalogue
accompanied by five lines from Thomson's
Seasons:

'All ether soft'ning sober evening takes
Her wonted station on the middle air;
A thousand shadows at her beck—
In circle following circle, gathers round,
To close the face of things.'

**239   Study in September in the fern house,
Mr. Lock's Park, Mickleham, Surry**
R.A. 1798 (640)

Watercolour, size unknown
Exh.: ? C.G. 1823 (102)
Provenance and whereabouts unknown

For Turner at Norbury Park see Nos 152–163.

241   Wakefield Bridge   *c.* 1798

Watercolour, 260 × 434
Prov.: George Salting, by whom bequeathed to the
museum, 1910
Coll.: Trustees of the British Museum (1910–
2–12–283)

Drawings of the Chantry on Wakefield Bridge occur
in the *North of England* sketchbook (T.B. XXXIV–10)
and the *Tweed and Lakes* sketchbook (T.B., XXXV–
1v); a loose sheet is T.B., XXXVI-A, the immediate
source for this design. Turner made a view of
Wakefield showing the bridge for the *Copper-Plate
Magazine* (see No. 101).

**242   Bedlington, on the River Blyth, near
Morpeth**   *c.* 1798

Watercolour, 477 × 660
Prov.: Mrs. Stern, sale Christie 19 June 1908 (54),
bt. Agnew; B. Chandler; Francis Izod Chandler;
Mrs. Chandler
Private collection, U.K.

243   Kilgarren Castle*   *c.* 1798

Watercolour, 267 × 365 (sight)
Sig. lower left: *W Turner*
Prov.: John Ruskin; Arthur Severn; Maxwell
Reekie; Agnew 1924; G. Beatson Blair 1924, by
whom bequeathed to the gallery, 1941
Coll.: City Art Gallery, Manchester (1947.114)

A drawing of the composition is on p. 88 of the
Hereford Court sketchbook (T.B. XXXVIII), where
Turner noted a commission for the subject from
'Mr. Woodhouse'. The same design was used for
the painting *Kilgarren Castle on the Twyvey* shown
at the Academy in 1799 (P11). It was taken up
again for an *England and Wales* subject
(No. 806).

237   Ambleside mill, Westmoreland   R.A. 1798
(408)

Watercolour, 368 × 254
Prov.: Agnew, 1905; Miss Emma Holt; Sir Charles
Sydney Jones, by whom bequeathed to the univer-
sity, 1947.
Coll.: University of Liverpool (Tate Hall)

A drawing inscribed *Ambleside Mill* occurs in the
Tweed and Lakes sketchbook (T.B., XXXV–51).

240   Sleaford Church, Lincolnshire
c. 1798–1800

Watercolour over pencil, 237 × 347
Engr.: by B. Howlett for *Selection of Views in the
County of Lincoln,* 1797–1801 (publ. 1801;
R. 33)
Prov.: White; Heugh, sale Christie 1874; Humph-
rey Roberts, sale Christie 23 May 1908 (288),

244   Pembroke Castle   *c.* 1798

Watercolour over pencil, 194 × 290
Prov.: Swinnerton; Parke Bernet, New York,

10–11 January 1946 (45); Lord Joicey; anon. sale
Christie 4 November 1975 (57), bt. MacInnes
Private collection

245 Kidwelly Castle *c.* 1798

Watercolour, 295 × 433
Prov.: ? Rodgett sale Christie 14 May 1859; Eric
W. Phipps, sale Christie 28 November 1978 (37),
bt. Gregory
Coll.: Martyn Gregory Gallery, London

A drawing of Kidwelly Castle from a different angle
is in the *South Wales* sketchbook (T.B., XXVI–16).

246 Caregcennan Castle, near Llandilo
c. 1798

Watercolour over pencil, 393 × 557
Prov.: ?Hon Edward Spencer Cowper, ?for whom
drawn (see T.B., XXXVII–17v); Eric W. Phipps, sale
Christie 28 November 1978 (38), bt. Arundale
Coll.: Dwight W. Arundale

247 Buildwas Abbey, Shropshire *c.* 1798

Watercolour over pencil, 480 × 327
Prov.: presented by the Council of the Guarantors
of the Royal Jubilee Exhibition, 1887
Coll.: Whitworth Art Gallery, University of Manchester (D.10.1887)

248 Richmond Bridge, Yorks *c.* 1798

Watercolour, 213 × 313
Prov.: ?Sir Westrow Hulse, Bt., sale Christie
10 July 1953 (80); W. B. Dalton, by whom given to
the gallery, 1959
Coll.: Art Gallery of Ontario, Toronto (58.43)

Possibly identifiable with the drawing sold at
Christie's in 1953, together with *Gillsborough*
[? *Guisborough*] *Abbey, Yorks,* same size. The pair
had been in the vendor's family since they were
drawn.

249 Durham Cathedral, from the river
c. 1799

Pencil and watercolour, 305 × 407
Sig. lower right: *W Turner*
Prov.: John Hoppner, R.A., for whom drawn; from
whom acquired by the Royal Academy
Coll.: Royal Academy of Arts, London

Farington (Diary, 24 October 1798) mentions that
Turner told him that Hoppner had chosen this
subject, to be executed as a present (see Finberg,
Life, p. 53). The drawing on which the watercolour
is based is in the *Tweed and Lakes* sketchbook
(T.B., XXXV–15). Finberg dated Hoppner's *Durham* to
about 1801, but it seems unlikely that Turner

would have delayed so long in making the drawing;
but see No. 282.

**250 Evening landscape, with castle and
bridge** *c.* 1798–9

Watercolour, 189 × 266
Prov.: Thomas Woolner, R.A.; Beaux-Arts Gallery,
from whom bt. by L. G. Duke, 1947, from whom bt.
by Paul Mellon, 1961
Coll.: Yale Center for British Art, Paul Mellon
Collection

251 Sunny morning—the cattle by *S. Gilpin,
R.A.* R.A. 1799 (325)

Watercolour, size unknown
Provenance and whereabouts unknown

A surviving example of Turner's collaboration with
Gilpin is No. 414.

**252 Abergavenny bridge, Monmouthshire,
clearing up after a showery day**
?R.A. 1799 (326)

Watercolour, 413 × 760
Prov.: Mr. Harvey; Henry Vaughan, by whom bequeathed to the museum, 1900
Coll.: Victoria and Albert Museum, London (978–1900)

This drawing is also known as *Bridge over the Usk* (see No. 253).

253 Bridge over the Usk, near Abergavenny 1799

Watercolour, 413 × 759
Sig.: *W Turner*
Prov.: J. Allnutt, Christie 1863; Abel Buckley
Coll.: untraced

This drawing is sometimes known as *Llangollen*. See No. 252. It is not certain which of these two very similar works is that shown at the R.A. in 1799.

254 Caernarvon castle* R.A. 1799 (340)

Watercolour over pencil, 570 × 825
Sig.: *Turner*
Exh.: R.A. 1974 (42)
Prov.: J. J. Angerstein; Daniel Thwaites 1887, and by descent to the present owner
Private collection

This drawing appeared in the R.A. catalogue accompanied by lines from Canto 1 of Mallet's *Amyntor and Theodora*:

'Now rose
Sweet Evening, solemn hour, the sun declin'd
Hung golden o'er this nether firmament,
Whose broad cerulean mirror, calmly bright,
Gave back his beamy visage to the sky
With splendour undiminish'd.'

The *Academical* sketchbook (T.B., XLIII) contains a series of studies in colour of Caernarvon Castle in a composition similar to this (pp. 39 verso, 41 verso, etc.). The first of these seems to have been preparatory for the finished drawing. There is a small panel in oil of the same subject in the Turner Bequest (P28). Turner modified the composition for use in his drawing of Caernarvon for the *England and Wales* series (No. 857).

255 Morning, from Dr. Langhorne's Visions of Fancy R.A. 1799 (356)

Watercolour, size unknown
Provenance and whereabouts unknown

Accompanied in the catalogue by the following lines from Langhorne's poem:

'Life's morning landscape gilt with orient light,
Where Hope and Joy, and Fancy hold their reign,
The grove's green wave the blue stream sparkling bright,
The blythe hours dancing round Hyperion's wain.
In radiant colours youth's free hand pourtrays,
Then hold the flattering tablet to his eye,
Nor thinks how soon the vernal grove decays,
Nor sees the dark cloud gathering o'er the sky.
Mirror of life thy glories thus depart.'

256 Warkworth Castle, Northumberland— thunder storm approaching at sun-set R.A. 1799 (434)

Watercolour, 521 × 749
Prov.: Ellison, by whom given to the museum
Coll.: Victoria and Albert Museum, London (Ellison gift 547)

Accompanied in the catalogue by the following lines from Thomson's *Seasons*:

'Behold slow settling o'er the lurid grove,
Unusual darkness broods; and growing, gains
The full possession of the sky; and on yon baleful cloud
A redd'ning gloom, a magazine of fate,
Ferment.'

The drawing on which this composition is based is on p. 40 of the *North of England* sketchbook (T.B., XXXIV). Turner used the design for a subject in the *Rivers of England* series, engraved in 1826 (R. 762). A corresponding watercolour is missing from the series (No. 742), and it is possible that the plate was engraved direct from this large watercolour.

257 Warkworth Castle, sunset *c.* 1799

Watercolour, 368 × 508
Prov.: J. Temple Leader, sale Christie 18 March 1834 (49), bt. Rought; John Dillon, sale Christie 29 April 1869 (132), bt. Agnew; Abel Buckley; T. W. Wright, sale Christie 27 April 1923 (96), bt. Leggatt; Appleby Bros., from whom bt. by Lord Beaverbrook, May 1957
Coll.: Beaverbrook Art Gallery, Fredericton, N.B., Canada (59/261)

Armstrong (p. 283) describes this as a 'Girtin-like drawing'. The castle appears in the centre instead of being to the right, as in No. 256. The composition is based on T.B., XXXIV-38.

258 ?Scene in North Wales *c.* 1799

Watercolour over pencil, 247 × 418
Prov.: R. W. Lloyd, by whom bequeathed to the museum, 1958
Coll.: Trustees of the British Museum (1958-7-12-405)

The size of this sheet is close to that of the *Smaller Fonthill* sketchbook (T.B., XLVIII); the drawing is probably related to a Welsh tour and resembles technically the large colour studies of scenes in Snowdonia (T.B., LX(a)).

259 Cader Idris* *c.* 1799

Watercolour, 578 × 788
Exh.: R.A. 1974 (ex cat.)
Prov.: Sir John Dean Paul
Private collection

Another version is No. 260.

260 Cader Idris *c.* 1799

Watercolour (varnished), 610 × 775
Prov.: W. G. Rawlinson
Coll.: untraced

According to Armstrong (p. 244) this is the same subject as No. 259.

261 Coniston Fells *c.* 1799

Pencil and watercolour, 252 × 415
Prov.: J. E. Taylor, by whom presented to the Whitworth Institute, 1892
Coll.: Whitworth Art Gallery, University of Manchester (D.93.1892)

This is a study. It is very likely a page from the *Smaller Fonthill* sketchbook (T.B., XLVIII). The identification of the subject is traditional, but seems to have little justification. Armstrong (p. 247) records

another drawing called *Coniston Fells,* which is similar in composition to the painting No. P5. It belonged to Horatio Micholls in 1899.

262 A lime-kiln by moonlight *c.* 1799

Watercolour, 165 × 240
Prov.: Sir Charles Robinson, anon. sale Christie 5 March 1974 (123), bt. Colnaghi
Coll.: Herbert Art Gallery and Museum, Coventry (5.74)

A note attached to the original backboard is said to have read: 'A drawing by W. Turner, R.A., to show the effect of moonlight on fire light made from the view of a lime kiln in Surrey when the moon was visible, 1799.' Compare the painting *Limekiln at Coalbrookdale* (P22).

263 Caernarvon castle, North Wales* R.A. 1800 (351)

Watercolour, 663 × 994
Exh.: R.A. 1974 (43)
Coll.: Trustees of the British Museum (T.B., LXX-M)

The following lines were appended to the title in the R.A. catalogue:

'And now on Arvon's haughty tow'rs
The Bard the song of pity pours,
For oft on Mona's distant hills he sighs,
Where jealous of the minstrel band,
The tyrant drench'd with blood the land,
And charm'd with horror, triumph'd in their cries,
The swains of Arvon round him throng,
And join the sorrows of his song.'

264 Ludlow Castle *c.* 1800

Watercolour, 527 × 768
Inscr. on label on back: *This original by Turner belongs to my son Charles P G to whom he gave it in the spring of 1837 PG*

Prov.: Charles Pascoe Grenfell; Desborough; Agnew, from whom bt., 1952
Coll.: Henry E. Huntington Library and Art Gallery, San Marino, California (52.1)

A smaller variant of the subject is No. 265. Compare also the composition of *Bridge over the Usk* (*Abergavenny Bridge,* No. 252). A partially coloured drawing of this view is in the *Hereford Court* sketchbook (T.B., XXXVIII–11). See No. 265 for a similar view.

265 Ludlow Castle 1800

Watercolour, 356 × 671
Prov.: Abel Buckley; Mrs. G. J. Gould, New York; Walter Jones
Coll.: Barber Institute of Fine Arts, University of Birmingham

See No. 264.

266 Llanrwst ?*c.* 1800

Watercolour, 292 × 457
Prov.: John Dillon, sale Foster & Son, 7 June 1856 (146); Pilkington; Fordham; Robert Stirling Newall; by descent to present owner
Private collection

Finberg (Index) dates this drawing to 1816. Its subject-matter and general treatment suggest a rather earlier period, but it is now so extremely faded that it is difficult to be certain.

267 Moel Siabod, Caernarvonshire *c.* 1800

Watercolour over pencil, 255 × 362
Prov.: E. J. Taylor, by whom presented to the Whitworth Institute, 1892
Coll.: Whitworth Art Gallery, University of Manchester (D.88.1892)

268 Conway Castle 1798–1800

Watercolour, 419 × 622
Sig.: *W Turner*
Prov.: William Blake, of Newhouse, for whom drawn; A. M. Blake; ?J. T. Leader, sale Christie 18 March 1843 (57), bt. Fuller
Coll.: untraced

Turner's drawing of Conway Castle in the *Hereford Court* sketchbook (T.B., XXXVIII–50v) is inscribed on the back with the names of 'Pope', 'Wm Blake', and 'Mr. Leader'. The painting of the subject executed for Leader is P141; the watercolour done for William Blake is presumably this one.

269 Conway Castle *c.* 1800

Watercolour, 399 × 610
Prov.: ?C. S. Bale; ?anon. sale Christie 5 June 1863 (104), bt. Agnew; Humphrey Roberts, sale Christie 23 May 1908 (290), bt. Boyd; Mrs. Charles Lupton; G. D. Lockett
Coll.: untraced

Like No. 268, based on T.B., XXXVIII–50. See also Nos 270, 271.

270 Conway Castle *c.* 1800

Watercolour, with scraping-out and stopping-out, 534 × 763 (sight)
Prov.: Buchanan sale, *c.* 1843, ?bt. Pascoe Grenfell; entered present collection 1954
Coll.: Viscount Gage

This and No. 271 seem to be variants of the composition sketched on T.B., XXXVIII–52; see No. 269. The sketch-sheet is inscribed with various names on the verso: 'Revd. Mr. Lancaster', 'Barrington' (?), Revd. Mr. Dunford' and 'Revd. Mr. Ogle'. These may be the names of prospective purchasers of versions of the subject. Other watercolour views of Conway are recorded, but not traced. A drawing of the castle from almost the

same viewpoint as No. 270, attributed to Turner, in the Huddersfield Libraries and Museums (acquired from the collection of Lord Northwick in 1946) appears to be too early to have been done by Turner after his first visit to Conway, and is either a copy after Dayes or perhaps by Dayes himself.

271 Conway Castle *?c.* 1800

Watercolour and surface scratching, 419 × 619
Sig. lower right: *JMWT RA*
Prov.: ?Dr. Thomas Monro; ?T. Graham; Mrs. Ashton; Mrs. P. W. Kessler, whose daughters presented it to the gallery, 1948
Coll.: Whitworth Art Gallery, University of Manchester (D.18.1948)

272 St. Agatha's Abbey, Easby, Yorkshire *c.* 1799–1800

Watercolour, with scratching-out, over pencil, 508 × 762
Sig. lower right: *W Turner*
Engr.: by J. Cousen (as 'The Abbey Pool') for Dr. Broadley's *Poems* (privately printed *c.* 1844); plate also used for *Art and Song,* 1867 (R. 640)
Prov.: Holloway, sale Christie 21 May 1864 (86),

bt. in; John Heugh, sale Christie 24 April 1874 (98), bt. Agnew: presented by the Council of Guarantors of the Royal Jubilee Exhibition, Manchester, 1887
Coll.: Whitworth Art Gallery, University of Manchester (D.15.1887)

273 St. Agatha's Abbey, Easby, from the River Swale *c.* 1800

Watercolour over traces of pencil, 629 × 889
Engr.: by J. Cousen for Dr. Broadley's *Poems* (privately printed *c.* 1844); plate also used for *Art and Song,* 1867 (R. 642)
Prov.: ?Wolffe, sale Christie 16 June 1832 (48), bt. Hixon; Mrs. Worthington, by whom bequeathed to the Whitworth Institute, 1904
Coll.: Whitworth Art Gallery University of Manchester (D.18.1904)

Based on a drawing in the *North of England* sketchbook (T.B., XXXIV–25); a similar composition was used for a plate in Whitaker's *History of Richmondshire* (No. 561). A view of the abbey from the opposite direction is No. 274; it may have been drawn a little later than 1800. A drawing of the same dimensions as No. 272, entitled *St. Agatha's Abbey,* appeared in the Bolckow sale, Christie's 2 May 1891 (51), bt. Agnew. This was presumably another treatment of the subject, now untraced. Finberg (Index) assumed that the Bolckow drawing was identical with No. 272, but as that was given to the Whitworth Institute in 1887 the sequence of events would be impossible. The Wolffe-Hixon drawing (see provenance for No. 273) is not certainly identified with any of these works.

274 St. Agatha's Abbey, Easby, Yorkshire *c.* 1800

Watercolour, with some pencil and scratching-out, 270 × 371
Sig. lower left: *W Turner*

Prov.: W. F. Morice; sale Christie 21 May 1922 (60), bt. Agnew; R. W. Lloyd, by whom bequeathed to the museum
Coll.: Trustees of the British Museum (1958-7-12–406)

275 York: looking along the River Ouse to the minster—twilight *c.* 1800

Watercolour, 508 × 717
Prov.: J. E. Taylor, sale Christie 5 July 1912 (55), bt. Agnew; E. Ruffer, sale 1924, bt. Messrs. Connell
Coll.: Theodore R. Bruen

A large atmospheric study which may have been executed a little later than 1800, but which perhaps belongs functionally with the experimental Welsh watercolours in the Turner Bequest (T.B., LX (a); LXX–O, X, , etc.).

276 Durham Cathedral—interior *c.* 1800

Watercolour, 241 × 162
Engr.: by S. Porter for Wharton's *Essay on Gothic Architecture,* 1802 (2nd ed.; R. 64)
Prov.: ?Mrs. Newall
Coll.: untraced

Finberg (Index) says that this drawing measures 9 1/2 × 6 3/8'' (241 × 162) and was in the collection of Mrs Newall. He gives its date as 1795–6, which is unlikely since the engraving by Porter was not made until 1802, and Turner did not visit Durham until 1797.
There is a large finished watercolour of the interior of Durham Cathedral, probably dating from about 1800, in the Turner Bequest, (T.B., XXXVI–G).

277 Norham Castle, on the Tweed *c.* 1800

Watercolour over pencil, 432 × 610
Prov.: Mrs. Worthington, by whom bequeathed to the Whitworth Institute, 1904
Coll.: Whitworth Art Gallery, University of Manchester (D.20.1904)

For other views of Norham see Nos 225, 226.

278 London: Autumnal morning R.A. 1801 (329)

Watercolour, 603 × 991
Exh.: ?C.G. 1824 (91)
Prov.: J. Burnett (the engraver; said to have been painted for him); J.T. Leader, sale Christie 18 March 1843 (59, as 'London from Wandsworth.—Cows in foreground'), bt. Graves; anon. sale Foster 19 November 1860 (111, as 'London from Battersea'), bt. White; C. F. Huth, sale Christie 6 July 1895 (60, as 'London from Battersea'), bt. Agnew; anon. sale Christie 18 May 1901 (73, as 'London from Lambeth'), bt. Ichenhauser; Ralph Brocklebank; Lady Brocklebank; by descent to the present owner
Private collection

A view of London, now in an American private collection, is a variant of this subject. It is possible that the provenance given above confuses the histories of the two versions.

279 St. Donat's castle, South Wales: Summer evening R.A. 1801 (358)

Watercolour, 584 × 851
Engr.: in lithograph by Gauci, 1852 (R. 841)
Prov.: John Green, sale Christie 26 April 1830 (16), bt. Smith; Thomas Ashton; Lord Ashton of Hyde; by descent to present owner
Private collection, England

280 Pembroke castle, South Wales: thunder storm approaching* R.A. 1801 (343)

Watercolour, 508 × 991
Exh.: R.A. 1974 (ex cat.)
Prov.: Earl of Harewood, sale Christie 1 May 1858 (56, as 'Pembroke Castle—Vessels at Anchor, Sun penetrating clouds') bt. T. Miller Webster; W. Pitt Miller; by descent to present owner
Private collection

There has been considerable confusion between this and No. 281, both as to subject and date, and as to provenance. Drawings for one or other of the two watercolours are T.B., LXIX–pp. 88, 89, in the *Studies for Pictures* sketchbook, in use shortly after 1800. The distinction indicated in Turner's titles suggests that the Toronto drawing is that of 1806: the fishing-boat on the extreme left shows that the wind is coming from the right, where a clearer sky is visible beyond a burst of sunshine. No such 'clearing-up' is apparent in the other drawing, which is executed in a manner more consistent with Turner's style about 1800. The Toronto drawing by contrast is more spaciously composed and balanced, as well as being more crisply executed. These observations are confirmed by a label on the back of the Toronto drawing, pertaining to its appearance in Messrs. Agnew's exhibition, *Turner, Cox and de Wint*, 1924 (115), under the title 'Clearing up after a Thunderstorm'.

281 Pembroke-castle: Clearing up of a thunder-storm R.A. 1806 (394)

Watercolour and body-colour over pencil, with scraping-out 670 × 1045 (sight)
Prov.: ? Charles Hoare, of Beckenham; Ralph Brocklebank
Coll.: Art Gallery of Ontario, Toronto (on loan from the Governing Council of the University of Toronto, Canada, 1976)

See No. 280 and the *England and Wales* subject No. 832.

282 Head of Derwentwater, with Lodore Falls 1801

Watercolour and scraping-out, 355 × 524
Signed and dated: lower left: *JMW Turner Keswick Augt 1801*
Inscr. verso: *To Joseph Farrington Esqre, with W. Turner's Respects*
Prov.: Joseph Farington, to whom given by the artist; the Farington family; Dr. A. V. Peatling; H. G. Spicer; O. E. C. Spicer, sale Sotheby 22 November 1961 (45), bt. Agnew; F. B. Hart-Jackson; Agnew 1977
Coll.: Thos. Agnew & Sons Ltd., London

Turner drew this subject on a page of the *Tweed and Lakes* sketchbook, of 1797 (T.B., XXXV–82). The drawing is inscribed on the back: *Mr. Farington.* A larger version of the subject in watercolour is T.B., XXXVI-H. Farington's account, in his *Diary* for 24 October 1798, of how Turner 'requested me to fix upon any subject which I preferred in his books, and begged to make a drawing or picture of it for me' is quoted in full by Finberg (*Life*, p. 53). See also No. 249, a drawing that Turner similarly made for Hoppner.

283 The Falls of Lodore and Derwentwater *c.* 1801

Watercolour and scraping-out, 220 × 315
Prov.: anon. sale Sotheby 7 July 1977 (141), bt. Smith
Private collection

284 Dunstanborough Castle *c.* 1801–2

Watercolour, 349 × 483
Prov.: Coll. Birchell; Sir Joseph Heron; Sir Donald Currie; Mrs. Craven
Private collection

Derived from drawings in the *North of England* sketchbook, T.B., XXXIV–45, 46, 46a; and a charcoal study for this subject is T.B., XXXVI–T.

IV(b) Nos 285–294
Drawings for the *History of the Parish of Whalley,* *c.* **1798–1801**

The drawings engraved in 1800 and 1801 by James Basire for two publications of Thomas Dunham Whitaker (1759–1821); the first of these was the *History of the Original Parish of Whalley and*

Honour of Clitheroe, in the Counties of Lancaster and York, issued in 1801; the second was a *History and Antiquities of the Deanery of Craven,* 1805. Farington (Diary, 11 September 1799) suggests that the commission was instigated by Charles Towneley (see Finberg, *Life,* pp. 61–2). The drawings are executed for the most part on sheets slightly smaller than the plates taken from them. Turner relied on studies made in the autumn of 1799 in the *Lancashire and North Wales* sketchbook (T.B., XLV), which he must have used with Whitaker's commission in mind, though one or two of the drawings may have been made before that tour.

285 Studies of seals from Whalley Abbey 1799–1800

Watercolour with pen and black ink over pencil, 267 × 194
Engr.: by J. Basire for Whitaker's *History of the Parish of Whalley,* 1800-1 (R. 52)
Prov.: Charles Stokes; John Ruskin (1852); presented by him to the museum 1861
Coll.: Syndics of the Fitzwilliam Museum, Cambridge (569; Cormack 9)

286 Ancient crosses, sedilia, etc. at Whalley Abbey 1799–1800

Watercolour, 260 × 191
Engr.: by J. Basire for Whitaker's *History of the Parish of Whalley,* 1800-1 (R. 53)
Prov.: John Ruskin, sale, Christie 15 April 1869 (2); J. Harrison sale Christie 2 May 1881 (107), bt. Agnew; J. E. Taylor sale, Christie 8 July 1912 (118), bt. Agnew; Agnew 1919, from whom bt. by Burnley Corporation, 1933
Coll.: Burnley Borough Council, Towneley Hall Art Gallery and Museums

287 Whalley Abbey (distant view) 1799–1800

Watercolour, 211 × 311
Engr.: by J. Basire for Whitaker's *History of the Parish of Whalley,* 1800-1 (R. 54)
Prov.: ? anon. sale Christie 29 April 1869 (120)
Coll.: untraced

The drawing for this is T.B., XLV–43. It is inscribed verso: 'Mr Sherlock & Tomkison'.

288 Cloisters of Whalley Abbey 1799–1800

Watercolour, 211 × 311
Engr.: by J. Basire for Whitaker's *History of the Parish of Whalley,* 1800-1 (R. 55)
Provenance and whereabouts unknown

289 Remains of Whalley Abbey (near view) *c.* 1800

Watercolour over pencil, 212 × 317
Engr.: by J. Basire for Whitaker's *History of the Parish of Whalley,* 1800-1 (R. 56)
Prov.: J. Harrison, sale Christie 2 May 1881 (108), bt. Agnew; W. Lees; Professor J. Hill Abram; Miss I. A. Abram, by whom bequeathed to the gallery, 1951
Coll.: Walker Art Gallery, Liverpool (1000)

The drawing for this is T.B., XLV–44.

290 Clitheroe, from Eadsford Bridge *c.* 1799

Watercolour, ? approx. 210 × 310
Inscr.: *Drawn by Wm Turner A*
Engr.: by J. Basire for Whitaker's *History of the Parish of Whalley,* 1800-1 (R. 57)
Provenance and whereabouts unknown

291 Browsholme Hall *c.* 1798–9

Pencil and watercolour, 210 × 311
Engr.: by J. Basire for Whitaker's *History of the Parish of Whalley,* 1800-1 (R. 58)
Prov.: J. Munn (1857); Andrew Wyld, 1974; Spink, 1975
Private collection

292 Towneley Hall 1799

Watercolour, 211 × 310

Inscr.: *Drawn by Wm Turner A*
Engr.: by J. Basire for Whitaker's *History of the Parish of Whalley,* 1800-1 (R. 59)
Prov.: Agnew 1912; Agnew 1913; Edward (?) Stocks Massey, by whom bequeathed to the museum
Coll.: Burnley Borough Council, Towneley Hall Art Gallery and Museums (102)

The drawing for this subject is T.B., XLV–45.

293 Stonyhurst College *c.* 1801

Watercolour, 210 × 305
Engr.: by J. Basire for Whitaker's *History of the Parish of Whalley,* 1800-1 (R. 60)
Prov.: C. F. Huth, sale Christie 6 July 1895 (58), bt. Vokins
Coll.: untraced

Turner's drawing of this subject is T.B., XLV–42. It was used again for the *England and Wales* series (see No. 820).

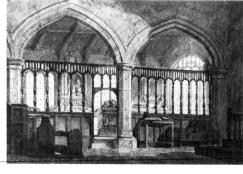

294 The Sherburne Chapel, Mitton Church *c.* 1799

Watercolour, 203 × 305
Inscr.: *Drawn by Wm Turner A*
Engr.: by J. Basire for Whitaker's *History of the Parish of Whalley,* 1800-1 (R. 61)
Prov.: Gen. Duncan, sale Christie 1890; Agnew 1901; Mrs. Rachel Beer; Agnew 1928
Coll.: Burnley Borough Council, Towneley Hall Art Gallery and Museums (51)

Turner's drawing of this subject is T.B., XLV–1. It is inscribed with a note of the inscription on the tomb of Sir Richard Sherburne. A drawing of the interior of Mitton Hall, also in the Towneley Hall Art Gallery and ascribed to Turner, is not by him; the subject was not engraved for Whitaker.

IV(c)   Nos 295–306
Drawings connected with the *Oxford Almanack,*
c. **1798–1804**

Ten watercolours were made by Turner to be engraved as head-pieces for the *Oxford Almanack.* They were deposited by the Delegates of the Clarendon Press, which had commissioned them, in the University Galleries in 1850. Turner made the drawings between 1798 and 1803–4, and they were used between 1799 and 1811. The designs were engraved by James Basire, with the exception of No. 303 (for the *Almanack* of 1810). Turner's drawing of this subject was rejected and another was made by Hugh O'Neill and engraved by J. Storer. In 1820–3 reduced versions of the plates were engraved by Joseph Skelton for his *Oxonia Antiqua Restaurata.* (See Herrmann 1968, pp. 55–63). A number of watercolour studies of Oxford subjects are in the Turner Bequest (T.B., L), but only one is directly related to the *Almanack* drawings (see No. 301).

295   South View of Christ Church, &c, from the Meadows   1798–9

Watercolour, with some pen and ink, over pencil, 315 × 451
Engr.: by J. Basire for the *Oxford Almanack,* 1799 (R. 38); by Joseph Skelton (reduced version of the design) for his *Oxonia Antiqua Restaurata,* 1823 (R. 38a)
Turner's drawing reproduced by chromo-lithography as the head-piece of the *Almanack* for 1913
Prov.: Deposited in the University Galleries by the Delegates of the Clarendon Press in 1850
Coll.: Visitors of the Ashmolean Museum, Oxford (Herrmann 1)

Compare the sketch, No. 408.

296   A View of the Chapel and Hall of Oriel College, &c.   1798–9

Watercolour over pencil, 312 × 440
Sig. lower left: *W Turner*
Engr.: by J. Basire for the *Oxford Almanack,* 1801 (R. 39); by Joseph Skelton (reduced version of the design) for his *Oxonia Antiqua Restaurata,* 1823 (R. 39a)
Prov.: deposited in the University Galleries by the Delegates of the Clarendon Press in 1850
Coll.: Visitors of the Ashmolean Museum, Oxford (Herrmann 2)

297   Inside View of the East end of Merton College Chapel   1801

Watercolour over pencil, with some scratching-out, 318 × 444
Engr.: by J. Basire for the *Oxford Almanack,* 1802 (R. 40); by Joseph Skelton (reduced version of the design) for his *Oxonia Antiqua Restaurata,* 1823 (R. 40a)
Prov.: deposited in the University Galleries by the Delegates of the Clarendon Press in 1850
Coll.: Visitors of the Ashmolean Museum, Oxford (Herrmann 3)

298   A View of Worcester College, &c.   1803–4

Watercolour over pencil, 320 × 443
Engr.: by J. Basire for the *Oxford Almanack,* 1804 (R. 41); by Joseph Skelton (reduced version of the design) for his *Oxonia Antiqua Restaurata,* 1823 (R. 41a)
Prov.: deposited in the University Galleries by the Delegates of the Clarendon Press in 1850
Coll.: Visitors of the Ashmolean Museum, Oxford (Herrmann 4)

299   A View from the Inside of Brazen Nose College Quadrangle   1803–4

Watercolour over pencil, 316 × 446
Engr.: by J. Basire for the *Oxford Almanack,* 1805 (R. 42); by Joseph Skelton (a reduced version of the design) for his *Oxonia Antiqua Restaurata,* 1823 (R. 42a)
Turner's drawing reproduced by chromo-lithography as the head-piece for the *Almanack* of 1917
Prov.: deposited in the University Galleries by the Delegates of the Clarendon Press in 1850
Coll.: Visitors of the Ashmolean Museum, Oxford (Herrmann 5)

300   View of Exeter College, All Saints Church &c. from the Turl   1802–4

Watercolour over pencil, 321 × 450
Engr.: by J. Basire for the *Oxford Almanack,* 1806 (R. 43); by Joseph Skelton (a reduced version of the design) for his *Oxonia Antiqua Restaurata,* 1823 (R. 43a)
Prov.: deposited in the University Galleries by the Delegates of the Clarendon Press in 1850
Coll.: Visitors of the Ashmolean Museum, Oxford (Herrmann 6)

301   Inside View of the Hall of Christ Church   1803–4

Watercolour over pencil, 329 × 448
Engr.: by J. Basire for the *Oxford Almanack,* 1807 (R. 44) after slight alterations had been made to the design (see Herrmann, p. 61); by Joseph Skelton (a reduced version of the engraving) for his *Oxonia Antiqua Restaurata,* 1823 (R. 44a); the drawing reproduced by chromolithography as the head-piece for the *Almanack* of 1916
Prov.: deposited in the University Galleries by the Delegates of the Clarendon Press in 1850

Coll.: Visitors of the Ashmolean Museum, Oxford (Herrmann 7)

A pencil drawing of this subject is T.B., L–J.

302 A View of Oxford from the South Side of Heddington [*sic*] Hill 1803–4

Watercolour over pencil, with some scratching-out, 316 × 448
Engr.: by J. Basire for the *Oxford Almanack*, 1808 (R. 45); by Joseph Skelton (a reduced version of the design) for his *Oxonia Antiqua Restaurata*, 1823 (R. 45a); the drawing reproduced by chromo-lithography as the head-piece for the *Almanack* of 1915
Prov.: deposited in the University Galleries by the Delegates of the Clarendon Press in 1850
Coll.: Visitors of the Ashmolean Museum, Oxford (Herrmann 8)

303 Part of Balliol College Quadrangle 1803–4

Watercolour over pencil, 318 × 447
Exh.: R.A. 1974 (40)

Prov.: deposited in the University Galleries by the Delegates of the Clarendon Press in 1850
Coll.: Visitors of the Ashmolean Museum, Oxford (Herrmann 9)

Turner's design was rejected; the head-piece for the *Almanack* of 1810 was engraved by J. Storer after a design by H. O'Neill, closely based on Turner's drawing (R. 46).

304 View of the Cathedral of Christ Church, and Part of Corpus Christi College 1803–4

Watercolour over pencil, 316 × 447
Engr.: by J. Basire for the *Oxford Almanack*, 1811 (R. 47); by Joseph Skelton (a reduced version of the design) for his *Oxonia Antiqua Restaurata*, 1823 (R. 47a)
Prov.: deposited in the University Galleries by the Delegates of the Clarendon Press in 1850
Coll.: Visitors of the Ashmolean Museum, Oxford (Herrmann 10)

The composition seems to have been developed from that of an earlier drawing (No. 133).

305 Christ Church Hall from the staircase *c.* 1800

Pencil and watercolour, 220 × 322
Prov.: Lord Mansfield; purchased through the Bilbrough Bequest 1924
Coll.: City Art Galleries, Leeds (514/24)

Not an *Oxford Almanack* design, but apparently executed at the time of Turner's most intensive preparation for the series.

306 Canterbury Gate, Christ Church, Oxford *c.* 1800

Watercolour over pencil, 250 × 333

Prov.: Lord Mansfield; Sir Leicester Harmsworth; Meatyard; Cotswold Gallery 1935; R. Stuart-Lomas, sale Sotheby 22 March 1979 (145), bt. Agnew
Private collection

The pencil drawing for this subject is T.B., XLVIII–5. The design was not engraved. The sheet is smaller than those used for the *Oxford Almanack*, but is not dissimilar in treatment.
See No. 165.

**IV(d) Nos 307–313
Drawings for Byrne's** *Britannia Depicta*, *c.* 1802–1810

William Byrne was assisted in his work on the plates by his daughter, Letitia, who is recorded as having contributed to No. 311. Although her father's name alone appears on the two later plates, he in fact died in 1805 and she may have had his name published with them as a memorial.

307 Wycombe, from the Marlow road *c.* 1802

Watercolour, 152 × 223
Engr.: by W. Byrne for Byrne's *Britannia Depicta*, 1803 (R. 65)
Prov.: W. G. Rawlinson; R. A. Tatton, sale 14 December 1928 (11), bt. Agnew; Paul Oppé, 1928; by descent to the present owner
Coll.: D. L. T. Oppé, London

308 Eton, from the Slough road *c.* 1802

Watercolour, ? approx. 150 × 220
Engr.: by W. Byrne for Byrne's *Britannia Depicta*, 1803 (R. 66)
Provenance and whereabouts unknown

309 Abington, from the Thames Navigation *c.* 1805

Pencil and watercolour, pen and black ink, 146 × 213
Engr.: by W. Byrne for Byrne's *Britannia Depicta*, 1805 (R. 67)
Prov.: Mrs. Woolner; Sir Charles Wakefield, 1911, bt. and sold to America; Monnell; Brian Pilkington; Agnew 1977
Private collection

310 Newbury, from Speen Hill *c.* 1805

Watercolour, ? approx. 150 × 220
Engr.: by W. Byrne for Byrne's *Britannia Depicta*, 1805 (R. 68)
Provenance and whereabouts unknown

311 Donnington Castle *c.* 1805

Watercolour, ? approx. 150 × 220
Engr.: by W. and L. Byrne for Byrne's *Britannia Depicta*, 1805 (R. 69)
Prov.: Revd. T. Case
Coll.: untraced

312 Chester—a distant view *c.* 1810

Watercolour, ? approx. 150 × 220
Engr.: by W. Byrne for Byrne's *Britannia Depicta*, 1810 (R. 70)
Provenance and whereabouts unknown

A drawing from which this subject was probably taken is in the *Chester* sketchbook (T.B., LXXXII–52); this is inscribed verso: *Mr Byrne*. Studies of the castle which were presumably used for No. 313 occur in the same book.

313 Chester Castle *c.* 1810

Watercolour over pencil, with some pen and ink and scratching-out, 153 × 216
Engr.: by W. Byrne for Byrne's *Britannia Depicta*, 1810 (R. 71)
Prov.: W. V. Paterson, by whom presented to the museum through the National Art-Collections Fund 1943
Coll.: Visitors of the Ashmolean Museum, Oxford (Herrmann 93)

See No. 312.

SECTION V
Nos 314–353   Fonthill and Scotland, *c.* 1799–1815

V(a)   Nos 314–326
Sheets from the *Smaller Fonthill* sketchbook, 1799–1801

The *Smaller Fonthill* sketchbook (T.B., XLVIII) was used by Turner between 1799 and 1802. Some of the drawings in it were made at Fonthill in preparation for the Beckford commission (see Nos 335–339); the rest of the book seems to have been used on Turner's journey to Edinburgh in 1801. Seven leaves remained in Turner's studio, but a large number of others have been scattered. Only those drawings which make use of watercolour are catalogued here; drawings in pencil only are distributed as follows: three at Leeds City Art Gallery; five at the Ashmolean Museum, Oxford (Herrmann 65–8, 70; two of these have some wash); fifteen at the Fogg Art Museum (one of Solway Moss, with grey wash, 1907.16); eight at the Museum of Fine Arts, Boston (one, 07.859, has a fine wash drawing verso); one at the Art Museum, Princeton University; two in a private collection in the United Kingdom. Others, no doubt, remain to be identified.

314 Durham Castle, with the cathedral beyond 1801

Pencil and watercolour, 392 × 268
Prov.: Sir Hickman Bacon, Bt.; by descent to present owner
Private collection

315 Durham Castle 1801

Watercolour over pencil, 405 × 250
Prov.: Thomas Griffith; A. J. Finberg; Miss Lupton, by whom bequeathed to the galleries, 1952
Coll.: City Art Galleries, Leeds (5.225/52)

316 Durham Cathedral *c.* 1801

Watercolour over traces of pencil, 410 × 248
Prov.: Henry Vaughan, by whom bequeathed to the gallery, 1900
Coll.: National Galleries of Scotland, Edinburgh (889)

317 Scarborough Castle 1801

Watercolour, 255 × 406
Prov.: E. J. Taylor; T. A. Tatton; Mrs. Crabtree; W. M. Williams (Yale)
Private collection

318 Scarborough 1801

Watercolour over pencil, 258 × 411
Prov.: John Ruskin; by whom given to the Ruskin School, Oxford, 1875; transferred to the museum, 1938

Coll.: Visitors of the Ashmolean Museum, Oxford (Herrmann 69)

book, (T.B., LVI-9v, etc.). See also the painting of 1810 (No. P104).

324   Fall of the Clyde c. 1801

Pencil and watercolour, 382 × 255 (sight)
Prov.: A. J. Rowe; Agnew 1971 (as 'A Waterfall');
Kurt Pantzer
Pantzer Collection, Indianapolis

319   Swaledale c. 1799

Watercolour over traces of pencil, 273 × 457
Prov.: Palser Gallery
Coll.: Governors of St. Olave's and St. Saviour's Grammar School Foundation

322   Fall of the Clyde 1801

Pencil and watercolour, 413 × 521 (two sheets joined down centre)
Prov.: Henry Vaughan, by whom bequeathed to the gallery, 1900
Coll.: National Galleries of Scotland, Edinburgh (886)

325   A canal tunnel near Leeds* c. 1799

Watercolour, pen and brown ink, 241 × 400
Prov.: Mrs. Newall; Mavis Strange
Coll.: Richard Ivor, London

326   Landscape   with   bridge   and   castle c. 1800

Pencil and watercolour, 265 × 413
Prov.: John Herron
Coll.: Indianapolis Museum of Art (John Herron Collection)

320   Edinburgh,   from   above   Duddingston c. 1800

Watercolour, 258 × 411
Prov.: Henry Vaughan, by whom bequeathed to the gallery, 1900
Coll.: National Gallery of Ireland, Dublin (2410)

321   Linlithgow Palace c. 1801

Watercolour, 245 × 400
Prov.: John Ruskin; Arthur Severn; Sir Thomas Barlow, Bt., by whom presented to the gallery through the National Gallery Society, 1953
Coll.: National Gallery of Victoria, Melbourne

Turner drew Linlithgow in the *Scotch Lakes* sketch-

323   Fall of the Clyde 1801

Pencil and watercolour, 415 × 259
Prov.: James Loeb, by whom given to the museum, 1907
Coll.: Fogg Art Museum, Harvard University, Cambridge, Mass. (1907.9)

**V(b)   Nos 327–334
Drawings of architectural projects,**
c. 1796–1799

Of these architectural views those connected with Fonthill were done for James Wyatt (1746–1813)—one, No. 333, was exhibited at the R.A. under Wyatt's name. It is possible that other drawings in the group also record Wyatt's designs: with the exception of the small neo-classical house in No. 328, all are of buildings in the gothic style practised by Wyatt. Wyatt also worked on the restoration of Salisbury Cathedral; Turner may have been introduced to him by Colt Hoare (see Nos 193–216). In October 1798 Turner made drawings of another Wyatt building, the Mausoleum on Lord Yarborough's estate at Brocklesby, in Lincolnshire (No. 330). No. 329 provides evidence that Turner did work for Joseph Bonomi (1739–1808), and it is possible that No. 328 shows another of Bonomi's projects. In several of these drawings the architecture itself is rendered very mechanically, presumably by assistants in the various architects' offices.

327 A castellated building *c.*1796–7

Pencil and watercolour, 319 × 422
Sig. lower left twice: *Turner*
Inscr. verso: *East Cliff House Ramsgate/The Residence of the Marquis Wellesley*
Prov.: Revd. W. Covington, sale Christie 18 May 1885 (169), bt. in
Private collection, England

The building is identifiable as East Cliff Lodge, Ramsgate, demolished probably in the early 1950s. According to Cotton's *History and Antiquities of the Church and Parish of St. Laurence, Thanet* the house was built *c.* 1800 by Boncey, of Margate, for Benjamin Bond Hopkins. A view of East Cliff House, from the other side, formerly attributed to Turner, is in the Victoria and Albert Museum (Dyce 963). It is now ascribed to Edward Hawke Locker (1777–1849).

328 A mansion in wooded grounds *c.* 1798

Watercolour, 356 × 407
Prov.: unknown
Coll.: Fogg Art Museum, Harvard University, Cambridge, Mass. (1900.9)

The title is misleading: the drawing appears to be a project for a small neo-classical house, surrounded by a few trees.

329 House of J. R. Leak, Esq., Longford *c.* 1797

Pen and ink and watercolour over pencil, 493 × 665
Inscr. recto lower left: *Joseph Bonomi/Architect 1792*
verso (in another hand): *South Front of House built at Longford near Newport, Shropshire for J. R. Leak, Esq. Started 1789, finished 1792. The house was designed by Joseph Bonomi (1739–1808)*
Prov.: Joseph Bonomi, the elder; Joseph Bonomi, the younger; Baroness Charles A. de Cosson; Claud A. de Cosson; Euretta de Cosson Rathbone; by descent to present owner
Coll.: Mr. Perry T. Rathbone

The date of the inscription seems to read '1792' rather than 1797, and so presumably refers to the year in which the house was completed. The style of the drawing indicates that it was made by Turner some five or six years afterwards. The house and drive appear to have been drawn and coloured by another hand, perhaps in 1792. Turner merely added figures, trees and perhaps sky. On the back of the frame is an old label: V/DESIGN FOR THE LIBRARY AT LAMBTON HALL DUR... [illeg.] /EXECUTED IN THE YEAR 1802/Joseph Bonomi, Architect/Nº 76 Great Tichfield Street, London.' This clearly refers to a different drawing. A twentieth-century label reads: 'The Landscape by Turner who was constantly employed by Bonomi.'

330 Brocklesby Mausoleum *?c.* 1799

Watercolour, size unknown
Engr.: in aquatint by F. C. Lewis *c.* 1800 (R. 812)
Prov.: the Earl of Yarborough, for whom drawn; destroyed

Towards the end of the century the Earl of Yarborough commissioned Turner to make a view (or possibly several) of a newly built mausoleum, designed by James Wyatt, in the grounds of Brocklesby Hall, near Crowle, in Lincolnshire. Seven drawings from a sketchbook used at Brocklesby are in the Turner Bequest (T.B., LXXXIII), on paper watermarked 1794. Finberg *(Inventory)* dates these to 1800–4, but the style of their pencil-work, still betraying the influence of Hearne and the Monro academy, suggests an earlier period; Wilkinson (1974, p. 64) probably correctly gives the date of the work as 1798, though without citing corroboration. The watercolour, or watercolours, that resulted perished in a fire at Brocklesby some time before 1909. Only one finished composition is now recorded. Turner made a further watercolour, of the interior of the mausoleum, for use as an illustration to one of his perspective lectures (T.B., CXCV-130).

The pencil drawing for this subject is T.B., LXXXIII-2. There is a large sketch in pencil and watercolour (T.B., CXXI-U), which shows a more distant view of the mausoleum, based on the pencil drawing T.B., LXXXIII-3.

331 Hafod *c.* 1798

Watercolour, 610 × 915
Prov.: unknown
Coll.: The Lady Lever Collection, Port Sunlight, Cheshire (328)

Turner is known to have visited Hafod 'in the days of my youth when I was in search of Richard Wilson's birthplace' (Finberg, *Life,* p. 419), and probably went there in 1798. The building shown in this drawing is apparently an architectural project and not a record of an existing structure, and John Harris is fairly certain that it represents a scheme by John Nash. This must have been rejected, and the plan was reconstituted and used for Corsham Court by 1797. The composition exists also in a small pencil and grey-wash sketch in the collection of Sir Edmund Bacon; although it is doubtful whether this is by Turner; and there is another on a loose leaf in the Turner Bequest which also does not appear to be by Turner. As in the case of No. 333, the drawing of the architecture is rather mechanical, and Turner may not have been responsible for it.

332 Perspective view of Fonthill Abbey from the south-west *c.* 1799

Watercolour, 493 × 758
Prov.: William Beckford; by descent to the Dukes of Hamilton; Hamilton Palace sale 1919; Ralph Brocklebank; Fine Art Society, London, from whom purchased 1948
Coll.: Bolton Museum and Art Gallery (P.2.1963)

The drawing represents an intermediate design by James Wyatt for Fonthill, which was replaced by the grander conception recorded in No. 333.

Turner's hand is apparent in the landscape detail of this drawing; he may not have been responsible for the outline of the architectural part (cf. No. 331).

333 North-west view of Fonthill Abbey
R.A. 1798 (955)

Watercolour, 670 × 1050
Prov.: ?Horatio, Lord Nelson; H. Nelson-Ward, of Bath; Roger Senhouse, sale Sotheby, 15 May 1957 (49), bt. Monier; C. A. Stonehill, New Haven, from whom bt. by Paul Mellon, 1960
Coll.: Yale Center for British Art, Paul Mellon Collection

Exhibited at the R.A. in 1798 as by James Wyatt.

334 Fonthill House, Wilts c. 1799

Watercolour, size unknown
Engr.: by W. Angus for *Angus' Seats*, 1800 (R. 62)
Provenance and whereabouts unknown

V(c) Nos 335–342
Drawings commissioned by William Beckford, 1799–1800

William Beckford (1760–1844) first commissioned his extravagant gothic abbey at Fonthill from James Wyatt in 1793. In 1799, when it was still in construction, Turner spent three weeks there with Henry Tresham, Benjamin West, William Hamilton and Wyatt. His studies are in the *Smaller Fonthill* sketchbook (T.B., XLVIII; see Nos 314–326) and the *Fonthill* sketchbook (T.B., XLVII). A large colour-beginning of Fonthill is T.B., LXX-P. The principal results of the commission were five very large watercolours showing the abbey at different times of the day, all exhibited at the Royal Academy in 1800. They all show the tower completed, though in fact Turner's working drawings indicate that it was unfinished while he was there; he probably had access to Wyatt's plans. A tall east wing, prominent in later views of the abbey, does not figure in the drawings. Beckford moved there in 1807 and the building was finished in 1813. It was sold in 1822, and in 1825 the central tower collapsed.
The identification and history of the five large exhibited drawings have occasioned much confusion, partly because a large copy of one them (see No. 338) has been taken for the original, and partly because the two acquired by John Allnutt (Nos 336 and 337) have been mixed up. Furthermore, serious fading has in almost every case destroyed Turner's intentions in differentiating the various light effects.

335 View of the Gothic Abbey (afternoon) now building at Fonthill, the seat of William Beckford Esq. R.A. 1800 (328)

Pencil and watercolour, 704 × 1053
Prov.: William Beckford, for whom drawn, 1800; John Heugh, sale Christie 24 April 1874 (100), bt. Agnew; C. J. Pooley; Sir Charles Tennant; Mrs. Geoffrey Lubbock; Hon. James D. G. Loder; Agnew 1977
Private collection, Japan

This drawing has faded to such an extent that the tower of Fonthill itself is no longer visible.

336 South-west view of a Gothic Abbey (Morning), now building at Fonthill, the seat of W. Beckford, Esq. R.A. 1800 (341)

Watercolour, 693 × 1029
Prov.: William Beckford, for whom drawn, 1800; J. Allnutt; John Heugh; Sir Henry Pellatt, of Toronto; John Paris Bickell, by whom bequeathed to the gallery, 1952
Coll.: Art Gallery of Ontario, Toronto (51/39)

337 South view of the Gothic Abbey (Evening) now building at Fonthill, the seat of W. Beckford, Esq.* R.A. 1800 (566)

Watercolour, 724 × 1060
Engr.: by T. Crostick, 1828, for *The Anniversary*, 1829 (R. 338)
Prov.: William Beckford, for whom drawn, 1800; J. Allnutt; M. Piers Watt Boulton; W. G. Rawlinson; bt. by the museum, 1963, through the Horsley and Annie Townsend Bequest
Coll.: Montreal Museum of Fine Arts, Quebec (963/1385)

338 East view of the Gothic Abbey (Noon) now building at Fonthill, the seat of W. Beckford, Esq. R.A. 1800 (663)

Watercolour, 685 × 1035
Prov.: William Beckford, for whom drawn, 1800; ?E. Bertram, sale Christie 3 March 1882 (92), bt. in; Ralph Brocklebank
Coll.: National Trust for Scotland (Brodrick Castle, Isle of Arran)

A small watercolour with a similar composition is No. 340 below. The large version of this view, now in the Whitworth Art Gallery, Manchester (D.4.1949, ex T.B. Barlow and Ralph Brocklebank) is a copy by another hand. The provenances of the two versions have become confused.

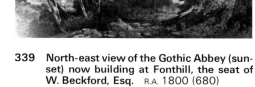

339 North-east view of the Gothic Abbey (sunset) now building at Fonthill, the seat of W. Beckford, Esq. R.A. 1800 (680)

Pencil and watercolour, 696 × 1035
Exh.: R.A. 1974 (39)
Prov.: William Beckford, for whom drawn; Agnew 1870; James Worthington; given by Mrs. Worthington to the Whitworth Institute, 1904
Coll.: Whitworth Art Gallery, University of Manchester (D.19.1904)

A watercolour study of this composition is in the *Fonthill* sketchbook (T.B., XLVII-11).

340 View of Fonthill from a stone quarry 1799

Watercolour over pencil, 298 × 442
Exh.: R.A. 1974 (38)
Prov.: Agnew and Norman Lupton Collection, bequeathed to Leeds, 1953
Coll.: City Art Galleries, Leeds (13.224/53)

See No. 338 above.

341   Fonthill *c.* 1799

Watercolour, 324 × 458
Prov.: Hugh Dobson, sale Christie 9 April 1920,
? bt. Sampson
Coll.: untraced

This may be a sheet from the *Fonthill* sketchbook
(T.B., XLVII).

342   Autumn morning, near Fonthill, Wiltshire
c. 1799

Watercolour over pencil, 321 × 465
Prov.: J. E. Taylor, by whom given to the Whitworth
Institute, 1892
Coll.: Whitworth Art Gallery, University of Man-
chester (D.97.1892)

This is possibly a page from the *Fonthill* sketchbook
(T.B., XLVII).

V(d)   Nos 343–353
Finished Scottish subjects, 1802–1815

Turner's visit to Scotland in 1801 resulted in five
watercolours shown at the Academy in 1802 and
1804 (Nos 343, 344, 346, 347, 348). Other
finished watercolours of Scottish subjects appeared at about the same time and at later dates.
There are several watercolour studies of Scottish
subjects in the Turner Bequest, together with the
series of elaborate 'Scottish Pencils' (T.B., LVIII).
Turner also used on the tour his *Smaller Fonthill*
sketchbook (T.B., XLVIII) and seven other sketchbooks (T.B., LII, LIII, LIV, LV, LVI, LVII and LIX).

343   The fall of the Clyde, Lanarkshire:
Noon.—Vide Akenside's Hymn to the
Naiads   R.A. 1802 (336)

Watercolour, 745 × 1058
Prov.: William Leech, sale Christie 21 May 1887
(75), bt. Agnew; Joseph Ruston, sale Christie
21 May 1898 (53), bt. Wallis; Robert Durning
Holt; D. Holt and R. D. Holt, by whom presented to
the gallery, 1909
Coll.: Walker Art Gallery, Liverpool (864)

Studies of the Fall of the Clyde occur on leaves from
the *Smaller Fonthill* sketchbook (see
Nos 322–324). Turner reinterpreted the subject
towards the end of his life in an oil-painting
(P510).

344   Kilchern castle, with the Cruchan Ben
mountains, Scotland: Noon*   R.A. 1802
(377)

Watercolour, 533 × 772
Prov.: George R. Burnett, sale Christie 24 March
1860 (60), bt. Flatou; Abel Buckley; Mrs. Beausire;
E. E. Cook, by whom bequeathed through the
National Art-Collections Fund, 1955
Coll.: City Museum and Art Gallery, Plymouth
(1955–44)

This drawing is sometimes known as 'Kilchern
Castle and Loch Awe, with rainbow'. There are
several drawings of Loch Awe and the Ben Cruchan
Mountains in the *Scotch Lakes* sketchbook (T.B., LVI,
42–63). Further drawings of the area are T.B., LVIII,
13–17.

345   Kilchurn Castle, Loch Awe *c.* 1802

Watercolour, size unknown
Engr.: by William Miller, 1847 (R. 664)
Prov.: Agnew 1904
Coll.: untraced

346   Ben Lomond Mountains, Scotland: The
Traveller—Vide Ossian's War of Caros
R.A. 1802 (862)

?Watercolour, ?241 × 292
Prov.: ? Wynn Ellis, sale Christie 6 May 1876
(110, as 'Mountain scene with cattle'); H. Darell
Brown, sale Christie 23 May 1924 (43, as 'A
Mountain Scene'), bt. Agnew; H. L. Fison
Coll.: untraced

Finberg records this subject as an oil-painting (*Life*,
p. 465); but Bell (63) suggests that it is probably a
watercolour, for it 'was exhibited in the Library of
the Academy along with oil pictures, engravings,
miniatures, enamels and even a model of a ship in
ivory... it does not seem probable that an oil picture
by an Academician would have found itself in such
mixed company.'

347   Edinburgh New Town, castle, &c; from the
Water of Leith   R.A. 1802 (424)

Watercolour, size unknown
Prov.: John Heugh, sale Christie 24 April 1874
(99), bt. Agnew; H. W. F. Bolckow, sale Christie
2 May 1891 (55), bt. Agnew
Coll.: untraced

The drawing of this subject in the Fowler sale,
Christie 6 May 1899 (32), bt. Agnew (repr.
Armstrong, p. 30) is not by Turner. The provenance
given here may apply in whole or in part to that
drawing. See Addenda, No. 347a.

348   Edinburgh, from Caulton-hill*   R.A. 1804
(373)

Watercolour, 660 × 1004
Coll.: Trustees of the British Museum (T.B., LX-H)

The pencil drawing for this subject was sold at
Christie's on 4 November 1975 (13), bt. Ahern. It is
probably a leaf taken from the *Smaller Fonthill*
sketchbook (T.B., XLVIII).

349   Loch Fyne, with Inverary Castle in the
distance 1802–5

Watercolour, 545 × 827
Engr.: etched and mezzotinted by the artist for the
Liber Studiorum (R. 65)
Prov.: Duke of Argyll, for whom drawn; Christie
17 March 1855 (36), bt. White; F. S. Ellis; Christie
13 December 1918 (46), bt. J. Magalhais; anon.
sale Christie 4 November 1975 (59), bt. Ahern
Private collection

Turner made several drawings at Inverary in the
Scotch Lakes sketchbook (T.B., LVI, 38–40). There
are watercolour studies of Inverary in T.B., LX-A, B, D,
J).

350 Loch Fyne 1810

Watercolour, 280 × 394
Signed and dated: *JMW Turner RA 1810*
Exh.: Turner's gallery 1810; Grosvenor Place 1819
(6); Leeds 1839 (21)
Prov.: Walter Fawkes; by descent; Sir Donald
Currie
Coll.: untraced

The drawing from which this watercolour was
developed occurs among the *Scottish Pencils*,
T.B., LVIII-8. There are other views of Loch Fyne in
the same group. See also No. 349.

351 Loch Fyne 1815

Watercolour and some scratching-out, 278 ×
388
Signed and dated: lower left: *JMW Turner RA
1815*
Prov.: George Salting, by whom bequeathed to the
museum, 1910
Coll.: Trustees of the British Museum (1910-
2-12-275)

352 Inverary, Loch Fyne *c.* 1803

Watercolour, 210 × 295
Sig. lower right: *JMW Turner RA*
Engr.: by J. Heath for Mawman's *Excursion to the
Highlands and the English Lakes,* 1805 (R. 73)
Prov.: anon. sale Christie 1863; Mrs. Stern, sale
Christie 19 June 1908 (53), bt. Vicars; from whom
bt. Agnew 1908; James Blair, by whom
bequeathed to the gallery, 1917
Coll.: City Art Gallery, Manchester (1917.108)

This and No. 353 appeared as engravings in the
same publication as the view of *Patterdale*
(No. 229).

353 Loch Lomond *c.* 1803

Watercolour, size unknown
Engr.: by J. Heath for Mawman's *Excursion to the
Highlands and the English Lakes,* 1805 (R. 74)
Provenance and whereabouts unknown

SECTION VI
Nos 354–406 Drawings of Swiss subjects, made during Turner's Swiss tour of 1802 and subsequently to 1832

Nos 354–362 are pages from the *St. Gothard and
Mont Blanc* sketchbook (T.B., LXXV), which Turner
used in Switzerland in 1802. The majority of the
pages in this book are prepared with a grey wash.
Many of the drawings in it were used as the bases
of finished watercolours, acquired between 1804
and about 1820 by Walter Fawkes, Sir John
Swinburne and others. Although most of the leaves
remained in the artist's studio, several escaped,
perhaps through Ruskin, who took a particular
interest in Turner's drawings of the Alps. The
following are dispersed sheets.

354 Bonneville, Savoy 1802

Watercolour and white body-colour, pencil and
scratching-out on white paper prepared with a grey
wash, 308 × 473
Prov.: Rev. Stopford Brooke; Mrs. L. Jacks, sale
Christie 17 December 1920 (51), bt. Agnew;
R. W. Lloyd, by whom bequeathed to the museum,
1958
Coll.: Trustees of the British Museum (1958-
7-12-407)

The subject is that of the untraced painting
P148.

355 Bonneville 1802

Watercolour and body-colour over pencil on white
paper prepared with a grey wash, 310 × 471
Prov.: John Ruskin, by 1878; Arthur Severn, 1900;
Revd. W. MacGregor, by 1902, sale Christie
23 April 1937 (9), bt. Cawston; anon. sale Christie
17 December 1937 (55), bt. Yates; Sir Stephen
Courtauld, and presented to the Institute in his
memory by his family, 1974
Coll.: Courtauld Institute of Art, University of
London (5.74; Kitson 2)

This drawing is the basis for the finished watercolour of the subject, 1817 (No. 400). Compare
the painting P 50.

356 Chamonix: Glacier des Bossons 1802

Pencil, watercolour and body-colour on white
paper prepared with a grey wash (both sides),
326 × 478
Prov.: John Ruskin; Sir Hickman Bacon, Bt.; by
descent to the present owner
Private collection

357 The Aiguillette, Valley of Cluses 1802

Pencil and watercolour, with scraping-out on white
paper prepared with a grey wash, 460 × 314
Exh.: R.A. 1974 (61)
Prov.: John Ruskin; Arthur Severn; purchased
1925

Coll.: Whitworth Art Gallery, University of Manchester (D.56.1925)

Used as the basis for the finished watercolour of ?1806 (No. 372).

358 Vevay, Switzerland 1802

Watercolour on white paper prepared with a grey wash, 305 × 482
Prov.: John Ruskin; Sir J. Gibson Carmichael
Coll.: untraced

May have been used as the basis for the finished watercolour of ?1810 (No. 392).

359 Lake of Thun, from Unterseen 1802

Watercolour and pencil, with surface scratching and blotting-out on white paper prepared with a grey wash, 315 × 470
Exh.: R.A. 1974 (63)
Prov.: ?John Ruskin; Arthur Severn; purchased 1925
Coll.: Whitworth Art Gallery, University of Manchester (D.58.1925)

360 Fortified pass, Val d'Aosta* 1802

Watercolour and scratching-out on white paper prepared with a grey wash, 309 × 474
Prov.: John Ruskin; Arthur Severn, sale Sotheby 10 May 1931 (109), bt. for the Friends of the Fitzwilliam, by whom given, 1931
Coll.: Syndics of the Fitzwilliam Museum, Cambridge (1585; Cormack 10)

The basis for the finished watercolour of ?1804 (No. 369).

361 The Great Fall of the Reichenbach* 1802

Pencil, watercolour and body-colour on white paper prepared with a grey wash, 473 × 312
Prov.: Henry Vaughan, by whom bequeathed to the gallery, 1900
Coll.: National Gallery of Ireland, Dublin (2431)

The basis for the finished watercolour of 1804 (No. 367).

362 The Upper Fall of the Reichenbach 1802

Pencil and watercolour, with scraping-out on white paper prepared with a grey wash, 312 × 467
Prov.: H. Virtue-Tebbs, by 1877, sale Christie 10 March 1900 (35), bt. Agnew; Mrs. Rachel Beer,

sale Christie 22 July 1927 (25), bt. A. J. Finberg; Sir Stephen Courtauld by 1929 and presented to the institute in his memory by his family, 1974.
Coll.: Courtauld Institute of Art, University of London (8.74; Kitson 3)

The basis for the finished watercolour of ?1810 (No. 396).

363 The Great St. Bernard Pass ?c. 1803

Pencil and watercolour, 664 × 990
Exh.: R.A. 1974 (66)
Coll.: Trustees of the British Museum (T.B., LXXX-D)

A large sheet from the Turner Bequest which may be a 'finished' drawing in an incomplete state, perhaps intended as a pendant to No. 365 (see *Turner in Switzerland*, p. 46).
Turner's study for this drawing is in the *Lake Thun* sketchbook (T.B., LXXVI-66).

364 St. Huges denouncing vengeance on the shepherd of Cormayer, in the valley of d'Aoust* R.A. 1803 (384)

Watercolour, 673 × 1010
Inscr. lower right: *JMW Turner* also monogram
Prov.: Sir John Soane
Coll.: Sir John Soane's Museum, London

The drawings used as an immediate source for this watercolour are in the *France Savoy Piedmont* sketchbook (T.B., LXXIII-62 verso, 63 verso).

365 Glacier and source of the Arveron, going up to the Mer de Glace* R.A. 1803 (396)

Watercolour, 685 × 1015
Exh.: Grosvenor Place 1819 (39); Leeds 1839 (61); R.A. 1974 (65)
Prov.: Walter Fawkes; and by descent until 1961; Agnew, from whom bt. by Paul Mellon, 1961
Coll.: Yale Center for British Art, Paul Mellon Collection

The drawing used as an immediate source for this watercolour is T.B., LXXIX-L.

366 The passage of Mount St. Gothard, taken from the centre of the Teufels Broch (Devil's Bridge), Switzerland* Turner's gallery 1804

Watercolour, with scraping-out, 985 × 685
Signed and dated top left: *IMW Turner RA 1804*
Exh.: R.A. 1815 (281); Grosvenor Place 1819 (4); Leeds 1839 (68); R.A. 1974 (67)

Prov.: Walter Fawkes; by descent to Walter R. Fawkes, sale Christie 2 July 1937 (36), bt. Esmond Morse, by whom given to the gallery
Coll.: Abbot Hall Art Gallery, Kendal, Cumbria

This watercolour is based on a drawing in the *St. Gothard and Mont Blanc* sketchbook (T.B., LXXV-33).

367 The great fall of the Riechenbach, in the valley of Hasle, Switzerland Turner's gallery 1804

Watercolour, 1022 × 689
Signed and dated lower right (on rock): *IMW Turner RA 1804*
Exh.: R.A. 1815 (292); Grosvenor Place 1819 (2); Leeds 1839 (23)
Prov.: Walter Fawkes; by descent to Walter R. Fawkes, sale Christie 2 July 1937 (37), bt. in; Miss F. M. C. Raymond; anon. sale Sotheby 13 October 1954 (29), bt. Agnew; sold to the gallery in the same year
Coll.: Cecil Higgins Art Gallery, Bedford (P.98)

This watercolour is based on the study in the National Gallery of Ireland (No. 361).

368 St. Gotthard: the Devil's Bridge ?1804

Watercolour, 1045 × 750
Prov.: W. Houldsworth, sale Christie 16 May 1896 (50), bt. McLean; Thomas McKenzie
Coll.: untraced

369 Mont Blanc, from Fort Roch, in the Val d'Aosta* ?1804

Watercolour, 660 × 1000
Sig. lower left: *IMW Turner RA*
Exh.: Grosvenor Place 1819 (33); Leeds 1839 (75, as 'Battle of Fort Rock')
Prov.: Walter Fawkes; by descent to Revd. Ayscough Fawkes, sale Christie 27 June 1890 (58), bt. Agnew; Sir Donald Currie; by descent to the present owner
Private collection

This drawing was tentatively dated in *Turner in Switzerland* to 1804; it may have been done somewhat later, perhaps nearer 1810.
The immediate source for the design is the drawing in the Fitzwilliam Museum (No. 360).

341

370 Lake of Geneva, with Mont Blanc from the lake ?1805

Watercolour with scraping-out, 715 × 1130
Sig. lower left: *JMW Turner RA* and on boat left: *JMWT*
Inscr. on wall at right: *CARRATE*
Exh.: ?Grosvenor Place 1819 (25)
Prov.: ?Walter Fawkes; John Ruskin; J. Budgett, by descent to R. A. Budgett; sale Sotheby 17 June 1970 (17), bt. John Baskett, from whom bt. by Paul Mellon, 1970
Coll.: Yale Center for British Art, Paul Mellon Collection

The immediate source of this watercolour is possibly the drawing on p. 35 of the *France Savoy Piedmont* sketchbook (T.B., LXXIII). See the smaller drawing of the subject, No. 382.

371 Mer de Glace, with Blair's Hut 1806

Watercolour, with some body-colour, 274 × 389
Exh.: ?Turner's gallery 1806; Grosvenor Place 1819 (38); Leeds 1839 (60 or 65, see No. 389 below)
Prov.: Walter Fawkes; bt. from the Fawkes family by Agnew 1912; A. H. Wild, sale Christie 16 June 1922 (125), bt. Mitchell; bt. from Agnew by Sir Stephen Courtauld 1927; presented to the institute in his memory by his family, 1974
Coll.: Courtauld Institute of Art, University of London (7.74; Kitson 4)

Based on the drawing in the *St. Gothard and Mont Blanc* sketchbook (T.B., LXXV–22).

372 L'Aiguillette, Valley of Cluses ?1806

Watercolour, 380 × 270
Prov.: John Ruskin; Lord Horder; Mrs. Doggett, sale Sotheby 20 November 1969 (93), bt. Agnew
Private collection

The immediate source of this watercolour is the drawing in the Whitworth Art Gallery, Manchester (No. 357).

373 The Lake of Thun, Switzerland* ?1806

Watercolour, 280 × 390
Exh.: Grosvenor Place 1819 (26); R.A. 1974 (68)
Prov.: Walter Fawkes; by descent to Walter R. Fawkes, sale Christie 2 July 1937 (41), bt. Fine Art Society, London; W. Newall
Private collection

Perhaps based on drawings in the *Lake Thun* sketchbook (T.B., LXXVI–60, 61).

374 Lake of Brienz, moonlight* ?1806

Watercolour, 277 × 392
Sig. lower right: *JMW Turner RA*
Exh.: Leeds 1839 (85)
Prov.: Walter Fawkes; by descent to Walter Ramsden Fawkes, sale Christie 2 July 1937 (56), bt. Walter Stoye; by descent to present owner
Private collection

The immediate source of this watercolour is on p. 34 of the *Rhine Strasbourg and Oxford* sketchbook (T.B., LXXVII); a watercolour study is T.B., LXXX-E. The subject may be identifiable with the *Town of Brienz*, exhibited by Fawkes in 1819 (No. 375 below).

375 Town of Brienz, Switzerland ?1806

Watercolour, 277 × 392
Exh.: Grosvenor Place 1819 (35)
Provenance and whereabouts unknown

It is possible that this untraced watercolour may be identified with the *Lake of Brienz, moonlight* (No. 374 above).

376 Montanvert, Valley of Chamouni ?1806

Watercolour and scraping-out over pencil, 278 × 395
Sig. lower left: *IMW Turner RA*
Exh.: Grosvenor Place 1819 (31)
Prov.: Walter Fawkes; by descent to Revd. Ayscough Fawkes, sale Christie 27 June 1890 (49,

as 'Source of the Avenon') bt. Pyke Thompson; bequeathed by him to the museum, 1898
Coll.: National Museum of Wales, Cardiff (3220)

The immediate source of this watercolour is p. 21 of the *St. Gothard and Mont Blanc* sketchbook (T.B., LXXV).

377 Lausanne, Lake of Geneva Turner's gallery 1807

Watercolour, 280 × 390
Signed and dated: *JMW Turner RA 1807*
Exh.: Grosvenor Place 1819 (40); Leeds 1839 (30)
Prov.: Walter Fawkes; by descent to Revd. Ayscough Fawkes, sale Christie 27 June 1890 (48), bt. Agnew; Sir A. J. Forbes-Leith, by descent to the present owner
Private collection

378 Lake of Lucerne, from the landing place at Fluelen, looking towards Bauen and Tell's chapel, Switzerland* ?1807

Watercolour, 673 × 1003
Signed and ?dated: *JMWT*
Exh.: R.A. 1815 (316); Grosvenor Place 1819 (3); Leeds 1839 (25)
Prov.: Walter Fawkes; by descent to Revd. Ayscough Fawkes, sale Christie 27 June 1890 (57), bt. Agnew; Sir Donald Currie; Major F. D. Mirrielees, sale Christie 20 March 1959 (55)
Private collection

This watercolour is based on the drawing on p. 41 of the *Lake Thun* sketchbook (T.B., LXXVI).

379 Mont Blanc, from the bridge of St. Martin, Sallenches ?1807

Watercolour, approx. 280 × 390
Prov.: ?Walter Fawkes; ?Humphrey Roberts
Private collection

The immediate source of this watercolour is the drawing in the *St. Gothard and Mont Blanc* sketchbook (T.B., LXXV–11).

380 St. Martin and Salenche, Savoy ?1807

Pencil and watercolour, with scraping-out, 281 × 399
Sig. lower left: *IMW Turner RA*
Exh.: Grosvenor Place 1819 (30); R.A. 1974 (69)
Prov.: Walter Fawkes; by descent to Revd. Ayscough Fawkes, sale Christie 27 June 1890 (46), bt. Agnew; London art market 1976

Coll.: Leger Galleries Ltd., London

The immediate source of this watercolour is the drawing on p. 12 of the *St. Gothard and Mont Blanc* sketchbook (T.B., LXXV).

381 Bonneville, Savoy ?1807

Watercolour, 280 × 381
Exh.: Grosvenor Place 1819 (29); Leeds 1839 (72)
Prov.: Walter Fawkes; Monnell, U.S.A.
Coll.: Brian Pilkington, London

This is the first version of the subject, repeated in No. 385.
The immediate source of this subject is the drawing on p. 7 of the *St. Gothard and Mont Blanc* sketchbook (T.B., LXXV).

382 Lake of Geneva, with Mont Blanc in the distance ?1808

Watercolour, 280 × 395
Sig.: *JMW Turner*
Inscr.: *Lac de Geneve*
Prov.: Laundy Walters; D. W. Freshfield, sale Christie 2 November 1934 (37), bt. Fine Art Society, London; London art market 1946
Coll.: untraced

The basis for this watercolour is probably the drawing on p. 35 of the *France Savoy Piedmont* sketchbook (T.B., LXXIII). See also the larger drawing, No. 370.

383 Source of the Arveiron (second version) ?1808

Watercolour, approx. 280 × 390
Prov.: ? Dillon, sale Christie 17 April 1869 (33)
Coll.: untraced

This untraced watercolour may have been the basis for the drawing (T.B., CXVIII-G) of this subject which was mezzotinted in 1816 for the *Liber Studiorum* (R. 60). It is a variant of the composition of No. 365.

384 Fall of the Staubach, in the Valley of Lauterbrunnen, Switzerland 1809

Watercolour, approx. 280 × 380
Signed and dated: *JMW Turner 1809*
Exh.: Grosvenor Place 1819 (27); Leeds 1839 (51)
Prov.: Walter Fawkes; Robinson sale, Christie 4 July 1967 (56), bt. Leger
Private collection, England

The drawing on which this watercolour is based is in the *St. Gothard and Mont Blanc* sketchbook (T.B. LXXV–32).

385 Bonneville 1809 (or 1808)

Watercolour, 277 × 394
Signed and dated: lower right: *JMW Turner RA 09* or *08*
Exh.: B.M. 1975 (37)
Prov.: Abel Buckley, 1904; Agnew, to George Salting 1906, by whom bequeathed to the museum, 1910
Coll.: Trustees of the British Museum (1910-2-12-284)

The immediate source of this watercolour is the drawing on p. 7 of the *St. Gothard and Mont Blanc* sketchbook (T.B., LXXV). The primary version of the subject is No. 381.

386 The Lake of Brienz 1809

Watercolour, 388 × 556
Signed and dated lower right: *JMW Turner RA PP 1809*
Exh.: B.M. 1975 (38, as 'The Lake of Thun')
Prov.: Sir John Swinburne, for whom drawn; by descent to Julia Swinburne, sale Christie 26 May 1916 (118); R. W. Lloyd, by whom bequeathed to the museum, 1958
Coll.: Trustees of the British Museum (1958-7-12-409)

This watercolour is based on p. 43 of the *Grenoble* sketchbook (T.B., LXXIV) and on p. 38 of the *Rhine Strasbourg and Oxford* sketchbook (T.B., LXXVII).

387 The Valley of Chamouni 1809

Watercolour, gouache and surface scratching, 280 × 395
Signed and dated: *JMW Turner 1809*
Exh.: Grosvenor Place 1819 (37); Leeds 1839 (57)
Prov.: Walter Fawkes; by descent to F. H. Fawkes; E. E. Cook; presented by his Executors through the National Art-Collections Fund, 1955
Coll.: Whitworth Art Gallery, University of Manchester (D.18.1955)

The immediate source of this watercolour is the drawing on p. 18 of the *St. Gothard and Mont Blanc* sketchbook (T.B., LXXV).

388 Chateau de Rinkenberg, on the Lac de Brientz, Switzerland* 1809

Watercolour, 281 × 394
Signed and dated lower right: *JMW Turner RA 1809*
Exh.: Grosvenor Place 1819 (32)

Prov.: Walter Fawkes; T. S. Kennedy, sale Christie 18 May 1895 (92), bt. H. Quilter; Charles P. Taft Coll.: Taft Museum, Cincinnati, Ohio (1931.388)

This watercolour is based on a drawing in the *Grenoble* sketchbook (T.B., LXXIV–46) and on two others in the *Rhine Strasbourg and Oxford* sketchbook (T.B., LXXVII–17 verso, inscr: *Ringenberg;* 23 verso).

389 Mer de Glace, in the Valley of Chamouni, Switzerland (Chamonix, looking down the valley) ?1809

Watercolour and scraping-out, 280 × 394
Exh.: Grosvenor Place 1819 (24); Leeds 1839 (60 or 65, see No. 371 above)
Prov.: Walter Fawkes; Humphrey Roberts; Charles P. Taft
Coll.: Taft Museum, Cincinnati, Ohio (1931.389)

The basis for this watercolour is possibly the drawing on p. 20 of the *St. Gothard and Mont Blanc* sketchbook (T.B., LXXV).

390 The Castle of Chillon* ?1809

Watercolour, with some scraping-out, 281 × 395
Sig. lower left: *JMW Turner RA*
Prov.: Sir John Swinburne, for whom drawn; by descent to Isobel Swinburne, sale Christie 26 May 1916 (119), bt. Agnew; R. W. Lloyd, by whom bequeathed to the museum, 1958
Coll.: Trustees of the British Museum (1958–7–12–410)

For a second version of this subject see No. 395.

391 Lake of Brienz *c.* 1809

Watercolour, approx. 305 × 432

Prov.: Thomas Wright, of Upton, sale Christie 7 June 1845 (46), bt. Lord Lansdowne; by descent to present owner
Coll.: Bowood Collection

Based on a monochrome drawing in the *Grenoble* sketchbook (T.B., LXXIV–50), and on a watercolour study (T.B., LXXX-C).

392 Lake of Geneva, from above Vevey ?1810

Watercolour, approx. 280 × 390
Exh.: Grosvenor Place 1819 (28); Leeds 1839 (33)
Prov.: Walter Fawkes; by descent to Revd. Ayscough Fawkes, sale Christie 27 June 1890 (45), bt. Agnew; Sir Donald Currie; by descent to the present owner
Private collection

393 Courmayeur ?1810

Watercolour, 275 × 389
Prov.: J. Dillon, sale, Christie 17 April 1869 (44, as 'Mont Blanc from Aosta'), bt. in; J. F. Haworth, bt. Agnew 1918 (as 'Valley of Aosta, with Mont Blanc in the distance, *c.* 1810'); Sir Stephen Courtauld, 1919; presented to the institute in his memory by his family, 1974
Coll.: Courtauld Institute of Art, University of London (6.74; Kitson 5)

The immediate source of this watercolour is in the *France Savoy Piedmont* sketchbook (T.B., LXXIII, 67v–68r). It is possible that it may be identified with the untraced *Valley of Aosta* (No. 394).

394 Valley of Aosta ?1810

Watercolour, 267 × 394
Prov.: ?Pilkington; Dillon
Coll.: untraced

It is possible that this untraced work could be identified with the drawing in the Courtauld Institute of Art (No. 393).

395 Castle of Chillon ?1810

Watercolour, approx. 280 × 380
Prov.: Mrs. Stern, sale Christie 19 June 1908 (52), bt. Vicars; S. S. Phipps
Coll.: untraced

A version of the subject of No. 390.

396 Upper Fall of the Reichenbach: rainbow ?1810

Watercolour, heightened with white, over pencil, 276 × 394
Exh.: Grosvenor Place 1819 (36); Leeds 1839 (29)
Prov.: Walter Fawkes; by descent until 1937; Agnew, bt. S. Girtin and T. Girtin, 1938; Tom Girtin; John Baskett, from whom bt. by Paul Mellon, 1970.
Coll.: Yale Center for British Art, Paul Mellon Collection

The immediate source of this watercolour is the drawing in the Courtauld Institute of Art (No. 362).

397 Valley of Aosta 1813

Watercolour, 384 × 263
Signed and dated lower left: *JMW Turner RA 1813*
Prov.: John Ruskin; J. Budgett, Stoke Park; Humphrey Roberts; Sir Donald Currie; by descent to the present owner
Private collection

The immediate source of this watercolour is the drawing on p. 5 of the *Grenoble* sketchbook (T.B., LXXIV).

398 Valley of the Var 1813

Watercolour, approx. 140 × 220
Signed and dated lower right: *JMW Turner RA 1813*

Prov.: H. A. J. Munro of Novar, sale Christie 6 April 1878 (76), bt. Agnew; W. Lee, 1883; Sir Donald Currie; by descent to the present owner
Private collection

399 The Battle of Fort Rock, Val d'Aouste, Piedmont 1796* R.A. 1815 (192)

Watercolour, 695 × 1010
Signed and dated lower left: *IMW Turner 1815*
Exh.: B.M. 1975 (43)
Coll.: Trustees of the British Museum (T.B., LXXX-G)

The title in the R.A. catalogue was accompanied by the following lines from Turner's M.S. poem *Fallacies of Hope*:

'The snow-capt mountain, and huge towers of ice,
Thrust forth their dreary barriers in vain:
Onward the van progressive forc'd its way,
Propell'd, as the wild Reuss, by native Glaciers fed,
Rolls on impetuous, with ev'ry check gains force
By the constraint uprais'd; till, to its gathering powers
All yielding, down the pass wide devastation pours
Her own destructive course. Thus rapine stalk'd
Triumphant; and plundering hordes, exulting, strew'd,
Fair Italy, thy plains with woe.'

This highly finished watercolour is based on the watercolour of ?1804 (No. 369), which in turn is based on the leaf from the *St. Gothard and Mont Blanc* sketchbook, now in the Fitzwilliam Museum, Cambridge (No. 360).

400 Bonneville 1817

Watercolour, approx. 300 × 430
Signed and dated lower left: *IMW Turner RA 1817*
Engr.: by Davies for *The Bijou,* 1829 (R. 313)
Prov.: Sir John Swinburne, for whom drawn; by descent to anon. sale, Christie 26 April 1902 (49), bt. Mallard; Miss Julia Swinburne; Lewis sale, Christie 28 February 1930 (50), bt. Leggatt; G. R. Stamp
Coll.: untraced

Based on the watercolour in the Courtauld Institute of Art (No. 355) and on T.B., LXXX-H.

401 Scene in the Savoy (Italy of the olden times) *c.* 1815–20

Watercolour. 281 × 393

Prov.: John Dillon; Pilkington; John Ruskin; Arthur Severn
Coll.: untraced

The subject is uncertain. The two given here were both used by Ruskin (*Ruskin on Pictures,* No. 68).

402 Snowstorm, Mont Cenis 1820

Watercolour, 292 × 400
Inscr. lower right: *PASSAGE of Mt Cenis Jan 15 1820 JMW Turner*
Engr.: by S. Fisher 1833
Exh.: Leeds 1839 (56); R.A. 1974 (B90)
Prov.: Walter Fawkes; by descent to W. R. Fawkes, sale Christie 2 July 1937 (39), bt. Colnaghi; J. Leslie Wright, by whom bequeathed to the art gallery, 1953
Coll.: City Museums and Art Gallery, Birmingham (409.53)

403 The Val d'Aosta *c.* 1820

Watercolour, 408 × 302
Sig. lower right: *JMW Turner*
Exh.: B.M. 1975 (96)
Prov.: ?J. Leigh Clarke, sale Christie 28 March 1868 (99, as 'Narni, Italy'), bt. Colngahi; Abel Buckley; Mrs. George J. Gould; Christie 26 November 1926 (25); R. W. Lloyd, by whom bequeathed to the museum, 1958
Coll.: Trustees of the British Museum (1958–7–12–425)

This composition is based on that of No. 397. The drawing may have been executed en suite with the *Marksburg* and *Biebrich* of the same date (Nos 692 and 691).

404 Grenoble Bridge 1824

Watercolour, 530 × 737
Sig. lower right: *JMWT*
Prov.: Charles Holford, for whom painted, sale Christie 24 June 1861 (28), bt. Broderip; sale Christie 6 February 1872 (626), bt. Agnew; Thomas Greenwood, sale Christie 12 March 1875 (282), bt. Agnew; Lord Dudley; Sir Donald Currie, by descent to Mrs. Craven; purchased by the Baltimore Museum through the Nelson and Juanita Greif Gutman Fund, 1968
Coll.: Baltimore Museum of Art, Maryland (68.28).

The basis for this watercolour is the drawing on p. 14 of the *Grenoble* sketchbook (T.B., LXXIV). Two colour-beginnings of the subject are T.B., CCLXIII-367, 368.

405 Messieurs les voyageurs on their return from Italy (par la diligence) in a snow drift upon Mount Tarrar—22nd of January, 1829* R.A. 1829 (520)

Watercolour and body-colour, 545 × 747
Exh.: B.M. 1975 (147)
Prov.: William Moir; Mrs. Moir; bt. Agnew 1899; S. G. Holland, sale Christie 26 June 1908 (259), bt. Agnew; Sir Joseph Beecham, sale Christie 4 May 1917 (157); R. W. Lloyd, by whom bequeathed to the museum 1958
Coll.: Trustees of the British Museum (1958–7–12–431)

406 Falls of the Rhine at Schaffhausen* 1831–2

Watercolour and body-colour, 309 × 457
Sig. (on stone in foreground): *JMWT*
Engr.: by J. B. Allen for *The Keepsake,* 1833 (R. 329)
Prov.: John Ruskin; bt. through the Art Gallery Purchase Fund, 1891
Coll.: City Museums and Art Gallery, Birmingham (31.91)

This design is based on the large pencil study of 1802, T.B., LXXIX-E.

SECTION VII
Nos 407–439
Views along the Thames and in Sussex, *c.* 1800–1820

VII(a) Nos 407–422
Unexhibited sketches, chiefly Thames subjects, *c.* 1800–1811; and the finished view of *Windsor Park,* shown R.A. 1811

The following drawings are grouped round sketches made along the Thames after Turner's move to Isleworth in about 1804. His characteristic style in these studies is recorded in the series of watercolour sketches in the *Thames from Reading to Walton* sketchbook (T.B., XCV). Some larger watercolours, probably done about the same date, are among the miscellaneous sheets in T.B., LXX; though these retain some of the characteristics of the large finished watercolours of about 1798–1800, they also seem to relate to the oil sketches on a white ground which Turner made along the Thames and Wey in the first decade of the century (see Nos P160–P170).

Other studies in this group are associated with the series by reason of their general style, though they are not necessarily Thames subjects.

407   A child giving money to a beggar at a cottage door   *c.* 1801

Pencil and watercolour, 188 × 321 (sight)
Prov.: unknown
Private collection

Similar in style to the Scottish figures studies of 1801.

408   Merton College, Oxford, from the meadows   *c.* 1801

Watercolour, 255 × 400

Prov.: J. E. Taylor, sale Christie 8 July 1912 (105), bt. Agnew; J. E. T. Allen; by descent to present owner
Private collection

Finberg (Index) dates this drawing to 1796–8, but it seems to have been done a little later.

409   Study of a group of cows   *c.* 1801

Watercolour over pencil, with some scratching-out, 216 × 324
Prov.: John Ruskin, by whom given to the Ruskin School, Oxford, 1875; transferred to the museum, 1938
Coll.: Visitors of the Ashmolean Museum, Oxford (Herrmann 71)

Herrmann associates this drawing with the *Cows* sketchbook (T.B., LXII), which Finberg tentatively dated to 1801. This study may relate to the large finished watercolours of *c.* 1798–1800 in which cows are prominent, e.g. Nos 235, 272; but perhaps it should rather be linked with the scenes of cattle watering in T.B., LXX. A colour study of cows beside a stream, which may be by Turner and date from about this time, is the *Cattle Watering* in the possession of the Clonterbrook Trustees.

410   Barges on a river   ?*c.* 1804

Pencil and watercolour, 203 × 265
Prov.: J. E. Taylor, sale Christie 8 July 1912 (137), bt. Agnew; Mr. and Mrs. Walter Stoye; by descent to the present owner
Private collection

411   On the Thames (? Sion House) ?*c.* 1804

Watercolour, 222 × 356
Prov.: ? William Leech, sale Christie 21 May 1887 (78), bt. Agnew

---

Coll.: Victoria and Albert Museum, London (208.1887)

412   Landscape, with trees by a river   *c.* 1805–07

Watercolour over traces of pencil, 235 × 356
Prov.: Lloyd Roberts, by whom bequeathed to the gallery, 1920
Coll.: City Art Gallery, Manchester (1920.638)

413   Eton College, from the Thames   *c.* 1805–7

Watercolour over traces of pencil, 247 × 342
Prov.: Mrs. Worthington, by whom bequeathed to the Whitworth Institute, 1904
Coll.: Whitworth Art Gallery, University of Manchester (D.14.1904)

414   Windsor Park: with horses by the late Sawrey Gilpin, Esq. R.A.   *c.* 1805–7

Watercolour and scraping-out, 548 × 756
Exh.: R.A. 1811 (295)
Coll.: Trustees of the British Museum (T.B., LXX-G)

The identification of the work shown at the R.A. with the drawing in the Turner Bequest was suggested

by Finberg (*Inventory*, I, p. 175); this seems highly plausible. Sawrey Gilpin had died in 1807 and this watercolour may have been executed shortly before that date.

415   The Thames   *c.* 1806

Watercolour, with some scratching-out, 251 × 353
Prov.: Joseph Gillott, sale Christie 4 May 1872 (504), bt. Agnew; Sir John Fowler, sale Christie 6 May 1899 (38). bt. Gooden; George Salting, by whom bequeathed to the museum, 1910
Coll.: Trustees of the British Museum (1910–2-12-285)

416   View along the Thames   *c.* 1807

Watercolour over faint traces of pencil, 244 × 354
Prov.: Private collection, England; Thomas Gibson Fine Art Co. Ltd., to present owner
Private collection, U.S.A.

417   View on the River Brent   ?*c.* 1807

? Watercolour, 394 × 686
Prov.: Henry James Wheeler, sale Foster 1 June 1864 (121), bt. in; by descent to Alfred L. Wheeler
Coll.: untraced

Apparently a subject similar to that of P198, which Butlin and Joll date to *c.* 1807–9. Armstrong (p. 243) gives a date of *c.* 1820. When the drawing was exhibited at the Royal Academy Winter Exhibition of 1887 it was dated to *c.* 1825; this seems unusually late for a repetition of an oil-painting in another medium.

418   River scene, with a bridge in the distance   *c.* 1808

Watercolour and oils on paper, 225 × 295
Prov.: T. W. Bacon, by whom given to the museum, 1950
Coll.: Syndics of the Fitzwilliam Museum, Cambridge (PD.110–1950; Cormack 12)

Possibly connected with Turner's work in the *Tabley No. 1* sketchbook (T.B., CIII), in use in about 1808.

419   Woodland scene*   *c.* 1810–15

Watercolour, 280 × 229
Prov.: ?J. E. Taylor, sale Christie 5 July 1912 (97), bt. Agnew
Coll.: Lady Monk Bretton

This sheet is possibly connected with Turner's work for Fuller on the views in Sussex (see Nos 423–439); it may date, therefore, from a few years later.

420   Warwick Castle   ?*c.* 1810

Watercolour, 229 × 353

Prov.: ? J. E. Taylor, sale Christie 12 July 1912 (134, as 'A Pool'), bt. Agnew; Herbert Powell; presented to the gallery by the National Art-Collections Fund from the Herbert Powell Bequest, 1968
Coll.: Tate Gallery, London (T.1021)

421   River landscape, with a castle on a hill   *c.* 1811

Watercolour and pencil, 167 × 228
Prov.: P. & D. Colnaghi, 1895, bt. T. W. Bacon, by whom given to the museum, 1950
Coll.: Syndics of the Fitzwilliam Museum, Cambridge (PD.112-1950; Cormack 24)

See No. 422.

422   River landscape, with a distant hill   *c.* 1811

Watercolour, 170 × 245
Prov.: John Ruskin, by whom given to the museum, 1861
Coll.: Syndics of the Fitzwilliam Museum, Cambridge (570; Cormack 23)

Cormack dates this and No. 421 to *c.* 1824–31, but this is perhaps a little late, though, as he says, the drawings do have points of similarity with Turner's work for the *Rivers of England* series of early 1820s. However, their technique is not far removed from that of Turner's Thames drawings of *c.* 1806; they may be connected with the West Country tours of 1811 and 1813.

**VII(b)   Nos 423–439
Drawings commissioned by John Fuller, and other Sussex subjects** *c.* 1815–1820

Turner was first engaged to do work for John Fuller, of Rosehill Park, Brightling, Sussex, in about 1810; Farington in his Diary for 21 April of that year records that 'Mr Fuller, member for Suffolk [READ:

Sussex], has engaged Turner to go into that County to make drawings of three or four views. He is to have 100 guineas for the *use* of his drawings, which are to be returned to him.' These drawings have not been identified, but about that time Turner executed an oil-painting of Rosehill (P211), and in about 1815 seems to have begun work on a series of watercolour views of the surrounding countryside which were engraved for Fuller by W. B. Cooke between 1816 and 1820. Of eight commenced plates only six were published, in Part I of *Views in Sussex*, for the cover of which Turner himself etched an emblematical design (R. 128). The watercolours were retained by Fuller, together with four others of slightly different format, aquatinted by Joseph Stadler, probably about 1818 (Nos 432–435). No. 438 is a further watercolour from the same group, which was not engraved. For these drawings Turner relied on material gathered together in three or possibly four sketchbooks: T.B., CXXXVII–CXL. The last of these, the *Hastings to Margate* book, reflects his concern to collect subject-matter for the *Southern Coast* series (see Nos 445–489).

423 Battle Abbey, the spot where Harold fell *c.* 1816

Watercolour, 375 × 552
Engr.: by W. B. Cooke for Cooke's *Views in Sussex*, 1816–20 (R. 129)
Prov.: John Fuller, of Rosehill Park; by descent to Sir Alexander Acland-Hood, sale Christie 4 April 1908 (95), bt. Levin.
Coll.: untraced

This composition is based on the drawing in the *Views in Sussex* sketchbook (T.B., CXXXVIII–11).

424 The Observatory at Rosehill Park, the seat of John Fuller, Esq. *c.* 1816

Watercolour, 381 × 559
Engr.: by W. B. Cooke for Cooke's *Views in Sussex*, 1816–20 (R. 130)
Exh.: C.G. 1824 (86)
Prov.: John Fuller, of Rosehill Park; by descent to Sir Alexander Acland-Hood, sale Christie 4 April 1908 (94), bt. Agnew
Coll.: untraced

This composition derives from a drawing in the *Hastings* sketchbook (T.B., CXXXIX, 34v–35).

425 The Vale of Ashburnham * 1816

Watercolour, 379 × 563
Signed and dated lower right: *IMW Turner RA 1816*
Engr.: by W. B. Cooke for Cooke's *Views in Sussex*, 1816–20 (R. 131)
Exh.: B.M. 1975 (45)
Prov.: John Fuller, of Rosehill Park; by descent to Sir Alexander Acland-Hood, sale Christie 4 April 1908 (91), bt. Agnew; George Salting by whom bequeathed to the museum, 1910
Coll.: Trustees of the British Museum (1910-2-12-272)

This composition is based on a drawing in the *Vale of Heathfield* sketchbook (T.B., CXXXVII, 68v–69).

426 Pevensey Bay, from Crowhurst Park *c.* 1816

Watercolour, 369 × 559

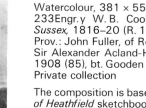

Engr.: by W. B. Cooke for Cooke's *Views in Sussex*, 1816–20 (R. 132)
Prov.: John Fuller, of Rosehill Park; by descent to Sir Alexander Acland-Hood, sale Christie 4 April 1908 (96), bt. Agnew
Coll.: Lady Monk Bretton

Based on the *Views in Sussex* sketchbook T.B., CXXXVIII–8, 9).

427 The Vale of Heathfield *c.* 1816

Watercolour, 379 × 562
Engr.: by W. B. Cooke for Cooke's *Views in Sussex*, 1816–20 (R. 133)
Exh.: B.M. 1975 (46)
Prov.: John Fuller, of Rosehill Park; by descent to Sir Alexander Acland-Hood, sale Christie 4 April 1908 (92), bt. Agnew; George Salting, by whom bequeathed to the museum, 1910
Coll.: Trustees of the British Museum (1910-2-12-273)

This composition is derived from a pencil drawing in the *Vale of Heathfield* sketchbook (T.B., CXXXVII, 41v–42).

428 Bodiam Castle, Sussex *c.* 1816

Watercolour, 381 × 559
233Engr.y W. B. Cooke for Cooke's *Views in Sussex*, 1816–20 (R. 134)
Prov.: John Fuller, of Rosehill Park; by descent to Sir Alexander Acland-Hood, sale Christie 4 April 1908 (85), bt. Gooden
Private collection

The composition is based on a drawing in the *Vale of Heathfield* sketchbook (T.B., CXXXVII–6v and 7).

429 Hurstmonceux Castle, Sussex 1817

Watercolour, 381 × 559
Signed and dated lower left: *JMW Turner 1817*
Engr.: by W. B. Cooke (open etching only) but not publ., for Cooke's *Views in Sussex*, 1816–20 (R. 135)
Exh.: C.G. 1823 (99)
Prov.: John Fuller, of Rosehill Park; by descent to Sir Alexander Acland-Hood, sale Christie 4 April 1908 (88), bt. Agnew
Coll.: Lady Monk Bretton

Based on a drawing in the *Views in Sussex* sketchbook (T.B., CXXXVIII–5).

430 Winchelsea, Sussex, and the Military Canal *c.* 1817

Watercolour, 127 × 203
Engr.: by W. B. Cooke (open etching only) but not publ. for Cooke's *Views in Sussex*, 1816–20 (R. 136)
Exh.: C.G. 1822 (91)
Prov.: H. A. J. Munro of Novar, sale Christie 2 June 1877 (19), bt. Gibbs; Abel Buckley
Coll.: untraced

A number of drawings of Winchelsea appear in the *Hastings to Margate* sketchbook (T.B., CXL), of about 1815.

431 Pevensey Castle, Sussex *c.* 1817

Watercolour, 375 × 559
Exh.: C.G. 1823 (15)
Prov.: John Fuller, of Rosehill Park; by descent to
Sir Alexander Acland-Hood, sale Christie 4 April
1908 (86), bt. Agnew
Coll.: Lady Monk Bretton

The drawing on which this composition is based
occurs in the *Views in Sussex* sketchbook
(T.B., CXXXVIII–7). The watercolour is uniform in size
with the 'Four large coloured Views in Sussex',
which follow (Nos 432–435).

432   The Vale of Pevensey, from Rosehill Park
c. 1816

Watercolour, 394 × 565
Aquatinted: by Joseph Stadler, *c.* 1816–8, and
privately printed *c.* 1818, *Four large coloured Views
in Sussex* (R. 822)
Exh.: R.A. 1974 (127)
Prov.: John Fuller, of Rosehill Park; by descent to
Sir Alexander Acland-Hood, sale Christie 4 April
1908 (93), bt. Agnew; C. Fairfax Murray 1910;
C. Morland Agnew, 1912; by descent
Coll.: the Executors of the late Vice-Admiral Sir
William Agnew, K.C.V.O., C.B., D.S.O.

This composition is based on a pencil drawing in
the *Views in Sussex* sketchbook (T.B., CXXXVIII–19).

433   The Vale of Ashburnham   *c.* 1816

Watercolour, 362 × 550
Sig. lower left: *JMW Turner RA*
Aquatinted: by Joseph Stadler *c.* 1816–8 and
privately printed *c.* 1818, *Four large coloured Views
in Sussex* (R. 823)
Prov.: John Fuller of Rosehill Park; by descent to Sir
Alexander Acland-Hood, sale Christie 4 April 1908
(87), bt. Agnew; C. Fairfax Murray; Sir Charles
Sydney Jones, by whom bequeathed to the univer-
sity, 1947
Coll.: University of Liverpool

The composition is based on a drawing in the *Views
in Sussex* sketchbook (T.B., CXXXVIII–17).

434   Beauport, near Bexhill   *c.* 1816

Watercolour over some pencil, with scratching-out,
378 × 546
Sig. lower right: *W. Turner RA* (?)
Aquatinted: by Joseph Stadler *c.* 1816–8 and
privately printed *c.* 1818, *Four large coloured Views
in Sussex* (R. 824)
Prov.: John Fuller, of Rosehill Park; by descent to
Sir Alexander Acland-Hood, sale Christie 4 April
1908 (89), bt. Willis; Grenville L. Winthrop, by
whom bequeathed to the university, 1943
Coll.: Fogg Art Museum, Harvard University,
Cambridge, Mass. (1943–508)

The composition is based on a drawing in the *Views
in Sussex* sketchbook (T.B., CXXXVIII–18).

435   Battle Abbey   *c.* 1816

Watercolour, 375 × 552
Aquatinted: by Joseph Stadler *c.* 1816–8 and
privately printed *c.* 1818, *Four large coloured Views
in Sussex* (R. 825)
Prov.: John Fuller, of Rosehill Park; by descent to
Sir Alexander Acland-Hood, sale Christie 4 April
1908 (90), bt. Agnew; C. Fairfax Murray
Coll.: Lady Monk Bretton

This watercolour is based on a drawing in the *Views
in Sussex* sketchbook (T.B., CXXXVIII, 2–3).

436   Battle Abbey   ?*c.* 1816

Watercolour, size unknown
Prov.: H. A. J. Munro of Novar; John Ruskin, sale
Christie 15 April 1869 (3), bt. Gambart
Coll.: untraced

437   Battle Abbey   ?*c.* 1816

Watercolour, 155 × 257
Prov.: E. Nettlefold
Coll.: untraced

438   Rosehill, Sussex   1816

Watercolour, 379 × 556
Exh.: B.M. 1975 (47)
Prov.: John Fuller, of Rosehill Park; by descent to
Sir Alexander Acland-Hood, sale Christie 4 April
1908 (97), bt. Colnaghi; Revd. J.W.R. Brockle-
bank, sale Christie 25 November 1927 (92);
R. W. Lloyd, by whom bequeathed to the museum,
1958
Coll.: Trustees of the British Museum (1958–
7–12–411)

Turner's study for this composition is in the
Hastings sketchbook (T.B., CXXXIX–32v, 33v, 34r).

439   Eridge Castle, East Sussex   *c.* 1815–20

Watercolour and body-colour, with pencil and
scratching-out, 369 × 543
Prov.: John Dillon, sale Christie 29 April 1869
(133, as 'Eridge Castle—Female and Sheep'), bt.
Agnew; ? H. W. F. Bolckow, sale Christie 2 May
1891 (52), bt. Agnew; presented by the Guarantors of the Royal Jubilee Exhibition, 1887
Coll.: Whitworth Art Gallery, University of Manchester (D.12.1887)

Not apparently connected with the Fuller commission, but executed at about the same time, and may
have been intended to form part of the set. The
watercolour of this subject in the Bolckow sale may
have been another version or a copy, since the
Whitworth drawing was acquired earlier. The provenance given here is that usually cited.

SECTION VIII
Nos 440–489 'Rivers of Devon' and 'Southern Coast', *c.* 1811–1824

VIII(a) Nos 440–444
Subjects related to Cooke's *Rivers of Devon,* *c.* 1813

Four subjects were engraved for a projected publication, *The Rivers of Devon,* by William Bernard Cooke, who first commissioned Turner to work on the *Picturesque Views on the Southern Coast of England* (Nos 445–484) in 1811 or shortly before. The *Southern Coast* project (see VIII(b)) involved the production of forty subjects depicting views between Whitstable, Kent, and Watchet, Somerset. Turner made a tour of Devon and Cornwall in 1811, and returned to that part of the country in 1813; his work along the Sussex and Kent coast has been referred to in connection with the Fuller drawings of *c.* 1816 (see Nos 423–439). The *Southern Coast* series was engraved by Cooke and his brother, George, with assistance from others, between 1814 and 1826. The work was issued in parts, each intended to contain three plates, with two vignettes and descriptive letter-press for the views. Other artists were intended to contribute, and Henry Edridge, William Alexander, Samuel Owen, William Westall, Peter de Wint, William Havell and Joshua Cristall supplied nine subjects in all. Turner originally contracted to make twenty-four drawings at £7.10s each, but after four issues his price was increased to ten guineas. Cooke received twenty-five guineas for engraving each plate, a fee increased to £40 in about 1816. As the work progressed relations between Cooke and his artists and the publisher, John Murray, deteriorated, but Turner continued to supply drawings, so that he was eventually responsible for almost the whole of the work. The series was reprinted in 1849 by Nattali, as *Antiquarian and Picturesque Tour round the Southern Coast* (2 vols); and in 1892 by Virtue & Co., with an introduction by Marcus B. Huish (see Finberg, *An Introduction to Turner's Southern Coast,* 1929). The four *Rivers of Devon* plates were never published as a series. A few other drawings of West Country or *Southern Coast* subjects, datable to these years, are included in the group.

440 Plymouth Citadel *c.* 1813

Watercolour, 178 × 292
Engr.: by W. B. Cooke for *Rivers of Devon* series. This design was publ. (R. 137) with *Plymouth Sound* (No. 441) as a pair in 1823
Prov.: George Hibbert, who purchased it from the artist, sale Christie 24 March 1860 (107), bt. Rought; Agnew 1862 (International Exhibition); Robert Thornton, sale Christie 15 May 1896 (115), bt. Agnew
Coll.: untraced

Studies of Plymouth appear in the *Ivy Bridge to Penzance* sketchbook (T.B., CXXV); drawings of the Sound and the Citadel probably used for this and No. 441 are in the *Plymouth, Hamoaze* sketchbook (T.B., CXXXI).

441 Plymouth Sound *c.* 1813

Watercolour, 178 × 280
Engr.: by W. B. Cooke for *Rivers of Devon* series.

This design was publ. (R. 138) with *Plymouth Citadel* (No. 440) as a pair in 1823
Provenance and whereabouts unknown

See No. 440.

442 Ivy Bridge *c.* 1813

Watercolour, 280 × 409
Engr.: by J. C. Allen for *Rivers of Devon* series. This design was publ. in 1821 (R. 139)
Coll.: Trustees of the British Museum (T.B., CCVIII-X)

A pencil drawing of this subject is in the *Devon Rivers No. 2* sketchbook (T.B., CXXXIII–45).

443 Dartmoor: the source of the Tamar and the Torridge *c.* 1813

Watercolour, 203 × 320
Engr.: by W. B. Cooke for *Rivers of Devon* series. This design was publ. *c.* 1850 (R. 140)
Prov.: J. Gillott, sale Christie 4 May 1872 (505), bt. Agnew; John Heugh, sale Christie 24 April 1874 (85); H. Gaskell, sale Christie 24 June 1909 (236), bt. Agnew; H. M. Robinson; R. Brocklebank; W. West; G. H. and R. H. Gaskell; Mrs. E. Walton-Brown; J. M. A. Day; Agnew 1962, bt. Mellon
Coll.: Yale Center for British Art, Paul Mellon Collection

444 Sunshine on the Tamar *c.* 1813

Pencil and watercolour, with scraping-out, 217 × 367
Engr.: chromolithograph by J. Coventry 1855 (R. 851), publ. by Gambart
Exh.: ? E.H. 1829 as 'River Tavey'
Prov.: John Ruskin; by whom given to the Ruskin School, Oxford 1875; transferred to the museum, 1938
Coll.: Visitors of the Ashmolean Museum, Oxford (Herrmann 76)

Based on a pencil study in the *Vale of Heathfield* sketchbook (T.B., CXXXVII–53v). Ruskin entitled this drawing 'Pigs in sunshine. Scene on the Tavey, Devonshire.'

VIII(b) Nos 445–489
Picturesque Views on the Southern Coast of England **and related subjects,** *c.* 1811–1824. See note to VIII(a).

445 St. Michael's Mount, Cornwall *c.* 1812

Watercolour, 140 × 222
Engr.: by W. B. Cooke, 1814, for *Southern Coast* (R. 88)
Exh.: C.G. 1822 (117)
Prov.: Agnew 1900; Sir A. de Rothschild, sale Christie 1923 (38), bt. Mitchell
Private collection

The drawing for this subject is in the *Ivy Bridge to Penzance* sketchbook (T.B., CXXV, 43v–44).

446 Poole and distant view of Corfe Castle, Dorsetshire *c.* 1812

Watercolour, 139 × 219
Engr.: by G. Cooke, 1814, for *Southern Coast* (R. 89)
Exh.: C.G. 1822 (92)
Prov.: John Dillon, sale Christie 17 April 1869 (42), bt. Agnew; John Farnworth, sale Christie 10 May 1874 (14), bt. Agnew; Holbrook Gaskell; Lt.-Col. James B. Gaskell, sale Christie 30 April 1926 (79), bt. in; by descent to the present owners
Coll.: Ernest and Roger Gaskell

Pencil drawings of Poole appear in the *Devonshire Coast No. 1* sketchbook (T.B., CXXIII).

---

447 Land's End, Cornwall: approaching thunderstorm *c.* 1813

Watercolour, size unknown
Engr.: by G. Cooke, 1814, for *Southern Coast* (R. 90)
Exh.: C.G. 1822 (31)
Prov.: T. E. Crawhall, sale Christie 11 March 1893 (114), bt. Agnew
Coll.: untraced

The drawing for this subject is on a leaf catalogued by Finberg with the *Ivy Bridge to Penzance* sketchbook (T.B., CXXV–50); it seems to be referred to in Turner's note on the *Corfe to Dartmouth* sketchbook (T.B., CXXIV): 'Lands End in Book with N Dev^n'.

448 Weymouth, Dorsetshire *c.* 1811

Watercolour and scraping-out, 140 × 213
Sig. lower right: *JMW Turner RA*
Engr.: by W. B. Cooke, 1814, for *Southern Coast* (R. 91)
Exh.: C.G. 1822 (111)
Prov.: B. G. Windus; C. S. Bale, sale Christie 14 May 1881 (196), bt. McLean; W. Hurdy; A. T. Hollingsworth; E. Bulmer; Agnew 1961, bt. Mellon
Coll.: Yale Center for British Art, Paul Mellon Collection

Turner made a drawing of Weymouth in the *Corfe to Dartmouth* sketchbook (T.B., CXXIV–24).

---

449 Lulworth Cove, Dorsetshire *c.* 1812

Watercolour, 147 × 203
Engr.: by W. B. Cooke, 1814, for *Southern* Coast (R. 92)
Prov.: ?John Morley, sale Christie 16 May 1896 (24), bt. Agnew; Francis Stevenson; T. A. Tatton, sale Christie 14 December 1928 (14), bt. Agnew
Coll.: untraced

Turner's drawing for this subject is in the *Corfe to Dartmouth* sketchbook (T.B., CXXIV–22). The view-point is identical to that chosen by William Daniell for his plate of Lulworth Cove in the *Voyage round Great Britain,* a rival publication to Cooke's *Southern Coast* issued between 1814 and 1825.

450 Corfe Castle *c.* 1812

Watercolour, 138 × 223
Engr.: by G. Cooke, 1814, for *Southern Coast* (R. 93)
Prov.: John Parker, sale Foster 12 December 1861 (274), ?bt. in; Sir Joseph Heron, sale Christie 9 June 1890 (78), bt. Agnew; Humphrey Roberts, sale Christie 23 May 1908 (291), bt. Agnew; E. J. Weldon; Thomson
Coll.: untraced

The drawing for this subject is in the *Corfe to Dartmouth* sketchbook (T.B., CXXIV–17).

451 Lyme Regis, Dorsetshire: a squall *c.* 1812

Watercolour, 153 × 217
Engr.: by W. B. Cooke, 1814, for *Southern Coast* (R. 94)
Exh.: C.G. 1822 (4)
Prov.: Moncure D. Conway, sale Christie 15 May 1880 (116), bt. in; C. S. Bale, sale Christie 14 May 1881 (195), bt. S. White; James Donald, by whom given to the gallery
Coll.: Art Gallery and Museum, Glasgow (1126)

The drawing for this subject is in the *Corfe to Dartmouth* sketchbook (T.B., CXXIV–29v).

452 Teignmouth, Devonshire *c.* 1813

Watercolour and body-colour, 149 × 222
Sig. lower left: *JMW Turner*
Engr.: by G. Cooke, 1815, for *Southern Coast* (R. 95)
Exh.: C.G. 1822 (112)

Prov.: A. E. Hollingsworth; L. F. Loyd, sale Christie 31 January 1913 (113), bt. Agnew; J. M. Harvey; Mrs. Nuttall; sale Christie 19 April 1929 (81), bt. Agnew; Baskett 1974, bt. Mellon
Coll.: Yale Center for British Art, Paul Mellon Collection

Turner's drawing of this subject is in the *Corfe to Dartmouth* sketchbook (T.B., CXXIV, 36–37). It served also as the basis for an oil-painting of 1812 (P120).

---

453 Dartmouth, Devon *c.* 1814

Watercolour, 140 × 126
Engr.: by W. B. Cooke, 1815, for *Southern Coast* (R. 96)
Exh.: C.G. 1822 (26)
Prov.: E. Rodgett, sale Christie 14 May 1859 (49), bt. Agnew; John Morley, sale Christie 16 May 1896 (20), bt. Vokins; Howard Morley, sale Christie 3 June 1920, bt. Agnew; C. Stokes, sale Christie April 1926, bt. Princess Obolensky (née Astor)
Coll.: untraced

454 The Mew-stone, at the entrance of Plymouth Sound *c.* 1814

Watercolour, 156 × 237
Engr.: by W. B. Cooke, 1816, for *Southern Coast* (R. 97)
Exh.: C.G. 1824 (32)
Prov.: C. Stokes; E. Rodgett, sale Christie 14 May 1859, bt. Agnew; Henry Vaughan, by whom bequeathed to the gallery, 1900
Coll.: National Gallery of Ireland, Dublin (2413)

A colour-beginning of this subject is T.B., CXCVI-F. Turner used the subject again for one of the plates of his *Little Liber* series (R. 804; see No. 773).

455 Falmouth Harbour *c.* 1812–14

Watercolour, with some body-colour, 152 × 229

Engr.: by W. B. Cooke, 1816, for *Southern Coast* (R. 98)
Exh.: R.A. 1974 (169)
Prov.: anon. sale, Christie 3 May 1918 (62), bt. Gooden & Fox; Viscount Leverhulme
Coll.: The Lady Lever Collection, Port Sunlight, Cheshire (3507)

Drawings of Falmouth Harbour appear in the *Ivy Bridge to Penzance* sketchbook (T.B., CXXV).

456 Plymouth Dock, from Mount Edgecumbe *c.* 1814

Watercolour, 156 × 241
Sig. lower right: *JMW Turner RA*
Engr.: by W. B. Cooke, 1816, for *Southern Coast* (R. 99)
Exh.: C.G. 1822 (113)
Prov.: Col. Meeking, 1886; anon. sale, Christie 6 March 1973 (72), bt. Leger
Private collection, England

The drawing for this composition is in the *Ivy Bridge to Penzance* sketchbook (T.B., CXXV–10v, 11).

457 Plymouth, with Mount Batten *c.* 1816

Watercolour, 146 × 235
Engr.: by W. B. Cooke, 1817, for *Southern Coast* (R. 100)
Prov.: William Smith, by whom bequeathed to the museum, 1876
Coll.: Victoria and Albert Museum, London (3035–1876)

Turner's drawing of Plymouth and Mount Batten, looking over Catwater from Turn Chapel is in the *Ivy Bridge to Penzance* sketchbook (T.B., CXXV–11v, 12).

458 Pendennis Castle, Cornwall: scene after wreck *c.* 1816

Watercolour, 155 × 235
Engr.: by G. Cooke, 1817, for *Southern Coast* (R. 101)
Exh.: C.G. 1822 (104)
Prov.: John Dillon, sale Christie 17 April 1869 (40), bt. Vokins; George Rennie, sale Christie 4 June 1870 (29), bt. Vokins; sale Robinson and Fisher 1928; H. L. Fison, sale Christie 6 November 1973 (147), bt. Leger
Coll.: R.A. Shuck, England

This view of Pendennis Castle and the entrance to Falmouth Harbour is recorded in a pencil drawing, partially worked up in watercolour, in the *Ivy Bridge to Penzance* sketchbook (T.B., CXXV–27).

459 Bow and Arrow Castle, Isle of Portland *c.* 1815

Watercolour, 152 × 230
Engr.: by W. B. Cooke, 1817, for *Southern Coast* (R. 102)
Exh.: C.G. 1822 (279)
Prov.: anon. sale Christie 8 May 1855 (77), bt. Agnew; E.F. White, sale Christie 12 December 1862 (93*), unsold; H. Burton, sale Christie 12 July 1890 (100), bt. Wigzell; G. R. Burnett 1900; Agnew 1912; Sir Charles Sydney Jones, by whom bequeathed to the university, 1947
Coll.: University of Liverpool

This view is recorded in the *Corfe to Dartmouth* sketchbook (T.B., CXXIV–27).

460 Martello Towers, Bexhill *c.* 1815

Watercolour, size unknown
Engr.: by W. B. Cooke, 1817, for *Southern Coast* (R. 103)
Provenance and whereabouts unknown

Another treatment of this subject was used by Turner for his *Liber Studiorum* (R. 34); the drawing is T.B., CXVII–K.

461 East and West Looe, Cornwall *c.* 1815

Watercolour and scratching-out, 159 × 241
Engr.: by W. B. Cooke, 1818, for *Southern Coast* (R. 104)
Exh.: C.G. 1822 (244)
Prov.: J. & W. Vokins; Agnew 1873; Andrew G. Kurtz, sale Christie 11 May 1891 (201), bt. Agnew; James Blair, by whom bequeathed to the gallery, 1917
Coll.: City Art Gallery, Manchester (1917.116)

This subject was recorded in the *Ivy Bridge to Penzance* sketchbook (T.B., CXXV–17v).

462 Ilfracombe, North Devon: storm and shipwreck *c.* 1813–6

Watercolour, 144 × 230
Sig. lower right: *JMW Turner*
Engr.: by W. B. Cooke, 1818, for *Southern Coast* (R. 105)
Exh.: C.G. 1822 (1)
Prov.: Mrs. C. Wheeley-Lea, sale Christie 11 May 1917 (40), bt. Ball; Sir Thomas Beecham; Christie 1 June 1956 (132), bt. Fine Art Society, London; Walter Brandt
Coll.: Trustees of the P. A. Brandt Settlement

Turner made drawings at Ilfracombe in the *Devonshire Coast No. 1* and *Somerset and North Devon* sketchbooks (T.B., CXXIII, CXXVI).

463 Tintagel Castle, Cornwall *c.* 1815

Watercolour and scratching-out, 156 × 237
Engr.: by G. Cooke, 1818, for *Southern Coast* (R. 106)
Exh.: C.G. 1822 (2)
Prov.: J. C. Robinson, sale Christie 23 April 1865 (50), bt. Agnew; John Knowles, sale Christie 19 May 1877 (95), bt. Agnew; William Lee, sale Christie 22 June 1888 (361), bt. Agnew; William Dell, sale, Christie 21 April 1899 (52, as 'The Sandpits'), bt. Agnew; C. Fairfax Murray; Ellen T. Bullard, at whose request given to the museum, 1959

Coll.: Museum of Fine Arts, Boston, Mass. (59.796)

464 Watchet, Somersetshire *c.* 1818

Watercolour, size unknown
Engr.: by G. Cooke, 1820, for *Southern Coast* (R. 107)
Exh.: C.G. 1822 (294)
Prov.: E. W. Cooke, R.A., sale Christie 22 May 1880 (166), bt. Philpot
Coll.: untraced

A drawing of Watchet occurs in the *Devonshire Coast No. 1* sketchbook (T.B., CXXIII–170v).

465 Bridport, Dorsetshire *c.* 1818

Watercolour, 152 × 235
Engr.: by W. B. Cooke, 1820, for *Southern Coast* (R. 108)
Exh.: C.G. 1824 (94)
Prov.: C. Stokes; A. C. Pilkington; Thomas Wrigley; presented by his children to the gallery, 1901
Coll.: Art Gallery and Museum, Bury, Lancashire (Wrigley donation)

Drawings made at Bridport occur in the *Devonshire Coast No. 1* and *Corfe to Dartmouth* sketchbooks (T.B., CXXIII, CXXIV).

466 Fowey Harbour, Cornwall *c.* 1818

Watercolour, 152 × 229
Engr.: by W. B. Cooke 1820, for *Southern Coast* (R. 109)
Exh.: C.G. 1824 (99)
Prov.: C. Stokes; A. H. Campbell, sale Christie 15 June 1869 (87), unsold; A. C. Pilkington
Coll.: untraced

The drawing for this composition is in the *Ivy Bridge to Penzance* sketchbook (T.B., CXXV–18v, 19).

467 Lulworth Castle, Dorsetshire *c.* 1820

Watercolour, with some scratching-out, 155 × 235
Engr.: by G. Cooke, 1821, for *Southern Coast* (R. 110)
Exh.: C.G. 1822 (103)
Prov.: John Dillon, sale Christie 17 April 1869 (41), bt. Agnew; J. Farnworth, sale Christie 10 May 1874 (19), bt. Vokins; J. Grant Morris, Liverpool, sale Christie 23 April 1898 (64), bt. Agnew; G. R. Burnett, sale Christie 21 March 1908 (26), bt. Agnew; Miss Schuster, 1908, afterwards Lady Jones, who bequeathed it to Capt. Francis Newbolt, from whose widow bt. Agnew, 1969; purchased from Agnew, 1970
Coll.: Yale Center for British Art, Paul Mellon Collection

This subject was recorded in the *Corfe to Dartmouth* sketchbook (T.B., CXXIV–19).

468 Tor Bay, from Brixham *c.* 1816–7

Watercolour, 158 × 240
Engr.: by W. B. Cooke, 1821, for *Southern Coast* (R. 111)
Exh.: C.G. 1822 (15)
Prov.: Sir William Knighton, sale Christie 23 May 1885 (410), bt. Vokins; Stephen G. Holland, sale Christie 26 June 1908 (263), bt. Robson; Arthur Young, by whom bequeathed to the museum, 1936
Coll.: Syndics of the Fitzwilliam Museum, Cambridge (1790; Cormack 13)

The view is recorded in T.B., CXXIV48.

469 Minehead, Somersetshire *c.* 1820

Watercolour over traces of pencil, 152 × 222
Engr.: by W. B. Cooke, 1821, for *Southern Coast* (R. 112)
Exh.: C.G. 1822 (94)

Prov.: J. Morley, sale Christie 16 May 1896 (21), bt. Agnew; Francis Stevenson; Agnew 1903; James Orrock, sale Christie 4 June 1904 (46), bt. A. Smith; Agnew, from whom purchased, 1907, by Lord Leverhulme
Coll.: The Lady Lever Collection, Port Sunlight, Cheshire (WHL 225)

Studies of Minehead with Dunster Castle are in the *Devonshire Coast No. 1* and *Somerset and North Devon* sketchbooks (T.B., CXXIII, CXXVI).

470 Margate *c.* 1822

Watercolour and scraping-out, 155 × 236
Engr.: by G. Cooke, 1824, for *Southern Coast* (R. 113)
Exh.: C.G. 1824 (93)
Prov.: L. F. Loyd, sale Christie 31 January 1913 (112), bt. Agnew; Rt. Hon. C. P. Allen; Commander Cecil Allen; Agnew 1973
Coll.: Yale Center for British Art, Paul Mellon Collection

Turner's drawing of this subject is in the *Hastings* sketchbook (T.B., CXXXIX–16, 17).

471 View of Rye *c.* 1820

353

Watercolour and scraping-out, 145 × 227
Engr.: by E. Goodall, 1824, for *Southern Coast*
(R. 114)
Prov.: John Miller, sale Christie 20 May 1858 (60),
bt. Farrer; Matthew Uzielli, sale Christie 12 April
1861 (236), bt. Mason; C. S. Bale, sale Christie
14 May 1881 (194), bt. Vokins; S. G. Holland, sale
Christie 26 June 1908 (262), bt. Blaker; Miss
Gwendoline Davies, by whom bequeathed to the
museum, 1952
Coll.: National Museum of Wales, Cardiff (2956)

Turner's drawing of this view is in the *Hastings*
sketchbook (T.B., CXXXIX–21v, 22).

472   Clovelly Bay *c.* 1822

Watercolour, 147 × 226
Engr.: by W. Miller, 1824, for *Southern Coast*
(R. 115)
Prov.: Henry Vaughan, by whom bequeathed to the
gallery, 1900
Coll.: National Gallery of Ireland, Dublin (2414)

Drawings of Clovelly occur in the *Devonshire Coast
No. 1* sketchbook (T.B., CXXIII).

473   St. Mawes, Cornwall *c.* 1823

Watercolour and scraping-out, 142 × 217
Sig. lower left: *JMW Turner*
Engr.: by J. C. Allen, 1824, for *Southern Coast*
(R. 116)
Prov.: McCranker (?McCracken), sale Christie
31 March 1855 (83), bt. in; A. T. Hollingsworth,
sale Christie 11 March 1882 (75), bt. in; Francis
Stevenson; James Orrock, sale 4 June 1904 (43),
bt. Edwards, of Geneva; Agnew, from whom
purchased by Paul Mellon, 1963
Coll.: Yale Center for British Art, Paul Mellon
Collection

474   Ramsgate, Kent *c.* 1822

Watercolour, 165 × 241
Engr.: by R. Wallis, 1824, for *Southern Coast*
(R. 117)
Prov.: A. Levy; Mr. and Mrs. Murray, of Pains-
wick
Coll.: untraced

The drawing which served as a basis for this design
is in the *Hastings to Margate* sketchbook (T.B.,
CXL–85). Turner made a variant of this subject for
the *Ports of England* series (No. 754).

475   Hythe, Kent 1824

Watercolour, 140 × 229
Engr.: by G. Cooke, 1824, for *Southern Coast*
(R. 118)
Exh.: R.A. 1974 (171)
Prov.: Thomas Plint, sale Christie 7 March 1862
(169), bt. Wallis; George Simpson, sale Christie
18 April 1896 (69), bt. Wallis
Coll.: Guildhall Art Gallery, London (1259)

This composition is based on a drawing in the
Hastings sketchbook (T.B., CXXXIX–19v, 20).

476   Combe Martin, Devonshire *c.* 1824

Watercolour over pencil, with pen, 146 × 232
Engr.: by W. Miller, 1825, for *Southern Coast*
(R. 119)
Prov.: McCracken; anon. sale Christie 8 May 1855
(79), bt. Wallis; John Ruskin, by whom given to the
museum, 1861
Coll.: Visitors of the Ashmolean Museum, Oxford
(Herrmann 24)

A drawing of this view occurs in the *Devonshire
Coast No. 1* sketchbook (T.B., CXXIII–147); other
drawings of Combe Martin are in the *Somerset and
North Devon* sketchbook (T.B., CXXVI).

477   Portsmouth *c.* 1824

Watercolour, 152 × 218
Engr.: by W. Miller, 1826, for *Southern Coast*
(R. 120)
Prov.: James Vine, sale Christie 25 April 1838
(491), bt. D. White; C. F. Huth, sale Christie 6 July
1895 (59), bt. Agnew; Francis Stevenson; Agnew
1903; James Orrock, sale Christie 4 June 1904
(45), bt. A. Smith; Agnew, from whom purchased
1907 by Lord Leverhulme
Coll.: The Lady Lever Collection, Port Sunlight,
Cheshire (WHL 226)

478   Boscastle, Cornwall *c.* 1824

Watercolour over pencil, with pen and ink,
142 × 231
Engr.: by E. Goodall, 1825, for *Southern Coast*
(R. 121)
Prov.: John Ruskin, by whom presented to the
museum, 1861
Coll.: Visitors of the Ashmolean Museum, Oxford
(Herrmann 25)

Turner drew Boscastle in the *Devonshire Coast
No. 1 sketchbook* (T.B., CXXIII–182).

479   Brighton 1823–4

Watercolour, 152 × 229
Engr.: by G. Cooke, 1825, for *Southern Coast*
(R. 122)
Prov.: John Morley, of Clapton, sale Christie
16 May 1896 (19), bt. Vokins; Mrs. Robinson, of
Sheffield
Coll.: untraced

For this drawing Turner may have used material
noted in the *Brighton and Arundel* sketchbook
(T.B., CCX).

480 Folkestone, Kent *c.* 1823

Watercolour, 150 × 242
Engr.: by R. Wallis, 1826, for *Southern Coast* (R. 123)
Prov.: John Ruskin, given by him to Sir John Simon; Agnew 1904; Scott and Fowles, New York; Charles P. Taft
Coll.: Taft Museum, Cincinnati, Ohio (1931.385)

This composition is based on drawings in the *Folkestone* sketchbook (T.B., CXCVIII–17v, etc.).

481 Deal, Kent *c.* 1824

Watercolour, 153 × 241
Engr.: by W. Radclyffe, 1826, for *Southern Coast* (R. 124)
Prov.: F. R. Leyland, sale Christie 9 March 1872 (40), bt. Agnew; Horatio Micholls; R. Beddington
Coll.: untraced

Turner's drawing of this subject is in the *Holland* sketchbook (T.B., CCXIV–273).

482 Mount Edgecombe, Plymouth *c.* 1824

Watercolour, size unknown
Engr.: by E. Goodall, 1826, for *Southern Coast* (R. 125)
Provenance and whereabouts unknown

483 Dover from Shakespeare Cliff *c.* 1824

Watercolour, 159 × 241
Engr.: by G. Cooke, 1826, for *Southern Coast* (R. 126)

Prov.: Matthew T. Shaw, sale Christie 20 March 1880 (51, as 'Dover') bt. Jervois; F. Nettlefold, sale Christie 5 June 1913 (42), bt. Agnew; J. F. Howarth; Nelson C. White; by descent to the present owner
Coll.: Mrs. Nelson H. White, Waterford, Conn. U.S.A.

484 Whitstable *c.* 1824

Watercolour, size unknown
Sig. lower left
Engr.: by J. Horsburgh, 1826, for *Southern Coast* (R. 127)
Prov.: G. F. Robson; J. E. Taylor; Vokins Gallery 1891
Private collection

485 Off Dover *c.* 1820

Watercolour, 165 × 267
Prov.: anon. sale Christie 22 June 1923 (24), bt. Gooden & Fox for Lord Leverhulme
Coll.: The Lady Lever Collection, Port Sunlight, Cheshire (WHL 4698)

486 Rye, Sussex *c.* 1820

Watercolour, 184 × 273
Prov.: Miss Carol N. Kay-Taylor, Toronto, sale Christie 3 March 1970 (101), unsold
Coll.: untraced

There is a pencil and wash drawing of this subject, *c.* 1795, similar in composition, in the National Gallery of Scotland, Edinburgh (Vaughan Bequest).

487 Plymouth Harbour: towing in French prizes *c.* 1820

Watercolour, 254 × 356
Prov.: Mrs. Hollis
Coll.: untraced

488 Coast scene, with white cliffs and boats ?*c.* 1815–20

Watercolour and stopping-out, 184 × 231
Prov.: Agnew *c.* 1880; Sir A. James; by descent; P. & D. Colnaghi, from whom purchased, 1966
Coll.: Mr. and Mrs. Paul Mellon, Upperville, Virginia

489 Margate Pier early 1820s

Watercolour over pencil, 128 × 193
Prov.: John Ruskin (who bought it from the artist), sale Christie 15 April 1869 (14), bt. Vokins; William Blodgett, of New York; by descent to Eleanor Blodgett, by whom given to Franklin D. Roosevelt, 1911; bequeathed by Mrs. Eleanor Roosevelt to her physician, Dr. A. David Gurewitsch; Mrs. Gurewitsch, until 1978; Agnew 1979
Private collection, U.S.A.

An unusual drawing, which may be connected with Turner's work for the *Southern Coast* series, or perhaps for the *Ports of England*. Ruskin noted: 'I have seen no other example of a drawing by Turner arrested so near completion'. Despite its lack of detail it is executed in a precise manner, unlike that of Turner's usual preparatory studies (see Francis Russell, 1975).

SECTION IX
Nos 490–523 Miscellaneous finished watercolours, *c.* 1809-1836

IX (a)   Nos 490–498
Miscellaneous finished watercolours, *c.* 1809–1819

490   Cottage Steps, Children feeding Chickens*   Turner's gallery 1809 (3)

Watercolour, 611 × 463
Sig.: *JMW Turner RA*
Exh.: R.A. 1811 (503); Grosvenor Place 1819 (5); Leeds 1839 (50)
Prov.: Walter Fawkes; Major Le G. G. W. Horton-Fawkes; Agnew; H. C. Green; Leger Galleries, London
Private collection, Japan

This drawing was exhibited at the R.A. in 1811 as 'May: Chickens', a title which suggests that it was conceived as a pair to No. 491.

491   November: Flounder-fishing   R.A. 1811 (312)

Watercolour, 642 × 477
Exh.: Grosvenor Place 1819 (1); Leeds 1839 (84)
Prov.: Walter Fawkes; Major Le G. G. W. Horton-Fawkes; Agnew; H. C. Green; Leger Galleries, London
Private collection, Japan

This drawing may be regarded as the pair to No. 490, and was therefore perhaps executed at about the same time, i.e. *c.* 1809.

492   Chryses*   R.A. 1811 (332)

Watercolour, 660 × 1004
Prov.: Thomas Griffith, from whom bt. Vokins; R. C. L. Bevan; sold by executors, Christie 4 July 1891 (53), bt. Agnew; Thomas Ashton; by descent to present owner
Private collection, England

The title in the R. A. catalogue was accompanied by the following lines from Pope's *Homer's Iliad*, Book 1:

'The trembling priest along the shore return'd,
And in the anguish of a father mourn'd;
Disconsolate, not daring to complain,
Silent he wander'd by the sounding main;
Till safe at distance to his God he prays;
The God who darts around the world his rays.'

For studies of this subject see the *Wey Guildford* sketchbook (T.B., XCVIII–3a, 4, ?5a).

493   Temple of Aegina   *c.* 1815

Watercolour, 267 × 432
Engr.: by T. Kelly for unknown annual (R. 347)
Prov.: ? C. R. Cockerell, for whom made; Allen, 1860; H. A. J. Munro of Novar, sale Christie 1867; ? H. W. F. Bolckow, sale Christie 2 May 1891 (54, as 'The Acropolis'), bt. Agnew
Coll.: Lord Joicey, Etal Manor, Berwick-upon-Tweed

Probably based on a drawing by C. R. Cockerell. Compare the two paintings of the Temple of Jupiter Panhellenius, in the Island of Aegina, which Turner exhibited in 1816 (P133 and P134).

494   The Field of Waterloo   *c.* 1817

Watercolour, 288 × 405
Exh.: Grosvenor Place 1819 (34)
Prov.: Walter Fawkes; Major Richard Fawkes; A. W. Fawkes, by whom bequeathed to the museum, 1942
Coll.: Syndics of the Fitzwilliam Museum, Cambridge (2476; Cormack 14)

Studies used for this watercolour are in the *Waterloo and Rhine* sketchbook (T.B., CLX). Turner was engaged about 1817 on a painting of *The Field of Waterloo*, shown at the R.A. in 1818 (P138).

495   Landscape: Composition   of   Tivoli*   1817   R.A. 1818 (474)

Watercolour, 676 × 1020
Signed and dated lower right: *IMW Turner 1817*
Engr.: by E. Goodall for Allnutt, 1827 (R. 207) for J. Burnet, *Turner and his Works*, 1859
Exh.: Society of Painters in Water Colours 1823 (loan exhibition; 88); R.A. 1974 (181)
Prov.: John Allnutt, for whom drawn, sale Christie 18 June 1863 (328), bt. Lord Ashburton; Lady Ashburton, sale Christie 1 June 1864 (22), bt. Sir John Fowler, sale Christie 6 May 1899 (31), bt. Agnew; Sir James Joicey; Agnew, to Miss Aguirre, Buenos Aires 1913; bt. Agnew from a South American collector, 1973
Private collection

A large colour-beginning for this subject is T.B., CXCVII–A. Turner is said to have made a companion, *The Rise of the River Stour at Stourhead* (No. 496) at about the same time, though it was not exhibited until 1825.

496   Rise of the River Stour at Stourhead   ?*c.* 1817

Watercolour, 673 × 1022
Exh.: R.A. 1825 (465)
Prov.: Charles Morrison; Simon Morrison
Coll.: Walter Morrison Collection, Sudeley Castle, Gloucestershire

The title in the R. A. catalogue was accompanied by the following lines:

'From his two springs in Stourton's woody glade,
Pure welling out — into the lake,
He pours his infant stream.'

This was painted as a pendant to *Landscape: Composition of Tivoli* (see No. 495).

497   Temple of Minerva Sunias, Cape Colonna   ?*c.* 1820

Watercolour, size unknown
Engr.: by J. T. Willmore, 1854 (R. 673)
Prov.: C. H. L. Wood, 1887
Coll.: untraced

Willmore's engraving was made 'exclusively for the Members of the Association for the Promotion of the Fine Arts in Scotland for the year 1854'.

498   London, from the windows of 45 Grosvenor Place, when in the possession of W. Fawkes   *c.* 1819

Watercolour, 248 × 388
Prov.: Walter Fawkes; by descent to Revd.

Ayscough Fawkes, sale Christie 27 June 1890 (36), bt. Agnew; Brocklebank; Vicars
Coll.: untraced

IX(b) Nos 499–512
Finished marine subjects, *c.* 1815–1832

499 A First-Rate taking in stores 1818

Pencil and watercolour, 286 × 397
Signed and dated lower right: *IMW Turner 1818*
Exh.: Grosvenor Place 1819 (20); Leeds 1839 (14); R.A. 1974 (194)
Prov.: Walter Fawkes, for whom drawn at Farnley Hall during the artist's stay there in November 1818; W. R. Fawkes sale, Christie 2 July 1937 (44), bt. Tooth; Viscount Eccles; Agnew, from whom bt. by the gallery, 1953
Coll.: Cecil Higgins Art Gallery, Bedford (P. 99)

The composition of this subject is anticipated in a study of *c.* 1797 (T.B., XXXIII–e). It is possible that the *Loss of a man-of-war* (No. 500) was conceived as the pair to this drawing, which is supposed to have been executed as 'a drawing of the ordinary dimensions that will give some idea of the size of a man of war' (typescript account of Edith Mary Fawkes, National Gallery, London).

500 Loss of a man-of-war *c.* 1818

Watercolour, 280 × 395
Exh.: Grosvenor Place 1819 (22); Leeds 1839 (15)
Prov.: Walter Fawkes; Major Le G. G. W. Horton Fawkes, bt. Agnew 1938; G. Mitchell; Agnew 1974
Private collection

See No. 499. The subject of this watercolour may be rather 'The wreck of an East Indiaman'. A colour-study for this composition is T.B., CXCVI–N; it is inscribed: 'Begun for Dear Fawkes of Farnley'.

501 Man-of-war, making a signal for a pilot off the Tagus *c.* 1819

Watercolour, 280 × 394
Sig. lower right: *IMW Turner*
Exh.: Grosvenor Place 1819 (18); Leeds 1839 (18)
Prov.: Walter Fawkes; Agnew 1913; bt. through the Maleham Bequest, 1943, when it entered the gallery collection
Coll.: Graves Art Gallery, Sheffield (2285)

It may be that this subject, acquired, like Nos 499, 500 by Fawkes, was executed *en suite* with them: the three drawings are similar in size as well as being linked by their concern with warships.

502 Bell Rock Lighthouse *c.* 1820

Watercolour, size unknown
Engr.: by J. Horsburgh 1824 (R. 201) as the frontispiece to Stevenson's *Account of the Bell Rock Lighthouse;* by W. Miller 1864 (R. 681)
Provenance and whereabouts unknown

This drawing was commissioned by Robert Stevenson in 1819 (see Finberg, *Life,* p. 257).

503 Hastings: fish-market *c.* 1810

Watercolour, 280 × 381
Sig.: *JMW Turner RA*
Exh.: Grosvenor Place 1819 (19)
Prov.: Walter Fawkes; Agnew 1913; Mrs. Ernest Agnew; by descent to the present owner
Private collection

504 Hastings: deep-sea fishing 1818

Watercolour, 398 × 591
Signed and dated lower right: *IMW Turner RA 1818*
Engr.: by R. Wallis 1851 (R. 665)
Exh.: C.G. 1822 (9); B.M. 1975 (54)
Prov.: ?W. B. Cooke; Charles Sackville Bale,

sale Christie 13 May 1881 (197), bt. Vokins; S. G. Holland, sale Christie 26 June 1908 (258), bt. Sir Joseph Beecham; sale Christie 3 May 1915 (150), bt. R. W. Lloyd, by whom bequeathed to the museum, 1958
Coll.: Trustees of the British Museum (1958–7–12–419)

Two colour-beginnings for the subject are T.B., CXCVII–J,K. Finberg (*Life,* p. 482) identifies the drawing shown at Cooke's gallery in 1822 as 'Hastings from the Sea' with the work now known as *Shipwreck off Hastings* (No. 511).

505 Dover from the sea 1822

Watercolour and body-colour, 432 × 629
Signed and dated lower right: *JMW Turner 1822*
Engr.: by J. T. Willmore 1851 (R. 666)
Exh.: C.G. 1823 (26)
Prov.: John Dillon; Chapman; W. Leech, sale Christie 21 May 1887 (69), bt. Agnew; Samuel Putnam Agery Jr., New York; David P. Kimball, by whom bequeathed in memory of his wife, Clara Bertram Kimball
Coll.: Museum of Fine Arts, Boston, Mass. (23.513)

The two following subjects were issued under the title 'Marine Views', by Turner himself, singly in paper wrappers decorated with a vignette engraved by W. B. Cooke. This was the design of 'Neptune's Trident' which Cooke thought the artist had presented to him, but which he was later asked to return with a two-guinea fee for the loan (see Thornbury, pp. 187–8). The drawing is T.B., CLXVIII–C. Other watercolours in the group catalogued here may have been intended for publication in the series.

506 Eddystone Lighthouse *c.* 1822

Watercolour, approx. 430 × 650
Engr.: in mezzotint by T. Lupton, 1824 (R. 771); a reduced plate was made of this subject (R. 773)
Prov.: ? John Dillon, sale Christie 17 April 1869 (35), bt. Agnew
Coll.: untraced

Finberg (*Index*) refers to a drawing of this subject (8 × 12 inches; 203 × 305) but doubts if this is the engraved design because it is too small. He gives the provenance as: ex Dillon; Leech; B. Macgregor (1901). A drawing of the subject is listed in the Dillon sale (Christie 17 April 1869 (35), bt. Agnew), with reference to an engraving (see above).

507 Margate from the sea: whiting fishing 1822

Watercolour, 426 × 648
Signed and dated: *JMW Turner 1822*
Engr.: in mezzotint by T. Lupton, 1825 (R. 772); a reduced plate was made of this subject (R. 774); chromolithograph by engraver unknown and publ. M. & N. Hanhart, probably 1852–6 (R. 853)
Exh.: C.G. 1823 (no number) as 'Margate: Sunrise'
Prov.: B. G. Windus; Mrs. Fordham; Mrs. Henry Folland; Christie 5 October 1945 (5), bt. Mitchell Gallery
Coll.: untraced

508 The storm ?1823

Watercolour, 434 × 632
Sig. lower right: *JMW Turner RA*
Exh.: C.G. 1823 (no number) as 'Shipwreck'; B.M. 1975 (87)
Prov.: W. B. Cooke; Lewis Loyd 1857; R. W. Lloyd, by whom bequeathed to the museum, 1958
Coll.: Trustees of the British Museum (1958–7-12–424)

Colour-beginnings for this subject are T.B., CCLXIII–371, 377, 379. This drawing is apparently the work executed in 1823, with a companion *Sunrise* (No. 507); the pair were exhibited at Cooke's exhibition in May of that year.

509 Twilight—smugglers off Folkestone fishing up smuggled Gin 1824

Watercolour, 432 × 648
Signed and dated: *JMW Turner 1824*
Engr.: in mezzotint by T. Lupton, 1830 (R. 798, unpubl.)
Exh.: C.G. 1824 (41)
Prov.: W. Leech, Christie 1887; Hollins; Hippisley; E. Nettlefold
Coll.: untraced

A related subject is No. 512 below.

510 Hastings: fish-market on the sands 1824

Watercolour, 339 × 667
Signed and dated: *JMW Turner 1824*
Exh.: C.G. 1824 (21)
Prov.: presented by Turner to Sir Anthony Carlisle, his doctor; Joseph Gillott, sale Christie 4 May 1872 (511), bt. Vokins; anon. sale, Christie 17 May 1873 (40), bt. Agnew; Cornelius Vanderbilt; Sotheby 29 May 1963 (60), bt. in; sold privately to the Leger Galleries
Coll.: untraced

A drawing entitled 'Fish Market at Hastings' was sold by H. Wallis at Winstanley's rooms, 28 May 1852 (62); its purchaser is not recorded.

511 Shipwreck off Hastings ?c. 1825

Watercolour, 190 × 285
Engr.: by W. Miller 1866 (R. 867)
Prov.: Henry Vaughan, by whom bequeathed to the gallery, 1900
Coll.: National Gallery of Ireland, Dublin (2411)

512 Folkestone from the sea c. 1832

Watercolour and body-colour, 487 × 691
Listed in the *Inventory* as one of the *Rivers and Ports* series, but not engraved
Exh.: B.M. 1975 (82)
Coll.: Trustees of the British Museum (T.B., CCVIII-Y).

A colour-beginning for this subject is T.B., CCLXIII–357.

IX(c) Nos 513–523
Finished watercolours of London and neighbourhood, c. 1824–1836

Turner made a number of finished watercolours of London subjects in the mid-1820s. They do not, however, appear to have been a series. His only previous important watercolour with a London subject had been his earliest R.A. exhibit (No. 10), and the *Autumn Morning* of 1801 (No. 278). The large 'sketch from memory' of Lawrence's funeral (No. 521) was the last watercolour that Turner showed at the Academy; he evidently sent it as a mark of respect for the deceased President, since it was not his custom to show such works at this date; and in any case it cannot be described as 'finished'. A few of these subjects were engraved for annuals, and some may have been executed specifically for that purpose.

513 View of London from Greenwich ?c. 1824

Watercolour, size unknown
Prov.: ?Arthur Severn
Private collection, U.S.A.

An elaborate subject with many figures in the foreground, holding rolls of paper; other rolls inscribed: *London 1526; London 1825; Designs of London; George IV; St. Paul's Cathedral*, etc.

514 The Port of London 1824

Watercolour and body-colour, 292 × 445
Signed and dated: *JMW Turner RA/24*
Inscr. on buoy: *PORT OF LONDON*
Engr.: by E. Goodall
Prov.: John Dillon sale, Foster & Son, 7 June 1856 (140); Jones, by whom bequeathed to the museum, 1882
Coll.: Victoria and Albert Museum, London (522–1882)

515 Tower of London c. 1825

Watercolour, 305 × 432
Engr.: by W. Miller for *The Literary Souvenir*, 1831 (R. 318)
Prov.: Birchall; John Knowles, sale Christie 19 May 1877 (99, as 'First Steamer on the Thames: Tower of London'), bt. Burchell; William Carver, sale Christie 22 March 1890 (114, as 'First Steamboat on the Thames'), bt. Innes; Leger, 1943
Coll.: untraced

516 The Custom House, London c. 1825

Watercolour, 127 × 229
Engr.: by J. C. Allen, 1827
Prov.: G. Hibbert, sale Christie 2 May 1860 (213), bt. Wallis; ?John Farnworth, sale Christie 18 May 1874 (13, as 'London Docks'), bt. Williams; ? A. G.

Kurtz, sale Christie 11 May 1891 (202, as 'London Docks'), bt. Williams; L. Butters; Vancouver Art Gallery, from where stolen
Coll.: untraced

517   London Docks   ? 1825

Watercolour, ? 127 × 229
Provenance and whereabouts unknown

518   Richmond Hill *   c. 1820–5

Watercolour and body-colour, 297 × 489
Engr.: by E. Goodall for *The Literary Souvenir,* 1826 (R. 314)
Exh.: R.A. 1974 (257)
Prov.: John Knowles, sale Christie, 19 May 1877 (97, as 'Richmond Hill—Boy and Kite'), bt. Agnew; Agnew 1902; Lord Leverhulme
Coll.: The Lady Lever Collection, Port Sunlight, Cheshire (743)

Compare the *England Wales* drawing of the same view (No. 879) and the large painting of 1819 (P140). Colour-beginnings of the subject are T.B., CCLXIII–348, 385.

519   Virginia Water *   c. 1829

Watercolour, 290 × 443
Engr.: by R. Wallis for *The Keepsake,* 1830 (R. 323)
Exh.: E.H. 1829; R.A. 1974 (258)
Prov.: C. Pemberton; W. J. Houldsworth, bt. Agnew 1881; Daniel Thwaites; by descent to present owner
Private collection, England

This and No. 520 were executed as a pair for George IV, who, in the event, refused to buy them. Turner's studies at Virginia Water are in the *Kenilworth* sketchbook (T.B., CCXXXVIII).

520   Virginia Water   c. 1829

Watercolour, 289 × 442
Engr.: by R. Wallis for *The Keepsake,* 1830 (R. 322)
Exh.: E.H. 1829
Prov.: C. Pemberton; W. Leech, sale Christie 21 May 1887 (70), bt. McLean
Coll.: untraced

A pair to No. 519.

521   Funeral of Sir Thomas Lawrence, a sketch from memory   R.A. 1830   (493)

Watercolour and body-colour, 616 × 825

Inscr. lower left: *Funeral of Sir Thos Lawrence PRA Jany 21 1830 SKETCH FROM MEMORY IMWT*
Coll.: Trustees of the British Museum (T.B., CCLXIII–344)

Turner's account of Lawrence's funeral, in a letter to George Jones of 22 January 1830, is published in Finberg's *Life,* p. 320. The event affected Turner deeply, and this large 'Sketch from memory', the only object of its kind ever exhibited by him at the Academy, was no doubt intended as a private homage to the President.

522   The Burning of the Houses of Parliament 1834

Watercolour and body-colour, 293 × 440 (sight)
Exh.: R.A. 1974 (456)
Coll.: Trustees of the British Museum (T.B., CCCLXIV–373)

Turner's pencil notes of the fire of 16 October 1834 are in a small sketchbook (T.B., CCLXXXIV); they are rapid and incomplete. A series of colour studies of the scene, possibly done on the spot but more probably made later, are from another sketchbook (T.B., CCLXXXIII). This larger drawing is not quite in a finished state; see also the vignette of the subject (No. 1306) and the two paintings (P359, P364).

523   Fire at Fenning's Wharf, on the Thames at Bermondsey 1836

Watercolour, pencil and body-colour, with scratching-out, 289 × 435
Prov.: J. E. Taylor; presented by him to the Whitworth Institute, 1892
Coll.: Whitworth Art Gallery, University of Manchester (D.100.1892)

This watercolour records a conflagration which occurred on the night of 30 August 1836; it can be seen as part of a sequence of drawings and paintings concerned with the theme of fire, which appeared in the mid-1830s.

SECTION X
Nos 524–635   Yorkshire and the North of England, *c.* 1809–1821

**X(a)   Nos 524–555
Miscellaneous North-Country subjects,**
c. 1809–1821

Several were acquired by Fawkes, and some, showing the area around his house, Tent Lodge, at Coniston (Nos 551–555), were commissioned by him. Another patron who bought drawings of views in the same area was Sir Henry Pilkington. The material for these drawings was gathered in a series of sketchbooks which Turner was using at the time for his work on various commissions; but a few of the subjects are drawn from the *Tweed and Lakes* sketchbook (T.B., XXXV) of 1797.

524   Distant view of Lowther Castle   1809

Watercolour and pencil, 224 × 352
Prov.: Revd. W. Kingsley; John Ruskin, by whom given to the Ruskin School, Oxford, 1875; transferred to the museum, 1938
Coll.: Visitors of the Ashmolean Museum, Oxford (Herrmann 72)

This and two pencil drawings of Lowther (Herrmann 73, 74) were done while Turner was collecting subjects for Lord Egremont around Egremont's north-country seat, Cockermouth, in 1809; there is a small *Lowther* sketchbook of this date (T.B., CXIII). The three Ashmolean sheets may have come from the *Petworth* sketchbook (T.B., CIX), which contains a number of views at Cockermouth, as well as at Petworth.
See also the painting of Cockermouth (P108).

525   Beeston Castle, Cheshire   ? 1809

Watercolour, 210 × 330
Prov.: John Dillon, sale Christie 29 April 1869 (123); John Heugh, sale Christie 24 April 1874 (91), bt. Colnaghi; F. J. Nettlefold
Private collection

526   Yorkshire coast   1805–10

Watercolour over pencil, 218 × 353
Prov.: ? Revd. Stopford A. Brooke; Sir E. Tootal Broadhurst, by whom bequeathed to the Whitworth Institute, 1922, and received on the death of Lady Broadhurst, 1924

Coll.: Whitworth Art Gallery, University of Manchester (D.52.1924)

The dating is Finberg's; the drawing is faded and not easy to assess. It is a study that does not fit readily into a sequence of other drawings, but may be connected with the series of Yorkshire subjects that Turner produced around 1809.

527 Scarborough Castle: boys crab-fishing 1809

Watercolour, 280 × 390
Signed and dated left (on bank): *JMW Turner RA 1809*
Prov.: Sir H. Pilkington, for whom drawn; E. Bicknell, sale Christie 29 April 1863 (268), bt. Wells for Lord Hertford
Coll.: Wallace Collection, London (P654)

Nos 527, 528, 529 are variants of a composition that Turner was to use again in a modified form in the *Ports of England* (No. 751). Several drawings of Scarborough Castle were made in the *Smaller Fonthill* sketchbook (T.B., XLVIII; see Nos 317, 318), and Finberg suggests that some sketches in the *Chester* sketchbook (T.B., LXXXII, 16–20) may also show Scarborough, though this is disputable. A colour-beginning for this subject is T.B., CXCVI-B.

528 Scarborough Town and Castle: Morning: Boys catching crabs* R.A. 1811 (392)

Watercolour, 687 × 1016
Exh.: Grosvenor Place 1819 (16); Leeds 1839 (17); R.A. 1974 (113)
Prov.: Walter Fawkes; W. R. Fawkes, sale Christie 2 July 1937 (35), bt. Sir Frederick Hamilton; by descent to present owner
Private collection, England

A larger treatment of the 1809 drawing (No. 527). A full-scale colour-beginning is T.B., CXCVI-C; the small colour-beginning associated here with No. 527 may also have been used in connection

with this drawing. A closer view of Scarborough from the same direction occurs in the *Ports of England* series (No. 751; see also No. 529).

529 Scarborough 1818

Watercolour and scraping-out, 278 × 394
Signed and dated lower right: *JMW Turner 1818*
Prov.: John Ruskin; Arthur Severn; C. Morland Agnew; by descent to Vice-Admiral Sir William Agnew
Coll.: Mr. and Mrs. Eugene Victor Thaw

Studies made at Scarborough in about 1817 and used for this drawing are in the *Scarborough 1* sketchbook (T.B., CL–8,31) and in the *Scarborough 2* sketchbook, T.B., CLI, where the whole view is outlined on p. 17 verso. See also No. 527.

530 The Strid, Bolton Abbey, Yorkshire c. 1809

Watercolour, 280 × 381
Sig.: *JMWT*
Exh.: Grosvenor Place 1819 (14); Leeds 1839 (22)
Prov.: Walter Fawkes; F. H. Fawkes; Agnew, 1938; Esmond Morse
Coll.: untraced

A large pencil study (T.B., CLIV-U) served as the basis for this drawing. The subject occurs in a list of drawings for Fawkes written out by Turner on p. 52 of the *Greenwich* sketchbook (T.B., CII).

531 Bolton Abbey, Yorkshire c. 1809

Watercolour, 278 × 387
Sig. lower left: *JMW Turner RA PP*
Exh.: Grosvenor Place 1819 (13); Leeds 1839 (76)
Prov.: Walter Fawkes; Sir C. Sydney Jones, 1939;

bequeathed by him to the university, 1947
Coll.: University of Liverpool

Turner made two views of Bolton Abbey, perhaps as a pair, from opposite directions in about 1809; both are mentioned in Turner's list in the *Greenwich* sketchbook (T.B., CII); see No. 530. The other Bolton view is No. 532.

532 Bolton Abbey, Yorkshire 1809

Watercolour and scraping-out, 278 × 395
Signed and dated lower right: *IMW Turner RA PP 1809*
Exh.: ? Grosvenor Place 1819 (23); B.M. 1975 (39)
Engr.: by E. Finden, 1826, for *The Literary Souvenir* (R. 315)
Prov.: ?Walter Fawkes; George Salting, by whom bequeathed to the museum, 1910
Coll.: Trustees of the British Museum (1910–2-12-282)

Perhaps the pair to No. 531. Some large pencil studies of Bolton Abbey are T.B., CLIV-Q,T; Finberg dates these to after 1816, but they may have been done in connection with these watercolours of c. 1809. See No. 547.

533 Malham Cove, Yorkshire c. 1810

Watercolour, 279 × 396
Sig. lower right: *IMW Turner RA*
Exh.: R.A. 1974 (123)
Prov.: Agnew 1908; George Salting, by whom bequeathed to the museum, 1910
Coll.: Trustees of the British Museum (1910–2-12-277)

The pencil sketch for this is in the *Tabley No. 1* sketchbook (T.B., CIII–10).

534 Woodcock shooting on the Chiver 1813

Watercolour, 280 × 400
Signed and dated lower left: *JMW Turner RA 1813*
Engr.: chromolithograph by B. & G. Leighton, publ. Hogarth, 1852 (R. 849)
Prov.: Sir H. Pilkington, for whom drawn; E. Bicknell, sale Christie 29 April 1863 (271), bt. Wells for Lord Hertford
Coll.: Wallace Collection, London

A pencil study for this subject is in the *Woodcock Shooting* sketchbook (T.B., CXXIX–47). It is a pair to No. 535; both were executed for Sir Henry Pilkington.

535 Grouse shooting *c.* 1813

Watercolour, 280 × 390
Sig. lower right: *JMW Turner RA PP* (?)
Engr.: chromolithograph by B. & G. Leighton, publ. Hogarth, 1852 (R. 848)
Prov.: Sir H. Pilkington, for whom drawn; E. Bicknell, sale Christie 29 April 1863 (270), bt. Wells for Lord Hertford
Coll.: Wallace Collection, London

See the companion to this, No. 534.

536 Mowbray Lodge, Ripon, Yorkshire *c.* 1815

Watercolour, 280 × 390
Sig. lower right: ... *Turner RA*
Prov.: Sir H. Pilkington, for whom drawn; E. Bicknell, sale Christie 29 April 1863 (269), bt. Wells for Lord Hertford
Coll.: Wallace Collection, London

This and No. 537 are almost identical; it is most

unusual for Turner to have repeated a subject so literally. It seems likely that the version at Port Sunlight is the replica.

537 Mowbray Lodge, Ripon *c.* 1815

Watercolour and scratching-out, 277 × 394
Prov.: James Orrock, from whom purchased by Lord Leverhulme, 1910
Coll.: The Lady Lever Collection, Port Sunlight, Cheshire (WHL 754)

See No. 536.

538 On the Washburn, under Folly Hall *c.* 1815

Watercolour, 277 × 393
Sig. lower left: *IMW Turner RA*
Exh.: B.M. 1975 (56)
Prov.: Sir H. Pilkington for whom drawn; John

Dillon, sale Christie 17 April 1869 (45), bt. Agnew; R. Leake; F. Stevenson; Agnew, 1903; James Orrock, sale Christie 4 June 1904 (40); George Salting, by whom bequeathed to the museum, 1910
Coll.: Trustees of the British Museum (1910–2-12-287)

A partly coloured study of this subject is in the *Large Farnley* sketchbook (T.B., CXXVIII–41).

539 On the Washburn (a study) *c.* 1815 or earlier

Pencil and watercolour, 286 × 457
Prov.: J. E. Taylor, who gave it to Sir Frank Short; Miss Dorothea Short, sale Christie 9 November 1971 (120), bt. Baskett, from whom bt. by Paul Mellon, 1971
Coll.: Yale Center for British Art, Paul Mellon Collection

This is apparently a leaf from the *Large Farnley* sketchbook (T.B., CXXVIII). It served as the basis for the finished watercolour (No. 540).

540 On the Washburn *c.* 1815

Watercolour over pencil, 272 × 391
Sig. lower left centre: *IMW Turner RA*
Prov.: ?Walter Fawkes; by descent to F. H. Fawkes, sale Christie 6 July 1872 (130), bt. Barns; Abel Buckley; Agnew, 1904; C. Fairfax Murray; Sir William Mills; N. H. Rollason; Agnew, from whom bt. by Paul Mellon, 1963
Coll.: Yale Center for British Art, Paul Mellon Collection

Based on the colour sketch No. 539.

Prov.: Hon. Emily Kitson, sale Sotheby 20 March 1963 (86), bt. Agnew
Private collection, England

For *Loidis and Elmete* see Nos 584, 585, 586.

sketchbook (T.B., XXXIV–35), on which the composition for the *England and Wales* series seems to have been based (see No. 827).

541 Weathercote Cave, Yorkshire *c.* 1815

Watercolour, 394 × 282
Sig.: *JMW Turn...*
Prov.: Agnew; bt. through the Maleham Bequest, 1942, when it entered the gallery collection
Coll.: Graves Art Gallery, Sheffield (2279)

The composition is based on the pencil drawing on p. 34 of the *Yorkshire 4* sketchbook (T.B., CXLVII). For another view of the Weathercote Cave see No. 580.

542 A rocky pool, with heron and kingfisher *c.* 1815

Watercolour, 309 × 400
Exh.: R.A. 1974 (193)
Prov.: John Knowles, sale Christie 5 June 1880 (485, as 'Wharfedale, Richmondshire'), bt. Fine Art Society, London; J. E. Taylor, sale Christie 5 July 1912 (49, as 'Dell near Wharfedale'), bt. Agnew; C.E. Fairfax-Murray; Asa Lingard; purchased by the gallery, 1957
Coll.: City Art Galleries, Leeds (5.57)

This drawing has a traditional title, 'A lonely dell, Wharfedale', which reinforces its resemblance in style and mood to the Wharfedale drawings made for Sir Henry Pilkington in about 1815.

544 Leeds 1816

Watercolour, 290 × 425
Signed and dated lower left: *JMW Turner RA 1816*
Engr.: as a lithograph by J. D. Harding, 1823, perhaps for a later edition of Whitaker's *Loidis and Elmete,* originally publ. 1816–20
Exh.: R.A. 1974 (186)
Prov.: John Allnutt, sale Christie 18 June 1863 (166), bt. Vokins; John Knowles, sale Christie 5 June 1880 (484), bt. Fine Art Society, London; ?John Ruskin, sale Christie 22 July 1882 (65), bt. McLean; Mrs. Lee; A. G. Turner, to his son, J. G. Turner; Agnew, from whom bt. by Paul Mellon, 1962
Coll.: Yale Center for British Art, Paul Mellon Collection

There are pencil sketches of views of Leeds and its environs in the *Devonshire Rivers No. 3 and Wharfedale* sketchbook (T.B., CXXXIV), and on pp. 79, 80 there is a sketch of the town which is identifiable with this composition.
For *Loidis and Elmete* see Nos 584, 585, 586.

545 Tynemouth Priory, Northumberland *c.* 1818

Watercolour, 159 × 241
Prov.: Mrs. Sara Austen, sale Christie 10 April 1889 (199, as 'Off Holy Island'), bt. Vokins; J. Vavasseur, sale Christie 23 April 1910 (21, as 'Off Holy Island'), bt. Vicars; Mrs. C. H. Barley
Private collection

A watercolour study of Tynemouth Priory is T.B., XXXIII-T; and there is a later study, with some colour, of the same subject in the *North of England*

546 Interior of Fountains Abbey, Yorkshire *c.* 1819

Watercolour, 280 × 394
Exh.: Grosvenor Place 1819 (7); Leeds 1839 (52)
Prov.: Walter Fawkes; by descent to Revd. Ayscough Fawkes, sale Christie 27 June 1890 (40), bt. Agnew; J. E. Taylor, sale Christie 5 July 1912 (50), bt. Agnew; J. E. T. Allen; by descent to present owner
Private collection

Turner made drawings of the interior of Fountains Abbey in the *Devonshire Rivers No. 3 and Wharfedale* sketchbook (T.B., CXXXIV).

547 Patterdale Old Church *c.* 1810–15

Watercolour and scratching-out, 279 × 395
Sig. lower left: *JMW Turner RA PP*
Prov.: J. Gillott, sale Christie 4 May 1872 (506), bt. Agnew; Albert Levy, sale 1 April 1876 (282), bt.

543 Gledhow, Yorkshire 1816

Watercolour, 280 × 406
Sig. lower right: *JMW Turner RA*
Engr.: by George Cooke for Whitaker's *Loidis and Elmete*, 1816–20 (R. 87)

Heugh; sale Christie 10 May 1878 (153), bt. Agnew; Sir William Agnew 1910; C. Morland Agnew; Hugh Agnew; Agnew, from whom bt. by Paul Mellon, 1965
Coll.: Yale Center for British Art, Paul Mellon Collection

Turner noted subjects in Patterdale in the *Tweed and Lakes* sketchbook, of 1797 (T.B., XXXV–44, 45). The mood and style of this drawing are close to those of Malham Cove (No. 533) and these may have been intended as a pair.

548 Arthington Mill, on the Wharfe *c.* 1815–20

Watercolour over pencil, 273 × 387
Engr.: by J. C. Allen, date unknown (R. 168); not publ.
Prov.: J. E. Taylor, sale Christie 5 July 1912 (54), bt. Agnew; H. J. Mullen; James Blair, by whom bequeathed, 1917
Coll.: City Art Gallery, Manchester (1917.98)

A large pencil drawing for this subject, inscribed 'Arthington' is T.B., CLIV-M. Among the drawings for Fawkes listed on p. 52 of the *Greenwich* sketchbook (T.B., CII) are noted 'Mill. finished Mill. sketch'. These may be connected with this drawing. Another version of the subject is No. 549.

549 Arthington Mill *c.* 1815

Watercolour over pencil, with some scraping-out, 275 × 385
Prov.: Revd. Richard Hall, of Harewood; by descent to Dr. James Braithwaite (by 1914); by descent; anon. sale Sotheby 16 March 1978 (137), bt. Love
Private collection

A note attached to this drawing claims that the first owner watched Turner while he made it. Apart from

a slight variation in the figures and general divergence of detail, this is exactly the same composition as No. 548. In view of Fawkes's comment that 'everybody is delighted with your Mill' (see *Life*, p. 228), it is likely that Turner was asked to repeat the subject for a friend of Fawkes (Hall was rector of the nearby parish of Harewood); but on stylistic grounds it seems possible that this is in fact an earlier treatment of the subject. It is less elaborate in its handling, preserving more of the characteristics of a study, and is rather difficult to date precisely.

550 Bardon Tower, on the Wharfe *c.* 1815

Watercolour, 279 × 350
Prov.: Mrs. Stern, sale Christie 19 June 1908 (51), bt. Gooden & Fox; J. D. Hughes, sale Christie 31 May 1912 (63), bt. Wyndham; by descent to the Hon. Mark Wyndham, sale Christie 7 March 1972 (77), bt. Wilberforce
Private collection, U.K.

551 Ullswater Lake, from Gowbarrow Park, Cumberland 1815–8

Watercolour and scratching-out, 280 × 413
Exh.: Grosvenor Place 1819 (8)
Prov.: Walter Fawkes; by descent to Revd. Ayscough Fawkes, sale Christie 27 June 1890 (38), bt. Agnew; presented by the Guarantors of the Royal Jubilee Exhibition, 1887
Coll.: Whitworth Art Gallery, University of Manchester (D.14.1887)

For this subject Turner seems to have had recourse to drawings made in the *Tweed and Lakes* sketchbook (T.B., XXXV–40, 43).

552 Coniston Water, with Tent Lodge 1818

Watercolour and body-colour on grey paper, 501 × 660
Exh.: Grosvenor Place 1819 (17)
Prov.: Walter Fawkes; Admiral Fawkes; A. W. Fawkes, by whom bequeathed to the museum, 1942
Coll.: Syndics of the Fitzwilliam Museum, Cambridge (2477; Cormack 19)

553 Tent Lodge, Coniston Water *c.* 1815

Body-colour on grey paper, 508 × 597
Prov.: Walter Fawkes; F. B. Hart-Jackson, Ulverston
Coll.: untraced

554 The Old Man, Coniston Lake (a sketch) *c.* 1815

Body-colour on grey paper, 508 × 597
Exh.: Grosvenor Place 1819 (15)
Prov.: Walter Fawkes; by descent to Major Le G. G. Horton-Fawkes and the present owner
Private collection

555 Windermere 1821

Watercolour, 292 × 407
Signed and dated lower right: *JMW Turner RA 1821*
Exh.: Leeds 1839 (62)
Prov.: Walter Fawkes; by descent to Revd. Ayscough Fawkes, sale Christie 27 June 1890 (37), bt. Agnew; Sir Donald Currie; Major F. D. Mirrielees, sale Christie 20 March 1959 (57), bt. Agnew
Private collection

X(b) Nos 556–558
Three designs for Surtees's *History of Durham,* *c.* 1817

These subjects were engraved by Samuel Rawle in 1819 and 1820 for Robert Surtees's *History of Durham,* Turner collected all the relevant material in the *Raby* sketchbook T.B., CLVI), which he used while staying in the north in the autumn of 1817. He was also working on the commission for a view of Raby to be painted for Lord Darlington (P136).

556 Hylton Castle, Durham *c.* 1817

Watercolour, 198 × 280
Engr.: by S. Rawle for Surtees's History of Durham 1816–23 (R. 141)
Prov.: Mrs. Bowes, Streatham Castle
Private collection

Turner's initial drawing of this view is in the *Raby* sketchbook (T.B., CLVI–10); a colour-beginning for the composition is T.B., CXCVII–P.

557 Gibside, Co. Durham *c.* 1817

Watercolour, 191 × 280
Engr.: by S. Rawle for Surtees's *History of Durham,* 1816–23 (R. 142)
Prov.: Mrs. Bowes, Streatham Castle
Private collection

The view is noted in the *Raby* sketchbook (T.B., CLVI, 3v–4). There is another watercolour of this subject in the same collection, made from a more distant viewpoint.

558 Raby Castle *c.* 1817

Watercolour, size unknown
Engr.: by S. Rawle for Surtees's *History of Durham,* 1816–23 (R. 143)
Provenance and whereabouts unknown

Turner made many drawings of Raby in the *Raby* sketchbook (T.B., CLVI); see also the painting of 1817–8 (P136).

X(c) Nos 559–581
Designs for Whitaker's *History of Richmond-shire, c.* 1816–1821

Thomas Dunham Whitaker, whose *History of Whalley* and *History of Craven* Turner had illustrated around 1800, projected his comprehensive history of Yorkshire in about 1816, when he approached Turner to make drawings for him. There were to have been some 120 subjects in the complete work, but only one part, *The History of Richmondshire,* was published by Longmans between 1819 and 1823. For this, between 1816 and 1818, Turner made twenty drawings for a fee of twenty-five guineas each. Turner gathered subject-matter in a series of sketchbooks, labelled *Yorkshire 1–6* (T.B., CXLIV, CXLV, CXLVI, CXLVII, CXLVIII, CXLIX), used on an industrious visit to Yorkshire in July and August 1816, and probably on other visits as well.

559 Richmond, Yorkshire *c.* 1818

Watercolour, 290 × 417
Engr.: by W. R. Smith, 1819, for Whitaker's *History of Richmondshire,* 1819–23 (R. 169)
Prov.: John Ruskin; given by the Executors of Robert Clarke Edwards to the museum, 1938
Coll.: Victoria and Albert Museum, London (P. 17–1938)

A pencil drawing for this subject is in the *Yorkshire 5* sketchbook (T.B., CXLVIII, 10v–11).

560 Richmond Castle and Town *c.* 1818

Watercolour, size unknown
Engr.: by J. Archer, 1820, for Whitaker's *History of Richmondshire,* 1819–23 (R. 170)
Prov.: John Ruskin
Coll.: untraced

A pencil drawing of this subject is in the *Yorkshire 5* sketchbook (T.B., CXLVIII–12v, continued on p. 41).

561 St. Agatha's Abbey, near Richmond, Yorkshire *c.* 1821

Watercolour over pencil, with scraping-out, 288 × 415
Engr.: by J. Le Keux, 1822, for Whitaker's *History of Richmondshire,* 1819–23 (R. 171)
Exh.: C.G. 1823 (152); B.M. 1975 (ex cat.)
Prov.: Sir Thomas Lawrence, P.R.A.; Revd. C. J. Sale; Mrs. Sale, by whom bequeathed to the museum, 1915
Coll.: Trustees of the British Museum (1915–3-13-48)

For this subject Turner used a view that he had treated in about 1800 (see No. 273); but he made a new pencil drawing on the spot in the *Yorkshire 2* sketchbook (T.B., CXLV–112). See also a later colour-beginning of the subject (No. 892).

562 Aske Hall *c.* 1820

Watercolour, 280 × 413
Engr.: by J. Scott 1820 for Whitaker's *History of Richmondshire,* 1819–23 (R. 172)
Prov.: Abel Buckley; Humphrey Roberts, ? sale Christie 23 May 1908 (284), bt. Gooden; Marchioness of Zetland, sale Sotheby's 30 November 1960 (91), bt. Pantzer, who later sold it back to the Marchioness of Zetland
Coll.: The Marchioness of Zetland, Aske, Richmond

There is a drawing of this title at the Astley Cheetham Art Gallery, Stalybridge, Cheshire, which has been generally accepted as Turner's original design for the *Richmondshire* plate; but although it is convincingly executed in parts, it does not altogether withstand scrutiny. It is presumably a close copy of the original drawing by another hand.

563 High Force or Fall of Tees 1816–8

Watercolour, 285 × 407
Engr.: by J. Landseer, 1822, for Whitaker's *History of Richmondshire,* 1819–23 (R. 173)
Prov.: H. A. J. Munro of Novar; T. S. Kennedy, sale Christie 18 May 1895 (93), bt. Agnew; Marshall; Sir A. J. Forbes–Leith; by descent to the present owner
Private collection

Turner made drawings along the Tees in the *Yorkshire 5* sketchbook (T.B., CXLVIII). No. 564 is another version of the same composition.

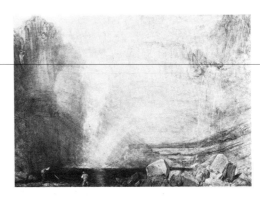

564 High Force, Fall of the Tees, Yorkshire 1816–8

Watercolour, 283 × 403
Exh.: Grosvenor Place 1819 (12); Leeds 1839 (66)

Prov.: Walter Fawkes; by descent to Revd. Ayscough Fawkes, sale Christie 27 June 1890 (39), bt. Sir H. Doulton, from whose daughter bt. Colnaghi, from whom bt. by gallery, 1947
Coll.: Art Gallery of New South Wales, Sydney

A version with some modifications of the *Richmondshire* subject, No. 563.

565 Egglestone Abbey, near Barnard Castle *c.* 1818

Watercolour, 286 × 419
Engr.: by T. Higham 1822 for Whitaker's *History of Richmondshire,* 1819–23 (R. 174)
Prov.: Thomas Brown, sale Christie 8 June 1869 (649), bt. Colnaghi; John Ruskin, sale 22 July 1882 (54), bt. in; A. Severn; Lord Derby
Private collection

Turner's original drawing of Egglestone for this composition is in the *North of England* sketchbook, of 1797 (T.B., XXXIV–27); but he made further studies of the subject in the *Yorkshire 4* sketchbook (T.B., CXLVII–31r and v).

566 Junction of Greta and Tees at Rokeby 1816–8

Watercolour over pencil, with scratching-out, 290 × 414
Engr.: by J. Pye 1819 for Whitaker's *History of Richmondshire,* 1819–23 (R. 175)
Exh.: Society of Painters in Water Colours 1850 (291)
Prov.: J. Dillon, sale Foster 7 and 9 June 1856 (141); John Ruskin, by whom given to the Ruskin School, Oxford 1875; transferred to the museum, 1938
Coll.: Visitors of the Ashmolean Museum, Oxford (Herrmann 79)

Herrmann identifies the rough sketch on p. 29v of the *Yorkshire 5* sketchbook (T.B., CXLVIII) as showing this composition. A fuller pencil note of the subject is T.B., CLIV–K.

567 Brignall Church, Yorkshire *c.* 1820

Watercolour, size unknown
Engr.: by S. Rawle, 1822, for Whitaker's *History of Richmondshire,* 1819–23 (R. 176)
Exh.: C.G. 1824 (155)
Prov.: J. Slegg; Thomas Griffith; C. S. Bale; destroyed by fire while in the possession of Bale (see Thornbury, p. 597)

Studies of Brignall and its church occur in the *Yorkshire 4* sketchbook (T.B., CXLVII–28, 30).

568 Wycliffe, near Rokeby *c.* 1820

Watercolour and body-colour, 292 × 430
Engr.: by J. Pye, 1823, for Whitaker's *History of Richmondshire,* 1819–23 (R. 177)
Prov.: Cosmo Orme (of Longman's), sale Christie 7 March 1884 (42), bt. Agnew; H. Roberts; Mrs. George Holt; Miss Eva Melly, by whom bequeathed to the gallery, 1944
Coll.: Walker Art Gallery, Liverpool (1096)

Turner's pencil study of this composition is in the *Yorkshire 4* sketchbook (T.B., CXLVII–26).

569 Merrick Abbey, Swaledale *c.* 1820

Watercolour, 282 × 413
Engr.: by J. C. Varrall, 1822, for Whitaker's *History of Richmondshire,* 1819–23 (R. 178)
Prov.: Thomas Brown, sale Christie 8 June 1869 (651), bt. Colnaghi; John Ruskin; J. Irvine Smith; A. Levy, sale Christie 1 April 1876 (280), bt.

Agnew; Revd. W. MacGregor, sale Christie 23 April 1937 (12), bt. Fine Art Society, London
Coll.: Major-Gen. and Mrs. J. H. S. Bowring

570 Aysgarth Force 1817

Watercolour over pencil, 280 × 404
Engr.: by J. Scott, 1820, for Whitaker's *History of Richmondshire,* 1819–23 (R. 179)
Prov.: W. T. Houldsworth; William Carver; Sir Donald Currie; Mrs. Walter James; L. Crispin Warmington, sale by order of the Executrix, Sotheby 14 March 1962 (120), bt. Mitchell
Coll.: Pantzer Collection, Indianapolis

Based on a pencil drawing in the *Yorkshire 4* sketchbook (T.B., CXLVII–11).

571 Simmer Lake, near Askrigg *c.* 1820

Watercolour, some scratching-out, 287 × 412
Sig. lower right: *IMW Turner RA*
Engr.: by H. Le Keux, 1822, for Whitaker's *History of Richmondshire,* 1819–23 (R. 180)
Prov.: Cosmo Orme (of Longman's), sale Christie 7 March 1884 (44), bt. Agnew; George Salting, by whom bequeathed to the museum, 1910
Coll.: Trustees of the British Museum (1910–2-12–280)

There are drawings of Simmer Lake, or 'Simmer Water', in the *Yorkshire 4* sketchbook (T.B., CXLVII, 2–4).

572 Mossdale Fall *c.* 1816–8

Watercolour with scraping-out, 291 × 418
Engr.: by J. Middiman, 1822, for Whitaker's *History of Richmondshire,* 1819–23 (R. 181)
Exh.: C.G. 1824 (164)
Prov.: J. Slegg; Revd. W. Kingsley; John Ruskin, who gave it to the museum, 1861

Coll.: Syndics of the Fitzwilliam Museum, Cambridge (571; Cormack 16)

The pencil drawing on which this watercolour is based occurs in the *Yorkshire 5* sketchbook (T.B., CXLVIII, 15v–16). For another version of the subject see No. 573.

---

573 Mossdale Fall *c.* 1816–8

Watercolour, 291 × 418
Prov.: Miss C. L. Adamson, 1951
Coll.: untraced

Cormack records this drawing as a version of No. 572.

574 Hardraw Fall *c.* 1816–8

Watercolour with scraping-out, 292 × 415
Engr.: by S. Middiman and J. Pye, 1818, for Whitaker's *History of Richmondshire,* 1819–23 (R. 182)
Prov.: William Quilter, sale Christie 18 May 1889 (95), bt. Vokins; E. Steinkopf, sale Christie 24 May 1935 (55), bt. Fine Art Society, London; Sir Jeremiah Colman, sale Christie 25 March 1955 (12), bt. Fine Art Society, London; J. E. Bullard, by whom bequeathed to the museum, 1961
Coll.: Syndics of the Fitzwilliam Museum, Cambridge (P.D., 227–1961; Cormack 17)

There are drawings of this subject in the *Yorkshire 5* sketchbook (T.B., CXLVIII–15, 28v).

---

575 Crook of Lune, looking towards Hornby Castle* 1816–8

Watercolour, 280 × 417
Engr.: by J. Archer, 1821, for Whitaker's *History of*

Richmondshire, 1819–23 (R. 183)
Prov.: Cosmo Orme (of Longman's), sale Christie 7 March 1884 (41), bt. Agnew; Revd. W. MacGregor, sale Christie 23 April 1937 (11), bt. Fine Art Society, London; Sir Stephen Courtauld, and presented to the institute in his memory by his family, 1974
Coll.: Courtauld Institute of Art, University of London (4.74; Kitson 6).

Turner made drawings of the Crook of Lune in the *Yorkshire 2* sketchbook (T.B., CXLV), and another, close to this subject, is on p. 4v of the *Yorkshire 5* sketchbook (T.B., CXLVIII). A colour-beginning is T.B., CXCVII–I, and two other colour-studies which are perhaps related are T.B., CXCVI, V and W.

---

576 Ingleborough, from Hornby Castle Terrace 1818

Watercolour, 286 × 419
Signed and dated: 1818
Engr.: by C. Heath, 1822, for Whitaker's *History of Richmondshire,* 1819–23 (R. 184)
Prov.: Bernal; C. S. Bale, sale Christie 14 May 1881 (192), bt. Agnew; W. Law, 1909; by descent to present owner
Private collection

There is a pencil study of this subject in the *Yorkshire 2* sketchbook (T.B., CXLV–62v).

577 Hornby Castle, from Tatham Church 1816–8

Watercolour, 292 × 419
Engr.: by W. Radclyffe, 1822, for Whitaker's *History of Richmondshire,* 1819–23 (R. 185)
Prov.: John Sheepshanks, by whom given to the museum
Coll.: Victoria and Albert Museum, London (88)

A pencil study for this composition is in the *Yorkshire 4* sketchbook (T.B., CXLVII–41v, 42).

---

578 Kirby Lonsdale Churchyard* *c.* 1818

Watercolour, 286 × 415
Engr.: by C. Heath, 1822, for Whitaker's *History of Richmondshire,* 1819–23 (R. 186)
Exh.: R.A. 1974 (180)
Prov.: Cosmo Orme (of Longman's), sale Christie 7 March 1884 (43), bt. Agnew; Sir Donald Currie, by descent to present owner
Private collection

There are drawings of Kirby Lonsdale in the *Yorkshire 2* sketchbook (T.B., CXLV), one of which, on pp. 58–58v, is inscribed: 'The Continuation of K. L. Cyd View'; but it does not correspond with this subject. Further drawings at Kirby Lonsdale are in the *Yorkshire 6* sketchbook (T.B., CXLIX).

579 Heysham and Cumberland Mountains 1818

Watercolour, some scraping-out, 290 × 424
Signed and dated: *JMW Turner 1818*
Engr.: by W. R. Smith, 1822, for Whitaker's *History of Richmondshire,* 1819–23 (R. 187)
Prov.: John Ruskin, sale Christie 22 July 1882 (53), bt. in; George Salting, by whom bequeathed to the museum, 1910
Coll.: Trustees of the British Museum (1910–2–12–274)

Turner made drawings at Heysham in the *Yorkshire 2* sketchbook (T.B., CXLV); the basis for this composition is the sketch on pp. 40v, 41 of the *Yorkshire 4* sketchbook (T.B., CXLVII).

580 Weathercote Cave *c.* 1818

Watercolour, 301 × 423
Engr.: by S. Middiman, 1822, for Whitaker's *History of Richmondshire,* 1819–23 (R. 188)
Exh.: B.M. 1975 (55)
Prov.: Abel Buckley; Agnew 1904; George Salting, by whom bequeathed to the museum, 1910
Coll.: Trustees of the British Museum (1910–2–12–281)

The pencil drawing which was the basis for this subject appears on p. 33v of the *Yorkshire 4* sketchbook (T.B., CXLVII). For another view of Weathercote Fall see No. 541.

581 Lancaster Sands c.1818

Watercolour, 280 × 366
Exh.: Grosvenor Place 1819 (21); Leeds 1839
(77); R.A. 1974 (179)
Prov.: Walter Fawkes; F. H. Fawkes, sale Christie
2 July 1937 (38), bt. Colnaghi; Leslie Wright, by
whom bequeathed to the gallery, 1953
Coll.: City Museums and Art Gallery, Birmingham
(406.53)

A design for Whitaker's *Richmondshire* series, but
not engraved. Studies made in the neighbourhood
of Lancaster occur in the *Yorkshire 5* sketchbook
(T.B., CXLVIII), though there is no sketch of this
subject. Another view of Lancaster Sands appears
in the *England and Wales* series (No. 803).

X(d) Nos 582–631
Views of Farnley and neighbourhood made for Walter Fawkes, c.1815–1819

Armstrong (p. 252) distinguishes thirteen views of
the house and garden at Farnley, all approx. 13 ×
17 inches (330 × 430), as forming a set, executed
between 1815 and 1820. One of these, 'Farnley,
Yorkshire, a sketch', was exhibited by Fawkes at his
exhibition in 1819 (10), but this is difficult to
identify. The whole set comprised Nos 583–586,
590–598. Here, the set is incorporated into the
group as a whole, which Fawkes seems to have
referred to as 'the Wharfedales'; though it is plain
from a reference in a letter to the drawing of
Arthington Mill (No. 548) in this context that other
subjects were also included under that heading
(see *Life*, p. 228). Of the drawings no longer in the
Fawkes collection several have been confused on
account of the similarity of their titles. Dating is also
a problem. The majority of the works catalogued
here have been assigned to the period about 1818,
since Turner is known to have executed some of
them in that year. In fact work on them probably
continued from 1815 until about 1819. The drawings vary from loose sketches, often executed on a
grey ground or grey paper in black chalk and
body-colour, to fully worked-up watercolours on
white paper. Many of them were shown at the
Holburne of Menstrie Museum, Bath, *J. M. W. Turner, Watercolours from Farnley Hall*, 1959.

582 At Farnley Hall (a frontispiece) 1815

Watercolour over pencil, with pen and ink and a
little scratching-out, 178 × 242

Signed and dated lower right: *JMW Turner RA
1815*
Prov.: Walter Fawkes; Charles Stokes; John
Ruskin; by whom given to the Ruskin School,
Oxford, 1875; transferred to the museum, 1938
Coll.: Visitors of the Ashmolean Museum, Oxford
(Herrmann 77)

The family of Walter Fawkes owned a collection of
relics of the Cromwellian general, Thomas Fairfax
(1612–71), and in about 1815 Turner made a
series of drawings depicting them and commemo-
rating Fairfax's involvement in the Civil War. These
drawings are contained in an album entitled *Fairfaxiana*. Some preliminary studies for the project
are in the Turner Bequest (T.B., CLIV–B, C, D, E). This
drawing, which seems to have been intended as a
frontispiece for the *Fairfaxiana*, left Fawkes's hands
at an early date, through Colnaghi's, who sold it to
Charles Stokes. It was acquired from Stokes by
Ruskin, to whom Stokes related that Turner told
him 'the helmet, drinking-cup, and sword were
those of a knight of that family [i.e. Fawkes's] who
was called Black Jack'. One of the *Fairfaxiana*
designs, *Drawings of the Swords of Cromwell,
Fairfax, Lambert, &c.*, was exhibited at the Leeds
exhibition of drawings from Fawkes's collection in
1839 (40). The album is not included in this
catalogue (for a drawing of the Fairfax Cabinet see
No. 583 below). In 1850 Hawksworth Fawkes
sent Turner a copy of a catalogue he had compiled
of all Turner's drawings at Farnley. In a letter to him
of 27 December Turner acknowledged the catalogue and added: 'Fairfax's Sword Black Jug and the
Warrant I do not find?', which suggests that the
frontispiece, which shows those items, had already
left Farnley (see Finberg, *Life*, p. 430).

583 Fairfax Cabinet, Farnley c.1815

Body-colour on grey paper, approx. 330 × 430
(opening doors pasted on)
Prov.: Walter Fawkes; by descent to present
owner
Private collection

Listed by Armstrong as one of the thirteen Farnley
subjects, but possibly executed as part of the
'Fairfaxiana' project, c. 1815 (see No. 582).

584 Front door and porch, Farnley c.1815

Body-colour on grey paper, 268 × 320 (sight)
Inscr.: *FARNLEY HALL*
Engr.: by engraver unknown for Whitaker's *Loidis
and Elmete*, 1816, and entitled 'Flower Garden
Porch at Farnley removed from Newhall
A.D. 1814' (R. 84)
Prov.: Walter Fawkes; by descent to present
owner
Private collection

T. D. Whitaker's *Loidis and Elmete* was published in
1816 with five plates after Turner (for two of these
see Nos 219, 543). Three were etched by an
unknown hand, possibly Turner's own, after views
taken at Farnley Hall. The full title of the work was:
'*LOIDIS AND ELMETE* or/an attempt to illustrate/
the/District described in those words by Bede:/
and supposed to embrace the/Lower Portions of
Airedale and Wharfedale,/together with/The
Entire Vale of Calder/in the/County of York/by
Thomas Dunham Whitaker, L. L. D., F. S. A. Vicar of
Whalley, and Rector of Heysham in Lancashire
1816.' These three drawings (Nos 584, 585, 586)
belong, however, to the larger group of Farnley
views catalogued below (Nos 587–631).

585 Gateway to the Flower Garden at Farnley c.1815

Body-colour and black chalk on grey paper,
320 × 406 (sight)
Engr.: by engraver unknown for Whitaker's *Loidis
and Elmete*, 1816, and entitled 'Gateway to the
Flower Garden at Farnley removed from Monston
Hall, formerly the seat of Col. Charles Fairfax A.D.
1814' (R. 85)
Prov.: Walter Fawkes; by descent to present
owner
Private collection

A drawing possibly of this gateway is on p. 1v of the
Devon Rivers No. 3 and Wharfedale sketchbook

(T.B., CXXXIV). Turner drew the entrance to the gardens in the *Devon Rivers No. 2* sketchbook (T.B., CXXXIII–5v and 6v). See No. 584.

586 Garden Front, with sundial, Farnley *c.* 1815

Body-colour and black chalk on grey paper, 303 × 403 (sight)
Engr.: by engraver unknown for Whitaker's *Loidis and Elmete*, 1816, and entitled 'Bay windows in the Flower Garden at Farnley removed from Lindley Hall, an ancient seat of the Palmes Family by W. Fawkes, Esq., A.D. 1814' (R. 86)
Prov.: Walter Fawkes; by descent to present owner
Private collection

See No. 584.

587 View of Farnley Hall *c.* 1818

Body-colour and black chalk on grey paper, 311 × 394
Prov.: Walter Fawkes; by descent to present owner
Private collection

Compare the composition of Turner's view of *Rosehill, Sussex* (No. 438 above).

588 The West Lodge, Farnley *c.* 1818

Body-colour on grey paper, 329 × 444
Exh.: R.A. 1974 (191)
Prov.: Walter Fawkes; by descent to present owner
Private collection

Turner's drawing of the West Lodge, used as the basis for this watercolour, is in the *Farnley* sketchbook (T.B., CLIII, 14v–15). The subject is also known as 'Otley Lodge and Bridge'.

589 Gate and Lodges, Farnley *c.* 1818

Body-colour on grey paper, 300 × 414 (sight)
Prov.: Walter Fawkes; by descent to the present owner
Private collection

This is East Lodge, known as 'Turner's Lodge', as he is said to have designed it. A drawing of the new lodge is on pp. 13v and 14 of the *Farnley* sketchbook (T.B., CLIII).

590 Grand Staircase, Farnley *c.* 1818

Body-colour on grey paper, 326 × 422 (sight)
Prov.: Walter Fawkes; by descent to present owner

Private collection

591 Morning-room, Farnley *c.* 1818

Body-colour on grey paper, 314 × 428 (sight)
Prov.: Walter Fawkes; by descent to present owner
Private collection

The room shown in the drawing was originally the dining-room designed by Robert Adam.

592 Drawing-room, Farnley 1818

Body-colour on grey paper, 315 × 412
Exh.: R.A. 1974 (189)
Prov.: Walter Fawkes; by descent to present owner
Private collection

The Music-room, with Turner's own *Dort* (P137) hanging above the fireplace.

593 Oak-panelled room, with Fairfax Chair, Farnley *c.*1818

Body-colour on grey paper, 283 × 400 (sight)
Prov.: Walter Fawkes; by descent to present owner
Private collection

594 Oak Staircase, Farnley *c.*1818

Body-colour on grey paper, 318 × 411 (sight)
Exh.: R.A. 1974 (190)
Prov.: Walter Fawkes; by descent to present owner
Private collection

595 Library, Farnley *c.*1818

Body-colour on grey paper, 323 × 429 (sight)
Prov.: Walter Fawkes; by descent to present owner
Private collection

A drawing of the Library is on pp. 15v–16 of the *Farnley* sketchbook (T.B., CLIII).

596 Library, with heraldic window, Farnley *c.*1818

Body-colour on grey paper, 310 × 405 (sight)
Prov.: Walter Fawkes; by descent to present owner
Private collection

597 Conservatory, with memorial window, Farnley *c.*1818

Pen and black ink and body-colour over black chalk on grey paper, 332 × 416 (sight)
Prov.: Walter Fawkes; by descent to present owner
Private collection

598 Memorial window, Farnley 1819

Body-colour on grey paper, 290 × 318 (sight)
Inscr. above, centre: *1819*
Prov.: Walter Fawkes; by descent to present owner
Private collection

599 The Old Dairy, Farnley *c.*1818

Body-colour on grey paper, 275 × 390 (sight)
Prov.: Walter Fawkes; by descent to present owner
Private collection

600 The Avenue, Farnley* *c.*1818

Black chalk, watercolour and body-colour on a ?grey ground, 311 × 419 (sight)
Prov.: John Ruskin, sale Christie 22 July 1882 (57), bt. in; Arthur Severn
Coll.: Mrs. Cecil Keith

A drawing of the Avenue at Farnley is in the *Devon Rivers No. 2* sketchbook (T.B., CXXXIII–78).

601 The Carriage Drive, Farnley *c.*1818

Body-colour on grey paper, 293 × 409 (sight)
Prov.: Walter Fawkes; by descent to present owner
Private collection

602 The Woodwalk, Farnley Hall *c.*1818

Watercolour and body-colour on grey paper, 292 × 400
Prov.: Walter Fawkes, by descent to Revd. Ayscough Fawkes (not in 1890 sale); F. Stevenson, 1912; R. Norton, sale Christie 26 May 1919

(130), bt. Sampson; Herbert Dean, sale, Sotheby 19 November 1947 (132), bt. Agnew; Major Horton-Fawkes; Agnew; Gilbert Davis, sale Sotheby 19 March 1958 (105), bt. Messrs. John Mitchell, from whom purchased by the museum (Fairhaven Fund), 1958
Coll.: Syndics of the Fitzwilliam Museum, Cambridge (PD. 50–1958; Cormack 18)

603 The Pheasant's Nest, Farnley Park *c.* 1818

Black chalk, watercolour and body-colour, 281 × 394
Prov.: Walter Fawkes; by descent to Mr. Justice Fawkes, by whom bequeathed to the gallery, 1942
Coll.: South African National Gallery, Cape Town

604 Farnley Park: the Pheasant's Nest *c.* 1818

Body-colour on grey paper, 305 × 413
Prov.: John Ruskin, sale Christie 22 July 1882 (56, as 'Farnley–Summer House'), bt. in; Arthur Severn; Lord Derby
Private collection

A drawing of this subject is in the *Hastings* sketchbook (T.B., CXXXIX–1 and inside cover).

605 Lake Plantation, Farnley *c.* 1818

Watercolour, 386 × 394
Prov.: Walter Fawkes; by descent to present owner
Private collection

606 Lake Tiny, Farnley Park *c.* 1818

Body-colour, 280 × 381
Exh.: Leeds 1839 (91)
Prov.: Walter Fawkes; by descent to present owner
Private collection

Drawings of Lake Tiny are in the *Hastings* sketchbook and in the *Farnley* sketchbook (T.B., CXXXIX, 36v–39, CLIII–1v, 2, 3).

607 Lake Tiny, with Almias Cliff in the distance *c.* 1818

Watercolour and body-colour on ? grey paper, 330 × 439
Prov.: Walter Fawkes; by descent to W. R. Fawkes, sale Christie 2 July 1937 (55), bt. Gooden & Fox; E. E. Cook, by whom bequeathed to the gallery through the National Art-Collections Fund, 1955
Coll.: Hereford City Museum and Art Galleries

The pencil drawing on which this watercolour is based is in the *Farnley* sketchbook (T.B., CLIII–1v, 2, 3).

608 Grounds of Farnley Hall *c.* 1818

Body-colour on grey paper, 330 × 439
Prov.: Walter Fawkes; by descent to Revd. Ayscough Fawkes, sale Christie 27 June 1890 (42, as 'In Wharfedale—ducks in a Pond'), bt. Donaldson; G. P. Wall, sale Christie 16 March 1912 (116, as 'Grounds of Farnley Hall'), bt. Agnew; Yates Thompson, sale by order of Executors of Mrs. Yates Thompson, Sotheby 2 July 1941 (222); Humphrey Neame, sale Sotheby 12 July 1967 (197), bt. Agnew
Private collection

609 The Wharfe, from Farnley Hall *c.* 1818

Body-colour on grey paper, 296 × 416 (sight)
Exh.: R.A. 1974 (192)
Prov.: Walter Fawkes; by descent to present owner
Private collection

610 Shooting party on Hawksworth Moor *c.* 1815

Watercolour with scratching-out, 280 × 397
Sig. lower left: *JMW* Turner
Prov.: Walter Fawkes; by descent to present owner
Private collection

Turner's pencil drawing of this subject is in the *Large Farnley* sketchbook (T.B. CXXVIII–10). Although the watercolour has always belonged with the

Farnley series (Nos 587–631), it is stylistically different from them and seems to date from slightly earlier.

611   Caley Park, Otley Chevin *c*. 1818

Body-colour on grey paper, 340 × 434
Prov.: Walter Fawkes; by descent to W. R. Fawkes, sale Christie 2 July 1937 (51), bt. in; by descent to present owner
Private collection

A drawing of Caley Park, Otley Chevin, is in the *Farnley* sketchbook (T.B., CLIII, 5v–6).

612   Caley Hall *c*. 1818

Body-colour on buff paper, 299 × 411
Prov.: Walter Fawkes; by descent to W. R. Fawkes; Sir Thomas Barlow; Helen Barlow, by whom bequeathed to the gallery, 1976
Coll.: National Galleries of Scotland, Edinburgh (05023-41)

613   Farnley Hall, from above Otley *c*. 1815

Watercolour, 280 × 398
Prov.: Walter Fawkes; John Ruskin; anon. sale Sotheby 18 July 1974 (123, as 'Wharfedale from the Chevin—Farnley from above Otley'), bt. Marshall Spink
Coll.: Brian Pilkington, London

614   View of Otley Mills *c*. 1815

Watercolour, size unknown
Prov.: Walter Fawkes; by descent to Revd. Ayscough Fawkes; sold anonymously to Sedelmeyer 28 June 1890
Coll.: untraced

615   Wharfedale, from the Chevin *c*. 1816

Body-colour, 264 × 369
Sig. lower right: *JMW Turner RA PP*
Exh.: Grosvenor Place 1819 (11)
Prov.: Walter Fawkes; John Ruskin; Fine Art Society, London, from whom bt. by donor, 1961, and donated anonymously to the museum, 1971
Coll.: Museum of Art, Rhode Island School of Design, Providence, R.I. (anon. gift 71.153.6)

616   The Deer Park, Caley Hall *c*. 1818

Watercolour, 280 × 381
Sig.: *JMW Turner RA PP*
Prov.: Walter Fawkes; by descent to W. R. Fawkes, sale Christie 2 July 1937 (47), bt. Allon Dawson; by descent to present owner
Private collection

Turner made a drawing of the deer park in the *Farnley* sketchbook (T.B., CLIII, 7v–8).

617   Valley of the Wharfe, from Caley Park *c*. 1815

Body-colour, 298 × 445
Exh.: Grosvenor Place 1819 (9); Leeds 1839 (26, as 'Wharfedale from Chevin Deer Park')
Prov.: Walter Fawkes; by descent to W. R. Fawkes, sale Christie 2 July 1937 (46), bt. Allon Dawson; by descent to present owner
Private collection

A pencil drawing of the Wharfe valley from Caley Park is in the *Hastings* sketchbook (T.B., CXXXIX, 39v–41).

618   View across the Wharfe, from Caley Park *c*. 1818

Body-colour on grey paper, 327 × 440 (sight)
Prov.: Walter Fawkes; by descent to present owner
Private collection

619 Farnley Hall, from the junction of the Wharfe and the Washburn *c.* 1818

Watercolour, 306 × 437
Exh.: Leeds 1839 (92)
Prov.: Walter Fawkes; by descent to W. R. Fawkes, sale Christie 2 July 1937 (45), bt. Colnaghi; Walter Stoye; by descent to present owner
Private collection

620 Valley of the Washburn and Leathly Church, Farnley *c.* 1818

Black and coloured chalks and ?body-colour, 272 × 385 (sight)
Exh.: ? Leeds 1839 (93)
Prov.: Walter Fawkes; by descent to present owner
Private collection

621 View across the Wharfe towards Lindley Hall *c.* 1818

Watercolour, 280 × 381

Prov.: Walter Fawkes; J. Leslie Wright, by whom bequeathed to the gallery, 1953
Coll.: City Museums and Art Gallery, Birmingham (404.53)

This drawing has hitherto been known as 'Landscape with a rainbow'. It is possible that this may be the same subject as that listed in Finberg's 'Index' as 'Wharfedale in flood', from the Farnley collection.

622 Lindley Hall *c.* 1818

Body-colour on grey paper, 265 × 387
Prov.: Walter Fawkes; by descent to present owner
Private collection

Drawings of Lindley Hall are in the *Munro* sketchbook, which was in use in the early 1820s (see Finberg, *The Connoisseur*, 1935), and this and some of the Lindley subjects listed here may have been executed rather later than the date suggested.

623 Lindley Hall, with Lindley Bridge *c.* 1818

Body-colour on grey paper, 398 × 445
Prov.: Walter Fawkes; by descent to present owner
Private collection

A large pencil study of this view is T.B., CLIV–W. A smaller sketch of the same subject occurs on another sheet, T.B., CLIV–X.

624 Lindley Bottom *c.* 1818

Watercolour, 330 × 451
Prov.: Walter Fawkes; by descent to W. R. Fawkes,

sale Christie 2 July 1937 (54), bt. Allon Dawson; by descent to present owner
Private collection

625 Valley of the Washburn and Lindley Bridge *c.* 1818

Body-colour, 280 × 381
Prov.: Walter Fawkes
Private collection, Canada

626 Banks of the Washburn? *c.* 1818

Watercolour, 330 × 407
Prov.: Walter Fawkes
Coll.: untraced

This drawing was exhibited at Agnew's, 1951 (33).

627 The Washburn, from Leathly Church *c.* 1818

Body-colour on brown paper, 298 × 426
Prov.: Walter Fawkes; by descent to W. R. Fawkes, sale Christie 2 July 1937 (49), bt. Allon Dawson; by descent to present owner
Private collection

628 Steeton Manor House, near Farnley *c.* 1815–8

Watercolour and scraping-out, 105 × 162 (sheet 114 × 170, with a ruled pen line round drawing)
Prov.: Walter Fawkes; J. Irvine Smith; C. Morland Agnew; Alan G. Agnew; Mrs. Desmond Whitaker; Agnew, from whom bt. by Paul Mellon, 1964
Coll.: Yale Center for British Art, Paul Mellon Collection

Dated by Finberg to about 1818, this drawing is quite exceptional in being so small in size; Turner did not make any other finished watercolours on this scale until his work for Cadell and Finden in the 1830s.

629   Farnley in olden time   *c.*1818

Body-colour on grey paper, 278 × 393 (sight)
Exh.: Leeds 1839 (19, as 'Old Farnley Hall')
Prov.: Walter Fawkes; by descent to present owner
Private collection

630   Newall Old Hall   *c.*1818

Body-colour on grey paper, 315 × 412 (sight)
Prov.: Walter Fawkes; by descent to present owner
Private collection

A drawing of Newall Old Hall is in the *Devon Rivers No. 2* sketchbook (T.B., CXXXIII, 4v–5); a colour-beginning of the subject is T.B., CLIV–P. The doorway shown here was removed to Farnley in 1814 (see No. 584).

631   Hawksworth Hall   *c.*1818

Body-colour on grey paper, 268 × 388 (sight)
Prov.: Walter Fawkes; by descent to present owner
Private collection

X(e)   Nos 632–635
Studies of game birds, *c.* 1815–1820

These studies all probably originated at Farnley, where Turner was a keen participant in shooting-parties (see No. 610). Fawkes's brother was an amateur ornithologist, and Turner compiled a 'Book of Birds', consisting of seventeen sheets with drawings of twenty birds (said to have been shot by the artist): Grouse; Dead Wood Pigeon; The Partridge (head); The Moor Game (head) and Green woodpecker (head); Guinea Fowl (head) and The Moor Hawk (head); Woodcock (head); White owl (head); Redbreast; The Jay; Heron eating Fish (head); Peacock (head and neck); Goldfinch; Game-Cock; Dead Kingfisher; Cuckoo (head) and Pheasant (head); Pheasant (head); Turkey.
A pencil study of the dead kingfisher is in the *Devonshire Rivers No. 3 and Wharfedale* sketchbook (T.B., CXXXIV–1; see Finberg, *Connoisseur*, 1912). Two studies of a teal are in the Turner Bequest (T.B., CCLXIII–340, 341). Two further sheets which appear to be connected with Farnley are the study of a pheasant hanging against a picture frame and the pheasant and woodpecker, both in the Turner Bequest, on paper watermarked *1818* (T.B., CCLXIII–358, 359).

632   A dead blackcock   *c.*1815–20

Watercolour and body-colour over pencil, on paper washed in pinkish-grey, 258 × 231
Prov.: given by the artist to Miss Fawkes (Mrs. Hotham); J. E. Taylor, sale Christie 8 July 1912 (122), bt. Brown & Phillips; R. W. Lloyd, by whom bequeathed to the museum, 1958
Coll.: Trustees of the British Museum (1958–7-12–408)

633   Study of a dead grouse   *c.*1815–20

Watercolour and pencil, 235 × 311
Inscr. lower right-hand margin in Ruskin's hand: *By J.M.W. Turner/Certified. John Ruskin, Brantd/ 24th July 1886*
Prov.: given by the artist to Miss Fawkes (Mrs. Hotham); J. E. Taylor, sale Christie 8 July 1912 (123), bt. Agnew; Major E. A. Mackay, sale Sotheby 14 February 1962 (89), bt. Pantzer, and given to the museum in memory of Dr. and Mrs. Hugo O. Pantzer by their children
Coll.: Indianapolis Museum of Art

634   Sketch of a pheasant   *c.*1815–20

Watercolour over pencil, 223 × 345
Prov.: ?Walter Fawkes; John Ruskin, by whom given to the Ruskin School, Oxford, 1875; transferred to the museum, 1938
Coll.: Visitors of the Ashmolean Museum, Oxford (Herrmann 78)

635   Dead pheasant   *c.*1815–20

Watercolour, 286 × 376
Prov.: Walter Fawkes; John Ruskin, sale Christie 15 April 1869 (11), bt. Vokins; J. E. Taylor, by whom presented to the Whitworth Institute, 1892

Coll.: Whitworth Art Gallery, University of Manchester (D.94.1892)

SECTION XI
Nos 636–696 Rhine subjects, c. 1817–1820

XI (a) Nos 636–686
The fifty-one Rhine drawings, 1817

In August and September of 1817 Turner toured Holland and Belgium and the Rhine between Cologne and Mainz. Preparatory notes for the journey fill the *Itinerary Rhine Tour* sketchbook (T.B., CLIX), which also contains a number of sketches of scenery. The majority of his studies however, are in the *Waterloo and Rhine, Rhine* and *Dort* sketchbooks (T.B., CLX, CLXI and CLXII). The first two of these were drawn on extensively for the subjects of a series of fifty-one small views in watercolour and body-colour on a grey ground, which Turner executed immediately after his return to England—either while he was working at Raby Castle for his oil-painting of that house (P136), or shortly afterwards at Farnley. All the subjects are of views along the Rhine and are characterized by great boldness of execution. They vary considerably in finish, from fairly fully worked-up designs to broad sketches; but Fawkes acquired the whole group, apparently for £500, and they are generally thought of as 'finished' works. In practice, nevertheless, Turner treated several of them as preparatory studies for more highly developed drawings which he produced in about 1820. These fall into two groups: a few larger watercolours on white paper, executed for the Swinburne family (probably Sir John Swinburne chose his subjects from those in Fawkes's hands); and an unfinished set of drawings of roughly the same dimensions as the original fifty-one, and carried out in similar media on a grey ground. These last were to have been published in a series of Rhine views by W. B. Cooke, who exhibited two of them at his gallery in 1823 (see Nos 687–9).

636 Mainz 1817

Body-colour on white paper prepared with a grey wash, 202 × 311
Prov.: Walter Fawkes; by descent to Revd. Ayscough Fawkes, sale Christie 27 June 1890 (1), bt. Vokins; sale Christie 20 March 1896 (177), bt. McLean
Coll.: untraced

637 Mainz 1817

Watercolour, 210 × 340
Prov.: Walter Fawkes; by descent to Revd. Ayscough Fawkes, sale Christie 27 June 1890 (2), bt. Agnew; J. E. Taylor sale, Christie 5 July 1912 (57), bt. Agnew; Walter J. Jones; sale Christie 3 July 1942 (44), bt. Agnew; Sir George F. Davies, from whom bt. Agnew 1956; R. E. Dangerfield; Agnew 1976
Private collection

638 The Bishop's Palace, Biebrich 1817

Watercolour and body-colour and scraping-out on white paper prepared with a grey wash, 229 × 343
Prov.: Walter Fawkes; by descent to Revd. Ayscough Fawkes, sale Christie 27 June 1890 (3), bt. J. Pyke Thompson, by whom bequeathed to the museum, 1898
Coll.: National Museum of Wales, Cardiff (3214)

639 Rudesheim, looking to Bingen Klopp 1817

Watercolour and body-colour and scraping-out on white paper prepared with a grey wash, 203 × 330

Exh.: R.A. 1974 (197)
Prov.: Walter Fawkes; by descent to Revd. Ayscough Fawkes, sale Christie 27 June 1890 (4), bt. J. Pyke Thompson, by whom bequeathed to the museum, 1898
Coll.: National Museum of Wales, Cardiff (3218)

640 Bausenberg in the Brohltal 1817

Body-colour on white paper prepared with a grey wash, 219 × 311
Prov.: Walter Fawkes; by descent to Revd. Ayscough Fawkes, sale Christie 27 June 1890 (5), bt. Agnew; Lloyd Roberts; Agnew 1914; G. Newhouse
Coll.: untraced

641 Furstenburg 1817

Watercolour and body-colour on white paper prepared with a grey wash, 235 × 311
Prov.: Walter Fawkes; by descent to Revd. Ayscough Fawkes, sale Christie 27 June 1890 (6), bt. McLean; anon. sale Christie 20 February 1904 (71), bt. McLean; James Blair, by whom bequeathed to the gallery, 1917
Coll.: City Art Gallery, Manchester (1917.118)

642 Bacharach and Stahleck 1817

Body-colour on white paper prepared with a grey wash, 202 × 311
Prov.: Walter Fawkes; by descent to Revd. Ayscough Fawkes, sale Christie 27 June 1890 (7), bt. McLean; Sir E. Durning Lawrence; anon. sale Christie 2 June 1939 (70), bt. Agnew; J. A. McCallum, 1944
Coll.: untraced

643 Pfalz on the Rhine 1817

Watercolour and body-colour on white paper prepared with a grey wash, 190 × 305
Prov.: Walter Fawkes; by descent to Revd. Ayscough Fawkes, sale Christie 27 June 1890 (8), bt. Hardy; anon. sale Christie 30 June 1939 (46), bt. in; Sir Rupert Hardy, sale Christie 1954 (5), bt. Agnew; J. C. Butterwick; Agnew, 1971
Private collection

644   Oberwesel and Schonberg Castle   1817

Body-colour on white paper prepared with a grey wash, 219 × 356
Prov.: Walter Fawkes; by descent to Revd. Ayscough Fawkes, sale Christie 27 June 1890 (9), bt. Henson; Mary Portman; Viscount Portman; Appleby, 1962, 1965
Coll.: untraced

645   St. Goarhausen and Katz Castle   1817

Watercolour and body-colour on white paper prepared with a grey wash, 193 × 304
Prov.: Walter Fawkes; by descent to Revd. Ayscough Fawkes, sale Christie 27 June 1890 (10), bt. Vokins; sale Christie 20 March 1896 (178), bt. G. R. Burnett, sale Christie 21 March 1908 (27), bt. Agnew; W. G. Rawlinson, 1917; T. A. Tatton, sale Christie 12–14 December 1928 (16); A. J. Finberg; Cotswold Gallery 1930; Sir Stephen Courtauld, and presented by his family to the institute in his memory, 1974
Coll.: Courtauld Institute of Art, University of London (10.74; Kitson 7)

646   Lurleiberg   1817

Watercolour and body-colour and scratching-out on white paper prepared with a grey wash, 197 × 305
Exh.: R.A. 1974 (198)
Prov.: Walter Fawkes; by descent to Revd.

Ayscough Fawkes, sale Christie 27 June 1890 (11), bt. Lord Penrhyn; purchased by the gallery, 1925
Coll.: Whitworth Art Gallery, University of Manchester (D.57.1925)

647   Lurleiberg   1817

Body-colour on white paper prepared with a grey wash, 188 × 300
Prov.: Walter Fawkes; by descent to Revd. Ayscough Fawkes, sale Christie 27 June 1890 (12), bt. Hardy; Sir Algernon Firth; Mrs. Dewar; Sir William Worsley; Agnew
Private collection

648   The Loreleiberg   1817

Watercolour and body-colour on white paper prepared with a grey wash, 202 × 302
Exh.: R.A. 1974 (199)
Prov.: Walter Fawkes; by descent to Revd. Ayscough Fawkes, sale Christie 27 June 1890 (13), bt. Doulton; Agnes and Norman Lupton, by whom bequeathed to the gallery, 1953
Coll.: City Art Galleries, Leeds (13.319/53)

649   Katz Castle and Rheinfels   1817

Watercolour and body-colour, with some scraping-out, on white paper prepared with a grey wash, 190 × 311
Prov.: Walter Fawkes; by descent to Revd. Ayscough Fawkes, sale Christie 27 June 1890 (14), bt. Agnew; H. G. Marquand, sale 1903; Doll & Richards, Boston; T. Jefferson Coolidge; by descent to Dr. Catherine Coolidge; Agnew, 1978
Coll.: Galerie Jan Krugier, Geneva

Armstrong (p. 259) refers to another version of this subject (305 × 425), which was in the L. B. Mozley sale of 1863.

650   Rheinfels looking to Katz and Goarhausen   1817

Watercolour and body-colour on white paper prepared with a grey wash, 200 × 315
Prov.: Walter Fawkes; by descent to Revd. Ayscough Fawkes, sale Christie 27 June 1890 (15), bt. Vokins; anon. sale Christie 5 March 1974 (149), bt. Baskett and Day; bt. by Paul Mellon, 1974
Coll.: Yale Center for British Art, Paul Mellon Collection

651   Bruderbergen on the Rhine   1817

Watercolour and body-colour on white paper prepared with a grey wash, 212 × 327
Prov.: Walter Fawkes; by descent to Revd. Ayscough Fawkes, sale Christie 27 June 1890 (16, as 'Castles of the Two Brothers'), bt. Agnew; J. F. Schwann, sale Christie 15 May 1925 (45), bt. Leggatt; the Hon. Mrs. Dighton-Pollock, who bequeathed it to the museum, 1929
Coll.: Syndics of the Fitzwilliam Museum, Cambridge (1520; Cormack 15)

652   Boppart   1817

Body-colour on white paper prepared with a grey wash, 188 × 311
Prov.: Walter Fawkes; by descent to Revd.

Ayscough Fawkes, sale Christie 27 June 1890 (17), bt. Salomans; Mrs. Mallmann; anon. sale Christie 27 April 1965 (9), bt. Colnaghi; from whom purchased, 1965
Coll.: Mr. and Mrs. Paul Mellon, Upperville, Virginia

653 Marksburg 1817

Watercolour, body-colour, with scraping-out on white paper prepared with a grey wash, 200 × 319
Exh.: R.A. 1974 (195)
Prov.: Walter Fawkes; by descent to Revd. Ayscough Fawkes, sale Christie 27 June 1890 (19), bt. Donaldson; Henry Lee Higginson; Betty Parsons Galleries, New York, 1960, bt. Pantzer; given to the museum in memory of Dr. and Mrs. Hugo O. Pantzer by their children
Coll.: Indianapolis Museum of Art

654 Oberlahnstein 1817

Watercolour and body-colour on white paper prepared with a grey wash, 198 × 316
Prov.: Walter Fawkes; by descent to Revd. Ayscough Fawkes, sale Christie 27 June 1890 (20), bt. Agnew; W. F. Morice, sale, Christie 21 May 1922 (61), bt. Agnew; R. W. Lloyd, by whom bequeathed to the museum, 1958
Coll.: Trustees of the British Museum (1958–7–12–413)

655 Junction of the Lahn and the Rhine 1817

Body-colour on white paper prepared with a grey wash, 196 × 314
Prov.: Walter Fawkes; by descent to Revd. Ayscough Fawkes, sale Christie 27 June 1890 (21), bt. Lord Penrhyn; Frank C. Parker; Sotheby 18 March 1971 (74), bt. Agnew
Private collection

656 Ehrenbreitstein (back view from the Zathel) 1817

Body-colour on white paper prepared with a grey wash, 197 × 311
Prov.: Walter Fawkes; by descent to Revd. Ayscough Fawkes, sale Christie 27 June 1890 (22), bt. Fine Art Society, London; Grenville L. Winthrop, by whom bequeathed to the museum, 1904
Coll.: Fogg Art Museum, Harvard University, Cambridge, Mass. (1904.35)

657 View from Ehrenbreitstein 1817

Body-colour on white paper prepared with a grey wash, 197 × 311
Prov.: Walter Fawkes; by descent to Revd. Ayscough Fawkes, sale Christie 27 June 1890 (23), bt. Agnew; C. F. Martin, Montreal
Coll.: untraced

658 Coblenz: the Quay 1817

Body-colour on white paper prepared with a grey wash, 197 × 311
Prov.: Walter Fawkes; by descent to Revd. Ayscough Fawkes, sale Christie 27 June 1890 (24), bt. McLean
Coll.: untraced

See No. 687.

659 Moselle Bridge at Coblenz 1817

Watercolour and body-colour on white paper prepared with a grey wash, 199 × 311
Prov.: Walter Fawkes; by descent to Revd. Ayscough Fawkes, sale, 27 June 1890 (25), bt. Agnew; Revd. W. MacGregor, sale Christie 23 April 1937 (14), bt. Fine Art Society, London; Lord Astor of Hever, until 1962
Coll.: untraced

660 Weissenthurm and the Hoch Monument 1817

Body-colour on white paper prepared with a grey wash, 197 × 311
Prov.: Walter Fawkes; bt. Agnew 1912 from Farnley; Sir Algernon Firth; Jane Taft Ingalls, by whom bequeathed to the museum, 1962
Coll.: Taft Museum, Cincinnati, Ohio (1962.8.67)

661 Neuwied and Weissenthurm 1817

Body-colour on white paper prepared with a grey wash, 197 × 311
Prov.: Walter Fawkes; by descent to Revd. Ayscough Fawkes, sale Christie 27 June 1890 (26), bt. Agnew; Agnew 1901, 1912; H. Collison 1926
Coll.: untraced

The later *Neuwied* in the National Galleries of Scotland (No. 689) presumably reproduces the composition of this drawing.

662 Andernach 1817

Watercolour and body-colour on white paper prepared with a grey wash, 200 × 312
Prov.: Walter Fawkes; by descent to Revd. Ayscough Fawkes, sale Christie 27 June 1890 (27), by Vokins; anon. sale Christie 5 March 1974 (150), bt. David Peel; bt. by Paul Mellon, 1974
Coll.: Yale Center for British Art, Paul Mellon Collection

663 Roman Tower at Andernach* 1817

Body-colour on white paper prepared with a grey wash, 197 × 311
Prov.: Walter Fawkes; by descent to Revd. Ayscough Fawkes, sale Christie 27 June 1890 (28), bt. Donaldson
Coll.: Isabella Stewart Gardner Museum, Boston, Mass.

664 Hammerstein, below Andernach 1817

Body-colour on white paper prepared with a grey wash, 195 × 320
Prov.: Walter Fawkes; by descent to Revd. Ayscough Fawkes, sale Christie 27 June 1890 (29), bt. T. Woolner, sale Christie 21 May 1895 (97), bt. Agnew; Agnew 1948, bt. A. S. Furner, from whose estate it came to the gallery
Coll.: Johannesburg Art Gallery (744)

665 Remagen and Linz 1817

Watercolour and body-colour on white paper prepared with a grey wash, 197 × 318
Prov.: Walter Fawkes; by descent to Revd. Ayscough Fawkes, sale Christie 27 June 1890 (30), bt. Agnew; Sir G. T. Gibson Carmichael, 1902; C. Fairfax Murray ? 1908; H. E. Lawley 1921; Sir Hugh Reid, or Sir James Roberts, sale Christie 20 March 1936 (19); anon. sale Sotheby 9 November 1955 (47); Kurt Pantzer; given to the museum in memory of Dr. and Mrs. Hugo O. Pantzer by their children
Coll.: Indianapolis Museum of Art

666 Rolandswerth Nunnery and Drachenfels 1817

Watercolour and body-colour on white paper prepared with a grey wash, 195 × 303
Prov.: Walter Fawkes; by descent to Revd. Ayscough Fawkes, sale Christie 27 June 1890 (31), bt. Vokins; Sir Donald Currie, from whose executors bt. Agnew 1907; C. Morland Agnew; Hugh L. Agnew; by descent to present owner
Private collection

667 Drachenfels 1817

Watercolour and body-colour on white paper prepared with a grey wash, 210 × 289
Prov.: Walter Fawkes; by descent to Revd. Ayscough Fawkes, sale Christie 27 June 1890 (32), bt. Fine Art Society, London; Mr. and

Mrs. W. W. Spooner, by whom bequeathed to the institute, 1967
Coll.: Courtauld Institute of Art, University of London

668 Godesberg 1817

Watercolour and body-colour, with some scraping-out, on white paper prepared with a grey wash, 195 × 303
Prov.: Walter Fawkes; by descent to Revd. Ayscough Fawkes, sale Christie 27 June 1890 (33), bt. Fine Art Society, London; R. Norton; C. Morland Agnew; Hugh L. Agnew; by descent to present owner
Private collection

669 Rhine Gate, Cologne 1817

Watercolour and body-colour on white paper prepared with a grey wash, 197 × 305
Prov.: Walter Fawkes; by descent to Revd. Ayscough Fawkes, sale Christie 27 June 1890 (34), bt. D. P. McEwen, sale Christie 1 April 1911 (79), bt. Eaton; D. C. Thomson; Miss Gwendoline E. Davies, by whom bequeathed to the museum, 1952
Coll.: National Museum of Wales, Cardiff (2953)

670 Cologne 1817

Body-colour on white paper prepared with a grey wash, 197 × 305
Prov.: Walter Fawkes; by descent to Revd. Ayscough Fawkes, sale Christie 27 June 1890 (35), bt. Agnew; W. S. Steel
Coll.: untraced

671 Sooneck, with Bacharach in the distance 1817

Watercolour and body-colour, with some scraping-out, on white paper prepared with a grey wash, 221 × 359
Prov.: Walter Fawkes; R. W. Lloyd, by whom bequeathed to the museum, 1958
Coll.: Trustees of the British Museum (1958-7-12-417)

See No. 693, a watercolour derived from this composition.

672 Abbey near Coblenz 1817

Watercolour on white paper prepared with a grey wash, 195 × 313
Exh.: B.M. 1975 (50)
Prov.: Walter Fawkes; Frederick H. Fawkes; Agnew 1912; R. W. Lloyd, by whom bequeathed to the museum, 1958
Coll.: Trustees of the British Museum (1958-7-12-412)

673 Johannisberg 1817

Watercolour on white paper prepared with a grey wash, 213 × 337
Exh.: B.M. 1975 (49)
Prov.: Walter Fawkes; Frederick H. Fawkes; Agnew 1912; H. E. Walters; Agnew 1918; A. E. Lawley, sale Christie 25 February 1921 (127); R. W. Lloyd, by whom bequeathed to the museum, 1958

Coll.: Trustees of the British Museum (1958–7-12–418)

Pencil, chalk or ink, watercolour and body-colour on white paper prepared with a grey wash, 235 × 292
Prov.: Walter Fawkes; by descent to Ayscough Fawkes; F. H. Fawkes, bt. Agnew 1912; E. D. Brandegee, 1915; James Lawrence, Brookline, Mass.; Christie 4 June 1974 (178), bt. Stanford University (gift of the Committee for Art)
Coll.: Stanford University Museum of Art, California (76.168)

Prov.: Walter Fawkes; F. H. Fawkes, from whom bt. Agnew 1912; Walter Jones; Christie, 3 July 1942 (51), bt. Gooden and Fox; Viscount Allendale; by descent to his son, Capt. the Hon. Nicholas Beaumont, from whom bt. Agnew, 1966
Private collection

674   Osterspey and Feltzen on the Rhine: rainbow 1817

Watercolour, 217 × 327
Prov.: Walter Fawkes; by descent to Revd. Ayscough Fawkes, sale Christie 27 June 1890 (18, as 'Peterhof'), bt. Agnew; Henry S. Marquand, sale American Art Association, 24–31 January 1903 (15); Parke Bernet, 3 November 1967 (81, as 'Peterhof'); Josephine Grant McCreery, by whom given in memory of her parents, Joseph and Edith Grant
Coll.: Stanford University Museum of Art, California (72.59)

Turner made a finished watercolour closely based on this composition in 1820 (see No. 688).

676   St. Goarhausen 1817

Pencil, watercolour on white paper prepared with a grey wash, 190 × 311
Prov.: Walter Fawkes; bt. Agnew 1912 from Farnley; Sir Algernon Firth; Agnew 1944; Miss B. M. Towlson, sale Sotheby 19 April 1961 (59), bt. Agnew, from whom bt. by the gallery
Coll.: Henry E. Huntington Library and Art Gallery, San Marino, California (62.2)

679   Bingen Lorch and the Mausethurm 1817

Body-colour on white paper prepared with a grey wash, 194 × 311
Prov.: Walter Fawkes; F. H. Fawkes, from whom bt. Agnew, 1912; T. A. Tatton, sale Christie 14 December 1928 (34), bt. Agnew; A. Roffe; Agnew; Mrs. Church 1943; Agnew 1966
Private collection

680   Abbey at Bingen 1817

Body-colour on white paper prepared with a grey wash, 194 × 309
Prov.: Walter Fawkes; by descent to Revd. Ayscough Fawkes; Agnew 1913, sold to G. W. Palmer
Coll.: untraced

677   From Rheinfels looking over St. Goar to Katz 1817

Watercolour and body-colour, with scraping-out, on white paper prepared with a grey wash, 195 × 313
Exh.: R.A. 1974 (196)
Prov.: Walter Fawkes; F. H. Fawkes, from whom bt. Agnew 1912; T. A. Tatton, sale Christie, 14 December 1928 (35), bt. Agnew; Lord Horder; anon. sale, Sotheby 10 December 1958 (102), bt. Agnew
Private collection

675   Drachenfels on the Rhine, from near Rhondorf 1817

678   Mainz and Kastel 1817

Watercolour and body-colour on white paper prepared with a grey wash, 208 × 365

681   Hirzenach, below St. Goar 1817

Watercolour and body-colour, with scraping-out, on white paper prepared with a grey wash, 210 × 325
Prov.: Walter Fawkes; F. H. Fawkes; R. W. Lloyd, by whom bequeathed to the museum, 1958
Coll.: Trustees of the British Museum (1958-7-12-415)

682   Bingen from the Lorch   1817

Watercolour and body-colour, with scratching-out, on white paper prepared with a grey wash, 198 × 318
Prov.: Walter Fawkes; Sir R. Hardy; R. W. Lloyd, by whom bequeathed to the museum, 1958
Coll.: Trustees of the British Museum (1958-7-12-414)

683   A view on the Rhine   1817

Watercolour and body-colour, with scraping-out on white paper prepared with a grey wash, 227 × 317
Prov.: Viscountess Wakefield, by whom given in memory of her husband, Viscount Wakefield of Hythe, 1943
Coll.: Victoria and Albert Museum, London (P.18-1943)

684   Lurleiberg and St. Goarhausen   1817

Watercolour and body-colour on white paper prepared with a grey wash, 197 × 309
verso: slight pencil sketch of mountains or clouds
Exh.: B.M. 1975 (48)

Prov.: Walter Fawkes; F. H. Fawkes; Agnew 1913; R. W. Lloyd, by whom bequeathed to the museum, 1958
Coll.: Trustees of the British Museum (1958-7-12-416)

685   Lurleiberg   1817

Body-colour on white paper prepared with a grey wash, 191 × 302
Prov.: Walter Fawkes; by descent to F. H. Hawkes; Agnew 1912; Matthews & Brookes 1923; F.V. Gill, sale Christie 2 June 1927 (257), bt. Agnew; Mostyn Owen; anon. sale Christie 20 March 1979 (137), bt. Agnew
Coll.: with Thos. Agnew & Sons Ltd., London

686   Lurleiberg   1817

Watercolour and body-colour over pencil, with scraping-out, on white paper prepared with a grey wash, 188 × 300
Prov.: Walter Fawkes; Agnew 1913; Agnew 1924; Agnew 1945; Sir Algernon Firth
Coll.: Mr. and Mrs. Eugene Victor Thaw

XI(b)   Nos 687–696
Finished drawings of Rhine subjects and related studies, *c.* 1820

687   Ehrenbreitstein, during the demolition of the fortress   1819–20

Watercolour and scraping-out, 177 × 286
Engr.: by J. C. Allen, 1824 (R. 202); a reduced version engr. by J. Pye, 1828, for *The Literary Souvenir* (R. 317a)
Prov.: Thomas Wrigley; presented by his children to the gallery, 1901
Coll.: Art Gallery and Museum, Bury, Lancashire (Wrigley Donation, 117)

Nos 687, 688, 689 are drawings for the engraved series of Rhine views, a W. B. Cooke project which did not materialize (see Finberg, *Life*, p. 256). This subject is probably derived from the Rhine drawing of 1817, No. 658.

688   Osterspey and Feltzen on the Rhine   *c.* 1820

Watercolour and body-colour on light-brown paper, 188 × 292
Engr.: by W. Miller, 1852 (R. 669)
Exh.: C.G. 1823 (21)
Prov.: W. B. Cooke; J. Slegg; B. G. Windus; A. C. Pilkington; Fine Art Society, London, from whom purchased by the donor to the museum
Coll.: Museum of Art, Rhode Island School of Design, Providence, R.I. (anon. gift)

See No. 687. The composition is derived from No. 674.

689   Neuwied and Weise Thurn, with Hoche's Monument, on the Rhine, looking towards Andernach   *c.* 1820

Watercolour and body-colour, with pen and black ink and scratching-out, on white paper partially prepared with grey wash, 184 × 286

Engr.: by R. Brandard 1852 (R. 670)
Exh.: C.G. 1823 (34)
Prov.: Henry Vaughan, by whom bequeathed to the gallery, 1900
Coll.: National Galleries of Scotland, Edinburgh (857)

See No. 687. The composition probably derives from No. 661.

690   Cologne, from the river*   1820

Watercolour, 308 × 463
Signed and dated lower left: *JMW Turner RA 1820*
Engr.: by E. Goodall 1824 (R. 203); by A. Willmore 1859 for *The Turner Gallery,* 1861
Exh.: C.G. 1822 (20)
Prov.: T. Tomkinson; B. G. Windus; Samuel Mendel; Agnew by 1872; Abel Buckley, from whom bt. Agnew 1904; George J. Gould, New York; Christie, 26 November 1926 (23), bt. Agnew; Walter H. Jones, sale Christie 3 July 1942 bt. Gooden and Fox; Viscount Allendale, by descent to the Hon. Richard Beaumont, from whom bt. Agnew 1970; Mr. and Mrs. Louis Brechemin, by whom given to the museum
Coll.: Seattle Art Museum, Washington (70.70)

See No. 696. This drawing perhaps uses the composition of No. 670 above.

691   Biebrich Palace   1820

Watercolour, 293 × 453
Exh.: Northern Academy of Arts, Newcastle 1828 (74); B.M. 1975 (79)
Prov.: 'A member of the Swinburne family' (? for whom drawn); Swinburne family; N. E. Hayman; Agnew 1912; R. W. Lloyd, by whom bequeathed to the museum, 1958
Coll.: Trustees of the British Museum (1958–7–12–420)

See No. 696.

692   Marksburg   1820

Watercolour, 291 × 458
Signed and dated lower right: *IMW Turner/1820*
Inscr.: *MARXBOURG and BRUGBERG* [Braubach] *on the RHINE*
Exh.: Northern Academy of Arts, Newcastle 1828 (71); B.M. 1975 (80)
Prov.: 'A member of the Swinburne family' (? for whom drawn); Swinburne family; sale Christie 17 March 1900 (78), bt. Vokins; C. Fairfax Murray; 1912 R. W. Lloyd, by whom bequeathed to the museum, 1958
Coll.: Trustees of the British Museum (1958–7–12–422)

See No. 696.

693   Bacharach on the Rhine   *c.*1820

Watercolour, 286 × 413
Prov.: Lewis Loyd; Capt. E. N. F. Loyd, sale Christie 30 April 1937 (62), bt. Rayner MacConnell; bt. by the gallery through the Webster Bequest, 1952
Coll.: Aberdeen Art Gallery (52.8)

This is based on the watercolour of *Sooneck, with Bacharach in the distance* (No. 671). See No. 696.

694   A bridge between trees (the Dark Bridge) ?*c.*1820

Watercolour, 292 × 457
Prov.: D. C. Thompson; Earl of Swinton; P. M. Turner; Sir Arthur Colgate; Spink
Coll.: formerly with Spink & Son Ltd., London

See No. 696.

695   Tivoli   ?*c.*1820

Watercolour, 303 × 436
Prov.: purchased 1922
Coll.: Whitworth Art Gallery, University of Manchester (D. 31.1922)

See No. 696.

696   Loch Katrine   ?*c.*1820

Watercolour, 232 × 457
Prov.: A. E. Anderson, and presented by him to the Whitworth Institute through the National Art-Collections Fund, 1922
Coll.: Whitworth Art Gallery, University of Manchester (D. 45.1922)

There is little evidence to corroborate the title traditionally given to this drawing. In style and format it is very like the 'Tivoli' colour-beginning acquired by the Whitworth Institute at the same time. It may well be, therefore, that this is another design for a continental subject of about 1820. A colour-beginning of a type similar to Nos 694, 695 is T.B., CXCVI-Q (repr. B.M. 1975, No. 75). It shows Martigny and seems to be a design for a finished watercolour like *Marksburg* (No. 692). These studies may also represent unrealized compositions in the same series, which perhaps includes Nos 690–3.

SECTION XII
Nos 697–731 Drawings of Italian subjects, *c.* 1816–1828, including designs for Hakewill's *Picturesque Tour in Italy, c.* 1816–1818

Shortly before his first visit to Italy Turner produced a number of topographical views of that country from sketches by others. The first of these may have been the frontispiece to T. Allason's *Antiquities of Pola,* executed perhaps in 1816 from Allason's own drawing, and engraved by George Cooke for the book which appeared in 1819 (R. 162). A study of the motif is T.B., CXCVI-T. In 1817 Turner made the large *Eruption of Vesuvius,* owned by Fawkes; this has been confused with a smaller drawing of a similar subject, made with a pair, *Vesuvius in Repose,* and engraved in *Friendship's Offering,* 1830. The imaginary composition of Tivoli (No. 495) also dates from 1817. In the following year Turner received from James Hakewill 200 guineas for ten watercolours derived from Hakewill's own *camera obscura* pencil outline drawings of Italian views; these, together with an additional eight, were engraved for Hakewill's *Picturesque Tour in Italy,* published in 1818–20 (Nos 700–717).

The drawings that Turner made in Italy in 1819 fill nineteen, or possibly twenty, sketchbooks (T.B., CLXXIV–CXCIII and CLVIII, the *Skies* notebook); most are pencil studies, but some fifty make use of watercolour, often to magnificent effect. A short series of finished watercolours were executed in 1820–21 (Nos 718–724) and acquired by Fawkes. Before he returned to Rome in 1828 Turner began work on a further series of Italian subjects for a projected *Picturesque Views in Italy,* referred to in the advertisement for Charles Heath's exhibition of drawings by Turner at the Egyptian Hall, London in 1829. The completed subjects that can be connected with this scheme, which came to nothing, are Nos 726–731.

697 Eruption of Vesuvius* 1817

Watercolour and scraping-out, 286 × 397
Inscr.: verso: *Mount Vesuvius in Eruption JMW Turner RA 1817*
Exh.: C.G. 1822 (8); Leeds 1839 (80); R.A. 1974 (184)
Prov.: Walter Fawkes; by descent to Revd. Ayscough Fawkes, sale Christie 27 June 1890 (52), bt. Davis; W. Newall, sale Christie 30 June 1922 (75); Sir Robert Hadfield, sale Christie 19 January 1945 (109); Brian Hamilton, sale Sotheby 22 November 1961 (48); Colnaghi, 1962; Mr. and Mrs. Mellon
Coll.: Yale Center for British Art, Paul Mellon Collection

Perhaps derived from a drawing by Hakewill, though no view of Vesuvius occurs in the *Picturesque Tour in Italy.*

698 Bay of Naples (Vesuvius angry) *c.* 1817

Watercolour, 176 × 284
Engr.: by T. Jeavons, 1830, for *Friendship's Offering* (R. 339); a small replica engraved by H. Adlard, 1830, for unknown annual (R. 346)
Exh.: Society of Painters in Water Colours 1850 (284 or 299)
Prov.: John Dillon, sale Christie 17 April 1869 (37), bt. Vokins; John Ruskin; Arthur Severn
Coll.: Williamson Art Gallery, Birkenhead

This and No. 699 seem to have been drawn as a pair, and this subject is said to have been engraved by Cooke for a work entitled *Delineations of Pompeii.* It is distinct from No. 697, though the two have been confused.

699 Bay of Naples (Vesuvius in repose) *c.* 1817

Watercolour, 181 × 286
Exh.: Society of Painters in Water Colours 1850 (284 or 299)
Prov.: John Dillon, sale Christie 17 April 1869 (36), bt. Vokins; John Ruskin
Coll.: Brian Pilkington, London

A pair to No. 698. It was reproduced by Ruskin in his *Lectures on Landscape,* 1897, facing p. 16. Like Nos 697 and 698 it may derive from a sketch by Hakewill, though it is also possible that an older drawing by, say, J. R. Cozens was used.

700 The Rialto, Venice *c.* 1818

Watercolour, 140 × 216
Engr.: by J. Pye, 1820, for Hakewill's *Italy* (R. 144); small replica of this design engraved by H. Adlard, 1830, for unknown annual (R. 342)
Exh.: C.G. 1824 (40); Liverpool Academy 1845 (58)
Prov.: ?anon. sale, Christie 5 June 1875 (31), bt. Lasalles; T. Laurie and Sons, sale Christie 21 June 1884 (116), bt. Permain; S. E. Kennedy; anon. sale, Christie 15 December 1916 (51), bt. Gillott
Coll.: untraced

701 Cascade of Terni *c.* 1817

Watercolour, 222 × 133
Sig. lower left: *JMW Turner*
Engr.: by J. Landseer, 1819, for Hakewill's *Italy* (R. 145); small replica of this design engraved by H. Adlard, 1830, for annual unknown (R. 343)
Prov.: John Dillon, sale Christie 17 April 1869 (39), bt. Vokins; John Ruskin; Arthur Severn; Miss G. Bickham; Agnew 1923, 1925; E. L. Hartley, by whom bequeathed to the museum, 1954
Coll.: Museum and Art Gallery, Blackburn, Lancashire

702 Bridge at Narni *c.* 1817

Watercolour, 140 × 216
Sig. lower right: *JMW Turner*
Engr.: by S. Middiman, 1819, for Hakewill's *Italy* (R. 146)
Prov.: H. A. J. Munro of Novar, sale Christie 2 June 1877 (39), bt. Arthur Severn; John Ruskin; Sir George Agnew; Agnew 1973
Private collection

703 Bridge and Castle of St. Angelo, Rome *c.* 1817

Watercolour, 140 × 216
Engr.: by G. Hollis, 1818, for Hakewill's *Italy* (R. 147)
Exh.: C.G. 1824 (20)
Prov.: J. Slegg; Mrs. Sara Austen, sale Christie 11 April (cat. printed as for 10 April) 1889 (198), bt. Agnew; Lady Tate; Christie 20 December 1946 (98), bt. Fine Art Society, London
Private collection, Hobart, Tasmania

704 Roman Forum, from the Capitol c. 1816

Watercolour, 140 × 216
Engr.: by G. Cooke, 1818, for Hakewill's *Italy* (R. 148)
Exh.: Liverpool Academy 1831 (231)
Prov.: John Dillon, sale Christie 29 April 1869 (143), bt. Vokins; William Dell, sale Christie 21 April 1899 (54, as 'Ancient Rome'), bt. Vokins; William Cooke
Private collection

705 Forum Romanum 1818

Watercolour, 140 × 216
Signed and dated lower right: *JMW Turner 1818*
Engr.: by G. Hollis and J. Mitan, 1820, for Hakewill's *Italy* (R. 149); a reduced replica of this plate by J. Henshall, 1830, for *The Rembrancer*, 1832 (R. 340) and some copies of *The Talisman*, 1831
Exh.: Liverpool Academy 1831 (222)
Prov.: John Dillon, sale Christie 29 April 1869 (142, as 'Forum'), bt. Vokins; Lord Justice Gifford, sale Christie 23 March 1889 (76), bt. Vokins; T. MacLean
Coll.: National Gallery of Canada, Ottawa (4920)

706 Rome from the Farnese Gardens c. 1818

Watercolour, 140 × 216
Engr.: by J. Le Keux, 1820, for Hakewill's *Italy* (R. 150)
Prov.: George Blood; T. MacLean; anon. sale Christie 25 April 1952 (24, with unframed print by Le Keux on reverse), bt. in
Private collection

707 Rome from Monte Testaccio c. 1818

Watercolour, 140 × 216
Engr.: by J. Byrne, 1819, for Hakewill's *Italy* (R. 151)
Provenance and whereabouts unknown

708 Rome from the Monte Mario* c. 1818

Watercolour, 137 × 213
Engr.: by J. Byrne, 1820, for Hakewill's *Italy* (R. 152)
Prov.: John Ruskin; Arthur Severn; Frank C. Parker; anon. sale Sotheby 18 March 1971 (76), bt. Baskett, from whom bt. by Paul Mellon, 1971
Coll.: Yale Center for British Art, Paul Mellon Collection

709 Rome: Tomb of Cecilia Metella c. 1818

Watercolour, 133 × 223
Engr.: by J. Byrne, 1819, for Hakewill's *Italy* (R. 153)
Prov.: H. A. J. Munro of Novar, sale Christie 1875; William Quilter, sale Christie 9 April 1875 (245), bt. in; sale, Christie 18 May 1889 (100), bt. Vokins; E. Steinkopf, sale, Christie 24 May 1935 (56), bt. Lady Hague; Sotheby 15 July 1959 (80), bt. Fine Art Society, London, from whom stolen in December 1960
Coll.: untraced

710 View of La Riccia c. 1816

Watercolour, 140 × 216
Sig. lower right: *JMW Turner RA*
Engr.: by J. Pye, 1819, for Hakewill's *Italy* (R. 154)
Exh.: C.G. 1824 (128)
Prov.: B. G. Windus; Mrs. Sara Austen, sale Christie 11 April (cat. printed as for 10 April) 1889 (197), bt. Vokins; Robert Struass; E. Steinkopf, sale Christie 24 May 1935 (57), bt. Thomson
Private collection

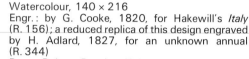

711 Lake Nemi c. 1818

Watercolour, 140 × 216
Sig. lower left: *JMW Turner RA*
Engr.: by S. Middiman and J. Pye, 1819, for Hakewill's *Italy* (R. 155)
Exh.: C.G. 1824 (153)

Prov.: B. G. Windus; John Dillon, sale Christie 17 April 1869 (38), bt. Vokins; John Ruskin; Agnew 1919; C. Morland Agnew; Christie 3 March 1970 (100), bt. Sanders
Coll.: The Hon. Christopher Lennox-Boyd, London

712 Naples, from the Mole c. 1818

Watercolour, 140 × 216
Engr.: by G. Cooke, 1820, for Hakewill's *Italy* (R. 156); a reduced replica of this design engraved by H. Adlard, 1827, for an unknown annual (R. 344)
Prov.: Robert Durning Holt; anon. sale, Christie 6 December 1935 (88, as 'The old harbour, Naples'), bt. in
Coll.: untraced

713 Florence, from the Ponte alla Carraia c. 1816–7

Watercolour, 140 × 210
Sig. lower right: *JMW Turner RA*
Engr.: by S. Rawle, 1818, for Hakewill's *Italy* (R. 157)
Prov.: A. O. Prior; sold Southgate & Barnet, 8 April 1853 (256); John Dillon, sale Christie 29 April 1869 (146, as 'Florence from the Ponte Alla'), bt. Agnew; John Farnworth, sale Christie 10 May 1874 (38, as 'Florence'), bt. Agnew; A. G. Kurtz, sale Christie 11 May 1891 (203, as 'Florence'), bt. Agnew; presented by the Guarantors of the Royal Jubilee Exhibition, 1887
Coll.: Whitworth Art Gallery, University of Manchester (D.13.1887)

714 Florence, from the Chiesa al Monte c. 1816–8

Watercolour, 133 × 213
Engr.: by G. Cooke, 1820, for Hakewill's *Italy* (R. 158); a reduced replica of this design engraved by E. Goodall, 1831, for *The Amulet* (R. 337)
Prov.: Major A. W. Foster; R. F. Goldschmidt
Private collection, England

715 Florence, from Fiesole *c.* 1818

Watercolour, 140 × 216
Sig. lower left: [?] *Turner RA*
Engr.: by W. R. Smith, 1819, for Hakewill's *Italy* (R. 159); a reduced replica of this design engraved by H. Adlard, 1830, for unknown annual (R. 345)
Prov.: John Dillon, sale Christie 29 April 1869 (145), bt. Vokins; John Ruskin; A. T. Hollingsworth; Humphrey Roberts, sale Christie 23 May 1908 (289), bt. Agnew; Lady Mayer; by descent to the present owner
Private collection

716 Isola Bella, on the Lago Maggiore *c.* 1817

Watercolour, 140 × 216
Engr.: by J. Fittler, 1818, for Hakewill's *Italy* (R. 160)
Prov.: John Ruskin; Rhode Island School of Design, Providence, R.I.; sold, 1949, to Gimbels, New York; Agnew, 1960
Coll.: untraced

717 Turin, from the portico of the Superga Church *c.* 1818

Watercolour, 140 × 216
Engr.: by J. Mitan, 1820, for Hakewill's *Italy* (R. 161)
Prov.: John Ruskin; C. Morland Agnew; Paul Nitze, Washington
Coll.: Dorothy and Sydney Spivack

718 The Rialto, Venice* *c.* 1820

Watercolour, 286 × 413
Inscr. lower right: *IMWT*
Exh.: Leeds 1839 (73)

Prov.: Walter Fawkes; F. H. Fawkes, sale Christie 2 July 1937 (42); Lockett Thomson; Lord Craigmyle; Christie 15 July 1964 (50), bt. Mitchell; Pantzer Collection, Indianapolis
Coll.: Indianapolis Museum of Art

This composition was drawn in pencil by Turner in his *Milan to Venice* sketchbook (T.B., CLXXV, 48v–49). He had already made a watercolour of a similar view, from a sketch by Hakewill (No. 700), and this sheet has been mistaken by Armstrong and Goldyne for that earlier work. The Hakewill drawings are, however, uniformly small in size, while this is the same format as the series of Italian views executed for Fawkes in about 1820.

719 Rome, from the Monte Mario *c.* 1820

Watercolour and scraping-out, 286 × 406
Inscr. lower right: *ROMA 1820 from Mt MARIO*
Exh.: Leeds 1839 (32)
Prov.: Walter Fawkes; by descent to Revd. Ayscough Fawkes, sale Christie 27 June 1890 (50), bt. Vokins; Sir Donald Currie; by descent to present owner
Private collection

Compare the view for Hakewill, No. 708. Drawings of Rome from Monte Mario occur in the *St. Peters* sketchbook (T.B., CLXXVIII) and in the *Rome: C. Studies* sketchbook (T.B., CLXXXIX, pp. 31, 33, 60).

720 Rome, from the Pincian Hill *c.* 1820–1

Watercolour, 286 × 419
Sig. lower right: *JMW Turner RA*
Inscr.: *Rome Pietro memorio*
Prov.: Walter Fawkes; by descent to Revd. Ayscough Fawkes, sale, Christie 27 June 1890 (51), bt. Obach; Agnew 1974
Private collection

721 Venice, from Fusina* 1821

Watercolour, 286 × 406
Inscr. lower left: *1821*; on bale to right: *T*; on awning right: *VENICE from FUSINA*
Exh.: Leeds 1839 (81)
Prov.: Walter Fawkes; by descent to Revd. Ayscough Fawkes, sale Christie 27 June 1890 (54), bt. Vokins; Sir Donald Currie; by descent to present owner
Private collection

722 Bay of Naples, with Vesuvius—morning* *1820*

Watercolour, 265 × 387
Signed and dated lower centre: *IMW Turner 1820*
Inscr.: *NAPOLI*
Exh.: C.G. 1822 (27); Leeds 1839 (69)
Prov.: Walter Fawkes; by descent to Revd. Ayscough Fawkes, sale Christie 27 June 1890 (53), bt. Gerald Hardy; anon. sale Sotheby 1 April 1976 (124), bt. Givaudon, Geneva
Private collection

723 Rome: the Colosseum* 1820

Watercolour, 277 × 293
Inscr. lower right: *Colliseum Rome W Turner 1820*
Exh.: Leeds 1839 (70); B.M. 1975 (74)
Prov.: W. Fawkes; Revd. J. W. R. Brocklebank; sale Christie 25 November 1927 (91); R. W. Lloyd, by whom bequeathed to the museum, 1958
Coll.: Trustees of the British Museum (1958–7–12–421)

Based on a drawing in the *Rome: C. Studies* sketchbook (T.B., CLXXXIX–23).

724 Interior of St. Peter's, Rome* 1821

Watercolour, 292 × 413
Signed and dated on pavement: *IMW Turner RA 1821*
Exh.: Leeds 1839 (27)
Prov.: Walter Fawkes; F. H. Fawkes, sale Christie 2 July 1937 (57); Mrs. E. L. Hedley; Sotheby 7 July 1965 (45), bt. Spink
Private collection

Based on the pencil drawing in the *St. Peters* sketchbook (T.B., CLXXXVIII–83).

725 Venice: the Rialto* *c.* 1820

Watercolour, 287 × 407
Prov.: Robert Dunthorne; Mr. Bryce, by whom presented to the nation, and entered the collection, 1972
Coll.: National Gallery of Ireland, Dublin (7512)

An unfinished drawing which may have been planned at the time of the Fawkes Italian series, but which is possibly connected with the *Picturesque Views in Italy* of *c.* 1828. Stylistically it seems to belong to the earlier group. It is based on the pencil drawing in the *Milan to Venice* sketchbook (T.B., CLXXV 80v–81r); compare the composition of the large oil-painting, also unfinished, P245.

726 Florence, from San Miniato *c.* 1827

Watercolour, 321 × 483
Engr.: by E. Goodall, 1828, for *The Keepsake* (R. 319)
Exh.: ? Birmingham Society of Artists 1830 (300)
Prov.: J. C. Grundy, sale Christie 4 November 1867 (112), bt. E. White; Miss Crofton; Sir Donald Currie; by descent to present owner
Private collection

This and the following three drawings are variants on the same view; one was presumably executed for Heath's *Picturesque Views in Italy,* and the others produced simply as varied repetitions for different patrons. Turner made several drawings of Florence from San Miniato in the *Rome and Florence* sketchbook (T.B., CXCI–62v, etc.).

727 Florence, from San Miniato *c.* 1827

Watercolour, 290 × 425
Prov.: Thomas Griffith; Lord Northbourne, *c.* 1840; Sir Walter James; Lord Kenilworth, by whom bequeathed to the gallery, 1954
Coll.: Herbert Art Gallery and Museum, Coventry (845)

728 Florence, from San Miniato *c.* 1828

Watercolour and body-colour, 286 × 418
Exh.: B.M. 1975 (145)
Prov.: H. A. J. Munro of Novar; ? Sir J. Pender, sale Christie 29 May 1897 (16), bt. Agnew; Hon. W. F. D. Smith; bt. Agnew 1908; Sir Joseph Beecham, sale Christie 4 May 1917 (149); R. W. Lloyd, by whom bequeathed to the museum, 1958
Coll.: Trustees of the British Museum (1958–7–12–426)

729 Florence, from San Miniato *c.* 1828

Watercolour, 335 × 495
Prov.: J. Vavasseur, ? sale Christie 23 April 1910 (20), bt. Agnew; Scott and Fowles, New York; Mrs. Joseph B. Schlotman, 1910; by whom bequeathed to present owner, 1974
Private collection, U.S.A.

A replica of No. 727.

730 Arona, Lago Maggiore* *c.* 1828

Watercolour, 292 × 422
Engr.: by W. R. Smith, 1829, for *The Keepsake* (R. 321)
Exh.: R.A. 1974 (466)
Prov.: John Ruskin; T. S. Kennedy, sale Christie 18 May 1895 (96), bt. Agnew
Coll.: Brian Pilkington, London

731 Lake Albano *c.* 1828

Watercolour, 286 × 412
Engr.: by R. Wallis, 1829, for *The Keepsake* (R. 320)
Exh.: E.H. 1829; Birmingham Society of Artists 1829 (412)
Prov.: F. R. Leyland, sale Christie 9 March 1872 (39), bt. Agnew; J. Pierpont Morgan
Coll.: untraced

Turner made several studies of Lake Albano in his *Albano, Nemi, Rome* sketchbook (T.B., CLXXXII, 3–26).

SECTION XIII
Nos 732–784 The 'Rivers', 'Ports' and 'Little Liber', *c.* 1823–1830

XIII(a) Nos 732–749
Designs for the *Rivers of England,* *c.* 1823–1824

These eighteen subjects were engraved in mezzotint for W. B. Cooke's *Rivers of England.* Fifteen were published between 1823 and 1825. All but one are extant as small, highly finished watercolours in the Turner Bequest (CCVIII); the missing subject is *Warkworth Castle* (No. 742), which is closely based on the large drawing of 1799 (No. 256). It is unlikely that Turner, having made a uniform set of drawings for the engravers, would have asked them to work from so different an original in this one case, and it must be assumed that the subject was executed with the rest; but it is not recorded. Turner kept all the drawings and loaned them to Cooke for eight guineas each. The publication also included four subjects after Girtin, and Turner is supposed to have worked on these plates himself. Another view was contributed by William Collins.

732 Shields on the River Tyne 1823

Watercolour, 154 × 216
Signed and dated lower left: *JMWT 1823*
Engr.: by C. Turner, 1823, for *Rivers of England* (R. 752)
Coll.: Trustees of the British Museum (T.B., CCVIII–V)

733 Newcastle on Tyne *c.* 1823

Pencil and watercolour, 152 × 215

Engr.: by T. Lupton, 1823, for *Rivers of England* (R. 753)
Exh.: B.M. 1975 (85)
Coll.: Trustees of the British Museum (T.B., CCVIII–K)

A pencil study of this view is in the *Scotch Antiquities* sketchbook (T.B., CLXVII–2).

734 More Park, near Watford, on the River Colne *c.* 1823

Watercolour, 157 × 221
Engr.: by C. Turner, 1824, for *Rivers of England* (R. 754)
Exh.: R.A. 1974 (240)
Coll.: Trustees of the British Museum (T.B., CCVIII–H)

The view is taken from a pencil study in the *River* sketchbook (T.B., XCVI, 76, 49).

735 Rochester on the Medway *c.* 1824

Watercolour, 152 × 219
Engr.: by T. Lupton, 1824, for *Rivers of England* (R. 755)
Coll.: Trustees of the British Museum (T.B., CCVIII–W)

Based on a pencil drawing in the *Medway* sketchbook (T.B., CXCIX, 18v–19).

736 Norham Castle, on the Tweed* *c.* 1823

Watercolour, 156 × 216
Engr.: by C. Turner, 1824, for *Rivers of England* (R. 756); by Percy Heath, 1827, perhaps for *The Literary Souvenir* (R. 317; unpubl.)
Exh.: R.A. 1974 (645)

Coll.: Trustees of the British Museum (T.B., CCVIII–O)

A colour-beginning specifically for this drawing seems to be T.B., CCLXIII–22; it derives from the *Liber Studiorum* subject, R. 57, which is itself modified from the early watercolours of the scene (Nos 225 and 226).

737 Dartmouth Castle, on the River Dart *c.* 1824

Watercolour, 159 × 224
Engr.: by T. Lupton, 1824, for *Rivers of England* (R. 757)
Coll.: Trustees of the British Museum (T.B., CCVIII–D)

Studies of Dartmouth Castle occur in the *Devonshire Coast No. 1* and in the *Devon Rivers No. 2* sketchbooks (T.B., CXXIII; CXXXIII, 53–5).

738 Okehampton, on the Okement *c.* 1824

Watercolour, 163 × 230
Engr.: by C. Turner, 1825, for *Rivers of England* (R. 758)
Coll.: Trustees of the British Museum (T.B., CCVIII–E)

Turner made drawings at Okehampton in the *Devon Rivers No. 1* and in the *Devonshire Rivers No. 3 and Wharfedale* sketchbooks (T.B., CXXXII, 43–50; CXXXIV, 23, 24, 67, 70, 71).

739 Dartmouth, on the River Dart *c.* 1824

Watercolour, 157 × 227
Engr.: by S. W. Reynolds, 1825, for *Rivers of England* (R. 759)

Coll.: Trustees of the British Museum (T.B., CCVIII–C)

740 Brougham Castle, near the junction of the Rivers Eamont and Lowther *c.* 1824

Watercolour, 161 × 228
Engr.: by W. Say, 1825, for *Rivers of England* (R. 760)
Coll.: Trustees of the British Museum (T.B., CCVIII–N)

Turner's drawing of this subject is in the *Vale of Heathfield* sketchbook (T.B., CXXXVII–70).

741 Kirkstall Abbey, on the River Aire *c.* 1824

Watercolour, 160 × 225
Engr.: by J. Bromley, 1826, for *Rivers of England* (R. 761)
Exh.: R.A. 1974 (239)
Coll.: Trustees of the British Museum (T.B., CCVIII–M)

The sketch which Turner apparently used in making this drawing is in the *Brighton and Arundel* sketchbook (T.B., CCX–48).

742 Warkworth Castle, on the Coquet
c. 1824

?Watercolour, size unknown
Engr.: by T. Lupton, 1826, for *Rivers of England* (R. 762)
Provenance and whereabouts unknown

This composition is closely based on that of the large watercolour exhibited in 1799 (No. 256).

Based on the study in the *Brighton and Arundel* sketchbook (T.B., CCX–60v).

748 Arundel Castle, on the River Arun, with rainbow *c*. 1823

Watercolour, 159 × 230
Engr.: by engraver unknown, for *Rivers of England* (R. 768; unpubl.)
Coll.: Trustees of the British Museum (T.B., CCVIII–F)

Drawings of this view are in the *Brighton and Arundel* sketchbook (T.B., CCX–66).

743 Mouth of the Humber *c*. 1824

Watercolour, 165 × 243
Engr.: by G. H. Phillips, 1826, for *Rivers of England* (R. 763)
Coll.: Trustees of the British Museum (T.B., CCVIII–R)

Finberg suggests that a watercolour study in the *Ports of England* sketchbook (T.B., CCII–20) is preparatory for this design; also some loose sheets (T.B., CCIII, E, F, G, H).

746 Stangate Creek, on the River Medway
c. 1824

Watercolour, 161 × 240
Engr.: by T. Lupton, 1827, for *Rivers of England* (R. 766); a chromolithograph published by Gambart, 1858 (R. 864)
Coll.: Trustees of the British Museum (T.B., CCVIII–A)

749 The Medway *c*. 1824

Pencil and watercolour, 156 × 218
Not engraved for *Rivers of England* (listed R. 769); a modified version of this design mezzotinted by Turner for the *Little Liber* series (R. 809a)
Exh.: R.A. 1974 (242)
Coll.: Trustees of the British Museum (T.B., CCVIII–P)

See No. 765.

744 Arundel Park, on the River Arun *c*. 1824

Watercolour, 159 × 228
Engr.: by G. H. Phillips, 1827, for *Rivers of England* (R. 764)
Exh.: B.M. 1975 (86)
Coll.: Trustees of the British Museum (T.B., CCVIII–G)

Drawings for this view are in the *Brighton and Arundel* sketchbook (T.B., CCX–69v, 70).

745 Kirkstall Lock, on the River Aire *c*. 1824

Watercolour, 160 × 235
Engr.: by W. Say, 1827, for *Rivers of England* (R. 765)
Coll.: Trustees of the British Museum (T.B., CCVIII–L)

747 Totnes, on the River Dart *c*. 1824

Watercolour, 162 × 230
Engr.: by C. Turner, 1827, for *Rivers of England* (R. 767); the plate was cancelled after *First Publication* and *Second State;* and publication was stopped before *Third State*
Coll.: Trustees of the British Museum (T.B., CCVIII–B)

Turner made drawings of Totnes in the *Corfe to Dartmouth* sketchbook (T.B., CXXIV–39, 40).

XIII(b)   Nos 750–768
Designs for the *Ports of England,* and related drawings, *c*. 1823–1828

The twelve designs for a sequel to the *Rivers of England* (Nos 732–749) were mezzotinted by Thomas Lupton, who had already made several prints after Turner (the wrapper-vignette is No. 750). Six of them were published under Lupton's name as *The Ports of England* between 1826 and 1828; they were reissued, with the remaining six, in 1856 as *Harbours of England,* for which Ruskin provided the text. Six of the drawings remained in the artist's possession; he presumably came to an arrangement with Lupton similar to that with Cooke for the *Rivers* series, and was probably himself responsible for disposing of the designs that are not in the Bequest. Several of the subjects are modifications of views that Turner had made for the

Southern Coast series; but there is no evidence that his work on this set was in any way hurried or unconcerned; Ruskin described the *Sheerness* as 'one of the noblest sea-pieces which Turner ever produced' (*Harbours of England,* p. 37).

750 Wrapper-design for 'Ports of England' 1825

Pencil and grey wash, 300 × 211, vignette
Inscr. in grey wash, top: *Harbours of England;* bottom: *1825*
Engr.: etched by engraver unknown, possibly Turner himself, 1826, for *Ports of England;* reissued in *Harbours of England, by Turner and Ruskin,* 1856 (R. 778)
Prov.: John Ruskin; presented by him to the museum, 1861
Coll.: Syndics of the Fitzwilliam Museum, Cambridge (567; Cormack 20)

751 Scarborough *c.* 1825

Watercolour over traces of pencil, 157 × 225
Engr.: by T. Lupton, 1826, for *Ports of England;* reissued in *Harbours of England, by Turner and Ruskin,* 1856 (R. 779)
Exh.: B.M. 1975 (91)
Coll.: Trustees of the British Museum (T.B., CCVIII–I)

This composition derives from the series of watercolour views of Scarborough that Turner had produced from 1809; especially from that of 1818 (No. 529). A colour study related to it is in the *Ports of England* sketchbook (T.B., CCII–18).

752 Whitby 1824

Watercolour, 158 × 225
Engr.: by T. Lupton, 1826, for *Ports of England;* reissued in *Harbours of England, by Turner and Ruskin,* 1856 (R. 780)
Coll.: Trustees of the British Museum (T.B., CCVIII–J)

A drawing used for this view is in the *King's Visit to Scotland* sketchbook (T.B., CC–84).

753 Dover *c.* 1825

Watercolour, 161 × 245
Engr.: by T. Lupton, 1827, for *Ports of England,* reissued in *Harbours of England, by Turner and Ruskin,* 1856 (R. 781)
Exh.: B.M. 1975 (92)
Coll.: Trustees of the British Museum (T.B., CCVIII–U)

A colour sketch for this subject is in the *Ports of England* sketchbook (T.B., CCII–14).

754 Ramsgate 1824

Watercolour, 161 × 232

Engr.: by T. Lupton, 1827, for *Ports of England;* reissued in *Harbours of England, by Turner and Ruskin,* 1856 (R. 782)
Coll.: Trustees of the British Museum (T.B., CCVIII–Q)

A variant of the subject drawn for the *Southern Coast* series (No. 474); both make use of a study in the *Hastings to Margate* sketchbook (T.B., CXL–85).

755 Sheerness 1824

Watercolour, 160 × 238
Engr.: by T. Lupton, 1828, for *Ports of England;* reissued in *Harbours of England, by Turner and Ruskin,* 1856 (R. 783)
Coll.: Trustees of the British Museum (T.B., CCVIII–T)

756 Portsmouth 1824

Watercolour, 160 × 240
Engr.: by T. Lupton, 1828, for *Ports of England;* reissued in *Harbours of England, by Turner and Ruskin,* 1856 (R. 784)
Exh.: R.A. 1974 (243)
Coll.: Trustees of the British Museum (T.B., CCVIII–S)

A colour study for this design is T.B., CCIII–A. Small pencil studies of Portsmouth occur in T.B., CCVI, 1–3, 5, 9.

757 Margate *c.* 1826–8

Watercolour with scraping-out, 154 × 255
Engr.: by T. Lupton, 1828, for *Ports of England,* but not used; publ. *Harbours of England, by Turner and Ruskin,* 1856 (R. 785)
Prov.: John Ruskin; presented by him to the museum, 1861

Coll.: Visitors of the Ashmolean Museum, Oxford (Herrmann 26)

758   Deal *c.* 1826–8

Watercolour and body-colour, 162 × 237
Engr.: by T. Lupton, 1828, for *Ports of England,* but not used; publ. *Harbours of England, by Turner and Ruskin,* 1856 (R. 786)
Prov.: A. R. Johnston; J. Hill Abram
Coll.: Walker Art Gallery, Liverpool (1001)

Compare the *Southern Coast* subject (No. 481).

759   Sidmouth *c.* 1824

Watercolour and scratching-out, 184 × 263
Engr.: by T. Lupton, 1828, for *Ports of England,* but not used; publ. *Harbours of England, by Turner and Ruskin,* 1856 (R. 787)
Prov.: H. W. F. Bolckow, sale Christie 2 May 1891 (50), bt. Reece; E. Nettlefold, sale Christie 11 June 1909 (171), bt. Agnew; Hollingworth; E. J. Nettlefold, by whom given to the gallery, 1948
Coll.: Whitworth Art Gallery, University of Manchester (D.8.1948)

760   Plymouth *c.* 1825

Watercolour, 160 × 245
Engr.: by T. Lupton, 1828, for *Ports of England,* but not used; publ. *Harbours of England, by Turner and Ruskin,* 1856 (R. 788)
Exh.: R.A. 1974 (173)
Prov.: John Dillon, sale Foster & Son, 7 June 1856 (143); Langton; J. Farnworth; William Quilter, sale Christie, 9 April 1875 (243), bt. Lane; J. Ruston, sale Christie 4 July 1913 (107), bt. Agnew
Coll.: Fundaçao Calouste Gulbenkian, Lisbon (374)

761   Catwater, Plymouth *c.* 1826

Watercolour, 159 × 229
Engr.: by T. Lupton, 1828, for *Ports of England,* but not used; publ. *Harbours of England, by Turner and Ruskin,* 1856 (R. 789)
Prov.: J. Price; Holbrook Gaskell, sale Christie 25 June 1909 (235), bt. Agnew: R. Brocklebank; Christie 7 May 1954 (68), bt. Fine Art Society, London
Private collection, Hobart, Tasmania

762   Falmouth *c.* 1825

Watercolour, 145 × 220

Engr.: by T. Lupton, 1828, for *Ports of England,* but not used; publ. *Harbours of England, by Turner and Ruskin,* 1856 (R. 790)
Prov.: Robert Stirling Newall; by descent to present owner
Private collection

763   Off Hastings *c.* 1820–5

Watercolour, 202 × 260
Exh.: C.G. 1822 (9)
Prov.: Henry Vaughan, by whom bequeathed to the gallery, 1900
Coll.: National Gallery of Ireland, Dublin (2412)

Similar in style and subject-matter to the study of the *Mew-Stone* associated with both the *Southern Coast* and the *Little Liber* series, No. 773 below; see also No. 764.

764   Shakespeare Cliff, Dover *c.* 1825

Watercolour, 181 × 245
Prov.: C. F. Huth, not traceable in sale Christie 1895; T. W. Bacon, by whom given to the museum, 1950
Coll.: Syndics of the Fitzwilliam Museum, Cambridge (P.D. 114–1950; Cormack 21)

Possibly a leaf from the *Ports of England* sketch-book (T.B., CCII). Compare also the colour study for the *Mew-Stone* (No. 773 below) and No. 763 above.

765   On the Medway ?*c.* 1823

Watercolour, 235 × 368
Prov.: J. E. Taylor, sale Christie 5 July 1912 (83), bt. Agnew; Ernest Debenham; Agnew 1947; Sir William Worsley; Agnew 1970
Private collection

A large sheet, related in general subject to the scene on the Medway with a rainbow which Turner made in connection with the *Rivers of England* (No. 749), and adapted for one of his *Little Liber* plates. This treatment, in very broad pale washes, is reminiscent of the colour-beginnings associated with the *England and Wales* project and executed in the early 1830s. It is possible, therefore, that this represents a further application of the subject for that work. Technically, however, a date in the early or mid-1820s seems appropriate.

766   Ship and sailing-boat at sea   *c.* 1825

Pencil and watercolour, 170 × 240
Prov.: unknown
Private collection

767   Rough sea, with a fishing-boat   *?c.* 1825

Watercolour, 198 × 294
Prov.: J. E. Taylor, sale Christie 8 July 1912 (?126); George Healing; Major-Gen. J. A. Robertson; Agnew, from whom purchased, 1967
Coll.: Mr. and Mrs. Paul Mellon, Upperville, Virginia

768   Storm off Margate   *?c.* 1825

Watercolour, 178 × 260
Prov.: John Ruskin, sale Christie 29 April 1869 (?15)
Coll.: Denys Sutton

III(c)   Nos 769–784
Studies connected with the *Little Liber* mezzotints, *c.* **1825–1830**

These colour studies are related to mezzotints made by Turner for the unpublished series of plates known as the *Little Liber Studiorum*, or are sheets which seem to have some connection with that work, either by virtue of their general style or mood, or because they may have been executed at about the same date and deal with comparable subject-matter. Turner's intention in this series seems to have been to explore dramatic effects of natural light in terms of the mezzotint medium, and all the subjects are storm- or night-scenes. Although the impulse to make the plates may have derived from Turner's experiments with some of the later mezzotints of the *Liber Studiorum*, he was perhaps directly inspired by the appearance of F. C. Lewis's mezzotint after Francis Danby's *Sunset at Sea after a Storm*, which appeared in 1826. It was presumably about this time that he was beginning to notice Danby's work: he is recorded as having answered one critic's comments on Danby by saying, 'Sir, Danby is a poetical painter' (*Life,* p. 290, note 1).

769   Paestum in a thunderstorm   *c.* 1825

Watercolour, with pencil, 213 × 305
Related to the mezzotint of this subject in the *Little Liber* series (R. 799)
Exh.: R.A. 1974 (252)
Coll.: Trustees of the British Museum (T.B., CCCLXIV–224)

770   The evening gun   *c.* 1825

Watercolour, size unknown
A preparatory drawing for the mezzotint of this subject in the *Little Liber* series (R. 800)
Prov.: J. E. Taylor
Coll.: untraced

771   Shields Lighthouse (Moonlight on calm sea)   *c.* 1825

Watercolour, with some body-colour, 195 × 245
Connected with the mezzotint of this subject in the *Little Liber* series (R. 801)
Coll.: Trustees of the British Museum (T.B., CCLXIII–308)

772   Ship in a storm   *c.* 1825

Watercolour and pencil, 216 × 290
Connected with the mezzotint of this subject in the *Little Liber* series (R. 803)
Coll.: Trustees of the British Museum (T.B., CCLXIII–309(a))

773   The Mew-stone   *c.* 1825

Watercolour and ?some body-colour, 242 × 384
Related to the mezzotint of this subject in the *Little Liber* series (R. 804).
Coll.: Trustees of the British Museum (T.B., CXCVI–F)

389

This design is a modification of that for the subject in the *Southern Coast* series (No. 454)

774 Catania, Sicily, in a storm *c.*1825

Watercolour, 212 × 283
Design (previously known as 'Storm over St. Peter's') for the mezzotint of this subject in the *Little Liber* series (R. 805)
Prov.: (?J.) E. Taylor; Ellen T. Bullard; given to the museum by the legatees under her will, in accordance with her request, 1959
Coll.: Museum of Fine Arts, Boston, Mass. (59.794)

775 Study of sea and sky *c.* 1825

Watercolour, size unknown
Connected with the mezzotint of this subject in the *Little Liber* series (R. 806)
Prov.: ?J. E. Taylor
Coll.: untraced

776 Bridge and monument *c.*1825

Watercolour, 211 × 292
Connected with the mezzotint of this subject for the *Little Liber* series (R. 807)
Exh.: R.A. 1974 (247, as 'A Stormy Landscape with an Obelisk and Classical Portico')
Coll.: Trustees of the British Museum (T.B., CCLXIII–252)

777 Ship and cutter *c.* 1825

Pencil and watercolour, 241 × 300
Connected with the mezzotint of this subject for the *Little Liber* series (R. 808)
Prov.: J. E. Taylor; William Norton Bullard, by whom given to the museum, 1923
Coll.: Museum of Fine Arts, Boston, Mass. (23.1240)

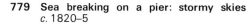

778 Gloucester Cathedral *c.*1825

Watercolour and pencil, 230 × 298
A preliminary drawing for the mezzotint of this subject (sometimes known as 'Boston Stump') in the *Little Liber* series (R. 809)
Exh.: R.A. 1974 (245)
Coll.: Trustees of the British Museum (T.B., CCLXIII–307)

A drawing closely related to this is T.B., CCLXIII–246.

779 Sea breaking on a pier: stormy skies *c.* 1820-5

Watercolour over traces of pencil, 158 × 230
Exh.: R.A. 1974 (265)

Prov.: Sir Hickman Bacon, Bt.; by descent to the present owner
Private collection

780 Cloud and sunlight at sea ?*c.* 1825

Watercolour, 192 × 242
Prov.: John Ruskin, by whom given to the Ruskin School, Oxford, 1875; transferred to the museum, 1938
Coll.: Visitors of the Ashmolean Museum, Oxford (293; Herrmann 85)

Herrmann dates this sheet to about 1840; it is probably earlier, and in both size and treatment resembles pages from the *Ports of England* sketchbook (T.B., CCII); cf. Nos 763, 764, 773, 777.

781 Sunset over the river *c.* 1825–30

Watercolour over pencil, 186 × 271
Prov.: Sir J. C. Robinson; W. G. Rawlinson; T. A. Tatton, sale Christie 14 December 1928 (28,

as 'A sketch on a Swiss, or North Italian, Lake'), bt. Agnew; from whom purchased by anon. donor to the museum
Coll.: Museum of Art, Rhode Island School of Design, Providence, R.I.

782   Study of Clouds over the sea   *?c.* 1825

Watercolour, 174 × 237
Verso: evening sky (watercolour)
Prov.: Mrs. Hubert Pryor, Los Angeles, Calif., sale Sotheby 5 August 1973 (106), bt. Colnaghi
Private collection, Germany

783   Farne Island   *c.* 1825

Watercolour, 140 × 203
Engr.: by J. T. Willmore, 1860 (R. 688, unpubl.)
Prov.: J. E. Taylor; Wallis & Son; anon. sale, Christie 30 June 1916 (122), bt. in; Barbizon House
Coll.: untraced

Reproduced in A. L. Baldry, 'British Marine Painting', *Studio,* 1919, p. 44.

784   Sunrise off Margate   *c.* 1825–30

Watercolour, 221 × 280 (sight)
Prov.: ? John Ruskin, sale 15 April 1869 (17), bt. Cassel; Denis Nahum, sale Sotheby 23 November 1967 (81), bt. Fine Art Society, London; Walter Brandt
Coll.: Trustees of the P. A. Brandt Settlement

SECTION XIV
Nos 785–929 'England and Wales' and Petworth, *c.* 1825–1840

XIV(a)   Nos 785–895
Designs for *Picturesque Views in England and Wales,* **with unused subjects and related colour-beginnings,** *c.* 1825–1838

The *Picturesque Views in England and Wales* were commissioned from Charles Heath in about 1825; 120 views were planned, but in the event only ninety-six were published. Turner was paid, according to Rawlinson, 'sixty to seventy guineas apiece' for his drawings, but this is possibly too high a figure; the team of experienced engravers engaged for the work received £100 per plate. The subjects appeared in serial issues between 1827 and 1838, and a first volume of sixty plates, with text by Hannibal Evans Lloyd, was published in 1832. A second volume containing thirty-six more subjects was also issued, but the project was never completed. It met with little success, and the plates, having been sold by Heath to another publisher, were eventually put up for auction, when Turner bought back the whole set, together with unsold impressions. The series was reprinted in two volumes of forty-eight plates each, in 1838. A few finished drawings which appear to have been intended for the work, together with some colour-beginnings associated with the enterprise, are listed as Nos 881–895.

785   Rivaulx Abbey, Yorkshire   *c.* 1826

Watercolour, 280 × 400
Engr.: by E. Goodall, 1827, for *England and Wales* (R. 209)
Prov.: John Dillon, sale Christie 17 April 1869 (43), bt. Agnew; Albert Levy, sale Christie 1 April 1876 (270), bt. Agnew; A. G. Kurtz, sale 11 May 1891 (204), bt. Agnew; Sir Donald Currie; by descent to the present owner
Private collection

786   Lancaster, from the Aqueduct Bridge   *c.* 1825

Watercolour, with some body-colour, 280 × 394
Inscr. on boat right: *LANCASTER*
Engr.: by R. Wallis, 1827, for *England and Wales* (R. 210)
Prov.: Charles Langton, sale Christie 17 May 1862 (104), bt. Agnew; William Leech, sale Christie

21 May 1887 (67), bt. Agnew; J. Orrock, sale Christie 4 June 1904 (42), bt. Boswell; Lord Leverhulme
Coll.: The Lady Lever Collection, Port Sunlight, Cheshire (277)

Turner's pencil drawing for this subject is in the *Yorkshire 5* sketchbook (T.B., CXLVIII–35v). Another version of the subject exists in the Cecil Higgins Art Gallery, Bedford; it is a very close copy and was apparently accepted by Finberg (MS. Index), but is perhaps a drawing in the same category as the elaborate copy of the 1843 *Faido* in the Rhode Island School of Design, executed by a member of Ruskin's circle (see Cormack, *Catalogue of Watercolours in the Museum of Art, Rhode Island School of Design,* 1972, No. 56).

787   Dartmouth Cove   *c.* 1826

Watercolour, 280 × 387
Engr.: by W. R. Smith, 1827, for *England and Wales* (R.211)
Exh.: M.B.G. 1833
Prov.: B. G. Windus; J. Heugh, sale Christie 24 April 1874 (93), bt. Agnew; Holbrook Gaskell, sale Christie 25 June 1909 (233), bt. King; Frank Gaskell, 1937; by descent to the present owners
Coll.: Ernest and Roger Gaskell

788   Bolton Abbey, Yorkshire   *c.* 1825

Watercolour, 280 × 394
Engr.: by R. Wallis, 1827, for *England and Wales* (R. 212)
Prov.: John Ruskin 1878; J. Orrock, sale Christie 4 June 1904 (40), bt. Agnew; Lord Leverhulme
Coll.: The Lady Lever Collection, Port Sunlight, Cheshire (228)

The pencil drawing of this view is in the *Devonshire Rivers No. 3 and Wharfedale* sketchbook (T.B., CXXXIV, 81–82).

789 Colchester, Essex *c.* 1826

Watercolour, with some body-colour, 283 × 404
Engr.: by R. Wallis, 1827, for *England and Wales*
(R. 213)
Exh.: E.H. 1829; Birmingham Society of Artists
1829 (388); M.B.G. 1833
Prov.: J. H. Maw, by 1829; Miss James, sale
Christie 22 June 1891 (160), bt. Agnew; Locket
Agnew; Thos. Agnew, sale Christie 16 June 1906
(58), bt. Agnew; Charles Fairfax Murray; Agnew
1908; Sir Stephen Courtauld, 1918, and pre-
sented to the institute in his memory by his family,
1974
Coll.: Courtauld Institute of Art, University of
London (Stephen Courtauld Bequest 11.74; Kitson
8)

A pencil study used for this design is in the *Norfolk,
Suffolk and Essex* sketchbook (T.B., CCIX–6v).

790 Fall of the Tees, Yorkshire *c.* 1825

Watercolour, 280 × 393
Engr.: by E. Goodall, 1827, for *England and* Wales
(R. 214)
Prov.: C. S. Bale, sale Christie 14 May 1881 (198),
bt. Brown; Hon. Francis Baring, sale Christie 3 June
1893 (1), bt. Agnew; J. E. Taylor, sale Christie
5 July 1912 (51), bt. Agnew
Private collection

791 Richmond, Yorkshire *c.* 1826

Watercolour, 275 × 397
Engr.: by W. R. Smith, 1827, for *England and Wales*
(R. 215)
Exh.: M.B.G. 1833; R.A. 1974 (421)
Prov.: B. G. Windus; John Leigh Clare, sale Christie
28 March 1868 (98), bt. Isaac; ?John Farnworth,
sale 10 May 1874 (49), bt. Agnew; ? A. G. Kurtz,
sale Christie 11 May 1891 (200), bt. Tooth;
George Salting, by whom bequeathed to the
museum, 1910

Coll.: Trustees of the British Museum
(1910–2–12–276)

The drawing for this subject is in the *Yorkshire No. 5*
sketchbook (T.B., CXLVIII–13v).

792 Launceston, Cornwall *c.* 1826

Watercolour, 279 × 394
Engr.: by J. C. Varrall, 1827, for *England and Wales*
(R. 216)
Verso: a watercolour sketch
Exh.: E.H. 1829; M.B.G. 1833
Prov.: T. Tomkison (1833); T. Birchall (1857); Mrs.
Moir; Mrs. E. C. Innes, sale Christie
13 December 1935 (53), bt. Polak; Beneficiaries of
a private collection, sale Christie 5 June 1973
(121), bt. Colnaghi
Private collection, Iran

Drawings made at Launceston appear in the *Devon
Rivers No. 1* and *Devon Rivers No. 3 and Wharfedale*
sketchbooks (T.B., CXXXII, CXXXIV).

793 Barnard Castle, Durham *c.* 1825

Watercolour, 292 × 419
Engr.: by R. Wallis, 1827, for *England and Wales*
(R. 217); a reduced version of this design engraved
by J. T. Willmore for *The Talisman*, 1831
(R. 341)
Prov.: Thomas Griffith; Major Pitt-Miller; Mrs. Pitt-
Miller; Paul Mellon, 1976
Coll.: Yale Center for British Art, Paul Mellon
Collection

A colour study perhaps of Barnard Castle is
No. 890.

794 Saltash, Cornwall 1825

Watercolour and body-colour, 273 × 408
Signed and dated lower right: *JMW Turner RA/
25*
Engr.: by W. R. Smith, 1827, for *England and Wales*
(R. 218)
Exh.: E.H. 1829; M.B.G. 1833; B.M. 1975 (90)
Prov.: B. G. Windus; J. H. Maw; R. R. Davies
(1857); anon. sale Christie 3 March 1862 (52), bt.
in; J. Knowles, sale Christie 7 April 1865 (122), bt.
Vokins; F. R. Leyland, sale Christie 9 March 1872
(36), bt. White; anon. sale Christie 10 March 1876
(130), bt. S. Addington, sale Christie 22 May 1886
(57), bt. Vokins; S. G. Holland, sale Christie
26 June 1908 (261), bt. Agnew; Sir Joseph
Beecham, sale Christie 4 May 1917 (152);
R. W. Lloyd, by whom bequeathed to the museum,
1958
Coll.: Trustees of the British Museum
(1958–7–12–427)

795 Aldeburgh, Suffolk *c.* 1826

Watercolour and body-colour, 280 × 400
Engr.: by E. Goodall, 1827, for *England and Wales*
(R. 219)
Prov.: John Dillon, sale 29 April 1869 (128), bt.
Agnew; William Quilter, sale Christie 9 April 1875
(242), bt. Isaac; Beresford Rimington Heaton, by
whom bequeathed to the gallery, 1940
Coll.: Tate Gallery, London (5236)

796 Orford, Suffolk c. 1828

Watercolour, 280 × 403
Engr.: by R. Brandard, 1827, for *England and Wales* (R. 220)
Exh.: M.B.G. 1833
Prov.: Thomas Griffith; George Young, sale Christie 19 May 1866 (29), bt. Agnew; John Knowles, sale Christie 19 May 1877 (98), bt. Newton; Mrs. McKenzie; S. G. Holland, sale Christie 26 June 1908 (260), bt. Agnew; Agnew 1913
Private collection, England

The drawing on which this design is based appears in the *Norfolk, Suffolk and Essex* sketchbook (T.B., CCIX–86v).

797 Straits of Dover c. 1827

Watercolour, size unknown
Engr.: by W. Miller, 1828, for *England and Wales* (R. 221)
Exh.: M.B.G. 1833
Prov.: B. G. Windus; David Reynolds Davies, sale Christie 31 March 1882 (42), bt. in; ? Nettlefold
Coll.: untraced

798 Prudhoe Castle, Northumberland* c. 1826

Watercolour, 292 × 408
Inscr. lower left: *JMW* [monogram] *Turner*
Engr.: by E. Goodall, 1828, for *England and Wales* (R. 222)
Exh.: B.M. 1975 (106)
Prov.: Revd. W. Kingsley; Agnew; R. W. Lloyd, by whom bequeathed to the museum, 1958
Coll.: Trustees of the British Museum (1958–7–12–428)

There is a drawing of this view in the *Durham, North Shore* sketchbook (T.B., CLVII, 77v–78). A 'Prudhoe Castle' (635 × 470) was sold by a 'Collector from the North', Christie, 8 May 1855 (62), bt. Wallis.

799 Valle Crucis Abbey, Denbighshire c. 1826

Watercolour and body-colour, some scratching-out, 285 × 410
Engr.: by J. C. Varrall, 1828, for *England and Wales* (R. 223)
Exh.: M.B.G. 1833
Prov.: Thomas Griffith; H. A. J. Munro of Novar, sale Christie 2 June 1877 (52), bt. Vokins; The French Gallery, 120 Pall Mall, 1912; James Blair, by whom bequeathed to the gallery, 1917
Coll.: City Art Gallery, Manchester (1917–93)

Turner sketched this view in the *Hereford Court* sketchbook, of 1798 (T.B., XXXVIII–55).

800 Buckfastleigh Abbey, Devonshire c. 1826

Watercolour, 274 × 394
Engr.: by R. Wallis, 1828, for *England and Wales* (R. 224); a reduced version of this design was engraved by R. Wallis for *The Literary Souvenir*, 1827 (R. 316)
Exh.: M.B.G. 1833
Prov.: Thomas Griffith; B. G. Windus; John Ruskin; Arthur Severn; anon. sale Christie 9 March 1901 (95), bt. Tooth; Barnet Lewis, sale Christie 28 February 1930 (48), bt. Agnew; Agnew 1936
Coll.: Executors of the late Vice-Admiral Sir William Agnew, K.C.V.O., C.B., D.S.O.

801 Entrance to Fowey Harbour, Cornwall c. 1827

Watercolour, 282 × 391
Engr.: by W. R. Smith, 1829, for *England and Wales* (R. 225)
Exh.: E.H. 1829; Birmingham Society of Artists 1829 (356); M.B.G. 1833

Prov.: B. G. Windus; Lowndes (1833); E. Atkinson; Marquess of Lansdowne; anon. sale Christie 22 July 1955 (83), bt. Fine Art Society, London; Knoedler, New York
Private collection, U.S.A.

Compare the view of the 'Entrance to Fowey Harbour' made for the *Southern Coast* series (No. 466).

802 Okehampton, Devonshire c. 1826

Watercolour, 280 × 406
Engr.: by J. T. Willmore, 1828, for *England and Wales* (R. 226)
Exh.: M.B.G. 1833
Prov.: Thomas Griffith; John Dillon; John Ruskin; James Orrock, sale Christie 4 June 1904 (44), bt. Agnew; C. Fairfax Murray; acquired by the gallery through the Felton Bequest, 1905
Coll.: National Gallery of Victoria, Melbourne

A pencil drawing used for this composition is in the *Devonshire Rivers No. 3 and Wharfedale* sketchbook (T.B., CXXXIV–70). Compare the *Rivers of England* view (No. 738).

803 Lancaster Sands c. 1826

Watercolour, 278 × 404
Engr.: by R. Brandard, 1828, for *England and Wales* (R. 227)
Exh.: M.B.G. 1833; R.A. 1974 (419)
Prov.: Tomkison (1833); H. A. J. Munro of Novar, sale Christie 2 June 1877 (43), bt. Agnew; J. Irvine Smith; F. Stevenson; George Salting, by whom bequeathed to the museum, 1910
Coll.: Trustees of the British Museum (1910–2–12–279)

See the study, No. 894, which may be connected with this subject.

804 Knaresborough, Yorkshire *c*. 1826

Watercolour, 289 × 413
Engr.: by T. Jeavons, 1828, for *England and Wales*
(R. 228)
Exh.: M.B.G. 1833
Prov.: Revd. E. Coleridge; H. A. J. Munro of Novar,
sale Christie 6 April 1878 (91), bt. Agnew;
J. F. White (1886); Laundy Walters (1899);
Agnew 1913
Private collection

Turner made drawings at Knaresborough in the
North of England sketchbook, of 1797 (T.B.,
XXXIV); also in the *Yorkshire No. 1* and in the *Yorkshire No. 3* sketchbooks (T.B., CXLIV, 50–58; CXLVI,
31–2).

805 Malmesbury Abbey, Wiltshire *c*. 1827

Watercolour, 289 × 416
Engr.: by J. C. Varrall, 1829, for *England and Wales*
(R. 229)
Exh.: M.B.G. 1833
Prov.: Tomkison; H. A. J. Munro of Novar, sale
Christie 6 April 1878 (93), bt. Vokins; J. Grant
Morris, sale Christie 23 April 1898 (63), bt.
Agnew; R. E. Tatham; C. Hiltermann, sale Christie
14 June 1977 (151), bt. Oscar & Peter Johnson
Coll.: Oscar & Peter Johnson Ltd., Lowndes Lodge
Gallery, London

Among the many early studies of Malmesbury, that
on p. 1 of the *Hereford Court* sketchbook (T.B.,
XXXVIII) was perhaps the basis of this design; see
also the *Dinevor Castle* sketchbook (T.B., XL–5, 6).

806 Kilgarren Castle, Pembroke *c*. 1828

Watercolour, 279 × 400
Engr.: by J. T. Willmore, 1829, for *England and
Wales* (R. 230)
Exh.: E.H. 1829; Birmingham Society of Artists
1829 (345); M.B.G. 1833

Prov.: Thomas Griffith; W. W. Pattinson; Marquess
of Lansdowne; by descent to present owner
Coll.: Bowood Collection

An adaptation of the design of the early watercolour and oil-painting of the castle (No. 243 and
P11 respectively).

807 Exeter *c*. 1827

Watercolour with some body-colour, 300 × 428
Engr.: by T. Jeavons, 1829, for *England and Wales*
(R. 231)
Exh.: M.B.G. 1833
Prov.: B. G. Windus; Sir H. H. Campbell, sale
Christie 24 March 1856 (45), bt. Cox Levy; Albert
Levy, sale Christie 1 April 1876 (281), bt. Goupil;
(? J. C. Ure, 1911); Anthony Gibbs, sale Christie
29 April 1911 (47), bt. Agnew; James Blair, by
whom bequeathed to the gallery, 1917
Coll.: City Art Gallery, Manchester (1917–107)

808 Richmond, Yorkshire (Richmond from the
Moors) *c*. 1826–8

Watercolour, 280 × 400
Engr.: by J. T. Willmore, 1829, for *England and
Wales* (R. 232)
Exh.: E.H. 1829; Birmingham Society of Artists
1829 (424, as 'Richmond Castle'); M.B.G. 1833
Prov.: B. G. Windus; John Ruskin, by whom given
to the museum, 1861
Coll.: Syndics of the Fitzwilliam Museum, Cam-
bridge (572; Cormack 25)

A colour-beginning of this subject is T.B., CXCVII–N;
and on pp. 11v–12 of the *Yorkshire 5* sketchbook
(T.B., CXLVIII) there is a pencil study of the same
view.

809 Louth, Lincolnshire* *c*. 1827

Watercolour and scraping-out, 285 × 420
Engr.: by W. Radclyffe, 1829, for *England and
Wales* (R. 233)
Exh.: E.H. 1829; M.B.G. 1833; R.A. 1974 (422)
Prov.: Thomas Griffith (1833); H. A. J. Munro of
Novar, sale Christie 2 June 1877 (50), bt. Severn;
John Ruskin; George Salting, by whom be-
queathed to the museum, 1910
Coll.: Trustees of the British Museum
(1910–2–12–278)

Based on a drawing in the *North of England*
sketchbook, of 1797 (T.B., XXXIV–80).

810 Great Yarmouth, Norfolk *c*. 1827

Watercolour, 279 × 394
Engr.: by W. Miller, 1829, for *England and Wales*
(R. 234)
Exh.: M.B.G. 1833
Prov.: B. G. Windus; Revd. W. Kingsley; Miss
L. L. A. Taylor; Mr. and Mrs. L. B. Murray; by
descent to present owner
Private collection

Turner made several studies at Yarmouth in the
Norfolk, Suffolk and Essex sketchbook (T.B., CCIX,
24–34); compare the smaller view of Yarmouth for
the 'East Coast' series, unpubl. (No. 904).

811 Stonehenge, Wiltshire *c*. 1827

Watercolour, 279 × 404
Engr.: by R. Wallis, 1829, for *England and Wales*
(R. 235)
Exh.: E.H. 1829; M.B.G. 1833
Prov.: Samuel Rogers, sale Christie 8 May 1856
(1255a), bt. Wallis; W. G. Rawlinson; Agnew
1924; T. A. Tatton, sale Christie 14 December
1928 (13), bt. Agnew; Lord Horder
Private collection, England

There are studies of Stonehenge in the *Studies for Pictures* sketchbook (T.B., LXIX–79, 80); and in the *Stonehenge* sketchbook (T.B., CXXV–B, not in *Inventory)*, and in the *Devonshire Coast No. 1* sketchbook (T.B., CXXIII–211, 212). Colour-beginnings related to the subject are T.B., CCLXIII–1, 37).

812 Hampton Court Palace *c.* 1827

Watercolour, size unknown
Engr.: by C. Westwood, 1829, for *England and Wales* (R. 236)
Exh.: M.B.G. 1833
Prov.: Thomas Griffith (1833); Edward Rodgett, sale Christie 14 May 1859 (44), bt. Dixon
Coll.: untraced

813 Devonport and Dockyard, Devonshire *c.* 1828

Watercolour, 287 × 439
Engr.: by T. Jeavons, 1830, for *England and Wales* (R. 237)
Exh.: M.B.G. 1833
Prov.: John Ruskin; Agnew; Charles Fairfax Murray, by whom given to the museum in memory of W. J. Stillman, 1903
Coll.: Fogg Art Museum, Harvard University, Cambridge, Mass. (1903–49)

814 Dunstanborough Castle, Northumberland *c.* 1828

Watercolour, 291 × 419 (sight)
Engr.: by R. Brandard, 1830, for *England and Wales* (R. 238)
Exh.: M.B.G. 1833; R.A. 1974 (423)
Prov.: T. Tomkison; ? Thomas Birchall, 1857; H. A. J. Munro of Novar, sale Christie 11 May 1867 (172), bt. John Heugh; sale Christie 24 April

1874 (94), bt. Agnew; Sir William Armstrong; W. A. Watson-Armstrong, 1902; sale Christie 24 June 1910 (38), bt. Agnew; James Blair, by whom bequeathed to the gallery, 1917
Coll.. City Art Gallery, Manchester (1917–110)

A reinterpretation of the view of Dunstanborough noted by Turner in the *North of England* sketchbook, of 1797 (T.B., XXXIV–45), used for an early watercolour (No. 284) and for the *Liber Studiorum* plate (R. 14), as well as for the paintings P 6, P 32.

815 Carisbrook Castle, Isle of Wight *c.* 1828

Watercolour, 292 × 412
Engr.: by C. Westwood, 1830, for *England and Wales* (R. 239)
Exh.: M.B.G. 1833
Prov.: B. G. Windus; John Ruskin; J. E. Taylor, sale Christie 5 July 1912 (44), bt. C. P. Allen; sale Christie 5 December 1930 (46), bt. Agnew
Coll.: Executors of the late Vice-Admiral Sir William Agnew, K.C.V.O., C.B., D.S.O.

Turner made a drawing, partly coloured, of the Gate of Carisbrook Castle in the *Isle of Wight* sketchbook (T.B., XXIV–25v).

816 Cowes, Isle of Wight *c.* 1828

Watercolour, body-colour and scraping-out, 286 × 419
Engr.: by R. Wallis, 1830, for *England and Wales* (R. 240); a chromolithograph of this subject (R. 852) by an engraver unknown and published probably 1852 by publisher unknown
Exh.: M.B.G. 1833
Prov.: T. Tomkison; J. H. Hawkins; William Leech, sale Christie 21 May 1887 (68), bt. Agnew; E. Atkinson; Agnew, 1905; William Yates; by descent; sale Sotheby 19 October 1967 (23), bt. Agnew

Private collection

This drawing was presumably made very shortly after Turner had collected material at Cowes while staying with Nash in the summer of 1827 (see T.B., CCXXVI).

817 Stamford, Lincolnshire* *c.* 1828

Watercolour, 293 × 420
Engr.: by W. Miller, 1830, for *England and Wales* (R. 241)
Exh.: M.B.G. 1833
Prov.: Thomas Griffith (1833); E. Crockford, sale Christie 24 February 1849 (70, as 'Stamford in a Storm'), bt. Rought; ? T. H. Burnett; Adam Fairrie, sale Christie 6 March 1861 (92), bt. Jones; Sir J. Fowler, sale Christie 6 May 1899 (35), bt. Lyons; Greenwood, sale Christie 9 May 1919 (75), bt. Sampson
Coll.: Usher Art Gallery, Lincoln

Based on a pencil drawing in the *North of England* sketchbook, of 1797 (T.B., XXXIV–86).

818 Alnwick Castle, Northumberland *c.* 1829

Watercolour, 283 × 483
Engr.: by J. T. Willmore, 1830, for *England and Wales* (R. 242)
Exh.: E.H. 1829; M.B.G. 1833; Royal Manchester Institution 1835 (260, as 'Moonlight')
Prov.: Thomas Griffith; F. N. Fordham; A. R. Fordham, sale Christie 12 July 1918 (105), bt. Leggatt; Mrs. M. P. Stamp, sale Christie 12 September 1941 (82), bt. Fine Art Society, London; Brian Hamilton; acquired by the gallery through a Government grant, 1958
Coll.: Art Gallery of South Australia, Adelaide

Based on a drawing in the *North of England* sketchbook, of 1797 (T.B., XXXIV–44).

819 Holy Island, Northumberland *c.*1829

Watercolour, with some body-colour and scraping-out, pen and black ink, 292 × 432
Engr.: by W. Tombleson, 1830, for *England and Wales* (R.243)
Exh.: E.H. 1829; M.B.G. 1833
Prov.: G. Lowndes (1833); B. G. Windus; D. R. Davies; anon. sale Christie 22 June 1917 (58), bt. Sampson; A. W. Nicholson; Lady Wakefield, by whom given to the museum, 1943
Coll.: Victoria and Albert Museum, London (P17–1943)

820 Stoneyhurst College, Lancashire *c.*1828

Watercolour, 280 × 419
Engr.: by J. B. Allen, 1830, for *England and Wales* (R.244)
Exh.: E.H. 1829; M.B.G. 1833
Prov.: B. G. Windus; F. Broderip, sale Christie 6 February 1872 (625), bt. McLean; J. A. Baumbach, sale Christie 2 June 1900 (35), bt. Agnew; anon. sale Christie 4 July 1913 (37), bt. Mullen
Coll.: Lord Joicey, Etal Manor, Berwick-upon-Tweed

Compare Turner's view of Stonyhurst for Whitaker's *History of the Parish of Whalley* (No. 293).

821 Winchelsea, Sussex, soldiers on the march *c.*1828

Watercolour and body-colour, with pencil and some scraping-out, 293 × 425
Engr.: by J. Henshall, 1830, for *England and Wales* (R.245)
Exh.: M.B.G. 1833
Prov.: Thomas Griffith; John Ruskin; Agnew 1913; R. W. Lloyd, by whom bequeathed to the museum, 1958
Coll.: Trustees of the British Museum (1958-7-12-429)

822 Trematon Castle, Cornwall *c.*1828

Watercolour, 280 × 407
Engr.: by R. Wallis, 1830, for *England and Wales* (R.246)
Exh.: E.H. 1829; M.B.G. 1833
Prov.: Greenwood; Ripp, sale Foster 13 May 1857; ? James Mason
Coll.: untraced

Turner made drawings of Trematon Castle in the *Plymouth, Hamoaze* sketchbook (T.B., CXXXI–37, 38).

823 St. Mawes, Cornwall *c.*1828

Watercolour, 292 × 419
Engr.: by J. H. Kernot, 1830, for *England and Wales* (R.247)
Prov.: James Bagnall, sale Christie 1 June 1872 (16), bt. Vokins; J. Harrison, sale Christie 2 May 1881 (111), bt. Wigzell; George James, sale Christie 10 April 1897 (92), bt. Tooth; Senator Clark, Washington, D.C.
Coll.: untraced

Compare the design of St. Mawes for the *Southern Coast* series (No. 473).

824 Walton Bridge on Thames, Surrey *c.*1828

Watercolour, 289 × 457
Engr.: by J. C. Varrall, 1830, for *England and Wales* (R.248)
Exh.: E.H. 1829; M.B.G. 1833
Prov.: Thomas Griffith; Thomas Ashton, by 1857; by descent to present owner
Private collection

Derived from the painting of about 1806 (P63).

825 Ludlow Castle, Shropshire *c.*1829

Watercolour, 305 × 457
Engr.: by R. Wallis, 1831, for *England and Wales* (R.249)
Exh.: M.B.G. 1833
Prov.: Thomas Griffith; George Morant, sale Christie 16 April 1847 (240), bt. Broderip; F. Broderip, sale Christie 6 February 1871 (624), bt. in; Hon. W. F. D. Smith; Sir Joseph Beecham, sale Christie 4 May 1917 (147), bt. Tooth; anon. sale Christie 10 May 1918 (88), bt. Baird Carler
Private collection

This composition is based on the pencil drawing in the *Hereford Court* sketchbook, of 1798 (T.B., XXXVIII–63); a large colour study of the view, made shortly after the drawing, is T.B., XLIV–i (repr. B.M. 1975, No. 17).

826 Folkestone Harbour and coast to Dover *c.*1829

Watercolour heightened with white, 292 × 451
Engr.: by J. Horsburgh, 1831, for *England and Wales* (R.250)
Exh.: E.H. 1829; M.B.G. 1833
Prov.: Thomas Griffith; John Dillon, sale Christie 29 April 1869 (131), bt. Tooth; Farnworth, sale Christie 10 May 1874 (39), bt. Vokins; C. L. Parker, sale Christie 15 May 1875 (109), bt. White; Humphrey Roberts, sale Christie 23 May 1908 (285), bt. Permain; Sir Joseph Beecham; Arthur Frisk, sale Sotheby 29 May 1963 (61); Oscar and Peter Johnson, from whom bt. Paul Mellon, 1965
Coll.: Yale Center for British Art, Paul Mellon Collection

827 Tynemouth, Northumberland *c.*1829

Watercolour, 280 × 407
Engr.: by W. R. Smith, 1831, for *England and Wales* (R.251)
Exh.: M.B.G. 1833

Prov.: B. G. Windus, sale Christie 14 February 1868 (262), bt. Vokins; H. W. F. Bolckow, sale Christie 18 June 1892 (140), bt. Ayles; ? Arthur William H. Gregson; destroyed by fire in February 1962

A pencil study, partly coloured, in the *North of England* sketchbook (T.B., XXXIV–35) seems to be the basis for this composition. A watercolour (T.B., XXXIII–T) is an earlier design of the same subject.

828 Gosport, entrance to Portsmouth Harbour *c.* 1829

Watercolour, 285 × 419
Engr.: by R. Brandard, 1831, for *England and Wales* (R. 252)
Exh.: M.B.G. 1833
Prov.: Thomas Griffith; John Ruskin; Sir Donald Currie; by descent to the present owner
Private collection

Drawings made at Gosport occur in the *London Bridge and Portsmouth* sketchbook and in the *Gosport* sketchbook (T.B., CCVI, CCVII).

829 Windsor Castle, Berkshire *c.* 1829

Watercolour, 288 × 437
Engr.: by W. Miller, 1831, for *England and Wales* (R. 253)
Exh.: E.H. 1829; M.B.G. 1833; B.M. 1975 (148)
Prov.: Thomas Tomkison; J. Smith, sale Christie 4 May 1870 (59), bt. Agnew; William Moir; Mrs. Moir; bt. Agnew 1899; R. E. Tatham, sale Christie 29 February 1908 (84), bt. Agnew; Sir Joseph Beecham, sale Christie 4 May 1917 (148), bt. in; sale Christie 10 May 1918 (85); R. W. Lloyd, by whom bequeathed to the museum, 1958
Coll.: Trustees of the British Museum (1958–7-12–432)

Based on drawings in the *Windsor and St. Anne's Hill* sketchbook (T.B., CCXXV–2).

830 Eton College, Berkshire *c.* 1829

Watercolour, 305 × 445
Engr.: by W. Radclyffe, 1831, for *England and Wales* (R. 254)
Exh.: E.H. 1829; M.B.G. 1833
Prov.: Thomas Griffith; the Marquess of Lansdowne; by descent to present owner
Private collection

831 Bedford *c.* 1829

Watercolour, 349 × 489
Engr.: by J. T. Willmore, 1831, for *England and Wales* (R. 255)
Exh.: M.B.G. 1833
Prov.: J. H. Maw; H. A. J. Munro of Novar, sale Christie 2 June 1877 (45), bt. Agnew; John Heugh, sale Christie 10 May 1878 (158), bt. Agnew; Agnew 1912; Davis Jardine, sale Christie 16 March 1917 (56), bt. Agnew; W. H. Barratt, 1924; Mark Fletcher, sale Sotheby 30 November 1960 (55), bt. Leggatt
Coll.: untraced

832 Pembroke Castle, Wales *c.* 1829

Watercolour and scraping-out, 298 × 426
Engr.: T. Jeavons, 1831, for *England and Wales* (R. 256)
Exh.: M.B.G. 1833
Prov.: Thomas Griffith; Earl of Harewood, sale Christie 1 May 1858 (56), bt. Webster; H. A. J. Munro of Novar, sale Christie 6 April 1878 (94), bt. Agnew; J. F. Haworth; Davis Jardine, sale Christie 16 March 1917 (57), bt. King; Ernest Cook, by whom bequeathed to the museum through the National Art-Collections Fund, 1955
Coll.: Holburne of Menstrie Museum, University of Bath

Adapted from the subject of the large watercolour of 1806 (No. 281).

833 Richmond Hill and Bridge, Surrey* *c.* 1831

Watercolour and some body-colour, 291 × 435
Engr.: by W. R. Smith, 1832, for *England and Wales* (R. 257)
Exh.: M.B.G. 1833; B.M. 1975 (174)
Prov.: John Ruskin; Agnew 1900; G. P. Dewhurst; Agnew 1916; R. W. Lloyd, by whom bequeathed to the museum, 1958
Coll.: Trustees of the British Museum (1958–7-12–435)

Perhaps related to the sketch in the *Hints River* sketchbook (T.B., CXLI–14). Compare also the painting by T. C. Hofland, exhibited R.A. 1815 (193), engraved by Charles Heath, 1822.

834 Malvern Abbey and Gate, Worcestershire *c.* 1830

Watercolour, with some scraping-out, 299 × 428
Engr.: by J. Horsburgh, 1832, for *England and Wales* (R. 258)
Exh.: M.B.G. 1833; R.A. 1974 (424)
Prov.: B. G. Windus (1833); W. Quilter, sale Christie 9 April 1875 (246), bt. Agnew; ?John Heugh; ?Agnew; W. Thompson (1877); Agnew 1902; James Blair, by whom bequeathed to the gallery, 1917
Coll.: City Art Gallery, Manchester (1917.104)

Derived from the early watercolour (No. 50).

835 Plymouth, Devonshire *c.* 1830

Watercolour and scraping-out, 280 × 412
Engr.: by W. J. Cooke, 1832, for *England and Wales* (R. 259)
Exh.: M.B.G. 1833
Prov.: W. Jones, by whom bequeathed to the museum, 1882
Coll.: Victoria and Albert Museum, London (521–1882)

836 Salisbury, Wiltshire *c.* 1828

Watercolour, 272 × 395
Engr.: by W. Radclyffe, 1830, for *England and Wales* (R. 260)
Exh.: M.B.G. 1833
Prov.: B. G. Windus; John Ruskin; George Coats; by descent
Private collection

It has been suggested (Hamburg 1976, 87) that the colour-beginning T.B., CCLXIII–304, 'A church spire', is related to this design; but the two buildings seem wholly different both in shape and proportion.

837 St. Catherine's Hill, Guildford, Surrey *c.* 1830

Watercolour and some scraping-out, 296 × 442
Engr.: by J. H. Kernot, 1832, for *England and Wales* (R. 261)
Exh.: M.B.G. 1833
Prov.: Thomas Griffith (1833); G. R. Burnett, sale 6 March 1872 (94), bt. in; Croal Thomson 1927; purchased from the Fine Art Society, London, by Paul Mellon, 1971
Coll.: Yale Center for British Art, Paul Mellon Collection

The ruins on top of St. Catherine's Hill were noted in the *Wey, Guildford* sketchbook, of about 1807 (T.B., XCVIII–110v).

838 Chatham, from Fort Pitt, Kent *c.*1830

Watercolour, 282 × 457
Engr.: by W. Miller, 1832, for *England and Wales* (R. 262)
Exh.: M.B.G. 1833
Prov.: J. H. Maw; H. A. J. Munro of Novar, sale Christie 2 June 1877 (47), bt. Agnew; G. Gurney, sale Christie 17 March 1883 (194), bt. in; George Gurney, sale Christie 11 July 1903 (41), bt.

Permain; Barnet Lewis, sale Christie 28 February 1930 (49); Lord Bilsland
Private collection

Probably designed with the aid of drawings in the *Medway* sketchbook, of 1821 (T.B., CXCIX).

839 Margate, Kent *c.* 1830

Watercolour and ? body-colour, 295 × 450
Engr.: by R. Wallis, 1832, for *England and Wales* (R. 263)
Exh.: M.B.G. 1833
Prov.: Lord Northbourne; Mrs. Crabtree; R. McConnell; Lord Kenilworth, by whom bequeathed to the gallery, 1954
Coll.: Herbert Art Gallery and Museum, Coventry (846)

840 Ashby-de-la-Zouch, Leicestershire *c.* 1830

Watercolour, 304 × 439
Engr.: by W. Radclyffe, 1832, for *England and Wales* (R. 264)
Exh.: M.B.G. 1833
Prov.: Thomas Griffith; H. A. J. Munro of Novar, sale Christie 6 April 1878 (88), bt. Agnew; Locket Agnew; sale Thos. Agnew Christie 16 June 1906 (59), bt. Agnew; J. B. Phipps; Agnew 1907
Coll.: untraced

Based on a drawing in the *Kenilworth* sketchbook (T.B., CCXXXVIII–22).

841 Warwick Castle, Warwickshire *c.* 1829

Watercolour and scratching-out, 297 × 451
Engr.: by R. Wallis, 1832, for *England and Wales* (R. 265)
Exh.: E.H. 1829; M.B.G. 1833
Prov.: Thomas Griffith; John Ruskin; J. E. Taylor,

sale Christie 25 April 1868 (136), bt. Baker; Abraham Haworth; Jesse Haworth, by whom bequeathed to the Whitworth Institute, 1937
Coll.: Whitworth Art Gallery, University of Manchester (D.22.1937)

842 View of Kenilworth Castle *c.* 1830

Watercolour and body-colour, with traces of pencil, 292 × 454
Engr.: by T. Jeavons, 1832, for *England and Wales* (R. 266)
Exh.: M.B.G. 1833
Prov.: Thomas Griffith (1833); John Ruskin; H. A. J. Munro of Novar, sale Christie 2 June 1877 (41), bt. Agnew; W. Tattersall; Agnew; Mrs. W. H. Crocker, California; Mrs. Henry Potter Russell; Osgood Hooker, by whom given to the Palace of the Legion of Honor, San Francisco, 1967
Coll.: Fine Arts Museums of San Francisco, Achenbach Foundation for Graphic Arts (1967.4)

Based on the pencil drawing in the *Kenilworth* sketchbook (T.B., CCXXXVIII, 29v–30).

843 Brinkburn Priory, Northumberland *c.* 1830

Watercolour, 292 × 463
Engr.: by J. C. Varrall, 1832, for *England and Wales* (R. 267)
Exh.: M.B.G. 1833
Prov.: B. G. Windus; Joseph Gillott, sale Christie 4 May 1872 (509), bt. W. Cox; sale Thomas & B., Birmingham, 8 April 1892 (89); Laurence W. Hodson, sale Christie 25 June 1906 (128), bt. Agnew; Sir Joseph Beecham; F. J. Nettlefold, by whom bequeathed to the gallery, 1948
Coll.: Graves Art Gallery, Sheffield (2260)

Based on a pencil study on a leaf from the *Smaller Fonthill* sketchbook, of *c.* 1801 (T.B., XLVIII), now in the Fogg Art Museum, Harvard (1907.12).

844 Tamworth Castle, Staffordshire *c.* 1830

Watercolour, 292 × 445
Engr.: by J. T. Willmore, 1832, for *England and Wales* (R. 268)
Exh.: M.B.G. 1833
Prov.: B. G. Windus; Capt. E. N. F. Loyd, sale Christie 30 April 1937 (60), bt. Frank Partridge & Sons
Private collection

The drawing on which this design is based is in the *Kenilworth* sketchbook (T.B., CCXXXVIII–51c); a colour-beginning is T.B., CCLXIII–184.

845 Ely Cathedral, Cambridgeshire* *c.* 1831

Watercolour, 302 × 410
Engr.: by T. Higham, 1833, for *England and Wales* (R. 269)
Exh.: M.B.G. 1833
Prov.: Thomas Griffith; L. Loyd; Capt. E. N. F. Loyd, sale Christie 30 April 1937 (61); Miss E. F. Jones; anon. sale Christie 16 June 1970 (119), bt. Leger
Private collection

The pencil drawing on which this composition is based dates from 1794; it is now in a private collection; compare the earlier 'Ely from the south-east' (No. 193).

846 Blenheim House and Park, Oxford* *c.* 1832

Watercolour, with some scraping-out, 296 × 468
Engr.: by W. Radclyffe, 1833, for *England and Wales* (R. 270)
Exh.: M.B.G. 1833; R.A. 1974 (427)
Prov.: Thomas Griffith: H. A. J. Munro of Novar, sale Christie 6 April 1878 (90), bt. Agnew; R. D. Holt; anon. sale, Christie 10 May 1918 (91), bt. Agnew; Sir E. E. Parkes, and, in accordance with his wishes, presented by his family to the gallery, 1920
Coll.: City Museums and Art Gallery, Birmingham (1.20)

This design makes use of drawings in the *Kenilworth* sketchbook, of 1830 (T.B., CCXXXVIII, 4–10, and especially pp. 11–12). A colour-beginning is T.B., CCLXIII–365.

847 Castle Upnor, Kent *c.* 1831

Watercolour and body-colour, with some scraping-out, 286 × 435
Engr.: by J. B. Allen, 1833, for *England and Wales* (R. 271)

Exh.: M.B.G. 1833; R.A. 1974 (425)
Prov.: Thomas Griffith; John Heugh; Mrs. E. T. Broadhurst, by whom bequeathed to the Whitworth Institute, 1924
Coll.: Whitworth Art Gallery, University of Manchester (D.41.1924)

The view was noted in a pencil sketch in the *Medway* sketchbook (T.B., CXCIX, 87v–88).

848 Laugharne Castle, Caermarthenshire *c.* 1831

Watercolour, 312 × 470
Engr.: by J. Horsburgh, 1833, for *England and Wales* (R. 272)
Exh.: M.B.G. 1833
Prov.: Thomas Griffith; McCrachen, sale Christie 8 May 1855 (86), bt. Rought; W. Minshill Bigg, sale Christie 22 February 1868 (110), bt. Vokins; John Ruskin; E. W. Cooke, R.A., sale Christie 22 May 1880 (167), bt. Grindley; F. Stevenson, sale Fine Art Society, London, April 1902, bt. Agnew, from whom bt. James Gresham, sale Christie 12 July 1917 (34), bt. in; anon. sale Christie 9 May 1919 (135), bt. J. W. R. Brocklebank; by descent to D. R. Brocklebank, sale Christie 25 November 1927 (87), bt. Vicars; K. M. Gallop, Frost & Reed, Bristol, from whom bt. Doll & Richards, Boston; from whom bt. Dr. John Dane, 1935; by descent to John Dane, jnr., from whom bt. John Schwartz, Brookline, Mass., 1946, sale Parke-Bernet Galleries, New York, 27 February 1947 (133), bt. Frederick W. Schumacker, by whom bequeathed to the gallery, 1957
Coll.: Columbus Gallery of Fine Arts, Columbus, Ohio ([57]47.73)

Turner made drawings of Laugharne Castle in his *South Wales* sketchbook, of 1795 (T.B., XXVI–19, 21). Another drawing of Laugharne Castle (241 × 343) appeared at Christie's, 19 December 1919 (78), bt. Morton.

849 Coventry, Warwickshire *c.* 1832

Watercolour, 288 × 437
Engr.: by S. Fisher, 1833, for *England and Wales* (R. 273)
Exh.: M.B.G. 1833; B.M. 1975 (197)
Prov.: Charles Heath (1833); H. A. J. Munro of Novar, sale Christie 2 June 1877 (49), bt. Wallis; C. Wheeley Lea; Mrs. Wheeley Lea, sale Christie 11 May 1917 (33), bt. Agnew; Agnew 1919; R. W. Lloyd, by whom bequeathed to the museum, 1958
Coll.: Trustees of the British Museum (1958-7-12-434)

Based on studies in the *Birmingham and Coventry* sketchbook (T.B., CCXL–15, 25–27).

850 Nottingham *c.* 1831

Watercolour, 305 × 463
Engr.: by W. J. Cooke, 1833, for *England and Wales* (R. 274)
Exh.: M.B.G. 1833
Prov.: Charles Heath (1833); ?John Knowles, sale 19 May 1877 (100), bt. Agnew; John Knowles, sale Christie 5 June 1880 (488), bt. Agnew; Sir E. H. Scott, Bt., sale Sotheby 19 June 1940 (31), bt. N. Mitchell
Coll.: City Museum and Art Gallery, Nottingham (40–18)

An adaptation of the composition of one of the views executed for the *Itinerant* (No. 89); see Ruskin's discussion of the two versions in *Works* (VI, pp, 42–4, Pls. 22, 23).

851 Carew Castle, Pembroke *c.* 1832

Watercolour, with body-colour and scratching-out, 305 × 457 (sight)
Engr.: by W. Miller, 1832, for *England and Wales* (R. 275)
Exh.: M.B.G. 1833
Prov.: Charles Heath: ? Thomas Birchall; John Heugh, sale Christie 24 April 1874 (95), bt.

Agnew; S. Addington, sale Christie 22 May 1886 (56), bt. Agnew; T. S. Kennedy, sale Christie 18 May 1895 (97), bt. Agnew; Joseph Ruston; Mrs. Ruston, sale Christie 4 July 1913 (105), bt. Wallis; James Blair, by whom bequeathed to the gallery, 1917
Coll.: City Art Gallery, Manchester (1917.99)

Turner draw Carew Castle in his *South Wales* sketchbook, of 1795 (T.B., XXVI, 24–6).

852 Penmaen Mawr, Caernarvonshire *c.* 1832

Watercolour and some white body-colour, 312 × 440
Inscr.: verso: *Pass of Penmanmawr, North Wales*
Engr.: by J. T. Willmore, 1832, for *England and Wales* (R. 276)
Exh.: M.B.G. 1833
Prov.: Charles Heath (1833); J. Leigh Clare, sale Christie 30 March 1868 (96), bt. McLean; Murrieta, sale Christie 30 April 1892 (51), bt. Agnew; Leopold Salomons, sale, Knight Frank & Rutley (at Norbury Park, Dorking), 11 September, 1916 (127, as 'A Mountainous Coast Scene'), bt. Agnew; R. W. Lloyd, by whom bequeathed to the museum, 1958
Coll.: Trustees of the British Museum (1958–7–12–437)

853 Christ Church College, Oxford *c.* 1832

Watercolour, with body-colour and scraping-out, 299 × 419
Engr.: by J. Redaway, 1832, for *England and Wales* (R. 277)
Exh.: M.B.G. 1833
Prov.: Charles Heath; H. A. J. Munro of Novar, sale Christie 2 June 1877 (48), bt. Vokins; Mrs. Morris; Haworth 1915; Mrs. Brocklehurst 1917; G. E. Leeming; Agnew 1920; S. A. Courtauld 1925; by descent to present owner
Private collection

854 Arundel Castle and Town, Sussex *c.* 1832

Watercolour and body-colour, with scratching-out, 296 × 434 (sight)
Engr.: by T. Jeavons, 1832, for *England and Wales* (R. 278)
Exh.: M.B.G. 1833
Prov.: Charles Heath (1833); anon. sale Christie 23 May 1866 (no lot), bt. Agnew; Pender; Mrs. Thwaites; by descent to present owner
Private collection

This composition is based on drawings in the *Brighton and Arundel* sketchbook, of about 1824 (T.B., CCX–63r and v).

855 Llanberis Lake, Wales* *c.* 1832

Watercolour, with some body-colour, 314 × 470
Engr.: by J. T. Willmore, 1832, for *England and Wales* (R. 279)
Exh.: M.B.G. 1833
Prov.: Charles Heath (1833); B. G. Windus; Henry Vaughan, by whom bequeathed to the gallery, 1900
Coll.: National Galleries of Scotland, Edinburgh (884)

856 Leicester Abbey, Leicestershire *c.* 1832

Watercolour, 296 × 457
Engr.: by W. R. Smith, 1832, for *England and Wales* (R. 280)
Exh.: M.B.G. 1833
Prov.: Charles Heath (1833); H. A. J. Munro of Novar, sale 2 June 1877 (44), bt. Severn; John Ruskin
Coll.: untraced

A drawing of Leicester Abbey occurs in the *Kenilworth* sketchbook, of 1830 (T.B., CCXXXVIII–20).

857 Caernarvon Castle, Wales* *c.* 1833

Watercolour over traces of pencil, 278 × 418
Engr.: by W. Radclyffe, 1835, for *England and Wales* (R. 281)
Exh.: B.M. 1975 (199)
Prov.: H. A. J. Munro of Novar, sale Christie 2 June 1877 (46), bt. Severn; John Ruskin; R. E. Tatham, sale, Christie 29 February 1908 (85), bt. Agnew; Walter Jones; Agnew, 1912; bt. 1913 R. W. Lloyd, by whom bequeathed to the museum, 1958
Coll.: Trustees of the British Museum (1958–7–12–439)

This composition is adapted from that of the large watercolour, 1799 (No. 254), which was based on the study T.B., XLIII–39v.

858 Dudley, Worcestershire* *c.* 1832

Watercolour and body-colour, 288 × 430
Engr.: by R. Wallis, 1835, for *England and Wales* (R. 282)
Exh.: M.B.G. 1833; R.A. 1974 (426)
Prov.: Charles Heath (1833); John Ruskin (1878); Sir George Drummond, Montreal, sale Christie 26 June 1919 (131), bt. Gooden & Fox; Lord Leverhulme
Coll.: The Lady Lever Collection, Port Sunlight, Cheshire (4030)

Studies made at Dudley in 1830 occur in the *Kenilworth* and *Birmingham and Coventry* sketchbooks (T.B., CCXXXVIII, CCXL).

859 Boston, Lincolnshire *c.* 1833

Watercolour, 280 × 419
Engr.: by T. Jeavons, 1835, for *England and Wales* (R. 283)
Prov.: J. Feetham, sale Christie 27 May 1895 (108), bt. Tooth; Mrs. Clayton; Mrs. J. V. Fisher, sale Christie 5 November 1974 (152), bt. Leger
Coll.: R. A. Shuck, England

Based on a drawing in the *North of England* sketchbook, of 1797 (T.B., XXXIV–82).

860 Ullswater, Cumberland* *c.* 1833

Watercolour, 330 × 426
Engr.: by J. T. Willmore, 1835, for *England and Wales* (R. 284)
Exh.: R.A. 1974 (428)
Prov.: H. A. J. Munro of Novar, sale Christie 6 April 1878 (95), bt. Agnew; Agnew 1911; Scott and Fowles; Monnell
Coll.: Brian Pilkington, London

Probably based on studies made at Ullswater in the *Tweed and Lakes* sketchbook, of 1797 (T.B., XXXV).

861 Powis Castle, Montgomery *c.* 1834

Watercolour and some pencil, 280 × 489 (sight)
Engr.: by J. T. Willmore, 1836, for *England and Wales* (R. 285)
Prov.: Joseph Gillott, sale Christie 4 May 1872 (507), bt. Agnew; J. Gillott, sale Christie 30 April 1904 (23), bt. McLean; Humphrey Roberts; Agnew, from whom bt. by James Blair, 1906, and bequeathed by him to the gallery, 1917
Coll.: City Art Gallery, Manchester (1917–117)

Based on a pencil drawing in the *Hereford Court* sketchbook, of 1798 (T.B., XXXVIII–62).

862 Worcester, Worcestershire *c.* 1833

Watercolour, 292 × 439
Engr.: by T. Jeavons, 1835, for *England and Wales* (R. 286)
Exh.: B.M. 1975 (200)
Prov.: Hon. W. F. D. Smith; Agnew 1908; Sir Joseph Beecham, sale Christie 4 May 1917 (151), bt. in; Christie 10 May 1918 (86); R. W. Lloyd, by whom bequeathed to the museum, 1958
Coll.: Trustees of the British Museum (1958–7–12–438)

Based on drawings in the *Worcester and Shrewsbury* sketchbook, of 1830 (T.B., CCXXXIX, 80–83).

863 Llanthony Abbey, Monmouthshire* *c.* 1835

Watercolour, with some body-colour, 298 × 426
Engr.: by J. T. Willmore, 1826, for *England and Wales* (R. 287)
Exh.: R.A. 1974 (430)
Prov.: John Ruskin; J. E. Taylor, sale Christie 5 July 1912 (48), bt. Agnew; Kurt Pantzer; given to the museum in memory of Dr. and Mrs. Hugo O. Pantzer by their children
Coll.: Indianapolis Museum of Art

Based on the pencil drawing of *c.* 1792 (T.B., XII–F) and early watercolours derived from it, e.g. No. 65.

864 Longships Lighthouse, Land's End *c.* 1835

Watercolour, 281 × 432
Engr.: by W. R. Smith, 1836, for *England and Wales* (R. 288)
Exh.: R.A. 1974 (431)
Prov.: H. A. J. Munro of Novar; Frederick Craven, by 1868, sale Christie 18 May 1895 (38), bt. Agnew; J. E. Taylor, sale Christie 5 July 1912 (42), bt. Agnew; C. Morland Agnew; C. Gerald Agnew
Coll.: Executors of the late Vice-Admiral Sir William Agnew, K.C.V.O., C.B., D.S.O.

865 Beaumaris, Isle of Anglesey *c.* 1835

Watercolour and body-colour, with scraping-out, 295 × 420
Engr.: by W. R. Smith, 1836, for *England and Wales* (R. 289)
Prov.: Arthur Street; Agnew 1965
Coll.: Henry E. Huntington Library and Art Gallery, San Marino, California (65.10)

866 Lyme Regis, Dorset *c.* 1834

Watercolour and body-colour, with scraping-out, 292 × 448
Engr.: by T. Jeavons, 1836, for *England and Wales* (R. 290)
Prov.: Isaac Cook; Pattinson; John Heugh, sale Christie 28 April 1860 (207), bt. Gambart; anon. sale Christie 21 June 1875 (27), bt. Harrison; John Wheeldon Barnes, sale Christie 7 April 1894 (136), bt. Wigzell; Emilie L. Heine, by whom given to the museum, 1940, in memory of Mr. and Mrs. John Hauck
Coll.: Cincinnati Art Museum, Ohio (1940.953)

Compare the view of Lyme Regis in the *Southern Coast* series (No. 451).

867 Harlech Castle, North Wales *c.* 1834

Watercolour, ? 356 × 482
Engr.: by W. R. Smith, 1836, for *England and Wales* (R. 291)
Prov.: F. R. Leyland, sale Christie 9 March 1872 (37), bt. White; John Ruskin; T. S. Kennedy, sale Christie 22 July 1882 (63), bt. McLean; George W. Vanderbilt
Coll.: untraced

Turner made drawings of Harlech Castle in the *Hereford Court* and *North Wales* sketchbooks, both of 1798 (T.B., XXXVIII, XXXIX).

868 Flint Castle, North Wales *c.* 1834

Watercolour, 265 × 391
Engr.: by J. R. Kernot, 1836, for *England and Wales* (R. 292)
Prov.: John Ruskin; George Coats; by descent
Private collection

869 Lowestoffe, Suffolk *c.* 1835

Watercolour, 275 × 427
Engr.: by W. R. Smith, 1837, for *England and Wales* (R. 293)
Exh.: B.M. 1975 (208)
Prov.: H. A. J. Munro of Novar; sale Christie 6 April 1878 (92), bt. Agnew; Revd. Charles Sale; Mrs. Sale, sale Christie 9 July 1915 (85), bt. Agnew; R. W. Lloyd, by whom bequeathed to the museum, 1958
Coll.: Trustees of the British Museum (1958–7–12–441)

870 Kidwelly Castle, South Wales *c.* 1832

Watercolour, 289 × 445
Engr.: by T. Jeavons, 1837, for *England and Wales* (R. 294)
Exh.: M.B.G. 1833
Prov.: Thomas Griffith (1833); H. A. J. Munro of Novar, sale Christie 2 June 1877 (42), bt. Agnew; Lord Armstrong; W. Watson-Armstrong; Agnew, 1911, 1913, 1924
Coll.: Harris Museum and Art Gallery, Preston, Lancashire

Turner drew Kidwelly Castle in the *South Wales* sketchbook, of 1795 (T.B., XXVI–16, 17).

871 Keswick Lake, Cumberland *c.* 1835

Watercolour, 276 × 438

Engr.: by W. Radclyffe, 1837, for *England and Wales* (R. 295)
Exh.: B.M. 1975 (203)
Prov.: John Ruskin; J. E. Taylor, sale Christie 5 July 1912 (43), bt. Agnew; Baron Goldschmidt Rothschild; H. E. Walters, 1914; A. E. Lawley, sale Christie 25 February 1921 (123); R. W. Lloyd, by whom bequeathed to the museum, 1958
Coll.: Trustees of the British Museum (1958–7-12–442)

Drawings of Keswick Lake (Derwentwater) which were probably used for this design are in the *Tweed and Lakes* sketchbook (T.B., XXXV–82) and among related sheets (T.B., XXXVI–H).

872 Llangollen, North Wales *c.* 1836

Watercolour, 267 × 419
Engr.: by J. T. Willmore, 1837, for *England and Wales* (R. 296)
Prov.: F. R. Leyland, sale Christie 9 March 1872 (35), bt. Agnew; H. W. F. Bolckow, sale Christie 2 May 1891 (53), bt. Vokins; C. F. H. Bolckow; Mrs. Taylor Whitehead, 1925, bt. Agnew; R. F. Goldschmidt, sale Christie 26 June 1941 (82), bt. de Casseras; E. P. Jones, sale Sotheby 19 April 1961 (73), bt. Leger
Private collection

Drawings of Llangollen with the new viaduct occur in the *North Wales* and *Hereford Court* sketchbooks (T.B., XXXIX, XXXVIII), both of 1798.

873 Durham Cathedral *c.* 1835

Watercolour, 295 × 442
Engr.: by W. Miller, 1836, for *England and Wales* (R. 297)
Prov.: Henry Vaughan, by whom bequeathed to the gallery, 1900
Coll.: National Galleries of Scotland, Edinburgh (883)

Probably based on drawings made at Durham in the *Helmsley* sketchbook, of 1801 (T.B., LIII, 20–25).

874 Winander-Mere, Westmoreland *c.* 1835

Watercolour, body-colour, wiping-out and pencil, 290 × 460
Engr.: by J. T. Willmore, 1837, for *England and Wales* (R. 298)
Prov.: Joseph Gillott, sale Christie 4 May 1872 (508), bt. Lane; Earl Dudley, sale Christie 11 June 1909 (184), bt. Agnew; James Blair, by whom bequeathed to the gallery, 1917
Coll.: City Art Gallery, Manchester (1917.109)

Probably based on drawings of Windermere made in the *Tweed and Lakes* sketchbook (T.B., XXXV, 52–55).

875 Whitehaven, Cumberland *c.* 1835

Watercolour and body-colour, with some scraping-out, 316 × 465
Engr.: by W. R. Smith, 1837, for *England and Wales* (R. 299)

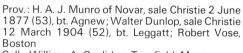

Prov.: H. A. J. Munro of Novar, sale Christie 2 June 1877 (53), bt. Agnew; Walter Dunlop, sale Christie 12 March 1904 (52), bt. Leggatt; Robert Vose, Boston
Coll.: William A. Coolidge, Topsfield, Mass.

A colour study of Whitehaven is No. 893.

876 Criccieth Castle *c.* 1835

Watercolour, 290 × 425
Sig. lower right: *IMW*
Engr.: by S. Fisher, 1937, for *England and Wales* (R. 300)
Exh.: B.M. 1975 (206)
Prov.: H. A. J. Munro of Novar, sale Christie 2 June 1877 (40), bt. Agnew; W. Dunlop; Col. H. J. Holdsworth, sale Christie 4 May 1889 (78), bt. Gooden; William Newall; sale, Christie 30 June 1922 (74), bt. King; J. B. Gaskell, sale 30 April 1926 (77), bt. Sampson; Gilbert Lees Hardcastle, sale Christie 4 May 1933 (34); R. W. Lloyd, by whom bequeathed to the museum, 1958
Coll.: Trustees of the British Museum (1958–7-12–440)

877 Rochester, Stroud and Chatham, Medway, Kent *c.* 1836

Watercolour, 286 × 439
Engr.: by J. C. Varrall, 1838, for *England and Wales* (R. 301)
Prov.: John Ruskin; George Schlotel, sale Christie 25 April 1885 (51), bt. Agnew; A. F. L. Wallace; destroyed by fire, 1955

Based on the early watercolour of Rochester, dated 1795 (No. 129).

878 Chain Bridge over the River Tees *c.* 1836

Watercolour, 278 × 426
Engr.: by W. R. Smith, 1838, for *England and Wales* (R. 302)
Prov.: H. A. J. Munro of Novar, sale Christie 6 April 1878 (89), bt. Cross; C. S. Bale, sale Christie 14 May 1881 (199), bt. Agnew; Abraham Howarth
Private collection

Derived from a pencil drawing in the *Yorkshire No. 5* sketchbook, of about 1816 (T.B., CXLVIII–6v).

879   Richmond Terrace, Surrey   *c.* 1836

Watercolour and body-colour and scratching-out, 280 × 435
Engr.: by J. T. Willmore, 1838, for *England and Wales* (R. 303)
Exh.: R.A. 1974 (434)
Prov.: H. A. J. Munro of Novar, sale Christie 2 June 1877 (51), bt. Agnew; A. G. Kurtz, sale Christie 11 May 1891 (200), bt. Tooth; Sir Durning Lawrence; anon. sale Christie 29 November 1946 (67); T. H. Farr; C. F. L. Beausire, by whom bequeathed to the gallery
Coll.: Walker Art Gallery, Liverpool (8142)

A variant of the view shown in an earlier watercolour (No. 518), and of a large oil-painting of 1819 (P140).

880   Mount St. Michael, Cornwall   *c.* 1836

Watercolour, with some body-colour, 305 × 439
Engr.: by S. Fisher, 1838, for *England and Wales* (R. 304)
Exh.: R.A. 1974 (433)
Prov.: Craven sale Christie 2 May 1866 (227), bt. Tooth; F. R. Leyland, sale Christie 9 March 1872 (38), bt. Agnew; Sir Robert Leake; Sir Charles Sydney Jones, by whom bequeathed to the university 1947
Coll.: University of Liverpool (214)

Compare the design for the *Southern Coast* series (No. 445) and the oil-painting of this subject (P358).

881   Northampton   *c.* 1830

Watercolour, 295 × 439
Exh.: M.B.G. 1833
Prov.: Charles Heath (1833); H. A. J. Munro of Novar, sale Christie 2 June 1877 (38), bt. White; R. D. Holland; Christie 17 December 1937 (57), unsold; Mrs. Young, from whom bt. Spink 1947
Private collection

Designed for *England and Wales* series, but not engraved.
Eric Shanes has suggested that the scene depicts the re-election on 6 December 1830 of Lord Althorp as the county member for Northamptonshire. A similar view of this subject, only from a more distant viewpoint, was made by Turner for the engraving published in *The Pocket Magazine* of 1795 (No. 118), and this was based on the pencil study in the *Matlock* sketchbook (T.B., XIX–12).

882   Lichfield   1830–5

Watercolour, 286 × 438
Prov.: H. A. J. Munro of Novar, sale Christie 6 April 1878 (80), bt. Agnew; Sir E. H. Scott, sale Sotheby 19 June 1940 (30), bt. Fine Art Society, London; anon. sale, Sotheby 14 November 1962 (55), bt. in
Private collection

A pencil drawing of Lichfield occurs in the *Kenilworth* sketchbook (T.B., CCXXXVIII–51b) and a colour-beginning based on it is T.B., CCLXIII–99.

883   Shoreham   *c.* 1830

Watercolour, 210 × 312
Prov.: J. Irvine Smith; Mrs. E. J. Gould, New York; Agnew, 1927, 1928; E. L. Hartley, by whom bequeathed to the museum
Coll.: Art Gallery and Museum, Blackburn, Lancashire

A much smaller sheet than the *England and Wales* drawings, this has points in common with the *Southern Coast* designs, but seems to be later.

884   A view of Folkestone, with beached fishing-boat   *?c.* 1830

Watercolour, 180 × 260
Sig. lower left: *Turner*
Prov.: Henry Vaughan, by whom bequeathed to the gallery, 1900
Coll.: National Gallery of Ireland, Dublin (2415)

885   Welsh Coast near Flint Castle   *?c.* 1830

Watercolour, 229 × 349
Inscr. lower left: *IMWT RA*

Prov.: John Knowles, sale Christie 19 May 1877 (96), bt. Smith; Mrs. Barrow, 1918; Mrs. Nuttall; Richard Green, 1974, by whom sold to present owner
Coll.: M. M. Yamanaka, Tokyo

A similar view to that of the *England and Wales* subject (No. 868), though with many important differences, especially of the figures.

---

886   Folkestone *?c.* 1830

Watercolour, size unknown
Engr.: by J. Cousen for *Dr Broadley's Poems* (privately printed *c.* 1844); plate also used for *Art and Song*, 1867 (R. 643)
Provenance and whereabouts unknown

---

887   Merton College, Oxford* *c.* 1830

Watercolour, 295 × 433
Coll.: Trustees of the British Museum (T.B., CCLXIII–349)

---

888   Tynemouth Priory *c.* 1830

Watercolour, size unknown
Engr.: by W. Miller for *Dr Broadley's Poems* (privately printed *c.* 1844); plate also used for *Art and Song*, 1867 (R. 641)
Prov.: anon. sale Christie 29 May 1873 (158), bt. Hinton; Agnew, 1912
Private collection

889   Oxford, from Boar's Hill *c.* 1835–40

Watercolour and body-colour, 352 × 516
Engr.: by E. Goodall 1841, with the title *Oxford from North Hinksey* (R. 651)
Prov.: H. A. J. Munro of Novar, sale Christie 6 April 1878 (81), bt. Agnew; J. S. Kennedy, sale Christie 18 May 1895 (94), bt. Tooth; Wallis & Son; The French Gallery; James Blair, by whom bequeathed to the gallery, 1917
Coll.: City Art Gallery, Manchester (1917–102)

A much larger sheet than any of the *England and Wales* drawings, and possibly executed considerably later, perhaps *c.* 1840. It was previously called *Oxford from Headington Hill*.

---

890   Barnard Castle *?c.* 1826

Watercolour, 165 × 235
Prov.: W. G. Rawlinson; R. A. Tatton; W. H. Jones;

Margaret Mostyn Owen, by whom given to present owner
Private collection

Possibly related to the *England and Wales* design (No. 793), although the identification of the scene is doubtful.

891   A Yorkshire river *?c.* 1827

Watercolour, 280 × 406
Prov.: ?W. Quarrell; Miss Margaret S. Davies, sale Sotheby 24 February 1960 (91), bt. Colnaghi, from whom purchased
Coll.: Mr. and Mrs. Paul Mellon, Upperville, Virginia

A colour-beginning possibly related to *Richmond from the Moors* (No. 808).

---

892   St. Agatha's Abbey, Easby, Yorkshire *?c.* 1830

Watercolour, 340 × 464
Prov.: Daniel Klein, New York
Private collection

Derived from the composition of the view of St. Agatha's used for Whitaker's *Richmondshire* (No. 561); another colour-beginning, perhaps for an *England and Wales* design, is T.B., CCLXIII–360, and T.B., CCLXIII–89 is possibly another.

---

893   Whitehaven *?c.* 1835

Watercolour, 222 × 358
Inscr. in pencil: *Wet Sand Water Yellow in Refd Light*
Prov.: C. T. Harris, sale Christie 27 November 1913 (56), bt. Wickham; Lord Brand; Agnew, 1973
Private collection

See *England and Wales* subject (No. 875).

894   Beach scene

Watercolour, 292 × 432
Prov.: Sir Stephen Courtauld; by descent to present owner
Private collection, Channel Islands

Compare the *England and Wales* subject No. 803.

---

895   Bamborough Castle *?c.* 1840

Watercolour, 508 × 711 approx.
Prov.: ?J. Heugh, sale Christie 28 April 1860 (203), bt. Pennell; or Revd. T. Coleridge (Manchester 1857); J. Gillott, sale Christie 4 May 1872 (514), bt. Lane; Lord Dudley; Mrs. Cornelius Vanderbilt, New York
Coll.: untraced

It is uncertain what purpose this drawing served. The date is that given by Armstrong (p. 241), though works of this size are unusual at this period.

XIV(b)   Nos 896–905
Designs for 'Picturesque Views on the East Coast of England' ('Holloway's Continuation of the England and Wales'), and associated drawings, *c.* 1830

These designs appear to have been conceived as a series of 'Picturesque Views on the East Coast of England', perhaps on the model of the *Southern Coast*. They have been known as 'Holloway's Continuation of the England and Wales', or 'the Supplement to the England and Wales'. But they are in no way connected with the *England and Wales* project, being much smaller in size and executed in the medium of watercolour and body-colour on toned paper, rather in the manner of the *Rivers of Europe* series. It is assumed that they date from about the period of that sequence, that is *c.* 1830. Many of the drawings are traditionally dated late in the 1830s, presumably on the ground that they were done as a sequel to the *England and Wales* set; such a late date seems unlikely. All the plates were engraved by J. C. Allen; some were not finished; and at least one subject (No. 904) was not engraved at all. No. 905 is apparently not part of the series and is rather more elaborate in treatment. It is placed here on account of its similar size and subject-matter; it no doubt dates from the same period.

896   Lowestoffe Lighthouse *c.* 1830

Body-colour on blue paper, approx. 125 × 95, vignette
Engr.: by J. C. Allen (R. 305; unpubl.)
Prov.: H. A. J. Munro of Novar, sale Christie 2 June 1877 (54), bt. Anthony Gibbs; by descent to Lord Wraxall; Christie 17 April 1964 (35), bt. Kurt Pantzer
Coll.: Pantzer Collection, Indianapolis

897   Orford Castle and Church *c.* 1830

Watercolour and body-colour on blue paper, approx. 120 × 190, vignette
Inscr. below: *Orford Haven*
Engr.: by J. C. Allen (R. 307; unpubl.)
Prov.: H. A. J. Munro of Novar, sale Christie 2 June 1877 (55), bt. Goupil; by descent to Lord Wraxall; Christie 17 April 1964 (34), bt. Kurt Pantzer
Coll.: Pantzer Collection, Indianapolis

898   Harborough Sands *c.* 1830

Body-colour on blue paper, 165 × 127, vignette
Inscr. below: *Harboro Sands* (or ? *Hasboro*)
Engr.: by J. C. Allen (R. 306; unpubl.)
Prov.: Lewis Loyd; Miss J. E. Stanier, sale Christie 5 March 1974 (190), bt. Agnew
Private collection

The subject is probably Happisburgh, Norfolk (pronounced Haysborough).

899   Aldborough, Suffolk *c.* 1830

Body-colour on blue paper, 172–254
Engr.: by J. C. Allen (R. 308; unpubl.)
Prov.: ?John Dillon, sale Christie 29 April 1869 (128), bt. Agnew; P. G. B. Westmacott, sale Christie 10 May 1918 (36, as 'Scarborough'), bt. Agnew; F. W. Smith 1920; Miss M. Smith; Agnew 1930
Private collection

900   Dunwich *c.* 1830

Body-colour on blue paper, 174 × 257
Engr.: by J. C. Allen (R. 309; unpubl.)
Prov.: Sir Joseph Heron, sale Christie 9 June 1890 (73, as 'Dymchurch'), bt. Agnew; F. Stevenson; Fine Art Society, London, 1902; Agnew;

T. Humphry Ward, 1903; James Blair, 1904, by whom bequeathed to the gallery, 1917
Coll.: City Art Gallery, Manchester (1917–94)

901   Orfordness *c.* 1830

Body-colour on blue paper, 165 × 254
Engr.: by J. C. Allen (R. 310; unpubl.)
Prov.: Abraham Haworth; by descent to present owner
Private collection

902   Lowestoffe *c.* 1830

Pencil, watercolour and body-colour on blue paper, 174 × 252
Engr.: by J. C. Allen (open etching only; R. 311)
Prov.: H. A. J. Munro of Novar, sale Christie 2 June 1877 (54), bt. Goupil; J. E. Taylor, sale Christie 5 July 1912 (62), bt. Agnew; Walter Stoye; by descent to present owner
Private collection

903   Whitby *c.* 1830

Body-colour on blue paper, 165 × 254
Engr.: J. C. Allen (open etching only; R. 312)
Prov.: John Dillon, sale Christie 29 April 1869 (129), bt. Agnew; F. N. Fordham
Coll.: untraced

904   Yarmouth Sands *c.* 1830

Watercolour and body-colour on blue paper, 185 × 245
Inscr. on verso in pencil: *NELSON'S COL[...]Yar*
Prov.: John Ruskin, by whom given to the museum, 1861

Coll.: Syndics of the Fitzwilliam Museum, Cambridge (576; Cormack 22)

905 Whitby, Yorks *c.* 1825–30

Watercolour, 159 × 248
Engr.: by J. Cousen, 1844, for *Dr. Broadley's Poems* (unpubl.); plate also used for *Art and Song,* 1867 (R. 639)
Prov.: F. N. Fordham; B. G. Fordham, sale Sotheby 6 June 1951 (13), bt. Apsley Cherry-Garrard; Mrs. Gordon Mathias, sale Sotheby 19 April 1961 (36), bt. Agnew; George Goyder; Agnew 1969
Private collection

XIV(c) Nos 906–929
English subjects on toned paper associated with Petworth and the south coast, *c.* **1828–1840**

The third Earl of Egremont had begun to acquire works by Turner very early in the century—perhaps in 1802, for he bought the painting of *Ships bearing up for Anchorage,* which was in the R.A. exhibition of that year. Turner visited Petworth in 1809, and again, after a long interval, in 1827, on his way home from East Cowes Castle. Thereafter Petworth became a regular retreat for him, at least partially replacing Farnley, to which he did not return after Fawkes's death in 1825. The majority of the drawings that Turner made at Petworth are in the Bequest. A few are pencil sketches in the *Petworth* sketchbook (T.B., CCXLIII), but the rest are in colour, on loose sheets of blue paper, torn from large sheets (T.B., CCXLIV). There are 116 of these drawings in the Bequest, and a few elsewhere which are listed below (Nos 906–912), together with other drawings on similar sheets of torn blue paper which seem to be of English subjects (Nos 913–929). For other works on this type of paper see the 'Rivers of Europe' series (Nos 930–1043).

906 Spilt milk *c.* 1828
Watercolour and body-colour on blue paper, 534 × 588
Exh.: R.A. 1974 (B139)
Prov.: Mrs. Hasler (the Earl of Egremont's granddaughter), for whom drawn; by descent to the present owner
Coll.: from the Petworth Collection

Although in the characteristic medium and format of Turner's Petworth drawings, this sheet does not belong with the set that he made and kept for his own use: it was drawn because the artist had spoiled the dress of the earl's grand-daughter at breakfast, and given to her as an apology.

907 Landscape near Petworth *c.* 1828
Body-colour on blue paper, 140 × 190
Prov.: given by Turner to Mrs. Hasler (granddaughter of the third Earl of Egremont); by descent to the present owner
Coll.: from the Petworth Collection

908 Petworth Park, Sussex *c.* 1828
Watercolour and body-colour on blue paper, 139 × 193

Prov.: Henry Vaughan, by whom bequeathed to the gallery, 1900
Coll.: National Gallery of Ireland, Dublin (2430)

909 Petworth Park, Sussex *c.* 1828
Watercolour and body-colour on blue paper, 139 × 194
Prov.: J. E. Taylor, by whom given to the Whitworth Institute, 1892
Coll.: Whitworth Art Gallery, University of Manchester (D.91.1892)

910 Sunset in Petworth Park: deer grazing on a ridge near the lake *c.* 1828
Watercolour and body-colour, on blue paper, 140 × 190
Prov.: unknown
Coll.: Andrew Wyld, London

911 The Lake, Petworth Park *c.* 1828
Watercolour and body-colour on blue paper, 139 × 190

Prov.: C. Dyson Perrins; Sotheby, 22 April 1959 (67); Agnew, from whom purchased by anon. donor to the museum
Coll.: Museum of Art, Rhode Island School of Design, Providence, R.I. (70.118.55)

The building by the water is the boathouse that can be seen in Turner's *Petworth: Dewy morning,* of 1810 (Cat. P113), and the tower on the ridge is the 'Monument' erected in about 1816, and perhaps by Soane (see Gervase Jackson-Stops, 'The Building of Petworth', *Apollo,* May 1977, pp. 324–33).

912 Petworth Park, sunset, with a cart *c.* 1828

Body-colour on blue paper, approx. 140 × 190
Prov.: Agnew
Private collection

913 Fishermen on a weir *c.* 1830

Pencil, watercolour and body-colour on grey paper, 136 × 187
Inscr. below: *Foul by God*
Prov.: sale Sotheby 14 July 1954 (21), bt. Spink; L. G. Duke, from whom bt. by Paul Mellon, 1961
Coll.: Yale Center for British Art, Paul Mellon Collection

The scene may be continental rather than English; Turner seems to have used his blue paper sheets either abroad or, generally, in south-east England: the scenery here, if English, is apparently either that of Yorkshire or, perhaps, Devon.

914 Boat and red buoy in a choppy sea *c.* 1828–30

Body-colour, with touches of pencil, on blue paper, 140 × 194

Prov.: Sir Hickman Bacon Bt.; by descent to the present owner
Private collection

915 Shipping *c.* 1828–30

Pen and brush and brown ink and white, with some body-colour over pencil, on blue paper, 136 × 187
Sig. with initials lower right: *JMWT*
Prov.: 'a lady from near Petworth', sale Messenger, May & Baverstock, Godalming, 12 October 1976 (164), bt. Leger, from whom purchased
Coll.: Yale Center for British Art, Paul Mellon Collection

Very similar to drawings in the Bequest: e.g. T.B., CCLIX–21; the signature with initials only is somewhat unusual, especially in a study such as this. Two comparable drawings, signed in the same way, were in the J. P. Heseltine sale, Sotheby 25 March 1920, formerly in the Greenwood Collection. The titles given then were *Fishing boats at sea: boarding a steamer* (183) and *View of a seaport* (182). These have much in common with the pen and ink drawings made by Turner at Cowes in 1827 (T.B., CCXXVII(a), CCXXVIII).

916 Cricket on the Goodwin Sands ?*c.* 1828–30

Body-colour with ?blue chalk, on grey-blue paper, 140 × 189
Prov.: Richard Johnson; Sir Alexander Bruce; Agnew, from whom purchased 1969
Coll.: Mr. and Mrs. Paul Mellon, Upperville, Virginia

917 Ship aground: Brighton ?*c.* 1828–30

Watercolour and body-colour on blue paper, 142 × 195

Prov.: J. E. Taylor, sale Christie 5 July 1912 (112), bt. Gooden & Fox; J. G. Griffiths, sale at 4 Hyde Park Gardens, 5 March 1923, bt. in; sale Christie 17 May 1923 (59), bt. Finberg; John Baskett, from whom purchased 1971
Coll.: Mr. and Mrs. Paul Mellon, Upperville, Virginia

918 Waves breaking on a beach *c.* 1830

Watercolour and body-colour on blue paper, 133 × 185
Prov.: W. E. A. Bull; Agnew, 1973
Coll.: Mr. and Mrs. Eugene Victor Thaw

919 Figures on the shore *c.* 1830

Watercolour and body-colour on grey paper, 136 × 184
Prov.: W. E. Bull; Agnew, 1975; Knoedler, New York
Private collection

920   Margate (?)   *?c.* 1830–40

Body-colour on blue paper, 127 × 178
Prov.: Gwendoline E. Davies, by whom bequeathed to the museum, 1951
Coll.: National Museum of Wales, Cardiff (2951)

923   Seascape with a boat   *?c.* 1835

Watercolour, chalk and body-colour on blue or grey paper, 142 × 193
Prov.: R. Nesham; entered the gallery collection through the Graves Gift, 1942
Coll.: Graves Art Gallery, Sheffield (874)

926   Effect of cloud and sunset over the sea   *?c.* 1830s

Pencil, watercolour and body-colour on grey paper, 139 × 187
Prov.: Sir Hickman Bacon, Bt.; by descent to the present owner
Private collection

921   Harbour view   *c.* 1830

Body-colour on blue paper, 140 × 190
Prov.: Henry Vaughan, by whom bequeathed to the gallery, 1900
Coll.: National Galleries of Scotland, Edinburgh (880)

924   Storm off the East Coast   *?c.* 1835

Watercolour, chalk and body-colour on blue or grey paper, 209 × 273
Prov.: Richardson; Johnson; Howard Bliss; purchased by the gallery, 1947
Coll.: Graves Art Gallery, Sheffield (2205)

927   The seashore from Hastings   *c.* 1830–5

Watercolour over pencil on buff paper, 133 × 178
Prov.: John Ruskin; Dr. Denman W. Ross, by whom given to the museum, 1917
Coll.: Fogg Art Museum, Harvard University, Cambridge, Mass. (1917.17)

922   Sea view   *c.* 1830

Body-colour on blue paper, 140 × 190
Prov.: Henry Vaughan, by whom bequeathed to the gallery, 1900
Coll.: National Galleries of Scotland, Edinburgh (881)

925   Sun and clouds over sea   *c.* 1830s

Body-colour and coloured chalks on grey paper, 132 × 180
Prov.: ?John Ruskin
Private collection

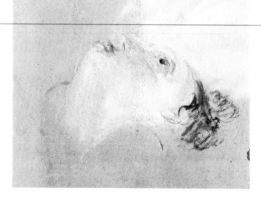

928   Head of a woman (A fishwife lying in the sun)   *?c.* 1830

Body-colour on brown paper, 216 × 260
Prov.: ?Mrs. Booth; A. G. B. Russell (the sheet bears his stamp); Mrs. J. B. Priestley, sale Sotheby 20 July 1972 (84), bt. Fry; R. M. M. Prior
Coll.: R. E. Moore, Ottawa

The erotic overtones of this study suggest a possible connection with Turner's work at Petworth.It is apparently one of a small group of such studies said to have been given by Turner to Mrs. Booth, three of which were subsequently in the Nettlefold collection. The group is traditionally connected either with an incident in which Turner drew a drowned girl at Chelsea, or with his visits to Margate. Butlin and Joll associate the subject with an oil sketch (P 452). See also No. 929.

929 Study of a fisherwoman ?c.1830

Body-colour, size unknown
Prov.: ?Mrs. Booth; ?Nettlefold; sale Sotheby 10 March 1965 (36)
Private collection

This study is said to have been made, with others, at Margate. See No. 928 above.

SECTION XV
Nos 930–1051 The 'Rivers of Europe' project, c. 1825–1834

In 1833 Charles Heath, promulgator of *The Keepsake* and other annuals, as well as the *England and Wales* series, advertised a new publication: 'GREAT RIVERS OF EUROPE. On June 1 will appear, elegantly bound, price One Guinea, TURNER'S ANNUAL TOUR; or, RIVER SCENERY OF EUROPE: containing twenty-one Plates, from Drawings by J. M. W. Turner, Esq. R.A. Engraved by the first Artists, under the superintendence of Mr. CHARLES HEATH...'. Turner's first activity in connection with the project, which was inspired by his *Rivers of England* and other earlier publications of the type, seems to have been the tour to Holland, the Meuse and the Moselle in 1825. Finberg dated this tour to 1826, the year given in all subsequent accounts; but notes in the *Rivers Meuse and Moselle* sketchbook (T.B., CCXVI, p. 270) indicate that 1825 was in fact the year of the journey. (I am indebted to Mr. Timothy Clifford for pointing out Finberg's miscalculation.) In 1826 Turner visited the Loire valley, returning through Paris. In 1827 he had definitely begun to use the small torn sheets of blue paper, on which nearly all the 'Rivers of Europe' designs are made: his drawings at East Cowes Castle can be firmly dated to that summer. It is likely that many of the Meuse, Moselle and Loire subjects were in hand by about this time, but he continued to make tours in connection with the project: in particular he collected material during his journey to Italy in 1828, concentrating on the southern French coast. In 1829 he visited Paris and travelled along the Seine; he toured in the same region in 1832. In 1833 he made a longer journey across Europe, visiting Venice and, perhaps, Vienna, Dresden and Berlin; though the northern part of this itinerary may belong to 1835. In 1834 he

revisited the Meuse-Moselle area, and returned along the Rhine. It may be presumed, therefore, that the Rhine, the Danube, the Meuse, the Moselle, and perhaps the Rhône, the Po and the Saône were included in Turner's list of rivers to be illustrated; but only the Seine and the Loire were published: the Loire in *Turner's Annual Tour* of 1833, with twenty-one views, and the Seine in two uniform volumes, issued in 1834 and 1835, each with twenty views. Those for the *Loire* (Nos 930–950) may have been finished shortly after the tour of 1826; the *Seine* drawings (Nos 951–990) were evidently not completed until just before they were engraved. Exact dating of these series is difficult; Finberg believed the *Loire* set to precede the rest. Ruskin acquired nearly all the *Loire* drawings, and gave them to Oxford; the *Seine* designs, with a few exceptions, remained in the artist's studio (T.B., CCLIX), with a series of pencil, pen and ink studies, apparently made on the spot like the sketches in the notebooks, but on individual sheets of torn blue paper (T.B., CCLX). There are, in addition, large numbers of colour studies, some of them virtually 'finished' works, relating to the completed and uncompleted parts of the project (Nos 991–1043); a few of these are scattered, but most remain in the Bequest (T.B., CCXX, CCXXI, CCXXII, CCXXIII, CCXXIV (pencil and chalks only), CCXCII).

XV(a) Nos 930–950
The Loire c. 1826–1830

930 Nantes c.1826–30

Watercolour and body-colour, with pen, on blue paper, 186 ×134, title-page vignette
Engr.: by W. Miller for *Turner's Annual Tour—the Loire,* 1833 (R.432)
Prov.: Thomas Griffith; Charles Stokes, 1850; by descent to Hannah Cooper, from whom bt. by Ruskin, February 1858; given by him to the University of Oxford, 1861
Coll.: Visitors of the Ashmolean Museum, Oxford (Herrmann 29)

A pencil sketch of the subject is in the *Morlaise to Nantes* sketchbook (T.B., CCXLVII-61v.).

931 Orléans c.1826–30

Watercolour and body-colour, with pen, on blue paper, 136 × 189
Engr.: by Thomas Higham for *Turner's Annual Tour—the Loire,* 1833 (R.433)
Prov.: Thomas Griffith; Charles Stokes, 1850; by descent to Hannah Cooper, from whom bt. by Ruskin, February 1858; given by him to the University of Oxford, 1861
Coll.: Visitors of the Ashmolean Museum, Oxford (Herrmann 48)

932 Beaugency c.1826–30

Watercolour and body-colour, with pen, on blue paper, 118 × 175
Engr.: by R. Brandard for *Turner's Annual Tour—the Loire,* 1833 (R.434)
Prov.: Thomas Griffith; Charles Stokes, 1850; by descent to Hannah Cooper, from whom bt. by Ruskin, February 1858; given by him to the University of Oxford, 1861
Coll.: Visitors of the Ashmolean Museum, Oxford (Herrmann 47)

933 Blois c.1826–30

Watercolour and body-colour, with pen, on blue paper, 135 × 183
Engr.: by R. Brandard for *Turner's Annual Tour — the Loire,* 1833 (R. 435)
Exh.: R.A. 1974 (386)
Prov.: Thomas Griffith; Charles Stokes, 1850; by descent to Hannah Cooper, from whom bt. by Ruskin, February 1858; given by him to the University of Oxford, 1861
Coll.: Visitors of the Ashmolean Museum, Oxford (Herrmann 42)

934   Palace at Blois   *c.* 1826–30

Pencil, watercolour and body-colour, with pen, on blue paper, 130 × 185
Engr.: by R. Wallis for *Turner's Annual Tour — the Loire,* 1833 (R. 436)
Prov.: Thomas Griffith; Charles Stokes, 1850; by descent to Hannah Cooper, from whom bt. by Ruskin, February 1858; given by him to the University of Oxford, 1861
Coll.: Visitors of the Ashmolean Museum, Oxford (Herrmann 44)

A pencil sketch of the Palace at Blois is in the *Loire, Tours, Orleans and Paris* sketchbook (T.B., CCXLIX-20).

935   Amboise   *c.* 1826–30

Watercolour and body-colour, with pen, on blue paper, 132 × 187
Engr.: by W. R. Smith for *Turner's Annual Tour — the Loire,* 1833 (R. 437)
Exh.: R.A. 1974 (384)
Prov.: Thomas Griffith; Charles Stokes, 1850; by descent to Hannah Cooper, from whom bt. by Ruskin, February 1858; given by him to the University of Oxford, 1861
Coll.: Visitors of the Ashmolean Museum, Oxford (Herrmann 38)

936   Château of Amboise   *c.* 1826–30

Watercolour and body-colour, with pen, on blue paper, 136 × 188
Engr.: by J. B. Allen for *Turner's Annual Tour — the Loire,* 1833 (R. 438)
Prov.: Thomas Griffith; Charles Stokes, 1850; by descent to Hannah Cooper, from whom bt. by Ruskin, February 1858; given by him to the University of Oxford, 1861
Coll.: Visitors of the Ashmolean Museum, Oxford (Herrmann 35)

937   The Canal of the Loire and Cher, near Tours   *c.* 1826–30

Watercolour and body-colour, with pen, on blue paper, 123 × 182
Engr.: by T. Jeavons for *Turner's Annual Tour — the Loire,* 1833 (R. 439)
Exh.: R.A. 1974 (387)
Prov.: Thomas Griffith; Charles Stokes, 1850; by descent to Hannah Cooper, from whom bought by Ruskin, February 1858; given by him to the University of Oxford, 1861
Coll.: Visitors of the Ashmolean Museum, Oxford (Herrmann 43)

A pencil sketch of this view is in the *Loire, Tours, Orleans and Paris* sketchbook (T.B., CCXLIX-8).

938   Tours   *c.* 1826–30

Pencil, watercolour and body-colour, with pen, on blue paper, 122 × 183
Engr.: by R. Brandard for *Turner's Annual Tour — the Loire,* 1833 (R. 440)
Prov.: Thomas Griffith; Charles Stokes, 1850; by descent to Hannah Cooper, from whom bt. by Ruskin, February 1858; given by him to the University of Oxford, 1861

Coll.: Visitors of the Ashmolean Museum, Oxford (Herrmann 46)

939   St. Julian's, Tours   *c.* 1826–30

Pencil, watercolour and body-colour, on blue paper, 120 × 184
Engr.: by W. Radclyffe for *Turner's Annual Tour — the Loire,* 1833 (R. 441)
Prov.: Thomas Griffith; Charles Stokes, 1850; by descent to Hannah Cooper, from whom bt. by Ruskin, February 1858; given by him to the University of Oxford, 1861
Coll.: Visitors of the Ashmolean Museum, Oxford (Herrmann 45)

A drawing that seems to be related to this design is that on p. 45 verso of the *Loire, Tours, Orleans and Paris* sketchbook (T.B., CCXLIX).

940   Tours—looking backwards   *c.* 1826–30

Body-colour, with some pen, on blue paper, 124 × 188
Engr.: by R. Brandard for *Turner's Annual Tour — the Loire,* 1833 (R. 442)
Prov.: Lewis Loyd; Capt. E. N. F. Loyd; Mrs. Jonas; T. E. Fattorini; Sir Steven Runciman; Dr. P. G. McEverdy; Agnew, from whom bt. by Paul Mellon, 1967
Coll.: Yale Center for British Art, Paul Mellon Collection

A pencil drawing of a similar view is in the *Loire, Tours, Orleans and Paris* sketchbook (T.B., CCXLIX-8v). Another view of Tours, from the collection of Rayner MacConnell, was with Agnew in 1949.

941   Saumur   *c.* 1826–30

Body-colour on blue paper, 123 × 185
Engr.: by J. T. Willmore for *Turner's Annual Tour — the Loire,* 1833 (R. 443)

Prov.: Lewis Loyd: Capt. E. N. F. Loyd; Rayner MacConnell
Private collection

Turner noted the subject in the *Nantes, Angers and Saumur* sketchbook (T.B., CCXLVIII-42).

942   Rietz, near Saumur *c.* 1826–30

Pencil, watercolour and body-colour, with pen, on blue paper, 124 × 181
Engr.: by R. Brandard for *Turner's Annual Tour—the Loire,* 1833 (R. 444)
Prov.: Thomas Griffith; Charles Stokes, 1850; by descent to Hannah Cooper, from whom bt. by Ruskin, Feburary 1858; given by him to the University of Oxford, 1861
Coll.: Visitors of the Ashmolean Museum, Oxford (Herrmann 49)

943   Montjen *c.* 1826–30

Watercolour and body-colour, with pen and scratching-out, on blue paper, 135 × 188
Engr.: by J.T. Willmore for *Turner's Annual Tour—the Loire,* 1833 (R. 445)
Prov.: Thomas Griffith; Charles Stokes, 1850; by descent to Hannah Cooper, from whom bt. by

Ruskin, February 1858; given by him to the University of Oxford, 1861
Coll.: Visitors of the Ashmolean Museum, Oxford (Herrmann 40)

Derived from pencil sketches in the *Nantes, Angers and Saumur* sketchbook, (T.B., CCXLVIII-20, 21).

944   St. Florent *c.* 1826–30

Body-colour on blue paper, approx. 140 × 190
Engr.: by R. Brandard for *Turner's Annual Tour—the Loire,* 1833 (R. 446)
Prov.: Lewis Loyd; Capt. E. N. F. Loyd, sale Christie 30 April 1937 (70), bt. Capt. Loyd
Private collection

Based on a drawing in the *Nantes, Angers and Saumur* sketchbook (T.B., CCXLVIII-18). Another view of St. Florent occurs among the colour studies for the series (T.B., CCLIX-9).

945   Between   Clairmont   and   Mauves *c.* 1826–30

Watercolour and body-colour, with pen and scratching-out, on blue paper, 138 × 189
Engr.: by W. Miller for *Turner's Annual Tour—the Loire,* 1833 (R. 447)
Prov.: Thomas Griffith; Charles Stokes, 1850; by descent to Hannah Cooper, from whom bt. by Ruskin, February 1858; given by him to the University of Oxford, 1861
Coll.: Visitors of the Ashmolean Museum, Oxford (Herrmann 31)

946   Château Hamelin, between Oudon and Ancenis *c.* 1826–30

Watercolour and body-colour, with pen and scratching-out, on blue paper, 137 × 189

Engr.: by R. Brandard for *Turner's Annual Tour—the Loire,* 1833 (R. 448)
Exh.: R.A. 1974 (385)
Prov.: Thomas Griffith; Charles Stokes, 1850; by descent to Hannah Cooper, from whom bt. by Ruskin, February 1858; given by him to the University of Oxford, 1861
Coll.: Visitors of the Ashmolean Museum, Oxford (Herrmann 39)

Based on a pencil sketch in the *Nantes, Angers and Saumur* sketchbook (T.B., CCXLVIII-13).

947   Scene on the Loire (near the Coteaux de Mauves) *c.* 1826–30

Watercolour and body-colour, with pen, on blue paper, 140 × 190
Engr.: by R. Wallis for *Turner's Annual Tour—the Loire,* 1833 (R. 449)
Prov.: Thomas Griffith; Charles Stokes, 1850; by descent to Hannah Cooper, from whom bt. by Ruskin, February 1858; given by him to the University of Oxford, 1861
Coll.: Visitors of the Ashmolean Museum, Oxford (Herrmann 50)

Herrmann suggests that the basis for this design was a pencil sketch in the *Nantes, Angers and Saumur* sketchbook (T.B., CCXLVIII-22v).

948   Clairmont *c.* 1826–30

Watercolour and body-colour, with scratching-out, on blue paper, approx. 140 × 190
Engr.: by J. T. Willmore for *Turner's Annual Tour—the Loire,* 1833 (R. 450)
Prov.: anon. sale Christie 23 February 1920 (23), bt. Sampson
Private collection, U.S.A.

Based on a pencil drawing in the *Nantes, Angers and Saumur* sketchbook (T.B., CCXLVIII-10v).

949 Coteaux de Mauves *c.* 1826–30

Watercolour and body-colour, with pen and scratching-out, on blue paper, 138 × 187
Engr.: by R. Wallis for *Turner's Annual Tour—the Loire*, 1833 (R. 451)
Prov.: Thomas Griffith; Charles Stokes, 1850; by descent to Hannah Cooper, from whom bt. by Ruskin, February 1858; given by him to the University of Oxford, 1861
Coll.: Visitors of the Ashmolean Museum, Oxford (Herrmann 41)

Based on a pencil sketch in the *Nantes, Angers and Saumur* sketchbook (T.B., CCXLVIII-9v).

950 Château de Nantes *c.* 1826–30

Watercolour and body-colour, with pen, on blue paper, 123 × 180
Engr.: by W. Miller for *Turner's Annual Tour—the Loire*, 1833 (R. 452)
Prov.: Thomas Griffith; Charles Stokes, 1850; by descent to Hannah Cooper, from whom bt. by Ruskin, February 1858; given by him to the University of Oxford, 1861
Coll.: Visitors of the Ashmolean Museum, Oxford (Herrmann 51)

**XV(b) Nos 951–990
The Seine,** *c.* 1832

951 Light-towers of the Heve *c.* 1832

Body-colour on blue paper, 189 × 134, title-page vignette
Engr.: by J. Cousen for *Turner's Annual Tour—the Seine,* 1834 (R. 453)
Coll.: Trustees of the British Museum
(T.B., CCLIX-136)

Turner made several studies for this design; pencil sketches are in the *Seine and Paris* sketchbook (T.B., CCLIV-87v, 88); colour studies are T.B., CCLIX-1, 2, 80; and Nos 1001–1004 below.

952 Havre: sunset in the port *c.* 1832

Body-colour on blue paper, 140 × 192
Engr.: by W. Miller for *Turner's Annual Tour—the Seine,* 1834 (R. 454)
Coll.: Trustees of the British Museum
(T.B., CCLIX-133)

953 Havre, Tower of Francis I: twilight outside the port *c.* 1832

Body-colour on blue paper, 140 × 192

Engr.: by R. Wallis for *Turner's Annual Tour—the Seine,* 1834 (R. 455)
Coll.: Trustees of the British Museum
(T.B., CCLIX-134)

954 Graville *c.* 1832

?Watercolour and body-colour on blue paper, approx. 135 × 185
Engr.: by R. Brandard for *Turner's Annual Tour—the Seine,* 1834 (R. 456)
Prov.: Heath; sold by order of the Court of Chancery (Evans v. Heath), Christie 22 May 1852 (56), bt. Lambe; R. Freeland; Robert Hanbury, sale Christie 13 May 1884 (130), bt. Permain; A. J. Finberg
Coll.: untraced

Based on a pencil drawing in the *Tancarville and Lillebonne* sketchbook (T.B., CCLIII-6v).

955 Harfleur *c.* 1832

Body-colour on blue paper, 139 × 191
Engr.: by J. Cousen for *Turner's Annual Tour—the Seine,* 1834 (R. 457)
Exh.: R.A. 1974 (397)
Coll.: Trustees of the British Museum
(T.B., CCLIX-102)

Based on a pencil drawing in the *Tancarville and Lillebonne* sketchbook (T.B., CCLIII-5v).

956 Tancarville *c.* 1832

Body-colour on blue paper, 140 × 194
Engr.: by J. T. Willmore for *Turner's Annual Tour—the Seine,* 1834 (R. 458)
Coll.: Trustees of the British Museum
(T.B., CCLIX-128)

Based on a pencil drawing in the *Tancarville and Lillebonne* sketchbook (T.B., CCLIII-54).

957 Tancarville, with the town of Quillebœuf *c.*1832

Body-colour on blue paper, 140 × 191
Engr.: by R. Brandard for *Turner's Annual Tour—the Seine,* 1834 (R. 459)
Coll.: Trustees of the British Museum
(T.B., CCLIX-130)

Based on a pencil drawing in the *Tancarville and Lillebonne* sketchbook (T.B., CCLIII-46v).

958 Lillebonne Château and Town *c.* 1832

Body-colour on blue paper, 140 × 190
Engr.: by T. Jeavons for *Turner's Annual Tour—the Seine,* 1834 (R. 460)
Coll.: Trustees of the British Museum
(T.B., CCLIX-110)

A pencil drawing of this view is in the *Tancarville and Lillebonne* sketchbook (T.B., CCLIII-37); and another from almost the same viewpoint is on p. 29 of the same sketchbook.

959 Lillebonne Château *c.* 1832

Body-colour on blue paper, 140 × 191
Engr.: by J. T. Willmore for *Turner's Annual Tour—the Seine,* 1834 (R. 461)
Coll.: Trustees of the British Museum
(T.B., CCLIX-111)

Based on pencil drawings in the *Tancarville and Lillebonne* sketchbook (T.B., CCLIII).

960 Caudebec *c.*1832

Body-colour on blue paper, 139 × 190
Engr.: by J. B. Allen for *Turner's Annual Tour—the Seine,* 1834 (R. 462)
Exh.: B.M. 1975 (190)
Coll.: Trustees of the British Museum
(T.B., CCLIX-105)

Turner's pencil drawing of this subject is in the *Guernsey* sketchbook (T.B., CCLII, 17v-18); other sketches for it are on pp. 17, 18 verso.

961 Jumièges *c.* 1832

Body-colour on blue paper, 140 × 190
Engr.: by J. C. Armytage for *Turner's Annual Tour—the Seine,* 1834 (R. 463)
Coll.: Trustees of the British Museum
(T.B., CCLIX-131)

Based on a pencil drawing in the *Tancarville and Lillebonne* sketchbook (T.B., CCLIII-59v).

962 La Chaire de Gargantua, near Duclair *c.*1832

Body-colour on blue paper, 137 × 188
Engr.: by R. Brandard for *Turner's Annual Tour—the Seine,* 1834 (R. 464)
Exh.: B.M. 1975 (191)

Coll.: Trustees of the British Museum
(T.B., CCLIX-106)

Drawings of this stretch of the Seine, with the 'Giant's Chair', are in the *Tancarville and Lillebonne* sketchbook (T.B., CCLIII, 67-70).

963 Rouen, looking up the Seine *c.* 1832

Body-colour, with some pen, on blue paper, 141 × 192
Engr.: by R. Brandard for *Turner's Annual Tour—the Seine,* 1834 (R. 465)
Exh.: R.A. 1974 (401)
Coll.: Trustees of the British Museum
(T.B., CCLIX-107)

964 Rouen, looking down the Seine *c.* 1832

Body-colour on blue paper, 140 × 192
Engr.: by W. Miller for *Turner's Annual Tour—the Seine,* 1834 (R. 466)
Exh.: R.A. 1974 (402)
Coll.: Trustees of the British Museum
(T.B., CCLIX-108)

965–972

965 Rouen: the west front of the cathedral *c.* 1832

Watercolour and body-colour, with some pen, on blue paper, 140 × 194
Engr.: by T. Higham for *Turner's Annual Tour—the Seine,* 1834 (R. 467)
Exh.: B.M. 1975 (192)
Coll.: Trustees of the British Museum
(T.B., CCLIX-109)

Probably based on a pencil sketch in the *Dieppe, Rouen and Paris* sketchbook (T.B., CCLVIII-22).

966 Rouen from St. Catherine's Hill *c.* 1832

?Watercolour and body-colour on blue paper, approx. 140 × 190
Engr.: by W. Miller for *Turner's Annual Tour—the Seine,* 1834 (R. 468)
Prov.: John Ruskin; H. Yates Thompson
Coll.: untraced

Several sketches of Rouen from St. Catherine's Hill occur in the *Rouen* sketchbook (T.B. CCLV) and in the *Dieppe, Rouen and Paris* sketchbook (T.B., CCLVIII), the closest to this composition is T.B., CCLV-8v.

967 Château de la Mailleraie *c.* 1832

?Watercolour and body-colour on blue paper, approx. 140 × 190
Engr.: by R. Brandard for *Turner's Annual Tour—the Seine,* 1834 (R. 469)
Prov.: Heath; sold by order of the Court of Chancery (Evans v. Heath), Christie 22 May 1852 (58), bt. Lambe; Robert Hanbury, sale Christie 13 May 1884 (129), bt. Capt. G. H.
Coll.: untraced

Apparently based on the pencil drawing on p. 72 verso of the *Seine and Paris* sketchbook (T.B., CCLIV).

968 Between Quillebœuf and Villequier *c.* 1832

Watercolour, body-colour and pen on blue paper, 138 × 190
Engr.: by R. Brandard for *Turner's Annual Tour—the Seine,* 1834 (R. 470)
Exh.: R.A. 1974 (400)
Coll.: Trustees of the British Museum
(T.B., CCLIX-104)

Based on a pencil drawing in the *Tancarville and Lillebonne* sketchbook (T.B., CCLIII-55v).

969 Quillebœuf *c.* 1832

Body-colour, with some pen, on blue paper, 140 × 189
Engr.: by R. Brandard for *Turner's Annual Tour—the Seine,* 1834 (R. 471)
Exh.: R.A. 1974 (398)
Coll.: Trustees of the British Museum
(T.B., CCLIX-103)

Pencil sketches of this subject are in the *Seine and Paris* sketchbook (T.B., CCLIV-77, 79v). Turner used the motif again in his oil-painting of 1833 (P353).

970 Honfleur *c.* 1832

Watercolour and body-colour, with some pen and brown colour on blue paper, 140 × 191

Engr.: by J. Cousen for *Turner's Annual Tour—the Seine,* 1834 (R. 472)
Exh.: B.M. 1975 (193)
Coll.: Trustees of the British Museum
(T.B., CCLIX-135)

971 Château Gaillard, from the south *c.* 1832

Body-colour on blue paper, 193 × 140, title-page vignette
Engr.: by J. Cousen for *Turner's Annual Tour—the Seine,* 1835 (R. 473)
Coll.: Trustees of the British Museum
(T.B., CCLIX-127)

Based on pencil sketches in the *Seine and Paris* sketchbook (T.B. CCLIV-40 to 58). Another design for this vignette of Château Gaillard is the very different *Nicholo Poussin's Birth-place* (No. 1006).

972 Château Gaillard, from the east *c.* 1832

Body-colour, with some pen, on blue paper, 140 × 191
Engr.: by J. Smith for *Turner's Annual Tour—the Seine,* 1835 (R. 474)
Exh.: B.M. 1975 (194)
Coll.: Trustees of the British Museum
(T.B., CCLIX-113)

Based on pencil sketches in the *Seine and Paris* sketchbook (T.B., CCLIV-55, 56).

973 Vernon *c.* 1832

Body-colour, with some pen, on blue paper, 138 × 194
Engr.: by J. T. Willmore for Turner's *Annual Tour—the Seine,* 1835 (R. 475)
Exh.: R.A. 1974 (403)
Coll.: Trustees of the British Museum
(T.B., CCLIX-129)

974 Pont de l'Arche *c.* 1832

Body-colour on blue paper, 139 × 192
Engr.: by J. T. Willmore for *Turner's Annual Tour—the Seine,* 1835 (R. 476)
Exh.: B.M. 1975 (195)
Coll.: Trustees of the British Museum
(T.B., CCLIX-112)

975 View of the Seine between Mantes and Vernon *c.* 1832

Body-colour, with some pen, on blue paper, 142 × 193
Engr.: by R. Brandard for *Turner's Annual Tour—the Seine,* 1835 (R. 477)

Exh.: R.A. 1974 (404)
Coll.: Trustees of the British Museum
(T.B., CCLIX-114)

976 Mantes *c.* 1832

Body-colour on blue paper, 140 × 193
Engr.: by W. Radclyffe for *Turner's Annual Tour—the Seine,* 1835 (R. 478)
Coll.: Trustees of the British Museum
(T.B., CCLIX-115)

977 Bridge at Meulan *c.* 1832

Body-colour on blue paper, 138 × 190
Engr.: by J. Cousen for *Turner's Annual Tour—the Seine,* 1835 (R. 479)
Coll.: Trustees of the British Museum
(T.B., CCLIX-116)

978 St. Germain *c.* 1832

Body-colour on blue paper, 138 × 192
Engr.: by J. B. Allen for *Turner's Annual Tour—the Seine,* 1835 (R. 480)
Exh.: R.A. 1974 (407)
Coll.: Trustees of the British Museum
(T.B., CCLIX-122)

Turner noted the panorama from the terrace of St. Germain-en-Laye on another sheet of blue paper (T.B., CCLX-59).

979 St. Denis (moonlight) *c.* 1832

Body-colour on blue paper, 138 × 192
Engr.: by S. Fisher for *Turner's Annual Tour—the Seine,* 1835 (R. 481)
Exh.: R.A. 1974 (408)
Coll.: Trustees of the British Museum
(T.B., CCLIX-121)

Turner's pencil sketch of the view is in the *Paris and Environs* sketchbook (T.B., CCLVII-154); the church of St. Denis is noted on pp. 152v, 153.

980 Bridges at St. Cloud and Sèvres *c.* 1832

Body-colour on blue paper, 137 × 189
Engr.: by J. Radclyffe for *Turner's Annual Tour—the Seine,* 1835 (R. 482)
Coll.: Trustees of the British Museum
(T.B., CCLIX-123)

A pencil sketch of the subject, in a different view, is in the *Dieppe, Rouen and Paris* sketchbook (T.B., CCLVIII-21v); and there is another on p. 25 verso of the same sketchbook.

981 The Lanterne at St. Cloud *c.* 1832

Body-colour on blue paper, 140 × 190
Engr.: by J. T. Willmore for *Turner's Annual Tour—the Seine,* 1835 (R. 483)

Coll.: Trustees of the British Museum
(T.B., CCLIX-132)

Turner's pencil sketch of this subject is in the *Seine and Paris* sketchbook (T.B., CCLIV-14v).

982   Bridge of St. Cloud from Sèvres *c.* 1832

Body-colour on blue paper, 140 × 192
Engr.: by S. Fisher for *Turner's Annual Tour—the Seine,* 1835 (R. 484)
Coll.: Trustees of the British Museum
(T.B., CCLIX-124)

Based on a pencil sketch in the *Paris and Environs* sketchbook (T.B., CCLVII-148).

983   Paris: view of the Seine from the Barrière de Passy, with the Louvre in the distance *c.* 1832

Body-colour, with some pen, on blue paper, 140 × 191
Engr.: by J.T. Willmore for *Turner's Annual Tour—the Seine,* 1835 (R. 485)
Exh.: R.A. 1974 (405)

Coll.: Trustees of the British Museum
(T.B., CCLIX-117)

Based on a pencil sketch in the *Paris and Environs* sketchbook (T.B., CCLVII-156).

984   Paris: the Pont Neuf and the Ile de la Cité *c.* 1832

Body-colour on blue paper, 141 × 188
Engr.: by W. Miller for *Turner's Annual Tour—the Seine,* 1835 (R. 486)
Exh.: R.A. 1974 (406)
Coll.: Trustees of the British Museum
(T.B., CCLIX-118)

Based on pencil sketches in the *Paris and Environs* sketchbook (T.B., CCLVII-55v, 56v).

985   Paris: Marché aux Fleurs and Pont-au-Change *c.* 1832

Watercolour and body-colour on blue paper, 139 × 190
Engr.: by W. Radclyffe for *Turner's Annual Tour—the Seine,* 1835 (R. 487)
Coll.: Trustees of the British Museum
(T.B., CCLIX-120)

Turner drew the Marché aux Fleurs and the Pont-au-Change in the *Paris and Environs* sketchbook (T.B., CCLVII-67v).

986   Paris: Hôtel de Ville and Pont d'Arcole *c.* 1832

Watercolour and body-colour on blue paper, 139 × 190
Engr.: by T. Jeavons for *Turner's Annual Tour—the Seine,* 1835 (R. 488)

Coll.: Trustees of the British Museum
(T.B., CCLIX-119)

A pencil sketch of this view of the Pont d'Arcole is in the *Paris and Environs* sketchbook (T.B., CCLVII-66).

987   Paris: Boulevard des Italiens *c.* 1832

Body-colour on (?) blue paper, 134 × 184
Engr.: by T. Higham for *Turner's Annual Tour—the Seine,* 1835 (R. 489)
Prov.: Heath; sold by order of the Court of Chancery (Evans v. Heath), Christie 22 May 1852 (59), bt. Lambe; Robert Hanbury, sale Christie 13 May 1884 (131), bt. Agnew; Sir Donald Currie
Private collection

988   Confluence of the Seine and the Marne *c.* 1832

Body-colour on blue paper, 135 × 187
Inscr. verso in brush and red colour by Turner: *Junction of Seine and Marne at Charenton*
Engr.: by J.C. Armytage for *Turner's Annual Tour—the Seine,* 1835 (R. 490)

Prov.: Heath; sold by order of the Court of Chancery (Evans v. Heath), Christie, 22 May 1852 (132), bt. Lambe; Robert Hanbury, sale Christie 13 May 1884 (132) bt. Walford; C. E. Hughes; by descent to present owner
Private collection

989 Melun *c.* 1832

Body-colour on blue paper, 140 × 192
Engr.: by W. Miller for *Turner's Annual Tour—the Seine,* 1835 (R. 491)
Coll.: Trustees of the British Museum
(T.B., CCLIX-125)

Based on a pencil sketch in the *Paris and Environs* sketchbook (T.B., CCLVII-76v).

990 Troyes *c.* 1832

Body-colour on blue paper, 142 × 192
Engr.: by C. Armytage for *Turner's Annual Tour—the Seine,* 1835 (R. 492)
Coll.: Trustees of the British Museum
(T.B., CCLIX-126)

XV (c) Nos 991–1043
Unused designs and studies for the 'Rivers of Europe' project, *c.* 1825–1834

991 Scene on the Loire 1826–30

Watercolour and body-colour on blue paper, 140 × 191
Prov.: Thomas Griffith; Charles Stokes, 1850; by descent to Hannah Cooper, from whom bt. by Ruskin, February 1858; given by him to the Ruskin

School of Drawing and Fine Art, Oxford, 1875; transferred to the museum, 1938
Coll.: Visitors of the Ashmolean Museum, Oxford (Herrmann 82)

992 Calm on the Loire (? near Nantes) *c.* 1832

Watercolour and body-colour, with pen, on blue paper, 138 × 188
Prov.: Thomas Griffith; Charles Stokes, 1850; by descent to Hannah Cooper, from whom bt. Ruskin, February 1858; given by him to the University of Oxford, 1861
Coll.: Visitors of the Ashmolean Museum, Oxford (Herrmann 33)

993 The Bridge at Blois: fog clearing *c.* 1826–30

Watercolour and body-colour, with pen, on blue paper, 131 × 187

Prov.: Thomas Griffith; Charles Stokes, 1850; by descent to Hannah Cooper, from whom bt. by Ruskin, February 1858; given by him to the University of Oxford, 1861
Coll.: Visitors of the Ashmolean Museum, Oxford (Herrmann 34)

994 The Bridge and Château at Amboise *c.* 1826–30

Pencil, watercolour and body-colour, with pen, on blue paper, 134 × 187
Prov.: Thomas Griffith; Charles Stokes, 1850; by descent to Hannah Cooper, from whom bt. by Ruskin, February 1858; given by him to the University of Oxford, 1861
Coll.: Visitors of the Ashmolean Museum, Oxford (Herrmann 36)

995 Angers *c.* 1826–30

Watercolour and body-colour, with pen, on blue paper, 136 × 187
Prov.: Thomas Griffith; Charles Stokes, 1850; by descent to Hannah Cooper, from whom bt. by Ruskin, February 1858; given by him to the University of Oxford, 1861
Coll.: Visitors of the Ashmolean Museum, Oxford (Herrmann 37)

996 Nantes 1826–30

Watercolour and body-colour, with pen, on blue paper, 142 × 193
Prov.: Thomas Griffith; Charles Stokes, 1850; by descent to Hannah Cooper, from whom bt. by Ruskin, February 1858; given by him to the museum, 1861

Coll.: Syndics of the Fitzwilliam Museum, Cambridge (580; Cormack 27)

997 Orléans, twilight 1826–30

Watercolour and body-colour, with pen, on blue paper, 140 × 195
Prov.: Thomas Griffith; Charles Stokes, 1850; by descent to Hannah Cooper, from whom bt. by Ruskin, February 1858; given by him to the museum, 1861
Coll.: Syndics of the Fitzwilliam Museum, Cambridge (579; Cormack 26)

998 Harfleur c. 1823

Watercolour and body-colour, with pen, on blue paper, 134 × 185
Prov.: Thomas Griffith; Charles Stokes, 1850; by descent to Hannah Cooper, from whom bt. by

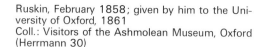

Ruskin, February 1858; given by him to the University of Oxford, 1861
Coll.: Visitors of the Ashmolean Museum, Oxford (Herrmann 30)

999 Tancarville c. 1832

Watercolour and body-colour, with pen, on blue paper, 135 × 188
Prov.: Thomas Griffith; Charles Stokes, 1850; by descent to Hannah Cooper, from whom bt. by Ruskin, February 1858; given by him to the University of Oxford, 1861
Coll.: Visitors of the Ashmolean Museum, Oxford (Herrmann 32)

1000 Rouen from St. Sever c. 1832

Watercolour and body-colour, with pen, on blue paper, 101 × 178
Inscr. in ? Ruskin's hand: *This is a leaf from a sketchbook*
Prov.: John Ruskin; Kurt Pantzer; given to the museum in memory of Dr. and Mrs. Hugo O. Pantzer by their children
Coll.: Indianapolis Museum of Art

1001 Study for 'Light-towers at La Hève' c. 1832

Watercolour over traces of pencil, 197 × 159, vignette
Prov.: Elhanan Bicknell, sale Christie 29 April 1863 (118), bt. Col. F. R. Leyland, sale Christie 9 March 1872 (43, as 'Light Towers of Le Havre'), bt. White; Mrs Newall; Phillips & MacConnell, from whom purchased by Lord Leverhulme, 1923
Coll.: The Lady Lever Collection, Port Sunlight, Cheshire (WHL 4715)

This and the following three drawings appear to be studies related to the design of the title vignette for *Wanderings by the Seine*, 1834 (No. 951, above); though Nos 1003, 1004 may possibly represent a different location. N.B. these designs are on white paper.

1002 La Hève: Light-towers c. 1832

Watercolour, 192 × 148, vignette
Prov.: ?H. A. J. Munro of Novar, sale Christie 2 June 1877 (22, as 'Havre——Sail on left Side'), bt. Kennedy; ?T. S. Kennedy, sale Christie 18 May 1895 (88, as 'Entrance to the Port of Le Havre'), bt. Agnew; Sir Donald Currie; by descent to present owner
Private collection

See No. 1001. The provenance of this drawing is uncertain (see Nos 1004, 1005).

1003 Study for 'Light-towers at La Hève' c. 1832

Pencil and watercolour, 170 × 145, vignette
Prov.: J. E. Taylor, by whom given to the Whitworth Institute, 1892
Coll.: Whitworth Art Gallery, University of Manchester (D.101.1892)

See No. 1001.

1004 Study for 'Light-towers at La Hève' *c.* 1832

Watercolour over pencil, 211 × 184, vignette
Inscr.: *Mar*
Prov.: Charles Stokes; ?T. S. Kennedy; Thomas Hughes; Mrs. F. Hughes, sale Sotheby 28 November 1922 (123), bt. Lord Leverhulme
Coll.: The Lady Lever Collection, Port Sunlight, Cheshire (WHL 4398).

This drawing is traditionally known as 'Margate', on account of the brief inscription.
See No. 1001.

1005 Havre *c.* 1832

Body-colour on blue paper, 140 × 191
Prov.: ?H. A. J. Munro of Novar, sale Christie 2 June 1877 (22, as 'Havre—Sail on left Side'), bt. J. Kennedy; ?T. S. Kennedy, sale Christie 18 May 1895 (88, as 'Entrance to the Port of Le Havre') bt. Agnew
Coll.: untraced

The provenance of the drawing, apparently a vignette, is confused with that of 1002, and it is possible they may be the same work.

1006 Château Gaillard: Nicolas Poussin's birthplace *c.* 1832

Watercolour and body-colour on blue paper, 181 × 127, vignette
Inscr. lower centre: *Nicholo Poussin's Birth-place*
Prov.: ? Elhanan Bicknell, sale Christie 25 April 1863 (262), bt. Agnew; John Ruskin; Sir James Knowles; Sotheby, 18 June 1970 (95), bt. Pantzer
Pantzer Collection, Indianapolis

Presumably a design for the *Seine* tour, showing as it does the Château Gaillard, above Andelys, in Normandy. This may have been intended as a title vignette; its relationship with the drawing of Claude's birthplace (No. 1007) is not entirely clear. Perhaps both designs were made independently of the 'Tours', as private tributes to the artists in question.
See No. 971.

1007 'Claude Lorraine's Birthplace', the Pont de Buzet? *c.* 1832

Watercolour and body-colour on blue paper, 180 × 130
Prov.: John Ruskin; Christie 13 July 1971 (92), bt. Pantzer
Coll.: Kurt Pantzer Collection, Indianapolis

See No. 1006.

1008 Pont de Buzet *c.* 1825–34

Watercolour, body-colour and chalk, with pen and brown ink on buff paper, 140 × 193
Inscr. lower left: *Pont de Buset* (?)
Prov.: John Ruskin, sale Christie 22 July 1882 (61), bt. in; G. Harland Peck; Agnew, from whom bt. by donor, 1960
Coll.: Museum of Art, Rhode Island School of Design, Providence, R.I. (anon. gift)

The location of this view is uncertain; but see No. 1007.

1009 Arles: Castle and Aqueduct ?*c.* 1828

Watercolour and body-colour on blue paper, 138 × 190
Prov.: Thomas Griffith; Charles Stokes, 1850; by descent to Hannah Cooper; Henry Vaughan; J. L. Roget; by descent to J. Romilly Roget, sale Sotheby 18 June 1970 (179 as '?Vernon sur Seine'), bt. Kurt Pantzer, by whom given to the museum
Coll.: Indianapolis Museum of Art

1010 Sisteron, Basses Alpes *c.* 1830

Watercolour and body-colour, with some pen, on blue paper, 140 × 191
Prov.: Henry Vaughan, by whom bequeathed to the gallery, 1900
Coll.: National Gallery of Ireland, Dublin (2429)

The identification of this subject, like that of others in this group, is traditional but dubious.

1011 Sisteron, Basses Alpes *c.* 1830

Body-colour on grey paper, 127 × 178
Prov.: John Ruskin, by whom given to J. W. Bunney; by descent; sale Christie 1 June 1956 (127), bt. Alfred Payton Jenkins
Coll.: untraced

1012 View in the Basses Alpes (Sisteron) *c.* 1830

Watercolour and body-colour, with some pen, on buff paper, 138 × 190
Prov.: Herbert Powell, by whom bequeathed to the museum 1973
Coll.: Victoria and Albert Museum, London (P16. 1973)

1013 Sisteron, France 1825-34

Body-colour, with some pen, on buff paper, 140 × 187
Prov.: J. E. Taylor, by whom given to the Whitworth Institute, 1892
Coll.: Whitworth Art Gallery, University of Manchester (D.115.1892)

Another drawing of *Sisteron,* of these dimensions, was in an anonymous sale, Christie 15 May 1896 (99), bt. Shepherd; this may be identifiable with the

Sisteron in the collection of G. R. Burnett, sale Christie 21 March 1908 (29), bt. Agnew, and with the drawing of the same title in the collection of G. P. Wall, sale Christie 16 March 1912 (117), bt. Bowden. Two drawings called 'Sisteron' were in the Thomas Greenwood sale, Christie 13 February 1875 (245, 247), the former bt. in, the latter bt. Vokins.

1014 On the south coast of France (?) *? c.* 1828

Watercolour and body-colour, with pencil and some pen, on blue paper, 137 × 190
Prov.: unknown
Private collection

1015 Coast of Genoa *c.* 1828

Watercolour and body-colour, with pen and scratching-out, on blue paper, 138 × 180
Verso: sketch of a town above and below cliffs
Pencil and white body-colour
Prov.: Thomas Griffith; Charles Stokes, 1850; by descent to Hannah Cooper; from whom bt. by Ruskin, February 1858; given by him to the University of Oxford, 1861
Coll.: Visitors of the Ashmolean Museum, Oxford (Herrmann 28)

1016 Genoa: looking down over the harbour *c.* 1828

Watercolour and body-colour on blue paper, 140 × 192
Prov.: C. S. Roundell; ? Christie 1901; W. G. Rawlinson; Mrs. Flora Koch; Gooden & Fox, from whom bt. by present owner

Private collection, U.S.A.

1017 Genoa *c.* 1828

Pencil, some pen, watercolour and body-colour on blue paper, 138 × 189
Prov.: Sir Hickman Bacon, Bt.; by descent to the present owner
Private collection

1018 Corsica *c.* 1828

Watercolour on brown paper, 139 × 187
Prov.: William Leech, sale Christie 21 May 1887 (74), ? bt. in; Van Ingen, New York, 1928; Agnew, from whom purchased, 1963
Coll.: Mr. and Mrs. Paul Mellon, Upperville, Virginia

The title is presumably inaccurate. The subject is probably a view along the Mediterranean coast, perhaps at Monaco, unless Turner made an unrecorded excursion to Corsica during his journey to Italy in 1828.

1019   Luxembourg *c.* 1825 or 1834

Body-colour, with pen and ? some chalk, on buff paper, 135 × 189
Prov.: ?Birket Foster, sale Christie 28 April 1894 (39), bt. Vokins; Sir Donald Currie; Lady Mirrielees; Mrs. Craven; Agnew, from whom bt. by Paul Mellon, 1968
Coll.: Yale Center for British Art, Paul Mellon Collection

1020   Luxembourg *c.* 1825 or 1834

Body-colour, with pen, on blue paper, 135 × 187
Exh.: R.A. 1974 (374)
Prov.: John Ruskin, sale Christie 1869 (23), bt. Vokins; J. E. Taylor, sale Christie 5 July 1912 (80), bt. Agnew
Private collection

1021   Luxembourg *c.* 1825 or 1834

Pencil, pen and body-colour on buff paper, 137 × 187

Prov.: ?Birket Foster, sale Christie 28 April 1894 (39), bt. Vokins; Sir Donald Currie; Agnew; Beresford Rimington Heaton, by whom bequeathed to the gallery, 1940
Coll.: Tate Gallery, London (5237)

1022   Luxembourg *c.* 1825 or 1834

Body-colour on blue paper, 140 × 187
Prov.: Beresford Rimington Heaton, by whom bequeathed to the gallery, 1940
Coll.: Tate Gallery, London (5240)

1023   Scene on the Meuse *c.* 1825–34

Watercolour and body-colour, with pen, on blue paper, 134 × 186
Prov.: Thomas Griffith; Charles Stokes, 1850; by descent to Hannah Cooper, from whom bt. by Ruskin, February 1858; given by him to the Ruskin School of Drawing and Fine Art, Oxford, 1875; transferred to the museum, 1938
Coll.: Visitors of the Ashmolean Museum, Oxford (Herrmann 27)

The scene is perhaps more likely to be a view on the Moselle.

1024   Huy on the Meuse* *c.* 1825–34

Watercolour and body-colour, with some pen, on blue paper, 140 × 194
Prov.: Thomas Griffith; Charles Stokes, 1850; by descent to Hannah Cooper, from whom bt. by Ruskin, February 1858; given by him to the museum, 1861
Coll.: Syndics of the Fitzwilliam Museum, Cambridge (578; Cormack 29)

1025   Namur on the Meuse *c.* 1825–34

Watercolour and body-colour, with pen, on blue paper, 140 × 190
Prov.: Thomas Griffith; Charles Stokes, 1850; by descent to Hannah Cooper, from whom bt. by Ruskin, February 1858; given by him to the museum, 1861
Coll.: Syndics of the Fitzwilliam Museum, Cambridge (577; Cormack 28)

1026   Dinant on the Meuse *c.* 1825–34

Body-colour, with pen, on blue paper, 133 × 190
Prov.: ?John Ruskin; Arthur Severn; Agnew, from whom purchased by the Trustees of the John Wigham Richardson Bequest to the Walker Mechanics Institute, 1925, and placed on permanent loan to the gallery
Coll.: Laing Art Gallery, Newcastle upon Tyne (Tyne and Wear Council Museums)

Based on the colour sketch T.B., CCXCII-37.

1027   Dinant (Rocher de Bayard) *c.* 1825–34

Watercolour and body-colour on blue paper, 127 × 184
Prov.: J. E. Taylor, sale Christie 5 July 1912 (92), bt. Blaker; Gwendoline E. Davies, by whom bequeathed to the museum, 1952
Coll.: National Museum of Wales, Cardiff (2957).

1028 Landscape (a town with a fortress on a high cliff) *c.* 1825–34

Body-colour, with pen, on ?buff paper, 132 × 182
Prov.: G. Beatson Blair, by whom bequeathed to the gallery, 1941
Coll.: City Art Gallery, Manchester (1947-109)

Perhaps a view in a town on the Meuse.

1029 On the Moselle* *c.* 1825–34

Body-colour, with pen, on blue paper, 137 × 184
Prov.: ?John Ruskin; by whom given to J. Bunney; Mrs. Bunney; T. A. Tatton, sale Christie 14 December 1928 (21), bt. Agnew; Agnew 1975
Private collection

1030 St. Goar on the Rhine *c.* 1825–34

Watercolour and body-colour on blue-grey paper, 133 × 184
Prov.: Birket Foster, sale Christie 28 April 1894 (40), bt. McLean; G. N. Stevens, sale Christie 14 June 1912 (70), bt. Wallis; Margaret S. Davies, sale Sotheby 24 February 1960 (89), bt. Agnew
Coll.: Mrs. Cecil Keith

1031 On the Rhine *c.* 1830

Body-colour over traces of pencil on blue paper, 133 × 190

Prov.: John Napier, sale Christie 6 March 1886 (42 or 43), bt. Permain; Sir James Knowles; Sir Edward Durning Lawrence; anon. sale Christie 2 June 1939 (71), bt. D. G. Thompson; Agnew; Lord Bilsland; Richard Ivor, 1975
Coll.: J. H. Silley, U.K.

1032 Sion *c.* 1825–34

Body-colour, with some pen, on ?buff paper, 140 × 190
Prov.: Charles Langton, sale Christie 20 April 1901 (104, as 'Evening sun—Sion, Rhone Valley'), bt. Agnew; J. Gresham, 1917; A. H. Wild, 1922, sale Sotheby 16 April 1958 (33), bt. back; anon. sale, Sotheby 16 March 1978 (155), bt. Stanhope Shelton
Coll.: Stanhope Shelton

This drawing is also known as 'Entrance to the Via Mala'. Its actual subject is doubtful.

1033 River landscape in France (?) *c.* 1830

Pencil, watercolour and body-colour on grey paper, 137 × 190
Inscr. on frame verso: *given to HDR 1878 by Frank Barnett*
Prov.: anon. sale Sotheby 26 January 1978 (214), bt. Andrew Wyld; anon. sale Christie 21 November 1978 (81), bt. Somerville & Simpson
Coll.: Somerville & Simpson, London

1034 Ehrenbreitstein *c.* 1825–34

Body-colour on blue paper, 140 × 190
Engr.: by R. Wallis, 1833, for *The Keepsake* (R. 328) and printed in Heath's *Gallery of British Engravings,* 1836
Prov.: Henry Vaughan, by whom bequeathed to the gallery, 1900
Coll.: National Galleries of Scotland, Edinburgh (879)

1035 St. Martin's Precipice, Innsbruck ?*c.* 1833

Body-colour over pencil on buff paper, 131 × 184 (sight)
Prov.: ?Fine Art Society, London, 1900; Agnew, 1903; ?Walter Dunlop, sale Christie 12 March 1904 (101), bt. McLean; James Blair, by whom bequeathed to the gallery, 1917
Coll.: City Art Gallery, Manchester (1917.115)

1036 Martinswand, near Innsbruck, in the Tyrol *c.* 1833

Body-colour on grey paper, 137 × 191
Prov.: John Ruskin, by whom presented to J. W. Bunney; anon. sale Christie 1 June 1956 (126), bt. Kurt Pantzer; presented to the museum in memory of Dr. and Mrs. Hugo Pantzer by their children

Coll.: Indianapolis Museum of Art

1037 Shipping, with buildings, (?) Venice
   ?c. 1833

Watercolour and body-colour over pencil, on grey paper, 140 × 190
Prov.: Lord Halifax, from whom purchased by the Rt. Hon. Professor Sir Clifford Allbutt, by whom bequeathed to the museum 1925, received 1935
Coll.: Syndics of the Fitzwilliam Museum, Cambridge (1764; Cormack 41)

1038 Lake Como, looking towards Lecco
   c. 1828

Body-colour on blue paper, 140 × 190
Prov.: Henry Vaughan, by whom bequeathed to the gallery, 1900
Coll.: National Galleries of Scotland, Edinburgh (878)

1039 Vesuvius in eruption   *?c.* 1828

Watercolour and body-colour on blue paper, 124 × 175
Prov.: sale Foster, 4 May 1921 (59), bt. A. P. Oppé; by descent to present owner
Coll.: D. L. T. Oppé, London

A weak drawing, which it is difficult to place precisely. Nos 1040, 1041 are from the same group, which also includes a study in similar format of *The smoke from the volcano* in black-and-white chalk.

1040 Vesuvius in eruption, from a point nearer the shore   *?c.* 1828

Watercolour and body-colour on blue paper, 124 × 175
Prov.: sale Foster, 4 May 1921 (?60), bt. A. P. Oppé; by descent to the present owner
Coll.: D. L. T. Oppé, London

See No. 1039.

1041 Distant view of Vesuvius by sunset
   ?c. 1828

Watercolour and body-colour on blue paper, 124 × 175
Prov.: sale Foster, 4 May 1921 (?61), bt. A. P. Oppé; by descent to present owner
Coll.: D. L. T. Oppé, London

See No. 1039.

1042 Boats on a lake   *c.* 1830

Watercolour and body-colour on blue paper, 140 × 193
Prov.: L. G. Duke; Colnaghi, London, 1960, from whom bt., 1961
Coll.: Mr. and Mrs. Paul Mellon, Upperville, Virginia

1043 A winding river   *c.* 1830

Watercolour and body-colour, with some pen, on blue paper, 140 × 190
Prov.: J. E. Taylor, sale Christie 8 July 1912 (132), bt. Agnew; G. E. T. Allen; by descent to present owner
Private collection

XV(d) Nos 1044–1051
Finished watercolours, derived from the 'Rivers of Europe' project, *c.* 1829–1833

Six engravings of French subjects after Turner appeared in *The Keepsake* between 1830 and 1834; at least one other design (No. 1050) seems to have been executed for a similar purpose, and it is possible that the drawings that Heath published in his 'Annual' were part of what was intended to be a longer series of 'Picturesque Views in France'. They make use of material gathered for the *Wanderings by the Seine,* and may simply be by-products of Turner's work on that project. They are not of uniform size.

1044 Nantes *c.* 1829

Watercolour, 280 × 419
Engr.: by J. T. Willmore, 1831, for *The Keepsake* (R. 325)
Prov.: John Dillon, sale Foster, 7 June 1856 (145)
Coll.: untraced

1045 St. Germain-en-Laye* *c.* 1830

Watercolour, 299 × 457
Engr.: by R. Wallis, 1832, for *The Keepsake* (R. 326)
Prov.: H. A. J. Munro of Novar, sale Christie 2 June 1877 (36), bt. McLean; J. A. Baumbach, sale Christie 2 June 1900 (34), bt. Tooth; Barnet Lewis, sale Christie 28 February 1930 (51), bt. Agnew; Agnew 1975
Coll.: Musée du Louvre, Paris (R.F. 36.057)

Based on T.B., CCLX-68.

1046 Saumur *c.* 1830

Watercolour, 283 × 423
Engr.: by R. Wallis, 1830, for *The Keepsake* (R. 324)
Exh.: B.M. 1975 (168)
Prov.: John Ruskin; H. A. J. Munro of Novar, sale Foster 1855; J. Dillon, sale Foster 7 June 1856 (144); J. H. Maw, 1857; Hon. W. F. D. Smith; Sir Joseph Beecham, sale Christie 4 May 1917 (153), bt. in; sale Christie 10 May 1918 (87); R. W. Lloyd, by whom bequeathed to the museum, 1958
Coll.: Trustees of the British Museum (1958-7-12-430)

Based on T.B., CCLIX-145.

1047 Marly* *c.* 1831

Watercolour and some body-colour, 286 × 426
Engr.: by W. Miller, 1832, for *The Keepsake* (R. 327)
Exh.: B.M. 1975 (175)
Prov.: H. A. J. Munro of Novar, sale Christie 2 June 1877 (37), bt. White; John Heugh, sale Christie 10 May 1878 (157), bt. C. Harrison; Revd. J. W. R. Brocklebank; R. W. Lloyd, by whom bequeathed to the museum, 1958
Coll.: Trustees of the British Museum (1958-7-12-433)

Based on T.B., CCLX-58; a colour-beginning of the subject is T.B., CCLXIII-30.

1048 Le Havre: sunset *c.* 1833

Watercolour over pencil, 172 × 254
Engr.: by R. Wallis, 1834, for *The Keepsake* (R. 330)
Prov.: F. R. Leyland, sale Christie 9 March 1872 (41), bt. Agnew; Albert Levy, sale Christie 31 March 1876 (279), bt. Agnew; ? sale Christie 13 June 1937, bt. Leggatt; Mrs. M. P. Stamp; her Executors, sale Christie 12 September 1941 (83), bt. Baer; J. Baer, sale Sotheby 9 November 1955 (48), bt. Agnew; bt. Pantzer, and given to the museum in memory of Dr. and Mrs. Hugo O. Pantzer by their children
Coll.: Indianapolis Museum of Art

Finberg thought the drawing that appeared in the 1937 sale to be either 'entirely repainted or a forgery'; the work catalogued here is certainly very weak, though possibly as a result of fading. The provenance may confuse two (or more) different objects.

1049 Palace of La Belle Gabrielle *c.* 1832

Watercolour, 318 × 426
Engr.: by W. Miller, 1834, for *The Keepsake* (R. 331)
Prov.: John Ruskin; Francis Stevenson
Coll.: untraced

1050 Grandville *c.* 1830

Watercolour, 178 × 267
Prov.: John Ruskin; Richard Martin, 1914; Charles Mason; Mrs. K. M. Dampier-Bennett, sale Sotheby 18 June 1970 (94), bt. in; anon. sale, Sotheby 20 April 1972 (56), bt. Everett
Private collection

1051 Ehrenbreitstein *c.* 1832

Watercolour, 305 × 451

Engr.: by R. Wallis, 1833, for *The Keepsake* (R. 328)
Prov.: Joseph Gillott, sale Christie 4 May 1872 (513), bt. Agnew; Thomas Wrigley; presented by his children to the gallery, 1901
Coll.: Art Gallery and Museum, Bury, Lancashire (Wrigley Donation; 115)

SECTION XVI
Nos 1052–1314
Book illustrations,
c. 1822–1840

XVI(a) Nos 1052–1057
Illustrations to Scott, Byron and Moore made for Fawkes, *c.* 1822

In about 1822 Walter Fawkes commissioned Turner to make six drawings illustrating lines from poems by Scott, Byron and Moore—oddly prophetic of the illustrative work that Turner was to undertake between 1823 and 1838. A 'frontispiece' to this group is also recorded (see Thornbury, p. 590).

1052 Norham Castle *c.* 1822

Watercolour, 190 × 143
Sig.: *JMW Turner*
Inscr.: *Day sat on Norham's Castled steep* (from Scott's *Marmion*)
Prov.: Walter Fawkes; by descent to present owner
Private collection

1053 Rokeby *c.* 1822

Watercolour, 202 × 142
Inscr.: *Here twixt Rock and River grew*
  A dismal grove of sable yew
  With whose sad tints were mingled seen
  The blighted firs sepulcharl [sic] green
and a second quatrain (from Scott's *Rokeby*)
Prov.: Walter Fawkes; by descent to F. H. Fawkes; Agnew, from whom purchased, 1952
Coll.: Cecil Higgins Art Gallery, Bedford (P.100)

1054 Glen Artney *c.* 1822

Watercolour, 203 × 146
Inscr. lower left: *Lone Glen Artney's Hazel Shade/ Lady of the Lake* (from Scott's *Lady of the Lake*)
Prov.: Walter Fawkes; by descent to F. H. Fawkes; Lord Bilsland; Agnew, 1972
Private collection

1055 The Acropolis, Athens 1822

Watercolour, 187 × 137
Signed and dated lower left: *JMW Turner RA 22*
Inscr. below: *T'is living Greece no more* (from Byron's *Giaour*)
Prov.: Walter Fawkes; by descent to F. H. Fawkes; Lord Bilsland; Agnew 1973
Private collection

1056 Melrose Abbey *c.* 1822

Watercolour, 184 × 133
Inscr.: *If you would view fair Melrose aright/You must view it by the pale moonlight* (from Scott's *Lay of the Last Minstrel*)
Prov.: Walter Fawkes; by descent to present owner
Private collection

1057 Lalla Rookh *c.* 1822

Watercolour, 184 × 133
Prov.: Walter Fawkes
Coll.: untraced

An illustration to Moore's poem *Lalla Rookh*.

XVI(b) Nos 1058–1069
Designs for *The Provincial Antiquities of Scotland,* *c.* **1818–1825**

In 1818 Turner was commissioned to make designs for a series of plates showing Scottish subjects, to accompany a text written by Walter Scott. He toured the neighbourhood of Edinburgh that autumn, collecting material; another visit, in 1822, also provided material for the work, which was issued in a set of ten paper-bound parts between 1819 and 1826. Turner contributed ten subjects, together with the title-page vignettes for the two volumes in which the work was planned finally to appear; these vignettes were executed in 1825, and are in the Turner Bequest (Nos 1058, 1063). Each part contained five plates; other artists involved were A. W. Calcott, H. W. Williams, J. Schetky, A. Geddes, the architectural draughtsman Edward Blore, and Scott's friend, the amateur landscape painter, the Revd. John Thomson of Duddingston. Although Scott formed a bad opinion of Turner during the venture (he had originally wanted Thomson to make all the designs), he had eight of Turner's watercolours mounted together in a frame made, it is said, from an oak-tree felled at Abbotsford. These were given to him by his publisher, Robert Cadell, and they remained together when they passed into the collection of Ralph Brocklebank.

1058 Edinburgh Castle *c.* 1825

Pencil and grey wash, 198 × 130, title-vignette, vol. I
Sig. lower right: *JMWT*
Inscr. above: *PROVINCIAL ANTIQUITIES/of Scotland/NEMO ME IMPUNE LACESSIT;*
below: *London*
Engr.: by G. Cooke, 1826, for *the Provincial Antiquities of Scotland,* 1819–26 (R. 189)
Coll.: Trustees of the British Museum
(T.B., CLXVIII-A)

Armstrong (p. 251) implies that the grey-wash drawings in the Turner Bequest which correspond with the subjects of the two title-vignettes (Nos 1058, 1063) are preparatory studies; no other designs for them have been traced and it is evident from the degree of finish they exhibit that these are the final designs.

1059 Crichton Castle *c.* 1818

Watercolour and scraping-out, 161 × 240
Engr.: by G. Cooke, 1819, for *The Provincial Antiquities of Scotland,* 1819–26 (R. 190); a reduced replica by W. B. Cooke for Tilt's *Illustrations to Scott's Poetical Works,* 1834 (R. 558)
Prov.: Sir Walter Scott; by descent to Mary Monica Scott, 1858; Ralph Brocklebank; by descent to Thomas Brocklebank, sale Christie 8 July 1938 (14), bt. Rayner MacConnell; Mrs. Francis Tompkins, sale Sotheby 13 October 1954 (30), bt. Callender; Viscountess Garnock, sale Christie 1 March 1977 (144), withdrawn; Viscountess Garnock, sale Christie 21 November 1978 (77), bt. Branson
Private collection

A colour-beginning of the subject is in the *Scotland and Venice* sketchbook (T.B., CLXX-4); another is No. 1143 below. A drawing entitled *Crichton Castle* was sold by Thomas Woolner, R.A., Christie 12 June 1875 (131), bt. Agnew; this may have been the *Crichton Castle,* measuring 686 × 1041, sold by Ralph Brocklebank, Christie 29 April 1893 (91), bt. Colnaghi.

1060 Borthwick Castle *c.* 1818

Watercolour and scraping-out, 160 × 249
Sig. lower left: *Turner*
Engr.: by H. Le Keux, 1819, for *The Provincial Antiquities of Scotland,* 1819–26 (R. 191)
Prov.: Sir Walter Scott; by descent to Mary Monica Scott, 1858; Ralph Brocklebank; by descent to

Thomas Brocklebank, sale Christie 8 July 1938 (14), bt. Rayner MacConnell; Mrs. Francis Tompkins, sale Sotheby 13 October 1954 (31), bt. Agnew; Kurt Pantzer, by whom given to the museum
Coll.: Indianapolis Museum of Art

Based on a pencil drawing in the *Scotch Antiquities* sketchbook (T.B., CLXVII-76). Two more studies are in the *Scotland and Venice* sketchbook (T.B., CLXX, pp. 1, 2).

1061   Edinburgh High Street *c.* 1818

Watercolour, 161 × 243
Engr.: by H. Le Keux and G. Cooke, 1819, for *The Provincial Antiquities of Scotland,* 1819–26 (R. 192)
Prov.: Sir Walter Scott; by descent to Mary Monica Scott, 1858; Ralph Brocklebank; by descent to Thomas Brocklebank, sale Christie 8 July 1938 (14), bt. Rayner MacConnell; Mrs. Francis Tompkins, sale Sotheby 13 October 1954 (33), bt. Lord Blackford; Mr. and Mrs. Paul Mellon
Coll.: Yale Center for British Art, Paul Mellon Collection

Based on a pencil drawing in the *Scotch Antiquities* sketchbook (T.B., CLXVII, 64v - 65).

1062   Edinburgh from the Calton Hill *c.* 1818

Watercolour, 162 × 254
Engr.: by G. Cooke, 1820, for *The Provincial Antiquities of Scotland,* 1819–26 (R. 193)
Prov.: Sir Walter Scott; by descent to Mary Monica Scott, 1858; Ralph Brocklebank; by descent to Thomas Brocklebank, sale Christie 8 July 1938 (14), bt. Rayner MacConnell
Coll.: untraced

Based on a pencil drawing in the *Scotch Antiquities* sketchbook (T.B., CLXVII, 39v–40).

1063   Edinburgh from Leith Harbour *c.* 1825

Pencil on grey wash, 206 × 157, title-vignette, vol. II
Sig. lower left: *JMWT*
Inscr. above: *PROVINCIAL ANTIQUITIES/of Scotland/with.../Vol. I TR 2/DIEU ET MON DROIT* (repeated)
Engr.: by R. Wallis, 1826, for *The Provincial Antiquities of Scotland,* 1819–26 (R. 194)
Coll.: Trustees of the British Museum (T.B., CLXVIII-B)

See No. 1058.

1064   Heriot's Hospital, Edinburgh 1816

Watercolour, 169 × 251
Signed and dated: *JMW Turner RA 1816*
Engr.: by H. Le Keux and G. Cooke, 1822, for *The Provincial Antiquities of Scotland,* 1819–26 (R. 195)
Prov.: Sir Walter Scott, by descent to Mary Monica Scott, 1858; Ralph Brocklebank; by descent to Thomas Brocklebank, sale Christie 8 July 1938 (14, as 'Grassmarket, Edinburgh'), bt. Rayner MacConnell
Coll.: untraced

1065   Roslyn Castle *c.* 1823

Watercolour, 175 × 265
Sig. lower right: *Turner*
Engr.: by W. R. Smith, 1822, for *The Provincial Antiquities of Scotland,* 1819–26 (R. 196); a reduced replica by W. R. Smith for Tilt's *Illustrations to Scott's Poetical Works,* 1834 (R. 557)
Exh.: R.A. 1974 (206)
Prov.: Sir Walter Scott; by descent to Mary Monica Scott, 1858; Ralph Brocklebank; by descent to Thomas Brocklebank, sale Christie 8 July 1938 (14 as 'Hawthornden'), bt. Rayner MacConnell; Mrs. Francis Tompkins, sale Sotheby 13 October 1954 (32), bt. Agnew; Kurt Pantzer, by whom given to the museum
Coll.: Indianapolis Museum of Art

This drawing presents a problem; the plate engraved from it is dated 1822, but the watermark in the sheet of paper on which it is drawn reads

'1823'. The design is based on a pencil sketch in the *Scotch Antiquities* sketchbook (T.B., CLXVII-66). The subject is also known as 'Hawthornden'.

1066   Dunbar *c.* 1823

Watercolour, 165 × 254
Engr.: by J. B. Allen, 1824, for *The Provincial Antiquities of Scotland,* 1819–26 (R. 197)
Prov.: Sir Walter Scott; K. E. Hughes, sale Sotheby 27 June 1956 (69), bt. Ford
Coll.: untraced

Based on pencil drawings made in 1818, especially T.B., CLXVII, 29v–30.

1067   Tantallon Castle   1821

Watercolour, 175 × 254
Signed and dated: *JMW Turner 1821*
Engr.: by E. Goodall, 1822, for *The Provincial Antiquities of Scotland,* 1819–26 (R. 198); a reduced replica by W. B. Cooke, 1834, for Tilt's *Illustrations to Scott's Poetical Works,* 1834 (R. 559)
Prov.: Sir Walter Scott; Thomas Brocklebank, sale Christie 8 July 1938 (14), bt. Rayner MacConnell
Coll.: untraced

Based on a pencil drawing in the *Scotch Antiquities* sketchbook (T.B., CLXVII, 5v–6). Compare also the sheet from the *Smaller Fonthill* sketchbook, now in the Princeton Art Museum; this may be the drawing entitled 'Tantallon Castle' put up for sale by 'Lesser', Christie 19 January 1878 (153), bt. in.

1068   Linlithgow Palace   1821

Watercolour, 172 × 254
Signed and dated: *JMW Turner RA Sept 14 1821*
Engr.: by R. Wallis, 1822, for *The Provincial Antiquities of Scotland,* 1819–26 (R. 199)
Prov.: Sir Walter Scott; Thomas Brocklebank, sale Christie 8 July 1938 (14), bt. Rayner MacConnell
Coll.: untraced

Based on pencil drawings in the *Scotch Antiquities* sketchbook (T.B., CLXVII, 52–4). The composition reiterates the view of Turner's painting of Linlithgow, exhibited 1810 (P104).

1069   The Bass Rock *   *c.* 1824

Watercolour, 159 × 254
Engr.: by W. Miller, 1826, for *The Provincial Antiquities of Scotland,* 1819–26 (R. 200)
Exh.: R.A. 1974 (205)
Prov.: Matthew Uzielli, sale Christie 12 April 1861 (235), bt. Vokins; C. F. Huth, sale Christie 6 July 1895 (57), bt. Vokins; Charles Maw; purchased by Lord Leverhulme, 1920
Coll.: The Lady Lever Collection, Port Sunlight, Cheshire (4696)

Based on a pencil drawing in the *King's Visit to Scotland* sketchbook (T.B., CC-79), and, probably on other studies in the *Bass Rock and Edinburgh* sketchbook (T.B., CLXV, 5–6, 37v, 38). A study of the Bass Rock was sold by Ruskin at Christie 15 April 1869 (8), bt. Agnew. Another, showing the rock by moonlight, was sold by Louis Huth, Christie, 20 May 1905 (23), bt. Agnew.

XVI(c) Nos 1070–1151
Illustrations to the works of Sir Walter Scott, and connected studies, *c.* **1832–1836**

Scott's publisher, Robert Cadell, commissioned Turner to illustrate the *Poetical Works* in 1831, and Turner spent several weeks that summer in Scotland making drawings both at Abbotsford, where he stayed with Scott, and on a lengthy tour of the country, as far as Staffa and Inverness. He returned to London in September and worked on the commission during the following year. The work consisted of twelve volumes, each with a frontispiece and title-page vignette. All the vignettes for the *Poetical Works* were designed with cartouches consisting of a simple line frame ornamented with figures on either side; this was not printed in the octavo editions, with the exception of that in the 'Abbotsford' design, vol. XII. Engraving was undertaken by a number of men who had collaborated with Turner on earlier projects, and continued until 1834, when the work appeared (though the date 1833 is engraved on several early title-pages). In that year Cadell also began to publish the *Prose Works* of Scott, for which Turner supplied designs similarly, drawing now on the material accumulated in sketchbooks from several continental tours as well as from the Scottish journey of 1831. The complete edition, consisting of forty volumes, was published between 1832 and 1836. Several of the finished drawings were exhibited by Cadell at the gallery of Moon, Boys and Graves in London in 1832 and 1833 (see Finberg, *Life,* pp. 492, 515).

1070 Carlisle *c.* 1832

Watercolour, 83 × 142
Engr.: by E. Goodall, 1833, for *Scott's Poetical Works,* 1834 (R. 493)
Exh.: M.B.G. 1832, 1833
Prov.: Robert Cadell; T. E. Plint, sale Christie 7 March 1862 (168), bt. Agnew; C. Langton, sale Christie 20 April 1901 (105), bt. Agnew for C. S. Gulbenkian, by whom given to Sir Nigel Ronald (Ambassador to Portugal); Agnew 1962; Edwin Brown; bt. from his nephew by Agnew, 1972, from whom bt. 1973
Coll.: Yale Center for British Art, Paul Mellon Collection

Published as the frontispiece to vol. I of Scott's 'Minstrelsy of the Scottish Border'. Drawings of Carlisle occur in the *Minstrelsy of Scottish Border* sketchbook (T.B., CCLXVI); pp. 42 verso–43 have the sketch used as the basis for this view.

1071 Smailholm Tower *c.* 1832

Watercolour, size unknown, vignette
Inscr. below: *Smailholme Tower*

Engr.: by E. Goodall, 1833, for *Scott's Poetical Works,* 1834 (R. 494)
Exh.: M.B.G. 1832, 1833
Prov.: Robert Cadell; T. E. Plint, sale Christie 7 March 1862 (171), bt. Smith; H. A. J. Munro of Novar, sale Christie 2 June 1877 (1), bt. Wallis; John Feetham, sale Christie 27 May 1895 (114), bt. H. Quilter; C. Wheeley Lea; Mrs. Wheeley Lea, sale Christie 11 May 1917 (37), bt. Agnew; W. F. Morrice; Martin; Rt. Hon. C. P. Allen
Coll.: untraced

The title-vignette for vol. I, 'Minstrelsy of the Scottish Border'. The sketch on which it is based is in the *Abbotsford* sketchbook (T.B., CCLXVII-84v).

1072 Jedburgh Abbey *c.* 1832

Watercolour, 94 × 159
Engr.: by R. Brandard, 1833, for *Scott's Poetical Works,* 1834 (R. 495)
Exh.: M.B.G. 1832, 1833
Prov.: Robert Cadell; John Feetham, sale Christie 27 May 1895 (111), bt. H. Quilter; Agnew 1904; Charles P. Taft
Coll.: Taft Museum, Cincinnati, Ohio (1931.383)

Published as the frontispiece to vol. II, 'Minstrelsy of the Scottish Border'. Sketches of Jedburgh occur in the *Abbotsford* sketchbook (T.B., CCLXVII, 62–5).

1073 Johnnie Armstrong's Tower *c.* 1832

Watercolour, 281 × 206, vignette
Inscr. above: *BORDER MINSTREL/Vol*; below: *Johnnie Armstrong's/Tower*
Engr.: by E. Goodall, 1833, for *Scott's Poetical Works,* 1834 (R. 496)
Exh.: M.B.G. 1832, 1833

Prov.: Robert Cadell; H. A. J. Munro of Novar, sale Christie 2 June 1877 (2), bt. Gibbs; Lady Ashburton; Charles P. Taft
Coll.: Taft Museum, Cincinnati, Ohio (1931.386)

Published as the title-vignette to vol. II, 'Minstrelsy of the Scottish Border'. A sketch used for this drawing is in the *Minstrelsy of the Scottish Border* sketchbook (T.B., CCLXVI-61v).

1074 Kelso *c.* 1832

Watercolour, 81 × 143
Engr.: by R. Wallis, 1833, for *Scott's Poetical Works,* 1834 (R. 497)
Exh.: M.B.G. 1832, 1833
Prov.: Robert Cadell; John Miller, sale Christie 20 May 1858 (54); G. R. Burnett, sale Christie 16 March 1872 (95), bt. Vokins; William Dell, sale Christie 21 April 1899 (53), bt. Vokins; Barnet Lewis, sale Christie 3 March 1930 (58), bt. Haworth
Private collection

Published as the frontispiece to vol. III, 'Minstrelsy of the Scottish Border'. The sketch on which the drawing is based is in the *Abbotsford* sketchbook (T.B., CCLXVII, 19v–20).

1075 Lochmaben Castle *c.* 1832

Watercolour, 273 × 193, vignette
Inscr. above: *BORDER MINSTRELSY/Vol*; below: *Lochmaben Castle*
Engr.: by J. T. Willmore, 1833, for *Scott's Poetical Works,* 1834 (R. 498)
Exh.: M.B.G. 1832
Prov.: Robert Cadell; John Ruskin; anon. sale Foster, bt. Greatorex; J. R. Williams, sale Christie

10 June 1865 (57), bt. Agnew; John Leigh Clare, sale Christie 28 March 1868 (95), bt. Colnaghi; Sir Donald Currie; by descent to present owner
Private collection

Published as the title-vignette to vol. III, 'Minstrelsy of the Scottish Border'.
See No. 1150.

1076   Caerlaverock Castle *c.* 1832

Watercolour, 83 × 140
Engr.: by E. Goodall, 1833, for *Scott's Poetical Works,* 1834 (R. 499)
Exh.: M.B.G. 1832, 1833
Prov.: Robert Cadell; H. A. J. Munro of Novar, sale Christie 2 June 1877 (4), bt. Agnew; anon. sale Christie, 18 March 1911 (47), bt. King
Private collection

Published as the frontispiece to vol. IV, 'Minstrelsy of the Scottish Border'. The sketch on which the design is based is in the *Minstrelsy of the Scottish Border* sketchbook (T.B., CCLXVI-49v).

1077   Hermitage Castle *c.* 1832

Watercolour, size unknown, vignette
Inscr. below: *Hermitage Castle*
Engr.: by R. Wallis, 1833, for *Scott's Poetical Works,* 1834 (R. 500)
Exh.: M.B.G. 1832, 1833
Prov.: Robert Cadell; H. A. J. Munro of Novar, sale Christie 2 June 1877 (3), bt. Agnew; John Knowles, sale Christie 5 June 1880 (483), bt. Lord Carysfort
Private collection

Published as the title-vignette to vol. IV, 'Minstrelsy of the Scottish Border'. The sketch of Hermitage Castle, in Lidderdale, occurs in the *Minstrelsy of the Scottish Border* sketchbook (T.B., CCLXVI-64).

1078   Dryburgh Abbey *c.* 1832

Watercolour, 78 × 147
Engr.: by W. Miller, 1833, for *Scott's Poetical Works,* 1834 (R. 501)
Exh.: M.B.G. 1832; R. A. 1974 (290)
Prov.: Robert Cadell; Beresford Rimington Heaton, by whom bequeathed to the gallery, 1940
Coll.: Tate Gallery, London (5241)

Published as the frontispiece to vol. V, 'Sir Tristrem'. The sketch on which the design is based is in the *Abbotsford* sketchbook (T.B., CCLXVII, 8v–9).

1079   Bemerside Tower *c.* 1832

Watercolour, 146 × 114, vignette
Engr.: by J. Horsburgh, 1833, for *Scott's Poetical Works,* 1834 (R. 502)
Exh.: M.B.G. 1832, 1833
Prov.: Robert Cadell; ?John Miller, sale Christie 20 May 1858; J. E. Taylor, sale Christie 5 July 1912 (75), bt. Agnew; Mrs. Thomas, 1913
Private collection

Published as the title-vignette to vol. V, 'Sir Tristrem'. A drawing of Bemerside occurs in the *Abbotsford* sketchbook (T.B., CCLXVII-82v).

1080   Melrose* *c.* 1832

Watercolour, 101 × 155
Engr.: by W. Miller, 1833, for *Scott's Poetical Works,* 1834 (R. 503)
Exh.: M.B.G. 1832
Prov.: Robert Cadell; Henry Vaughan, by whom bequeathed to the gallery, 1900
Coll.: National Galleries of Scotland, Edinburgh (860)

Published as the frontispiece to vol. VI, 'Lay of the Last Minstrel'. Turner's drawing of the subject is in the *Abbotsford* sketchbook (T.B., CCLXVII, 14v–15).

1081   Newark Castle *c.* 1832

Watercolour, 115 × 146, vignette
Engr.: by W. J. Cooke, 1833, for *Scott's Poetical Works,* 1834 (R. 504)
Exh.: M.B.G. 1832, 1833
Prov.: Robert Cadell; E. J. Taylor, sale 5 July 1912 (70), bt. Agnew
Private collection

Published as the title-vignette to vol. VI, 'Lay of the Last Minstrel'. Turner's pencil drawing is in the *Abbotsford* sketchbook (T.B., CCLXVII-78v).

1082   Edinburgh from Blackford Hill *c.* 1832

Watercolour, 86 × 146
Engr.: by W. Miller, 1833, for *Scott's Poetical Works,* 1834 (R. 505)
Prov.: Robert Cadell
Private collection

Published as the frontispiece to vol. VII, 'Marmion'.

1083   Ashestiel *c.* 1832

Pencil and watercolour, 287 × 223, vignette
Inscr. above: *MARMION/VOL*; below: *Ashistiel*
Engr.: by J. Horsburgh, 1833, for *Scott's Poetical Works*, 1834 (R. 506)
Prov.: Robert Cadell; John Ruskin, by whom presented to the museum, 1861
Coll.: Syndics of the Fitzwilliam Museum, Cambridge (573; Cormack 30)

Published as the title-vignette to vol. VII, 'Marmion'. Turner's pencil drawing of the subject is in the *Abbotsford* sketchbook (T.B., CCLXVII, 89v–90).

1084 Loch Katrine *c.* 1832

Watercolour, 96 × 149
Engr.: by W. Miller, 1833, for *Scott's Poetical Works*, 1834 (R. 507)
Exh.: B.M. 1975 (178)
Prov.: Robert Cadell; H. A. J. Munro of Novar, sale Christie 6 April 1878 (73), bt. Agnew; C. Wheeley Lea; Mrs. Wheeley Lea, sale Christie 11 May 1917 (39) bt. Agnew; R. W. Lloyd, by whom bequeathed to the museum, 1958
Coll.: Trustees of the British Museum (1958-7-12-436)

Published as frontispiece to vol. VIII, 'The Lady of the Lake'. Turner's pencil drawing of the subject is in the *Stirling and West* sketchbook (T.B., CCLXX-47).

1085 Loch Achray *c.* 1832

Pencil and watercolour, 170 × 200, vignette
Inscr. above: *LADY of the LAKE/Vol*;
below: *Trossacs/from/Loch Achray*

Engr.: by W. Miller, 1833–4, for *Scott's Poetical Works*, 1834 (R. 508)
Prov.: Robert Cadell; J. E. Fordham; Mrs. Fordham; Iolo Williams; Mrs. Williams, from whom bt. by Paul Mellon, 1977
Coll.: Yale Center for British Art, Paul Mellon Collection

Published as the title-vignette to vol. VIII, 'The Lady of the Lake'. Turner made drawings of Loch Achray in the *Stirling and West* sketchbook (T.B., CCLXX).

1086 Junction of the Greta and the Tees *c.* 1832

Watercolour, 82 × 146
Engr.: by John Pye, 1833, for *Scott's Poetical Works*, 1834 (R. 509)
Exh.: M.B.G. 1833
Prov.: Robert Cadell; J. E. Fordham; Mrs. Fordham
Private collection

Published as frontispiece to vol. IX, 'Rokeby'. Turner's pencil drawing of the subject is in the *Minstrelsy of the Scottish Border* sketchbook (T.B., CCLXVI-35v).

1087 Bowes Tower *c.* 1832

Watercolour, size unknown, vignette
Engr.: by E. Webb, 1833, for *Scott's Poetical Works*, 1834 (R. 510)
Exh.: M.B.G. 1833
Prov.: Robert Cadell; anon. sale Christie 2 June 1939 (69), bt. Agnew
Coll.: untraced

Published as title-vignette to vol. IX, 'Rokeby'.

1088 Loch Coriskin *c.* 1832

Watercolour, 89 × 143
Engr.: by H. Le Keux, 1834, for *Scott's Poetical Works*, 1834 (R. 511)

Prov.: Robert Cadell; Henry Vaughan, by whom bequeathed to the gallery, 1900
Coll.: National Galleries of Scotland, Edinburgh (861)

Published as frontispiece to vol. X, 'The Lord of the Isles'.

1089 Fingal's Cave, Staffa *c.* 1832

Pencil and watercolour, 135 × 87, vignette
Inscr. above: *LORD of the Isles/Vol*;
below: *Fingals Cave*
Engr.: by E. Goodall, 1833–4, for *Scott's Poetical Works*, 1834 (R. 512)
Prov.: Robert Cadell; H. A. J. Munro of Novar, sale Christie 2 June 1877 (5), bt. Fine Art Publishing Co., London; John Ruskin; the Storey family; the Hon. Gavin Astor; sale Christie 1 March 1977 (143), bt. Somerville & Simpson
Private collection, U.S.A.

Published as title-vignette to vol. X, 'The Lord of the Isles'. Turner's pencil drawings of Fingal's Cave occur in the *Staffa* sketchbook, T.B., CCLXXIII; that on p. 29 was used as the basis for the vignette.

1090 Skiddaw *c.* 1832

Watercolour, 101 × 152
Engr.: by W. Miller, 1833, for *Scott's Poetical Works*, 1834 (R. 513)
Prov.: Robert Cadell; F. N. Fordham
Coll.: untraced

Published as frontispiece to vol. XI, 'The Bride of Triermain'. Turner noted Skiddaw in the *Rokeby and Appleby* sketchbook (T.B., CCLXIV, 44v–45).

1091 Mayburgh *c.* 1832

Watercolour, size unknown, vignette
Engr.: by J. Horsburgh, 1833, for *Scott's Poetical Works*, 1834 (R. 514)
Prov.: Robert Cadell; H. A. J. Munro of Novar, sale Christie 2 June 1877 (6), bt. Lady Ashburton
Coll.: untraced

Published as title-vignette to vol. XI, 'The Bride of Triermain'.

1092   Berwick upon Tweed   c. 1832

Watercolour, 87 × 152
Engr.: by W. Miller, 1833, for *Scott's Poetical Works,* 1834 (R. 515)
Exh.: M.B.G. 1833
Prov.: Robert Cadell; J. R. Findlay; anon. sale Christie 5 June 1875 (32), bt. 'Lasalles'; Lady Lucas Tooth, sale Sotheby 15 August 1960 (75), bt. Fine Art Society, London; Vose Galleries, Boston, from whom bt. by present owner 1967
Private collection, U.S.A.

Published as frontispiece to vol. XII, 'Dramatic Pieces'. Turner made pencil drawings at Berwick in the *Berwick* sketchbook (T.B., CCLXV); the study used for this subject is in the *Abbotsford* sketchbook (T.B., CCLXVII, 48v–49).

1093   Abbotsford   c. 1832

Watercolour, 115 × 147, vignette
Engr.: by H. Le Keux, 1834, for *Scott's Poetical Works,* 1834 (R. 516) and by W. Miller, 1841, for the Library Edition (R. 569)
Prov.: Robert Cadell; ?John Dillon, sale 29 April 1869 (134), bt. Agnew; ?John Ruskin; J. E. Taylor, sale Christie 5 July 1912 (68), bt. Agnew
Private collection

Published as title-vignette to vol. XII, 'Dramatic Pieces'. Drawings of Abbotsford are in the *Abbotsford* sketchbook (T.B., CCLXVII). Another view of the house was engraved for Lockhart's *Life of Scott* (R. 568; No. 1142).

1094   Dryden's Monument   c. 1833

Watercolour, size unknown, vignette
Engr.: by J. Horsburgh, 1834, for *Scott's Prose Works.* 1834–6 (R. 517)

Prov.: H. A. J. Munro of Novar, sale Christie 2 June 1877 (7), bt. McLean; ?McLean sale Christie 1 April 1881 (37), bt. in
Coll.: untraced

Published as title-vignette to vol. I, 1834, 'Life of Dryden'. Turner's drawing for the subject is in the *Mouth of the Thames* sketchbook (T.B., CCLXXVIII-6).

1095   Dumbarton Castle and River Leven   c. 1833

Watercolour, 181 × 184, vignette
Inscr.: *Dumbarton*
Engr.: by W. Miller, 1834, for *Scott's Prose Works,* 1834–6 (R. 518)
Prov.: H. A. J. Munro of Novar, sale Christie 2 June 1877 (8), bt. Rutley; Mrs. Mary Morgan; Christie 4 March 1975 (86), bt. Albany Gallery, London, from whom bt. by present owner
Private collection, U.S.A.

Published as title-vignette to vol. III, 1834, 'Biographical Memoirs'. A drawing of Dumbarton Rock occurs in the *Stirling and West* sketchbook (T.B., CCLXX-82v).

1096   Brussels—distant view   c. 1833

Watercolour, 82 × 143
Engr.: by W. Miller, 1834, for *Scott's Prose Works,* 1834–6 (R. 519)
Prov.: H. A. J. Munro of Novar, sale Christie 2 June 1877 (9), bt. Cox
Coll.: untraced

Published as frontispiece to vol. V, 1834, 'Paul's Letters'.

1097   Hougoumont   c. 1833

Watercolour, 175 × 146, vignette
Engr.: by W. Miller, 1834, for *Scott's Prose Works,* 1834–6 (R. 520)
Prov.: John Miller, sale Christie 20 May 1858 (53), bt. in; Agnew, 1907; anon. sale Sotheby 12 July 1967 (269)
Coll.: untraced

Published as title-vignette to vol. V, 1834, 'Paul's Letters'. For a possible provenance for this drawing see No. 1229 (R. 425) below.

1098   New Abbey, near Dumfries   c. 1833

Watercolour, size unknown, vignette
Engr.: by W. Miller, 1834, for *Scott's Prose Works,* 1834–6 (R. 521)
Prov.: H. A. J. Munro of Novar, sale Christie 2 June 1877 (11), bt. Agnew; Miss Dennistoun; anon. sale Christie 30 June 1916 (53), bt. Vicars
Coll.: untraced

Published as title-vignette to vol. VII, 1834, 'Provincial Antiquities of Scotland'. Turner's sketch of this subject occurs in the *Minstrelsy of the Scottish Border* sketchbook (T.B., CCLXVI-46).

1099   Norham Castle—moonrise   c. 1833

Watercolour, 89 × 140
Engr.: by W. Miller, 1834, for *Scott's Prose Works,* 1834–6 (R. 522)
Prov.: H. A. J. Munro of Novar, sale Christie 2 June 1877 (10), bt. Wallis; George Vanderbilt
Coll.: untraced

Published as frontispiece to vol. VII, 1834, 'The Provincial Antiquities of Scotland'. Turner revisited Norham on his tour of 1831 and made sketches there in the *Abbotsford* sketchbook (T.B., CCLXVII-59v).

1100   Jerusalem   c. 1833

Watercolour, 89 × 140
Engr.: by W. Miller, 1834, for *Scott's Prose Works,* 1834–6 (R. 523)
Prov.: John Dillon, sale Christie 29 April 1869 (140), bt. Agnew; Murrieta, sale Christie 2 May 1892 (311), bt. Leggatt; Sir Donald Currie; by descent to present owner
Private collection

Published as frontispiece to vol. VI, 1834, 'Essays on Chivalry, Romance and the Drama'.

1101   Shakespeare's Monument   c. 1833

Watercolour, size unknown vignette
Engr.: by J. Horsburgh, 1834, for *Scott's Prose Works,* 1834–6 (R. 524)
Prov.: J. E. Fordham; Mrs. Fordham
Coll.: untraced

Published as title-vignette to vol. VI, 1834, 'Essays on Chivalry, Romance and the Drama'. Turner's sketch for the subject is in the *Val d'Aosta* sketchbook (T.B., CCXCIII-82v).

1102   Hotel de Ville, Paris   c. 1833

Watercolour, 110 × 95, vignette
Engr.: by J. Horsburgh, 1834, for *Scott's Prose Works,* 1834–6 (R. 525)
Prov.: H. A. J. Munro of Novar, sale Christie 6 April 1878 (67), bt. Wertheimer; L. Deighton, sale Sotheby 23 January 1957 (76), bt. Pantzer, by whom given to the museum
Coll.: Indianapolis Museum of Art

Published as title-vignette to vol. VIII, 1834, 'Life of Napoleon', I. The sketch for the subject occurs in the *Paris and Environs* sketchbook (T.B., CCLVII-65 verso). The engraver's name as given on the plate, and as recorded by Rawlinson, is W. Miller; but an erratum slip in early editions states that this was an error for J. Horsburgh.

Watercolour, 90 × 145
Engr.: by W. Miller, 1835, for *Scott's Prose Works,*
1834–6 (R. 532)
Prov.: John Ruskin, by whom presented to the
museum, 1861
Coll.: Syndics of the Fitzwilliam Museum,
Cambridge (574; Cormack 31)

Published as frontispiece to vol. XII, 1835, 'Life
of Napoleon', V. Turner's sketch of the subject
occurs in the *Paris and Environs* sketchbook
(T.B., CCLVII–84v).

1103 Napoleon's Logement, Quai Conti *c.* 1833

Watercolour, size unknown, vignette
Engr.: by J. Horsburgh, 1834, for *Scott's Prose
Works,* 1834–6 (R. 526)
Prov.: S. Addington, sale Christie 22 May 1886
(547), bt. Permain; J. Miller; sale Sotheby 26 July
1922 (117), bt. Agnew; J. E. W. Astley
Coll.: untraced

Published as title-vignette for vol. IX, 1835, 'Life
of Napoleon', II. Turner's sketch of the subject
occurs in the *Paris and Environs* sketchbook
(T.B., CCLVII–62).

1104 Brienne *c.* 1833

Watercolour, 76 × 152
Engr.: by W. Miller, 1834, for *Scott's Prose Works,*
1834–6 (R. 527)
Prov.: John Dillon, sale Christie 29 April 1869
(138), bt. Vokins; G. R. Burnett, sale Christie 16
March 1872 (96), bt. McLean; Murrieta sale,
Christie 23 May 1873 (143), bt. Calcott; K. Mac-
Kinlay, sale Christie 24 June 1879 (134), bt. in;
K. MacKinlay, sale Christie 9 April 1880 (103), bt.
White
Coll.: untraced

Published as frontispiece to vol. IX, 1835, 'Life of
Napoleon', II.

1105 Venice: the Campanile *c.* 1833

Watercolour, 211 × 178 (sheet), vignette
Engr.: by W. Miller, 1835, for *Scott's Prose Works,*
1834–6 (R. 528)
Prov.: John Feetham, sale Christie 27 May 1895
(110, as 'The Piazzetta, Venice'), bt. Vokins; Sir
Donald Currie; by descent to present owner
Private collection

Published as title-vignette to vol. X, 1835, 'Life of
Napoleon', III.

1106 Piacenza *c.* 1833

Watercolour, 76 × 152
Engr.: by W. Miller, 1835, for *Scott's Prose Works,*
1834–6 (R. 529)

Prov.: John Dillon, sale Christie 29 April 1869
(136), bt. McLean; Murrieta, sale Christie 2 May
1892 (313), bt. Vokins; Sir Donald Currie; Howard
Bliss, sale 12 March 1947 (78), bt. W. C. C. Quar-
rell, sale Sotheby 22 April 1959 (35), bt. Truman;
Sotheby 27 February 1960 (87), bt. Walker
Gallery, London; Walter Brandt
Coll.: Trustees of P. A. Brandt Settlement

Published as frontispiece to vol. X, 1835, 'Life of
Napoleon', III.

1107 Verona *c.* 1833

Watercolour, 86 × 143
Engr.: by W. Miller, 1835, for *Scott's Prose Works,*
1834–6 (R. 530)
Prov.: John Miller, sale Christie 20 May 1858 (57),
bt. Gambart; Sir Charles Robinson; John Knowles,
sale Christie 7 April 1865 (112), bt. Agnew; James
Gresham, sale Christie 12 July 1917 (35), bt. King;
Christie 30 July 1924 (194), bt. Sampson
Coll.: untraced

Published as frontispiece to vol. XI, 1835, 'Life of
Napoleon', IV.

1108 Vincennes *c.* 1833

Watercolour, 89 × 89, vignette
Engr.: by W. Miller, 1835, for *Scott's Prose Works,*
1834–6 (R. 531)
Prov.: H. A. J. Munro of Novar, sale Christie 2 June
1877 (12), bt. Agnew; John Heugh, sale Christie
10 May 1878 (156), bt. Agnew; C. W. Wheeley
Lea; Mrs. Wheeley Lea, sale Christie 11 May 1917
(35), bt. Leggatt; Mr. Justice McCardie, sale
Sotheby 28 June 1933 (107), bt. Turner
Coll.: untraced

Published as title-vignette to vol. XI, 1835, 'Life
of Napoleon', IV. Turner's sketch for this subject
is in the *Paris and Environs* sketchbook
(T.B., CCLVII–47).

1109 St. Cloud *c.* 1833

1110 Mayence *c.* 1833

Watercolour, 112 × 150, vignette
Inscr. below in pencil: *May[ence]*
Engr.: by W. Miller, 1834, for *Scott's Prose Works,*
1834–6 (R. 533)
Prov.: John Heugh, 1892; J. E. Taylor, sale Christie
5 July 1912 (69), bt. Agnew; E. L. Hartley, by
whom bequeathed to the museum, 1954
Coll.: Museum and Art Gallery, Blackburn, Lancashire

Published as title-vignette to vol. XII, 1835, 'Life of
Napoleon', V.

1111 Milan *c.* 1833

Watercolour, 89 × 146
Engr.: by J. Horsburgh, 1835, for *Scott's Prose
Works,* 1834–6 (R. 534)
Prov.: John Miller, sale Christie 20 May 1858 (56),
bt. Gambart; ?John Mitchell, sale Christie 28 May
1860, bt. Gambart; Thomas Plint, sale Christie 7
March 1862 (167), bt. Crofts; McLean, sale Chris-
tie 12 March 1881 (22), bt. in
Coll.: untraced

Published as frontispiece to vol. XIII, 1835, 'Life of
Napoleon', VI. Sketches of Milan cathedral occur in
the *Milan to Venice* sketchbook (T.B., CLXXV, 1v–2, 4,
5, etc.).

1112 The Simplon *c.* 1833

Watercolour, size unknown, vignette
Engr.: by W. Miller, 1834, for *Scott's Prose Works,*
1834–6 (R. 535)
Prov.: H. A. J. Munro of Novar, sale 6 April 1878
(65), bt. H. Martineau, sale Christie 2 March 1901

(61), bt. Colnaghi; Agnew 1944; Heffer; Agnew, 1949; Charles Russell
Coll.: untraced

Published as title-vignette to vol. XIII, 1835, 'Life of Napoleon', VI. A colour study entitled by Finberg 'The Simplon' is in the Turner Bequest, CCLXXX–8.

1113 Paris, from Père la Chaise, Massena's Monument *c*.1833

Watercolour, 89 × 127
Engr.: by W. Miller, 1835, for *Scott's Prose Works*, 1834–6 (R. 536)
Prov.: F. R. Leyland, sale Christie 9 March 1872 (42), bt. McLean; anon. sale Christie 15 May 1891 (46), bt. McLean; sale Christie 23 May 1947 (24), bt. in
Coll.: untraced

Published as frontispiece to vol. XIV, 1835 'Life of Napoleon', VII. The subject is probably based on sketches made in the *Dieppe, Rouen and* Paris sketchbook (CCLVIII–28v). In addition to the tomb of Massena, an inscription to Le Fabre is also conspicuous in the design.

1114 Malmaison *c*.1833

Watercolour, size unknown, vignette
Engr.: by W. Miller, 1835, for *Scott's Prose Works*, 1834–6 (R. 537)
Prov.: H. A. J. Munro of Novar, sale Christie 2 June 1877 (13), bt. Agnew; Francis Stevenson; Agnew 1903
Coll.: untraced

Published as title-vignette to vol. XIV, 1835, 'Life of Napoleon', VII.

1115 Fontainebleau *c*.1833

Watercolour, 195 × 180, vignette
Engr.: by W. Miller, 1835, for *Scott's Prose Works*, 1834–6 (R. 538)
Prov.: L. Deighton, sale Sotheby 23 January 1957 (77), bt. Kurt Pantzer, by whom given to the museum
Coll.: Indianapolis Museum of Art

Published as title-vignette to vol. XV, 1835, 'Life of Napoleon', VIII. A sketch of the subject is in the *Paris and Environs* sketchbook (T.B., CCLVII–149).

1116 The Field of Waterloo. From the Picton Tree *c*.1833

Watercolour, 83 × 140
Engr.: by W. Miller, 1835, for *Scott's Prose Works*, 1834–6 (R. 539)
Prov.: John Dillon, sale Christie 29 April 1869 (139), bt. Agnew; Marquis de Santurce, sale Christie 16 June 1883 (124), bt. in; Sir John Fowler, sale Christie 6 May 1899 (36), bt. Agnew; Francis Stevenson; E. G. Poole; Christie 1 October 1948 (20), bt. Agnew; Miss J. E. Stanier, sale Christie 5 March 1974 (189), bt. Leger
Private collection, U.K.

Published as frontispiece to vol. XVI, 1835, 'Life of Napoleon', IX.

1117 The Bellerophon, Plymouth Sound *c*.1833

Watercolour, 130 × 100, vignette
Engr.: by E. Goodall, 1835, for *Scott's Prose Works*, 1834–6 (R. 540)
Prov.: H. A. J. Munro of Novar, sale Christie 6 April 1878 (66), bt. Agnew; Miss E. H. Borough; Christie 20 October 1970 (133), bt. for anon. client
Private collection

Published as title-vignette to vol. XVI, 1835, 'Life of Napoleon', IX.

1118 Chiefswood Cottage, near Abbotsford *c*.1833

Watercolour, with some pen, 140 × 95, vignette
Engr.: by W. Miller, 1835, for *Scott's Prose Works*, 1834–6 (R. 541)
Prov.: Henry Vaughan, by whom bequeathed to the gallery, 1900

Coll.: National Galleries of Scotland, Edinburgh (859)

Published as title-vignette to vol. XVIII, 1835, 'Periodical Criticism'. Turner's sketch of the subject is in the *Edinburgh* sketchbook (T.B., CCLXVIII–52).

1119 The Rhymer's Glen, Abbotsford *c*.1833

Watercolour, with some pen and scraping-out, 127 × 82, vignette
Engr.: by W. Miller, 1835, for *Scott's Prose Works*, 1834–6 (R. 542)
Prov.: Henry Vaughan, by whom bequeathed to the gallery, 1900
Coll.: National Galleries of Scotland, Edinburgh (858)

Published as title-vignette to vol. XXL, 1836, 'Periodical Criticism'. Turner made a sketch of the subject in the *Edinburgh* sketchbook (T.B., CCLXVIII–50v).

1120 Edinburgh, from St. Anthony's Chapel *c*.1833

Watercolour, body-colour and scraping-out, 97 × 149
Engr.: by W. Miller, 1836, for *Scott's Prose Works*, 1834–6 (R. 543)
Prov.: H. A. J. Munro of Novar, sale Christie 6 April

1878 (70), bt. Durlacher; Scott & Fowles, 1905; P. A. Valentine, Chicago; Kurt Pantzer, 1948, by whom given to the museum
Coll.: Indianapolis Museum of Art

Published as frontispiece to vol. XXII, 1836, 'Tales of a Grandfather'. Turner's sketch of this subject is in the *Stirling and Edinburgh* sketchbook (T.B., CCLXIX–88v).

1121 Dunfermline *c.* 1833

Watercolour, 159 × 140, vignette
Engr.: by J. Horsburgh, 1836, for *Scott's Prose Works,* 1834–6 (R. 544)
Prov.: H. A. J. Munro of Novar, sale Christie 2 June 1877 (14), bt. Sir Donald Currie; by descent to present owner
Private collection

Published as title-vignette to vol. XXII, 1836, 'Tales of a Grandfather'.

1122 Stirling *c.* 1833

Watercolour, 89 × 165
Engr.: by W. Miller, 1836, for *Scott's Prose Works,* 1834–6 (R. 545)
Prov.: H. A. J. Munro of Novar, sale Christie 6 April 1878 (69), bt. George Gurney, sale 17 March 1883 (195), bt. in; Gurney, sale Christie 11 July 1903 (44), bt. Wallis
Coll.: untraced

Published as frontispiece to vol. XXIII, 1836, 'Tales of a Grandfather'. Several studies of Stirling Castle occur in the *Stirling and Edinburgh* sketchbook (T.B., CCLXIX, 47v–48, etc.).

1123 Craigmillar Castle *c.* 1833

Watercolour, size unknown, vignette
Engr.: by W. Miller, 1836, for *Scott's Prose Works,* 1834–6 (R. 546)
Prov.: H. A. J. Munro of Novar, sale Christie 2 June 1877 (15), bt. Agnew; Miss Dennistoun; anon. sale Christie 30 June 1916 (54), bt. Vicars
Coll.: untraced

Published as title-vignette to vol. XXIII, 1836, 'Tales of a Grandfather'. Turner's study of this subject is in the *Abbotsford* sketchbook (T.B., CCLXVII–24v).

1124 Dunstaffnage *c.* 1833

Watercolour and body-colour, 121 × 152
Engr.: by W. Miller, 1836, for *Scott's Prose Works,* 1834–6 (R. 547)
Prov.: John Dillon, sale Christie 29 April 1869 (135), bt. Agnew; Heimendahl, sale Christie 24 June 1879 (135), bt. Agnew; Pritchard; Abraham Haworth; by descent to Miss Haworth, sale, Christie 21 November 1952 (119), bt. Newman; sale Christie 2 November 1956 (31), bt. Kurt Pantzer, by whom given to the museum
Coll.: Indianapolis Museum of Art

Published as frontispiece to vol. XXIV, 1836, 'Tales of a Grandfather'. Turner's study for this subject is in the *Staffa* sketchbook (T.B., CCLXXIII–89).

1125 Linlithgow *c.* 1833

Watercolour over pencil, 105 × 108, vignette
Engr.: by W. Miller, 1836, for *Scott's Prose Works,* 1834–6 (R. 548)
Prov.: John Ruskin, by whom given to M. C. Churchill: Mrs. Eileen Bernard, by whom given to the museum, 1945

Coll.: Victoria and Albert Museum, London (P6–1945)
Published as title-vignette to vol. XXIV, 1836, 'Tales of a Grandfather'.

1126 Glencoe *c.* 1833

Watercolour, 94 × 143
Engr.: by W. Miller, 1836, for *Scott's Prose Works,* 1834–6 (R. 549)
Prov.: H. A. J. Munro of Novar, sale Christie 6 April 1878 (72), bt. Durlacher; Francis Stevenson; Mrs. Gustav Radeker, by whom given to the School of Design, 1972
Coll.: Museum of Art, Rhode Island School of Design, Providence, R.I. (72.087)

Published as a frontispiece to vol. XXV, 1836, 'Tales of a Grandfather'. Armstrong (p. 255) records a vignette design of a 'Mountain Pass', with the queried title 'Glencoe', from J. E. Taylor's collection; this is presumably the drawing sold under the title 'Glencoe', 114 × 76, Christie 5 July 1912 (73), bt. Agnew.

1127 Killiecrankie *c.* 1833

Watercolour, 184 × 133, vignette
Engr.: by W. Miller, 1836, for *Scott's Prose Works,* 1834–6 (R. 550)
Prov.: H. A. J. Munro of Novar, sale Christie 2 June 1877 (16), bt. Pilgeram and Lefevre; anon. sale Christie 14 January 1893 (116), bt. Vokins; Lawrence W. Hodson, sale 25 June 1906 (130), bt. Agnew
Coll.: untraced

Published as title-vignette to vol. XXV, 1836, 'Tales of a Grandfather'. The drawing published under this title in Berkeley 1975 (30), is a copy by an unidentified hand.

1128 Inverness *c.* 1833

Watercolour, 92 × 159

Engr.: by W. Miller, 1836, for *Scott's Prose Works*, 1834–6 (R. 551)
Prov.: H. A. J. Munro of Novar, sale Christie 6 April 1878 (71), bt. Agnew; C. W. Wheeley Lea; Mrs. Wheeley Lea, sale Christie 11 May 1917 (38), bt. King; Frank Gaskell, 1937, by descent to the present owners
Coll.: Ernest and Roger Gaskell

Published as frontispiece to vol. XXVI, 1836, 'Tales of a Grandfather'. Turner's study for the subject is in the *Inverness* sketchbook (T.B., CCLXXVII–5).

1129 Fort Augustus, Loch Ness *c.* 1833

Watercolour, size unknown, vignette
Engr.: by W. Miller, 1836, for *Scott's Prose Works*, 1834–6 (R. 552)
Prov.: J. E. Fordham
Coll.: untraced

Published as title-vignette to vol. XXVI, 1836, 'Tales of a Grandfather'. Turner's study of the subject is in the *Fort Augustus* sketchbook (T.B., CCLXXVI–18).

1130 Rouen—a distant view *c.* 1834

Watercolour and body-colour, with some scratching-out over traces of pencil, 83 × 147
Engr.: by W. Richardson, 1836, for *Scott's Prose Works*, 1834–6 (R. 553)
Exh.: R.A. 1974 (292)
Prov.: H. A. J. Munro of Novar, sale Christie 2 June 1877 (17), bt. Arthur Severn; John Ruskin; Francis Stevenson; Fine Art Society, London, 1902; Agnew; James Blair, by whom bequeathed to the gallery, 1917
Coll.: City Art Gallery, Manchester (1917–95)

Published as frontispiece to vol. XXVIII, 1836, 'Tales of a Grandfather'.

1131 Calais *c.* 1834

Watercolour, size unknown, vignette
Engr.: by J. Horsburgh, 1836, for *Scott's Prose Works*, 1834–6 (R. 554)
Prov.: J. E. Taylor, ?sale 5 July 1912 (78), bt. Agnew; Barnet Lewis, sale, Christie 28 February 1930 (57), bt. Vicars; Mr. Mason Pearson; Dr. Robert Pearson, 1968
Coll.: untraced

Published as title-vignette to vol. XXVII, 1836, 'Tales of a Grandfather'.

1132 Château d'Arques, near Dieppe *c.* 1834

Watercolour, 104 × 155
Engr.: by W. Forrest, 1836, for *Scott's Prose Works*, 1834–6 (R.555)

Prov.: John Dillon, sale 29 April 1869 (137), bt. Vokins; Albert Levy, sale Christie 1 April 1876 (271), bt. White; Fine Art Society, London, 1950; Alan D. Pilkington, by whom bequeathed to the college, 1973
Coll.: Provost and Fellows of Eton College, Berkshire (Pi.274)

Published as frontispiece to vol. XXVII, 1836, 'Tales of a Grandfather'. Several pencil studies of the castle are in the *Rivers Meuse and Moselle* sketchbook (T.B., CCXVI–237, etc.); and a colour study is T.B., CCXX–E. A colour-beginning related to the engraved subject is No. 1147 below.

1133 Abbeville *c.* 1834

Watercolour, 135 × 105, vignette
Engr.: by J. Horsburgh, 1836, for *Scott's Prose Works*, 1834–6 (R. 556)
Prov.: ?John Heugh; H. A. J. Munro of Novar, sale Christie 2 June 1877 (18), bt. Agnew; C. W. Wheeley Lea; Mrs. Wheeley Lea, sale Christie 11 May 1917 (36), bt. Agnew; Sotheby 25 March 1975 (242), bt. D. Gowan
Coll.: untraced

Published as title-vignette to vol. XXVIII, 1836, 'Tales of a Grandfather'. A drawing of the market-place at Abbeville, related to this design, occurs in the *Rivers Meuse and Moselle* sketchbook (T.B., CCXVI–192v).

The following six drawings (Nos 1134–1139) are designs for Fisher's collection of *Illustrations to the Waverley Novels*, which appeared in 1836 and 1837.

1134 Edinburgh Castle: March of the Highlanders *c.* 1835

Watercolour, 86 × 140

Engr.: by T. Higham, 1836, for *Fisher's Illustrations to the Waverley Novels*, 1836–7 (R. 560)
Exh.: R.A. 1974 (289)
Prov.: ?John Morley, sale Christie 16 May 1896 (23), bt. McLean; Humphrey Roberts, sale Christie 23 May 1908 (293), bt. Leggatt; R. H. Williamson, by whom bequeathed to the gallery, 1938
Coll.: Tate Gallery, London (4953)

An illustration to 'Waverley'.

1135 Col. Mannering, Hazlewood, and smugglers *c.* 1835

Watercolour, 80 × 140
Engr.: by W. Finden, 1836, for *Fisher's Illustrations to the Waverley Novels*, 1836–7 (R. 561)
Prov.: Thomas E. Plint, sale Christie 7 March 1862 (173); Alfred Brooks, sale Christie 17 May 1879 (57), bt. Vokins; Mrs. Lewis Hill, sale Christie 20 April 1907 (22), bt. Agnew; Brown & Rose, 1909; anon. sale Christie 28 November 1930 (35), bt. Permain; L. H. Hayter, sale Sotheby 15 April 1953 (34), bt. Agnew
Private collection, U.S.A.

An illustration to 'Guy Mannering'.

1136 Ballyburgh Ness *c.* 1835

Watercolour and scraping-out, 79 × 150
Engr.: by E. Finden, 1836, for *Fisher's Illustrations to the Waverley Novels*, 1836–7 (R. 562)
Prov.: Revd. W. Kingsley; Grenville L. Winthrop, by whom bequeathed to the museum, 1943
Coll.: Fogg Art Museum, Harvard University, Cambridge, Mass. (1943–509)

An illustration to 'The Antiquary'.

1137 'It's auld Ailie hersell' *c.* 1835

Watercolour, size unknown
Engr.: by J. C. Armytage, 1836, for *Fisher's Illustrations to the Waverley Novels*, 1836–7 (R. 563)
Prov.: Thomas E. Plint, sale Christie 7 March 1862 (172); Mrs. Lewis Hill, sale Christie 20 April 1907; Agnew, 1907
Coll.: untraced

An illustration to 'The Black Dwarf'.

1138 Wolfe's Hope *c.* 1835

Watercolour, 102 × 165
Engr.: by J. H. Kernot, 1836, for *Fisher's Illustrations to the Waverley Novels*, 1836–7 (R. 564)
Prov.: John Ruskin; J. R. Williams, sale Christie 10 June 1865 (35), bt. Shaw; Matthew T. Shaw, sale Christie 20 March 1880 (52), bt. Theodore

Lloyd, sale Christie 4 February 1911 (17), bt. James King; Lieut.-Col. James B. Gaskell; by descent to the present owners
Coll.: Ernest and Roger Gaskell

An illustration to 'The Bride of Lammermoor'.

1139 Loch Leven Castle *c.* 1835

Watercolour, 102 × 158
Engr.: by J. B. Allen, 1837, for *Fisher's Illustrations to the Waverley Novels,* 1836–7 (R. 565)
Prov.: John Morley, sale Christie 16 May 1896 (26), bt. Agnew; Sir Donald Currie; by descent to present owner
Private collection

An illustration to 'The Abbot'.

Nos 1140–1142 are illustrations to John Gibson Lockhart's *Life of Sir Walter Scott,* intended for the first edition, which appeared in 1837, but not actually published until the issue of the second edition in 1839.

1140 Sandy Knowe, or Smailholm Tower *c.* 1836

Watercolour, 110 × 90, vignette
Engr.: by W. Miller, 1839, for Lockhart's *Life of Scott* (R. 566)
Prov.: Sir Walter Scott; John Ruskin; Dr. Elias Magoon (*c.* 1856); Matthew Vassar, by whom given to the college, 1864
Coll.: Vassar College Art Gallery, Poughkeepsie, New York (864.1.221)

Published as title-vignette to vol. II. The figure of the boy with a stick is that of Scott when a child, seen here with his nurse. Turner made another, unpub-

lished, design of this subject, in which Scott and his nurse are replaced by a carriage, in which are three figures, probably Scott, Cadell and Lockhart.

1141 Sir Walter Scott's birthplace, No. 39 Castle Street, Edinburgh *c.* 1836

Watercolour and pencil, 141 × 83, vignette
Engr.: by W. Miller, 1830, for Lockhart's *Life of Scott* (R. 567)
Prov.: Charles Eliot Norton (through John Ruskin, 1855); Miss Sarah Norton; De Coursey Fales; purchased as the gift of De Coursey Fales, 1953
Coll.: Pierpont Morgan Library, New York (1953.1)

Published as title-vignette to vol. IV.

1142 Abbotsford from the Northern Bank of the Tweed *c.* 1836

Watercolour, 89 × 139
Engr.: by W. Miller, 1839, for Lockhart's *Life of Scott* (R. 568)
Prov.: John Dillon, sale Christie 29 April 1869 (134), bt. Agnew; Sir Donald Currie; Murrieta, sale Christie 20 March 1959 (60), bt. Leggatt
Private collection, England

Published as frontispiece to vol. VIII. The subject was copied in the painting of Abbotsford on a

tea-tray (P524) which is supposed to be the work of Turner, but is almost certainly by another hand.

The following drawings (Nos 1143–1151) are studies or finished designs which seem to relate to Turner's work on the poetical and prose works of Scott, including *The Provincial Antiquities of Scotland* (see above).

1143 Crichton Castle, with rainbow *c.* 1818

Watercolour, with traces of pencil, 173 × 239
Prov.: L. Crispin Warmington; Spink, from whom purchased by Paul Mellon, 1962
Coll.: Yale Center for British Art, Paul Mellon Collection

See No. 1059.

1144 Loch Awe, with a rainbow *?c.* 1831

Pencil and watercolour, with some scraping-out, 224 × 285 (sight)
Exh.: R.A. 1974 (51)
Prov.: Sir Hickman Bacon, Bt.; by descent to present owner
Private collection

A study that is difficult to place; Turner had made a large watercolour of Loche Awe with a rainbow in 1802 (No. 344), but this sheet is stylistically incompatible with that early date. Studies of this type occur in connection with the 'Antiquities' project of about 1818, but this slightly larger sheet is perhaps more likely to belong to the Scottish tour of 1831; it seems to come from a roll sketch-book.

1145 A mountain pass *?c.* 1833

Watercolour over pencil, 177 × 127 (sight), vignette
Prov.: J. E. Taylor, sale Christie 5 July 1912 (120), bt. Agnew; Dr. Lloyd Roberts, by whom bequeathed to the gallery, 1920
Coll.: City Art Gallery, Manchester (1920.583)

Perhaps a study for the vignette of the *Simplon*, engraved for Scott's 'Life of Napoleon' in 1834 (No. 1112).

1146 Hotel de Ville, Brussels *c.* 1833

Watercolour, approx. 82 × 143, vignette
Prov.: H. A. J. Munro of Novar, sale Christie 6 April 1878 (68), bt. Wertheimer
Coll.: untraced

Presumably a projected illustration to the 'Life of Napoleon', but not used.

1147 Château d'Arques-la-bataille, near Dieppe *c.* 1834

Watercolour, 160 × 230
Prov.: A. G. E. Godden, by whom bequeathed to the gallery, 1933
Coll.: Art Gallery and Museums, Royal Pavilion, Brighton (853)

A colour study for the finished illustration (No. 1132).

1148 Kenilworth: moonlight *c.* 1835

Watercolour, 86 × 134
Prov.: H. A. J. Munro of Novar, sale Christie 6 April 1878 (75), bt. Gurney; George Gurney, sale Christie 17 March 1883 (196, as 'Kenilworth en fête'), bt. de la Penha; ? Reginald Graham
Coll.: untraced

Possibly intended for use in *Fisher's Illustrations to the Waverley Novels.*

1149 Whitehall *c.* 1835

Watercolour and body-colour over pencil, 89 × 150 (sight)
Prov.: ? Vokins; Wallis & Son, The French Gallery, 1912; James Blair, by whom bequeathed to the gallery, 1917
Coll.: City Art Gallery, Manchester (1917.114)

Possibly intended for use in *Fisher's Illustrations to the Waverley Novels.*

1150 Kilchurn Castle and Loch Awe *c.* 1835

Watercolour, 79 × 143
Prov.: Charles Langton, sale 20 April 1901 (106), bt. Wallis; Lady Patricia Ramsay, sale Christie

4 June 1974 (176), bt. Gerald M. Norman Gallery
Coll.: Gerald M. Norman Gallery

Possibly intended for use in *Fisher's Illustrations to the Waverley Novels.* Armstrong (p. 260) notes that the view is close to that in the vignette of *Lochmaben Castle* (No. 1075).

1151 Rivaulx Abbey *c.* 1835

Watercolour, 122 × 207
Engr.: by J. Bentley for *Gallery of Modern British Artists,* 1835 (R. 571)
Exh.: R.A. 1974 (291)
Prov.: Mrs. F. Hughes; Travers Buxton, by whom bequeathed to the gallery, 1945
Coll.: Tate Gallery, London (5615)

Possibly intended as an illustration to one of Scott's novels.

XVI(d) Nos 1152–1209
Illustrations to Samuel Rogers's *Italy* and Poems, c. 1826–1832

Samuel Rogers (1763–1855) published his long poem *Italy* in two parts, the first in 1822 and 1824, the second in 1828. Neither was attended with any success, and, before the second part had been issued, he invited Turner to design vignette illustrations for a new edition, offering him £50 for each design. In the end it was arranged that he should merely hire the drawings at a fee of £5 each, Turner to receive them again when engraving was completed. Work was apparently begun on the designs in 1826 (see No. 1176), and most were probably completed by the end of 1827—the set was certainly finished before Turner's departure for Rome in the early autumn of 1828, though Omer suggests that his tour of that year furnished 'some details'; this is unlikely. Engraving was under way in 1827, and the work published in 1830. It was immediately successful: Ruskin claimed that it was by means of its engraved vignettes that he first came to know Turner well. The book was an important agent in spreading Turner's popular reputation. Almost immediately Rogers asked the artist for a similar set of designs for a volume of his collected *Poems,* which was already in print in an edition of 1827 illustrated by Stothard. Turner's copy is now in the Turner Bequest (T.B., CCCLXVI). Stothard contributed some designs to the new edition; it appeared in 1834, the vignettes having been engraved almost entirely in 1833. A preponderance of the designs was executed by Edward

Goodall, especially in the volume of *Poems,* but several other engravers, all of whom had already collaborated with Turner, contributed to the two books. In all, fifty-eight engraved vignettes after Turner were published, twenty-five in *Italy* and thirty-three in the *Poems.* They are often cited as the finest of all Turner's book illustrations. On account of the unusual agreement that the drawings were to be hired out by the artist, both sets remained in his studio and are now in the Bequest, together with many studies for them (T.B., CCLXXX). One drawing escaped: the *Hospice of the Great St. Bernard II—the Dead-House,* which was acquired by John Dillon and shortly afterwards became one of the first watercolours by Turner to reach America (see also Nos 1140, 1222, 1226).

1154 St. Maurice *c.* 1827

Pencil and watercolour, 165 × 220, vignette
Engr.: by R. Wallis, 1827–9, for Rogers's *Italy,* 1830, p. 9 (R. 350)
Coll.: Trustees of the British Museum
(T.B., CCLXXX–147)

A watercolour sketch for this subject is T.B., CCLXXX–1.

Stothard (1755–1834) and Edwin Landseer (1802–73); that of the figure on the stretcher being signed by the former, those of the two dogs at the right and bottom by the latter. Ruskin (*Works,* XIII, p. 514) suggests that these 'improvements' of Turner's oddly feeble drawing of the figures and dogs were not followed by the engraver, since Rogers wished him to adhere to the original design; but it is evident that, in fact, Landseer's dogs were used by Smith, though Stothard's figure seems to have been rejected. For another contribution by Landseer, see *Valombré,* No. 1191 below. A story that may have been confused with this is that of Landseer's adding the dog to Turner's picture of *Mortlake Terrace* (P239), related by Frederick Goodall, R.A., son of the engraver of *Valombré* (see W. T. Whitley, *Art in England, 1821–37,* 1930, p. 282).

1152 The Lake of Geneva *c.* 1827

Pencil and watercolour, 215 × 146, vignette
Engr.: by E. Goodall, 1829, for Rogers's *Italy,* 1830, p. 1 (R. 348)
Coll.: Trustees of the British Museum
(T.B., CCLXXX–152)

1155 Hospice of the Great St. Bernard I *c.* 1827

Pencil and watercolour, 244 × 304, vignette
Engr.: by W. R. Smith, 1829, for Rogers's *Italy,* 1830, p. 11 (R. 351)
Coll.: Trustees of the British Museum
(T.B., CCLXXX–153)

A study of the subject, made in 1802, is in the *Grenoble* sketchbook (T.B., LXXIV–4). The dog in the left-hand foreground of the design is omitted in the engraving.

1156 Hospice of the Great St. Bernard II (the Dead-House) *c.* 1827

Pencil and watercolour, 215 × 269, vignette
Engr.: by W. R. Smith, 1829, for Rogers's *Italy,* 1830, p. 16 (R. 352)
Inscr. lower left: *TS;* lower right: *EL* (monogram)
Prov.: John Dillon, sale Foster 7 June 1856 (137); Dr. Elias Magoon, New York; Matthew Vassar, by whom given to the college, 1864
Coll.: Vassar College Art Gallery, Poughkeepsie, New York (864.1.220)

The distant view of the Hospice is recorded in the *Grenoble* sketchbook (T.B., LXXIV–55 and 61). See also the note introducing this group, above. The marginal sketches on this sheet are by Thomas

1157 Marengo *c.* 1827

Pencil and watercolour, with some pen and brown ink, 125 × 200, vignette
Inscr.: *Battle MARENGO 18...* and *LODI*
Engr.: by E. Goodall, 1829, for Rogers's *Italy,* 1830, p. 17 (R. 353)
Exh.: R.A. 1974 (273)
Coll.: Trustees of the British Museum
(T.B., CCLXXX–146)

1158 Aosta *c.* 1827

Pencil and watercolour, 140 × 172, vignette
Inscr. on cross in foreground: *1826*
Engr.: by H. Le Keux, 1829, for Rogers's *Italy,* 1830, p. 25 (R. 354)
Exh.: R.A. 1974 (272)
Coll.: Trustees of the British Museum
(T.B., CCLXXX–145)

1153 William Tell's Chapel *c.* 1827

Pencil and watercolour, 240 × 305, vignette
Engr.: by R. Wallis, 1827–9, for Rogers's *Italy,* 1830, p. 8 (R. 349)
Coll.: Trustees of the British Museum
(T.B., CCLXXX–155)

In the engraving the date on the cross in the foreground is 1814. The '1826' in Turner's drawing may well be the date of its execution.

1159   Martigny   *c.* 1827

Pencil and watercolour, 254 × 286, vignette
Engr.: by W. Cooke, 1829, for Rogers's *Italy*, 1830, p. 28 (R. 355)
Coll.: Trustees of the British Museum
(T.B., CCLXXX–154)

1160   Hannibal passing the Alps   *c.* 1827

Pencil and watercolour, 140 × 205, vignette
Engr.: by W. R. Smith, 1830, for Rogers's *Italy*, 1830, p. 29 (R. 356)
Coll.: Trustees of the British Museum
(T.B., CCLXXX–149)

A watercolour study for this subject is T.B., CCLXXX–6.

1161   Lake of Como   *c.* 1827

Pencil and watercolour, 160 × 202, vignette
Engr.: by E. Goodall, 1829, for Rogers's *Italy*, 1830, p. 32 (R. 357)
Coll.: Trustees of the British Museum
(T.B., CCLXXX–157)

1162   Venice: the Ducal Palace   *c.* 1827

Pencil and watercolour, 127 × 184
Engr.: by E. Goodall, 1830, for Rogers's *Italy*, 1830, p. 47 (R. 358)
Coll.: Trustees of the British Museum
(T.B., CCLXXX–193)

1163   Florence   *c.* 1827

Pencil and watercolour, 123 × 170, vignette
Engr.: by E. Goodall, 1829, for Rogers's *Italy*, 1830, p. 102 (R. 359)
Coll.: Trustees of the British Museum
(T.B., CCLXXX–156)

1164   Galileo's Villa   *c.* 1827

Pencil and watercolour, 115 × 140, vignette
Engr.: by E. Goodall, 1830, for Rogers's *Italy*, 1830, p. 115 (R. 360)
Exh.: B.M. 1975 (114)
Coll.: Trustees of the British Museum
(T.B., CCLXXX–163)

1165   Villa Madama—moonlight   *c.* 1827

Watercolour, pen and black and brown ink, 115 × 115, vignette
Engr.: by H. Le Keux, 1829, for Rogers's *Italy*, 1830, p. 135 (R. 361)
Exh.: R.A. 1974 (277)
Coll.: Trustees of the British Museum
(T.B., CCLXXX–159)

1166   Rome, Castle of St. Angelo   *c.* 1827

Pencil and watercolour, 90 × 159, vignette
Engr.: by R. Wallis, 1829, for Rogers's *Italy*, 1830, p. 158 (R. 362)

Coll.: Trustees of the British Museum
(T.B., CCLXXX–160)

1167   The Forum   *c.* 1827

Pencil and watercolour, with pen and brown ink, 135 × 150, vignette
Engr.: by E. Goodall, 1829, for Rogers's *Italy,* 1830, p. 137 (R. 363)
Exh.: R.A. 1974 (276)
Coll.: Trustees of the British Museum
(T.B., CCLXXX–158)

1168   The Campagna of Rome   *c.* 1827

Pencil and watercolour, 70 × 185, vignette
Engr.: by E. Goodall, 1829, for Rogers's *Italy,* 1830, p. 153 (R. 364)
Coll.: Trustees of the British Museum
(T.B., CCLXXX–161)

1169   Tivoli   *c.* 1827

Pencil and watercolour, 115 × 120, vignette
Engr.: by J. Pye, 1830, for Rogers's *Italy,* 1830, p. 166 (R. 365)
Coll.: Trustees of the British Museum
(T.B., CCLXXX–166)

1170   Perugia   *c.* 1827

Pencil and watercolour, 115 × 155, vignette
Engr.: by E. Goodall, 1830, for Rogers's *Italy,* 1830, p. 168 (R. 366)
Coll.: Trustees of the British Museum
(T.B., CCLXXX–144)

1171   Banditti   *c.* 1827

Pencil and watercolour, 170 × 184, vignette
Engr.: by R. Wallis, 1830, for Rogers's *Italy,* 1830, p. 183 (R. 367)

Coll.: Trustees of the British Museum
(T.B., CCLXXX–164)

The three figures in the extreme left-hand foreground of the design are omitted in the engraving.

1172   Naples   *c.* 1827

Pencil and watercolour, 70 × 158, vignette
Engr.: by E. Goodall, 1829, for Rogers's *Italy,* 1830, p. 189 (R. 368)
Coll.: Trustees of the British Museum
(T.B., CCLXXX–143)

1173   Paestum   *c.* 1827

Pencil and watercolour, 88 × 172, vignette
Engr.: by J. Pye, 1830, for Rogers's *Italy,* 1830, p. 207 (R. 369)
Exh.: R.A. 1974 (274)
Coll.: Trustees of the British Museum
(T.B., CCLXXX–148)

A preliminary sketch for this subject is T.B., CCLXXX–92.

1174   Amalfi   *c.* 1827

Pencil and watercolour, 95 × 133, vignette
Engr.: by R. Wallis, 1829, for Rogers's *Italy,* 1830,
p. 216 (R. 370)
Coll.: Trustees of the British Museum
(T.B., CCLXXX–167)

1175   Padua: a villa on the night of the Festa di Ballo   *c.* 1827

Pencil and watercolour, pen and brown ink,
95 × 115, vignette
Engr.: by E. Goodall, 1829, for Rogers's *Italy,* 1830,
p. 223 (R. 371)
Exh.: B.M. 1975 (115)
Coll.: Trustees of the British Museum
(T.B., CCLXXX–165)

1176   A farewell: Lake of Como II   *c.* 1827

Pencil and watercolour, with pen and brown ink,
130 × 200, vignette
Engr.: by R. Wallis, 1830, for Rogers's *Italy,* 1830,
p. 233 (R. 372)
Exh.: R.A. 1974 (275)
Coll.: Trustees of the British Museum
(T.B., CCLXXX–150)

Ruskin recounts (M.S. 54 1 C, Bembridge Collection) that Rogers told him how he had asked Turner to draw this subject while they were both staying at Petworth; this was probably in 1826. See Omer, 1975.

1177   A garden   *c.* 1832

Watercolour, 121 × 133, vignette
Engr.: by W. Miller, 1833, for Rogers's *Poems,*
1834, frontispiece (R. 373)

Coll.: Trustees of the British Museum
(T.B., CCLXXX–162)

Illustrating Part I of 'The Pleasures of Memory'.

1178   A village evening—twilight   *c.* 1832

Watercolour, 80 × 108, vignette
Engr.: by E. Goodall, 1833, for Rogers's *Poems,*
1834, p. 7 (R. 374)
Exh.: B.M. 1975 (183)
Coll.: Trustees of the British Museum
(T.B., CCLXXX–168)

Published as head-piece to Part I of Rogers's poem 'The Pleasures of Memory'.

1179   The Gipsy   *c.* 1832

Watercolour, 80 × 100, vignette

Engr.: by E. Goodall, 1833, for Rogers's *Poems,*
1834, p. 12 (R. 375)
Coll.: Trustees of the British Museum
(T.B., CCLXXX–173)

Illustrating Part I of 'The Pleasures of Memory'.

1180   Leaving home   *c.* 1832

Watercolour, 95 × 130, vignette
Engr.: by E. Goodall, 1833, for Rogers's *Poems,*
1834, p. 16 (R. 376)
Coll.: Trustees of the British Museum
(T.B., CCLXXX–169)

Illustrating Part I of 'The Pleasures of Memory'.

1181   Greenwich Hospital   *c.* 1832

Pencil and watercolour, 100 × 152, vignette
Engr.: by E. Goodall, 1833, for Rogers's *Poems,*
1834, p. 33 (R. 377)
Exh.: R.A. 1974 (279)
Coll.: Trustees of the British Museum
(T.B., CCLXXX–176)

Illustrating Part II of 'The Pleasures of Memory'. A preliminary sketch of the subject is T.B., CCLXXX–94.

1182   Keswick Lake   *c.* 1832

Watercolour, 112 × 140, vignette
Engr.: by E. Goodall, 1833, for Rogers's *Poems,*
1834, p. 36 (R. 378)
Exh.: B.M. 1975 (188)
Coll.: Trustees of the British Museum
(T.B., CCLXXX–181)

Illustrating Part II of 'The Pleasures of Memory'.

1183 St. Herbert's Isle, Derwentwater *c.* 1832

Watercolour, 105 × 120, vignette
Engr.: by H. Le Keux, 1833, for Rogers's *Poems*, 1834, p. 40 (R. 379)
Coll.: Trustees of the British Museum
(T.B., CCLXXX–180)

Illustrating Part II of 'The Pleasures of Memory'.

1184 An old manor house *c.* 1832

Pencil and watercolour, 105 × 95, vignette
Engr.: by W. Miller, 1833, for Rogers's *Poems*, 1834, p. 63 (R. 380)
Exh.: B.M. 1975 (180)
Coll.: Trustees of the British Museum
(T.B., CCLXXX–201)

The design is also known as 'The English Manor House'. It was published as the head-piece to Rogers's poem 'Human Life'.

1185 Tornaro *c.* 1832

Pencil and watercolour, 185 × 160, vignette
Engr.: by R. Wallis, 1833, for Rogers's *Poems*, 1834, p. 80 (R. 381)
Coll.: Trustees of the British Museum
(T.B., CCLXXX–172)
An illustration to 'Human Life'.

Studies for this design are T.B., CCLXXX–86, 89.

1186 A village fair *c.* 1832

Pencil and watercolour, 115 × 120, vignette
Engr.: by E. Goodall, 1833, for Rogers's *Poems*, 1834, p. 84 (R. 382)
Exh.: B.M. 1975 (179)
Coll.: Trustees of the British Museum
(T.B., CCLXXX–200)

An illustration to 'Human Life'.

1187 Traitor's Gate, Tower of London *c.* 1832

Pencil and watercolour, 125 × 135, vignette
Engr.: by E. Goodall, 1833, for Rogers's *Italy*, 1834, p. 88 (R. 383)
Exh.: R.A. 1974 (278)

Coll.: Trustees of the British Museum
(T.B., CCLXXX–177)

An illustration to 'Human Life'. A preliminary sketch of the subject is T.B., CCLXXX–93.

1188 St. Anne's Hill I (the house) *c.* 1832

Pencil and watercolour, 100 × 175, vignette
Engr.: by E. Goodall, 1833, for Rogers's *Poems*, 1834, p. 91 (R. 384)
Exh.: B.M. 1975 (181)
Coll.: Trustees of the British Museum
(T.B., CCLXXX–170)

An illustration to 'Human Life'. The subject is based on a pencil drawing in the *Windsor and St. Anne's Hill* sketchbook (T.B., CCXXV–26). See No. 1201.

1189 A hurricane in the desert (the Simoom) *c.* 1832

441

Watercolour, 127 × 127, vignette
Engr.: by E. Goodall, 1833, for Rogers's *Poems*,
1834, p. 94 (R. 385)
Coll.: Trustees of the British Museum
(T.B., CCLXXX–195)

An illustration to 'Human Life'.

Engr.: by E. Goodall, 1833, for Rogers's *Poems*,
1834, p. 145 (R. 388)
Coll.: Trustees of the British Museum
(T.B., CCLXXX–183)

The design is more usually known as 'Jacqueline's
Cottage'; it was published as the head-piece to
'Jacqueline', II.

Watercolour, 128 × 130, vignette
Engr.: by E. Goodall, 1833, for Rogers's *Poems*,
1834, p. 172 (R. 390)
Coll.: Trustees of the British Museum
(T.B., CCLXXX–187)

An illustration to 'Captivity'.

1190   Venice: the Rialto—moonlight *c.* 1832

Watercolour, 120 × 135, vignette
Engr.: by W. Miller, 1833, for Rogers's *Poems*,
1834, p. 95 (R. 386)
Exh.: R.A. 1974 (281)
Coll.: Trustees of the British Museum
(T.B., CCLXXX–196)

An illustration to 'Human Life'. A preliminary study
for the subject is T.B., CCLXXX–108.

1195   An old oak *c.* 1832

Pencil and watercolour, 110 × 133, vignette
Engr.: by E. Goodall, for Rogers's *Poems*, 1834,
p. 176 (R. 391)
Exh.: B.M. 1975 (184)
Coll.: Trustees of the British Museum
(T.B., CCLXXX–174)

Published as head-piece to the poem 'To an Old
Oak'.

1193   St. Julienne's Chapel *c.* 1832

Watercolour, 143 × 86, vignette
Engr.: by E. Goodall, 1833, for Rogers's *Poems*,
1834, p. 151 (R. 389)
Coll.: Trustees of the British Museum
(T.B., CCLXXX–186)

Published as the head-piece to 'Jacqueline', III.

1196   Shipbuilding (an old oak dead) *c.* 1832

Pencil and watercolour, 100 × 140, vignette
Engr.: by E. Goodall, 1833, for Rogers's *Poems*,
1834, p. 178 (R. 392)
Exh.: R.A. 1974 (280)
Coll.: Trustees of the British Museum
(T.B., CCLXXX–175)

Published as tail-piece to the poem 'To an Old
Oak'.

1191   Valombré *c.* 1832

Watercolour, 122 × 90, vignette
Engr.: by E. Goodall, 1833, for Rogers's *Poems*,
1834, p. 144 (R. 387)
Coll.: Trustees of the British Museum
(T.B., CCLXXX–185)

An illustration to 'Jacqueline', I. The stag in this
design is said to have been drawn by Landseer; see
No. 1156 above.

1197   The Boy of Egremond *c.* 1832

Watercolour, 100 × 120, vignette
Engr.: by E. Goodall, 1833, for Rogers's *Poems*,
1834, p. 184 (R. 393)
Coll.: Trustees of the British Museum
(T.B., CCLXXX–178)

1192   St. Pierre's Cottage *c.* 1832

Watercolour, 235 × 303. vignette

1194   Captivity *c.* 1832

Watercolour, 241 × 303, vignette
Engr.: by E. Goodall, 1833, for Rogers's *Poems*, 1834, p. 192 (R. 395)
Coll.: Trustees of the British Museum
(T.B., CCLXXX–184)

Published as the head-piece to 'The Alps at Daybreak'.

Published as the head-piece to 'The Boy of Egremond'.

Engr.: by E. Goodall, 1833, for Rogers's *Poems*, 1834, p. 219 (R. 398)
Coll.: Trustees of the British Museum
(T.B., CCLXXX–188)

This and the following six designs are vignettes for the poem 'The Voyage of Columbus'. This design was published as the head-piece to Rogers's note, 'Inscribed on the original manuscript'.

1200 Loch Lomond *c.*1832

Watercolour, 85 × 150, vignette
Engr.: by W. Miller, 1833, for Rogers's *Poems*, 1834, p. 203 (R. 396)
Exh.: B.M. 1975 (187)
Coll.: Trustees of the British Museum
(T.B., CCLXXX–182)

Published as head-piece to lines 'Written in the Highlands of Scotland, September 2, 1812'.

1198 Bolton Abbey *c.*1832

Watercolour, 122 × 150, vignette
Engr.: by R. Wallis, 1833, for Rogers's *Poems*, 1834, p. 186 (R. 394)
Coll.: Trustees of the British Museum
(T.B., CCLXXX–179)

Published as the tail-piece to 'The Boy of Egremond'.

1203 Departure of Columbus *c.*1832

Pencil and watercolour, 100 × 147, vignette
Engr.: by E. Goodall, 1833, for Rogers's *Poems*, 1834, p. 227 (R. 399)
Coll.: Trustees of the British Museum
(T.B., CCLXXX–189)

Published as the head-piece to Canto I of 'The Voyage of Columbus'.

1201 St. Anne's Hill II (the garden) *c.*1832

Pencil and watercolour, 150 × 165, vignette
Engr.: by E. Goodall, 1833, for Rogers's *Poems*, 1834, p. 214 (R. 397)
Exh.: B.M. 1975 (182)
Coll.: Trustees of the British Museum
(T.B., CCLXXX–171)

Published as tail-piece to the lines 'Written in Westminster Abbey' (after the funeral of Charles James Fox, 10 October 1806). St. Anne's Hill was Fox's home (see No. 1188).

1202 Columbus at La Rabida, and his son *c.*1832

Pencil and watercolour, 122 × 133, vignette

1199 The Alps at daybreak *c.*1832

1204 The Vision *c.*1832

443

Pencil and watercolour, 108 × 133, vignette
Engr.: by E. Goodall, 1833, for Rogers's *Poems,*
1834, p. 233 (R. 400)
Coll.: Trustees of the British Museum
(T.B., CCLXXX–197)

Published as the tail-piece to Canto II of 'The
Voyage of Columbus'. Based on two preparatory
studies (T.B., CCLXXX–203, 204).

**1205 Dawn on the last day of the
voyage** *c.* 1832

Pencil and watercolour, 125 × 110, vignette
Engr.: by E. Goodall, 1833, for Rogers's *Poems,*
1834, p. 248 (R. 401)
Coll.: Trustees of the British Museum
(T.B., CCLXXX–190)

Published as the head-piece to Canto VIII of 'The
Voyage of Columbus'.

1206 Landing in America *c.* 1832

Pencil and watercolour, 80 × 140, vignette
Engr.: by E. Goodall for Rogers's *Poems,* 1834,
p. 251 (R. 402)
Coll.: Trustees of the British Museum
(T.B., CCLXXX–191)

Published as the head-piece to Canto IX of 'The
Voyage of Columbus'.

1207 The Evil Spirit *c.* 1832

Pencil and watercolour, 125 × 110, vignette
Engr.: by E. Goodall, 1833, for Rogers's *Poems,*
1834, p. 264 (R. 403)

Exh.: R.A. 1974 (283)
Coll.: Trustees of the British Museum
(T.B., CCLXXX–202)

Published as tail-piece to Canto XII of 'The Voyage
of Columbus'. There are pencil studies for the
design in the *Berwick* sketchbook (T.B., CCLXV–20
verso, 30).

1208 Cortes and Pizarro *c.* 1832

Pencil and watercolour, 126 × 95, vignette
Engr.: by E. Goodall, 1833, for Rogers's *Poems,*
1834, p. 265 (R. 404)
Coll.: Trustees of the British Museum
(T.B., CCLXXX–192)

Published as the head-piece to 'some stanzas in the
romance or ballad measure of the Spaniards' which
follow the poem 'The Voyage of Columbus'.

1209 Datur Hora Quieti *c.* 1832

Watercolour, 96 × 130, vignette
Engr.: by E. Goodall, 1833, for Rogers's *Poems,*
1834, p. 296 (R. 405)
Exh.: R.A. 1974 (282)
Coll.: Trustees of the British Museum
(T.B., CCLXXX–199)

Published as a *cul-de-lampe* or tail-piece to the
volume.

**XVI(e) Nos 1210–1235
Illustrations to the works of Lord Byron,**
c. 1823–1832

Turner made twenty-six designs illustrating the life
and works of Lord Byron. The drawings belong to
two distinct periods, the first being in fact the
earliest time when he worked as a book-illustrator,
about 1823–4. He produced then seven full-page
subjects which appeared in Murray's eleven-
volume edition of *Lord Byron's Works,* 1825. The
second period was the early 1830s, when he made
seventeen vignettes for the seventeen volumes of
Murray's complete duodecimo edition of Byron,
with a *Life* by Thomas Moore; these were probably
executed in about 1830–2. They were reprinted in
Finden's *Landscape and Portrait Illustrations to the
Life and Works of Lord Byron,* published in three
volumes by Murray and Tilt; this also included the
seven plates for the 1825 edition and two new
plates (Nos 1210, 1217). Most of the engravings
were done by Edward Finden. As with the *Bible*
illustrations (Nos 1236–1263), Turner relied to a
great extent on the drawings of artists who had
visited Greece and other parts of the Mediterranean that he had not seen; in this case, his principal
source was a minor professional topographer,
William Page (1794–1872).

1210 Gibraltar *c.* 1832

Watercolour, 94 × 143
Engr.: by E. Finden for *Landscape and Portrait
Illustrations to the Life and Works of Lord Byron,*
1833–4 (R. 406)
Prov.: R. Durning Holt
Coll.: untraced

Based on a sketch by George Reinagle. An illustration to 'Childe Harold', Canto II.

1211 Malta *c.* 1823–4

Watercolour, 165 × 267
Engr.: by E. Finden for *Lord Byron's Works,* 1825
(R. 407); the plate was used again for Finden's
Landscape Illustrations ... of Lord Byron, 1833–4

Prov.: John Ruskin; James Knowles, sale Christie 7 April 1865 (117, as 'Valetta Harbour'), bt. G. White; R. Durning Holt
Coll.: untraced

It is not known which draughtsman supplied Turner with the drawing used for this design; Turner himself did not visit Malta. The subject illustrates 'Childe Harold', Canto II (though Malta is not specifically mentioned there).

1212 The Acropolis of Athens *c.* 1823–4

Watercolour, 152 × 222
Engr.: by J. Cousen for *Lord Byron's Works,* 1825 (R. 408); the plate was used again for Finden's *Landscape Illustrations ... of Lord Byron,* 1833–4
Prov.: H. A. J. Munro of Novar, sale Christie 6 April 1878 (79), bt. Lewis Powell; anon. sale Christie 25 July 1947 (87), bt. in; anon. sale Sotheby 14 March 1962 (32), bt. Fine Art Society, London
Private collection

Based on a sketch by Thomas Allason. The design illustrates 'Childe Harold', Canto II. Studies of the subject, in colour alone, are T.B., CCLXIII–253, CCCLXIV–402.

1213 Temple of Minerva, Cape Colonna *c.* 1823–4

Watercolour, 160 × 219
Engr.: by E. Finden for *Lord Byron's Works,* 1825 (R. 409); the plate was used again for Finden's *Landscape Illustrations ... of Lord Byron,* 1833–4
Prov.: H. A. J. Munro of Novar, sale Christie 2 June 1877 (21), bt. Agnew; George Gurney, sale Christie 17 March 1883 (192), bt. Agnew; A. Pilkington; H. L. Fison

Coll.: Burnley Borough Council, Towneley Hall Art Gallery and Museums (CO. 162)

Based on a sketch by Thomas Allason. The subject illustrates 'Childe Harold', Canto II.

1214 Tomb of Cecilia Metella, Rome *c.* 1823–4

Watercolour, 111 × 216
Engr.: by E. Finden, for *Lord Byron's Works,* 1825 (R. 410); the plate was used again for Finden's *Landscape Illustrations ... of Lord Byron,* 1833–4
Prov.: John Dillon, sale Christie 29 April 1869 (144), bt. Vokins; Frederick Nettlefold, sale Christie 5 June 1913 (44), bt. Agnew; F. Whalley, 1914; G. Beatson Blair, by whom bequeathed to the gallery, 1941
Coll.: City Art Gallery, Manchester (1947.58)

The subject illustrates 'Childe Harold', Canto IV. Compare Turner's previous treatment of the Tomb of Metella for Hakewill, No. 709.

1215 Rhodes* *c.* 1823–4

Watercolour and body-colour, with scraping-out, 133 × 226
Engr.: by W. Finden for *Lord Byron's Works,* 1825 (R. 411); the plate was used again for Finden's *Landscape Illustrations ... of Lord Byron,* 1833–4
Prov.: H. A. J. Munro of Novar, sale Christie 6 April 1878 (78), bt. S. H. Fraser; sale Christie 7 May 1904 (9), bt. Wallis; Valentine, by 1963; R. Sterling, New York; Sotheby Parke Bernet 14 January 1977 (214), bt. Leger; Paul Mellon, 1977
Coll.: Yale Center for British Art, Paul Mellon Collection

1216 The Drachenfels *c.* 1823–4

Watercolour and scraping-out over pencil, 128 × 204 (sight)
Engr.: by W. Finden for *Lord Byron's Works,* 1825 (R. 412); the plate was used again for Finden's

Landscape Illustrations ... of Lord Byron, 1833–4
Exh.: R.A. 1974 (288)
Prov.: ? Thomas Brown, sale Christie 8 June 1869 (650), bt. Vokins; Sir W. Cunliffe Brooks, sale Phillips, 1901; Lady Cunliffe Brooks, sale Phillips, 8 July 1903, bt. Agnew; J. Blair, by whom bequeathed to the gallery, 1917
Coll.: City Art Gallery, Manchester (1917.113)

An illustration to 'Childe Harold', Canto IV.

1217 Cephalonia *c.* 1832

Watercolour, 95 × 140
Engr.: by E. Finden for Finden's *Landscape Illustrations ... of Lord Byron,* 1833–4 (R. 413)
Prov.: A. E. Jones, sale Christie 14 June 1946 (44), bt. Leger; Sir Thomas Baring
Coll.: untraced

Based on a sketch by William Page. It was on the island of Cephalonia that Byron began his operations in connection with the Greek war of independence.

1218 Negropont *c.* 1823–4

Watercolour, size unknown
Engr.: by E. Finden for *Lord Byron's Works,* 1825 (R. 414); the plate was used again for Finden's *Landscape Illustrations... of Lord Byron,* 1833–4
Prov.: James Wadmore, sale Christie 5 June 1863 (102), bt. Agnew; Agnew, 1904; A. Buckley; W. F. Morice
Private collection

Based on a sketch by Thomas Allason.

1219 Santa Maria della Spina, Pisa *c.* 1832

Watercolour, 190 × 173, vignette
Engr.: by E. Finden, 1832, for *The Works of Lord Byron: with his Letters and Journals and his Life,* by Thomas Moore, 1832–4 (R. 415); the plate was used again for Finden's *Landscape Illustrations... of Lord Byron,* 1833–4
Prov.: John Ruskin, by whom presented to the University of Oxford, 1861
Coll.: Visitors of the Ashmolean Museum, Oxford (Herrmann 52)

Based on a sketch by W. Page; but Turner visited Pisa in 1828 and made a pencil drawing of the same view (T.B., CCXXXIII–55). Published as frontispiece-vignette to vol. V.

1220   The Gate of Theseus, Athens   *c*. 1832

Watercolour, size unknown, vignette
Engr.: by E. Finden, 1832, for *The Works of Lord Byron...*, 1832–4 (R. 416); the plate was used again for Finden's *Landscape Illustrations... of Lord Byron*, 1833–4 ;
Prov.: John Ruskin
Coll.: untraced

Published as frontispiece-vignette to vol. VII.

1221   The Plain of Troy   *c*. 1832

Watercolour, size unknown, vignette
Engr.: by E. Finden, 1832, for *The Works of Lord Byron...*, 1832–4 (R. 417); the plate was used again for Finden's *Landscape Illustrations... of Lord Byron*, 1833–4
Prov.: John Ruskin, 1878; Leggatt Bros., 1926; H. H. McLeod
Coll.: untraced

Based on a sketch by William Page. Published as title-vignette to vol. VII.

1222   Bacharach on the Rhine   *c*. 1832

Watercolour, 225 × 273, vignette
Engr.: by E. Finden, 1832, for *The Works of Lord Byron...*, 1832–4 (R. 418); the plate was used again for Finden's *Landscape Illustrations... of Lord Byron*, 1833–4
Prov.: John Ruskin; Elias L. Magoon; Matthew Vassar, by whom given to the college, 1864
Coll.: Vassar College Art Gallery, Poughkeepsie, New York (864.1.2.7)

First publ. as frontispiece-vignette to vol. VIII.

1223   The Castle of St. Angelo   *c*. 1832

Watercolour, 171 × 210, vignette
Engr.: by E. Finden, 1832, for *The Works of Lord Byron...*, 1832–4 (R. 419); the plate was used again for Finden's *Landscape Illustrations... of Lord Byron*, 1833–4
Exh.: R.A. 1974 (285)
Prov.: Beresford Rimington Heaton, by whom bequeathed to the gallery, 1940

Coll.: Tate Gallery, London (5243)

First publ. as title-vignette to vol. VIII.

1224   Corinth from the Acropolis   *c*. 1832

Watercolour over pencil, 210 × 267, vignette
Engr.: by E. Finden, 1832, for *The Works of Lord Byron...*, 1832–4 (R. 420); the plate was used again for Finden's *Landscape Illustrations... of Lord Byron*, 1833–4
Prov.: H. A. J. Munro of Novar, sale Christie 2 June 1877 (77), bt. Agnew; William Lee, sale Christie 28 May 1883 (174), bt. in; Lee sale, Christie 22 June 1888 (363), bt. Tooth; Rt. Hon. Professor Sir Thomas Clifford Albutt, by whom bequeathed to the museum, 1935
Coll.: Syndics of the Fitzwilliam Museum, Cambridge (1762; Cormack 32)

Based on a sketch by William Page. First publ. as frontispiece-vignette to vol. X.

1225   The Bridge of Sighs, Venice   *c*. 1832

Watercolour, size unknown, vignette
Engr.: by E. Finden, 1832, for *The Works of Lord Byron...*, 1832–4 (R. 421); the plate was used again for Finden's *Landscape Illustrations ... of Lord Byron*, 1833–4
Prov.: B. G. Windus, sale Christie 26 March 1859 (II), bt. Holloway; Agnew, 1890; Sir Geoffrey Watson
Coll.: untraced

Based on a sketch by T. Little. First publ. as frontispiece-vignette to vol. XI. A drawing entitled *The Bridge of Sighs*, 178 × 203, was sold anonymously at Foster's, 19 November 1860 (128).

1226   The Bernese Alps   *c*. 1832

Watercolour, 223 × 277, vignette
Engr.: by E. Finden, 1832, for *The Works of Lord Byron...*, 1832–4 (R. 422); the plate was used again for Finden's *Landscape Illustrations ... of Lord Byron*, 1833–4
Prov.: T. Griffith, 1834 (?); John Ruskin; Elias L. Magoon, 1856; Matthew Vassar, by whom given to the college, 1864
Coll.: Vassar College Art Gallery, Poughkeepsie, New York (864.1.218)

First publ. as title-vignette to vol. XI.

1227   The Walls of Rome with the Tomb of Caius Sestus   *c*. 1832

Watercolour, 146 × 197, vignette
Engr.: by E. Finden, 1833, for *The Works of Lord Byron...*, 1832–4 (R. 423); the plate was used again for Finden's *Landscape Illustrations ... of Lord Byron*, 1833–4
Exh.: R.A. 1974 (286)
Prov.: H. A. J. Munro of Novar, sale 6 April 1878 (77), bt. Makins; Beresford Rimington Heaton, by whom bequeathed to the gallery, 1940
Coll.: Tate Gallery, London (5242)

First publ. as title-vignette to vol. XIII.

1228   Parnassus and Castalian Spring   *c*. 1832

Watercolour and body-colour, 184 × 140, vignette
Engr.: by E. Finden, 1833, for *The Works of Lord Byron...*, 1832–4 (R. 424); the plate was used again for Finden's *Landscape Illustrations ... of Lord Byron*, 1833–4

Watercolour, with some pen, 210 × 200, vignette
Engr.: by E. Finden, 1833, for *The Works of Lord Byron ...*, 1832–4 (R. 430); the plate was used again for Finden's *Landscape Illustrations ... of Lord Byron,* 1833–4
Prov.: John Ruskin, by whom given to the University of Oxford, 1861
Coll.: Visitors of the Ashmolean Museum, Oxford (Herrmann 53)

Based on a sketch by William Page. First publ. as frontispiece-vignette to vol. XVII.

Prov.: Beresford Rimington Heaton, by whom bequeathed to the gallery, 1940
Coll.: Tate Gallery, London (5238)

Based on a sketch by William Page. First publ. as frontispiece-vignette to vol. XIV.

1229   The Field of Waterloo from Hougoumont *c.* 1832

Watercolour, size unknown, vignette
Engr.: by E. Finden, 1833, for *The Works of Lord Byron ...*, 1832–4 (R. 425); the plate was used again for Finden's *Landscape Illustrations ... of Lord Byron,* 1833–4
Prov.: ? W. Dallas O. Grieg, sale Christie 12 March 1887 (74), bt. in; ? sale Christie 28 April 1890 (56), bt. in; ? Sir Charles Butt, sale Christie 1 July 1892 (217), bt. Richardson
Private collection, U.S.A.

First publ. as title-vignette to vol. XIV. The queried entries in the provenance refer to a drawing sold under the title 'La Haye Sainte'. This may have been the illustration to Scott's *Prose Works,* No. 1097 above.

1230   Scio (Fontana de Melek Mehmet, Pasha) *c.* 1832

Watercolour, size unknown, vignette
Engr.: by E. Finden, 1833, for *The Works of Lord Byron ...*, 1832–4 (R. 426); the plate was used again for Finden's *Landscape Illustrations ... of Lord Byron,* 1833–4
Prov.: John Ruskin, 1878
Coll.: untraced

Based on a sketch by William Page. First publ. as frontispiece-vignette to vol. XV.

1231   Genoa *c.* 1832

Watercolour, 109 × 190, vignette
Engr.: by E. Finden, 1833, for *The Works of Lord Byron ...*, 1832–4 (R. 427); the plate was used again for Finden's *Landscape Illustrations ... of Lord Byron,* 1833–4
Prov.: J. E. Taylor; A. A. Allen; sale Christie 19 March 1968 (106), bt. Hazlitt, Gooden and Fox; Oscar & Peter Johnson
Private collection

First publ. as title-vignette to vol. XV.

1232   Cologne *c.* 1832

Watercolour, 229 × 190, vignette
Engr.: by E. Finden, 1833, for *The Works of Lod Byron ...*, 1832–4 (R. 428); the plate was used again for Finden's *Landscape Illustrations ... of Lord Byron,* 1833–4
Prov.: William Leech, sale Christie 21 May 1887 (73), bt. Agnew; T. F. Blackwell; sale Christie 29 November 1946 (68), bt. Mitchell; anon. sale Christie 14 June 1966 (179), bt. Daly; anon. sale Christie 21 November 1978 (80), bt. in
Coll.: Leger Galleries, London

First publ. as frontispiece-vignette to vol. XVI.

1233   St. Sophia, Constantinople *c.* 1832

Watercolour, size unknown, vignette
Engr.: by E. Finden, 1833, for *The Works of Lord Byron ...*, 1832–4 (R. 429); the plate was used again for Finden's *Landscape Illustrations ... of Lord Byron,* 1833–4
Prov.: John Farnworth, sale Christie 18 May 1874 (12), bt. Agnew; Holbrook Gaskell, sale Christie 25 June 1909 (237), bt. Agnew
Private collection

Based on a sketch by C. Barry; first publ. as title-vignette to vol. XVI.

1234   The School of Homer, Scio *c.* 1832

1235   The Castellated Rhine *c.* 1832

Watercolour, 165 × 211, vignette
Engr.: by E. Finden, 1833, for *The Works of Lord Byron ...*, 1832–4 (R. 431); the plate was used again for Finden's *Landscape Illustrations ... of Lord Byron,* 1833–4
Prov.: William Leech, sale Christie 21 May 1887 (72), bt. Sir Donald Currie; by descent to Major F. D. Mirrielees, sale Christie 20 March 1959 (58), bt. Beit
Coll.: Beit Collection, Blessington, Co. Wicklow, Ireland

First publ. as title-vignette to vol. XVII.

XVI(f)   Nos 1236–1263
Designs for Finden's *Landscape Illustrations of the Bible, c.* **1832–1835**

The following twenty-eight drawings are designs made for, or arising out of, a joint commission by the engravers Edward and William Finden, and the publisher John Murray, which Turner probably received in 1832. The Finden brothers wished to publish a series of small plates showing biblical scenery, after a number of artists, including Clarkson Stanfield, James Duffield Harding and Sir Augustus Wall Callcott. Their views were based on studies made on the spot in the Middle East by various hands, notably the architect Sir Charles Barry, who had travelled in the Levant between 1817 and 1820. Turner made outline tracings of the sketches that he was to use for his subjects; these belonged to Mr. C. W. M. Turner, but are now untraced. The plates (R. 572–597) were first issued in parts; later they appeared in Murray's two-volume edition of *The Biblical Keepsake, or Landscape Illustrations of the Most Remarkable Places mentioned in The Holy Scriptures ... with descriptions of the Plates by the Rev. Thomas*

Hartwell Horne, B. D., 1835–6. This was advertised as being sold also by Charles Tilt, who had published three replicas of Turner's views for *The Provincial Antiquities of Scotland* in 1834 (R. 557–559; see Nos 1059, 1065, 1067).

1236   Mount Moriah   1832–4

Watercolour, 152 × 202
Engr.: by E. Finden, 1834, for Finden's *Bible*, 1835–6 (R. 572)
Prov.: Wyatt, sale Christie 13 May 1869 (288), bt. McLean; Murrieta, sale Christie 2 May 1892 (312), bt. Sir Donald Currie; by descent to present owner
Private collection, U.K.

Based on a drawing by Charles Barry.

1237   Red Sea and Suez   1832–4

Watercolour, 140 × 202
Engr.: by E. Finden, 1835, for Finden's *Bible*, 1835–6 (R. 573)
Prov.: Albert Levy, sale Christie 1 April 1876 (272), bt. Sir Donald Currie; by descent to present owner
Private collection, U.K.

Based on a drawing by J. G. Wilkinson.

1238   Mount Sinai, the Valley in which the Children of Israel were Encamped 1832–4

Watercolour, 127 × 202
Engr.: by J. B. Allen, 1834, for Finden's *Bible*, 1835–6 (R. 574)
Prov.: George Hibbert, sale Christie 2 May 1860 (347), bt. Agnew; Thomas Plint, sale Christie 7 March 1862 (184), bt. Vokins; G. W. Moss, by 1868, sale Christie 28 April 1900 (119), bt. Barnet Lewis; sale Christie 28 February 1930 (55), bt. Agnew
Coll.: untraced

Based on a drawing by H. Gally Knight, whose sketch of the Temple of Jupiter Panhellenius on Ægina, of 1810, had supplied Turner with the subject of his painting of the temple, R.A. 1816 (P134).

1239   The Desert of Sinai   1832–4

Watercolour, 140 × 202
Engr.: by E. Finden, 1834, for Finden's *Bible*, 1835–6 (R. 575)
Prov.: ? anon. sale, Foster 19 November 1860

(118), ? bt. in; Albert Levy, sale Christie 1 April 1876 (273), bt. Agnew; Agnew, 1919; Mrs. K. M. Dampier-Bennett, sale Sotheby 18 June 1970 (96), bt. Leger
Private collection, England

Based on a drawing by Major Felix.

1240   Jericho   1832–4

Watercolour over pencil, with pen and some scraping-out, 122 × 198
Engr.: by W. Finden, 1835, for Finden's *Bible*, 1835–6 (R. 576)
Prov.: John Ruskin, who gave it to J. F. Lewis, 1858; returned by him to Ruskin, 1859, by whom presented to the University of Oxford, 1861
Coll.: Visitors of the Ashmolean Museum, Oxford (Herrmann 55)

Based on a drawing by Revd. R. Master.

1241   The Dead Sea   1832–4

Watercolour, 127 × 202
Engr.: by E. Finden, 1834, for Finden's *Bible*, 1835–6 (R. 577)
Prov.: John Heugh; G. W. Moss, by 1868, sale Christie 28 April 1900 (118), bt. Barnet Lewis, sale Christie 28 February 1930 (56), bt. Agnew
Coll.: untraced

Based on a drawing by Revd. R. Master.

1242   The Wilderness of Engedi and the Convent of Santa Saba   1832–4

Watercolour, 127 × 202
Engr.: by J. B. Allen, 1834, for Finden's *Bible*, 1835–6 (R. 578)
Prov.: R. B. Preston by 1857; Mrs. E. L. Berthon, sale Christie 15 May 1891 (112), bt. Vokins; Sir Donald Currie; by descent to present owner
Private collection

Based on a drawing by Charles Barry.

1243   Joppa   1832–4

Watercolour, 121 × 203
Engr.: by E. Finden, 1834, for Finden's *Bible*, 1835–6 (R. 579)
Prov.: Albert Levy, sale Christie 1 April 1876 (274), bt. Sir Donald Currie; by descent to present owner
Private collection

Based on a drawing by Sir A. Edmonstone.

1244   Jerusalem: Solomon's Pools *c.* 1832–4

Watercolour, 142 × 206
Engr.: by J. Stephenson, 1834, for Finden's *Bible*, 1835–6 (R. 580)
Prov.: John Ruskin, who gave it to J. F. Lewis, 1858, returned by him to Ruskin, 1859, by whom presented to the museum, 1861
Coll.: Syndics of the Fitzwilliam Museum, Cambridge (575; Cormack 33)

Based on a drawing by Charles Barry.

1245 Ramah and Rachel's Tomb 1832–4

Watercolour and body-colour, 140 × 197
Engr.: by W. Finden, 1835, for Finden's *Bible*,
1835–6 (R. 581)
Prov.: William Quilter, sale Christie 9 April 1875
(232), bt. Permain; E.L. Hartley, by whom
bequeathed to the museum, 1954
Coll.: Museum and Art Gallery, Blackburn, Lancashire (566)

Based on a drawing by Sir A. Edmonstone.

1246 Babylon 1832–4

Watercolour, 140 × 202
Engr.: by J. Cousen, 1834, for Finden's *Bible*,
1835–6 (R. 582)
Prov.: Henry Vaughan, by whom bequeathed to the
museum, 1900
Coll.: Victoria and Albert Museum, London
(982–1900)

Based on a drawing by Sir Robert Ker Porter.

1247 Egypt: the Pyramids of Gizeh 1832–4

Watercolour, 137 × 210

Engr.: by E. Finden, 1836, for Finden's *Bible*,
1835–6 (R. 583)
Prov.: John Dillon, sale Foster 7 June 1856 (138);
Earl of Effingham, sale Christie 11 October 1957
(10), bt. Kurt Pantzer, by whom given to the
museum
Coll.: Indianapolis Museum of Art

Based on a drawing by Charles Barry. A larger
drawing of 'The Pyramids' (210 × 276) was
executed by Turner for Fawkes as a frontispiece to
his 'Chronology of Ancient History'; this was sold in
1890 and subsequently belonged to Sir R. Hardy
(see Armstrong, p. 272).

**1248 Mount Lebanon and the Convent of
St Antonio** 1832–4

Watercolour over pencil, with some pen,
146 × 200
Engr.: by W. Finden, 1834, for Finden's *Bible*,
1835–6 (R. 584)
Prov.: Charles Stokes; Hannah Cooper, from whom
purchased by John Ruskin, by whom presented to
the University of Oxford, 1861
Coll.: Visitors of the Ashmolean Museum, Oxford
(Herrmann 54)

Based on a drawing by Charles Barry.

1249 Nineveh, Moussul on the Tigris
c. 1832–4

Watercolour, 127 × 202
Engr.: by W. Radclyffe, 1835, for Finden's *Bible*,
1835–6 (R. 585)
Provenance and whereabouts unknown

Based on a drawing by C.J. Rich.

1250 Lebanon from Tripoli 1832–4

Watercolour, 140 × 202
Engr.: by E. Finden, 1835, for Finden's *Bible*,
1835–6 (R. 586)
Prov.: ? James Wadmore, by 1862; John Morley,
sale Christie 16 May 1896 (22), bt. Agnew;
? Leonard Brassey, sale Christie 20 February 1904
(120, as 'A town on the Bosphorus'), bt. Vokins
Coll.: untraced

Based on a drawing by Charles Barry. Wadmore
contributed a view of 'Tripoli and Mount Lebanon'
to the International Exhibition of 1862, but the
drawing sold by him at Christie, 5 June 1863 (101)
as 'Lebanon in a Thunderstorm' does not seem to
be the same subject. This may have been No. 1263
below.

1251 Jerusalem from the Mount of Olives
c. 1832–4

Watercolour, 134 × 203 (sight)
Engr.: by J.B. Allen, 1835, for Finden's *Bible*,
1835–6 (R. 587)
Prov.: ? Wyatt, sale Christie 13 May 1869 (189),
bt. Hall; Lady Battersea; Ellen, Countess of Hard-
wicke, sale Sotheby 24 February 1937 (16), bt.
Fine Art Society, London; Professor E. Harold
Hughes; by descent to present owner
Private collection

Based on a drawing by Charles Barry. For the
provenance of a drawing or drawings of Jerusalem
see No. 1254 below.

1252 Bethlehem 1832–4

Watercolour, 114 × 181
Engr.: by E. Finden, 1836, for Finden's *Bible*,
1835–6 (R. 588)
Prov.: Emil Reiss; anon. sale Christie 12 December
1913 (111), bt. Agnew; anon. sale Sotheby
29 July 1953 (20), bt. Humphrey
Coll.: untraced

Based on drawings by Charles Barry and Revd.
R. Master.

1253 Nazareth 1832–4

Watercolour, 127 × 202
Engr.: by E. Finden, 1834, for Finden's *Bible*,
1835–6 (R. 589)
Prov.: John Dillon, sale Foster 7 June 1856
(139); A.W. Foster; Sampson
Private collection, Montreal

Based on a drawing by Charles Barry.

1254 Jerusalem, with the Walls 1832–4

Watercolour, 127 × 202
Engr.: by W. Finden, 1834, for Finden's *Bible*,
1835–6 (R. 590)

Prov.: ? Wyatt, sale Christie 13 May 1869 (289), bt. Hall; Myles Kennedy, sale Christie 16 March 1889 (48), bt. Agnew; C. S. Hayne, sale Christie 16 April 1904 (39), bt. Permain; Barnet Lewis, sale Christie 28 February 1930 (52), bt. Agnew; Frost & Reed, 1931; Major Cecil M. Wills; anon. sale Christie 23 May 1952 (75), bt. Cain; S. A. Cave, sale Christie 25 May 1961 (107), bt. Tishoff
Coll.: untraced

Based on a drawing by Charles Barry. The provenance given for this drawing brings together several sales of a drawing or drawings referred to as 'Jerusalem', apparently not the subject drawn for Scott (No. 1100), but not necessarily the view of Jerusalem from the north-west catalogued here. Armstrong lists six of the Bible subjects under the title 'Jerusalem' (p. 259), Finberg (Index) gives seven; but the others are of particular spots or from particular viewpoints; this is the only design which one might expect to find referred to simply as 'Jerusalem'.

1255   Jerusalem, Pool of Bethesda   1832–4

Watercolour, 133 × 202
Engr.: by E. Finden, 1834, for Finden's *Bible*, 1835–6 (R. 591)
Prov.: John Ruskin; Arthur Severn
Coll.: untraced

Based on a drawing by Charles Barry.

1256   Valley of the Brook Kedron   1832–4

Watercolour, 140 × 203
Engr.: by E. Finden, 1836, for Finden's *Bible*, 1835–6 (R. 592)
Prov.: John Morley, sale Christie 16 May 1896 (25, as 'Absolom's Tomb'), bt. Agnew; G. P. Dewhurst; Agnew 1916; Mark Fletcher, by order of Executors, sale Sotheby 30 November 1960 (56), bt. Agnew
Private collection

Based on a drawing by Charles Barry. One of the subjects often referred to as 'Jerusalem' (see No. 1254 above), this design is commonly known as 'Absolom's Tomb'.

1257   Corinth, Cenchrea   1832–4

Watercolour, size unknown
Engr.: by E. Finden, 1836, for Finden's *Bible*, 1835–6 (R. 593)
Prov.: George Hibbert, sale Christie 2 May 1860 (215), bt. Gambart; John Ruskin, by whom given to Arthur Severn
Coll.: untraced

Based on a drawing by Charles Robert Cockerell. A drawing of 'Corinth', measuring 203 × 267 (larger than this series), was in the collection of William Lee, sale Christie 22 June 1888 (363), bt. Tooth.

1258   Assos   1832–4

Watercolour, 140 × 205
Engr.: by W. Finden, 1834, for Finden's *Bible*, 1835–6 (R. 594)
Prov.: Henry Vaughan, by whom bequeathed to the gallery, 1900
Coll.: National Gallery of Ireland, Dublin (2424)

Based on a drawing by Charles Barry. A weaker version of this subject is No. 1262 below.

1259   Rhodes   1832–4

Watercolour, 127 × 211
Engr.: by S. Fisher, 1835, for Finden's *Bible*, 1835–6 (R. 595)
Prov.: John Ruskin; Mozley, sale Christie 27 May 1865 (182), ? bt. in; J. Leigh Clare, sale Christie 28 March 1868 (101), bt. Cox
Coll.: untraced

Based on a drawing by Charles Barry.

1260   Sidon   1832–4

Watercolour, 127 × 202
Engr.: by W. Finden, 1834, for Finden's *Bible*, 1835–6 (R. 596)
Prov.: ? James Wadmore, sale Christie 5 June 1863 (101, as 'Lebanon in Thunderstorm'), bt. Wallis; Birket Foster, sale Christie 28 April 1894 (43), bt. Wallis
Coll.: untraced

Based on a drawing by Charles Barry. The drawing is stated by Armstrong (p. 277) to be that sold from the Wadmore collection in 1863, but it is likely that the title 'Lebanon in Thunderstorm' is that of an unpublished view of Lebanon (see No. 1263 below). Rawlinson (vol. II, R. 596) refers to 'a small vignette replica', 108 × 70, of Sidon, with 'several variations in details'. He cites no collection, and there is no other record of the drawing.

1261   Jerusalem, from the Latin Convent   1832–3

Watercolour, 127 × 202
Engr.: by E. Finden, 1833, for Finden's *Bible*, 1835–6 (R. 597) but not used

Prov.: Lady Mayer; by descent to present owner
Private collection, London

Based on a drawing by Charles Barry. See No. 1254 above for comment on the Jerusalem subjects in the sales.

1262   Assos   c. 1835

Watercolour, 133 × 202
Prov.: E. L. Hartley, by whom bequeathed to the museum, 1954
Coll.: Museum and Art Gallery, Blackburn, Lancashire

A somewhat perfunctory replica of the design made for Finden's *Bible*, No. 1258 above.

1263   The Cedars of Lebanon   1832–4

Watercolour and scraping-out, 130 × 203
Prov.: James Wadmore, sale Christie 5 June 1863 (101, as 'Lebanon in Thunderstorm'), bt. Wallis; Myles Kennedy, sale Christie 16 March 1889 (49); Arthur Samuel
Coll.: Richard Nathanson, London

Evidently an unused design for Finden's *Bible*. For comment on the Wadmore provenance see *Sidon*, No. 1260 above.

XVI(g)   Nos 1264–1270
Illustrations to Milton's *Poetical Works*, c. 1834

Seven designs that Turner made for vignettes illustrating an edition of Milton's *Poetical Works* published by John Macrone in 1835, which is also the year in which all the engravings were completed.

1264 Mustering of the Warrior Angels *c.* 1834

Watercolour, size unknown, vignette
Engr.: by R. Brandard, 1835, for Milton's *Poetical Works,* 1835 (R. 598)
Prov.: H. A. J. Munro of Novar, sale Christie 2 June 1877 (27), bt. Bromley (?Bromley-Davenport); W. Bromley-Davenport, sale Christie 13 May 1878 (118), bt. in; Agnew, 1928; Mrs. A. E. Clapham
Coll.: untraced

An illustration to 'Paradise Lost', Book V.

1265 The Fall of the Rebel Angels *c.* 1834

Watercolour, size unknown, vignette
Engr.: by E. Goodall, 1835, for Milton's *Poetical Works,* 1835 (R. 599)
Prov.: H. A. J. Munro of Novar, sale Christie 2 June 1877 (28), bt. Bromley (?Bromley-Davenport); W. Bromley-Davenport, sale Christie 13 May 1878 (119), bt. in; George Harwood
Coll.: untraced

An illustration to 'Paradise Lost', Book VI.

1266 The Expulsion from Paradise *c.* 1834

Watercolour, 193 × 140, vignette
Engr.: by E. Goodall, 1835, for Milton's *Poetical Works,* 1835 (R. 600)
Prov.: H. A. J. Munro of Novar, sale Christie 2 June 1877 (26), bt. George Boulton; sale Christie 13 December 1902 (43), bt. McLean; Sir Donald Currie; by descent to present owner
Private collection

An illustration to 'Paradise Lost', Book XI.

1268 The Temptation on the Pinnacle *c.* 1834

Watercolour, 193 × 140, vignette
Engr.: by F. Bacon, 1835, for Milton's *Poetical Works,* 1835 (R. 602)
Prov.: H. A. J. Munro of Novar, sale Christie 2 June 1877 (30), bt. Bromley (?Bromley-Davenport); George Gurney, sale Christie 17 March 1883 (193), bt. in; sale Christie 11 July 1903 (43), bt. Agnew; J. E. Taylor; J. E. T. Allen; by descent to present owner
Private collection

An illustration to 'Paradise Regained', Book IV.

1267 The Temptation of Christ on the Mountain *c.* 1834

Watercolour, 193 × 140, vignette
Engr.: by J. Cousen, 1835, for Milton's *Poetical Works,* 1835 (R. 601)
Prov.: H. A. J. Munro of Novar, sale Christie 2 June 1877 (29), bt. Agnew; A. T. Hollingsworth, sale Christie 11 March 1882 (74), bt. in; S. Sandars; H. L. Fison
Coll.: Mrs. E. A. G. Manton, New York

An illustration to 'Paradise Regained', Book III.

1269 St. Michael's Mount—Shipwreck of Lycidas *c.* 1834

Watercolour, 199 × 148, vignette
Engr.: by W. Miller, 1835, for Milton's *Poetical Works,* 1835 (R. 603)
Prov.: H. A. J. Munro of Novar, sale Christie 2 June 1877 (31), bt. Bromley (?Bromley-Davenport); George Gurney, sale Christie 17 March 1883 (198), bt. in; sale Christie 11 July 1903 (42), bt. Agnew; Charles P. Taft
Coll.: Taft Museum, Cincinnati, Ohio (1931.384.77)

An illustration to 'Lycidas'.

1270 Ludlow Castle—Rising of the Water Nymphs *c.* 1834

Watercolour, size unknown, vignette
Engr.: by E. Goodall, 1835, for Milton's *Poetical Works,* 1835 (R. 604)
Prov.: H. A. J. Munro of Novar, sale Christie 2 June 1877 (32), bt. George Gurney; sale Christie 17 March 1883 (197), bt. Agnew; Mrs. Ismay, sale Christie 4 April 1908 (24), bt. Sampson; Sir Charles Wakefield, sale Christie 30 June 1911 (29), bt. Agnew; Scott & Fowles, New York
Coll.: untraced

An illustration to 'Comus'.

XVI(h) Nos 1271–1290
Illustrations to the poems of Thomas Campbell, *c.* 1835

Twenty illustrations to an edition of the poetical works of Thomas Campbell were published by Edward Moxon. By the original agreement Turner was to receive £30 each for the designs; these, according to one account (Frederick Goodall, *Reminiscences,* 1902, p. 44), were to be engraved by Edward Goodall, who contracted with Moxon to share costs and profits equally, but who was dissatisfied with the agreement he had signed. He tried to persuade Turner to withdraw his designs, but Turner replied: 'You ask me too much—see what a sum I lose!' When he eventually allowed himself to be persuaded, he said, 'This is the greatest act of generosity I have ever done in my life.' Finally, however, he made the drawings, which were loaned to Moxon at £5 each, and returned to the artist, who kept them until his death. Another story states that Campbell became the possessor of the drawings and that, being short of money, he wished to sell them. In about 1842 Turner met him by chance and offered to purchase them from him which he duly did. This account seems to chime more accurately with Turner's character (see Finberg, *Life,* p. 391).

1271 Summer Eve—the Rainbow *c.* 1835

Watercolour, 130 × 130, vignette
Sig. lower right: *JMW Turner RA*
Engr.: by E. Goodall for Campbell's *Poetical Works,* 1837 (R. 613)
Prov.: Thomas Campbell; J. M. W. Turner; Sir Donald Currie; by descent to present owner

On loan to the National Galleries of Scotland, Edinburgh, from Mrs. M. D. Fergusson

An illustration to 'The Pleasures of Hope', p. 1.

1272   The Andes Coast *c.* 1835

Watercolour, 120 × 110, vignette
Sig. lower right: *JMW Turner RA*
Engr.: by E. Goodall for Campbell's *Poetical Works,* 1837 (R. 614)
Prov.: Thomas Campbell; J. M. W. Turner; Sir Donald Currie; by descent to the present owner
On loan to the National Galleries of Scotland, Edinburgh, from Mrs. M. D. Fergusson

An illustration to 'The Pleasures of Hope', p. 3.

1274   Sinai's Thunder *c.* 1835

Watercolour, 130 × 100, vignette
Inscr. below: *Like Sinai's Thunder, pealing from the cloud/Pleasures of Hope*
Engr.: by E. Goodall for Campbell's *Poetical Works,* 1837 (R. 616)
Prov.: Thomas Campbell; J. M. W. Turner; Sir Donald Currie; by descent to present owner
On loan to the National Galleries of Scotland, Edinburgh, from Mrs. M. D. Fergusson

An illustration to 'The Pleasures of Hope', p. 31.

1276   O'Connor's Child *c.* 1835

Watercolour, 130 × 100, vignette
Inscr. below: *A bolt that overhung our dome/ O'Connor's Child*
Engr.: by E. Goodall for Campbell's *Poetical Works,* 1837 (R. 618)
Prov.: Thomas Campbell; J. M. W. Turner; Sir Donald Currie; by descent to present owner
On loan to the National Galleries of Scotland, Edinburgh, from Mrs. M. D. Fergusson

An illustration to 'O'Connor's Child, or the Flower of Love Lies Bleeding', p. 66.

1273   Prague—Kosciusko *c.* 1835

Watercolour, 120 × 120, vignette
Inscr. lower right: *KOSCISKO* [sic]
below: *The sun went down, nor ceased the carnage there/ Pleasures of Hope*
Engr.: by E. Goodall for Campbell's *Poetical Works,* 1837 (R. 615)
Prov.: Thomas Campbell; J. M. W. Turner; Sir Donald Currie; by descent to present owner
On loan to the National Galleries of Scotland, Edinburgh, from Mrs. M. D. Fergusson

An illustration to 'The Pleasures of Hope', p. 14.

1275   A Swiss Valley *c.* 1835

Watercolour, 150 × 120, vignette
Inscr. lower centre (on stone): *JULIA;* below: *Twas Sunset,/Theodric*
Engr.: by E. Goodall for Campbell's *Poetical Works,* 1837 (R. 617)
Prov.: Thomas Campbell; J. M. W. Turner; Sir Donald Currie; by descent to present owner
On loan to the National Galleries of Scotland, Edinburgh, from Mrs. M. D. Fergusson

An illustration to 'Theodric', p. 39.

1277   Lochiel's Warning *c.* 1835

Watercolour, 150 × 130, vignette
Engr.: by E. Goodall for Campbell's *Poetical Works,* 1837 (R. 619)
Prov.: Thomas Campbell; J. M. W. Turner; Sir Donald Currie; by descent to present owner
On loan to the National Galleries of Scotland, Edinburgh, from Mrs. M. D. Fergusson

An illustration to 'Lochiel's Warning', p. 77.

1278   Battle of the Baltic *c.* 1835

Watercolour, with some pen over traces of pencil,
150 × 130, vignette
Engr.: by E. Goodall for Campbell's *Poetical Works*,
1837 (R. 620)
Exh.: R.A. 1974 (293)
Prov.: Thomas Campbell; J. M. W. Turner; Sir
Donald Currie; by descent to present owner
On loan to the National Galleries of Scotland,
Edinburgh, from Mrs. M. D. Fergusson

An illustration to 'Battle of the Baltic', p. 81.

1280   Lord Ullin's Daughter *c.* 1835

Watercolour, 120 × 100, vignette
Inscr. below: *And by my word! the bonny bird/In
danger shall not tarry/So though the waves are
raging white/Ill row you o'er the ferry*
*By this the storm grew loud apace/The water wraith
was shrieking/And in the scowl of heaven each
face/Grew dark as they were speaking/Lord Ullin's
Daughter*
Engr.: by R. Wallis for Campbell's *Poetical Works*,
1837 (R. 622)
Prov.: Thomas Campbell; J. M. W. Turner; Sir
Donald Currie; by descent to present owner
On loan to the National Galleries of Scotland,
Edinburgh, from Mrs. M. D. Fergusson

An illustration to 'Lord Ullin's Daughter', p. 92.

1282   The Last Man *c.* 1835

Watercolour, 120 × 90, vignette
Inscr. below: *Evn I am weary in yon skies/to watch
thy fading fire/Test of all sumless agonies/Behold
not me expire*
Engr.: by E. Goodall for Campbell's *Poetical Works*,
1837 (R. 624)
Prov.: Thomas Campbell; J. M. W. Turner; Sir
Donald Currie; by descent to present owner
On loan to the National Galleries of Scotland,
Edinburgh, from Mrs. M. D. Fergusson

An illustration to 'The Last Man', p. 104.

1279   Hohenlinden *c.* 1835

Watercolour, 150 × 100, vignette
Inscr. below: *But redder yet that light shall glow/On
Linden's hills of staned snow/And bloodier yet the
torrent flow/Of Iser rolling rapidly*
*'Tis morn, but scarce yon level sun/Can pierce the
war-clouds roling [sic] dun/Where furious Frank and
fiery Hun/Shout in their sulphrous canopy*
Engr.: by R. Wallis for Campbell's *Poetical Works*,
1837 (R. 621)
Prov.: Thomas Campbell; J. M. W. Turner; Sir
Donald Currie; by descent to present owner
On loan to the National Galleries of Scotland,
Edinburgh, from Mrs. M. D. Fergusson

An illustration to 'Hohenlinden', p. 87.

1281   The Soldier's Dream *c.* 1835

Watercolour, 120 × 80, vignette
Inscr. below: *I dremt [sic] of the pleasant fields
traversed so oft/in lifes morning march when my
bosom was young*
Engr.: by E. Goodall for Campbell's *Poetical Works*,
1837 (R. 623)
Prov.: Thomas Campbell; J. M. W. Turner; Sir
Donald Currie; by descent to present owner
On loan to the National Galleries of Scotland,
Edinburgh, from Mrs. M. D. Fergusson

An illustration to 'The Soldier's Dream', p. 100.

1283   Gertrude   of   Wyoming—the   Valley
c. 1835

Watercolour, 140 × 110, vignette
Engr.: by E. Goodall for Campbell's *Poetical Works*,
1837 (R. 625)
Prov.: Thomas Campbell; J. M. W. Turner; Sir
Donald Currie; by descent to present owner
On loan to the National Galleries of Scotland,
Edinburgh, from Mrs. M. D. Fergusson

An illustration to 'Gertrude of Wyoming', Part I,
p. 115.

1284 Gertrude of Wyoming—the Waterfall
*c.*1835

Watercolour, 130 × 120, vignette
Inscr. below: *It was in this lone Valey [sic] she would charm/The lingering noon where flowers a couch had strown/Gertrude of Wyoming*
Engr.: by E. Goodall for Campbell's *Poetical Works,* 1837 (R. 626)
Prov.: Thomas Campbell; J. M. W. Turner; Sir Donald Currie; by descent to present owner
On loan to the National Galleries of Scotland, Edinburgh, from Mrs. M. D. Fergusson

An illustration to 'Gertrude of Wyoming', Part II, p. 129.

1285 Rolandseck *c.*1835

Watercolour, 120 × 100, vignette
Inscr. below: *The Brave Roland/ But why so rash has she taken the veil/In yon Nonenwerden's cloister, pale/Theres one window yet of that pile/He built above the nun's green isle/When the chant and organ sounded slow/On the mansion of his love below/for herself he might not see*
Engr.: by E. Goodall for Campbell's *Poetical Works,* 1837 (R. 627)
Prov.: Thomas Campbell; J. M. W. Turner; Sir Donald Currie; by descent to present owner

On loan to the National Galleries of Scotland, Edinburgh, from Mrs. M. D. Fergusson

An illustration to 'The Brave Roland', p. 170.

1286 The Beech Tree's Petition *c.*1835

Watercolour, 130 × 110, vignette
Inscr. above *The Beech tree's Petition;* below: *Carved many a long forgotten name/Spare woodman spare the beechen tree*
Engr.: by E. Goodall for Campbell's *Poetical Works,* 1837 (R. 628)
Prov.: Thomas Campbell; J. M. W. Turner; Sir Donald Currie; by descent to present owner
On loan to the National Galleries of Scotland, Edinburgh, from Mrs. M. D. Fergusson

An illustration to 'The Beech Tree's Petition', p. 203.

1287 Camp Hill, Hastings *c.*1835

Watercolour, 140 × 130, vignette
Inscr. below: *Oer Hauberk and helm/As the sun's setting splendour was thrown/Thence th[e]y looked o'er a realm/And tomorrow beheld it their own*
Engr.: by E. Goodall for Campbell's *Poetical Works,* 1837 (R. 629)
Exh.: R.A. 1974 (294)

Prov.: Thomas Campbell; J. M. W. Turner; Sir Donald Currie; by descent to present owner
On loan to the National Galleries of Scotland, Edinburgh, from Mrs. M. D. Fergusson

An illustration to 'Lines on the Camp Hill, near Hastings', p. 216.

1288 The Death-Boat of Heligoland *c.*1835

Watercolour, 130 × 120, vignette
Inscr. below: *But her beams on a sudden grew sick-like and grey/And the mews that had slept clangd and shrieked far away/The Death Boat of Heligoland*
Engr.: by E. Goodall for Campbell's *Poetical Works,* 1837 (R. 630)
Prov.: Thomas Campbell; J. M. W. Turner; Sir Donald Currie; by descent to present owner
On loan to the National Galleries of Scotland, Edinburgh, from Mrs. M. D. Fergusson

An illustration to 'The Death-Boat of Heligoland', p. 237.

1289 Ehrenbreitstein *c.*1835

Watercolour, 130 × 120, vignette

Inscr. below: *Whilst your Broad Stone of Honour/ Ode to the Germans*
Engr.: by E. Goodall for Campbell's *Poetical Works*, 1837 (R. 631)
Prov.: Thomas Campbell; J. M. W. Turner; Sir Donald Currie; by descent to present owner
On loan to the National Galleries of Scotland, Edinburgh, from Mrs. M. D. Fergusson

An illustration to 'Ode to the Germans', p. 254.

1291 Part of the Ghaut at Hurdwar *c.* 1835

Watercolour, 140 × 211, the sheet made up with added strips at top and right
Engr.: by T. Higham, 1836, for *Views in India*, 1838 (R. 606)
Exh.: R.A. 1974 (299)
Prov.: William Wells, sale Christie 12 May 1890 (181), bt. Agnew; purchased from the Bilborough Bequest Fund, 1925
Coll.: City Art Galleries, Leeds (594/25)

In the reprinted edition of White's *Views in India*, 1845, this subject was renamed 'Pilgrims at the Sacred Fair of Hurdwar', under which title it was sold in 1890.

1294 View near Jubberah *c.* 1835

Watercolour, 127 × 203
Engr.: by J. Cousen, 1836, for *Views in India*, 1838 (R. 609)
Prov.: Mrs. R. B. Dodgson, by whom bequeathed to the museum, 1884
Coll.: Museum and Art Gallery, Blackburn, Lancashire (37)

1290 The Dead Eagle—Oran *c.* 1835

Watercolour, 120 × 100, vignette
Inscr. below: *Fallen as he is, this king of birds still seems/Like royalty in ruins. Though his eyes/are shut that looked undazzled on the sun/He was the sultan of the sky/The dead Eagle*
Engr.: by W. Miller for Campbell's *Poetical Works*, 1837 (R. 632)
Prov.: Thomas Campbell; J. M. W. Turner; Sir Donald Currie; by descent to present owner
On loan to the National Galleries of Scotland, Edinburgh, from Mrs. M. D. Fergusson

An illustration to 'The Dead Eagle. Written at Oran', p. 263.

1292 Mussooree and the Dhoon from Landour *c.* 1835

Watercolour, 127 × 200
Engr.: by J. B. Allen, 1836, for *Views in India*, 1838 (R. 607)
Prov.: Robert Strauss; Sotheby, 27 July 1960 (73), bt. Fine Art Society, London
Private collection

1293 Snowy Range from Tyne or Marma *c.* 1835

Watercolour, size unknown
Engr.: by E. Goodall, 1836, for *Views in India*, 1838 (R. 608)
Prov.: ? Elhanan Bicknell, sale Christie 25 April 1862 (114 or 115), bt. Vokins; ? Joseph Harrison, sale Christie 2 May 1881 (109 or 110), bt. Agnew or bt. in; S. W. R. Brocklebank
Coll.: untraced

The queried sales refer to drawings catalogued as 'The Himalaya Mountains' or 'Scene in the Himalayas', which have been tentatively identified here with this subject and No. 1296. They could apply almost as well to others in this group.

1295 Falls near the source of the Jumna *c.* 1835

Watercolour, 137 × 202
Engr.: by J. Cousen, 1836, for *Views in India*, 1838 (R. 610)
Prov.: Henry Vaughan, by whom bequeathed to the gallery, 1900
Coll.: National Galleries of Scotland, Edinburgh (862)

XVI(i) Nos 1291–1297
Designs for White's *Views in India*, *c.* 1835

Seven designs that Turner made for Lieut. George Francis White to illustrate White's *Views in India, chiefly among the Himalaya Mountains*. White himself provided sketches which formed the bases of all these watercolours. (In general format Turner followed the precedent of his work for Finden's *Bible* illustrations, Nos 1236–1263.) The first published state of each plate is 1836, with later states dated 1838, in which year the whole work appeared. Another edition was issued in 1845. The history of the drawings is rather obscure; they were evidently dispersed at an early date.

1296 Valley of the Dhoon *c.* 1835

Watercolour, size unknown
Engr.: by W. Floyd, 1836, for *Views in India*, 1838 (R. 611)
Prov.: ? Elhanan Bicknell, sale Christie 25 April 1862 (114 or 115), bt. Vokins; ? Joseph Harrison, sale Christie 2 May 1881 (109 or 110), bt. Agnew or bt. in; S. W. R. Brocklebank
Coll.: untraced

See No. 1293.

1297 Rocks at Colgong on the Ganges *c.* 1835

Watercolour, size unknown
Engr.: by E. Goodall, 1836, for *Views in India*, 1838 (R. 612)
Provenance and whereabouts unknown

XVI(j) Nos 1298–1301
Illustrations to Thomas Moore's *The Epicurean*, *c*.1838

The four vignette designs that Turner made for Moore's poem *The Epicurean* were commissioned probably in the early part of 1837. The poem had first appeared in 1827; the new edition, with vignettes, was published by John Macrone in 1839. Moore stated in an introduction that 'The idea of calling in the magic pencil of Mr. Turner, to illustrate some of the scenes of the following story, was first suggested by the late Mr. Macrone … His original wish had been that I should undertake for him some new poem, or story, to be thus embellished by the artist. But other tasks and ties having rendered my compliance with this wish impracticable, he proposed to purchase of me the copyright of the Epicurean, for a single ''illustrated'' edition; and hence the appearance of the work under its present new auspices and format.' Turner made a number of designs for this project, several of them brought to a high degree of finish, apart from the small group that were finally engraved by Goodall. These studies are in the artist's bequest, T.B., CCLXXX, 113–138 (two of them repr. B.M. 1975, 214, 215). None of the final designs is now traced.

1298 The Garden *c*.1838

Watercolour, size unknown, vignette
Engr.: by E. Goodall for Moore's *Epicurean,* 1839 (R. 634)
Prov.: H. A. J. Munro of Novar, sale Christie 2 June 1877 (25), bt. Agnew; Mrs. Prater, sale Christie 9 May 1879 (88, as 'Moors'; the identification is not certain), bt. in; Mrs. Prater, sale Christie 9 April 1880 (95), bt. White
Coll.: untraced

Published as the frontispiece.

1299 The Ring *c*.1838

Watercolour, size unknown, vignette
Engr.: by E. Goodall for Moore's *Epicurean,* 1839 (R. 635)
Prov.: H. A. J. Munro of Novar, sale 2 June 1877 (23), bt. Metzler; anon. sale Christie 29 May 1908 (421), bt. Betts; anon. sale Christie 27 March 1909 (81), bt. Knity
Coll.: untraced

Published on p. 58.

1300 The Nile *c*.1838

Watercolour, size unknown, vignette
Engr.: by E. Goodall for Moore's *Epicurean,* 1839 (R. 636)
Prov.: H. A. J. Munro of Novar, sale Christie 6 April 1878 (74, as 'Moonlight on the Rhine'), bt. Agnew; Fowler, 1899
Coll.: untraced

Published on p. 148.

1301 The Chaplet *c*. 1838

Watercolour, size unknown, vignette
Engr.: by E. Goodall for Moore's *Epicurean,* 1839 (R. 637)
Prov.: H. A. J. Munro of Novar, sale Christie 2 June 1877 (24), bt. Fine Art Publishing Co., London
Coll.: untraced

Published on p. 206.
A study for this subject, considerably different from the engraved design, is T.B., CCLXXX–138.

XVI(k) Nos 1302–1314
Miscellaneous designs for illustrations, *c*.1835–1840

Many of these drawings were not engraved. Those that were appeared as individual items; but some may have belonged to sets or groups related to particular works of literature.

1302 Greatheart conducted through the River *c*.1835

Watercolour, size unknown, vignette
Engr.: by E. Goodall for Fisher's *Pilgrim's Progress,* 1836 (R. 605)
Provenance and whereabouts unknown

Turner's design was first published as frontispiece to Fisher's 1836 edition of Bunyan's *Pilgrim's Progress,* and almost immediately transformed by the addition of an engraved title above the subject into a title-page vignette. It was used as such in a volume of *Illustrations of the Pilgrim's Progress.* This was also issued by Fisher in 1836; it contained a Sonnet on the Vignette Frontispiece which includes the following lines: 'But vain the painter's or the poet's skill,/That heavenly city's glory to declare;–/All such can furnish is a vision fair,/And gorgeous; having, as its centre still,/His cross who died on Calvary's holy hill;/Man's only title to admittance there.' Turner's subject shows the cross in radiant light, but it is apparently not the same design as that described by Armstrong (p. 271) as 'Vignette. Figure stretching out arms to a cross, lost in blaze of light. Probably Turner's last work for the engraver.' (This subject seems to have been known as 'Faith of Perrin'.) Armstrong dates the drawing to 1840–5, and states that it was engraved by E. Goodall as frontispiece to Fisher's 1847 edition. This is not referred to by Rawlinson. Armstrong says that the drawing belonged to Munro of Novar and E. M. Micholls [*sic*].

The following four designs were engraved for *The Keepsake* between 1835 and 1837. Some of them may have been intended for use in other projects on which Turner was engaged at that time, but none was published elsewhere. The subjects involving ships and the sea may all have been envisaged as contributing to a single work.

1303 The Sea! the Sea! *c*.1835

Watercolour, 184 × 152, vignette
Engr.: by J. T. Willmore, 1836, for *The Keepsake,* 1837 (R. 335)

Prov.: H. A. J. Munro of Novar, sale Christie 6 April 1878 (64), bt. Agnew; William Lea, sale Christie 28 May 1883 (175), bt. in; sale Christie 22 June 1888 (362), bt. Agnew; John Dent, sale Christie 9 April 1892 (142), bt. A. W. Cox
Private collection

Illustrates 'The Sea! the Sea!', an account of an event at sea by Lord Nugent.

1304 The Wreck *c*.1835

Watercolour, 211 × 152, vignette
Engr.: by H. Griffiths, 1835, for *The Keepsake,* 1836 (R. 334)
Prov.: Thomas Plint, sale Christie 7 March 1862 (170), bt. Smith; John Feetham, sale Christie 27 May 1895 (116), bt. Gribble; sale Christie 20 September 1946 (18), bt. Leger; Major Ewing, U.S.A.
Private collection U.S.A.

Illustrates 'The Wreck', a poem by E. Howard.

1305 A fire at sea *c*.1835

Watercolour, size unknown, vignette
Engr.: by J. T. Willmore, 1835, for *The Keepsake,* 1836 (R. 333)

Prov.: John Feetham, sale Christie 27 May 1895 (109), bt. Vokins; Sir Donald Currie; by descent to present owner
Private collection

Illustrates 'A fire at sea', an account of such a happening by Captain Frederic Chamier. Compare the subject of the large painting of about this date, P460.

1306 Destruction of both Houses of Parliament by Fire Oct[r] 16, 1834 *c.* 1835

Watercolour, 140 × 110, vignette
Engr.: by J. T. Willmore, 1835, for *The Keepsake*, 1836 (R. 332)
Prov.: Charles Sackville Bale, sale Christie 14 May 1881 (187), bt. Agnew; Sir Charles Tennant; by descent to present owner
Private collection

Illustrates a poem 'The Burning of the Houses of Lords and Commons' (no author named).

1307 The Great Whale *?c.* 1839

Watercolour, 100 × 143, vignette
Prov.: John Feetham, sale Christie 27 May 1895 (112), bt. H. Quilter; Horace P. Taft
Coll.: Taft Museum, Cincinnati, Ohio (1931.382)

This and the following three drawings may have been intended to illustrate the same work, although they vary considerably in style and in degree of finish. It is possible that the group was not executed on commission but was a project of Turner's own, inspired by his interest in Thomas Beale's *The*

Natural History of the Sperm Whale, 1839, to which his attention may have been drawn, as John Gage suggested (R.A. 1974, p. 189), by his patron, Elhanan Bicknell.

1308 Death of the whale *?c.* 1839

Watercolour and body-colour over pencil, 105 × 70, vignette
Prov.: unknown
Private collection

See comments under No. 1307 above.

1309 Ship and iceberg *?c.* 1839

Watercolour, 140 × 115, vignette
Prov.: J. E. Taylor, sale Christie 8 July 1912 (115 or 116), bt. Agnew; J. E. T. Allen; by descent to present owner
Private collection

See comments under No. 1307 above.

1310 Ship among icebergs *?c.* 1839

Watercolour, 140 × 115, vignette
Prov.: J. E. Taylor, sale Christie 8 July 1912 (115 or 116), bt. Agnew; anon. collection, Germany; Sotheby 1 April 1976 (125), bt. anonymously
Private collection

One of two studies for vignettes from the J. E. Taylor collection; see No. 1309 above, and comments under No. 1307 above.

1311 Lake Nemi *?c.* 1835–40

Watercolour and body-colour over pencil, 185 × 145, vignette
Engr.: by E. Goodall (R. 638) apparently for Dr. Broadley's *Poems* (privately printed *c.* 1844); plate also used for *Art and Song,* 1867
Prov.: Edward Fordham; sale Christie 30 April 1904 (48), bt. McLean; Charles P. Taft
Coll.: Taft Museum, Cincinnati, Ohio (1931.387)

Dr. Broadley's *Poems* are supposed to have been privately printed about 1844 (see Rawlinson, II, pp. 324–5); the six designs engraved for the publication were apparently not made specifically for it; the remainder are catalogued here in their chronologically or thematically appropriate places, Nos 272, 273, 886, 888, 905. This vignette of Lake Nemi is reminiscent in mood and technique of the large watercolour of the same lake, No. 1381.

1312 Classical vignette *?c.* 1835

Watercolour over pencil, 120 × 115, vignette
Prov.: W. Jones, by whom bequeathed to the museum, 1882

Coll.: Victoria and Albert Museum, London (583–1882)

Not published; possibly a design for Moore's *Epicurean*.

1313 Lake Leman ?*c.* 1835–40

Watercolour over pencil, sheet 158 × 237, vignette
Prov.: ?Thomas Greenwood, sale Christie 13 February 1875 (260, as 'Lake Leucan'), bt. Addington; sale Christie 22 May 1886 (54), bt. McGrath; E. H. Van Ingen; Eaton, 1937; Walter J. Noonan, by whom bequeathed to the museum, 1954
Coll.: Museum of Fine Arts, Boston, Mass. (54.1415)

Executed in a coarser, bolder style than the majority of the vignettes, this design does not fall naturally into any of the known series of Turner's illustrations; its authenticity has been doubted, but despite its unusual handling the drawing seems genuine.

1314 Venice* ?*c.* 1835–40

Pencil and watercolour, approx. 145 × 140, vignette
Prov.: Thomas Plint, sale Christie 7 March 1862 (183, as 'Venice—Sunset'), bt. Smith; John Feetham, sale Christie 27 May 1895 (115, as 'Venice—Sunrise'), bt. Gribble; anon. sale Christie 20 September 1946 (17), bt. Leger; Major Ewing, U.S.A.
Private collection, U.S.A.

SECTION XVII
Nos 1315–1381
European subjects (other than Switzerland), *c.* 1833–1844

XVII(a) Nos 1315–1351
German subjects from roll sketchbooks *c.* 1833–1844

Turner travelled frequently in Germany; his four principal tours of the 1830s, those of 1833, 1834, 1835 and 1836, all probably took him along the Rhine, and in either 1833 or 1835, and again in 1840, he certainly explored the Neckar and further east along the Danube. His tour of 1834 included the Meuse and Moselle as well as the Rhine; and that of 1836 may have involved a return journey along the Rhine. Precise itineraries are usually lacking; and exact identifications of many of the drawings have yet to be made. In the 1840s he again travelled frequently along the Rhine, and in 1844, returning from Switzerland, he visited Heidelberg. Stylistic variations are scarcely adequate to allocate the drawings to a clear sequence; but one group, principally of views along the Rhine and Moselle, is in a rather perfunctory style, using thin, pale washes and rough pencil outlines, which suggests a late date; though no journey along the Moselle is recorded for the 1840s. Finberg and others have assumed that Turner must have been there in either 1843 or 1844. Several of the sheets listed below are of a smaller size than the regular roll sketchbook leaf, and they may all belong to one or two books used on a late journey (Nos 1327–1348). A few of them are on a prepared grey ground, unusual at this date, though Turner employed it in 1825, and in views of the Rheinfall at Schaffhausen known to have been made in 1841. In default of firm evidence they have been placed together under a tentative date of 1844. By the 1830s Turner invariably travelled with soft-bound, rollable sketchbooks with sheets measuring about 230 × 300 mm. Most of the studies catalogued from this point on were made in such books.

1315 Valley with poplars and distant castle ?1834

Pen and brown ink, watercolour and scraping-out on paper prepared with a grey wash, 154 × 226
Prov.: Sir Hickman Bacon, Bt.; by descent to the present owner
Private collection

The identification of this view as a scene in Germany is entirely speculative; no definite evidence concerning its location has come to light.

1316 Lake and mountains under a crescent moon ?1834

Pencil, watercolour and body-colour, some touches of pen, on paper prepared with a grey wash, 153 × 224
Prov.: Sir Hickman Bacon, Bt.; by descent to the present owner
Private collection

Like No. 1315 above, this scene is not necessarily a German one.

1317 Passau on the Danube 1840

Watercolour, 241 × 303
Prov.: Henry Vaughan, by whom bequeathed to the gallery, 1900
Coll.: National Gallery of Ireland, Dublin (2418)

Another, rather similar, view of Passau is in the Turner Bequest (T.B., CCCXL–3).

1318 Andernach ?*c.* 1840

Watercolour, 241 × 299
Prov.: ?J. E. Taylor, sale Christie 5 July 1912 (79), bt. Agnew; L. K. Elmhirst; Walter F. Wedgwood
Private collection

1319 Andernach *c.* 1840

Watercolour, 222 × 292
Prov.: J. E. Taylor, Christie 5 July 1912 (79), bt.

Agnew; Sir Stephen Courtauld, by whom given to the university, 1947
Coll.: Fine Arts Collection of the University of Melbourne, Australia

1320   (?) Ehrenbreitstein *c.* 1840

Watercolour, 229 × 280 (sight)
Prov.: J. P. Heseltine; Sotheby 28 June 1944, bt. Willoughby; Sir Thomas Barlow
Coll.: untraced

1321   Ehrenbreitstein and Coblenz* *c.* 1840

Watercolour, 229 × 280
Prov.: Thomas Greenwood, sale Christie 13 February 1875 (255), bt. Tooth; ? J. E. Taylor, sale Christie 5 July 1912 (56), bt. Agnew; Sir Donald Currie; by descent to present owner
Private collection

1322   Ehrenbreitstein and Coblenz *c.* 1841

Watercolour, some pen and brown ink or colour, 229 × 292
Prov.: ? Thomas Greenwood, sale Christie 13 February 1875 (251), bt. Palmer or (269), bt. Noseda; C. F. Huth, sale Christie 6 July 1895 (62), bt. Agnew; J. P. Thompson; Gwendoline E. Davies, by whom bequeathed to the museum, 1952
Coll.: National Museum of Wales, Cardiff (2952)

1323   Coblenz—evening *c.* 1841

Pencil and watercolour, 232 × 287
Prov.: Thomas Greenwood, sale Christie 13 February 1875 (278), bt. Agnew; Sotheby 28 Nov-

ember 1974 (119 as 'Castle on the Moselle'), bt. in; anon. sale, Sotheby 15 July 1976 (73), bt. Agnew
Private collection

Evidently not a view of Coblenz; perhaps a castle on the Rhine or Moselle, it has been suggested that it is Braubach, with the Castle of Marksburg.

1324   Bacharach *c.* 1840

Watercolour and body-colour over pencil on white paper, 184 × 241
Prov.: John Ruskin, by whom given to the museum, 1861
Coll.: Syndics of the Fitzwilliam Museum, Cambridge (581; Cormack 49)

1325   On the Moselle, near Traben Trarbach *c.* 1841

Pencil and watercolour, with scraping-out, 230 × 286
Prov.: Anthony Jakins; Agnew, from whom bt. by Paul Mellon, 1966
Coll.: Yale Center for British Art, Paul Mellon Collection

Stylistically this sheet seems to belong with the finest roll sketchbook Swiss drawings of *c.* 1841; it may be misidentified.

1326   Heidelberg ? 1844

Watercolour, 236 × 295
Prov.: Palser Gallery, 1937; bt. by the Friends of the Fitzwilliam Museum and presented by them, 1937
Coll.: Syndics of the Fitzwilliam Museum, Cambridge (2284; Cormack 51)

1327   A castle in the mountains ? 1844

Pencil and watercolour, 184 × 242
Prov.: Sir Hickman Bacon, Bt.; by descent to the present owner
Private collection

1328   On the Rhine ? 1844

Pencil and watercolour, 184 × 241
Verso: another study on the Rhine, pencil, watercolour and scraping-out on paper prepared with a grey wash, 184 × 241
Prov.: John Ruskin; Mr. Forster, by whom bequeathed to the museum

Coll.: Victoria and Albert Museum, London (103)

1329   On the Rhine: looking over St. Goar to Katz, from Rheinfels   ?1844

Watercolour over pencil, 181 × 237
Prov.: John Ruskin, by whom given to the Ruskin School, Oxford, 1875; transferred to the museum, 1938
Coll.: Visitors of the Ashmolean Museum, Oxford (Herrmann 84)

1330   On the Rhine   ?1844

Watercolour and pencil, 151 × 230
Inscr. centre left: *Luhen* (?)
Prov.: John Ruskin, by whom given to the Ruskin Scholl, Oxford, 1875; transferred to the museum, 1938
Coll.: Visitors of the Ashmolean Museum, Oxford (Herrmann 83)

In view of the similarity of this drawing to the *Dieblich* (No. 1331), it may depict a Moselle view; the inscription may refer to Lehmen, near Cobern.

1331   Dieblich on the Moselle   ?1844

Pencil and watercolour, 156 × 232
Inscr. lower left: *Dib*
Prov.: John Ruskin; ?Agnew 1914; Kurt Pantzer, by whom given to the museum
Coll.: Indianapolis Museum of Art

1332   On the Rhine: the Katz   ?1844

Pencil and watercolour on paper prepared with a grey wash, 183 × 241
Verso: slight pencil sketch
Prov.: Denman W. Ross, by whom given to the museum, 1906
Coll.: Museum of Fine Arts, Boston, Mass. (06.124)

1333   Schloss Eltz on the Moselle   ?1844

Watercolour, pencil and pen and red ink, with some scratching-out on paper prepared with a grey wash, 159 × 232
Prov.: ? anon. sale, Christie 29 May 1908 (468), bt. Ross; Holbrook Gaskell, sale Christie 25 June 1909 (147), bt. Agnew; Walter Jones; Fine Art

Society, London, 1942 (as from the Ruskin collection); Christie, 4 June 1974 (181), bt. Agnew
Private collection

1334   Schloss Eltz   ?1844

Watercolour, pencil, pen and ink and scraping-out on paper prepared with a grey wash, 159 × 229
Prov.: ? J. E. Taylor, sale Christie 5 July 1912 (89), bt. Gibbs; anon. sale Christie 22 November 1977 (146), bt. Agnew
Private collection

1335   Schloss Eltz   ?1844

Pencil, body-colour and scraping-out on paper prepared with a grey wash, 158 × 228
Prov.: Elhanan Bicknell, sale Christie 29 April 1863 (260), bt. Agnew; John Smith, sale Christie 4 May 1870 (51), bt. Agnew; J. E. Taylor, sale Christie 5 July 1912 (89), bt. Gibbs; Mrs. Elmhirst, sale Parke Bernet, New York, 27 May 1942 (185), bt. Victor Spark; Walter Wedgwood; Agnew, 1979
Private collection

1336   'The Yellow Castle', Beilstein on the Moselle   ?1844

Watercolour, with a little scraping-out,
160 × 235
Prov.: John Ruskin; Palser Gallery; Cotswold Gallery, from whom purchased by the Friends of the Fitzwilliam Museum; given by them to the museum, 1933
Coll.: Syndics of the Fitzwilliam Museum, Cambridge (1725; Cormack 34)

From the collection of the late C. E. Hughes

This subject appears to have been known as 'Castle Sooneck'.

1343   Landscape on the Moselle or Rhine ?1844

Watercolour, with some pen, 183 × 242
Prov.: Miss Anne Callwell, by whom bequeathed to the gallery, 1904
Coll.: National Gallery of Ireland, Dublin (3776)

1337   Cochem on the Moselle ?1844

Pencil and watercolour, ?172 × 235
Prov.: ?John Ruskin; Sir J. C. Robinson; T. A. Tatton, sale Christie 14 December 1928 (19), bt. Agnew
Coll.: City Museums and Art Gallery, Birmingham (56.45)

1341   A castle on a river (? the Moselle) ?1844

Watercolour, 152 × 229
Provenance unknown
Private collection

1338   Traben Trarbach on the Moselle ?1844

Pencil and watercolour on cartridge paper, 181 × 240
Prov.: Agnes and Norman Lupton, by whom bequeathed to the gallery, 1953
Coll.: City Art Galleries, Leeds (13.222/53)

1342   St. Goar looking towards St. Goarhausen ?1844

Pencil and watercolour on paper prepared with a grey ground, 178 × 235

1344   Castle of Sonneck on the Rhine ?1844

Pencil and watercolour, 176 × 235
Inscr. lower right (in pencil): *Lorch [?]Sonnebg*
Verso: pencil sketch of a castle on the Rhine
Prov.: John Ruskin, ?sale 15 April 1869 (see lots 24–32); Sir David Young Cameron; E. Proctor Nowell; Ian MacNicol, Glasgow, by whom sold to Fine Art Society, London 1960, from whom bt. Walter Brandt, 1961
Coll.: Trustees of the P. A. Brandt Settlement

1339   A bridge over the Moselle ?1844

Watercolour, 229 × 330
Prov.: Charles E. Lees, and presented by him to the gallery in 1888
Coll.: Art Gallery and Museum, Oldham, Lancashire

1340   A fort on the Moselle or Rhine(?) ?1844

Watercolour on white paper, 148 × 219
Prov.: ?H. Finberg, by whom sold to the Fine Art Society, London, 1942; C. E. Hughes; by descent to present owner

Verso: *Katz* pencil and watercolour inscr.: *Cox at/Katz* (?)
Prov.: Major L. M. E. Dent; Spink, from whom bt. by present owner, 1967
Private collection, England

1345   Ehrenbreitstein ?1844

Pencil and watercolour, 175 × 241
Prov.: J. Pyke Thompson, by whom bequeathed to the museum, 1898
Coll.: National Museum of Wales, Cardiff (3063)

1346   The Mouse Tower   ?1844

Watercolour and pencil, 154 × 222
Prov.: Gwendoline E. Davies, by whom bequeathed to the museum, 1952
Coll.: National Museum of Wales, Cardiff (2958)

1347   Rheinfels   ?1844

Pencil and watercolour, 172 × 229
Prov.: Ronald Horton, sale Sotheby 20 March 1963 (56), bt. Mitchell; Kurt Pantzer, by whom given to the museum
Coll.: Indianapolis Museum of Art

1348   Coblenz   ?1844

Pencil and watercolour, 231 × 292
Inscr. lower right: *Coblenz*
Prov.: Sir Hickman Bacon, Bt.; by descent to the present owner
Private collection

1349   Heidelberg   ?1840

Watercolour and body-colour with pen and ink on grey paper, 175 × 267
Prov.: Sir Donald Currie; Lord Carmichael, 1918; S. L. Courtauld, 1927; Miss Deakin; Capt. R. H. Peters; Agnew, 1973
Private collection

Nos 1349–1351, which use body-colour on sheets of grey paper, are apparently related to a series of drawings in the Turner Bequest which have similar features and dimensions. Many of these are of Venetian subjects: T.B., CCCVII, 1–5, 19–34; others appear to show views on the Rhine and at Botzen—on the route that Turner probably took when he visited Venice in 1840. The three sheets that are not in the Bequest are, however, rather different from these series, and at the same time have much in common with each other. All show a building with an onion-shaped dome and it is possible that they were all made at the same place. Their present titles are not necessarily correct.

1350   View of Locarno   ?1840

Pencil, watercolour and body-colour on grey paper, 182 × 282
Prov.: W. W. Spooner, by whom bequeathed to the institute, 1967
Coll.: Courtauld Institute of Art, University of London (72)

See No. 1349.

1351   Rappersweil   ?1840

Pencil, watercolour and body-colour on grey paper, 187 × 280
Prov.: H. W. Sewening; Mr. Bryce, by whom presented to the nation, and entered the collection 1972
Coll.: National Gallery of Ireland, Dublin (7511)

See No. 1349.

XVII(b)   Nos 1352–1375
Venetian subjects, 1840

No finished watercolours resulted from the visits that Turner made to Venice in the later part of his life, but many Venetian subjects exist on the leaves of roll sketchbooks. The majority are in the Turner Bequest: one complete book (T.B., CCCXV) is watermarked 1834. Loose sheets from similar books are grouped together as T.B., CCXVI, 1–42 (of which pp. 11–15 are on rough, creamy paper as opposed to the usual smooth white Whatman). A further group is on grey paper (T.B., CCCXVII) and another (T.B., CCCXVIII) on brown paper. Several sheets, however, were extracted from the artist's collection and dispersed to various owners, probably through the agency of Thomas Griffith. It is these drawings which are catalogued here.
There is much debate as to the dating of the Venetian watercolours. Armstrong distributed them widely to the periods 1830–5, 1835–40, and 1840–5. Finberg allocated some more precisely to specific visits, in 1835 and 1840, and to years in the early 1840s. It is now reasonably certain that Turner's only visit in the 1830s was made in 1833, which means that the watermarked roll sketchbook must belong to a subsequent visit. Turner's next visit was in 1840, and it is arguable, from the evidence of the roll sketchbook, that all the studies were executed then or shortly afterwards. Despite considerable differences of treatment between individual drawings, there are clear interrelationships, in terms of palette, themes and handling, which suggest that the whole group is an extended series, perhaps partly made on the spot, and partly worked up in England, but most of them probably completed within a short period of time. The drawings on grey and brown paper, although obviously different in some respects, share themes and subject-matter with the white-paper drawings, and it seems best to give all of them the schematic date of 1840, with the proviso that the actual execution of the series may have extended into the following years. See Hardy George, 'Turner in Venice', *Art Quarterly*, LIII, 1971, pp. 84–7, and R.A. 1974, pp. 154–5.

1352 Venice: storm in the Piazzetta 1840

Watercolour, body-colour and scraping-out, with some pen and red colour, 219 × 321
Prov.: Henry Vaughan, by whom bequeathed to the gallery, 1900
Coll.: National Galleries of Scotland, Edinburgh (871)

1355 Venice: storm approaching San Giorgio and the Dogana 1840

Watercolour, 220 × 320
Exh.: R.A. 1974 (551)
Prov.: Revd. A. Stopford Brooke; by descent to the present owner
Private collection

1358 Venice: the Grand Canal 1840

Watercolour, 218 × 319
Prov.: Henry Vaughan, by whom bequeathed to the gallery, 1900
Coll.: National Gallery of Ireland, Dublin (2426)

1353 Venice: storm at sunset 1840

Watercolour and body-colour, with scratching-out, 222 × 320
Inscr. on verso: eight lines of verse (illegible)
Prov.: John Ruskin, by whom given to the museum, 1861
Coll.: Syndics of the Fitzwilliam Museum, Cambridge (590; Cormack 38)

1356 Venice: the Ducal Palace 1840

Watercolour, 240 × 304
Prov.: Henry Vaughan, by whom bequeathed to the gallery, 1900
Coll.: National Gallery of Ireland, Dublin (2423)

1359 Venice: the Grand Canal, looking towards the Dogana 1840

Watercolour, 221 × 320
Exh.: B.M. 1975 (259)
Prov.: Hon. W. F. D. Smith; Sir Joseph Beecham sale Christie 4 May 1917 (156), bt. Agnew; R. W. Lloyd, by whom bequeathed to the museum, 1958
Coll.: Trustees of the British Museum (1958–7–12–443)

1354 Venice: a storm 1840

Watercolour, 218 × 318
Exh.: B.M. 1975 (260)
Prov.: William Quilter, sale Christie 8 April 1875 (240, as 'Storm in the Lagunes'), bt. Agnew; Revd. C. J. Sale, by whom bequeathed to the museum, 1915
Coll.: Trustees of the British Museum (1915–3–13–50)

1357 Venice: San Giorgio Maggiore 1840

Watercolour, 225 × 290
Prov.: Henry Vaughan, by whom bequeathed to the gallery, 1900
Coll.: National Gallery of Ireland, Dublin (2417)

1360 Venice: the mouth of the Grand Canal

Watercolour, 219 × 317
Prov.: Rt. Hon. W. H. Smith; Sir Joseph Beecham, sale Christie 4 May 1917 (155); W. H. Jones; Gilbert Davis; Colnaghi, from whom bt. by Paul Mellon, 1966
Coll.: Yale Center for British Art, Paul Mellon Collection

463

1361   Venice: calm at sunrise   1840

Watercolour, with some pen, 222 × 325
Prov.: John Ruskin, by whom given to the museum,
1861
Coll.: Syndics of the Fitzwilliam Museum, Cambridge (591; Cormack 39)

1362   Venice: from the Lagoon   1840

Pencil, watercolour, and body-colour, with some
pen, 230 × 305
Prov.: John Ruskin, by whom given to the museum,
1861
Coll.: Syndics of the Fitzwilliam Museum, Cambridge (589; Cormack 40)

1363   Venice: the Grand Canal   1840

Pencil, watercolour and body-colour, with some
pen, 215 × 315
Exh.: R.A. 1974 (552)
Prov.: John Ruskin, by whom given to the Univer-
sity of Oxford, 1861
Coll.: Visitors of the Ashmolean Museum, Oxford
(Herrmann 56)

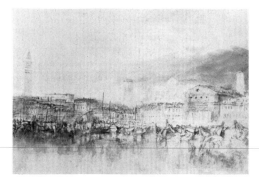

1364   Venice: the Riva degli Schiavoni   1840

Watercolour,   with   pen   and   scraping-out,
217 × 318
Exh.: R.A. 1974 (553)
Prov.: John Ruskin, by whom given to the Univer-
sity of Oxford, 1861
Coll.: Visitors of the Ashmolean Museum, Oxford
(Herrmann 58)

1365   Venice: the new moon   1840

Watercolour, 238 × 303
Prov.: Thomas Griffith; Revd. J. F. Griffith; L. Fried-
lander, who bequeathed it to the present owner
Private collection

1366   Venice: the Accademia   1840

Watercolour over pencil, with pen and scraping-
out, 217 × 318
Exh.: R.A. 1974 (554)
Prov.: John Ruskin, by whom given to the Univer-
sity of Oxford, 1861
Coll.: Visitors of the Ashmolean Museum, Oxford
(Herrmann 57)

**1367   Venice: San Giorgio Maggiore and the
Zitelle from the Giudecca**   1840

Watercolour, 184 × 273
Prov.: Thomas Greenwood, sale Christie 13 Fe-
bruary 1875 (261), bt. Albert Levy, sale Christie
1 April 1876 (275), bt. Galland; A. A. Allen; Walter
Stoye; by descent to the present owner
Private collection

**1368   Venice: the Grand Canal with the
Salute**   1840

Watercolour, with some body-colour and scraping-
out over traces of pencil, 218 × 318
Exh.: R.A. 1974 (555)
Prov.: Thomas Griffith; by descent to the present
owner
Private collection

1369   Venice: the Rialto   1840

Pencil, watercolour and body-colour, 206 × 299
Prov.: Henry Vaughan, by whom bequeathed to the
gallery, 1900
Coll.: National Galleries of Scotland, Edinburgh
(874)

**1370   Venice: Sta. Maria della Salute, from the
canal**   1840

Watercolour, with pen, 219 × 321
Prov.: Henry Vaughan, by whom bequeathed to the
gallery, 1900
Coll.: National Galleries of Scotland, Edinburgh
(888)

1371   Venice from the Laguna   1840

Watercolour and body-colour, 222 × 321
Prov.: Henry Vaughan, by whom bequeathed to the
gallery, 1900

Coll.: National Galleries of Scotland, Edinburgh (872)

1372 Venice: the Palazzo Balbi 1840

Pencil, watercolour and body-colour, 206 × 299
Prov.: Henry Vaughan, by whom bequeathed to the gallery, 1900
Coll.: National Galleries of Scotland, Edinburgh (873)

1373 Venice: the Ducal Palace from the Giudecca 1840

Watercolour, pen and brownish-red colour, 222 × 323
Prov.: R. R. Meade-King, by whom bequeathed to the gallery, 1934
Coll.: Walker Art Gallery, Liverpool (999)

1374 The Sun of Venice* 1840

Watercolour, with pen, 219 × 317
Prov.: Henry Vaughan, by whom bequeathed to the gallery, 1900
Coll.: National Galleries of Scotland, Edinburgh (875)

1375 Red sails at Chioggia 1840

Watercolour and body-colour on brown paper, 172 × 248
Prov.: A. P. Oppé; by descent to the present owner
Coll.: D. L. T. Oppé, London

XVII(c) Nos 1376–1381
Finished watercolours of European subjects, c. 1840

These six finished watercolours were probably executed in the years around 1840; one of them, the *Oberwesel,* is dated to that year, and the others conform to it, more or less, stylistically. For a detailed commentary on the group see Chapter 10, pp. 229–31.

1376 Heidelberg: sunset c. 1840

Watercolour, with scraping-out, 380 × 552
Exh.: R.A. 1974 (588)
Prov.: J. Price; William Quilter, sale Christie 9 April 1875 (247), bt. in; William Quilter, sale Christie 18 May 1889 (101), bt. Agnew; Mrs. Ruston, sale Christie 4 July 1913 (104), bt. Agnew; Baron Goldschmidt Rothschild; Agnew 1914; J. Blair, by whom bequeathed to the gallery, 1917
Coll.: City Art Gallery, Manchester (1917.106)

1377 Heidelberg, with a rainbow* c. 1841

Watercolour, 311 × 521
Engr.: by T. A. Prior, 1846 (R. 663)
Sig. (on mile-post): *JMW Turner*
Prov.: B. G. Windus; Joseph Gillott, sale Christie 4 May 1872 (512), bt. Lane; Lord Dudley; Stephen G. Holland, sale Christie 26 June 1908 (257), bt. Agnew; Sir Donald Currie; by descent to the present owner
Private collection

A large drawing in the Turner Bequest, T.B., CCCLXV–34, is apparently a study for this composition. It bears a date 1841, but the finished watercolour has many of the characteristics of earlier work, such as *England and Wales* views of c. 1830–5. It will be noted that the figures are in what appears to be medieval costume; compare the painting of *Heidelberg in the olden time* (P440).

1378 Caub and the Castle of Gutenfels on the Rhine c. 1840

Watercolour, 305 × 419
Sig.: *J M W Turner RA*
Prov.: J. Dugdale, sale Christie 24 June 1927 (117), bt. Leggatt; G. R. Stamp; Arthur Maiden
Private collection

A colour-beginning of this subject is T.B., CCLXIII–387 (repr. B.M. 1975 (84)).

1379 Tancarville on the Seine c. 1840

Watercolour, with scraping-out, 344 × 477
Exh.: B.M. 1975 (264)
Prov.: ? Edward Swinburne, for whom drawn; by descent to Julia Swinburne; H. E. Hayman; Agnew, 1912; R. W. Lloyd, by whom bequeathed to the museum, 1958
Coll.: Trustees of the British Museum (1958–7–12–423)

A composition study for this subject is T.B., CCLIX–169, and a colour-beginning is T.B., CCLXIII–17.

1380 Oberwesel* 1840

Watercolour and body-colour, with scraping-out, 345 × 530
Inscr. lower right: *IMWT. 1840*
Exh.: R.A. 1974 (583)
Engr.: by J. T. Willmore for Finden's *Royal Gallery of British Art,* 1842 (R. 660)
Prov.: B. G. Windus; Oldham; Whitaker; John Leigh Clare, sale Christie 28 March 1868 (100), bt. Agnew; William Quilter, sale Christie 9 April 1875 (248), bt. in; William Quilter, sale Christie 18 May 1889 (102), bt. Vokins; Andrew G. Kurtz, sale Christie 11 May 1891 (195), bt. McLean; E. Steinkopff, sale Christie 24 May 1935 (54), bt. Mitchell; anon. sale Christie 6 June 1972 (145), bt. Leger
Private collection, Switzerland

1381 Lake Nemi* *c.* 1840

Watercolour, with scraping-out, 347 × 515
Engr.: by R. Wallis for Finden's *Royal Gallery of British Art*, 1842 (R. 659)
Exh.: B.M. 1975 (263)
Prov.: B. G. Windus; J. E. Fordham; Sir John Fowler, sale Christie 6 May 1899 (29), bt. Vokins; William Cooke, sale Christie 8 June 1917 (66); R. W. Lloyd, by whom bequeathed to the museum, 1958
Coll.: Trustees of the British Museum (1958-7-12-444)

SECTION XVIII
Nos 1382–1429
Marine studies, including drawings of fish, *c.* 1830–1850; and *Dawn after the wreck, c.* 1841

The drawings listed in this group are all of marine or shore subjects, some extremely slight and difficult to identify. They are divided into four sections: studies that seem to have been done in the 1830s, often on a toned paper—usually buff, not the blue or grey of the 'Rivers of Europe' and related sheets (Nos 1382–1397); studies of fish (Nos 1399–1404); studies known as views at Yarmouth, all apparently done at the same time (?1840; Nos 1405–1410); and studies of the 1840s, including whaling scenes (Nos 1411–1429). A single finished drawing is catalogued here, *Dawn after the wreck*, of *c.* 1841 (No. 1398), as its subject-matter corresponds closely with that of these studies.

1382 Waves ?1830s

Body-colour and watercolour on grey paper, 187 × 273 (sight)
Prov.: Sir Hickman Bacon, Bt.; by descent to the present owner
Private collection

A very similar study is in the Fogg Art Museum, Harvard, but it appears to be a copy rather than an original drawing by Turner himself. Compare the oil study P457.

1383 Sunset at sea ?1830s

Body-colour on buff paper, 76 × 184
Prov.: ?John Ruskin; Sir Hickman Bacon, Bt.; by descent to the present owner
Private collection

This is the top study of three originally on one sheet; see Nos 1384, 1385.

1384 Beach, breakwater and distant headland in a rainstorm ?1830s

Watercolour and white chalk (or body-colour) on buff paper, 89 × 191
Prov.: John Ruskin; Sir Hickman Bacon, Bt.; by descent to the present owner
Private collection

One of three studies originally on one sheet; see Nos 1383, 1385.

1385 Waves breaking against a wooden groin ?1830s

Watercolour, body-colour and ? white chalk on buff paper, 114 × 191
Prov.: Sir Hickman Bacon, Bt.; by descent to the present owner
Private collection

The bottom study of three originally on one sheet; see Nos 1383, 1384.

1386 Figures on the shore ?1830s

Body-colour on coarse buff paper, 223 × 292
Exh.: R.A. 1974 (439)
Prov.: Sir Hickman Bacon, Bt.; by descent to the present owner

Private collection

1387 Sunset over a beach ?1830s

Body-colour on coarse buff-grey paper, 224×293
Exh.: R.A. 1974 (438)
Prov.: Sir Hickman Bacon, Bt.; by descent to the present owner
Private collection

1388 Shore scene: sunset ?1830s

Watercolour and body-colour, 97 × 189
Prov.: Robert Clarke Edwards; Mrs. Edwards; given by her executors to the museum, 1938
Coll.: Victoria and Albert Museum, London (P.19.1938)

1389 Study of sunlight ?1830s

Watercolour and body-colour, 89 × 190
Prov.: Robert Clarke Edwards; Mrs. Edwards; given by her executors to the museum, 1938

Coll.: Victoria and Albert Museum, London (P.20.1938)

1390 Study of sea: stormy sky ?1830s

Watercolour and body-colour, 91 × 189
Prov.: Robert Clarke Edwards; Mrs Edwards; given by her executors to the museum, 1938
Coll.: Victoria and Albert Museum, London (P.21.1938)

1391 A storm on Margate Sands ?1830s

Watercolour and body-colour on buff paper, 205 × 278
Prov.: Mrs. Booth; John Ruskin, sale Christie 15 April 1869 (15), bt. White; Revd. F. A. Armitage; his son, the Rev. A. L. Armitage; S. F. Armitage, sale Christie 18 April 1913 (79), bt. Agnew; Miss Bickham, sale Christie 25 November 1928 (29), bt. Agnew; Sir Stephen Courtauld; presented to the institute in his memory by members of his family, 1974
Coll.: Courtauld Institute of Art, University of London (2.74; Kitson 13)

1392 Heaped thundercloud over sea and land ?1830s

Watercolour and body-colour, with touches of black and red chalk, on buff paper, 214 × 284
Prov.: Mrs. Booth; John Ruskin, 1878; Arthur Severn, 1900; Sir Frederick Wigan, Bt., sale Christie 9 December 1915 (58), bt. Agnew; Sir Stephen Courtauld 1916; presented to the insti-

tute in his memory by members of his family, 1974
Coll.: Courtauld Institute of Art, University of London (3.74; Kitson 12)

1393 Sunset over a lake ?1830s

Watercolour, 215 × 254
Prov.: J. E. Taylor, sale Christie 8 July 1912 (?114, as 'A Lake Scene'), bt. Agnew; G. M. Booth; Miss Bickham; Kenneth Bird; John O'Gordon, sale Christie 14 March 1967 (122), bt. Agnew
Private collection

1394 Sunset over the sea ?1830s

Watercolour, 241 × 356
Prov.: ?John Ruskin; W. G. Rawlinson, bt. Agnew, 1906; Sir Hickman Bacon, Bt.; by descent to the present owner
Private collection

1395 A Sea-piece—squall c. 1835

Watercolour, 172 × 280
Prov.; J. E. Taylor; sale Christie 8 July 1912 (127), bt. Brown and Phillips
Coll: untraced

1396 Sunset at sea, with gurnets c. 1836

Watercolour, body-colour, black chalk, with scratching-out on buff paper, 218 × 284
Exh.: R.A. 1974 (437)
Prov.: ?John Ruskin, sale Christie 1869 (20, as 'Two Gurnets and a grey storm off Margate'); J. E. Taylor; presented to the institute in his memory by A. A., C. P., J. E. T., and R. E. T. Allen, his nephews, 1912

Coll.: Whitworth Art Gallery, University of Manchester (D.8.1912)

This drawing has been associated with the late oil study P481.

1397 Boats off Margate Pier ?c. 1840

Body-colour on buff-grey paper (discoloured), 210 × 277
Prov.: John Ruskin (who bt. it from the artist), sale Christie 15 April 1869 (13), bt. Colnaghi; William Blodgett, of New York; by descent to Eleanor Blodgett, by whom given to Franklin D. Roosevelt, 1911; Mrs. Eleanor Roosevelt, by whom bequeathed to her physician, Dr. A. David Gurewitsch; Mrs. Gurewitsch, until 1978; Agnew, 1979
Private collection, U.K.

See Francis Russell, 1975, for comment on this drawing.

1398 Dawn after the wreck c. 1841

Watercolour, 245 × 362
Prov.: Revd. W. Kingsley; Mrs. Kingsley, sale Christie 14 July 1916 (27), bt. Agnew; Sir Stephen Courtauld, 1917; presented to the institute in his memory by members of his family, 1974.
Coll.: Courtauld Institute of Art, University of London (9.74; Kitson 11)

Nos 1399–1404 are studies of fish. They are difficult to date, but Ruskin (Works, XIII, p. 469) refers to fish on the sideboard at Mrs. Booth's: '... [Mackerel] Study on his kitchen dresser at Margate, splendid. [Mackerel] Just a dash for three more. Cook impatient'. So it may be assumed that the mackerel studies at least date from the late 1830s, if not later. Other studies of fish, more meticulous in their treatment, and possibly datable to the late 1820s, are in the Turner Bequest (T.B., CCLXIII–338, 339); while a further drawing of three fish, in body-colour on a grey ground, is T.B., CCLXIII–342. This seems to date from somewhat later, and may come from the same period as the Study of a gurnard (No. 1404).

1399 Sketch of three mackerel c. 1835–40

Pencil and watercolour, 224 × 287
Exh.: R.A. 1974 (269)
Prov.: John Ruskin; by whom given to the Ruskin School, Oxford, 1875; transferred to the museum, 1938
Coll.: Visitors of the Ashmolean Museum, Oxford (Herrmann 80)

1400 Mackerel c. 1835–40

Pencil and watercolour, 133 × 254
Prov.: J. E. Taylor, sale 8 July 1912 (146), bt. Gooden & Fox; anon. sale Christie 4 June 1974 (179)
Private collection, U.S.A.

1401 Mackerel c. 1835–40

Watercolour and body-colour, 181 × 273
Inscr. verso in pencil: 'By J.M.W. Turner/Given to me by Mrs Booth Augt 1855/Sketched from Fish brought in for dinner/at Margate of which Fish Mr Turner partook of for his dinner (sic) N./Bartlett who attended Mr Turner for six months before his death and closed/his eyes in death at 9 a.m. (Aug^t)' (crossed out).
Prov.: Mrs. Booth; W. Bartlett; Count Antoine Sale, from whom inherited by present owner
Private collection

1402 Mackerel and prawns c. 1835–40

Watercolour and body-colour and white chalk on grey paper, 133 × 254
Prov.: J. E. Taylor, sale Christie 8 July 1912 (124), bt. Gooden and Fox; R. L. Harmsworth; Sir Harold Harmsworth; anon. sale Christie 4 June 1974 (180), bt. Leger
Private collection, Switzerland

1403 Study of fish with three prawns c. 1835–40

Watercolour over pencil, 244 × 302
Prov.: John Ruskin; by whom given to the Ruskin School, Oxford, 1875; transferred to the museum, 1938

Coll.: Visitors of the Ashmolean Museum, Oxford (Herrmann 81)

1404 Study of a gurnard c. 1840

Watercolour and body-colour, 193 × 276
Prov.: John Ruskin; Arthur Severn, 1900; Fine Art Society, London, 1900; given by the Executors of Robert Clarke Edwards, 1938
Coll.: Victoria and Albert Museum, London (P.18–1938)

Nos 1405–1410 fall together; not only because they are all traditionally known as Yarmouth subjects, but because they have much in common stylistically. The majority are similar in size and it is likely that these are all leaves from the same sketchbook. Owing to technical features that they have in common with some of the Venetian colour studies, they are dated here to 1840, but this is a conjecture. It is not known for certain that Turner visited Yarmouth after his voyage along the east coast in 1824. Compare the paintings P336, P387.

1405 ?Yarmouth, Norfolk ?c. 1840

Pencil and watercolour, with some scratching-out, 242 × 358
Prov.: John Ruskin; presented by him to the University of Oxford, 1861
Coll.: Visitors of the Ashmolean Museum, Oxford (Herrmann 23)

1406 Yarmouth Sands ?1840

Watercolour, 248 × 362
Prov.: ?Thomas Greenwood, sale Christie 13 February 1875 (252), bt. Agnew; J. Hamilton Houldsworth; G. F. Sullivan; Sotheby 26 July 1961 (118), bt. Colnaghi, from whom bt. by Paul Mellon, 1961

Coll.: Yale Center for British Art, Paul Mellon Collection

1407 Wreckers: (?) Yarmouth ?c. 1840

Pencil and watercolour, 222 × 289
Inscr. lower left: *Wreckers*
Prov.: Sir Hickman Bacon, Bt.; by descent to the present owner
Private collection

1408 Yarmouth c. 1840

Watercolour, 248 × 365
Prov.: Henry Vaughan, by whom bequeathed to the gallery, 1900
Coll.: National Gallery of Ireland, Dublin (2425)

1409 Yarmouth Roads c. 1840

Pencil and watercolour, with scraping-out, 241 × 356
Exh.: R.A. 1974 (626)

Prov.: Revd. W. Kingsley; Mrs. Newall; Phillips & MacConnell, from whom purchased by Lord Leverhulme, 1923
Coll.: The Lady Lever Collection, Port Sunlight, Cheshire (WHL 4716)

1410 Off Yarmouth ?c. 1840

Watercolour, 136 × 184
Prov.: J. E. Taylor; E. R. Debenham; Agnew 1929; Frank C. Parker; anon. sale Sotheby 18 March 1971 (77), bt. Agnew
Private collection

The following drawings (Nos 1411–29) are distinguished by their slightness, or by a general perfunctoriness of handling which suggests a very late date. They are mostly notes or reminiscences of effects of cloud or light over the sea and shore, and may have been made at Margate (Finberg's *Life*, p. 418, indicates that Turner continued to visit Margate until the late 1840s), or perhaps, in some cases, on the Thames. They need not be studies direct from nature. Their provenance is usually obscure: they emanate, probably, either from Mrs. Booth, or from Ruskin, who, no doubt, like Charles Stokes, acquired them through Mrs. Booth. These late scraps seem to have been regarded as legitimate plunder by those who had access to Turner's studio after his death. Many subsequently entered the collection of J. E. Taylor, and a large group was acquired by Sir Hickman Bacon.

1411 The Whaler: 'He breaks away' 1845

Pencil and watercolour, 227 × 325
Inscr. lower right: *He breaks away*
Prov.: William Ward; Messrs. Wm. B. Paterson, from whom purchased by T. W. Bacon, 1907; presented by him to the museum, 1950
Coll.: Syndics of the Fitzwilliam Museum, Cambridge (PD.116.1950; Cormack 52)

This and the next are perhaps sheets from the *Whalers* sketchbook, of 1845 (T.B., CCCLIII), or another of the books used in that year: the *Ambleteuse and Wimereux* sketchbook has a study of a stranded whale inscribed: *I shall use this* (T.B., CCCLVII–6).

1412 The Whaler: 'Hurrah boys' 1845

Watercolour (approx.) 227 × 325
Inscr.: *Hurrah boys*
Prov.: William Ward
Coll.: untraced

The inscription suggests a connection with the painting *Hurrah! for the Whaler Erebus! Another fish!,,,* of 1846 (P423), though that work seems in fact to be based on a drawing in the *Whalers* sketchbook (T.B., CCCLIII–14). See No. 1411.

1413 Fire at sea c. 1845

Watercolour, 230 × 312
Prov.: Sir Hickman Bacon, Bt.; by descent to the present owner
Private collection

Although not obviously a whaling subject, this drawing is close in mood and treatment to Nos 1411, 1412 and those in the *Whalers* sketchbook (T.B., CCCLIII). See also the various canvases that use the theme of fire at sea (P325, P460, P462).

1414 Sunset c. 1840–5

Watercolour, 222 × 298 (sight)
Prov.: J. E. Taylor, sale Christie 8 July 1912 (117), bt. Agnew; Lloyd Roberts, by whom bequeathed to the gallery, 1920
Coll.: City Art Gallery, Manchester (1920.594)

1415 Sunset on wet sand *c.* 1840–5

Watercolour and pencil, 229 × 292
Prov.: ?John Ruskin; J. E. Taylor; presented in memory of him by A. A., C. P., J. E. T. and R. E. T. Allen, his nephews, 1912
Coll.: Whitworth Art Gallery, University of Manchester (D.7.1912)

1416 Red and blue sunset sky *c.* 1845–50

Watercolour, 243 × 357
Exh.: R.A. 1974 (637)
Prov.: Sir Hickman Bacon, Bt.; by descent to the present owner
Private collection

1417 Sunset over water *c.* 1845–50

Watercolour, 185 × 268
Inscr.: *Given to me by Mrs. Booth August 1855. W. Bartlett 1 Bratton Terrace, Chelsea*
Exh.: R.A. 1974 (B151)
Prov.: Mrs. Booth; W. Bartlett; Sir Hickman Bacon Bt.; by descent to the present owner
Private collection

1418 Sunset 1845–50

Watercolour and body-colour on grey paper, 178 × 264
Prov.: Mrs. Booth; W. Bartlett; Messrs. Shepherd Bros., from whom purchased by T. W. Bacon, 1905; given by him to the museum, 1950
Inscr. on back of old mount: *Given to me by Mrs. Booth/August 1855/W. Bartlett M. P. S./ 1 Bretton Terrace, Chelsea* and *who attended Mr. B/during the last six months/of his existence*
Coll.: Syndics of the Fitzwilliam Museum, Cambridge (PD.113–1950: Cormack 54)

1419 Clouds over sand *c.* 1845–50

Watercolour over pencil, 228 × 295
Prov.: Sir Hickman Bacon, Bt.; by descent to the present owner
Private collection

1420 Sunset *c.* 1845–50

Watercolour, 229 × 327
Prov.: Mrs. Henry Lee Higginson, by whom bequeathed to the museum, 1935
Coll.: Museum of Fine Arts, Boston (35.1217)

1421 Grey sea—a boat running ashore *c.* 1845–50

Watercolour, 251 × 362
Prov.: Norman and Agnes Lupton, by whom bequeathed to the gallery, 1953
Coll.: City Art Galleries, Leeds (13.215/53)

1422 Study of sky and shore *c.* 1845–50

Watercolour, 228 × 393
Prov.: Sir Hickman Bacon, Bt.; by descent to the present owner
Private collection

1423 A steamboat and crescent moon *c.* 1845–50

Pencil and watercolour, 229 × 327
Prov.: Sir Hickman Bacon, Bt.; by descent to the present owner
Private collection

1424 'Fox Lugger' c. 1845–50

Pencil and watercolour, 229 × 327
Inscr. lower left: *Fox Lugger* and with other notes (illegible)
Prov.: Sir Hickman Bacon, Bt.; by descent to the present owner
Private collection

1425 'Lost to all Hope…'* c. 1845–50

Watercolour and pencil, 229 × 324
Inscr. at bottom: *Lost to all Hope she lies/each sea breaks over a derelict [?]/on an unknown shore/the sea folk[?]only sharing[?] the triumph*
Prov.: J. R. Reid; Appleby Bros.; Squire Gallery, from whom bt. by L. G. Duke, 1945, from whom bt. by Paul Mellon, 1961
Coll.: Yale Center for British Art, Paul Mellon Collection

1426 Wreck on the Goodwin Sands: sunset
c. 1845–50

Watercolour, 229 × 333
Inscr.: (in Turner's hand) across lower half of sheet:*Wreck on the Goodwins/And Dolphins [?] play around the wreck/The man's [?] hope holding all that hoped/Admits the work [? mark] of the almighty's hand fallacy [? falling] Hope/for sail*
Prov.: Agnew, 1973
Private collection, U.S.A.

1427 Storm-cloud over a river 1845–50

Watercolour, 233 × 286
Inscr. on verso by Turner in pencil: *Sept 12/45 (or* just possibly *46)*
Prov.: Messrs. Shepherd Bros., from whom purchased by T. W. Bacon, 1905; presented by him to the museum, 1950
Coll.: Syndics of the Fitzwilliam Museum, Cambridge (PD.115–1950; Cormack 53)

1428 A jetty: (?) Margate c. 1845–50

Pencil and watercolour, 229 × 327
Prov.: Denman W. Ross, by whom given to the museum, 1906
Coll.: Museum of Fine Arts, Boston, Mass. (06.125)

This sheet has been rechristened 'Calais sands', but there seems no justification for the title.

1429 Sunset over the coast c. 1845–50

Watercolour, 235 × 350
Prov.: John Smith, by descent to Sir Leslie Farrer, sale, Sotheby 15 July 1959 (82), bt. D. Carritt
Private collection

This is a very weak drawing. Compare the *Sun set at sea* in the British Museum (1953–4–11–34), which is excluded from this catalogue as of dubious authenticity.

SECTION XIX
Nos 1430–1522
Swiss subjects from roll sketchbooks, *c.* 1836–1844

XIX(a) Nos 1430–1456
The tour of 1836

These subjects are grouped together under the date of Turner's tour of 1836, when he accompanied H.A.J. Munro of Novar to Geneva, Bonneville, Chamonix and the Val d'Aosta; partly on account of traditional identifications, and principally because they seem to conform to a type that is possibly identifiable as characteristic of that year. Many of the sheets used are rather square in format (though this is also true of sheets from 1841 and later), and the colour is applied in a rich, almost unctuous way, with highlights scraped out with the blunt end of a brush. Colour is strong and the tonality rather dark. There are exceptions, of course: the *Aosta*, No. 1438, for instance, is on a prepared ground, unlike anything of 1836, and altogether unusual among late Swiss drawings. Some studies allocated here to a later date on the evidence of subject-matter seem to belong stylistically to the 1836 tour, and it may be that they represent localities different from those traditionally assigned to them (e.g. No. 1493).

1430 A scene in the Val d'Aosta ?1836

Watercolour and body-colour, with some pen and scraping-out over traces of pencil, 237 × 298
Prov.: W. G. Rawlinson by 1902; Agnew; R. A. Tatton, 1917; T. A. Tatton, sale Christie 14 December 1928 (27), bt. Lockett Thompson, from whom purchased and given to the museum by the Friends of the Fitzwilliam, 1932
Coll.: Syndics of the Fitzwilliam Museum, Cambridge (1612; Cormack 35)

1431 Swiss mountains ?1836

Watercolour, 230 × 343
Prov.: Gwendoline Davies, by whom bequeathed to the museum, 1952

Coll.: National Museum of Wales, Cardiff (2954)

1432   View down the Val d'Aosta   ?1836

Watercolour, 222 × 280
Prov.: Mrs. Leonard Elmhirst, sale New York 27 May 1942; Walter Wedgwood, Long Island; Agnew 1960; Boyd Alexander, sale Sotheby 24 November 1965 (66), bt. Agnew
Private collection

1433   Monte Rosa   ?1836

Watercolour, 241 × 336
Prov.: Henry Vaughan, by whom bequeathed to the gallery, 1900
Coll.: National Galleries of Scotland, Edinburgh (887)

1434   Hotel   Argent,   at   Villeneuve,   Val d'Aosta   ?1836

Watercolour,   body-colour   and   scraping-out, 247 × 302

Prov.: Henry Vaughan, by whom bequeathed to the gallery, 1900
Coll.: National Galleries of Scotland, Edinburgh (870)

1435   View in the Val d'Aosta (Verrès) ?1836

Watercolour, with pen and red ink, 256 × 280
Prov.: Henry Vaughan, by whom bequeathed to the gallery, 1900
Coll.: National Galleries of Scotland, Edinburgh (865)

1436   Val d'Aosta   ?1836

Watercolour and pen, 232 × 330
Prov.: entered the collection through the Olivia Shaler Swan Memorial Collection, 1950
Coll.: Art Institute of Chicago (1950.1366)

1437   An Alpine pass   c. 1836

Watercolour, 229 × 286
Prov.: Mrs. Thatcher (whose great-grandfather acquired it from the artist); Mrs. Eileen Young; Spink, London; Mount Trust Coll., sale Christie, 14 November 1972 (100), bt. Harris
Private collection, U.S.A.

1438   Aosta   ?1836

Pencil and watercolour, with scraping-out, on beige-grey prepared ground, 228 × 315
Provenance and whereabouts unknown

1439   Aosta   ?1836

Watercolour, 247 × 273
Prov.: J. E. Taylor, sale Christie 5 July 1912 (63), bt. Agnew; purchased by the museum 1942
Coll.:   Museum   of   Fine   Arts,   Boston,   Mass. (42.306)

1440   Glacier des Bossons   ?1836

Watercolour, with some scratching-out, 231 × 331
Prov.: ?Thomas Greenwood, sale Christie 13 February 1875 (272), bt. Albert Levy; sale Christie 1 April 1876 (277), bt. Seele (?Sale); Revd. C. J. Sale, by whom bequeathed to the museum, 1915
Coll.: Trustees of the British Museum (1915-3-13-49)

1441   Tête Noire   ?1836

Watercolour, 256 × 283
Prov.: Henry Vaughan, by whom bequeathed to the gallery, 1900
Coll.: National Gallery of Ireland, Dublin (2421)

1442   Landscape with river   ?1836

Pencil and watercolour, 240 × 300
Prov.: Henry Vaughan, by whom bequeathed to the gallery, 1900
Coll.: National Gallery of Ireland, Dublin (2416)

1443   Stelvio Pass (?)   ?1836

Watercolour, 242 × 305

Prov.: Henry Vaughan, by whom bequeathed to the gallery, 1900
Coll.: National Gallery of Ireland, Dublin (2419)

Turner visited Stelvio only in 1842, as far as can be judged. The style of this drawing is sufficiently like that of the Aosta subjects to justify a dating of 1836, but the proper location remains unclear.

1444   Brenva Glacier, from near Courmayeur   ?1836

Watercolour, 201 × 315
Prov.: ?Sir Cecil Harcourt Smith; ?Cotswold Gallery, as 'Alpine Pass', 1928
Coll.: Williamson Art Gallery and Museum, Birkenhead, Cheshire

1445   Brenva Glacier, with Entrèves and Mont Chétif   ?1836

?Watercolour, size unknown
Prov.: unknown
Coll.: ?Williamson Art Gallery and Museum, Birkenhead, Cheshire

Recorded by Finberg (Index) but not traced.

1446   Sion (Rhône)   ?1836

Watercolour, 247 × 277
Prov.: Henry Vaughan, by whom bequeathed to the gallery, 1900
Coll.: National Galleries of Scotland, Edinburgh (876)

This drawing is now known as *Splügen,* but does not seem to have anything to do with that region. It is apparently a view of Sion, as indicated by its earlier title (used here), and may date from Turner's tour of 1836.

1447   Sion (Valais)   ?1836

Watercolour and body-colour, 240 × 302
Prov.: Henry Vaughan, by whom bequeathed to the gallery, 1900
Coll.: National Galleries of Scotland, Edinburgh (864)

1448   Afterglow—Sierre—Rhône Valley (Sion)   ?1836

Watercolour, 235 × 299
Prov.: Gen. Rawdon; William Quilter, sale Christie 8 April 1875 (238), unsold; Quilter sale, Christie 18 May 1889 (98, as 'Sion'), bt. Innes; Lt.-Col. J. A. Innes
Private collection

The present title appears in the Leggatt 1960 catalogue (21); the drawing appeared in the Quilter sale as *Sion.*

1449   Couvent du Bonhomme, Chamonix   ?1836

Watercolour, with some pen and scraping-out, 242 × 302
Prov.: Thomas Greenwood, sale Christie 13 February 1875 (279), bt. White; T. M. Shuttleworth, sale Branch & Leete, 12 June 1890 (73), bt. White; T. W. Bacon, by whom given to the museum, 1950
Coll.: Syndics of the Fitzwilliam, Cambridge (PD. 111–1950; Cormack 37)

1450   Sisteron, Basses Alpes   ?1836

Watercolour, 197 × 280
Prov.: J. E. Taylor, sale Christie 5 July 1912 (53),
bt. Agnew; Mrs. A. A. Allen, sale Sotheby 15 May
1957 (63), bt. Agnew; Walter C. Baker, by whom
bequeathed to the museum
Coll.: Metropolitan Museum of Art, New York
(Walter C. Baker Bequest)

Compare the group of views of Sisteron made in
connection with the 'Rivers of Europe' project
(Nos 1010–1013).

1451   Alpine Valley   ?1836

Watercolour, 185 × 267
Prov.: John Ruskin; J. E. Taylor, sale Christie 5 July
1912 (87), bt. Gibbs; Mrs. Leonard K. Elmhirst;
Edward Pugliese, 1942; acquired for the museum
through the Ernest W. Longfellow Fund, 1942
Coll.: Museum of Fine Arts, Boston, Mass.
(42.305)

1452   Swiss valley, with bridge and town
?1836

Watercolour, 227 × 337
Prov.: unknown
Private collection

1453   A mountain gorge   ?1836

Watercolour, 229 × 292
Prov.: J. E. Taylor, sale Christie 5 July 1912 (95),
bt. Agnew: H. Gibbs; Mrs. Leonard K. Elmhirst;
Walter F. Wedgwood, Lond Island; Agnew, from
whom purchased by anon. donor to the museum

Coll.: Museum of Art, Rhode Island School of
Design, Providence, R. I. (69.154.58)

1454   A castle in the ?Italian Alps   ?1836

Pencil and watercolour, with pen and scratching-
out on paper prepared with a grey wash,
161×233
Prov.: Thomas Greenwood, sale Christie 13 February 1875 (244, as 'Castle on Height near
Genoa'), bt. Agnew; Spink, 1974
Private collection

1455   A conflagration, Lausanne   ?1836

Watercolour and body-colour, 241 × 305
Exh.: R.A. 1974 (590)
Prov.: J. E. Taylor; presented in memory of him by
his nephew, A. A. Allen, 1912
Coll.: Whitworth Art Gallery, University of
Manchester (D.6.1912)

1456   The Castle of Chillon   ?1836

Watercolour and pencil, 222 × 317
Prov.: ?Thomas Greenwood, sale Christie 13 Feb-
ruary 1875 (280), bt. Agnew; A. G. Kurtz, sale
Christie 11 May 1891 (192), bt. Agnew; presented
by the Guarantors of the Royal Jubilee Exhibition,
1887
Coll.: Whitworth Art Gallery, University of
Manchester (D.17.1887)

**XIX(b)   Nos 1457–1518
The tours of 1841–1844**

These subjects are sheets from roll sketchbooks
used in Switzerland or adjacent Alpine regions
between 1841 and 1844. A few items are on
sheets larger than the normal sketchbook size, but
they probably come from a book or books, unlike
the very large separate sheets catalogued as
Nos 1519–1522.
There is no conclusive evidence as to the dates at
which these drawings were made; some, like the
views of Bellinzona, must have been done in the
years that Turner is known to have gone to a
specific place, though even here we can choose
between two dates—1842 and 1843. It is possible that Turner's approach changed with each
locality—certainly his views of Brunnen, for
instance, are remarkably consistent in style.
However, some rough system of dating is required,
and it seems generally true that the colouring of the
drawings becomes less rich and various over the
period of the four tours, 1841, 1842, 1843 and
1844; by 1843 some of the studies are executed in
an almost monochrome ochre heightened with red
pen-strokes; and in 1844 colour is frequently pale
and pen outlines are very prominent; but there are
drawings undoubtedly made in 1841 which use
pen outline alone, so this rule of thumb must be at
best a very crude guide. One group of drawings,
that of the Rheinfall at Schaffhausen
(Nos 1460–1469), include several made on a
prepared ground, most unusual at this late date,
and one sheet is actually dated—an even rarer
occurrence. On the basis of this, the group is given a
provisional overall date of 1841, although there is
considerable variation within the group. These
studies may be leaves from the *Fribourg, Lausanne
and Geneva* sketchbook (T.B., CCCXXXII).

1457 St. Michael's Castle, Chamonix (Bonneville?) *c.* 1841

Pencil and watercolour, with pen and brown and black ink, 217 × 280 (sight)
Inscr. verso (not in Turner's hand): *Bellinzona No. 10*
Prov.: Kurt Pantzer, by whom given to the museum
Coll.: Indianapolis Museum of Art

'Chamonix' is the present identification of this subject, but it seems almost certainly to show the same structure that appears in Turner's early views of Bonneville. The inscription on the verso is evidently mistaken.

1460 Schaffhausen—moonlight 1841

Watercolour, pen and scratching-out, 230 × 284
Inscr. lower right: *Falls of the Rhine 1841*
Prov.: Henry Vaughan, by whom bequeathed to the gallery, 1900
Coll.: National Galleries of Scotland, Edinburgh (869)

Although there is considerable stylistic variation within the group, all the late Schaffhausen drawings (Nos 1460–1469) are provisionally dated to 1841 on the strength of the inscription on this sheet. They may be leaves from the *Fribourg, Lausanne and Geneva* sketchbook (T.B., CCCXXXII).

Coll.: Courtauld Institute of Art, University of London (12.74; Kitson 9)

1463 Schaffhausen—side view ?1841

Watercolour and body-colour, with pen and scratching-out, 229 × 286
Prov.: Henry Vaughan, by whom bequeathed to the gallery, 1900
Coll.: National Galleries of Scotland, Edinburgh (868)

1458 Lausanne, from Le Signal 1841

Watercolour, 235 × 330
Prov.: J. E. Taylor, sale Christie 7 July 1912 (64), bt. Agnew; C. P. Allen, sale Christie 5 December 1930 (48), bt. in
Private collection

1461 Falls of the Rhine, Schaffhausen ?1841

Watercolour, pen and scraping-out on white paper prepared with a grey wash, 226 × 286
Prov.: Walter Jones; Sir Donald Currie; Hugh Blaker; Margaret S. Davies, sale Sotheby 24 February 1960 (92), bt. Mitchell; Kurt Pantzer
Coll.: Pantzer Collection, Indianapolis

1462 Falls of the Rhine, Schaffhausen ?1841

Watercolour with some pen and scraping-out on white paper prepared with a grey wash, 227 × 284
Prov.: Revd. W. Kingsley; Mrs. Kingsley, sale Christie 14 July 1916 (28), bt. Agnew; Sir Stephen Courtauld, 1917; presented to the institute in his memory by members of his family, 1974

1459 Lausanne, from Le Signal 1841

Watercolour, 230 × 330
Prov.: Thomas Greenwood; W. G. Rawlinson; T. A. Tatton, sale Christie 14 December 1928 (29), bt. Harrison (repr. *Studio,* 1909, Pl. xxv)
Coll.: untraced

1464 Falls of the Rhine, Schaffhausen—front view ?1841

Watercolour, with pen and red colour, 229 × 292
Prov.: Henry Vaughan, by whom bequeathed to the gallery, 1900
Coll.: National Galleries of Scotland, Edinburgh (867)

1465 Schaffhausen ?1841

Pencil and watercolour, with pen and scraping-out, on white paper with a grey wash, 232 × 295
Prov.: ?H. B. Brabazon, by 1902; Herbert Powell; presented to the gallery by the National Art-Collections Fund from the Herbert Powell Bequest, 1968
Coll.: Tate Gallery, London (1022)

1466 Falls of Schaffhausen ?1841

Watercolour, 222 × 298
Prov.: Sir Donald Currie, by 1902; by descent to present owner
Private collection

1467 Falls of Schaffhausen ?1841

Pencil, watercolour, pen and scraping-out on white paper prepared with a grey wash, 219 × 281

Prov.: Sir Donald Currie, by 1902; by descent to present owner
Private collection

1468 Schaffhausen ?1841

Watercolour with pen, 235 × 325
Prov.: John Ruskin, by whom given to the museum, 1861
Coll.: Syndics of the Fitzwilliam Museum, Cambridge (583; Cormack 50)

1469 Falls of Schaffhausen on the Rhine (from below the fall) ?1841

Pencil and watercolour, with scraping-out, on a grey prepared ground, 222 × 280
Prov.: Maas; Walter Brandt
Coll.: Trustees of the P. A. Brandt Settlement

This sheet is similar in style to some of the German drawings, dated here to ?1844 (Nos 1327–1348).

1470 Lucerne ?1841

Watercolour and pencil, 235 × 358 (sight)
Prov.: Albert Wood; S. Addington, sale Christie 22 May 1886 (55), bt. Agnew; Sir James Knowles, sale Christie 28 May 1908 (363), bt. Colnaghi; Wallis & Son; James Blair, by whom bequeathed to the gallery, 1917
Coll.: City Art Gallery, Manchester (1917.112)

1471 Lucerne c. 1842

Watercolour, with some body-colour, 233 × 292
Inscr. lower right: *I don't know the place/(J. [?] Ruskin 1880/JMWT Late Time/and very bad (for him [?])*
Prov.: John Ruskin; J. B. MacGeorge, sale Morrison McLeary, Glasgow, 16 May 1958 (85, as 'Zurich'), bt. Fine Art Society, London; Sir Robert Abdy; Margaret Mower; given by her to the institute in memory of her mother, Elsa Durand Mower, 1960
Coll.: Art Institute of Chicago (1960.10)

The identification of the view was given by Gowing (1966, p. 62) and followed by me in *Turner in Switzerland,* (1976, p. 97), but Ruskin's uncertainty seems justified. This is clearly not the same scene as that recorded in T.B., CCCLXIV–324, and worked up in 1843 (see No. 1536). The distant towers on the left suggest Bellinzona, but in other respects this seems to be a view in a town on the Rhine.

1472 The Rigi, Lake Lucerne: sunset c. 1841

Watercolour, 242 × 356
Prov.: Revd. W. Kingsley, sale Christie 14 July

1916 (26), bt. Agnew; G. E. Leeming, from whom bt. Agnew, 1922
Private collection

Larger than the regular roll sketchbook format, this drawing is on a sheet similar in size to those of Thun (Nos 1503, 1504) and other drawings made in Switzerland at this date.

1473   The Rigi, Lake Lucerne: sunrise *c.* 1841

Watercolour, 241 × 309
Prov.: ?Thomas Greenwood, sale Christie 13 February 1875 (281), bt. Vokins; W. G. Rawlinson, by 1902; R. A. Tatton, 1917; T. A. Tatton, sale Christie 14 December 1928 (32), bt. Agnew; Miss Deakin; by descent to present owner
Private collection

1474   Evening: cloud on Mont Rigi, seen from Zug *c.* 1841

Watercolour, 218 × 267
Exh.: R.A. 1974 (592)
Prov.: John Ruskin, by whom given to the Ruskin School, Oxford, 1875; transferred to the museum, 1938
Coll.: Visitors of the Ashmolean Museum, Oxford (Herrmann 86)

1475   Lake Lucerne   ?1841

Watercolour, 225 × 289
Prov.: Henry Vaughan, by whom bequeathed to the gallery, 1900

Coll.: National Gallery of Ireland, Dublin (2422)

1476   Lake Lucerne   ?1841

Watercolour over pencil, 230 × 292
Prov.: Henry Vaughan, by whom bequeathed to the gallery, 1900
Coll.: National Gallery of Ireland, Dublin (2427)

1477   Lake Lucerne   ?1841

Pencil and watercolour, 214 × 282
Prov.: Henry Vaughan, by whom bequeathed to the gallery, 1900
Coll.: National Gallery of Ireland, Dublin (2428)

1478   Lake Lucerne, the Rigi in the distance —moonlight   ?1841

Watercolour, 229 × 306 (sight)
Prov.: presented by the Guarantors of the Royal Jubilee Exhibition, 1887
Coll.: Whitworth Art Gallery, University of Manchester (D.16.1887)

1479   Seelisberg by moonlight   ?1841

Watercolour and pencil, 222 × 283
Prov.: Henry Vaughan; Louis Huth, sale Christie 20 May 1905 (23, as 'The Bass Rock—moonlight'), bt. Agnew; W. G. Rawlinson, from whom bt. Agnew, 1917; R. A. Tatton; T. A. Tatton, sale Christie 14 December 1928 (31), bt. Agnew; Landon K. Thorne, New York; Agnew 1973
Private collection

1480   Tell's Chapel, Lake Lucerne   ?1841

Watercolour and pen and red colour, with scraping-out, 227 × 285
Prov.: John Ruskin; W. Sopper; W. G. Rawlinson; T. A. Tatton; Walter Jones; Lord Horder; George Goyder; Agnew, from whom purchased 1965
Coll.: Yale Center for British Art, Paul Mellon Collection

1481   ?Lake Lucerne   ?1841

Watercolour, with scratching-out, 217 × 268
Prov.: W. G. Rawlinson; Sir Hickman Bacon, Bt.; by descent to present owner
Private collection

1482   The first steamer on Lake Lucerne*   ?1841

Watercolour, with some scraping-out, over traces of pencil, 231 × 289
Prov.: Henry Vaughan, by whom bequeathed to the college, 1900
Coll.: University College, London

1483   Fluelen, from the lake   ?1841

Watercolour, with some pen, 232 × 290
Prov.: John Ruskin, by whom given to the museum, 1861
Coll.: Syndics of the Fitzwilliam Museum, Cambridge (585; Cormack 44)

A view very similar, except for the stormy conditions, to T.B., CCCLXIV–381, used as the basis for a finished watercolour of 1845 (No. 1549).

1484   Steamboat in a storm   ?1841

Watercolour 232 × 289
Prov.: Thomas Greenwood, sale Christie 13 February 1875 (267), bt. Agnew; James Houldsworth; by descent to Col. J. F. H. Houldsworth; anon. sale Sotheby 28 November 1974 (118), bt. Baskett & Day, from whom purchased
Coll.: Yale Center for British Art, Paul Mellon Collection

There is no explicit indication that this drawing shows a Lucerne Lake steamer, but the treatment of the sheet is very close to that of Lucerne drawings from the roll sketchbooks of about 1841.

1485   Brunnen, Lake Lucerne   ?1843

Pencil and watercolour, with some pen and red ink, 234 × 290
Prov.: ?J. Irvine Smith; Agnew, 1907; C. Fairfax Murray; Costwold Gallery, 1925; Sir Stephen Courtauld; presented to the institute in his memory by his family 1974
Coll.: Courtauld Institute of Art, University of London (13.74; Kitson 10)

1486   Brunnen, with Lake Lucerne in the distance   ?1843

Pencil and watercolour with pen, 225 × 290
Inscr.: by Turner in pencil verso: *Brennern/Lake of Lucern* and *15 18 X8*
Prov.: John Ruskin, by whom given to the museum, 1861

Coll.: Syndics of the Fitzwilliam Museum, Cambridge (584; Cormack 43)

1487   Schwytz   ?1843

Pencil, watercolour and pen, 229 × 286
Prov.: Henry Vaughan, by whom bequeathed to the gallery, 1900
Coll.: National Galleries of Scotland, Edinburgh (863)

1488   The Lowerzersee, with Schwytz and the Mythen   ?1843

Pencil and watercolour, 229 × 286
Prov.: Mrs. Booth, by descent to her son, D. J.

Pound; A. Austin, sale Christie 6 June 1909 (186, as 'A view on the Rhine'), bt. Agnew; Walter H. Jones; Christie 3 July 1942 (49, as 'The Lake of Lucerne: Brunnen in the distance'), bt. Agnew: L. B. Murray
Private collection

1489   Bellinzona   ?1843

Watercolour and pencil, 230 × 287
Prov.: B. G. Windus, sale Christie 26 March 1859 (17), bt. Pritchard; John Ruskin, sale Christie 15 April 1869 (35), bt. Vokins; Wallis & Son; The French Gallery, from whom bt. by James Blair, 1912, and bequeathed by him to the gallery, 1917
Coll.: City Art Gallery, Manchester (1917.100)

1490   Bellinzona   ?1843

Watercolour and pencil, 228 × 287
Prov.: George Salting, by whom bequeathed to the museum 1910
Coll.: Trustees of the British Museum (1910–2–12–288)

1491   Bellinzona   ?1843

Watercolour, with some pen, 225 × 280
Prov.: Henry Vaughan, by whom bequeathed to the gallery, 1900
Coll.: National Gallery of Ireland, Dublin (2420)

1492   Dazio Grande   ?1843

Watercolour, 229 × 277
Prov.: John Ruskin; Arthur Severn; R. C. Edwards
Private collection

1493   Faido   ?1843

Watercolour over faint pencil, 232 × 278
Prov.: J. S. Kennedy, by whom given to the Rt. Hon. Professor Sir Clifford Albutt, by whom bequeathed to the museum, 1925 (received 1935)
Coll.: Syndics of the Fitzwilliam Museum, Cambridge (1763; Cormack 48)

Stylistically similar to drawings of 1836, but evidently later, if the identification of the scene is correct. Another sheet very like this is T.B., CCCLXIV–128.

1494   An Italian town (in the Alps)   ?1843

Pencil, watercolour and pen, 229 × 292
Prov.: John Fleming, sale Christie 22 March 1879 (57, as 'Italian Tower'), bt. Agnew, and entered the museum's collection that year
Coll.: Victoria and Albert Museum, London (85–1879)

Compare the composition of the late finished drawing, *Sion near the Simplon Pass* (No. 1553).

1495   The   Domleschg   Valley,   Grisons, Switzerland   ?1843

Watercolour, 226 × 282
Prov.: C. S. Bale, sale Christie 14 May 1881 (193),

bt. James; Laundy Walters by 1902; by descent to his grand-daugther; Agnew 1975
Private collection

1496   The Rhine Valley, above Coire   ?1843

Watercolour over pencil, 230 × 289
Prov.: E. F. Nettlefold, sale Christie 5 June 1913 (43), bt. Agnew; Lloyd Roberts, by whom bequeathed to the gallery, 1920
Coll.: City Art Gallery, Manchester (1920.587)

1497   St. Gothard   ?1843

Pencil and watercolour on white paper prepared with a cream ground, 230 × 292
Prov.: Henry Vaughan, by whom bequeathed to the gallery, 1900
Coll.: National Galleries of Scotland, Edinburgh (877)

1498   The Blue Stream, St. Gothard ?1843

Watercolour and pencil, 232 × 295
Prov.: Norman and Agnes Lupton, by whom
bequeathed to the gallery, 1953
Coll.: City Art Galleries, Leeds, Yorkshire (13.223/
53)

1499   The Devil's Bridge, St. Gothard *c.* 1843

Watercolour, pen and grey and brown colour over
traces of pencil, 238 × 305
Inscr. in pencil by Turner verso: *Devil's Bridge
No. 8 04X* and *20*
Prov.: John Ruskin, by whom given to the museum,
1861
Coll.: Syndics of the Fitzwilliam Museum,
Cambridge (586; Cormack 45)

**1500   Hospenthal, Fall of St. Gothard—
morning** ?1843

Pencil, watercolour and body-colour, with some
pen and blue-black colour, 226 × 285
Prov.: John Ruskin, by whom given to the museum,
1861
Coll.: Syndics of the Fitzwilliam Museum,
Cambridge (588; Cormack 47)

1501   Hospenthal, Fall of St. Gothard—sunset
 ?1843

Pencil, watercolour and body-colour, with pen and
grey and purple colour, 227 × 286
Prov.: John Ruskin, by whom given to the museum,
1861
Coll.: Syndics of the Fitzwilliam Museum,
Cambridge (587; Cormack 46)

1502   Valley of St. Gothard ?1841

Pencil and watercolour with some scraping-out,
220 × 290
Prov.: R. Norton, Boston, U.S.A.; J. Leslie Wright;
Mrs. Dorian Williamson; anon. sale Sotheby,
24 November 1977 (119), bt. Agnew
Private collection

1503   Lake Thun: the Niessen ?1841

Watercolour, 254 × 355
Prov.: John Ruskin, sale Christie 15 April 1869
(33)
Coll.: untraced

Another drawing of this subject was also in
Ruskin's 1869 sale (34). One of the two may just
possibly be identifiable with the late view of *Lake
Thun* (No. 1504 below).

1504   Thun ?1841

Pencil and watercolour, with pen and red, blue and
yellow colour, 248 × 367
Prov.: Henry Vaughan, by whom bequeathed to the
gallery, 1900
Coll.: National Galleries of Scotland, Edinburgh
(866)

See No. 1503.

1505   Town and Lake of Thun ?1841

Watercolour, 227 × 287
Prov.: J. E. Taylor, by 1899; Agnew, 1913; Agnew,
1924; Mrs. A. A. Allen, sale Sotheby 15 May 1957
(64), bt. Agnew for the gallery
Coll.: Cecil Higgins Art Gallery, Bedford (P.122)

1506   Lake Brienz 1841

Watercolour and body-colour, 231 × 288

Exh.: R.A. 1974 (589)
Prov.: John Ruskin, ?sale Christie 15 April 1869 (40), bt. Agnew; Sir Hickman Bacon, Bt.; by descent to present owner
Private collection

1507   The Reichenbach   ?1844

Black chalk, pen and watercolour, 330 × 230
Prov.: C. J. Hegan, by whom presented to the school, 1935
Coll.: Harrow School, Middlesex (176)

1508   A view in Switzerland   ?c.1841

Watercolour, 232 × 292
Prov.: C. S. Bale, sale Christie 14 May 1881 (193, as 'Mountain torrent in Switzerland'), bt. Innes
Private collection

1509   River Scene (fort on a rock above a river) ?c.1841

Watercolour, 154 × 224
Prov.: John Ruskin, ?sale 15 April 1869 (5, as 'River Scene'), bt. Colnaghi; Bernard Buchanan McGeorge; Agnew, by whom sold 1958 to the Fine Art Society, London, from whom bt. Walter Brandt, 1959
Coll.: Trustees of the P. A. Brandt Settlement

Possibly a view at Sion or Bellinzona, this sheet is difficult to place. It may be related to the 'Rivers of Europe' project, and so date from the early 1830s.

1510   Swiss lake scene with bridge ('Bellinzona')   ?c.1840–2

Watercolour, 235 × 295 (sight)
Prov.: anon. sale Sotheby, 18 March 1964 (20); anon. sale Sotheby, 22 March 1979 (101, as 'A bridge over a river in the Alps')
Private collection

1511   Alpine landscape   ?1843

Watercolour over pencil, with some pen, 228 × 291
Prov.: John Ruskin, by whom given to the museum, 1861
Coll.: Syndics of the Fitzwilliam Museum, Cambridge (582; Cormack 42)

The subject was formerly known as *Scene in the Tyrol.* It may well depict a road in the Grisons.

1512   Alpine stream   c.1843

Watercolour, 229 × 286
Prov.: John Ruskin, ?sale Christie 15 April 1869 (36 or 37); Mrs. Walter Jones, by 1934
Private collection, U.S.A.

1513   A Swiss pass   ?1843

Watercolour and pencil, with some scratching-out, 232 × 291
Prov.: sale at 91 Eaton Square, 1906, bt. Vicars; Agnew; James Blair, by whom bequeathed to the gallery, 1917
Coll.: City Art Gallery, Manchester (1917.111)

1514   An Alpine Valley   c.1843

Watercolour, 229 × 292
Prov.: Mrs. J. W. Bunney; by descent to present owner
Private collection, U.S.A.

A slighter version of the same subject as No. 1512

1515   Swiss valley scene   ?c.1841–3

Watercolour over some pencil, 248 × 273
Prov.: F. Stevenson; Christie 22 June 1923 (23), bt. Gooden & Fox, for Lord Leverhulme
Coll.: The Lady Lever Collection, Port Sunlight, Cheshire (WHL 4697)

Perhaps a drawing from Turner's 1836 tour. See above Nos 1430–1456.

1516   Pass of St. Bernard *?c.* 1844

Watercolour and brown ink over pencil, 225 × 286
Prov.: D. J. Pound; W. Quilter, sale Christie 8 April 1875 (234), bt. White; H. L. Fison; Christie 6 November 1959 (6), bt. Fine Art Society, London, from whom purchased by anonymous donor to the museum
Coll.: Museum of Art, Rhode Island School of Design, Providence, R.I. (69.154.59)

See No. 1552 below.

1517   Looking towards Brunnen and the Seelisberg from Lake Zug *?* 1840s

Watercolour, 292 × 470
Prov.: Croal Thomson, from whom bt. by Walter Jones; anon. sale, Sotheby 26 March 1975 (216, as 'A mountain lake'), bt. C. Curtis
Coll.: Hinderton Trust, Wirral, Cheshire

This drawing is on a larger sheet than the usual roll-sketchbook size; but it does not belong with the big studies (Nos 1519–1522). The identification of the subject is uncertain.

1518   Castle on a river or lake *c.* 1841–4

Watercolour, 222 × 287 (sight)
Prov.: John Hay; by descent to present owner
Private collection, U.S.A.

The subject has not been identified; it may be a view of Ringgenberg on Lake Brienz, seen from the west.

XIX(c)   Nos 1519–1522
Large studies, *c.* **1842**

Large sheets, apparently of Swiss subjects, which Serota has suggested were made in Lucerne in 1842. It seems likely that they were done about that date, for they differ considerably from the large colour-beginnings of the later 1840s. Their function is not clear, however, and not all of them relate to the finished drawings of 1842–5.

1519   A valley in Switzerland *c.* 1842

Watercolour, 457 × 603
Prov.: Henry Vaughan, by whom bequeathed to the museum, 1900
Coll.: Victoria and Albert Museum, London (981–1900)

1520   The Moselle Bridge, Coblenz *c.* 1842

Pencil and watercolour, 454 × 592
Prov.: Pierre Bordeaux-Groult, Paris, from whom bt. by Paul Mellon, 1965
Coll.: Yale Center for British Art, Paul Mellon Collection

Hitherto known as *Le Pont, Lyon.* This colour-beginning—presumably not done on tour—may relate to the finished watercolour of 1842 (No. 1530).

1521   Mountainous landscape, with a lake *c.* 1842

Watercolour and pencil, 458 × 592
Inscr. lower right: *Dark* and *2nd Zut* (?) *2nd/Dark(?*

Prov.: Pierre Bordeaux-Groult, Paris, from whom bt. by Paul Mellon, 1965
Coll.: Yale Center for British Art, Paul Mellon Collection

Like No. 1520 this drawing seems to have been misnamed. The water is apparently a river, not a lake. The subject may be related to that of the finished watercolour of *Faido,* 1843 (No. 1538).

1522   The foot of the St. Gothard *c.* 1842

Watercolour, 440 × 570 (sight)
Prov.: ?Thomas Greenwood, sale Christie 13 February 1875 (275), bt. in; H. M. Hepworth, by whom given to the gallery 1943
Coll.: City Art Galleries, Leeds, Yorkshire (11.2/34)

SECTION XX
Nos 1523–1569
The late finished watercolours, 1842–1851

XX(a)   Nos 1523–1552
The finished Swiss subjects of 1842–1848, and related drawings

There are four series of finished watercolours that Turner made between 1841 and 1848, of which Ruskin gives lists or other explicit information; they are catalogued here with the few preliminary studies that do not still form part of the Turner Bequest, which are placed, in each case, immediately after the finished works to which they belong. The correspondence of study to final drawing is uniquely clear-cut in the watercolours of this period, and all those studies that are in the Bequest are referred to in the relevant entries. With the exception of the *Coblenz* (No. 1530) of 1842, all the subjects are Swiss, and the studies occur on sheets presumably removed from roll-sketchbooks used during Turner's tours of 1841, 1842, 1843 and 1844. They were presented by the artist to Thomas Griffith as 'samples' of compositions that he proposed to realise for any patrons who could be prevailed on to commission finished works (see chapter X). The dating of the 'samples' is simple for the series of 1842, which was completed between 1841 and 1842, from studies made on the Continent during the tour of 1841. It is probable that the subjects of the 1843 set derive from studies made in 1842; thereafter it becomes more dangerous to assert that 'samples' must belong to the tour preceding the execution of the finished drawings, and it may be that some of the 1845 subjects were taken from sketches made much earlier in the decade. The two drawings of 1847–8, however, seem likely to have been developed from studies of 1844, the year of Turner's final Swiss tour.

Nos 1523–1533: the ten drawings of 1842 (see Ruskin, *Works,* XIII, pp. 477–84)

1523   The Splügen Pass   1842

Watercolour, 292 × 451
Inscr. lower right: *BAINS*
Prov.: H. A. J. Munro of Novar (from T. Griffith, 1842), sale Christie 6 April 1878 (83, as 'Baths of Pfeffers; Ragatz, Pass of Splügen'), bt. Agnew; John Ruskin (presented to him by a group of friends, 1878); Arthur Severn, from whom bt. Agnew, 1923; Alexander T. Hollingsworth; Christie, 19 April 1929 (79), bt. Leggatt; F. J. Nettlefold, from whom bt. Agnew
Private collection

Based on the 'sample' study T.B., CCCLXIV–277.

1524   The Blue Rigi: Lake of Lucerne— sunrise*   1842

Watercolour, 297 × 450
Exh.: R.A. 1974 (601)
Prov.: Elhanan Bicknell, sale Christie 29 April 1863 (125), bt. Holmes; J. E. Taylor (by 1886), sale Christie 5 July 1912 (46), bt. Agnew; Walter H. Jones, sale Christie, 3 July 1942 (42), bt. Agnew; sold to uncle of present owner
Private collection

The 'sample' study on which this was based is possibly T.B., CCCLXIV–330.

1525   The Red Rigi*   1842

Watercolour, 305 × 458
Exh.: R.A. 1974 (603)
Prov.: H. A. J. Munro of Novar (from T. Griffith 1842); John Ruskin from whom bt. Colnaghi by 1878; J. E. Taylor, sale Christie 5 July 1912 (47); bt. Agnew; R. A. Tatton; T. A. Tatton, sale Christie 14 December 1928 (36), bt. Agnew; Walter H. Jones, sale Christie 3 July 1942 (41), bt. Fine Art Society, London; R. H. Turner; acquired by Felton Bequest, 1947
Coll.: National Gallery of Victoria, Melbourne (1704/4)

Based on the 'sample' study T.B., CCCLXIV–275.

1526   Lake Lucerne: Bay of Uri from above Brunnen*   1842

Watercolour over pencil, 292 × 457
Prov.: H. A. J. Munro of Novar, sale Christie 6 April 1878 (85), bt. Agnew; W. A. Watson Armstrong; Scott and Fowles, New York; Mrs. Joseph B. Schlotman, 1910, by whom bequeathed to present owner, 1974
Private collection, U.S.A.

The 'sample' study on which this composition was based is probably T.B., CCCLXIV–354.

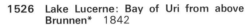

1527   Brunnen, Lake Lucerne   1842

Watercolour, 302 × 464
Exh.: R.A. 1974 (608)
Prov.: Elhanan Bicknell, sale Christie 30 April 1863 (265), bt. Colnaghi; J. Smith, sale Christie 15 April 1869 (51), bt. Lord Dudley; J. Irvine Smith, from whom bt. Agnew, 1907; C. Fairfax Murray, from whom bt. Agnew; Sir Donald Currie; by descent to Major L. K. Wisely; Mrs. Wisely; Agnew
Private collection, U.K.

The 'sample' study on which this design is based is No. 1528 below.

1528   Brunnen, with a steamer   c. 1841

Watercolour, 248 × 304
Prov.: Miss Griffith (daughter of T. Griffith), sale Christie 4 July 1887 (196), bt. Agnew; T. S. Kennedy; Mrs. T. S. Kennedy, sale Christie 22 February 1908 (69), bt. Agnew; Charles Fairfax Murray; E. D. Brandegee; James Lawrence, of Brookline, Mass., sale Christie 2 March 1976 (124), bt. Agnew
Private collection, U.S.A.

The 'sample' study for No. 1527 above.

1529   Lucerne from the Walls*   1842

Watercolour, with scraping-out, 295 × 455
Exh.: R.A. 1974 (607)
Prov.: John Ruskin; sold Vokins, c. 1875; Sir John Fowler, sale Christie 6 May 1889 (34), bt. Agnew; Edward Nettlefold; sale Christie 11 June 1909 (167), bt. Agnew; Sir Jeremiah Colman, sale Christie 2 May 1919 (136), bt. Sampson; D. Stoner Crowther; Christie 2 May 1924 (12), bt. Gooden and Fox; Viscount Leverhulme
Coll.: The Lady Lever Collection, Port Sunlight, Cheshire (4743)

Based on the 'sample' study T.B., CCCLXIV–290, which is inscribed verso: *J. Ruskin Junr Esqre; 17.*

1530   Coblenz   1842

Watercolour, ?303 × 467
Prov.: John Ruskin
Coll.: untraced

Based on the 'sample' study T.B., CCCLXIV–286, which is inscribed verso: *J. Ruskin Junr Esqre.* Another colour sketch of the Moselle Bridge at Coblenz is T.B., CCCLXIV–2; and for a large colour study apparently of this composition see No. 1520 above. At an early date the *Coblenz* was confused with a copy, perhaps made for Ruskin by William Ward, which was acquired by J. F. Haworth and listed as the original by Armstrong in his catalogue. It was reproduced by Cook and Wedderburn in their edition of Ruskin's *Works* (XIII, Pl. XXII), and the error has remained uncorrected ever since. I am grateful to Mr. Joseph Goldyne for kindly drawing my attention to this grave and long-standing misapprehension. Another good copy, also perhaps by Ward, is in an American private collection, and was referred to as the original by Clarence King, to whom Ruskin apparently gave it, in King's *Memoirs,* 1904 (pp. 129–30). A drawing called

'Bridge at Coblenz' was in Thomas Greenwood's collection; this was sold by Christie 12 April 1878 (51), and bt. F.A.S.; it was probably a study. The Haworth copy is now in the Art Museum, Cincinnati.

1531 Constance 1842

Watercolour, 304 × 454
Prov.: John Ruskin, from whom bt. Agnew, 1900; J. Irvine Smith, from whom bt. Agnew, 1903; R. E. Tatham, sale Christie 29 February 1908 (86), bt. Agnew; Sir Joseph Beecham, sale Christie 3 May 1917 (146), bt. Agnew; Sir Jeremiah Colman; by descent to present owner
Private collection

Based on the 'sample' study T.B., CCCLXIV–288.

1532 The Dark Rigi 1842

Watercolour, 305 × 455
Prov.: H. A. J. Munro of Novar, sale Christie 6 April 1878 (85), bt. Agnew; W. G. Cassels; Charles Alfred Swinburne, sale Christie 2 July 1904 (53), bt. Colnaghi; Sir Max Wachter; by descent, sale Sotheby 16 July 1975 (152), bt. Leggatt
Private collection

Based on the 'sample' study T.B., CCCLXIV–279, which is inscribed verso: *J A Munro Esq 31*.

1533 Zurich 1842

Watercolour, 300 × 456
Exh.: B.M., 1975 (286)
Prov.: H. A. J. Munro of Novar, sale Christie 6 April 1878 (87), bt. Agnew; J. Irvine Smith; Agnew, 1907; Sir George Drummond, sale Christie 27 June 1919 (129), bt. Agnew; C. Morland Agnew; R. W. Lloyd, 1924, by whom bequeathed to the museum, 1958
Coll.: Trustees of the British Museum (1958–7-12-445)

Based on the 'sample' study T.B., CCCLXIV–291, which is inscribed verso: *J A Munro Esqre; 16*.

Nos 1534–1539: the six drawings of 1843 (see Ruskin, *Works*, XIII, pp. 209, 477–84)

1534 Kussnacht, Lake of Lucerne 1843

Watercolour, 305 × 473
Signed and dated lower right: *JMWT 1843*
Prov.: H. A. J. Munro of Novar, sale Christie 6 April 1878 (86), bt. Goupil; C. A. Swinburne, sale Christie 2 July 1904 (52), bt. Smith; Sir John D. Milburn, Bt., sale Christie 11 June 1909 (152), bt. Wallis & Son; James Blair, by whom bequeathed to the gallery, 1917
Coll.: City Art Gallery, Manchester (1917.103)

Based on the 'sample' study T.B., CCCLXIV–208, which is inscribed verso: *Kusnacht and Tell's Church and Gessler's Castle—Lake of Lucerne No. 2* and *Mr Munro*.

1535 Lake of Zug: early morning 1843

Watercolour, 298 × 466

Prov.: H. A. J. Munro of Novar; John Ruskin (1878); Lord Dudley; T. W. Kennedy, sale Christie 15 May 1895 (95), bt. Agnew; Sir Donald Currie; by descent to Major F. D. Mirrielees, sale Christie 20 March 1959 (56), bt. Agnew, from whom purchased by the museum through the Marquand Fund, 1959.
Coll.: Metropolitan Museum of Art, New York (Marquand Fund; 59.120)

Based on the 'sample' study T.B., CCCLXIV–280, which is inscribed verso: *Art—Lake of Zug. No. 9; X810; Mr Munro*.

1536 Lucerne: moonlight 1843

Watercolour, 290 × 476
Exh.: B.M. 1975 (292)
Prov.: H. A. J. Munro of Novar, sale Christie 2 June 1877 (34), bt. Agnew; J. Irvine Smith; R. E. Tatham, by whom bequeathed to W. G. Gibbs; Agnew, 1920; R. W. Lloyd, by whom bequeathed to the museum, 1958
Coll.: Trustees of the British Museum (1958–7-12-446)

Based on the 'sample' study T.B. CCCLXIV–324.

1537 Goldau* 1843

Watercolour, 305 × 470
Exh.: R.A. 1974 (611)
Prov.: John Ruskin; George Coats (by 1901); by descent until 1978; Agnew 1978
Private collection, U.S.A.

Based on the 'sample' study T.B. CCCLXIV–281, which is inscribed verso: *Goldau-Rigi—and the Lake of Zug*.

1538 The Pass of Faido* 1843

Watercolour and scraping-out over pencil, 305 × 470
Exh.: R.A. 1974 (612)
Prov.: John Ruskin; George Coats (by 1901); by descent to the present owner
Private collection

Based on the 'sample' study T.B., CCCLXIV–209, which is inscribed verso: *Pass Piolano Tessin No 14*.

1539 Bellinzona, from the road to Locarno 1843

Watercolour, with scraping-out, 292 × 457
Exh.: R.A. 1974 (613)
Prov.: H. A. J. Munro of Novar; sale 'property of a gentleman' Christie 28 May 1920 (150, as 'Ehren-

breitstein'), bt. Cooling; Vicars Bros., 1927; Mark Fletcher, sale Sotheby 30 November 1960 (57), bt. Agnew; purchased by the gallery from the Edmond and Webster Bequests with a grant from the National Art-Collections Fund (Ramsay–Dyce Bequest), 1960
Coll.: Art Gallery, Aberdeen, Scotland (60.63)

Based on the 'sample' study T.B., CCCXXXII–25, which is inscribed verso: *Bellinzona No 12* and *Mr Munro*. This drawing is not listed in Ruskin's principal account of the drawings of 1842–3, but is referred to by him elsewhere (*Works*, XIII, p. 209).

Nos 1540–1549: the ten drawings of 1845 (see Ruskin, *Works,* XIII, pp. 194, 199, 200, 205, 476 note).

1540 Schaffhausen: the town and castle 1845

Watercolour, 292 × 477
Prov.: John Ruskin; H. A. J. Munro of Novar; Ralph Brocklebank; A. T. Hollingsworth: Walter Wedgwood
Coll.: Toledo Museum of Art, Toledo, Ohio (54.26)

Based on the 'sample' study T.B., CCCLXIV–337, which is inscribed verso: *Munro. Schaffhausen. 30.*

1541 Fluelen: morning (looking towards the lake) 1845

Watercolour, 299 × 481
Prov.: H. A. J. Munro of Novar; John Ruskin; Pattinson, sale Christie 21 June 1875 (26), bt. Agnew; John Hetherington until 1903; Cornelia Sage, Albany, New York; Agnew, from whom bt., 1974
Coll.: Yale Center for British Art, Paul Mellon Collection

Based on the 'sample' study T.B., CCCLXIV–282, which is inscribed verso *Munro*. The subject has since at least 1875 been mistitled 'Brunnen and the Schwytz Mountains'.

1542 Lake Lucerne 1845

Watercolour, size unknown
Prov.: ?John Ruskin; Mrs. Newall
Coll.: untraced

This is the only one of the late Swiss drawings recorded by Ruskin to be untraced today, unless it is in fact the drawing catalogued here as *Lucerne Town* (No. 1544 below).

1543 Lake of Lucerne—sunset 1845

Watercolour, 292 × 477
Prov.: John Ruskin; Holdsworth; Sir John Pender, from whom bt. Agnew, 1882; A. Haworth; by descent to present owner
Private collection

Based on the 'sample' study T.B., CCCLXIV–338, which is inscribed verso: *Ruskin, Lucerne*.

1544 Lucerne Town 1845

Pencil and watercolour, with some body-colour and scraping-out, 292 × 464

Prov.: John Ruskin (who bt. it from the artist), who sold it to Mrs. Newall, 1865; by descent until 1978; Agnew 1979
Private collection, Federal Republic of Germany

Based on the 'sample' study T.B., CCCLXIV–386. The drawing was identified by Joll (1967, No. 94) as the *Lake of Lucerne* listed by Ruskin as No. 3, of the 1845 set; but the same catalogue entry also quoted Ruskin's mention of *Lucerne Town, from the Lake* which must be the *Lucerne Town* he lists as No. 5. *Lake Lucerne* is apparently lost (see No. 1542 above).

1545 Brunnen, from the Lake of Lucerne 1845

Watercolour, 290 × 477
Prov.: John Ruskin; H. A. J. Munro of Novar; A. Haworth (?); John Yates; J. F. Talmage, sale New York 20 February 1913 (20); J. William Clark; Margaretta C. Clark (?); sale Parke Bernet 23 October 1941 (30), bt. Scott & Fowles, New York; D. R. S. Clark, 1941
Coll.: Sterling and Francine Clark Art Institute, Williamstown, Mass. (1865)

Based on the 'sample' study T.B., CCCLXIV–375, which is inscribed verso: *Lucerne looking towards Schwitz* and *Ruskin,* with notes and sketches; it is on paper watermarked *1822*.

1546 Storm in a Swiss pass ('First bridge above Altdorf') 1845

Watercolour and surface scratching, 290 × 470
Prov.: John Ruskin; H. A. J. Munro of Novar; F. R. Leyland; Abraham Haworth; Jesse Haworth, by whom bequeathed to the Whitworth Institute 1920; entered the collection on the death of Mrs. Jesse Haworth, 1937
Coll.: Whitworth Art Gallery, University of Manchester (D.23.1937)

Based on the 'sample' study T.B., CCCLXIV–283, which is inscribed verso: *Altorf* (*sic*).

1547   Lake of Lucerne, from Brunnen   1845

Watercolour, 279 × 464
Engr.: by R. Wallis, 1854 (R. 671)
Prov.: B. G. Windus; Mrs. de Patron; Mrs. Williams;
C. W. Dyson Perrins, sale, Sotheby 24 April 1959
(69), bt. Kurt Pantzer
Coll.: Pantzer Collection, Indianapolis

Based on the 'sample' study T.B., CCCLXIV–385,
which is inscribed verso: *Lucerne.*

1548   Zurich: fête, early morning*   1845

Watercolour, some pencil, with scraping-out,
293 × 475
Engr.: by T. A. Prior, 1854 (R. 672)
Prov.: B. G. Windus; Gillott, sale Christie 4 May
1872 (510, as 'Zurich'), bt. Vokins; R. E. Tatham,
sale Christie 7 March 1908 (87), bt. Wallis;
D. Course (?); with Wallis & Son, 1908; Robert
Paterson, sale Parke Bernet 19 March 1938,
bt. Knoedler; Agnew; Rayner MacConnell;
W. A. Locker; Mrs. W. A. Locker, sale Louis Taylor,
Stoke-on-Trent, 28 January 1976 (728), bt.
Leger
Coll.: Kunsthaus, Zurich (1976/14)

Based on the 'sample' study T.B., CCCLXIV–289,
which is inscribed verso: *Windus Zurich.*

1549   Fluelen, from the Lake of Lucerne
1845

Watercolour, 290 × 482
Prov.: H. A. J. Munro of Novar; Revd. C. U. Barry;
Mrs. P. G. Hewitt; R. Brocklebank; Grace Rainey
Rogers; Walter Wedgwood; purchased through
the Mr. and Mrs. William H. Marlatt Fund
Coll.: Cleveland Museum of Art, Ohio, U.S.A.

Based on the 'sample' study T.B., CCCLXIV–381,
which is inscribed verso: *Altorf* and *Windus.*

Nos 1550, 1552: the two drawings made for
Ruskin about January 1848 (see Ruskin, *Works,*
XIII, p. 194, and Finberg, *Life,* p. 420).

1550   The Brunig Pass, from Meiringen*
1847–8

Watercolour, 318 × 527
Prov.: John Ruskin; sale Christie 22 May 1852
(61), bt. in; ?Thomas Greenwood, sale Christie
13 February 1875 (277), bt. in; sale Christie
12 April 1878 (49), bt. Fine Art Society, London;
Richard S. Davis, Minneapolis
Private collection, U.S.A.

Based on the drawing No. 1551 below. Ruskin
annotated a letter to him from Turner, dated
13 January 1848, as referring to this and the
Descent of the St. Gothard (No. 1552 below). The
pair were presumably executed late in 1847 or
early in January 1848.

1551   Brunig Pass (from Meiringen)   ?1844

Watercolour, 252 × 362
Prov.: Leger Galleries, London, 1968; U.S.A.
?Private collection, U.S.A.

This roll sketchbook sheet is the source for the
finished *Brunig Pass* of 1847–8 (No. 1550 above).
It was probably noted when Turner visited Meiringen in 1844; see the *Meiringen and Grindelwald*
sketchbook (T.B., CCCXLVII), to which this page may
belong.

1552   The Descent of the St. Gothard (Valley of
the Ticino)   1847–8

Watercolour, 318 × 527
Prov.: John Ruskin; H. A. J. Munro of Novar, sale
Christie 6 April 1878 (84), bt. Agnew; A. G. Kurtz,

sale 9 May 1891 (205), bt. Agnew; Sir Donald
Currie; by descent to the present owner
Private collection

Executed at the same date as No. 1550 above. No
'sample' study is known for this composition,
though it is similar in many respects to the drawing
in the Rhode Island School of Design called *Pass of
St. Bernard* (No. 1516).

XX(b)   Nos 1553–1569
The 'Final Set', c. 1846–1851

These are drawings either executed between 1846
and 1851, or connected (as preparatory studies,
etc.) to works of that period. Some are similar to the
finished drawings of 1848 (Nos 1550, 1552) or to
the study related to one of them; but nearly all the
items listed here are compositions that Turner
worked out, or evidently planned, on the larger
scale of sheets measuring approximately 370 ×
540 mm. They exhibit a continuous progression
from the style of the 1845 drawings (e.g. the *Storm
in a Swiss Pass* or the *Zurich: fête* Nos 1546, 1548)
to a wholly different manner, seen at its most
pronounced in the *Lake of Thun, Florence* and *Genoa*
(Nos 1567, 1568, 1569), which, it is conceivable,
were made immediately before Turner's death in
1851. Unlike the drawings listed in the preceding
section, none of these appears to have been known
to Ruskin. Titles have been confused, and consequently provenances are also muddled. Whether
Turner intended to complete a further set of ten
drawings, or whether these should be regarded as
independent exercises, is not clear; but the general
uniformity of size suggests that a set was planned.
In fact, there are more than ten subjects in all,
counting those for which colour studies only exist.
The size is that of the *Heidelberg—sunset,* of
c. 1840 (No. 1376), and like the finished drawings
of c. 1840, this group is not confined to Swiss
themes.

1553   Sion, near the Simplon Pass   c. 1846

Watercolour with traces of pencil, 374 × 553
Prov.: L. B. Mozley, sale Christie 27 May 1865
(184), bt. Agnew; John Fowler; E. F. White;
Agnew, 1887; Lloyd Roberts, 1890; Dr. D. Lloyd
Roberts, by whom bequeathed to the gallery,
1920
Coll.: City Art Gallery, Manchester (1920.591)

Evidently a late drawing, with some characteristics
of the 1845 set, but in the large format of the last
group. It appears to be a restatement of the
principal motif of the great *Splügen* of 1842
(No. 1523). A study that may relate to the design is
No. 1494.

Watercolour, 246 × 365
Prov.: Vernon Wethered by 1936; by descent to his son, sale Christie 2 March 1976 (125), bt. Agnew
Private collection

1554 Heidelberg* *c.* 1846

Watercolour, 372 × 557
Prov.: Henry Vaughan, by whom bequeathed to the gallery, 1900
Coll.: National Galleries of Scotland, Edinburgh (885)

Compare the two earlier views of Heidelberg, Nos 1376, 1377.

1555 Lyons* ?*c.* 1846

Watercolour with some body-colour, 241 × 305
Prov.: Henry Vaughan, by whom bequeathed to the museum, 1900
Coll.: Victoria and Albert Museum, London (977–1900)

This is perhaps a motif collected by Turner when he toured the Loire or the Seine—possibly a view of Troyes. In conception and style, however, the sheet evidently belongs to a later period; it is from a roll sketchbook, but seems unlikely to have been made on the spot. It has features in common with the late drawing of Heidelberg (No. 1554) and perhaps dates from the same time, intended, possibly, as a further subject in the same group.

1556 Pallanza, Lago Maggiore 1848–50

Watercolour, 368 × 540
Exh.: R.A. 1974 (615)
Prov.: L. B. Mozley, sale Christie 21 May 1865 (186); Sir John Fowler, sale Christie 6 May 1899 (30), bt. Agnew; Sir Donald Currie; by descent to the present owner
Coll.: Mrs. J. H. S. Bowring

The identification of this scene has been questioned; Bellinzona has been suggested (see *Turner in Switzerland*, p. 124). The colouring and general handling of this drawing are very similar to those of the *Oberhofen* (No. 1557).

1557 Oberhofen, on Lake Thun *c.* 1848–50

Watercolour, with some body-colour, 368 × 540
Exh.: R.A. 1974 (616)
Prov.: ?Gen. Rawdon; ?W. Quilter, sale Christie 18 May 1889 (96), bt. Colnaghi; Joseph Ruston; John Smith; by descent to Sir Leslie Farrer, sale Sotheby 15 July 1959 (83), bt. Verney
Coll.: Pantzer Collection, Indianapolis

Very possibly developed from the roll sketchbook drawing (No. 1558), though likely to be rather later in date; an alternative source for this design (though probably not for No. 1558) is a pencil sketch in the *Lake of Thun* sketchbook

(T.B., LXXVI–67), inscribed *Oberhofen;* Turner could well have had recourse, as in other works of his last years, to a motif from his youth. The subject was previously known as 'Geneva', and its provenance has been confused with that of No. 1569.

1558 Oberhofen, on Lake Thun ?1844

Watercolour, with some pen, 245 × 356
Exh.: R.A. 1974 (591)
Prov.: John Leigh Clark, sale Christie 28 March 1868 (97, as 'Lago di Garda'), bt. Agnew; James Worthington; by descent until 1917; R. A. Tatton; T. A. Tatton, sale Christie 14 December 1928 (30), bt. Agnew; Lord Horder, sale Sotheby 12 December 1958 (104), bt. Agnew; George Goyder; Agnew
Coll.: Mrs. Cecil Keith

The assured, crisp finish of this drawing suggests a date earlier than 1844, and it may belong to Turner's 1841 tour; its connection with the large, evidently late, watercolour of Oberhofen (No. 1557) is not entirely established, but seems likely. The view has been known as 'Lake Garda' and 'Spiez on Lake Thun'.

1559 The Lake of Thun ?1844 or later

1560 Lake Nemi *c.* 1848–50

Watercolour, 369 × 540
Prov.: John Heugh, sale Christie 24 April 1874 (83), bt. Agnew; J. Knowles, sale Christie 19 May 1877 (92), bt. Agnew; Mrs. Williams; C. W. Dyson Perrins; Sotheby 26 April 1959 (68)
Private collection

Close in general treatment to *Oberhofen* and *Pallanza*, though evidently not so near to completion as those drawings. No. 1561 may be connected with this subject.

1561 A Swiss subject (Lake Nemi) ?1844

Watercolour and body-colour, 229 × 320
Prov.: Sir Abe Bailey, by whom bequeathed to the gallery, 1946
Coll.: South African National Gallery, Cape Town (1517)

Possibly a leaf from the *Meiringen and Grindelwald* sketchbook (T.B., CCCXLVII), from which the study for the *Brunig Pass* may have come (see Nos 1550, 1551). It may be related to the large unfinished watercolour known as *Lake Nemi* (No. 1560).

1562 Lake Brienz *c.* 1848–50

Watercolour, some pen and red ink, with scratching-out, 337 × 545
Prov.: Henry Vaughan, by whom bequeathed to the museum, 1900

Coll.: Victoria and Albert Museum, London (980–1900)

Similar in treatment to the *Lake with hills* (No. 1563) and *Swiss Pass* (No. 1565).

1563 Lake with hills (?Brienz) *c.* 1848–50

Watercolour, 353 × 527
Prov.: J. E. Taylor, by whom given to the museum, 1894
Coll.: Victoria and Albert Museum, London (124–1894)

Compare the *Lake Brienz* and *Swiss Pass* (Nos 1562, 1565).

1564 Swiss lake scene *c.* 1848

Watercolour, pen and red colour and scraping-out on flecked white paper, 272 × 388
Prov.: J. B. MacGeorge, sale Morrison McLearly, Glasgow, 16 May 1958 (86), bt. Fine Art Society, London; Agnew 1978
Coll.: Jan Krugier, Geneva

Apparently a sample study of the composition for which No. 1563 is a colour-beginning. The rich colour, especially the dense turquoise of the lake, is similar to that in the study of *Oberhofen* (No. 1558), although this drawing, with its more generalized design and rather crude indications of figures, seems to be later than that.

1565 A Swiss pass *c.* 1848–50

Watercolour, 359 × 508
Prov.: J. E. Taylor, by whom given to the museum, 1894
Coll.: Victoria and Albert Museum, London (125–1894)

This sheet has been known simply as *A mountainous landscape;* it may be a reworking of the *Faido* subject of 1843 (No. 1538), since the central feature, the cleft in the hills, is similar in both designs. It occurs also in an earlier study, on an even larger sheet (No. 1521); and also see No. 1562.

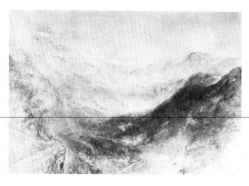

1566 Simplon Pass *c.* 1850

Watercolour over traces of pencil, 380 × 552
Inscr. lower right with calculations
Prov.: L. B. Mozley, sale Christie 27 May 1865 (185), bt. Agnew; Sir John Fowler, sale Christie 6 May 1899 (33), bt. Gooden; Edward W. Forbes, by whom given to the museum, 1954
Coll.: Fogg Art Museum, Harvard University, Cambridge, Mass. (1954.133)

1567 Lake of Thun* *c.* 1850–1

Watercolour, 369 × 541
Prov.: Gen. Rawdon; William Quilter, sale Christie 9 April 1875 (237), bt. in; sale Christie 18 May 1889 (97), bt. Agnew; Joseph Ruston, sale Christie 4 July 1913 (106), bt. Agnew; Charles P. Taft
Coll.: Taft Museum, Cincinnati, Ohio

1568 Florence *c.* 1850–1

Pencil and watercolour, 342 × 431
Prov.: ?William Houldsworth, sale Christie 23 May 1891 (31), bt. Duncan; ?William Houldsworth, sale Christie 16 May 1896 (51), bt. Wallis; Charles Hosmer; by descent to Olive Hosmer, from whom bt. by present owner, 1960
Private collection, U.S.A.

Very close in type to Nos 1567 and 1569, this drawing is, however, on a smaller sheet; it is possible that it has been cut down from a size uniform with the others in the group. If so, it may be identifiable with the drawing of Florence measuring 356 × 533 (the standard dimensions of this late series) sold twice by William Houldsworth in the 1890s.

1569 Genoa* *c.* 1850–1

Watercolour, blotting-out and pencil, 370 × 543
Prov.: ?Gen. Rawdon; ?William Quilter, sale Christie 9 April 1875 (236), bt. in; sale Christie 18 May 1889 (96), bt. Colnaghi; Mrs. Lees; Agnew, 1910; James Blair, by whom bequeathed to the gallery, 1917
Coll.: City Art Gallery, Manchester (1917.101)

This drawing appeared in the Quilter sales as 'Geneva'.

Addenda to the Watercolour Catalogue

These additional watercolours have been allotted numbers distinguished by the letter 'a'. The numbers themselves will enable the reader to place each drawing in its proper context in the catalogue; that is, immediately following the same number there, and subject to the comments applying to other items in the same section or sub-section.

Coll.: H. Schickman Gallery, New York

chell's—Size of Landilio Bridge'. This is probably a reference to the drawing exhibited in 1796 (No. 140).

13a Interior of King John's Palace, Eltham *c.* 1793

Watercolour, 388 × 260
Prov.: unknown
Private collection, U.K.

A variant of the subject of No. 13.

40a Finchley Church *c.* 1793–4

Pencil and watercolour with some body-colour, 240 × 310
Inscr. on reverse of old mount: *Original Drawing by Turner of Finchley Church made for my father in 1793 or 4 – Charles Monro*
Prov.: Thomas Monro; by descent to Charles Monro; Mrs. Stotherd; Lady Howard Dobson and R. A. Mills, sale Sotheby 22 March 1979 (132), bt. Schickman

56a Battle Abbey *c.* 1794

Pencil and watercolour, 305 × 222
Prov.: D. Thompson
Coll.: Williamson Art Gallery, Birkenhead

169a Aberdulais Mill *c.* 1796

Watercolour, approx. 356 × 502
Prov.: Col. A. T. Utterson by 1945
Coll.: Wernher Collection, Luton Hoo

A study of the subject is in the *South Wales* sketchbook (T.B., XXVI-6); on p. 49 of the same book Turner noted: 'Aberdillias Mill—Mr. Mit-

347a Edinburgh Castle (Edinburgh from the Water of Leith) *c.* 1802

Watercolour and scraping-out over pencil, 610 × 673
Prov.: ?Mrs. Worthington; Captain and Mrs. Johnson, by whom presented to the gallery, 1945
Coll.: Graves Art Gallery, Sheffield

Apparently a contemporary version of the subject of No. 347. Finberg (Index) notes that Mrs. Worthington's drawing was smaller than the exhibited work, as is this sheet. But the watercolour is in poor condition and may have been trimmed (top and left sides) from the full size at some point in its history; the composition as it is now does not seem complete.

689a Cologne *c.* 1820

Watercolour and body-colour, with some scraping-out, 241 × 336
Sig. lower right: *IMW Turner* and again faintly lower centre
Prov.: T. F. Blackwell, sale Christie 19 June 1979 (124), bt. Mitsukoshi
Private collection, Tokyo

Similar in type to the drawings made for Cooke's projected Rhine series (see No. 687), though this sheet is slightly larger than the identified designs for the series. Like No. 690 it may repeat the composition of No. 670.

997a Chateau Hamelin *c.* 1826–30

Watercolour and body-colour with scraping-out on blue paper, 133 × 183
Prov.: Lewis Loyd; Capt. E. N. F. Loyd, sale Christie 30 April 1937 (65); Thomson; Professor E. Harold Hughes; by descent to the present owner

Private collection, U.K.

1344a Castle of Sooneck on the Rhine ? 1844

Pencil and watercolour with some scraping-out on paper prepared with a grey wash, 170 × 230
Prov.: A. J. Finberg; Professor E. Harold Hughes; by descent to the present owner
Private collection, U.K.

1378a Berncastel *c.* 1835

Watercolour, 290 × 420
Prov.: A. Harris; Mrs. Benson Rathbone; Mrs. F. M. Peel, sale Sotheby 14 December 1972 (100), bt. Noble
Private collection, U.K.

This drawing, together with Nos. 406, 1051 and 1378, seems to belong to a sequence of finished Rhine subjects of the mid-1830s, though it is uncertain whether they were conceived as a set.

APPENDICES

BIBLIOGRAPHY

This bibliography contains the principal works on Turner and those which include significant material relating to him. Abbreviations used in this book are indicated in square brackets after the relevant entries.

A.   UNPUBLISHED MATERIAL

Agnew, M., List of seventeen drawings formerly in the collection of Mr. Morland Agnew (d. 1931), afterwards divided between his son and daughter. Typescript, 1932

Bell, C. F., MS. notes in *The Exhibited Works of J. M. W. Turner, R.A.* Victoria and Albert Museum Library

— —, MS. notes in 'Turner and his Engravers', *The Genius of Turner,* ed. C. Holme, The Studio Ltd., 1903. Victoria and Albert Museum Library

— —, MS. notes in A. J. Finberg, *A Complete Inventory of Drawings in the Turner Bequest,* 1909, Print Room, British Museum

— —, MS. notes in A. J. Finberg, *In Venice with Turner,* 1930, Victoria and Albert Museum Library

— —, MS. notes in A. J. Finberg, *Life of J. M. W. Turner,* 1939, Victoria and Albert Museum Library

Farington, J., Manuscript diary, 1793–1821, in the Royal Library, Windsor; selection published as *The Farington Diary,* ed. James Greig, 8 vols., London, 1922–8 [Farington, *Diary*]. A complete new edition is in progress, eds. K. Garlick and A. Macintyre. First 2 vols., London, New Haven, 1979

Fawkes, F. H., MS. catalogue of oil-paintings and watercolour drawings and sketches in watercolour in the possession of F. H. Fawkes, of Farnley Hall, 1850. Victoria and Albert Museum Library

Finberg, A. J., Index (on cards) of Turner's watercolours in private and public collections. Print Room, British Museum [Finberg, Index]

— —, Turner's Work, 1787–1851. Ten vols. of photographs compiled by Finberg. Print Room, British Museum, B.M. 182* b. 2–11

— —, Reviews of Thornbury's *Life,* compiled by Finberg. 2 vols., Print Room, British Museum, MM.5.34, 35

— —, Notes on four pencil drawings made by J. M. W. Turner in May or June 1793. Print Room, British Museum, MM.5.6

— — and Bell, C. F., Notes on two of Turner's sketchbooks and other papers. Print Room, British Museum, MM.5.4

— — — —, Turner Papers. A volume of cuttings and articles on J. M. W. Turner. Print Room, British Museum, MM.5.6

Jones, G., R.A., MS. reminiscences. Bodleian Library, Oxford

Pye, J., MS. collection of John Pye's correspondence and papers relating to Turner etc., 1813–84. Victoria and Albert Museum Library

Rawlinson, W. G., MS. letters to Rawlinson relating to Turner's *Liber Studiorum.* Print Room, British Museum, MM.5.24

Serota, N., J. M. W. Turner's Alpine Tours. Unpublished thesis, Courtauld Institute of Art, University of London, 1970

Stuckey, C. F., Turner: his Birthday and Related Matters. Unpublished article

Wunder, R. P., A Catalogue of Some Early Turner Drawings in New England. Unpublished thesis, Harvard, 1953

B.   BOOKS AND ARTICLES

[Amsterdam], *Light and Sight,* an Anglo-Netherlands Symposium, 22 May 1973, Amsterdam, 1974

Antal, F., 'Reflections on Classicism and Romanticism', *Burlington Magazine,* LXVI, April 1935, pp. 159–68; LXVIII, March 1936, pp. 130–9; LXXVII, September 1940, pp. 72–80; December, pp. 188–92; LXXVIII, January 1941, pp. 14–22

Armstrong, Sir W., *Turner,* 2 vols., 1902

Arnoult, L., *Turner, Wagner, Corot,* Paris, 1930

Ashby, T., 'Turner in Rome', *Burlington Magazine,* XXIV, January 1914, pp. 218–24; XXV, May 1914, pp. 98–104

—, 'Turner in Tivoli', *Burlington Magazine,* XXV, July 1914, pp. 241–7

—, 'Turner ed i suoi predecessori a Roma', *Congresso internazionale de Storia dell'Arte, 1912,* 1922, p. 438

—, *Turner's Vision of Rome,* London–New York, 1925

Bachrach, A. G. H., *Turner and Rotterdam, 1817, 1825, 1841,* 1974

—, 'J. M. W. Turner's "This made me a painter": a note on visual perception and representational accuracy', *Light and Sight,* 1974 (reprinted in *Koninklijke Nederlandse Akademie van Wetenschappen,* Amsterdam), pp. 41–58

Baldry, A. L., *British Marine Painting,* Studio, London, 1919

Bayes, W., *Turner: a Speculative Portrait,* London, 1931

Bazalgette, L., 'Crome et Turner, peintres de Paris', *L'Art et les Artistes,* XII, 1910, p. 124

Bega, *The Turner Spell: its Influence and Significance,* London, 1931

Beckett, R. B., '"Kilgarren Castle", a Link between Turner and Wilson', *Connoisseur,* CXX, September 1947, pp. 10–15

Bell, C. F., *The Exhibited Works of J. M. W. Turner, R.A.,* London, 1901

—, 'The Oxford Almanacks', *Art Journal,* LXVI, 1904

Binyon, R. L., *English Watercolours,* London, 1933; 2nd ed., 1934

—, *English Watercolours from the Work of Turner, Girtin, Cotman, Constable and Bonington,* London, 1949

Boase, T. S. R., 'English Artists and the Val d'Aosta', *Journal of the Warburg and Courtauld Institutes,* XIX, July 1956, pp. 283–93

—, 'Shipwrecks in English Romantic Painting', *Journal of the Warburg and Courtauld Institutes,* XXII, July–December 1959, pp. 332–46

—, *English Art, 1800–70,* Oxford, 1959 [Oxford History of English Art]

Bolt, T., 'New Leaves in Turner's Life', *Connoisseur,* XV, June 1906, pp. 111–16

Bonacina, L. C. W., 'Turner's Portrayal of Weather', *Quarterly Journal of the Royal Meteorological Society,* LXIV, 1938

Bouvy, E., 'Turner et Piranesi', *Etudes italiennes,* I, 1919

Brill, F., *Turner's 'Peace—Burial at Sea',* 1969

British Museum, *J. M. W. Turner: Twelve Watercolours in the British Museum,* London, 1976

Brock, A. C., 'The Weakness and Strength of Turner', *Burlington Magazine*, XVIII, October 1910, pp. 21–3

Brooke, S., *Notes on the Liber Studiorum of J. M. W. Turner, R.A.*, 1885

Brown, D., 'Turner, Callcott and Thomas Lister Parker: New Light on Turner's "Junction of the Thames and Medway" in Washington', *Burlington Magazine*, CXVII, 1975, pp. 719–22

Bullard, F., 'Thoughts Suggested by the Study of Turner's *Liber Studiorum*', appendix to catalogue of *Exhibition of the Liber Studiorum of J. M. W. Turner and a few Engravings after his Drawings*, Boston, Mass., 1904

—, *A Catalogue of the Engraved Plates for Picturesque Views in England and Wales, with notes and commentaries*, Boston, Mass., 1910

Bunt, C. G. E., *J. M. W. Turner: Poet of Light and Colour*, Leigh-on-Sea, 1948

Burnet, J., *Turner and his Works*, with a 'Memoir' by Peter Cunningham, London, 1852; 2nd ed., London, 1859

Butlin, M., *Turner Watercolours*, 1962 [Butlin, 1962]

—, *The Later Works of J. M. W. Turner*, Tate Gallery, London, 1965

—, *Watercolours from the Turner Bequest, 1819–1845*, 1968

—, see Rothenstein, J.

Butlin, M., and Joll, E., *The Paintings of J. M. W. Turner*, 2 vols., London—New Haven, 1977 [Butlin and Joll, 1977]

Carendente, G., 'Un viaggio di Turner in Umbria', *Spoletium*, Anno XI, 13, April 1968, pp. 13–24

Carey, C. W., 'The "Van Tromp" Pictures of J. M. W. Turner, R.A.', *Magazine of Art*, 1899, pp. 173–5

Chamot, M., *The Early Works of J. M. W. Turner*, London, 1965

Chignell, R., *J. M. W. Turner, R.A.*, London, 1902

Clare, C., *J. M. W. Turner, His Life and Work*, London, 1951

Clark, Sir K., 'Turner at Petworth', *Ambassador*, 8, 1949, pp. 75–90

—, 'Turner, the Snowstorm', *Looking at Art*, London, 1960

Clifford, T., *Vues pittoresques de Luxembourg: dessins et aquarelles par J. M. W. Turner 1775–1851*, Luxembourg, 1977

Colvin, S., 'Turner's Evening Gun', *The Portfolio*, 1872, pp. 75–6

—, 'The Sun of Venice going to Sea', *The Portfolio*, 1874, pp. 161–2

Coode, C. E., 'Turner's First Patron', *Art Journal*, 1901

Cook, Sir E. T., *Hidden Treasures at the National Gallery*, London, 1905

Cornwell-Clyne, A., 'The Birth of a Masterpiece: Crossing the Brook', *Country Life*, 14 April 1955, pp. 974–6

Crawford, H. J., *Turner's Sketches and Drawings of Stirling and Neighbourhood*, Stirling, 1936

Croft Murray, E., 'An Unpublished Early Watercolour by J. M. W. Turner: "Cote House, Bristol"', *Burlington Magazine*, XC, April 1948, pp. 106–9

Cundall, E. G., *Fonthill Abbey: A Descriptive Account of Five Watercolour Drawings by J. M. W. Turner, R.A.*, privately printed for Ralph Brocklebank, Tarporley, 1915

—, 'Turner Drawings of Fonthill Abbey', *Burlington Magazine*, XXIX, April. 1916, pp. 16–21

Cunningham, C. C., 'Van Tromp's shallop, at the entrance of the Scheldt', *Wadsworth Atheneum Bulletin*, 2nd series, No. 30, February 1952

—, 'Turner's Van Tromp Paintings', *Art Quarterly*, XV, Winter 1952, pp. 322–30

Cunningham, P., 'Memoir', prefixed to John Burnet's *Turner and his Works* [see above]

Cust, Sir L. H., 'The Portraits of J. M. W. Turner', *Magazine of Art*, 1895, pp. 248–9

—, 'J. M. W. Turner: an Episode in Early Life', *Burlington Magazine*, XXI, May 1912, pp. 109–10

Dafforne, J., *The Works of J. M. W. Turner, R.A., with a Biographical Sketch and Critical and Descriptive Notes*, London, [1877]

Davies, R., *Turner and Girtin's Watercolours*, 1926

[Dayes, E.,] *The Works of the late Edward Dayes...*, ed. E. W. Brayley, London, 1805

Dillon, E., 'Turner's Last Swiss Drawings', *Art Journal*, 1902, pp. 329, 362

Eastlake, Lady, *Journals and Correspondence*, ed. C. E. Smith, 1895

Eitner, L., '"The Open Window and the Storm-tossed Boat", an Essay in the Iconography of Romanticism', *Art Bulletin*, XXXVII, December 1955, pp. 281–90

Falk, B., *Turner the Painter: His Hidden Life*, London, 1938

Finberg, A. J., 'Some so-called Turners in the Print Room', *Burlington Magazine*, IX, 1906, pp. 191–5

—, *Turner's Sketches and Drawings*, 1910; paperback ed. with an introduction by L. Gowing, New York, 1968 [Finberg, 1910]

—, 'Turner's Isle of Wight Sketchbook', *Walpole Society*, I, 1911–12, pp. 85–91

—, *Turner's Watercolours at Farnley Hall*, Studio, London, n. d. [1912]

—, 'Some of the Doubtful Drawings in the Turner Bequest at the National Gallery', *Walpole Society*, II, 1912–13, pp. 127–32

—, 'Turner's South Wales Sketchbook', *Walpole Society*, III, 1913–14, pp. 87–97

—, 'Further Leaves from Turner's South Wales Sketchbook', *Walpole Society*, VI, 1917–18, pp. 95–103

—, *Early English Water-colour Drawings by Great Masters*, ed. G. Holme, *Studio*, special winter No., London, 1919

—, *Notes on Three of Turner's Earliest Architectural Drawings*, London, 1928

—, *Notes on Four Pencil Drawings made by J. M. W. Turner in May or June 1793* rev. ed., London, 1922

—, 'With Turner at Geneva', *Apollo*, January 1925, pp. 38–42

—, *The History of Turner's Liber Studiorum. With a new Catalogue Raisonné*, London, 1924

—, *An Introduction to Turner's 'Southern Coast'*, London, 1929

—, *In Venice with Turner*, London, 1930

—, 'Turner's Newly Identified Yorkshire Sketchbook', *Connoisseur*, XCVI, October 1935, pp. 184–7

—, *The Life of J. M. W. Turner, R.A.*, Oxford, 1939; 2nd ed., revised and with a supplement by Hilda F. Finberg, Oxford, 1961 [Finberg, Life]

Finberg, H. F., 'Turner's Gallery in 1810', *Burlington Magazine*, XCIII, 1951, pp. 383–6

—, 'Turner's View of Caernarvon Castle', *Connoisseur*, CXXIX, March 1952, pp. 32, 58

—, 'Turner to Mr. Dobree', *Burlington Magazine*, XCV, March 1953, pp. 98–9

—, 'With Mr. Turner in 1797', *Burlington Magazine*, XCIX, February 1957, pp. 48–51

Finley, G. E., 'An Early Experiment with Colour Theory', *Journal of the Warburg and Courtauld Institutes*, XXX, Turner, 1967, pp. 357–66

—, 'J. M. W. Turner and Sir Walter Scott: Iconography of a Tour', *Journal of the Warburg and Courtauld Institutes*, XXXV, 1972, pp. 359–85

—, 'Two Turner Studies: a "new Route" in 1822, and Turner's Colour and Optics', *Journal of the Warburg and Courtauld Institutes*, XXXVI, 1973, pp. 385–90

—, 'Turner's Illustrations to Napoleon', *Journal of the Warburg and Courtauld Institutes*, XXXVI, 1973, pp. 390–6

—, 'J. M. W. Turner's Proposal for a "Royal Progress"', *Burlington Magazine*, CXVII, 1975, pp. 27–35

Foss, K., *The Double Life of J. M. W. Turner*, London, 1938; new ed., London, 1951

Francis, H. S. A., 'A Water Color by J. M. W. Turner ('Fluelen, Lake of Lucerne'), *Bulletin of the Cleveland Museum of Art*, November 1954, pp. 201–3

Gage, J., 'Turner and the Society of Arts', *Journal of the Royal Society of Arts*, CXI, September 1963, pp. 842–6

—, 'Turner and the Picturesque', *Burlington Magazine*, CVII, January 1965, pp. 16–26; February, pp. 75–81

—, 'Turner's Academic Friendships: C. L. Eastlake', *Burlington Magazine*, CX, 1968, pp. 677–85

—, *Colour in Turner. Poetry and Truth*, London, 1969 [Gage, 1969]

—, *Turner—'Rain, steam and speed'*, London, 1972 [Gage, 1972]

—, 'Turner and Stourhead: the Making of a Classicist?', *Art Quarterly*, XXXVII, 1974, pp. 59–87 [Gage, 1974]

—, 'The Distinctness of Turner', *Journal of the Royal Society of Arts*, CXXIII, July 1975, pp. 448–58

Gaunt, W., *Turner*, London, 1971

—, *L'Univers de Turner: les carnets de dessins*, Paris, 1974

George, H., 'Turner in Venice', *Art Bulletin*, LIII, 1971, pp. 84–7

Goodall, F. C., *The Reminiscences of Fredrick Goodall, R.A...*, London—Newcastle-on-Tyne, 1902

Gowing, L., 'Turner's "Pictures of Nothing"', *Art News*, 62, October 1963, pp. 30–3

Graham, A., 'A National Gallery Controversy of a Century Ago and its Disastrous Consequences for the Turner Bequest', *Connoisseur*, special No., June 1959, pp. 14–17

—, 'The R. W. Lloyd Collection of Turner Watercolours', *Connoisseur*, CXLIII, February 1959, pp. 9–13

Gray, R. D., 'J. M. W. Turner and Goethe's Colour Theory', *German Studies presented to W. H. Bruford*, London, 1962

Grundy, C. R., 'Turner's Triumph', *Connoisseur*, LXXXVII, September 1931, pp. 192–5

H., M., [W. L. Leitch], 'The Early History of Turner's Yorkshire Drawings', *Athenaeum*, 8 September 1894, pp. 326–8

Hall, D., 'The Tabley House Papers', *Walpole Society*, XXXVIII, 1960–2, pp. 59–122

Hall, S. C. (ed.), *The Vernon Gallery of British Art*, 3 vols., London, 1849–54

—, *Catalogue of the Vernon Gallery of Paintings by British Artists...*, London, 1851

Hamerton, P. G., *The Life of J. M. W. Turner, R.A.*, London, 1879

Hanson, N. W., 'Some Painting Materials of J. M. W. Turner', *Studies in Conservation*, I, October 1954, pp. 162–73

Hardie, M., *Water-colour Painting in Britain*, II, *The Romantic Period*, London, 1967; 2nd ed., 1970

Harvey, F., *M. Halsted's celebrated collection of Turner's engravings in various states ... on sale*, London, n. d. [1876]

Hawes, L., 'Turner's "Fighting Temeraire"', *Art Quarterly*, XXXV, 1972, pp. 23–48 [Hawes, 1972]

Herrmann, L., *J. M. W. Turner, 1775–1851*, London, 1963

—, 'A Riddle Resolved', *Burlington Magazine*, CXII, October 1970, pp. 696–9

—, *Turner: Paintings, Watercolours, Prints and Drawings*, London, 1975 [Herrmann, 1975]

Hewison, R., *John Ruskin: the Argument of the Eye*, London, 1976

Hind, C. L., *Turner: Five Letters and a Postcript*, London, 1907

Hirsh, D., *The World of Turner, 1775–1851*, New York, 1969

Holcomb, A. M., 'A Neglected Classical Phase of Turner's Art: his Vignettes of Rogers's "Italy"', *Journal of the Warburg and Courtauld Institutes*, XXXII, 1969, pp. 405–10

—, 'The Vignette and the Vertical Composition in Turner's Oeuvre', *Art Quarterly*, XXII, 1970, pp. 16–29

—, '"Indistinctness is my fault". A Letter about Turner from C. R. Leslie to James Lenox', *Burlington Magazine*, CXIV, 1972, pp. 557–8

—, 'The Bridge in the Middle Distance: Symbolic Elements in Romantic Landscape', *Art Quarterly*, XXXVII, 1974, pp. 31–58

Holme, C. (ed.), *The Genius of J. M. W. Turner, R.A.*, *Studio*, special winter No., London, 1903–4

Holmes, C. J., 'Turner's Theory of Colouring', *Burlington Magazine*, VII, September 1905, pp. 409–15

—, 'Three Pictures by Turner', *Burlington Magazine*, XIV, 1908, pp. 17–25

Hughes, C. E., *Early English Water-Colours*, London, 1913; revised and ed. by J. Mayne, London, 1950

Huish, M. B., *The Seine and the Loire*, London, 1890

Hussey, C., 'Turner at Petworth', *Country Life*, VIII, 1925, pp. 974–8

Joll, E., 'Painter and Patron: Turner and the Third Earl of Egremont', *Apollo*, CV, May 1977, pp. 374–9

see Butlin, M.

Jones, G., R. A., *Sir Francis Chantrey: Recollections of his Life*, London, 1849

Kitson, M., *J. M. W. Turner*, London, 1964

—, 'Snowstorm: Hannibal Crossing the Alps', *Listener*, LXXIV, 12 August 1965, pp. 240–1

—, 'Un nouveau Turner au Musée du Louvre', *La Revue du Louvre*, XIX, 1969, pp. 247–56

—, 'Nouvelles précisions sur le "Paysage" de Turner au Musée du Louvre', *La Revue du Louvre*, XXI, 1971, pp. 89–94

Leclercq, J. 'William Turner', *Gazette des Beaux-Arts*, XXXI, 1904, pp. 485–94; XXXII, 1904, pp. 245–54

Leitch, W. L.: see H., M.

Leslie, C. R., *Autobiographical Recollections*, ed. T. Taylor, 2 vols., London, 1860

Lindsay, J., *J. M. W. Turner. His Life and Work. A Critical Biography*, London, 1966 [Lindsay, 1966]

— (ed.), *The Sunset Ship. The Poems of J. M. W. Turner*, Lowestoft, 1966

—, 'Turner and Music', *Turner Society Journal*, pt. I, 1975; pt. II, 1976

Livermore, A., 'Sandycombe Lodge', *Country Life*, 6 July 1951, pp. 40–7

—, 'J. M. W. Turner's Unknown Verse-book', *Connoisseur Year Book*, 1957, pp. 78–86

—, 'Turner and Music', *Music and Letters*, XXXVIII, London, 1957, pp. 170–9

—, 'Turner and Children', *Country Life*, 25 December 1958, pp. 1528–9

Lloyd, H. E., *Turner's Picturesque Views in England and Wales... with Descriptive and Historic Illustrations*, 3 pts., London, 1827–8

MacColl, D. S., 'Turner's Lectures at the Academy', *Burlington Magazine*, XII, March 1908, pp. 343–6

Malvezzi, P., *Viaggiatori inglesi in Valle d'Aosta (1800–60)*, Milan, 1972

Mauclair, C., *Turner*, 1938; Eng. transl. E. B. Shaw, 1939

Maurer, E., 'William Turners Laufenburger Zeichnungen', *Festgabe für Otto Mittler*, 1960, pp. 217–26

Mayne, J., 'Review of Exhibition of Turner Watercolours at Agnew's', *Burlington Magazine*, XCIII, April 1951, pp. 129–30

Miller, T., *Turner and Girtin's Picturesque Views sixty years since*, London, 1854

Monkhouse, W. C., *Turner Gallery.* [The descriptive text.] London, 1878

—, *Turner*, London, 1879

—, 'Some Portraits of J. M. W. Turner', *Scribner's Magazine*, July 1896

—, *The Earlier English Watercolour Painters*, London, 1890

Nekrasova, E. A., *Turner*, Moscow, 1970

Norton, C. E., *Catalogue of the Plates of Turner's Liber Studiorum*, with an introduction and notes, Cambridge, 1874

Norton, R., 'The *Liber Studiorum* and other Mezzotints', *Print Collector's Quarterly*, III, 1913, p. 415

Omer, M., 'Turner and "The Buildings of the Ark" from Raphael's third vault of the Loggia', *Burlington Magazine*, CXVII, November 1975, pp. 694–702

Oppé, A. P., 'Talented Amateurs: Julia Gordon and her Circle', *Country Life*, LXXXVI, 18 July 1939, pp. 20–2

Paulson, R., 'Turner's Graffiti: the Sun and its Glosses', *Images of Romanticism: Verbal and Visual Affinities*, ed. K. Kroeber and W. Walling, New Haven, 1978, pp. 167–88

Pianzola, M., 'William Turner et Genève', in *Pour une histoire qualitative: études offertes à Sven Stelling-Michaud*, 1976

Polak, A., 'Turner Påny', *Kunst Kultur*, Saertrykk av. 58, Årgang 1975, pp. 219–38

Priestley, E. J., 'Artists' Views of a Kentish Palace', *Country Life*, CXXXVII, 3 June 1965, p. 1342

Pye, J.: see Roget, J. L.

Quennel, P., 'Petworth', *L'Œil*, 83, November 1961, pp. 38–45

Quilter, H., *Sententiae Artis: First Principles of Art for Painters and Picture Lovers*, London, 1886

Rawlinson, W. G., *Turner's Liber Studiorum*, 2nd ed., London, 1906 [R.]

—, *The Engraved Work of J. M. W. Turner, R.A.*, 2 vols., London, 1908, 1913 [R.]

Rawlinson, W. G. and Finberg, A. J., *The Watercolour Drawings of J. M. W. Turner*, London, 1909

Redding, C., 'The Late J. M. W. Turner', *Fraser's Magazine*, XLV, 1852

—, *Past Celebrities whom I have known*, 1856

—, *Fifty Years' Recollections, Literary and Personal*, London, 1858

Redgrave, R. & S., *A Century of Painters of the English School*, London, 1866, vol. 2, pp. 80–135; new ed., London, 1947 [Redgrave, 1866]

Redgrave, S., *Dictionary of Artists of the English School*, 2nd ed., London, 1878

[Reeve, L.?], 'J. M. W. Turner, R.A.' [anonymous memoir], *Literary Gazette*, 27 December 1851, pp. 923–4; 3 January 1852, pp. 19–21

Reynolds, G., *Turner*, London, 1969 [Reynolds, 1969]

—, 'British Artists Abroad', IV: 'Wilson and Turner in Italy', *Geographical Magazine*, XXI, No. 2, 1948

—, 'Turner at East Cowes Castle', *Victoria and Albert Museum Yearbook*, I, 1969, pp. 67–69

Ritchie, L., *Wanderings by the Loire*, with Twenty-one Engravings from Drawings by J. M. W. Turner, London, 1833

—, *Liber Fluviorum;* or River Scenery in France depicted in Sixty-one Line Engraving from Drawings by J. M. W. Turner, with a biographical sketch by A. A. Watts, London, 1853

—, *Turner's Rivers of France*, with an introduction by John Ruskin and a biography of the artist by A. A. Watts, London, 1887

Roberts, W., 'Turner's "Winchester Cross"', *Art in America*, April 1915

Robinson, H. C., *Diary, Reminiscences and Correspondence of H. C. Robinson*, ed. T. Sadler, 3 vols., London, 1869

Roget, J. L., *A History of the 'Old Water-Colour Society'...*, 2 vols., London, 1891

Roget, J. L., and Pye, J., *Notes and Memoranda respecting the Liber Studiorum of J. M. W. Turner*, London, 1879 [Roget, 1879]

Rosny, J. H., *Turner*, 1925

Rothenstein, Sir J., 'J. M. W. Turner', British Painters Series, London, 1960

—, *Turner*, London, 1962

—, *An Introduction to English Painting*, rev. ed., London, 1965

Rothenstein, Sir J. and Butlin, M., *Turner*, London, 1964

Ruskin, J., *Modern Painters*, London, 1843–60; complete ed., 6 vols., Orpington, 1888

—, *Pre-Raphaelitism*, London, 1851

—, *Lectures on Architecture and Painting delivered in 1853*, London, 1854

—, *Notes on the Turner Gallery...*, London, 1856–7

—, *Works* (Library Edition), ed. Sir E. T. Cook and A. Wedderburn, 39 vols., London, 1903–12 [Ruskin, *Works*]

Russell, F., 'Turner in his Perfect Time', *Antique Collector*, May 1975, p. 46

Russell, J. and Wilton, A., *Turner in Switzerland*, ed. W. Amstutz, with a checklist of Turner's finished Swiss watercolours, Zurich, 1976 [Russell and Wilton, 1976]

Russell, R., 'Turner and Wilson Country', *Listener*, 23 August 1962

Salmon, T., 'The Watercolour Art of Turner', *Good Words*, 1896

Sandby, W., *The History of the Royal Academy of Arts from its Foundation in 1768 to the Present Time*, London, 1862

Sandilands, G. S., 'J. M. W. Turner', *Famous Water-colour Painters*, III, Studio, London, 1928

Schefold, M., 'William Turner in Heidelberg und am Neckar', *Jahrbuch der Staatlichen Kunstsammlungen in Baden-Württemberg*, V, 1968, pp. 131–50

Selz, J., *Turner*, Paris, 1975 (English transl. by E. B. Hennessey, 1975)

Shapiro, H., *Ruskin in Italy: Letters to his Parents, 1845*, Oxford, 1972

Shipp, H., 'Turner: the Background of Aesthetic Theory', *Apollo Miscellany*, 1951

Skene J., *The Skene Papers. Memories of Sir Walter Scott...*, ed. B. Thomson, London, 1909

Sparrow, W. S., 'Turner's Monochromes and Early Water-Colours'; 'The

Later Water-Colours', *The Genius of Turner*, ed. C. Holme, London, 1903

Stokes, A., *Painting and the Inner World ...*, London, 1963

Stokes, F. A., *J. M. W. Turner, Liber Studiorum*, New York, n. d.

Strzygowski, J., 'Turner's Path from Nature to Art' (transl. L. I. Armstrong), *Burlington Magazine*, XII, March 1908, pp. 335–42

Stuckey, C. F., 'Turner, Massaniello and the Angel', *Jahrbuch der Berliner Museen*, vol. 18, 1976, pp. 155–75 [Stuckey, 1976]

Swinburne, C. A., *Life and Works of J. M. W. Turner, R.A.*, London, 1902

Thomas, D., 'Watercolours from the Turner Bequest', *Connoisseur*, December 1968, pp. 244–5

Thornbury, W., *The Life of J. M. W. Turner, R.A.*, 2 vols., [1862] (with catalogues of Turner's works in vol. II, Appendix, pp. 352–408); rev. ed., London, 1876 [Thornbury]

Tinker, C. B., *Painter and Poet. Studies in the Literary Relations of English Painting*, Cambridge, Mass., 1938

[Turner, J. M. W.], *Catalogue of Photographs taken from the Turner Pictures in the National Gallery*, London, 1866

[Turner, J. M. W.], *The Farnley Hall Collection of Turner Drawings, in the possession of F. H. Fawkes, Esq.*, photographed by L. Caldesi & Co., London, 1864

[—], *J. M. W. Turner's Vignette Drawings, Series 1 & 2*, 1884–5, chromolithography by M. H. Long

Tyrrell-Gill, F., *Turner*, London, 1904

Underdown, H. W., *Five Turner Water-colours*, [London], 1923

Virch, C., 'Ye Mists and Exhalations That Now Rise', *The Metropolitan Museum of Art Bulletin*, n. s., XX, No. 8, April 1962, pp. 248–56

Walker, J., *Joseph Mallord William Turner*, New York, 1976

Walker, R., 'The Third Earl of Egremont, Patron of the Arts', *Apollo*, LVII, January 1953, pp. 11–13

Warner, O., 'Turner and Trafalgar', *Apollo*, LXII, October 1955, p. 104

Watts, A.: see Ritchie

Wedmore, Sir F., *Studies in English Art*, London, 1876–80

—, *Turner and Ruskin. An Exposition of the Work of Turner from the Writings of Ruskin*, 2 vols., London, 1900

Whitley, W. T., 'Turner as a Lecturer', *Burlington Magazine*, XXII, January 1913, pp. 202–8; February 1913, pp. 255–9

—, *Art in England: I, 1800–1820*, Cambridge, 1928

—, *Art in England: II, 1821–1837*, Cambridge, 1930 [Whitley, 1930]

—, 'Relics of Turner', *Connoisseur*, LXXXVIII, September 1931, p. 198

Whittingham, S., *Constable and Turner at Salisbury*, Salisbury, 1973

—, 'Turner, Ruskin and Constable at Salisbury', *Burlington Magazine*, CXIII, May 1971, p. 272

Wilkinson, G., *Turner's Early Sketchbooks. Drawings in England, Wales and Scotland, 1789–1802*, London, 1972

—, *The Sketches of Turner, R.A., 1802–20; Genius of the Romantic*, London, 1974 [Wilkinson, 1974]

—, *Turner's Colour Sketches, 1820–34*, London, 1975 [Wilkinson, 1975]

Willetts, P., 'Letters of J. M. W. Turner', *British Museum Quarterly*, XXII, Nos. 3–4, April 1960, pp. 59–62

Williams, I. A., *Early English Watercolours*, London, 1952

Wilton, A., 'Turner as a Watercolourist', *British Museum Bulletin*, March 1975

—, *British Watercolours, 1750 to 1850*, Oxford, 1977

—: see Russell, John

Woodbridge, K., 'Henry Hoare's Paradise', *Art Bulletin*, 1965

—, *Landscape and Antiquity: Aspects of English Culture at Stourhead, 1718–1838*, 1970

Wornum, R. N., 'The Sun of Venice going to sea', *The Portfolio*, 1874, pp. 161–2

— —, 'The Approach to Venice', *The Portfolio*, 1875, pp. 129–30

—, *The Turner Gallery ...*, with a memoir and illustrative text, 1875

Wroot, H. E., 'Turner in Yorkshire', *Miscellanies of the Thoresby Society*, XXVI, 1924

Wyllie, W. L., *J. M. W. Turner*, London, 1905

Ziff, J., 'Turner and Poussin', *Burlington Magazine*, CV, July 1963, pp. 315–21

—, '"Backgrounds, Introduction of Architecture and Landscape": a Lecture by J. M. W. Turner', *Journal of the Warburg and Courtauld Institutes*, XXVI, 1963, pp. 124–47

—, 'Proposed Studies for a Lost Turner Painting', *Burlington Magazine*, CVI, July 1964, pp. 328–33

—, 'J. M. W. Turner on Poetry and Painting', *Studies in Romanticism*, III, No. 4, Summer 1964, pp. 193–215

—, 'John Langhorne and Turner's "Fallacies of Hope"', *Journal of the Warburg and Courtauld Institutes*, XXVIII, 1964, pp. 340–2

—, 'Copies of Claude's Paintings in the Sketch Books of J. M. W. Turner', *Gazette des Beaux-Arts*, LXV, No. 1, January 1965, pp. 51–64

Zink, F., 'Turner in Heilbronn am Neckar', *Zeitschrift für Kunstwissenschaft*, VIII, 1954, pp. 225 et seq.

C. PUBLICATIONS OF PUBLIC AND PRIVATE COLLECTIONS

A. A. Allen's Collection: *Catalogue of Mr. A. A. Allen's Collection of Turner's Liber Studiorum*, London, 1914

Ashmolean Museum, Oxford: Herrmann, Luke, *Ruskin and Turner: a Study of Ruskin as a Collector of Turner, based on his gifts to the University of Oxford: incorporating a Catalogue Raisonné of the Turner Drawings in the Ashmolean Museum*, 1968

British Museum, London: Finberg, A. J., *Complete Inventory of the Drawings of the Turner Bequest, arranged chronologically: with which are included the twenty-three drawings bequeathed by Mr. Henry Vaughan*, 2 vols., London, 1909 [Finberg, Inventory]

— —, *British Museum Guide*, London, 1976

Cathcart Collection: Cathcart, Earl and others, *Caxton Head Catalogue: Turner's Liber Studiorum. Plates from the well known collection formed by the late Earl Cathcart and other owners*, London, n.d.

Courtauld Institute of Art, London: Kitson, M., *Watercolours by J. M. W. Turner from the Collection of Sir Stephen Courtauld*, University of London, 1974 [Kitson]

Fitzwilliam Museum, Cambridge: Cormack, M., *J. M. W. Turner, R.A. 1775–1851. A Catalogue of Drawings and Watercolours in the Fitzwilliam Museum, Cambridge*, 1975

—, Ruskin, J., *Drawings by the late J. M. W. Turner Presented to the Fitzwilliam Museum, Cambridge*, 1861

Frick Collection, New York: Davidson, B., *The Frick Collection: an Illustrated Catalogue*, 2 vols., New York, 1968

Harewood House: Borenius, T., *Catalogue of Pictures and Drawings at Harewood House*, Oxford, 1936

Leeds City Art Gallery: *The Lupton Collection*, Leeds, n.d.

— —, *Watercolours and Drawings*, Leeds, n.d.

Leicester Collection: Carey, W. P., *A Descriptive Catalogue of a Collection of Paintings by British Artists in the possession of Sir John Fleming Leicester, Bart.*, 1819

— —, Young, J., *A Catalogue of Pictures by British Artists in the Possession of Sir J. Fleming Leicester, Bart.*, London, 1821

Loyd Collection: Parris, L., *The Loyd Collection of Paintings and Drawings*, London, 1967

Manchester City Art Gallery: *English Paintings, 1800–1870*, Manchester, 1951

Munro Collection: Frost, W., A.R.A., *A Complete Catalogue of the Paintings, Water-colour Drawings, Drawings and Prints in the Collection of the late Hugh Andrew Johnstone Munro, Esq., of Novar...*, rev. H. Reeve, [London?], 1865

Museum of Fine Arts, Boston: Bullard, F., *A Catalogue of the Collection of Prints from the Liber Studiorum of J. M. W. Turner formed by the late Francis Bullard, of Boston, Mass., bequeathed by him to the Museum*, Boston, Mass., 1916

National Gallery, London: Cook, T. A., *The Watercolour Drawings of J. M. W. Turner in the National Gallery: Descriptive List*, London, 1904

— —, Davies, M., *The British School* (National Gallery Catalogues), London, 1946, rev. ed., 1959

— —, *General Catalogue*, London, 1973

National Gallery of South Australia, Adelaide: *Bulletin of the National Gallery of South Australia*, October 1958

National Gallery of Victoria, Melbourne: *European Painting and Sculpture before 1800 at the National Gallery of Victoria*, 3rd. ed., Melbourne, 1972

National Museum of Wales, Cardiff: *British Watercolour School: Handbook to the Pyke Thompson Gallery*, Cardiff, 1939

— —, Steegman, J., *Catalogue of the Gwendoline E. Davies Bequest of Paintings, Drawings and Sculpture*, Cardiff, 1952

— —, *Catalogue of the Margaret S. Davies Bequest: Paintings, Drawings and Sculpture*, Cardiff, 1963

Petworth Collection: Collins Baker, C. H., *Catalogue of the Petworth Collection of Pictures in the Possession of Lord Leconfield*, London, 1920 [Collins Baker]

— —, Sockett, Revd. T., *Inventory of the Petworth Collection of Pictures*, n.p., 1856. [All those pictures which were in the collection at Lord Egremont's death in 1837 are marked by an asterisk.]

— —, *Petworth House: Paintings and Sculpture*, n.p., 1964

— —, *Pictures at Petworth*, n.p., n.d.

Rawlinson Collection: *Catalogue of Mr. W. G. Rawlinson's Collection of Turner's Liber Studiorum*, London, 1887

Tate Gallery, London: Chamot, M., *The Tate Gallery, British School: a Concise Catalogue*, London, 1953

— —, MacColl, D. S., *National Gallery, Millbank: Catalogue: Turner Collection*, London, 1920

— —, *A Guide to the Tate Gallery, London: an Introduction to British and Foreign Art*, London, 1959

— —, *National Gallery, Millbank (Tate Gallery), London, Illustrated: Paintings and Drawings*, Glasgow, 1928

— —, *Official Guide to the Tate Gallery*, London, 1967

Turner House, Penarth: *A Descriptive Catalogue of Drawings, Prints, Pictures and Porcelain Collected by J. Pyke Thompson and Placed in the Turner House, Penarth*, 1888

Victoria and Albert Museum, London: *Catalogue of Prints: the Liber Studiorum of J. M. W. Turner*, London, 1908

— —, *Illustrative Catalogue (with Turner Supplement)* (National Gallery of British Art), London, 1908

— —, Strange, E. F., *Catalogue of Prints: the Liber Studiorum of J. M. W. Turner, R.A., in the Victoria and Albert Museum*, London, 1908

— —, *Summary Catalogue of British Paintings*, London, 1973

Walker Art Gallery, Liverpool: Bennet, M. and Morris, E., *Catalogue of the Emma Holt Bequest, Sudley*, Liverpool, 1971

— —, *Early English Drawings and Watercolours in the Walker Art Gallery*, Liverpool, 1968

Wallace Collection, London: *Wallace Collection Catalogues: Pictures and Drawings*, 15th ed., London, 1928

Wantage Collection: Temple, Sir A. G., *A Catalogue of Pictures Forming the Collection of Lord and Lady Wantage*, London, 1902

D. CATALOGUES OF TEMPORARY EXHIBITIONS DEVOTED WHOLLY OR LARGELY TO TURNER, HELD AFTER HIS DEATH

1854	*Pictures Exhibited at a Soirée given by John Buck Lloyd Esq., Mayor of Liverpool, at the Town Hall on Saturday Evening, September 23*
1856	*Notes on the Turner Gallery at Marlborough House, 1856*, by John Ruskin, M. A., author of 'Modern Painters', 'Stones of Venice', 'Seven Lamps of Architecture', etc. Five editions, published in 1856 and 1857
1857	Clarke, H. G., *The Turner Gallery, with a Catalogue of the Vernon Collection of Paintings and Sculpture, now on View at Marlborough House*, London
1857	Ruskin, J., *Catalogue of the Turner Sketches in the National Gallery*, Part I. For private circulation. Two editions, the latter containing 'Notes on One Hundred Drawings'
1857–8	Ruskin, J., *Catalogue of the Sketches and Drawings by J. M. W. Turner, R.A., Exhibited in Marlborough House in the Year 1857–8*. Accompanied with Illustrative Notes. 1857; enlarged edition 1858
1872	*Exhibition of Turner's Liber Studiorum*, Burlington Fine Arts Club, London. Reprinted Cambridge, Mass., 1874
1881	Ruskin, J., *Catalogue of Drawings and Sketches by J. M. W. Turner, R.A., at Present Exhibited in the National Gallery. Revised and Cast into Progressive Groups, with Explanatory Notes*. 3rd edition 1899

1881   Ruskin, J., *Ruskin on Pictures. A Collection of Criticisms by John Ruskin not heretofore re-printed and now re-edited and re-arranged*, ed. E. T. Cook: Vol. I, *Turner at the National Gallery and in Mr. Ruskin's Collection*, 1902 [*Ruskin on Pictures*]

1881   *Description of Proofs showing the different states of Plates 52 and 69 of Turner's 'Liber Studiorum'*

1882   *Eleven plates from the 'Liber Studiorum' engraved throughout by Turner*

1886   *Catalogue of Engravings and Drawings Illustrative of the Drawings by J. M. W. Turner, R.A., in the Winter Exhibition at the Royal Academy*, Burlington Fine Arts Club

1888   *Catalogue of an Exhibition of the 'Liber Studiorum' of J. M. W. Turner*, Grolier Club, New York

1896   *Engraved Works by J. M. W. Turner, also Watercolour Drawings and Other Works by the same Artist*, City Art Galleries, Leeds

1897   *The Liber Studiorum of J. M. W. Turner, R.A.*, new mezzotints by Frank Short, completing the book as arranged by Turner, with an introductory note by W. G. Rawlinson, Rembrandt Gallery, London

1898   *Turner and Claude*, University Galleries, Oxford

1899   *Loan Collection of Pictures and Drawings by J. M. W. Turner, R.A., and of a Selection of Pictures by some of his Contemporaries*, with descriptive and biographical notes by A. G. Temple, Corporation of London Art Gallery, Guildhall, April–July

1899   *Pictures and Drawings by J. M. W. Turner*, Birmingham Museums and Art Gallery

1902   *Art and Industrial Exhibition: Fine Art Section*, Wolverhampton, May–November

1902   *The Farnley Hall Collection of Pictures and Drawings by J. M. W. Turner, R.A., etc.*, Messrs. Lawrie & Co., London, May

1902   *The 'Liber Studiorum'*, Corporation Art Gallery, Bury

1904   *Exhibition of the 'Liber Studiorum' of J. M. W. Turner and a few Engravings after his Drawings*, Museum of Fine Arts, Boston, Mass.

1906   *Handbook to Exhibition of Line Engravings after Watercolours by J. M. W. Turner*, Fogg Art Museum, Boston, Mass.

1906   *Studies and Drawings by F. Shields. Drawings and Sketches by J. M. W. Turner*, Manchester School of Art

1908   *Autumn Exhibition of Modern Oil-Paintings and Watercolour Drawings, including works by J. M. W. Turner, etc.*, Municipal Art Gallery, Wolverhampton

1910   *The 'Liber Studiorum' of J. M. W. Turner*, Victoria and Albert Museum, London

1911   *Original Drawings, Etchings and Mezzotints of Turner's 'Liber Studiorum'*, Rembrandt Gallery, London

1912   *Original Drawings in Water Colour, etc., by J. M. W. Turner, R.A.*, Laing Art Gallery, Newcastle

1913   *Exhibition of Watercolour Drawings by J. M. W. Turner, R.A.*, Thos. Agnew & Sons Ltd., London

1914   *Loan Exhibition of Paintings by Thomas Gainsborough and J. M. W. Turner, R.A.*, Knoedler, New York, January

1914   *Welsh Drawings by J. M. W. Turner, R.A.: Loan Exhibition*, National Museum of Wales, Cardiff

1914–15   *Third National Loan Exhibition: Pictures from the Basildon Park and Fonthill Collections*, Grosvenor Gallery, London

1916   *Catalogue of the Collection of Prints from the 'Liber Studiorum' of Joseph Mallord William Turner, formed by the late Francis Bullard, of Boston, Massachusetts, and bequeathed by him to the Museum of Fine Arts, Boston*, by Grenville Lindall Winthrop

1918   *'Liber Studiorum' Prints by J. M. W. Turner*, Cartwright Memorial Hall, Bradford

1923   *Turner's Works shown at the Cotswold Gallery, London* [also in 1924, 1925, 1926, 1927 and 1929]

1924   *Special Loan Collection of Paintings in Oil, Water Colour, etc. by J. M. W. Turner, R.A.*, Laing Art Gallery, Newcastle

1924   *Watercolours by Turner, Cox and de Wint*, Thos. Agnew & Sons Ltd., London

1928   *A Selection of Mezzotints from Turner's 'Liber Studiorum'*, Colnaghi's Gallery, London

1931   *Turner's Early Oil-Paintings (1796–1815)*, with preface by J. B. Manson and introduction by A. J. Finberg, Tate Gallery, London, July–September

1933–4   *Engravings from Turner's 'Liber Studiorum'*, Cotswold Gallery, London

1936   *Drawings and Sketches by J. M. W. Turner*, National Museum of Wales, Cardiff

1937   *Aquarelles de Turner: Œuvres de Blake*, préface de Laurence Binyon, rédigée par Campbell Dodgson, Bibliothèque Nationale, Paris, 15 January–15 February

1937   *Ausstellung von englischen Gemälden und Aquarellen, W. Blake und J. M .W. Turner*, Verein der Museumfreunde, Vienna

1937   *Aquarelle von J. M. William Turner*, mit einer Einleitung von Campbell Dodgson, Albertina, Vienna

1946   *An Exhibition of Paintings, Drawings and Prints by J. M. W. Turner, John Constable, R. P. Bonington*, Museum of Fine Arts, Boston, March–April

1946–7   *Masterpieces of English Painting: William Hogarth, John Constable, J. M. W. Turner*, Metropolitan Museum of Art, New York; Art Institute, Chicago; Art Gallery of Ontario, Toronto

1947   *Exposición — homenaje a Turner (Collección Lazzaro)*, Museo de Arte Moderno, Barcelona

1947–8   *Turner, 1775–1851*, British Council tour to Stedelijk Museum, Amsterdam; Kunstmuseum, Bern; Orangerie, Paris; Palais voor Schone Kunst, Brussels; Museum voor Schone Kunst, Liège; British Pavilion, XXIV Venice Biennale; and Palazzo Venezia, Rome

1948   *Turner Watercolours from Farnley Hall*, City Art Galleries, Leeds, January–February

1949   *J. M. W. Turner, 1775–1851*, an exhibition of watercolours arranged by the Chelsea Society, 96 Cheyne Walk, London, May–June

1949–50   *British Painting from Hogarth to Turner*, British Council tour to Kunsthalle, Hamburg; Kunsternernes Hus, Oslo; Nationalmuseum, Stockholm; Statens Museum for Kunst, Copenhagen

1950–1   *Aquarelle aus dem Turner-Nachlass im Britischen Museum*, organized by the British Council, Düsseldorf, Wiesbaden, Mannheim, Munich and Nuremberg, October–March

1951   *J. M. W. Turner, the Collection from Petworth*, with notes based on the catalogue of the Petworth Collection by C. H. Collins Baker, 1920, Tate Gallery, May–July

1951   *J. M. W. Turner, 1775–1851,* loan collection of watercolour drawings, Thos. Agnew & Sons Ltd., London, February–March

1951   *Exhibition of Paintings by J. M. W. Turner,* Art Gallery of Ontario, Toronto, and National Gallery of Canada, Ottawa, October–December

1951   *Celebration of the Centenary of Turner's Death,* National Museum of Wales, Cardiff, February–March [no catalogue issued]

1951–2   *The First Hundred Years of the Royal Academy, 1769–1868,* Royal Academy of Arts, London, December–March [R.A. 1951–2]

1952   *Turner Watercolours,* Henry E. Huntington Art Gallery, San Marino, Calif., January–March

1952–3   *J. M. W. Turner, R.A., Exhibition of Watercolours,* Manchester City Art Gallery, December–January

1952–3   *J. M. W. Turner, R.A., 1775–1851: A Selection of Twenty-four Oil Paintings from the Tate Gallery,* travelling exhibition organized by the Arts Council of Great Britain, with introduction by K. Clark

1953   *J. M. W. Turner, R.A., an Exhibition of Pictures from Public and Private Collections in Great Britain,* with introduction by Sir John Rothenstein, Whitechapel Art Gallery, London, 5 February–15 March

1954   *Pictures and Works of Art from Petworth House,* Wildenstein & Co. Ltd., London, February–March

1955   *Turner in America, Oils, Watercolours, Drawings and some Engraved Work,* John Herron Art Museum, Indianapolis, 12 November–25 December

1955   *Engelse Landschapschilders von Gainsborough tot Turner,* British Council, Museum Boymans–van Beunigen, Rotterdam

1957   *Exhibition of Watercolours by J. M. W. Turner, R.A.,* King's Lynn, 27 July–10 August

1959   *J. M. W. Turner, Watercolours from Farnley Hall,* introduction by Denys Sutton, Holburne of Menstrie Museum, Bath

1960   *Exhibition of Paintings by J. M. W. Turner, R.A., 1775–1851, lent by the Tate Gallery, London,* National Gallery of South Australia, Adelaide; Art Gallery of New South Wales, Sydney; National Gallery of Victoria, Melbourne; Queensland Art Gallery, Brisbane; Art Gallery of Western Australia, Perth, March–September

1960   *Autumn Exhibition: J. M. W. Turner, R.A.,* introduction by Basil Taylor, Leggatt Bros., London, 14 October–4 November

1960   *J. M. W. Turner, Watercolours and Drawings,* introduction by Katherine Kuh, Otto Gerson Gallery, New York, 9 November–10 December

1961   *J. M. W. Turner, Watercolours on loan ... from the Turner Bequest,* National Gallery of Victoria, Melbourne, 12 September–1 October; Art Gallery of New South Wales, Sydney, October–November

1962   *J. M. W. Turner, Oil-sketches in the British Museum, c. 1820–30,* British Museum, London, 1962 [note issued with exhibition]

1963   *Turner in Indiana: Pencil Sketches, Watercolor Drawings and some Oils and Engraved Works,* text by Kurt Pantzer, Art Gallery, University of Notre Dame, Notre Dame, Indiana

1963   *J. M. W. Turner,* organized by the British Council, Bridgestone Museum of Art, Tokyo, and Fine Arts Museum, Osaka, 21 September–20 October and 1–30 November respectively

1963–4   *Turner Watercolors from the British Museum,* organized by the Smithsonian Institution, Washington; also Houston, San Francisco, Cleveland, Kansas City and Brooklyn, September–May

1964   *J. M. W. Turner on Poetry and Painting,* University of California, Los Angeles

1964   *Turner: an Exhibition of Watercolours from the British Museum,* organized by the British Council, City Hall Art Gallery, Hong Kong, 3–29 January

1964   *Ruskin and his Circle,* organized by the Arts Council of Great Britain, introduction by Kenneth Clark, Arts Council Gallery, London, January–February

1965   *Exhibition at Farnley Hall,* City Art Gallery, Bradford, 2–31 October

1966   *Turner Watercolours,* New Metropole Art Centre, Folkestone, 20 January–18 February

1966   *Turner: Imagination and Reality,* text by Lawrence Gowing, Museum of Modern Art, New York, 1966 [Gowing, 1966]

1966   *Exhibition of Watercolours of J. M. W. Turner,* introduction by Francis Hawcroft, Whitworth Art Gallery, University of Manchester

1966   *Turner Watercolours from the R. W. Lloyd Bequest,* British Museum, 1966 [typewritten leaflet]

1966–7   *Painting from Hogarth to Turner,* British Council tour to Wallraf-Richartz-Museum, Cologne; Palazzo Venezia, Rome; Muzeum Narodowe, Warsaw, October–March

1967   *Loan Exhibition of Paintings and Watercolours by J. M. W. Turner, R.A.,* 150th annivers. Agnew & Sons Ltd., London, introduction by Evelyn Joll, November–December

1968   *J. M. W. Turner (1775–1851),* National Galleries of Scotland, Edinburgh

1968   *Finished Watercolors of J. M. W. Turner, R.A., from the Collection of Mr. and Mrs. Kurt F. Pantzer,* Fort Wayne Museum of Art, Texas, September–October

1968–9   *J. M. W. Turner: a Selection of Paintings from the Paul Mellon Collection,* introduction by Ross Watson, National Gallery of Art, Washington, D.C., 31 October–21 April

1969–79   *A Decade of English Naturalism, 1810–20,* Norwich Castle Museum; Victoria and Albert Museum, London, November–February

1970   *Turner at Petworth, Watercolours from the Turner Bequest, CCXLIV, 1–114,* introduction by K. Clark, Petworth House, Sussex, June–August

1970–1   *Turner Watercolours Lent by the British Museum,* Musées Royaux des Beaux-Arts de Belgique, Brussels, 28 November–10 January

1972   *La Peinture romantique anglaise et les préraphaélites,* organized by the British Council, Petit Palais, Paris, January–April (introduction to the Turner section—Nos. 258–310—and catalogue entries by John Gage) [Paris, 1972]

1972   *William Turner, 1775–1851,* Gemäldegalerie Neuer Meister,

Dresden; Nationalgalerie, Staatliche Museen Preussischer Kulturbesitz, Berlin, July–November

1972 *Turner — Maler des Lichts,* ed. H. Bock and U. Prinz. [Includes two articles by Andrew Wilton.] Nationalgalerie, Berlin, September–November

1973 *Turner: Drawings, Watercolours and Oil-paintings,* introduction by Andrew Wilton and Luke Herrmann, Fundaçao Calouste Gulbenkian, Lisbon, June–July

1974 *J. M. W. Turner, 1775–1851: Watercolours, Influence in Britain,* British Council tour to Bridgestone Museum of Art, Tokyo; Fine Arts Museum, Osaka; City Hall Art Gallery, Hong Kong, February–April

1974 *Turner and Watercolour, Exhibition of Watercolours from the Turner Bequest,* travelling exhibition organized by the Arts Council of Great Britain, catalogue compiled and introduced by John Gage

1974 *J. M. W. Turner — Bonneville, Savoy,* special exhibition, with leaflet by Evelyn Joll, Thos. Agnew & Sons Ltd., London, 1–19 July

1974 *Perth Festival of Arts,* exhibition of Turner watercolours, Perth Art Gallery, 19 May–9 June

1974–5 *Turner 1775–1851,* bicentenary exhibition celebrating the artist's birth, introductions by Martin Butlin and Andrew Wilton, and 'Turner: Life and Times' by John Gage, Royal Academy of Arts, London, November–March [R.A. 1974]

1975 *Turner and the Poets,* exhibition organized by the Greater London Council, with introduction and catalogue notes by Mordechai Omer, Marble Hill House, Twickenham, 12 April–1 June

1975 *J. M. W. Turner: Illustrations for Books,* by Paula Lee Platt and Stephen Carpenter, Baltimore Museum of Art, April–May

1975 *Richmondshire and Other Engraved Works by J. M. W. Turner,* Bruce Castle, Lordship Lane, London, 14 August–9 September

1975 *Turner's 'Liber Studiorum',* P. & D. Colnaghi & Co. Ltd., London, 4–28 November

1975 *The 'Liber Studiorum' of J. M. W. Turner,* Fitzwilliam Musem, Cambridge [with duplicated list], November–December

1975 *One Hundred English Watercolours,* Spink & Sons Ltd., London, autumn

1975 *J. M. W. Turner — Works on Paper from American Collections,* introduction and text by J. R. Goldyne, University Art Museum, Berkeley, Calif., 30 September–23 November

1975–6 *Turner in the British Museum, Drawings and Watercolours,* introduction and catalogue by Andrew Wilton, British Museum, May–January [B.M. 1975]

1975–6 *Turner: Oils and Watercolours,* Hermitage Museum, Leningrad and Pushkin Museum, Moscow, October–January

1976 *Turner, R. A.: Watercolours in the North West,* Museum and Art Gallery, Blackburn, January

1976 *Dr. Thomas Monro and the Monro Academy,* with an introduction by F. J. G. Jefferiss, Victoria and Albert Museum, February–May

1976 *J. M. W. Turner — akvareller og tegninger fra British Museum,* with an introduction by D. Loshak, Statens Museum for Kunst, Copenhagen, 28 February–2 May

1976 *William Turner und die Landschaft seiner Zeit (Kunst um 1800),* introductions by Werner Hofman and Andrew Wilton, Kunsthalle, Hamburg, 19 May–18 July

1976 *Turner und die Dichtkunst: Aquarelle Graphik,* Bayerische Staatsgemäldesammlungen, Munich

1976 *William Turner: Aquarelle,* mit einer Einführung von Paul Vogt, Pipe Galerie, Munich

1976 *Turner and Ruskin,* Brantwood, Coniston, August–September

1976–7 *Turner und die Schweiz,* introduction by Andrew Wilton, Kunsthaus, Zurich, 5 October–2 January

1977 *English Landscape, 1630–1850,* drawings, prints and books from the Paul Mellon Collection, exhibition catalogue by Christopher White, Yale Center for British Art, New Haven, April–July

1977 *English Watercolours and Drawings from the Manchester City Art Gallery,* Thos. Agnew & Sons Ltd., London, October

1977 *London and the Thames: Paintings of Three Centuries,* organized by the National Maritime Museum, Greenwich, for the Department of the Environment, Somerset House, London, July–October

1977 *Turner,* special loan exhibition of 20 rarely seen paintings, Tate Gallery, London, October–December

1977–8 *Turner Watercolors from the British Museum,* and exhibition of works loaned by the Trustees of the British Museum, organized by the International Exhibitions Foundation, 1977–8, introduction and catalogue by Andrew Wilton, Cleveland Museum of Art; Detroit Institute of Arts, Detroit; Philadelphia Museum of Art, Philadelphia

1978 *Turner Watercolours* (from the Turner Bequest at the British Museum), introduction by Timothy Clifford, Sofia, 13–20 April; Belgrade, 10–30 May; Bucharest, 9 June–2 July

1978 *Turner's Illustrations to Campbell's Poems from the Fergusson Collection,* National Galleries of Scotland, Edinburgh, December

1978–9 *Turner in The Hague,* 19 oil-paintings on loan from the Tate Gallery, London, and other English collections, and 90 watercolours from the British Museum, Gemeentemuseum, The Hague, 16 December–26 February

1979 *The Vaughan Bequest: Turner Watercolours, 1800–1840,* National Galleries of Scotland, Edinburgh, 3–31 January

WATERCOLOUR CATALOGUE CONCORDANCES

I Finberg's Inventory (British Museum). This list includes items from the oil-paintings catalogue which are listed in the Inventory and therefore in the Turner Bequest at the British Museum.

Inventory No.	Cat. No.	Inventory No.	Cat. No.	Inventory No.	Cat. No.	Inventory No.	Cat. No.
I–A	5	CCVIII–K	733	CCLIX–131	961	CCLXXX–176	1181
I–B	6	CCVIII–L	745	CCLIX–132	981	CCLXXX–177	1187
III–C	9	CCVIII–M	741	CCLIX–133	952	CCLXXX–178	1197
III–D	8	CCVIII–N	740	CCLIX–134	953	CCLXXX–179	1198
IX–A	27	CCVIII–O	736	CCLIX–135	970	CCLXXX–180	1183
XXVII–R	65	CCVIII–P	749	CCLIX–136	951	CCLXXX–181	1182
XXVIII–A	143	CCVIII–Q	754	CCLXIII–252	776	CCLXXX–182	1200
XXIX–X	141	CCVIII–R	743	CCLXIII–307	778	CCLXXX–183	1192
LX–H	348	CCVIII–S	756	CCLXIII–308	771	CCLXXX–184	1199
LXX–G	414	CCVIII–T	755	CCLXIII–309(a)	772	CCLXXX–185	1191
LXX–M	263	CCVIII–U	753	CCLXIII–344	521	CCLXXX–186	1193
LXXX–D	363	CCVIII–V	732	CCLXIII–349	887	CCLXXX–187	1194
LXXX–G	399	CCVIII–W	735	CCLXXX–143	1172	CCLXXX–188	1202
XCV(a)–A	P154	CCVIII–X	442	CCLXXX–144	1170	CCLXXX–189	1203
XCV(a)–B	P157	CCVIII–Y	512	CCLXXX–145	1158	CCLXXX–190	1205
XCV(a)–C	P155	CCLIX–102	955	CCLXXX–146	1157	CCLXXX–191	1206
XCV(a)–D	P156	CCLIX–103	969	CCLXXX–147	1154	CCLXXX–192	1208
XCV(a)–E	P158	CCLIX–104	968	CCLXXX–148	1173	CCLXXX–193	1162
XCV(a)–F	P159	CCLIX–105	960	CCLXXX–149	1160	CCLXXX–195	1189
XCV(a)–G	P35	CCLIX–106	962	CCLXXX–150	1176	CCLXXX–196	1190
CIII–18	P208	CCLIX–107	963	CCLXXX–152	1152	CCLXXX–197	1204
CXXX–A	P213	CCLIX–108	964	CCLXXX–153	1155	CCLXXX–199	1209
CXXX–B	P214	CCLIX–109	965	CCLXXX–154	1159	CCLXXX–200	1186
CXXX–C	P215	CCLIX–110	958	CCLXXX–155	1153	CCLXXX–201	1184
CXXX–D	P216	CCLIX–111	959	CCLXXX–156	1163	CCLXXX–202	1207
CXXX–E	P217	CCLIX–112	974	CCLXXX–157	1161	CCCLXIV–224	769
CXXX–F	P218	CCLIX–113	972	CCLXXX–158	1167	CCCLXIV–373	522
CXXX–G	P219	CCLIX–114	975	CCLXXX–159	1165	1972.U.738	P487
CXXX–H	P220	CCLIX–115	976	CCLXXX–160	1166	1972.U.739	P489
CXXX–I	P221	CCLIX–116	977	CCLXXX–161	1168	1972.U.740	P492
CXXX–J	P222	CCLIX–117	983	CCLXXX–162	1177	1972.U.741	P491
CXXX–K	P223	CCLIX–118	984	CCLXXX–163	1164	1972.U.742	P493
CXXX–Add L	P224	CCLIX–119	986	CCLXXX–164	1171	1972.U.743	P490
CXCVI–F	773	CCLIX–120	985	CCLXXX–165	1175	1972.U.744	P494
CCVIII–A	746	CCLIX–121	979	CCLXXX–166	1169	1972.U.745	P485
CCVIII–B	747	CCLIX–122	978	CCLXXX–167	1174	1972.U.746	P488
CCVIII–C	739	CCLIX–123	980	CCLXXX–168	1178	1972.U.747	P499
CCVIII–D	737	CCLIX–124	982	CCLXXX–169	1180	1972.U.748	P498
CCVIII–E	738	CCLIX–125	989	CCLXXX–170	1188	1974.U.848	P497
CCVIII–F	748	CCLIX–126	990	CCLXXX–171	1201	1974.U.849	P500
CCVIII–G	744	CCLIX–127	971	CCLXXX–172	1185	1974.U.850	P486
CCVIII–H	734	CCLIX–128	956	CCLXXX–173	1179	1974.U.851	P495
CCVIII–I	751	CCLIX–129	973	CCLXXX–174	1195	1974.U.852	P496
CCVIII–J	752	CCLIX–130	957	CCLXXX–175	1196		

II Luke Herrmann, *Ruskin and Turner... Catalogue Raisonné of the Turner Drawings in the Ashmolean Museum, Oxford*

Herrmann No.	Cat. No.	Herrmann No.	Cat. No.	Herrmann No.	Cat. No.	Herrmann No.	Cat. No.
1	295	29	930	45	939	72	524
2	296	30	998	46	938	76	444
3	297	31	945	47	932	77	582
4	298	32	999	48	931	78	634
5	299	33	992	49	942	79	566
6	300	34	993	50	947	80	1399
7	301	35	936	51	950	81	1403
8	302	36	994	52	1219	82	991
9	303	37	995	53	1234	83	1330
10	304	38	935	54	1248	84	1329
23	1405	39	946	55	1240	85	780
24	476	40	943	56	1363	86	1474
25	478	41	949	57	1366	88	29
26	757	42	933	58	1364	90	39
27	1023	43	937	60	73	91	58
28	1015	44	934	69	318	93	313
				71	409	99	131

III Malcolm Cormack, *Turner: A Catalogue of Drawings and Watercolours in the Fitzwilliam Museum, Cambridge*

Cormack No.	Cat. No.	Cormack No.	Cat. No.	Cormack No.	Cat. No.	Cormack No.	Cat. No.
1	34	16	572	29	1024	43	1486
4	72	17	574	30	1083	44	1483
6	148	18	602	31	1109	45	1499
7	224	19	552	32	1224	46	1501
8	228	20	750	33	1244	47	1500
9	285	21	764	34	1336	48	1493
10	360	22	904	35	1430	49	1324
11	208	23	422	37	1449	50	1468
12	418	24	421	38	1353	51	1326
13	468	25	808	39	1361	52	1411
14	494	26	997	40	1362	53	1427
15	651	27	996	41	1037	54	1418
		28	1025	42	1511		

IV *Turner 1775–1851.* Exhibition catalogue, Royal Academy, London, 1974–5

R.A. 1974–5	Cat. No.	R.A. 1974–5	Cat. No.	R.A. 1974–5	Cat. No.	R.A. 1974–5	Cat. No.
1	8	28	221	51	1144	127	432
2	10	36	149	61	357	169	455
7	27	38	340	63	359	171	475
10	55	39	339	65	365	173	760
11	65	40	303	66	363	179	581
13	195	42	254	67	366	180	578
14	141	ex cat.	259	68	373	181	495
15	203	43	263	69	380	184	697
16	227	ex cat.	280	113	528	185	582
27	217	ex cat.	281	123	533	186	544

R.A. 1974–5	Cat. No.	R.A. 1974–5	Cat. No.	R.A. 1974–5	Cat. No.	R.A. 1974–5	Cat. No.
189	592	276	1167	403	973	555	1368
190	594	277	1165	404	975	583	1380
191	588	278	1187	405	983	588	1376
192	609	279	1181	406	984	589	1506
193	542	280	1196	407	978	590	1455
194	499	281	1190	408	979	591	1558
195	653	282	1209	419	803	592	1474
196	677	283	1207	421	791	601	1524
197	639	285	1223	422	809	603	1525
198	646	286	1227	423	814	607	1529
199	648	288	1216	425	847	608	1527
205	1069	289	1134	426	858	611	1537
206	1065	290	1078	427	846	612	1538
239	741	291	1151	428	860	613	1539
240	734	292	1130	430	863	615	1556
242	749	293	1278	431	864	616	1557
243	756	294	1287	433	880	626	1409
245	778	299	1291	434	879	637	1416
247	776	374	1020	436	521	640	225
252	769	384	935	437	1396	645	736
257	518	385	946	438	1387	B9	11
258	519	386	933	439	1386	B16	57
265	779	387	937	456	522	B20	40
269	1399	397	955	466	730	B90	402
272	1158	398	969	551	1355	B139	906
273	1157	400	968	552	1363	B151	1417
274	1173	401	963	553	1364		
275	1176	402	964	554	1366		

V *Turner in the British Museum*. Exhibition catalogue, British Museum, London, 1975

B.M. 1975	Cat. No.	B.M. 1975	Cat. No.	B.M. 1975	Cat. No.	B.M. 1975	Cat. No.
6	71	55	580	145	728	192	965
7	124	56	538	147	405	193	970
9	138	74	723	148	829	194	972
10	143	79	691	168	1046	195	974
22	206	80	692	174	833	197	849
23	205	82	512	175	1047	199	857
37	385	85	733	178	1084	200	862
38	386	86	744	179	1186	203	871
39	532	87	508	180	1184	206	876
43	399	ex cat.	561	181	1188	208	869
45	425	90	794	182	1201	259	1359
46	427	91	751	183	1178	260	1354
47	438	92	753	184	1195	263	1381
48	684	96	403	187	1200	264	1379
49	673	106	798	188	1182	286	1533
50	672	114	1164	190	960	292	1536
54	504	115	1175	191	962		

(Numbers in brackets refer to the two catalogues, or to the *Inventory* of the Turner Bequest.)

507

(67) 41, Pl. 16
Wreck buoy 1849 (P428) 222, 223, 227
Wreck of a transport ship c. 1810 (P210) 153, Pl. 164

Wreck on the Goodwin Sands: sunset *c.* 1845–50 (1426) 249
Wreck, with fishing-boats c. 1840–5 (P470) Pl. 238

Zurich 1842 (1533) 241, 242
Zurich: fête, early morning 1845 (1548) 241, 242, 244, 245, 249, Pl. 254

TOPOGRAPHICAL INDEX OF PLACES DEPICTED IN CATALOGUED WORKS

GENERAL INDEX OF PEOPLE, PLACES AND INSTITUTIONS REFERRED TO IN THE MAIN TEXT

LISTS OF OWNERS

CATALOGUE OF PAINTINGS

CATALOGUE OF WATERCOLOURS

AUSTRALIA

CANADA

EIRE

FRANCE

JAPAN

PORTUGAL

SOUTH AFRICA

SWITZERLAND

UNITED KINGDOM

PHOTOGRAPHIC ACKNOWLEDGEMENTS

The publishers wish to thank all those who have supplied photographs for this book, including the following institutions and individuals:

Aberdeen, Studio Morgan: Cat. W/C: 195, 693, 1539
Aberystwyth, University College of Wales: Cat. W/C: 96, 132
Adelaide, Art Gallery of South Australia: Cat. W/C: 818
Alnwick, D.M. Smith: Cat. W/C: 493, 820

Baltimore, Museum of Art: Cat. W/C: 404
— Walters Art Gallery: Pl. 131
Bath, Holburne of Menstrie Museum, University of Bath: Cat. W/C: 832
Belfast, Ulster Museum: Cat. P: 394
Bilston, Camera Craft: Cat. W/C: 446, 787, 1128, 1138
Birkenhead (Cheshire), Williamson Art Gallery and Museum: Cat. W/C: 1444
Birmingham, The Barber Institute of Fine Arts: Cat. W/C: 265; Cat. P: 95
— Museums and Art Gallery: Pls. 194, 206; Cat. W/C: 200, 402, 581, 1337
Blackburn, North Western Museum and Art Gallery Service: Cat. W/C: 332, 545, 701, 883, 1110, 1245, 1262, 1294
Bloomington, Indiana University Art Museum: Cat. P: 345
Boston, Isabella Stewart Gardner Museum: Pl. 130
— Museum of Fine Arts: Pl. 94; Cat. W/C: 189, 329, 463, 505, 774, 777, 1313, 1332, 1420, 1428, 1439, 1451
— Robert L. Scott: Cat. W/C: 875
Brighton, The Royal Pavilion, Art Gallery and Museums: Cat. W/C: 1147
Bristol, Derek Balmer: Cat. W/C: 117
— Brian Middlehurst: Cat. W/C: 19
— Museum and Art Gallery: Pl. 8; Cat. W/C: 16
Burnley, Alan Marsden: Cat. W/C: 292, 294, 1213
Bury, Art Gallery: Cat. W/C: 26, 465, 687, 1051; Cat. P: 334

Calne, Bowood Collection: Cat. W/C: 391, 806
Cambridge, Fitzwilliam Museum: Pls. 42, 103, 183; Cat. W/C: 34, 72, 112, 148, 208, 224, 228, 285, 418, 421, 422, 468, 494, 572, 574, 651, 652, 750, 764, 808, 904, 996, 997, 1025, 1037, 1083, 1109, 1224, 1244, 1324, 1326, 1336, 1353, 1361, 1362, 1411, 1427, 1430, 1449, 1468, 1493, 1499–1501, 1511; photos Stearn & Sons: Cat. W/C: 552, 602, 1418, 1483, 1486
— Edward Leigh: Cat. W/C: 78
Cambridge (Mass.), Fogg Art Museum: Cat. W/C: 323, 328, 434, 656, 813, 927, 1136, 1566; Cat. P: 238
Cape Town, South African National Gallery: Cat. W/C: 603, 1561
Cardiff, National Museum of Wales: Pl. 28; Cat. W/C: 81, 97, 125, 137, 140, 376, 471, 638, 639, 669, 920, 1027, 1322, 1345, 1346, 1431
Cheltenham, Central Photographic Studios: Cat. W/C: 496
Chicago, Art Institute of Chicago: Cat. W/C: 1436, 1471; Cat. P: 371, 372

Cincinnati, Art Museum: Cat. W/C: 866, 1530
— Taft Museum: Pls. 87, 258; Cat. W/C: 389, 480, 660, 1072, 1073, 1269, 1307, 1311; Cat. P: 514
Cleveland, Museum of Art: Cat. W/C: 1549; Cat. P: 364
Cockermouth, National Trust, Wordsworth's House; Pl. 43
Columbus, Gallery of Fine Arts: Cat. W/C: 848
Coventry, Herbert Art Gallery and Museum: Cat. W/C: 262, 727, 839

Dublin, National Gallery of Ireland: Pls. 27, 88, 160; Cat. W/C: 56, 155, 320, 454, 472, 511, 763, 884, 908, 1010, 1258, 1317, 1343, 1351, 1356–1358, 1408, 1441–1443, 1475–1477, 1491

Edinburgh, Tom Scott: Pls. 192, 207, 233, 245, 253, 255; Cat. W/C: 36, 316, 322, 338, 398, 612, 689, 836, 873, 921, 922, 987, 1034, 1038, 1082, 1088, 1118, 1119, 1121, 1139, 1243, 1271–1290, 1295, 1306, 1352, 1369–1372, 1433–1435, 1446, 1447, 1460, 1463, 1464, 1487, 1497, 1504; Cat. P: 513

Fredericton, Beaverbrook Art Gallery: Cat. W/C: 257; Cat. P: 354

Geneva, Editions Claude Givaudan: Pl. 155
— Galerie Jan Krugier: Cat. W/C: 1564
Glasgow, Annan Photographer: Pl. 121
— Art Gallery and Museum: Cat. W/C: 451; Cat. P: 374
Greenwich, National Maritime Museum: Cat. P: 252

Headley Bordon, Jeremy Whitaker: Cat. P: 77, 120, 289, 290, 333
Hessle, Donald I. Innes: Pls. 1, 2; Cat. W/C: 3, 4
Heversham, Graham Edwards: Cat. W/C: 30
Hexham, William Pattinson: Cat. W/C: 266, 762

Indianapolis, Museum of Art: Pls. 3, 156, 198; Cat. W/C: 91, 326, 633, 653, 665, 1000, 1036, 1048, 1060, 1065, 1102, 1115, 1120, 1124, 1247; photos Robert Wallace: Cat. W/C: 135
— Pantzer Collection: Cat. W/C: 110, 570, 1006, 1007, 1331, 1347, 1461, 1547, 1557

Johannesburg, Art Gallery: Cat. W/C: 664

Kansas City, Nelson Gallery – Atkins Museum: Cat. P: 105
Kelso, Hector Innes: Cat. W/C: 1074
Kendal, Abbot Hall Art Gallery: Pl. 93

Leeds, Art Galleries: Cat. W/C: 542, 648, 1291, 1421, 1498
— West Park Studios: Cat. W/C: 340, 1522
Lewes, Edward Reeves: Pl. 120; Cat. W/C: 426, 429, 431, 435
Lincoln, Usher Gallery: Pl. 189
Lisbon, Fundaçao Calouste Gulbenkian: Pl. 164; Cat. W/C: 760; Cat. P: 353
Liverpool, John Mills Photography Ltd.: Cat. P: 517